Lecture Notes in Computer Science

Commenced Publication in 1973
Founding and Former Series Editors:
Gerhard Goos, Juris Hartmanis, and Jan van Leeuwen

Milan Šonka   Ioannis A. Kakadiaris
Jan Kybic (Eds.)

Computer Vision and Mathematical Methods in Medical and Biomedical Image Analysis

ECCV 2004 Workshops CVAMIA and MMBIA
Prague, Czech Republic, May 15, 2004
Revised Selected Papers

 Springer

Volume Editors

Milan Šonka
University of Iowa, Department of Electrical and Computer Engineering
Iowa City IA 52242, USA
E-mail: milan-sonka@uiowa.edu

Ioannis A. Kakadiaris
University of Houston, Deaprtment of Computer Science and ECE
Visual Computing Lab, MS CSC 3010
Houston, TX 77204-3010, USA
E-mail: ioannisk@uh.edu

Jan Kybic
Czech Technical University, Faculty of Electrical Engineering
Department of Cybernetics
Technick 2, Praha 6, 166 27, Czech Republic
E-mail: kybic@fel.cvut.cz

Library of Congress Control Number: 2004111941

CR Subject Classification (1998): I.4, I.2.10, I.3.5, I.5, J.3

ISSN 0302-9743
ISBN 3-540-22675-3 Springer Berlin Heidelberg New York

Springer is a part of Springer Science+Business Media

springeronline.com

© Springer-Verlag Berlin Heidelberg 2004
Printed in Germany

Typesetting: Camera-ready by author, data conversion by Boller Mediendesign
Printed on acid-free paper   SPIN: 11301004   06/3142   5 4 3 2 1 0

Preface

Medical imaging and medical image analysis are rapidly developing. While medical imaging has already become a standard of modern medical care, medical image analysis is still mostly performed visually and qualitatively. The ever-increasing volume of acquired data makes it impossible to utilize them in full. Equally important, the visual approaches to medical image analysis are known to suffer from a lack of reproducibility. A significant research effort is devoted to developing algorithms for processing the wealth of data available and extracting the relevant information in a computerized and quantitative fashion.

Medical imaging and image analysis are interdisciplinary areas combining electrical, computer, and biomedical engineering; computer science; mathematics; physics; statistics; biology; medicine; and other fields. Medical imaging and computer vision, interestingly enough, have developed and continue developing somewhat independently. Nevertheless, bringing them together promises to benefit both of these fields. We were enthusiastic when the organizers of the 2004 European Conference on Computer Vision (ECCV) allowed us to organize a satellite workshop devoted to medical image analysis.

In a short time after the announcement, we received 60 full-length paper submissions, out of which 13 were accepted for oral and 25 for poster presentation after a rigorous peer-review process. The workshop included a keynote lecture and two invited talks. The keynote, entitled *Progress in Quantitative Cardiovascular Imaging*, was presented by Prof. Johan H.C. Reiber from the Leiden University Medical Center, The Netherlands. The first invited talk was given by Prof. Michael Unser from the Swiss Federal Institute of Technology, Lausanne (EPFL), Lausanne, Switzerland – titled *Wavelets, Fractals and Medical Image Analysis*. The second invited talk dealt with *Inverse Consistent Medical Image Registration* and was presented by Prof. Gary E. Christensen from the University of Iowa, Iowa City IA, USA.

The workshop logistics were handled by the organizers of the ECCV 2004, associated with the Centre for Machine Perception of the Czech Technical University in Prague, Czech Republic. We are grateful to all Centre members and students for the smooth organizational support during the entire workshop, as well as for providing a friendly working atmosphere. Finally, we extend our sincere thanks to the program committee members, to the reviewers, and to everyone else who made this workshop possible.

May 2004

Milan Šonka
Ioannis A. Kakadiaris
Jan Kybic

Organization

The 2004 *Computer Vision Approaches to Medical Image Analysis* (CVAMIA) and *Mathematical Methods in Biomedical Image Analysis* (MMBIA) Workshop was held in conjunction with the 8th *European Conference on Computer Vision* (ECCV) in Prague, on May 15, 2004. The ECCV conference was organized by the Centre for Machine Perception, Department of Cybernetics, Faculty of Electrical Engineering, Czech Technical University, Prague, Czech Republic.

Executive Committee

General Chair   Milan Šonka (University of Iowa)
Program Chair   Ioannis A. Kakadiaris (University of Houston)
Organizing Chair   Jan Kybic (Czech Technical University)

Program Committee

Amir Amini	Washington University
Nicholas Ayache	INRIA, France
Faisal Beg	Simon Fraser University
Mike Brady	University of Oxford
Gary Christensen	University of Iowa
Christos Davatzikos	University of Pennsylvania
Herve Delingette	INRIA Sophia Antipolis
James Duncan	University of Southern California
Guido Gerig	University of North Carolina at Chapel Hill
Dmitry Goldgof	University of South Florida
Tomas Gustavsson	Chalmers University of Technology
Thomas Huang	University of Illinois
Ghassan Hamarneh	Simon Fraser University
Ioannis A. Kakadiaris	University of Houston
Ron Kikinis	Harvard Medical School
Ben Kimia	Brown University
Andrew Laine	Columbia University
Tim McInerney	University of Toronto
Dimitris Metaxas	University of Pennsylvania
Erik Meijering	Biomedical Imaging Group, Rotterdam
Nikos Paragios	École Nationale de Ponts et Chaussées
Steve Pizer	University of North Carolina at Chapel Hill
Joseph Reinhardt	University of Iowa
Gabor Szekely	Computer Vision Laboratory, ETH Zurich
Demetri Terzopoulos	University of Toronto
Michael Unser	Swiss Federal Institute of Technology
Michael Vannier	University of Iowa
Max Viergever	Utrecht University
Andreas Wahle	University of Iowa
James Williams	Siemens
Terry Yoo	National Institutes of Health

Table of Contents

Medical Image Segmentation

Ultrasound Stimulated Vibro-acoustography

James F. Greenleaf[1], Mostafa Fatemi[1], and Marek Belohlavek[2]

[1]Department of Physiology and Biomedical Engineering, Mayo Clinic College of Medicine
(jfg@mayo.edu and Fatemi@mayo.edu)
[2]Department of Internal Medicine, Division of Cardiovascular Diseases
Mayo Clinic, Rochester, MN, USA, 55905
(belohlavek.marek@mayo.edu)

Abstract. Vibro-acoustography is a method of imaging and measurement that uses ultrasound to produce radiation force to vibrate objects. The radiation force is concentrated laterally by focusing the ultrasound beam. The radiation force is limited in depth by intersecting two beams at different frequencies so that there is interference between the beams at the difference frequency only at their intersection. This results in a radiation stress of limited spatial extent on or within the object of interest. The resulting harmonic displacement of the object is detected by acoustic emission, ultrasound Doppler, or laser interferometery. The displacement is a complicated function of the object material parameters. However, significant images and measurements can be made with this arrangement. Vibro-acoustography can produce high resolution speckle free images of biologically relevant objects such as breast micro-calcification and vessel calcifications, heart valves, and normal arteries. Vibro-acoustography can also make spot measurements such as microbubble contrast agent concentration in vessels. Several examples of these results will be described.

1 Introduction

It is well known that changes in the elasticity of soft tissues are often related to pathology. Traditionally, physicians use palpation as a simple method for estimating the mechanical properties of tissue. Physicians use a static force applied with their hands and obtain a crude estimation of tissue elasticity the sense of touch. Thus, the force is applied on the body surface and the result is a collective response of all the tissues below. Clinicians can sense abnormalities if the response to palpation is sufficiently different from that of normal tissue. However, if the abnormality lies deep in the body, or if is too small to be resolved by touch, then palpation fails. The dynamic response of soft tissue to a force is also valuable in medical diagnosis. For instance, rebound of tissue upon sudden release of pressure exerted by the physician's finger on the skin provides useful diagnostic information about the tissue.

Quantitative measurement of the mechanical properties of tissues and their display in raster format is the aim of a class of techniques generally called elasticity imaging, or elastography. The general approach is to measure tissue motion caused by an external (or, in some methods, internal) force and use the degree of displacement to reconstruct the elastic parameters of the tissue. The excitation stress can be either

M. Šonka et al. (Eds.): CVAMIA-MMBIA 2004, LNCS 3117, pp. 1-10, 2004.
© Springer-Verlag Berlin Heidelberg 2004

static or dynamic (vibration). Dynamic excitation is of particular interest because it provides more comprehensive information about tissue properties over a spectrum of frequencies. In many elasticity imaging methods, ultrasound is used to detect the motion or displacement resulting from the applied stress. Magnetic resonance elastography is a recently developed method [1] that employs a mechanical actuator to vibrate the body surface and then measures the resulting strain waves with a phase sensitive magnetic resonance imaging (MRI) machine.

The majority of elasticity imaging methods is based on an external source of force in which the object is pressed by a known amount of force or displacement, and the resulting internal deformations are measured by means of pulse-echo ultrasound. The elasticity of the region of interest is then calculated based on the resulting deformation in relation to the magnitude of the applied force (or displacement). Normally, the region of interest rests deep in the body and away from the source of the force. The problem with this method, termed elastography, is that the force actually exerted on the region of interest depends on the elastic properties of the tissues located between the source and the region of interest. Hence, the deformation and the estimated elasticity of the region of interest are subject to the variability of the intervening tissues.

An alternative strategy is to apply a localized stress directly in the region of interest. One way to accomplish this is to use the radiation pressure of ultrasound. Acoustic radiation force is the time average force exerted by an acoustic field on an object. This force is produced by a change in the energy density of an incident acoustic field [2]; for example, due to absorption or reflection. The use of ultrasound radiation force for evaluating tissue properties has several benefits, for example:

(a) Acoustic (ultrasound) energy is a non-invasive means of exerting force.
(b) Existing ultrasound technology and devices can be readily modified for this purpose, thus eliminating the need for developing a new technology.
(c) Radiation force can be generated remotely inside tissue without disturbing superficial layers.
(d) The radiation stress field can be highly localized, thus allowing for interrogation of a small excitation point.
(e) Radiation force can be produced in a wide range of frequencies or temporal shapes.

These features make radiation force methods highly attractive compared to other, mostly mechanical excitation methods used in elasticity imaging. Tissue probing with the radiation force of ultrasound can be accomplished with a variety of methods depending on the excitation and detection methods used. Similar to elasticity imaging methods with mechanical excitation, radiation force methods can use either a static or dynamic stress.

Using a dynamic radiation force to remotely probe tissue has certain unique characteristics and capabilities that can provide a new family of methods in the field of tissue characterization and imaging. It is insightful to set this new field apart from conventional ultrasound tissue characterization imaging. A major difference is that the dynamic radiation stress allows one to analyze the object based on its low frequency structural vibration properties as opposed to its ultrasonic parameters.

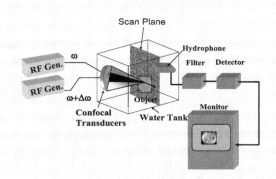

Fig. 1. Schematic of experiment setup

The dynamic radiation force methods may be categorized as:

(a) Transient methods, where an impulsive radiation force is used and the transient response of the tissue is detected by Doppler ultrasound [3].

(b) Shear-wave methods, where an impulsive or oscillating radiation is applied to the tissue and the resulting shear wave is detected by ultrasound or other methods [4,5,6].

(c) Vibro-acoustography, a method recently developed by the authors, where a localized oscillating radiation force is applied to the tissue and the acoustic response of the tissue is detected by a hydrophone or microphone [7].

Fig. 2. Vibro-acoustic image of US quarter obtained with the setup of Fig. 1.

2 Theory

Acoustic radiation force is a time average force exerted by a propagating acoustic wave on an object. This force is an example of a universal phenomenon in any wave motion that introduces some type of unidirectional force on absorbing or reflecting targets in the wave path. For a review of this topic the reader may refer to [2].

Consider a plane ultrasound beam interacting with a planar object of zero thickness and arbitrary shape and boundary impedance that scatters and absorbs. The radiation force vector, F, arising from this interaction has a component in the beam direction and another transverse to it. The magnitude of this force is proportional to the average energy density of the incident wave E at the object, where $<>$ represents the time average, and S the area of the projected portion of the object [8]:

$$F = drS <E> . \qquad (1)$$

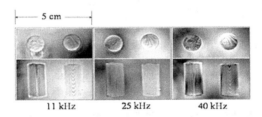

|——— 5 cm ———|

11 kHz   25 kHz   40 kHz

Fig. 3. Vibro-acoustic image of a hard (left) and a soft (right) urethane cylinder embedded within agar gel. Top row are images from the ends of the cylinders and bottom row are imaged from the side of the cylinders. The low difference frequencies, 11 kHz and 25 kHz. show the difference in stiffness of the two cylinders.

Here dr is called the vector drag coefficient with a component in the incident beam direction and another transverse to it. The coefficient dr is defined per unit incident energy density and unit projected area. For a planar object, the magnitude of dr is numerically equal to the force on the unit area of the object per unit energy density. Physically, the drag coefficient represents the scattering and absorbing properties of the object. The drag coefficient can also be interpreted as the ratio of the radiation force magnitude on a given object to the corresponding value if the object were replaced by a totally absorbing object of similar size. For simplicity, we assume a planar objected oriented perpendicular to the beam axis. In this case, the transverse component vanishes, thus, the drag coefficient (force) will have only a component normal to the target surface which we denote by scalar $dr(F)$. To produce a time-varying radiation force, the intensity of the incident beam can be modulated in various ways.

For example, a short ultrasound pulse can produce a transient pulsed radiation force, and a sinusoidally modulated beam can result in a sinusoidally varying force.

3 Experimental Setup for Imaging

The experimental setup is shown in Fig. 1. The experiments were conducted in a water tank. (In a system designed for *in vivo* imaging the transducers can be placed in contact with the skin instead of using water. The hydrophone would also be placed in contact with the skin. At low frequencies the sound wave propagates almost uniformly in all directions. Hydrophone position is not critical, as long as it is relatively close to the exposure site but not in the ultrasound path.) A two-element confocal ultrasound transducer array was positioned such that the beams meet the object at their joint focal point. Transducer was a confocal 38mm diameter transducer with a center frequency of 3MHz. The elements were driven by two stable RF synthesizers (HP 33120A) at frequencies of 3 MHz and 3 MHz+Δf. Sound produced by the object vibration was detected by a submerged hydrophone (ITC model 680) placed within the water tank. The received signal was filtered and amplified by a programmable filter (Stanford Research Systems, SR650) to reject the noise, then digitized by a 12-bits/sample digitizer (National Instruments VXI-1000) at a rate sufficiently higher than the Nyquist rate. Data are recorded on a computer disc.

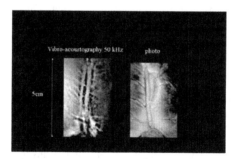

Fig. 4. Vibro-acoustic images of coronary vessels of an excised pig heart, left, compared to photograph, right.

4 Vibro-acoustography Results

An example of resolution is shown in Fig. 2 in which a US quarter was scanned with the set up of Fig. 1. The resolution of the method depends on the power point source function of the ultrasound transducers used to produce the ultrasound beam at the intersection of the confocal beams. To test the ability of vibro-acoustography to de-

tect differences in stiffness we prepared a phantom consisting of a block of agar gel
with two urethane cylinders about 2.5 cm in diameter and 4 cm in length. One of the
cylinders was stiffer than the other. We scanned the phantom using the setup of Fig.
1. The resulting images at three separate difference frequencies are shown in Fig. 3.
At the two lowest frequencies the difference in hardness is shown by the variation in
brightness of the cylinders. Fig. 4 illustrates the capability of vibro-acoustography to
image vessels on the surface of a heart. Of course this could not be done in the intact
chest but the image illustrates the capability of the method to obtain very high resolution images of vessels with no speckle.

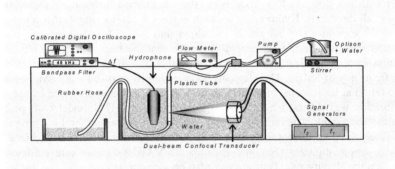

Fig. 5 Set up for measuring acoustic emission from contrast microbubbles.

5 Contrast Vibro-acoustography and the Experimental Setup

We used a customized dual-beam confocal transducer, 25 mm in diameter, to intersect 2 ultrasound beams at 7-cm focal distance. Bursts of 40-kHz vibrations   were
obtained from interference of 3.48-MHz and 3.52-MHz frequencies, calibrated to a
peak negative pressure of 350 kPa at 3.5 MHz and originating from 2 separate signal
generators (Model 33120A, Agilent Technologies, Palo Alto, CA).   Each tone burst
formed a narrow, approximately cylindrical (2 mm in diameter, 10 mm in length)
region of radiation force. In a water tank, a thin (0.25 mm) plastic tube (11 mm in
diameter) was centered at the beam intersection Fig. 5. Using rubber conduits, diluted
contrast agent was continuously run through the plastic tube by means of a peristaltic
flow pump (Model 7518-10, Cole-Parmer Instrument Co., Vernon Hills, IL). A flow
meter (Model T106, Transonic Systems Inc., Ithaca, NY) was used to set and maintain a constant flow rate. An underwater microphone (Model 8106, Bruel & Kjaer,
Naerum, Denmark) detected the emitted audio signals via a band-pass filter (Model
SR650, Stanford Research Systems, Sunnyvale, CA) centered at 40 ± 4 kHz for a -6
dB cutoff. The filter eliminated confounding audio signals from the surrounding environment, while passing the emitted audio signal. A digital oscilloscope (Model 3014,
Tektronix Inc., Beaverton, OR) measured the peak amplitude of the stimulated audio
signals.

A suspension of Optison™ (Mallinckrodt Inc., St. Louis, MO) is provided in 3 mL vials at a concentration of approximately 6.0×10^8 bubbles/mL and with 3.8-µm mean diameter. Using a tuberculin syringe, small amounts of the pre-mixed Optison were subsequently diluted in degassed distilled water to achieve the desired incremental testing concentrations.

6 Agent Vibrometry Results

We found that with increasing concentration of Optison, the amplitude of the stimulated audio signal reached a plateau. However, for concentrations of Optison less than about 4.0×10^5 bubbles/ml, the peak audio signal amplitude was linear (Fig. 6). We related pulsing intervals of the radiation force bursts to the peak audio signal amplitude for various flow rates (Fig. 7). Quantitative analysis of flow was based on the replenishment method described by Wei et al.[10]. Briefly, contrast microbubbles administered in a continuous infusion can be destroyed by a burst of ultrasound energy. The replenishment rate of the bubbles then provides a relative measure of mean microbubble velocity. Higher pulsing rates destroy more bubbles and the acoustic emission would be expected to decrease. Greater flow rate or bubble concentration will increase the acoustic emission. The relationship between the pulsing interval and the peak acoustic amplitude is described by a least-square fitted exponential function $y = A(1-e^{-\beta t})$, where y is the resulting peak acoustic amplitude, A represents the plateau value of the peak amplitude, β is the rate constant of the peak amplitude, and t is the pulsing interval [10,11].

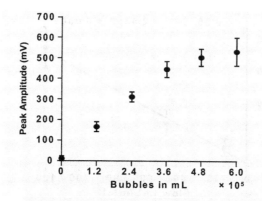

Fig. 6 Acoustic emission from contrast microbubbles is linear with concentration up to about 4×10^5 bubbles/mL.

Using a least-square exponential curve fit, we obtained values of A and β. The A-value, which is a function of microbubble concentration, ultimately reached a plateau that was similar for all testing flow rates, because microbubble concentration was kept constant. The value of β is proportional to volumetric flow. Figure 8 shows data that demonstrate that β is highly correlated with flow, as expected, because the cross-sectional area of the flow conduit was unchanged in our model.

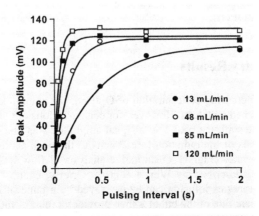

Fig. 7. Variation of Acoustic emission peak amplitude as function of pulsing rate and flow. Higher pulsing rates cause lower emission because fewer bubbles have traversed into the intersection of the two beams.

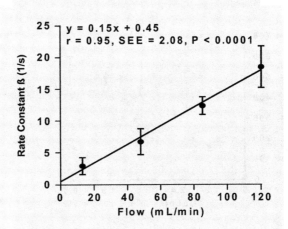

Fig.. 8. Rate constant versus flow from the bubble destruction/Vibro-acoustic flow curves of Fig. 5. Highly linear flow measurements are possible with Vibro-acoustographic point measurements within a vessel.

7 Discussion

Vibro-acoustography provides high contrast, high resolution and speckle free images that are related to object stiffness and acoustic characteristics. The format is the C-scan mode. Rather than obtaining a line in the image for each transmit Vibro-acoustography requires one transmit per pixel. The range of audio frequencies that can be used is very broad, as broad as the bandwidth of the ultrasound transducer, e.g., from DC to several hundred kilohertz. Vibro-acoustography provides objective, quantitative, and highly-localized assessment of contrast microbubble concentration and flow. The signal exhibits a linear response to low concentrations of microbubbles over a range applicable to *in vivo* use. The rate constant of a model of the response to varying pulsing intervals correlates with flow.

8 Summary

Vibro-acoustography can provide images of vessels within tissue and of objects with differing stiffness. The resolution of vibro-acoustography is similar to that of the ultrasound used to produce the radiation pressure. The images are free of speckle rivaling those of MRI in quality and time of acquisition. We demonstrate for the first time that contrast microbubbles can be detected and flow quantitated based on localized "remote tapping" of bubbles rather than on their harmonic response to high-frequency ultrasound. Additional work must concentrate on development of more realistic models and - ultimately - tests in humans before the technique can be introduced to a clinical environment.

9 Acknowledgment

This work was funded in part by grants EB2640 and EB2167 from the National Institute of Biomedical Imaging and Bioengineering.

References

1. Muthupillai, R., Lomas, D.J., Rossman, P.J., Greenleaf, J.F., and R. L. Ehman: Magnetic resonance elastography by direct visualization of propagating acoustic strain waves. Science 269 (Sept 29, 1995) 1854-1857,.
2. Chu, B.T., Apfel, R.E.: Acoustic radiation pressure produced by a beam of sound. J. Acoust. Soc. Am. 72 (1982) 1673-1687.
3. Sugimoto, T., Ueha, S., Itoh, K.: Tissue hardness measurement using the radiation force of focused ultrasound. Proc. Ultrason. Symp., eds. B. R. McAvoy, IEEE, NY (1990) 1377-1280.

4. Andreev, V., Dmitriev, V., Rudenko, O.V., Sarvazyan, A.: A remote generation of shear-wave in soft tissue by pulsed radiation pressure. J. Acoust. Soc. Am. 102 (1997) 3155.
5. Sarvazyan, A., Rudenko, O.V., Swanson, S.D., Fowlkes, B.J., Emelianov, Y.: Shear wave elasticity imaging: a new ultrasonic technology of medical diagnostics. Ultrasound Med. Biol. 24(9) (1998) 1419-1435.
6. Walker, W.F.: Internal deformation of a uniform elastic solid by acoustic radiation. J. Acoust. Soc. Am. 105 (1999) 2508-2518.
7. Fatemi, M., Greenleaf, J.F.: Vibro-acoustography: An imaging modality based on ultrasound-stimulated acoustic emission. Proc. Natl. Acad. Sci. USA 96 (June 1999) 6603-6608.
8. Westervelt, P.J.: The theory of steady force caused by sound waves. J. Acoust. Soc. Am. 23(4) (May 1951) 312-315.
9. Wei, K., Jayaweera, A.R., Firoozan, S, et al.: Quantification of myocardial blood flow with ultrasound-induced destruction of microbubbles administered as a constant venous infusion. Circulation 97 (1998) 473-483.
10. Belohlavek, M., T. Asanuma, R. R. Kinnick, and J. F. Greenleaf: Vibro-acoustography: Quantitation of flow with highly-localized low-frequency acoustic force. Ultrasonic Imaging 23:249-256, October 2001.

CT from an Unmodified Standard Fluoroscopy Machine Using a Non-reproducible Path

Chris Baker[1], Chris Debrunner[1], Mohamed Mahfouz[2,3],
William Hoff[1], Jamon Bowen[1]

[1]Colorado School of Mines, Golden, Colorado
[2]University of Tennessee at Knoxville
[3]Oak Ridge National Laboratory

Abstract. 3D reconstruction from image data is required in many medical procedures. Recently, the use of fluoroscopy data to generate these 3D models has been explored. Most existing methods require knowledge of the scanning path either from precise hardware, or pre-calibration procedures. We propose an alternative of obtaining this needed pose information without the need of additional hardware or pre-calibration so that many existing fluoroscopes can be used.

Our method generates 3D data from fluoroscopy collected along a non-repeatable path using cone-beam tomographic reconstruction techniques. The novelty of our approach is its application to imagery from existing fluoroscopic systems that are not instrumented to generate pose information or collect data along specific paths. Our method does not require additional hardware to obtain the pose, but instead gathers the needed object to camera pose information for each frame using 2D to 3D model matching techniques [1-3]. Metallic markers are attached to the object being imaged to provide features for pose determination. Given the pose, we apply Grangeat's cone-beam reconstruction algorithm to recover the 3D data.

In developing this approach, several problems arose that have not been addressed previously in the literature. First, because the Radon space sampling is different for each scan, we cannot to take advantage of a known Radon space discretization. Therefore we have developed a matching score that will give the best Radon plane match for the resampling step in Grangeat's approach [4]. Second, although we assume Tuy's condition [5] is satisfied, there are sometimes data gaps due to discretization. We have developed a method to correct for these gaps in the Radon data.

1 Introduction

Many medical procedures require three dimensional (3D) imaging of the human body. For example, when planning or executing surgical procedures, 3D imaging yields tremendous advantages over conventional 2D static radiographs. 3D image data can be obtained from CT and MRI, but these procedures may not be available in many clinics and operating rooms, and are therefore not as convenient as 3D from a fluoroscopy machine.

Fluoroscopy machines are much less expensive than CT or MRI instruments, and are widely available in operating rooms and clinics. However, a fluoroscopy image is

M. Šonka et al. (Eds.): CVAMIA-MMBIA 2004, LNCS 3117, pp. 11-23, 2004.

only a single plane projection, similar to a 2D X-ray. To obtain 3D data, the fluoroscope can be rotated in order to get multiple views of the object, and these projections can be processed using cone-beam tomographic reconstruction methods [4] to produce a 3D volumetric image similar to that obtained from CT.

Recently, Siemens has created a 3D fluoroscope using cone-beam tomography, called the SIREMOBIL Iso-C 3D. This instrument has a fluoroscope on a mobile C-arm that rotates automatically in a 190-degree arc around the patient. General Electric has produced a similar 3D fluoroscopic imaging and navigation system called FluoroCAT, an add-on for their OEC® 9800 Plus fluoroscope.

Although the method used in these systems gives good results, it requires a specialized fluoroscope that is designed to precisely and automatically rotate the source/detector (*SD*) around an axis, along with instrumentation to accurately measure the rotation. There are a great numbers of existing fluoroscopes in use that do not have this capability.

We have developed a method of generating 3D volumetric intensity data from fluoroscopy x-ray projections collected along a non-repeatable path using exact cone-beam reconstruction techniques. The novelty of our approach is that it can be applied to imagery from existing fluoroscopic systems that are not instrumented to reproduce specific paths or to generate accurate pose information for each image. Therefore our method does not require the addition of any external hardware to control or sense the motion of the fluoroscopy unit, but instead gathers the needed object to camera pose information for each frame using 2D to 3D model matching techniques [1-3]. In developing this method, several problems arose that have not been addressed previously in the literature. First, because the discrete sampling of the Radon space is different for each set of fluoroscopy images, we are not able to take advantage of a known discretization of our Radon space. Therefore we have developed a Radon plane matching score that will find the best matching plane during the resampling step in Grangeat's approach [4]. Second, although we assume that Tuy's condition [5] is satisfied, in practice there are sometimes gaps in the data due to discretization. We have developed a method to correct for any such missing Radon data. Although our implementation assumes that internal camera parameters are fixed, it could easily be modified to remove this assumption as was done in [6]

This approach allows much greater flexibility in imaging configurations, even allowing reconstruction from images collected as the patient moves in the field of view of a fixed fluoroscope. Variations of this approach could also be applied to 3D imaging using highly portable systems such as might be used in field hospitals in disaster relief or combat situations, as well as applications in non-destructive testing.

2   Previous Work

2.1   Pose Estimation

Tomographic reconstruction from projections requires accurate knowledge of the position and orientation (referred to collectively as the pose) of the *SD* relative to the object being scanned. A standard technique of determining the pose of a 3D object from a two dimensional image is to incorporate a set of fiducial markers of known 3D structure into the object. Once the images of these fiducial markers are correctly associated with their 3D counterparts, the pose of the object with respect to the imaging sensor can be determined using an "absolute orientation" algorithm [7]. Examples of 2D-to-3D registration in X-ray images using the fiducial technique include [1-3].

2.2 Cone Beam Tomographic Reconstruction

The Siemens SIREMOBIL Iso-C^{3D} mentioned in Section 1 is an example of a commercial cone-beam tomography unit. In addition, many approaches to cone-beam tomography have been developed or enhanced in earlier work including many specific path algorithms [4, 5, 8-18]. Whereas most commercial systems use the Feldkamp method [8], we have selected the method of Grangeat [4] as the most suitable for our problem since it is an exact cone-beam reconstruction method. We have modified the common resampling step of Grangeat's algorithm in a way similar to [19] to allow it to be applied to arbitrary discrete sets of SD locations. Because our path may be different for each scan, our sampling of the Radon space will be different for each scan. We therefore have developed a new method of choosing the best-matching Radon plane.

3   Approach

The processing required for reconstruction from an arbitrary path consists of two steps: recovery of the unknown pose of the SD, and cone-beam tomographic reconstruction. We assume that the images being used to perform this reconstruction have already been calibrated in such a way that the common pinhole camera model is an acceptable projection model [6] which removes the geometric distortions such as pincushion or barrel distortions We also assume that the pixel values have been calibrated to be proportional to the integral of the density along the 3D ray projecting to each pixel. The details of these calibration methods are available in [20]. The first step, recovery of the unknown pose is described in Section 3.1, followed by the description of the reconstruction process in Section 3.2.

3.1   Pose Estimation

In order to estimate the pose of the sensor in each image from the image data, we use markers at known 3D locations relative to the object and perform 2D to 3D model matching techniques. We use 2mm steel ball bearings rigidly attached to the object and uniformly distributed to cover the entire field of view.

To compute the pose of the sensor, we first find the correct associations (or correspondences) between image points and the 3D fiducial locations using an interpretation tree search method [21]. The correspondences are used to calculate a pose solution which is used to project the object points back onto the image to determine how accurately the pose solution fits the data. Once a set of correct correspondences is found, we compute the pose using a non-linear least squares method [22]. The solution minimizes the squared error between the observed image points and the expected position of those points, based on the projected model and the hypothesized pose. Once this process is complete, the pose of the SD for each image can be used in Grangeat's tomographic reconstruction algorithm to reconstruct the 3D volume.

3.2   Tomographic Reconstruction

The second step, cone-beam tomographic reconstruction, uses the algorithm developed by Grangeat [4]. Tomographic reconstruction using Grangeat's method has been well published and so we will not provide the details of his process here [4, 12, 13, 18, 19, 23]. Grangeat provides us with a method of computing 3D Radon data from the 2D detector data of a cone beam scan by way of the first derivative of the detector plane Radon data. This 3D Radon data must then be resampled to a spherical coordinate system. More specifically, it is resampled from the available planes (AP) in the sensor coordinate system, which is attached to the SD, to the desired planes (DP) in the 3D spherical object coordinate system where the backprojections can be computed. Using the pose found for the SD for each image in the previous pose estimation step, we can resample our Radon data collected on our sensor array into 3D Radon data using a method similar to [18, 19]. However, unlike methods with fixed paths, we cannot take advantage of any regularity in the path to reduce computation or to precompute the resampling coefficients. One issue that must be addressed in resampling is how to find the DP closest to a particular AP. Unlike [19], we define the closeness entirely in terms of the distance between the planes in the reconstruction volume. The available planes are parameterized by the 2D Radon parameters (A, α) in the image plane, and the image number, $inum$. The desired planes are given in the object coordinate system, whose axis are $(\hat{i}, \hat{j}, \hat{k})$ with coordinates (x, y, z). In the object coordinate space, we parameterize the DP by its unit normal $\hat{n}$ and its distance, ρ, from the origin. In order to get accurate reconstruction, it is crucial to match these two planes in the reconstruction volume as well as possible.

In [19] the plane matching method is based on the assumption that the DP should pass as close as possible to the vertex of the SD. Once the SD vertex position has been identified for each frame of the fluoroscopic image sequence the distance to the DP can be calculated and minimized to obtain the 2D Radon plane giving the best estimate of the plane. Then, within that image a search will determine which 2D Radon plane will match best. However, due to the discretization of the available 2D Radon dataset (the 2D Radon is typically computed on a discrete set of (A, α) values), there may be cases where the best AP will not be associated with the closest to the SD vertex. Fig. 1 helps to illustrate one situation where this could arise. Two consecutive SD positions are shown looking along the edge of the planes of interest. The first SD position is labeled $SD - A$ and the second $SD - B$. Because of the discretization of the 2D Radon transforms, the closest two APs for $SD - A$ are $AP - A1$ and $AP - A2$ shown as the dotted lines in Fig. 1, and similarly for $SD - B$

shown as the solid lines. Notice that in this case, the vertex for $SD - B$ is closer to the DP, however, $SD - A$ will give a better approximation of the DP by using $AP - A1$. Similar situations can arise due to the limited field of view of the sensor. Even if the desired plane passes close to the SD vertex, the sensor's field of view might not cover that desired plane. For these reasons we chose to develop a new plane matching method that finds the closest plane in the reconstruction volume rather than the SD vertex location [19].

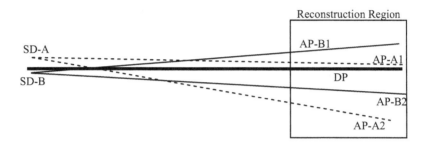

Fig. 1. The best matching AP may not always be found from the SD vertex position which is closest to the DP. This figure illustrates a case in which the discretization of the actual planes may be such that a plane whose SD vertex is closest to the DP does not contain the best estimate of the DP in the reconstruction volume. Notice how the Radon planes for SD-A are closer to the DP, but the vertex position of SD-B is closer. Here, most existing algorithms would choose SD-B as the source location from which to get the Radon data, however it is clear that SD-A would provide more accurate data.

Depending on our path taken during the data collection, we will have a set of images providing available Radon planes, AP, indexed by $(A, \alpha, inum)$. From these we must determine the appropriate $(\rho \hat{n})$ of the closest DP. Using similar triangles we compute the distance ρ as

$$\rho = \frac{AD}{\sqrt{A^2 + D^2}} , \tag{1}$$

where D is the perpendicular distance between the SD vertex and the image plane. We can write the AP normal in the image coordinates, (u, v, w) as

$$[\rho \hat{n}_u, \rho \hat{n}_v, \rho \hat{n}_w] = \left[\frac{\rho^2}{A} \cos \alpha, \frac{\rho^2}{A} \sin \alpha, \frac{A\rho}{\sqrt{A^2 + D^2}} \right]. \tag{2}$$

With the AP defined in the image coordinate system, we can use the pose of the SD to transform this vector to AP_O, which is the available plane in object coordinates. Now we can directly compare AP_O and the DP, which is also in object coordinates.

Our criterion for measuring the closeness of two Radon planes is related to the squared distance between the two planes within the reconstruction volume. We define two planes we would like to match (both in object coordinates) as

$$DP_i : [x, y, z] \bullet \hat{n}_{DP_i} = \rho_{DP_i} \qquad (3)a$$

$$AP_i : [x, y, z] \bullet \hat{n}_{AP_i} = \rho_{AP_i} . \qquad (3)b$$

We can write the signed perpendicular distance from an arbitrary point $[x, y, z]$ in DP_i to AP_i as

$$[x, y, z] \bullet \hat{n}_{AP_i} - \rho_{AP_i} . \qquad (4)$$

Solving Equation (3a) for z [1], substituting into (4), squaring to get the squared distances, and integrating within the reconstruction volume over $-d$ to d in x and y, gives us our match score, (MS), correlating to how well the two planes are aligned.

$$MS = \int_{-d}^{d} \int_{-d}^{d} \left\{ x\hat{n}_{AP_{ix}} + y\hat{n}_{AP_{iy}} + \hat{n}_{AP_{iz}} \left[\frac{\rho_{DP_i} - x\hat{n}_{DP_{ix}} - y\hat{n}_{DP_{iy}}}{\hat{n}_{DP_{iz}}} \right] - \rho_{AP_i} \right\}^2 dxdy \qquad (5)$$

Each time a new plane is found that will project into a particular DP, we calculate the MS given by (5), compare it to the currently stored MS in the destination array (the distances are initialized to infinity) and keep the best match.

Because our source data is generated along an arbitrary non-repeatable path and therefore, the discretization of the Radon space may be different for each scan, we may have cases where there is no AP to support a particular DP. Tuy's data sufficiency criterion [5] is not strictly met in this case, and we refer to this case as "missing data." In order to handle any missing data that may arise from an arbitrary non-repeatable path, we use a binary array to record whenever a DP bin is filled, defined as $N(\rho\hat{n})$. After the complete dataset has been resampled from the detector coordinate system to the world coordinate system, we can backproject the array N along with the resampled data as described in [4]. Once N has been processed it will be a reconstructed volume weighted according to which portions of the volume have the most supporting data. We can then use N as a normalization factor for our reconstructed volume to help account for missing data artifacts.

---

[1] In general we need to solve for whichever variable, (x, y, z) is most aligned with the normal $\hat{n}$. However, for simplicity of the discussion, we just use z. Note also that this will avoid division by zero in (5) since the coefficient in the divisor will always be the greatest in magnitude of the three (i.e. not equal to zero).

4 Results

Since the accuracy of our reconstruction relies heavily on the computation of the pose of the SD for each image, we first quantify the error in the pose calculation by comparing estimated poses to ground truth measurements collected with an optical tracker. Then we present the tomographic reconstructions of synthetic and real data sets to characterize the quality of the reconstructions.

4.1 Pose Estimation Compared to an Optical Tracker

To test the pose estimation accuracy, we used an Optotrak optical tracker[2] to record ground truth poses during an image data collection of a physical phantom constructed of PVC and acrylic. The various coordinate systems we used are illustrated in Fig.2. There are four coordinate systems that we must be concerned with in order to perform the verification in this way. First, we refer to the Optotrak probe coordinate system as P and the Optotrak base coordinate system as our world coordinate system, or W since it is the reference from for the ground truth measurements from the Optotrak. Finally, we refer to the SD coordinate system of the fluoroscope as F and the object coordinate system origin as O.

In order to measure the pose accuracy, we compare the motion of the object from frame 0 to frame i using two different transform paths. The paths are illustrated in Fig. 3. The first path (shown on the bottom of Fig. 3) takes us from the P coordinate system's initial pose through the world reference coordinate system (W) to the ith frame of P. The second path (shown across the top of Fig. 3) takes us from the same starting reference coordinate system of P through the initial frame of O to the SD reference frame, (F) (which is fixed during the data collection) back through the ith frame of O, and into the ith frame of P.

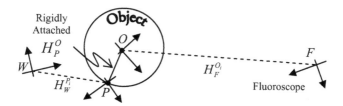

Fig. 2. Top view of Pose estimation verification setup. The P is attached to the outside of the phantom whose origin, O, is defined in the center of all the beads.

---

[2] The Optotrak used is the Northern Digital model #3020.

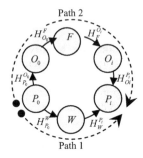

Fig. 3. The two paths used to verify the pose finding algorithm.

The transforms between W and P are calculated from the Optotrak data. The transforms between F and O are given from the pose estimation algorithm, which is the transform we wish to verify. The transform from P to O can be found with physical measurements since P and O are rigidly attached as Fig. 2 suggests. We denote the transform between O and P as H_O^P. Note also that because the probe is rigidly attached to the object, we know that $H_O^P = H_{O_i}^{P_i} = H_{O_0}^{P_0}$ and these notations will be used interchangeably to make consecutive transform cancellations more clear. We define the transformation from the F to O at the time of the ith image as $H_F^{O_i}$, and the transform between W and P at the time of the ith image as $H_W^{P_i}$.

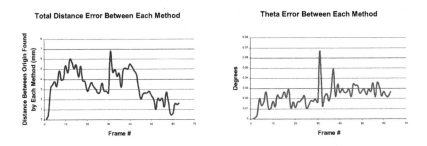

Fig. 4. The Euclidean distance between the probe origin found from the pose finding algorithm to the origin found using the Optotrak method (left). The error in the rotation angle between two consecutive image frames for 67 frames in the sequence. This error is calculated as the rotational error from the angle-axis representation of the residuals from the two pose calculation paths (right).

We measure our pose error by finding the change in the pose of P relative to its initial position, or $H_{P_0}^{P_i}$, in two ways, one using the Optotrak and the other using our pose estimation algorithm, or the two paths shown in Fig. 3. Then we compare the results to measure our error. We call the result of the first (using the Optotrak) $^{O}H^{P_i}_{P_0}$, and readily see that it can be computed as

$$^{O}H^{P_i}_{P_0} = H^{P_i}_{W} H^{W}_{P_0} \tag{6}$$

We call the result of the second method (using our pose estimation algorithm) $^{A}H^{P_i}_{P_0}$. Given the transform H^{O}_{P} from the physical measurements, we see that we can compute $^{A}H^{P_i}_{P_0}$ from the transforms $H^{F}_{O_0}$ and $H^{O_i}_{F}$ computed by our pose estimation algorithm as

$$^{A}H^{P_i}_{P_0} = H^{P_i}_{O_i} H^{O_i}_{F} H^{F}_{O_0} H^{O_0}_{P_0} . \tag{7}$$

By comparing these two results we can analyze the error in our pose finding method. We compare these two paths by computing

$$\left[^{O}H^{P_i}_{P_0} \right]^{-1} {}^{A}H^{P_i}_{P_0} . \tag{8}$$

If the two transforms were equal this would produce an identity matrix. We convert the relative rotation from this transform to angle-axis form and use the magnitude of the angle as our orientation error measure, and the magnitude of the translation as our position error measure. The position errors are shown in Fig. 4 (left), while the orientation errors are shown in Fig. 4 (right) for 63 frames. The mean translation error is 3.37mm, with a standard deviation of 1.53. The mean error in the angular deviation is 0.023 degrees, with a standard deviation of 0.0104.

These results demonstrate that our pose recovery algorithm is accurate when compared to a commercial optical tracker. Because the accuracy of our reconstruction depends primarily on the accuracy of pose, this result is critical to the success of our approach. Next we consider the reconstruction of various objects using our proposed method.

4.2   Tomographic Reconstruction Results

The next step in the analysis of our method is to evaluate the results of the complete reconstruction process. First we evaluate reconstructions from a set of synthetic phantom images and then from real imagery of a cadaver knee.

Synthetic Phantom Reconstruction. In order to verify the reconstruction algorithm independently of the pose finding algorithm, we generated synthetic data by integrating densities along a cone-beam projection pattern through a synthetically created 3D volume. The synthetic volumetric data used was a set of ellipsoids. Fig. 5 shows the rendered reconstructed volumetric results on the right with the original data on the left. The boundaries of the various ellipsoids can be seen clearly.

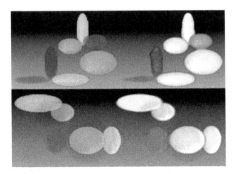

Fig. 5. Images taken of the reconstructed synthetic phantom. There are two different views of the same reconstructed volume with the original volume displayed next to it. The original volumes are shown on the left while the reconstructed volumes are shown on the right.

We used these synthetic reconstruction results to analyze the accuracy of the recovered densities relative to the original volumetric data, and to measure the geometric accuracy of our reconstruction algorithm.

Density analysis. In order to test the accuracy of our reconstructed voxel density information we can compare the final reconstructed voxel values with the density values of the original data. Since the most common use of the 3D density data is segmentation, ensuring accurate reconstructed density values is not as important as verifying relative density information. Therefore we fit a linear function to transform our reconstructed density information to the original density information and then compare to the linearly transformed data. We found the mean signed deviation to be 3.64 (from a range of zero to 255), and the standard deviation was 2.62.

Geometric accuracy analysis. In order to determine whether the reconstruction algorithm introduced any geometric errors (e.g., position offsets and scaling), we compared the position and size of each reconstructed ellipsoid to those of the corresponding ellipsoid in the original volume. We first found the three axes of each reconstructed ellipsoid by measuring the extremities of the segmented ellipsoid in the x, y, and z-directions. We then found the center of the ellipsoid by averaging the axis endpoints. The average of the absolute deviations of the center positions for the ellipsoids was 0.163 voxels, while the average of the absolute deviations from the axis lengths was 1.303 voxels. The errors in the axis lengths are larger than the error in the positions which is probably due to the blurring effect of the algorithm (accurate segmentation is very difficult with blurred edges, and a different segmentation method might reduce these errors). However, note the positions of the ellipsoids were found very accurately.

Cadaver Reconstruction. Fig. 6 shows our algorithm's reconstruction of a cadaver knee from 596 fluoroscopic images taken at 30 frames per second. Some noise can be seen at the top and bottom of the reconstruction due to parts of the cadaver being in the field of view during only part of the scan, thus these portions of the reconstructed volume do not satisfy Tuy's condition and are not a part of our supported reconstruction area. This effect has been addressed in the literature [24] and we do not address it here as it is out of the scope of this particular paper. We also notice some metal artifacts from the marker beads which are also addressed extensively in the literature (e.g. [25-27]). Further refinements to our algorithms could incorporate these enhancements and remove these artifacts. However, this demonstrates that our method can tomographically reconstruct a volume from real fluoroscopic imagery with quality sufficient to allow segmentation (e.g., to produce a 3D model of the bone for surgical planning or surgical navigation).

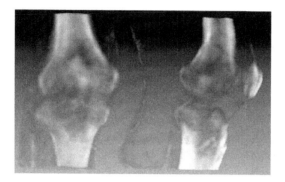

Fig. 6. The reconstructed volume from projections generated along an arbitrary path using our proposed algorithm.

5   Conclusions and Discussion

This paper presents results of a method of generating 3D volumetric data from fluoroscopy using image-based pose estimation and cone-beam reconstruction methods. The novelty of our approach is that it can be used with existing generic fluoroscopic systems that produce scans along a new path for each scan, and that have no hardware to control or sense the movement of the fluoroscopy system.

Because the discrete sampling of the Radon space is different for each scan of images, we are not able to take advantage of a known discretization of our Radon space, which has led us to develop a Radon plane matching score that will give the best plane match for the resampling step in Grangeat's approach. This allows any arbitrary and non-repeatable sensor path that meets Tuy's condition to be used to generate the source data for reconstructions. Because of the arbitrary discretization of the Radon space we have also developed a method to help correct for any missing Radon data. We have demonstrated the feasibility of our approach through accurate preliminary reconstructions of phantom data and a cadaver knee and have as well performed analysis of the accuracy of our pose finding method and the reconstruction.

The results from this work have the potential to provide an inexpensive and readily available 3D imaging capability that can benefit many medical applications. Advances in visualization and localization based on this method will allow minimally invasive procedures to be used more frequently, thus reducing the trauma to the patient. This 3D imaging capability can also make computer-aided procedures more accessible. It is expected that long term health care costs will be reduced because of the high efficiency of computer-aided procedures, and from the shorter hospitalization and recovery times that will be required [28].

References

1. Kall, B.K., *Comprehensive multimodality surgical planning and interactive neurosurgery*, in *Computers in Stereotactic Neruosurgery*, P.J. Kelly and B.K. Kall, Editors. 1992, Blackwell Scientific: Boston. p. 209-229.
2. Penney, G., et al., *A comparison of similarity measures for use in 2D-3D medical image registration*. IEEE Trans. on Medical Imaging, 1998. **1496**: p. 586-595.
3. Weese, J., et al., *Voxel-based 2D/3D registration of fluoroscopy images and CT scans for image-guided surgery*. IEEE Trans. Information Technology in Biomedicine, 1997. **1**(4): p. 284-293.
4. Grangeat, P., *Mathematical Framework of Cone Beam 3D Reconstruction via the First Derivative of the Radon Transform*, in *Mathematical Methods in Tomography*. 1992: Springer Verlag. p. 66.
5. Tuy, H.K., *INVERSION FORMULA FOR CONE-BEAM RECONSTRUCTION*. SIAM Journal on Applied Mathematics, 1983. **43**(3): p. 546-552.
6. Mitschke, M. and N. Navab, *Recovering the X-ray projection geometry for three-dimensional tomographic reconstruction with additional sensors: Attached camera versus external navigation system*. Medical Image Analysis, 2003. **7**: p. 65-78.
7. Horn, B.K.P., *Closed-form solution of absolute orientation using unit quaternions*. Journal Optical Soc. of America, 1987. **4**(4): p. 629-642.
8. Feldkamp, L.A., L.C. Davis, and J.W. Kress, *Practical cone-beam algorithm*. Journal of the Optical Society of America A: Optics and Image Science, 1984. **1**(6): p. 612-619.
9. Mueller, K., R. Yagel, and J.J. Wheller, *Anti-aliased three-dimensional cone-beam reconstruction of low-constrast objects with algebraic methods*. IEEE Trans. on Medical Imaging, 1999. **18**(6): p. 519-537.
10. Mueller, K., R. Yagel, and J.J. Wheller, *Fast implementations of algebraic methods for three-dimensional reconstruction from cone-beam data*. IEEE Trans. on Medical Imaging, 1999. **18**(6): p. 538-548.
11. Noo, F., M. Defrise, and R. Clack, *Direct reconstruction of cone-beam data acquired with a vertex path containing a circle*. IEEE Trans. on Image Processing, 1998. **7**(6): p. 854-867.
12. Schaller, S., T. Flohr, and P. Steffen, *Efficient Fourier method for 3-D Radon inversion in exact cone-beam CT reconstruction*. IEEE Transactions on Medical Imaging, 1998. **17**(2): p. 244-250.
13. Axelsson, C. and P.E. Danielsson, *Three-dimensional reconstruction from cone-beam data in O(N^3log N) time*. Physics in Medicine and Biology, 1994. **39**(3): p. 477.
14. Jacobson, C., *Fourier Methods in 3D-Reconstruction from Cone-Beam Data*. Linkoping Studies in Science and Technologry Dissertations, 1996. **427**.
15. Kudo, H., et al., *Performance of Quasi-Exact Cone-Beam Filtered Backprojection Algorithm for Axially Truncated Helical Data*. IEEE Transactions on Nuclear Science, 1999. **46**(3): p. 608-617.
16. Turbell, H. and D. Per-Erik, *Helical cone-beam tomography*. International Journal of Imaging Systems and Technology, 2000. **11**(1): p. 91-100.
17. Wang, G., et al., *A General Cone-Beam Reconstruction Algorithm*. IEEE Transactions on Medical Imaging, 1993. **12**(3): p. 486-496.
18. Wang, X. and R. Ning, *Cone-beam reconstruction algorithm for circle-plus-arc data-acquisition geometry*. IEEE Transactions on Medical Imaging, 1999. **18**(9): p. 815-824.

19. Noo, F., R. Clack, and M. Defrise, *Cone-beam Reconstruction from General Discrete Vertex Sets using Rdon Rebinning Algorithms.* IEEE Transactions on Nuclear Science, 1997. **44**(3): p. 1309-1316.
20. Baker, C., *Computed Tomography from Imagery Generated by Fluoroscopy along an Arbitrary Path*, in *Engineering.* 2004, Colorado School of Mines: Golden. p. 115.
21. Grimson, W.E.L., *Object recognition by Computer.* 1990, Cambridge, Massachusetts: MIT Press.
22. Haralick, R. and L. Shapiro, *Computer and Robot Vision.* 1993: Addison-Wesley Inc.
23. Kudo, H. and T. Saito, *Derivation and implementation of a cone-beam reconstruction algorithm for nonplanar orbits.* IEEE Transactions on Medical Imaging, 1994. **13**(1): p. 196-211.
24. Hsieh, J., *Reconstruction Algorithm for Single Circular Orbit Cone Beam Scans.* IEEE, 2002: p. 836-838.
25. Benac, J., *Alternating Minimization Algorithms for Metal Artifact Reduction in Transmission Tomography.*, in *Electrical Engineering.* 2002, Washington University: St. Louis, Missouri.
26. Wang, G., et al., *Iterative Deblurring for CT Metal Artifact Reduction.* IEEE Transactions on Medical Imaging, 1996. **15**(5): p. 657-664.
27. Zhao, S., et al., *X-Ray CT Metal Artifact Reduction Using Wavelets: An Application for Imaging Total Hip Prostheses.* IEEE Transactions on Medical Imaging, 2000. **19**(12).
28. Jolesz, F., Kikinis, and F. Shtern, *The Vision of Image-Guided Computer Surgery.* The High Tech Operating Room in Computer Integrated Surgery - Technology and Clinical Applications, ed. e.a. R. Taylor. 1996, Cambridge, Massachusetts: MIT Press. 717-721.

Three-Dimensional Object Reconstruction from Compton Scattered Gamma-Ray Data

Mai K. Nguyen[1], T.T. Truong[2], J.L. Delarbre[1], and N. Kitanine[2]

[1] Equipes de Traitement des Images et du Signal,
CNRS UMR 8051/E.N.S.E.A/Université de Cergy-Pontoise,
6 avenue du Ponceau, 95014 Cergy-Pontoise, France.
{nguyen,delarbre}@ensea.fr
[2] Laboratoire de Physique Théorique et Modélisation,
CNRS UMR 8089/Université de Cergy-Pontoise,
5 mail Gay Lussac, 95031 Cergy-Pontoise, France.
{tuong.truong,nikolai.kitanine}@ptm.u-cergy.fr

Abstract. A new imaging principle for object reconstruction is proposed in Single Photon Emission Computer Tomography (SPECT) which is widely used in nuclear medicine. The quality of SPECT images is largely affected by many adverse factors among which chiefly Compton scattering of gamma rays. Recently we have proposed to exploit Compton scattered radiation to generate *new data* necessary for object reconstruction, instead of discarding it as usually done. This has led us to a new underlying imaging principle based on the inversion of a generalized Radon transform. In this new three-dimensional reconstruction method both signal to noise ratio and image quality are improved. Remarkably the *complete* data, collected at various angles of scattering, can be obtained by a *motionless* data taking gamma camera. Examples of object reconstruction are presented as illustrations.

1 Introduction

In nuclear medicine, a gamma camera records images of body organs created by gamma rays emitted from a radiopharmaceutical (e.g. ^{99m}Tc) distributed unevenly inside a patient body after its ingestion. The different grey levels in the observed image, corresponding to a specific activity distribution of the radiopharmaceutical, give valuable functional information on the organ. This helps in localizing lesions, in detecting cancer metastasis at the cellular level and most importantly in achieving early accurate diagnosis.

But generally the quality of the gamma images is quite poor since it is affected by a number of degrading factors: Poisson noise of the gamma-ray emitters, absorption of the gamma rays by the biological medium, poor energy and space resolutions of the detector, low performance of the gamma "optics", measuring electronics and above all Compton scattering of the gamma photons by the electrons in the surrounding medium. This last factor causes a blurring of the image as well as a delocalization of the activity sources (see figure 1). Consequently

M. Šonka et al. (Eds.): CVAMIA-MMBIA 2004, LNCS 3117, pp. 24–34, 2004.

the detection of small structures (e.g. "cold" or "hot" nodules of the thyroid) becomes difficult. This is particularly very penalizing when one seeks to localize small spots of low activity in the midst of highly active areas (e.g. small tumor detection) in medical imaging.

Up to now efforts are generally concentrated in eliminating scattered photons. In most commonly used techniques scattered photons are separated from the non-scattered (or primary) ones. Whatever the method used, scattered photons are either eliminated from the overall counts or filtered by narrow energy windows around the photopeak energy. But is discarding Compton scattered photons *necessarily the best idea*?

A primary (direct) image of an object is obtained when gamma photons emitted from this object have gone through the medium without being deflected by Compton scattering and entered directly the collimator along the axis of the camera (see figure 1). The number of such photons is unfortunately very small compared to the total number of emitted photons in all directions by the object. This ideal image although in one-to-one correspondence with the object is quite faint and also blurred by noise, secondary scattering against the collimator walls, fluctuations of measurement electronics, etc. In currently used gamma cameras, typically 70 % to 80 % of the incident photons are discarded by the photopeak energy window. Moreover, among those retained roughly 30 % to 40 % should not have been taken because they have suffered from scattering. So this kind of separation technique leads to a net loss of photons collected and a very bad signal-to-noise ratio. This is especially unfavorable for detecting of small spots and for medical applications where both accuracy and low dose of emitted radiation are required.

Although scattered photons carry less information regarding their source than primary ones, they may turn out to be useful for improving image quality. This is particularly true for back scattered photons (i.e. photons which go back along the original path after scattering). From the camera point of view, these photons appear to come from the right location of the object. Hence accounting correctly for scattered photons may lead to an improvement of the image resolution and most likely also to a significant reduction of noise affecting the images.

In this work, instead of discarding the scattered photons it is proposed to take them into account in image processing from formation to restoration. Actually we exploit scattered photons, not only to improve the image quality, as done at first in [1], but also to propose an original new imaging principle. In fact, we establish a new integral relation between the object radioactivity density and the scattered photon flux density received on the detector. In addition we observe that Compton scattering properties allow to generate series of images at various angles of scattering (or equivalently at various scattering energies) from *single*-scattered photons. Interestingly these images can be recorded by a motionless camera. We have also shown that such sequences of *parametric* images constitute a *complete set of data* for the reconstruction of the object in three dimensions. Moreover they can be simulated within a reasonable computation time as opposed to Monte Carlo simulations [5] which require both excessive computing time and considerable memory and which must be performed anew for each patient. The proposed imaging procedure is particularly suited for the last generation of medical SPECT cameras operating in "list" mode whereby both energy and location of the detected photon are recorded simultaneously.

This paper is organized as follows. By performing a careful analysis on single Compton-scattered photons we establish first, in section 2, the so-called *image formation equation* which relates the single scattered photon flux density to the radioactive volume density of the object. This is an integral mathematical transform generalizing the Radon transform in imaging science. In section 3 we establish its invertibility, a crucial property which lends support to an analytical reconstruction method. This new imaging process presents a remarkable innovative advantage: the series of images necessary for the three-dimensional reconstruction can be obtained by a *motionless* data taking detector. This is not so in usual tomographic modalities based on primary gamma rays. We close with some examples of object reconstruction (section 4) and give some concluding remarks in the last section.

2   Image Formation by Compton-Scattered Radiation

To facilitate the reading let us introduce our notations:

$\mathbf{D}$	: detection site on detector.
$f(\mathbf{V})$	: object activity density function.
$F(u,v;z)$	: two-dimensional Fourier transform of $f(\mathbf{V})$.
$\bar{F}(u,v,w)$	: three-dimensional Fourier transform of $f(\mathbf{V})$.
$g(\mathbf{D},t)$	: photon flux density function on detector.
$G(u,v;t)$	: two dimensional Fourier transform of $g(\mathbf{D},t)$
$J_0(z)$	: Bessel function of zeroth order.
$\mathbf{M}$	: scattering site.
l	: distance detector-object.
n_e	: electron density in medium.
$P(\theta)$	: Klein-Nishina probability at angle of scattering θ.
r_e	: classical radius of the electron.
$RMSE$	: Root mean square error.
S/N	: signal-to-noise ratio.
θ	: Compton scattering angle.
$t = \tan\theta$	: tangent of the scattering angle θ.
2D/3D	: two/three-dimensional.
$\mathbf{V}$	: object emission site.
$Y(s)$	: Heaviside unit step function.

The activity volume density of the object under study $f(\mathbf{V}) = f(\xi_V, \eta_V, \zeta_V)$ represents the number of photons emitted per unit time and per unit object (or source) volume, uniformly distributed around a site $\mathbf{V}$. A primary photon

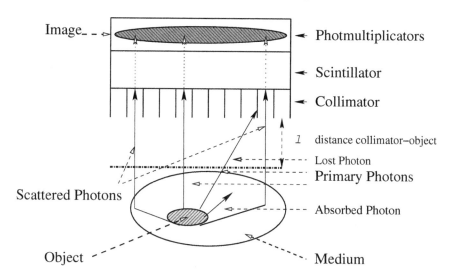

Fig. 1. Structure of a gamma camera

emitted at $\mathbf{V}$ would scatter an electron at site $\mathbf{M}$ in the surrounding medium and enter the collimated detector along its axis only if the scattering angle θ and the given photon energy E at detection site $\mathbf{D}$ fulfill the Compton relation [2]:

$$E = E_0 \frac{1}{1 + \varepsilon(1 - \cos\theta)}. \tag{1}$$

Thus the totality of such points $\mathbf{V}$ on the object lie on a circular cone of apex $\mathbf{M}$ and opening angle θ having an axis parallel to the camera collimator axis (see figure 2). So when the scattering contributions of these points are summed up, one would get at the detector site $\mathbf{D}$ a photon flux density $g(\mathbf{D}, t)$ given by an integral of $f(\mathbf{V})$ on a cone surface followed by an integral on all scattering sites of the cone axis:

$$g(\mathrm{D}, t) = K(t) \int_l^{\blacksquare} \frac{d\zeta_M}{\zeta_M^2} \int_0^{2\pi} d\phi \int_{0_+}^{\blacksquare} \frac{dr}{r} f(\xi_D + r\sin\theta\cos\phi, \eta_D + r\sin\theta\sin\phi, \zeta_M + r\cos\theta),$$

$$\tag{2}$$

where

$$K(t) = \frac{n_e}{4\pi} \frac{r_e^2}{2} P(\theta)\sin\theta \tag{3}$$

$$P(\theta) = \frac{1}{[1 + \varepsilon(1 - \cos\theta)]^2} \left[1 + \cos^2\theta + \frac{\varepsilon^2(1 - \cos\theta)^2}{1 + \varepsilon(1 - \cos\theta)} \right]. \tag{4}$$

Equation (2) describes the image formation by single scattered radiation and is called the *image formation equation*. As one add up contributions of point sources on a cone surface, one is doing a cone surface integral generalizing the integral on plane surfaces in the definition of the Radon transform. But here it is necessary to sum up also on all scattering sites on the cone axis. This is why we have called this entire procedure a Compound Conical Radon transform.

In this expression of $g(\mathbf{D}, t)$, the integral on r is formally divergent near the origin since $f(\mathbf{V})$, the activity density, is everywhere finite. A mathematical regularization procedure (e.g. cut-off) should be applied to give it a sense [3]. In numerical calculations a cut-off can be easily realized by choosing an appropriate discretization of the integration range.

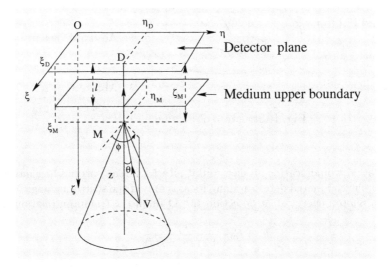

Fig. 2. Coordinate system used for calculations

Physically $g(\mathbf{D}, t)$ represents the data acquired on the detector at a given scattering angle (or outgoing photon energy). As the list mode of a gamma camera can record simultaneously at detection site the photon flux density and the deposited energy, this data is collected without having to move the detector as in a conventional tomographic procedure. Thus collecting data in this new modality can be done more rapidly at a much less equipment cost. Note that the scattering angle which labels each "image" of the object may be compared to the spatial rotation angle of a gamma camera in tomography.

3   Three-Dimensional Analytical Object Reconstruction

In this section we show that the Compound Conical Radon transform admit an inverse transform: the volume activity density $f(\mathbf{V})$ of an object may be expressed in terms of the measurements $g(\mathbf{D}, t)$, which form, *only for $0 < \theta < \pi$ a complete set of data* for the 3D reconstruction of $f(\mathbf{V})$ [3]. The mathematical proof of the inversion is given in [4].

The inversion is most conveniently done in Fourier space of the detector. Equation (2) is then converted to a zeroth order Hankel transform between $G(u, v; t)$ and the function $H(u, v; r\cos\theta)$ defined as:

$$H(u, v; r\cos\theta) = \int_l^\infty \frac{d\zeta_M}{\zeta_M^2} F(u, v, \zeta_M + r\cos\theta), \tag{5}$$

where ζ_M is the altitude of the apex of the cones.

$H(u, v; r\cos\theta)$ is a weighted average of the Fourier component $F(u, v, \zeta_M + r\cos\theta)$ of the object activity density. It has the form of a convolution product and may be reexpressed in terms of the 3D Fourier transform $\bar{F}(u, v, w)$ of $f(\mathbf{V})$ and $\mathcal{J}_l(w)$, the truncated Fourier transform of ζ^{-2} given by:

$$\mathcal{J}_l(w) = 2i\pi w\{e^{2i\pi lw}\left[Ci(2\pi l|w|) - i\,\epsilon(w)\,Si(2\pi l|w|)\right] - \frac{i}{2\pi wl}\}. \tag{6}$$

where $Ci(x)$ and $Si(x)$ are integral cosine and sine defined in [7].

Hence an inversion of the Hankel transform followed by a subsequent deconvolution yields the object activity density (in 3D Fourier space) in terms of the complete set of data $G(u, v; t)$, parameterized by the angle of scattering:

$$\bar{F}(u, v, w) = \frac{1}{\mathcal{J}_l(w)} \int_{-\infty}^\infty dz\, e^{2i\pi w(z+l)}\,(u^2 + v^2)\,z^2$$

$$2\pi \int_{0_+}^\infty t\, dt\, J_0(2\pi|z|t\sqrt{u^2 + v^2})\left[Y(z)\frac{G(u, v; t)}{K(t)} + Y(-z)\frac{G(u, v; -t)}{K(-t)}\right]. \tag{7}$$

Finally the object activity density $f(\mathbf{V})$ may be recovered by inverse 3D Fourier transform.

4   Examples of Object Reconstruction

As an illustration of the proposed inversion procedure using equation (7), we present the numerical computations for the reconstruction of two objects (a homogeneous and an inhomogeneous cubes) as examples. The working conditions are the following:

-   The gamma detector is a SPECT-camera. It is a discretized square of dimensions $N \times N$ length units with $N = 128$.
-   The pixel size is 1 mm^2.
-   The scattering medium is represented by a cube of dimensions $N \times N \times N$. To avoid boundary effects as much as possible, emission sites with non zero activity density are assumed to be localized inside a cube of size $64 \times 64 \times 64$ of same center as the larger cube with size $N = 128$.

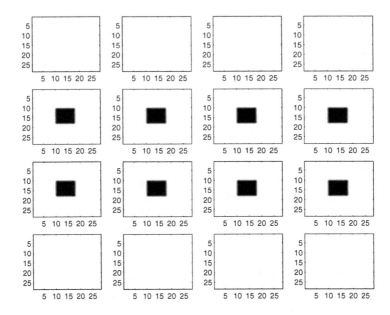

Fig. 3. Original homogeneous object (cube of 8 pixels per side) presented plane by plane

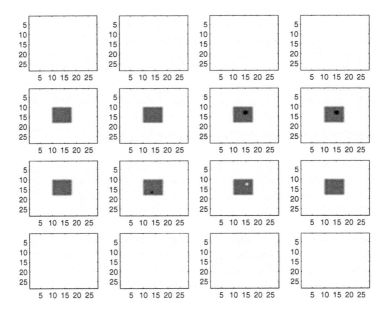

Fig. 4. Original inhomogeneous object (cube with 2 hot nodules and 1 cold nodule)

- The electron density in biological medium is $n_e = 3.510 \times 10^{23}$ electrons/cm^3.
- The radio pharmaceutical employed is Technecium 99 with an activity density 2.210 $\times 10^{-2}$ Ci/cm^3.
- The acquisition time per image is about 0.1 sec.
- The 3D original objects (cubes with 8 pixels per side) are placed at the center of the cubical scattering medium. Figures 3 and 4 represent respectively the original objects: a homogeneous cube and an inhomogeneous cube with two "hot" nodules and one "cold" nodule.
- The distance from camera to the upper face of the scattering medium cube is $l = 80$ units.
- Two series of images corresponding to the two objects at various scattering angles θ ($0.4^0 < \theta < 171.^0$) have been simulated as examples. They are presented in figures 5 and 6 respectively for homogeneous and inhomogeneous objects.

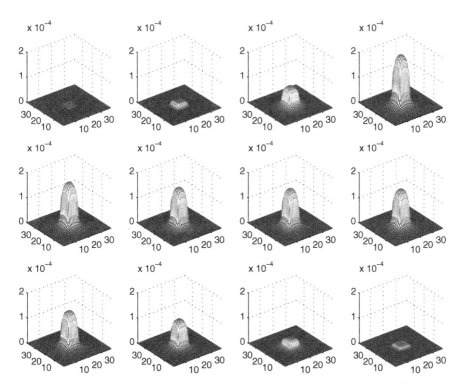

Fig. 5. Series of images of the original homogeneous cube labelled by θ ($0.4^0 < \theta < 171^0$)

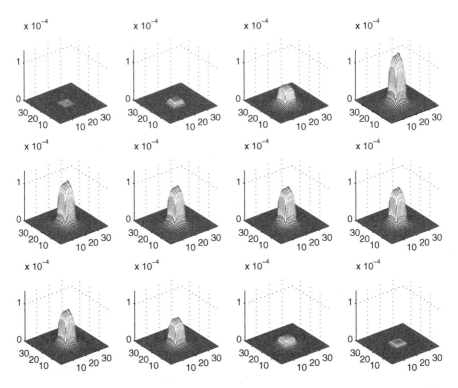

Fig. 6. Series of images of the original inhomogeneous cube labelled by θ ($0.4^0 < \theta < 171^0$)

The reconstructed objects are in figures 7 and 8. In the absence of noise, one can observe a good agreement with the original objects, in particular the small structures (nodules) are well recovered. The root mean square errors (RMSE) are respectively for the reconstructed homogeneous and inhomogeneous objects equal to $12, 4\%$ and 13%. Thus we observe a good performance of the Compound Conical Radon Transformation for modelling the new imaging process based on scattered radiation.

Since our main objective is to show how to exploit advantageously Compton scattered radiation to generate a new imaging principle we present only results on image formation as well as object reconstruction from scattered rays.

In real situations, of course, one must take into account other factors such as absorption by the medium, Poisson emission noise and the imperfections of the detector (collimator and measuring electronics).

Concerning emission noise there are well known methods to deal with it such as the method of Maximum Likelihood or the methods of wavelets. They may be used for "denoising" the measured data beforehand or jointly with the inversion process.

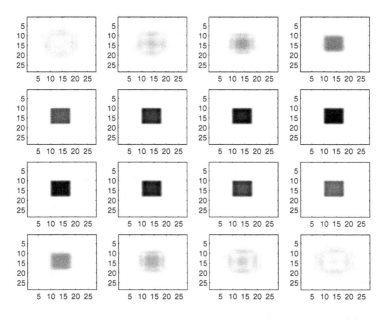

Fig. 7. Reconstructed homogeneous object (RMSE = 12.4%)

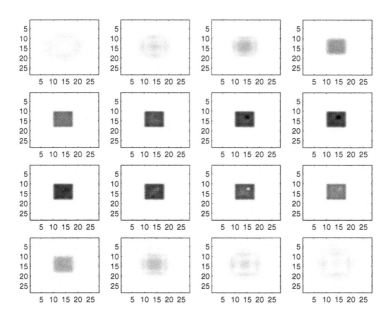

Fig. 8. Reconstructed inhomogeneous object (RMSE = 13%)

As for the imperfections of the detector, the standard way for treating this problem is to make use of a response function of the Gaussian type operating with spatial coordinates as well as with energy coordinate. These issues are discussed in detail in references [1], [6].

5   Conclusion

In this work the feasibility of 3D object reconstruction using Compton-scattered rays in gamma emission imaging is derived from a new linear integral transform directly from a Compton-scattering analysis of the image formation [3]. The proposed new imaging principle takes advantage of properties of scattered rays instead of rejecting them as usually done in most actual scatter correction methods. It improves the signal-to-noise ratio, and consequently the contrast. Moreover on one hand, in this procedure the angle of scattering appears as a free parameter and serves to label the collected data, on the other hand the multi-views of the object are obtained without the need of moving the detector. This possibility is particularly interesting in applications where the number of measurements is very limited, e.g. in non-destructive evaluation. Several perspectives of the proposed approach are possible: for example extension to transmission imaging and to prospective higher order Compton scattering imaging processes.

References

1. Nguyen Mai K., Faye C., Eglin L., Truong T. T.: Apparent Image Formation by Compton Scattered Photons in Gamma-ray Imaging. IEEE Signal Processing Letters. 8 (2001) 248-251
2. Barrett, H. H., Swindell W.: Radiological Imaging I and II. Academic Press, New York (1981)
3. Nguyen Mai K., Truong T. T.: On an Integral Transform and its Inverse in Nuclear Imaging. Inverse Problems. 18 (2002) 265-277
4. Nguyen Mai K., Truong T. T.: Exact Inversion of a Compounded Conical Radon Transform and a Novel Nuclear Imaging Principle. C.R. Acad. Sci. Paris Ser. I 335 (2002) 213-219
5. Zaidi H.: Relevance of Accurate Monte Carlo Modeling in Nuclear Medical Imaging. Med. Phys. 26 (1999) 574-608
6. Eglin L.: Imagerie Scintigraphique: Modélisation et Restauration Multiénergétiques, Ph.D Thesis, Université de Cergy-Pontoise (2002)
7. Lavoine J.: Transformation de Fourier. CNRS, Paris (1963)

Cone-Beam Image Reconstruction by Moving Frames

Xiaochun Yang[1] and Berthold K.P. Horn[2]

[1] Biovisum, Inc., Boston MA 02116, USA
xiaochun@biovisum.com
[2] MIT EECS and CSAIL, Cambridge MA 02139, USA
bkph@csail.mit.edu

A bstract. In this paper, we present a new algorithmic paradigm for cone-beam image reconstruction. The new class of algorithms, referred to as cone-beam reconstruction by moving frames, enables numerical implementation of exact cone-beam inversion using its intrinsic geometry. In particular, our algorithm allows a 3-D discrete approach to the differentiation-backprojection operator on the curved manifolds appearing in all analytical cone-beam inverse formulations. The enabling technique, called the method of moving frames, has been popular in the computer vision community for many years [3]. Although cone-beam image reconstruction has come from a different origin and has been until now developed along very different lines from computer vision algorithms, we can find analogies in their line-and-plane geometry. We demonstrate how the moving frame technique can be made into a ubiquitous and powerful computational tool for designing and implementing more robust and more accurate cone-beam reconstruction algorithms.

1 Introduction

As innovations in X-ray detector technology made it to the front lines of computerized tomography (CT) in the late 1980s, the idea of 3-D cone-beam CT triggered the dramatic onset of a new revolution in volumetric imaging. Facilitated by the slip-ring technology and detector advances, the cone-beam system is able to use multi-row area detectors rather than detectors aligned on a single linear array in the older, slice-at-a-time 2-D machines, significantly increasing the information throughput and leading to faster, more nearly isotropic data collection. As a result, the cone-beam CT has a great potential to dramatically improve the speed and accuracy of CT imaging while lowering the hazardous radiation exposure. Accurate imaging ensures better diagnosis; high throughput leads to more efficient use of CT machines and hence lowers scan costs. As the CT industry works towards achieving its next milestone, cone-beam CT is now at the center of attention and the subject of intensive study.

A typical cone-beam imaging system generates a set of cone-beam projections from a radiation source to an area detector. Each cone-beam projection image provides the integral of the object density, denoted by f, along the straight lines

M. Šonka et al. (Eds.): CVAMIA-MMBIA 2004, LNCS 3117, pp. 35–47, 2004.

from the source to points on the detector surface. As the source-detector pair rotates and translates around the object, a collection of line integrals with the source point moving along a curve are obtained. The curve followed by the source relative to the scanned object is called the source orbit or the scan path. The task of cone-beam reconstruction is to invert the line integrals obtained from a series cone-beam projections and recover the density distribution f.

Approaches to cone-beam reconstruction can be categorized as either approximate or exact. Approximate reconstruction methods, such as Feldkamp's algorithm [4], are usually extensions of 2-D fan-beam or parallel-beam reconstruction methods. They are simpler to implement, but have serious limitation in reconstruction accuracy. Exact reconstruction methods are instead based on exact cone-beam inversion formula. Before 1991, three inversion formulae had been derived by Tuy [15], Smith [14] and Grangeat [5]. For a decade, engineers and researchers worked to reduce the above mathematical formulism into practical implementation but encountered many difficulties. The most complex and expensive computational step, the differentiation-backprojection operation, acts on curved surface in a fashion that was not completely understood.

In 2001, cone-beam inversion formulae derived by Katsevich [9] and Yang [16] considerably simplified cone-beam reconstruction. Katsevich gave the first helical cone-beam inversion formula as an iterated 2-D integral which suggests the minimum use of data. With this formulation, however, some integral parameter has implicit dependency on the scanning geometry and a set of nonlinear equations need to be solved. Yang instead reformulated the 3-D Radon inverse for general trajectories. The result is a reduction of the 3-D backprojection into a series of 2-D backprojections – it is the first explicit cone-beam inverse. More recently, Katsevich extended his original formulation to general trajectories [10].

Underlying Katsevich and Yang's cone-beam inverse reconstructions are two intrinsic vector spaces: one is the projective space of lines or planes passing through a point, called a fiber; the other is the fiber bundle constituting all the fibers emitting from a 3-D curve. These vector spaces are curved, differentiable manifolds. Inverse reconstruction integrates and differentiates functions defined on said vector spaces. Currently, there is no general theory for numerical calculus on curved manifold. In this paper, we explore the mechanism for integration and differentiation on the manifolds of lines and planes described above and provide a new computational framework for cone-beam image reconstruction.

The remainder of this paper is organized as follows. Section 2 studies the topological structure and varied coordinate representations of the vector spaces arising in cone-beam image reconstruction. Section 3 presents a novel reconstruction algorithm using the method of moving frames. In particular, implementation of the exterior derivative in Katsevich and Yang's formulae is discussed in detail.

2   Integral Geometry in Cone-Beam CT

There are three distinguished spaces when we process cone-beam image data. First is the object space in which the 3-D density function f is to be evaluated. The object space is an Euclidean space, denoted by $\mathbf{E}^3$.

Next is the source orbit, assumed to be a smooth and differentiable 3-D curve, is a 1-D manifold, denoted by $\mathbf{C}^1$. Assume that the source orbit is parameterized in the Euclidean coordinate by $\mathbf{\Phi}(\lambda) = (\phi_1(\lambda), \phi_2(\lambda), \phi_3(\lambda))$ with $\lambda \in \Lambda$. Given λ, one can determine not only the position of the source in the Euclidean space $\mathbf{E}^3$, but also the local properties, such as the tangent and curvature, of the manifold $\mathbf{C}^1$ at $\mathbf{\Phi}(\lambda)$. In this sense, λ also acts as a local coordinate of the source orbit when viewed on the 1-parameter manifold $\mathbf{C}^1$.

A third space is the space constituting all the projective lines emitting from a 3-D curve, denoted by $\mathbf{T} := \sum_{\lambda \in \Lambda} \mathbf{P}_\lambda^2$ where $\mathbf{P}_\lambda^2$ stands for the 2-D projective line-space projected from a single source point $\mathbf{\Phi}(\lambda)$. According to the line-and-plane duality in 2-D projective space [12], the projective space of lines, $\mathbf{P}_\lambda^2$, is interchangeable with the projective space of planes with the same projection center. Denote the projective space of planes with center at $\mathbf{\Phi}(\lambda)$ by $\widehat{\mathbf{P}}_\lambda^2$. Denote the total space of projective planes intersecting $\mathbf{C}^1$ by $\widehat{\mathbf{T}} := \sum_{\lambda \in \Lambda} \widehat{\mathbf{P}}_\lambda^2$.

Note that $\mathbf{E}^3$, $\mathbf{C}^1$, $\mathbf{P}_\lambda^2$ and $\widehat{\mathbf{P}}_\lambda^2$ are all embedded in the Euclidean 3-space. Points in these spaces and their geometric relationship can be described in the language of coordinates.

2.1   Euclidean Moving Frames

The object space $\mathbf{E}^3$ can be represented in the Cartesian coordinate with an origin denoted by O. This coordinate system will be referred to as the global Euclidean frame – it is fixed with respect to the object.

As the radiation source moves around the object, the orientation of the detector surface changes accordingly. In practice, the detector surface may be curved. For convenience of exposition, we replace the detector array with an image plane that closely approximates the detector surface. A coordinate transformation is needed to map every point on the real detector surface onto the image plane.

Moving Frames and Local Coordinates. Assume that the source-to-detector distance is fixed. Also assume that the two perpendicular axes on the image plane evolve smoothly during the source-detector motion. A local Euclidean coordinate can be conveniently set up for each projection with the origin at the source point, two axes aligned with the axes of the image plane, and the third axis aligned with the perpendicular line from the source to the image plane. Let O_I be the intersecting point where the perpendicular line from the source to the image plane meets the image plane.

Denote by $\big\{ \mathbf{\Phi}(\lambda) : \boldsymbol{u}(\lambda), \boldsymbol{v}(\lambda), \boldsymbol{w}(\lambda) \big\}$ $(\lambda \in \Lambda)$ the series of local Euclidean frames attached to the source orbit where λ is considered as an index and $\boldsymbol{u}(\lambda)$,

$v(\lambda)$, $w(\lambda)$ are the three orthonormal basis vectors expressed in the global Euclidean coordinate. As λ ranges in Λ, the smooth evolution of u and v ensures the smooth evolution of w, since w can be computed from $u \times v$.

The sequence of orthonormal local coordinates described above are called the Euclidean moving frames. Construction of the moving frame bases generates a set of 3-by-3 orthonormal matrices, *i.e.*, $\mathbf{R}(\lambda) = \big(u(\lambda), v(\lambda), w(\lambda)\big)$ $(\lambda \in \Lambda)$, which are associated with a set of consecutive rotations. Given a point $x \in \mathbf{E}^3$, assume x' is the corresponding local coordinate in the Euclidean frame indexed by λ. The coordinate transform from x' to x and its inverse are given by

$$x = \mathrm{R}\,(\lambda)x^\square + \square\,(\lambda), \tag{1}$$

$$x^\square = \mathrm{R}\,(\lambda)^{\square\,1}\Big(x - \square\,(\lambda)\Big). \tag{2}$$

It is clear that every point in the object space has simultaneously a global Euclidean coordinate as well as a series of local Euclidean coordinates.

Construction of Moving Frames. Construction of the moving frames is fairly general, flexible and can be applied to a wide selections of source orbits and detector orientations. However, in practice, detector orientations are constrained in the sense that its movement needs to be synchronized with the source and the synchronized motion is under the control of rigid translation and rotation.

To produce a smooth evolution of the moving frame bases as the source-detector moves around the object, we can make use of the source orbit equation and express the local Euclidean bases in terms of the vector components of $\mathbf{\Phi}(\lambda)$. For example, if the rotational axis of the source orbit is fixed, as in traditional CT where source and detector are mounted on a cylindrical gantry that rotates around a fixed axis, we can align one of the basis vectors, say v, to the rotational axis (shown as the vertical axis in Fig. 1) and let the other two axes synchronize with the rotation of the source when viewed from a plane perpendicular to the rotational axis. This yields the following orthonormal basis:

$$\begin{cases} u(\lambda) = \dfrac{1}{\sqrt{\phi_1^2(\lambda) + \phi_2^2(\lambda)}}\Big(-\phi_2(\lambda), \phi_1(\lambda), 0\Big) \\[2mm] v(\lambda) = \Big(0,\, 0,\, 1\Big) \\[2mm] w(\lambda) = \dfrac{1}{\sqrt{\phi_1^2(\lambda) + \phi_2^2(\lambda)}}\Big(\phi_1(\lambda), \phi_2(\lambda), 0\Big) \end{cases} \tag{3}$$

Alternatively, if spherical symmetry characterizes the scanning geometry, such as in C-arm CT where the radiation source is confined on a spherical surface, then one of the moving frame basis vectors, say w, can be aligned with the position vector, $\mathbf{\Phi}(\lambda)$, and the other two axes are made dependent on both the position vector and the local tangent of the source orbit (see Fig. 2), *i.e.*,

$$\begin{cases} w(\lambda) = \dfrac{\square\,(\lambda)}{|\square\,(\lambda)|} \\[2mm] v(\lambda) = \dfrac{w \times \square^\square(\lambda)}{|w \times \square^\square(\lambda)|} \\[2mm] u(\lambda) = v \times w \end{cases} \tag{4}$$

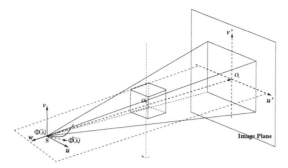

Fig. 1. *Moving frame (a).*

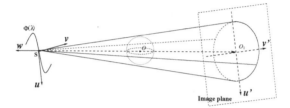

Fig. 2. *Moving frame (b).*

In both cases, cone-beam system design includes an alignment step to align the axes of the image plane with the designated axes.

Coordinate of Lines and Planes. In a local projection frame, we consider only the lines and planes passing through the source point $\Phi(\lambda)$ and the support of f. In the case of lines, the global Euclidean coordinates of the intersecting points between the lines and the image plane can be obtained from their local Euclidean coordinates via Eqn. (1). Consequently, the directions of the lines, denoted by $\alpha \in \mathbf{S}^2$, can also be expressed in the global Euclidean coordinates. We refer to (λ, α) as the projective coordinate of lines emitting from $\Phi(\lambda)$.

In the case of the planes, we note that a plane can be identified by two distinctive lines on that plane. Assume P_1 and P_2 are two points on the intersecting line between a given plane and the image plane. The projective coordinates of two lines connecting the source to P_1 and P_2 can be calculated as previously described. Denote the projective coordinates of the said lines by (λ, α_1) and (λ, α_2) respectively. The unit normal of the given plane, denoted by β, is perpendicular to both α_1 and α_2. Therefore, $\beta = \alpha_1 \times \alpha_2 / |\alpha_1 \times \alpha_2|$. The radial distance of the plane, denoted by l, can be evaluated as $l = \Phi(\lambda) \cdot \beta$. The coordinate (l, β) determines the position of a plane seen in the global Euclidean coordinate.

2.2   Integral Transforms on Projective Spaces

Each cone-beam projection consists of rays emitting from a source point. The pencil of rays forms a 2-D projective space. Two integral transforms can be defined on the projective 2-space of lines and its dual, namely the projective 2-space of planes, respectively. Inverting integral transforms on various geometric spaces is the main subject of study in integral geometry.

Divergent Ray Transform. For a fixed source position, say $\mathbf{\Phi}(\lambda)$, cone-beam projection maps points in $\mathbf{E}^3$ onto $\mathbf{P}^2_\lambda$ with the equivalence relation:

$$\mathbf{\Phi}(\lambda) + \boldsymbol{\alpha} \sim \mathbf{\Phi}(\lambda) + r\boldsymbol{\alpha} \quad \text{for } \boldsymbol{\alpha} \in \mathbf{S}^2,\ r \in \mathbb{R} \text{ and } r \neq 0. \tag{5}$$

The pair $(\lambda, \boldsymbol{\alpha})$ identifies a line in the Euclidean 3-space.

Assume that the density function f has a finite support, $\Omega \in \mathbb{R}^3$, and the source orbit $\mathbf{\Phi}(\lambda)$ is outside the convex hull of Ω. The *divergent ray transform* of f is by definition the integrals of f along the half-lines starting at $\mathbf{\Phi}(\lambda)$ which is a measurement available from the cone-beam image:

$$Df(\lambda, r\boldsymbol{\alpha}) := \int_0^{+\infty} f(\mathbf{\Phi}(\lambda) + t\boldsymbol{\alpha})\, dt, \quad \boldsymbol{\alpha} \in \mathbf{S}^2,\ r \in \mathbb{R}. \tag{6}$$

Cone-beam reconstruction is to recover f from Df.

Radon Transform. In the 2-D projective space of lines, every two distinctive lines determine a unique plane; every two distinctive planes determine a unique line. Thus, lines and planes are *dual* in the 2-D projective space. This duality relation is important in that it makes the integral transform along the lines interchangeable with some integral transform over the planes.

We can write a plane in $\mathbb{R}^3$ as

$$\mathbf{L}_{l,\boldsymbol{\beta}} := \left\{ \mathbf{x} \in \mathbb{R}^3 \mid \mathbf{x} \cdot \boldsymbol{\beta} = l,\ l \geq 0,\ \boldsymbol{\beta} \in \mathbf{S}^2 \right\}, \tag{7}$$

where $\boldsymbol{\beta}$ is the unit normal of the plane and l is the perpendicular distance of the plane from the origin. The space of all the planes in $\mathbb{R}^3$ is called the Radon space. Radon space is a projective 3-space, denoted by $\mathbf{P}^3$.

The *Radon transform* of f is defined as the set of integrals of f over all the planes in $\mathbb{R}^3$ which can be expressed as a function of two parameters (l and $\boldsymbol{\beta}$):

$$Rf(l, \boldsymbol{\beta}) := \int_{\mathbf{x} \in \left\{ \mathbf{x} \mid \mathbf{x} \cdot \boldsymbol{\beta} = l \right\}} f(\mathbf{x})\, d\mathbf{x}. \tag{8}$$

If Rf is known on all the planes passing by the support of f, then f can be reconstructed from the 3-D Radon inverse [6,13]:

$$f(\mathbf{x}) = -\frac{1}{8\pi^2} \int_{\mathbf{S}^2} \left. \frac{\partial^2 Rf(l, \boldsymbol{\beta})}{\partial l^2} \right|_{l = \mathbf{x} \cdot \boldsymbol{\beta}} d\boldsymbol{\beta}. \tag{9}$$

However, in cone-beam projection, only the divergent ray transform is available, not the Radon transform. In order to use Eqn. (9) to recover the function value at point x, the second-order radial derivative of the Radon transform needs to be obtained on all or almost all planes through x. Grangeat's Fundamental Relation [5] provides an important link from the divergent ray transform to the Radon transform. According to the Fundamental Relation, the first-order radial derivative of the Radon transform on a plane can be calculated from the weighted integral of the divergent ray transform along projective lines on the given plane as well as its adjacent planes within the same projection. The second radial derivative of the Radon transform can then be evaluated by differentiating the first radial derivative of the Radon transform over parallel planes.

Cone-beam inversion formulae earlier derived by Tuy [15] and Smith [14] have also been linked to Eqn. (9) [2,16]. It turns out that exact cone-beam reconstruction based on Eqn. (9) requires source orbit to meet the data sufficiency condition, *i.e.*, all or almost all planes passing by the support of f intersect with the source orbit [5,14,15,16].

Transform Spaces T and $\widehat{\mathbf{T}}$ as Fiber Bundles. From each point lying on the source orbit grows a 2-D projective space of lines, $\mathbf{P}_\lambda^2$, as well as a 2-D projective space of planes, $\widehat{\mathbf{P}}_\lambda^2$. The transform spaces $\mathbf{T}$ and $\widehat{\mathbf{T}}$ are unions of all $\mathbf{P}_\lambda^2$ and all $\widehat{\mathbf{P}}_\lambda^2$ projected from the source orbit respectively. The geometric structure of $\mathbf{T}$ and $\widehat{\mathbf{T}}$ is called a *fiber bundle* in differential geometry [11]. The source curve $\mathbf{C}^1$ is called the base space and $\mathbf{P}_\lambda^2$ or $\widehat{\mathbf{P}}_\lambda^2$ are the fibers. Points in $\mathbf{T}$ and $\widehat{\mathbf{T}}$ correspond to lines and planes when viewed in the Euclidean space.

Recall from our earlier discussion, lines and planes emitting from $\mathbf{\Phi}(\lambda)$ ($\lambda \in \Lambda$) can be identified by the direction of the lines, $\boldsymbol{\alpha} \in \mathbf{S}^2$, and the normal direction of the planes, $\boldsymbol{\beta} \in \mathbf{S}^2$, respectively. Assume $(\mathbf{S}^2; \ \alpha^i)$ is a basis for the fiber of lines, and $(\mathbf{S}^2; \ \beta^i)$ is a basis for the fiber of planes. Then, the Cartesian product of the bases from the base space and the fiber space, namely $(\Lambda; \ \lambda) \times (\mathbf{S}^2; \ \alpha^i)$ and $(\Lambda; \ \lambda) \times (\mathbf{S}^2; \ \beta^i)$, are local bases for $\mathbf{T}$ and $\widehat{\mathbf{T}}$.

Fiber bundle captures the underlying cone-beam scanning geometry concisely and precisely. Moreover, if the source orbit satisfies the data sufficiency condition, then $\widehat{\mathbf{T}} = \sum_{\lambda \in \Lambda} \widehat{\mathbf{P}}_\lambda^2$ is a covering space of the Radon space, $\mathbf{P}^3$ (reduced to contain only the planes intersecting the support of f). The *inclusion map* from each fiber $\widehat{\mathbf{P}}_\lambda^2$ to $\mathbf{P}^3$ is given by $\Pi_\lambda : \boldsymbol{\beta} \longrightarrow (l, \boldsymbol{\beta})$ with $l = \mathbf{\Phi}(\lambda) \cdot \boldsymbol{\beta}$. Note that the same map transforms the local coordinate in $\widehat{\mathbf{T}}$ to the global coordinate in $\mathbf{P}^3$. However, the above mapping is not bijective, because some planes in the Radon space are repeated multiple times in $\widehat{\mathbf{T}}$. Denote by $M(\lambda, \boldsymbol{\beta})$ the number of times that the 2-D plane $\boldsymbol{L}_{\mathbf{\Phi}(\lambda) \cdot \boldsymbol{\beta}, \boldsymbol{\beta}}$ intersects with the source orbit. Then the same function $M(\lambda, \boldsymbol{\beta})$ depicts the number of times that the plane $\boldsymbol{L}_{\mathbf{\Phi}(\lambda) \cdot \boldsymbol{\beta}, \boldsymbol{\beta}}$ is repeated in $\widehat{\mathbf{T}}$. This $M(\lambda, \boldsymbol{\beta})$ is called the *redundancy function*.

Differential Structure and Connection. Both the base space and the fiber space are differentiable manifolds. Therefore, the fiber bundles $\mathbf{T}$ and $\widehat{\mathbf{T}}$ are differentiable. The coordinate from the base space, λ, serves as a *connection* in the fiber bundles in the following sense: as λ smoothly varying in a neighborhood, the disjoint fibers get connected and the result is a smooth manifold. For fixed $\alpha \in \mathbf{S}^2$ and $\beta \in \mathbf{S}^2$, displacement in λ indicates parallel translation of a line (with direction α) or a plane (with normal direction β).

In $\widehat{\mathbf{T}}$, the first local coordinate λ relates to the first global coordinate l by the differentiable map $l = \mathbf{\Phi}(\lambda) \cdot \beta$. Hence, $\partial/\partial l = (1/\mathbf{\Phi}'(\lambda) \cdot \beta)\partial/\partial\lambda$. We can visualize the differentiation process over parallel planes by taking an infinitesimal step along the tangent direction of the source orbit – almost always we can find a plane parallel to the one we start from, except if the initial plane contains the tangent line. We call these exceptional planes the *defects* in the structure of the fiber bundle $\widehat{\mathbf{T}}$. Although differentiation over parallel planes breaks at the defective planes in $\widehat{\mathbf{T}}$, it can still be carried out in the Radon space, $\mathbf{P}^3$, with respect to the radial distance l. In the Radon space, the global coordinate l is a more stable benchmark for parallelism in planes than the local coordinate λ.

3 Exact Cone-Beam Reconstruction

Early algorithm development for exact cone-beam reconstructions is heavily based on inversion formulae derived by Tuy [15], Smith [14] and Grangeat [5]. Although varying in computational cost and stability, they share an important structural similarity in that they all inherited the differentiation-backprojection operator from the 3-D Radon inverse. They differ in the underlying intermediate functions linking the divergent ray transform to the Radon transform [2,16].

For nearly ten years, exact and efficient implementation of the three inversion formulae has encountered difficulties. This is mainly because the 3-D differentiation-backprojection operation has implicit dependency on the scanning parameter, λ, and discretization can not be easily introduced.

3.1 Inversion Formulae by Yang and Katsevich

Motivated by the similarity displayed in Tuy, Smith and Grangeat's inverse formulations, Yang investigated the topological structure of the Radon space, which is the transform space, and discovered two prevailing geometric constraints underlying cone-beam reconstruction [16]:

- First, within each cone-beam projection, all the planes passing through a particular projection line have normals perpendicular to that line; therefore, backprojection orientation is confined to a unit circle. The reduction of backprojection from 3-space to 2-space simplifies the reconstruction.
- Second, as the source moves along the orbit, backprojection orientation on the unit circle undergoes a rigid rotation. As long as the source orbit satisfies the data sufficiency condition, one can decompose 3-D backprojection into a series of 2-D backprojections in accordance with the scanning geometry.

This leads to the following decomposed 3-D Radon inverse:

$$f(\boldsymbol{x}) = -\frac{1}{8\pi^2} \int_\Lambda \left\{ \int_{\boldsymbol{\beta}\Box \left\{ \boldsymbol{x}\Box \ \Phi(\lambda) \right\}^\perp, \ \boldsymbol{\beta}\Box \mathrm{S}^2} R^\Box f(\Box(\lambda)\cdot\boldsymbol{\beta},\boldsymbol{\beta}) \frac{|\Box^\Box(\lambda)\cdot\boldsymbol{\beta}|}{M(\lambda,\boldsymbol{\beta})} \, d\boldsymbol{\beta} \right\} \, d\lambda, \quad (10)$$

in which, $\left\{ \boldsymbol{x}-\Phi(\lambda) \right\}^\perp$ denotes the plane perpendicular to the projection ray $\boldsymbol{x}-\Phi(\lambda)$ and through the origin. The outer integral integrates over the source orbit; the inner integral is a 2-D backprojection – with each cone-beam projection, there is only one 2-D backprojection that needs to be performed along each projection ray and the resulting value is assigned to all the points lying on that ray with the same weight. Coupled with Grangeat's Fundamental Relation, Eqn. (10) provides an explicit solution for cone-beam reconstruction.

More recently, Katsevich derived a new general cone-beam inversion formula which is extended from his inverse formulation for truncated helical cone-beam problem [9]. The new inverse is an iterated double integral [10]:

$$f(\boldsymbol{x}) = -\frac{1}{8\pi^2} \int_\Lambda \left\{ \frac{\sum c_m(\lambda,\boldsymbol{x})}{|\boldsymbol{x}-\Box(\lambda)|} \int_0^{2\pi} \frac{\partial}{\partial\lambda^\Box} Df(\Box(\lambda^\Box),\cos\gamma\boldsymbol{\alpha}(\lambda,\boldsymbol{x}) + \right.$$

$$\left. \sin\gamma\boldsymbol{\alpha}^\Box(\lambda,\boldsymbol{x},\theta_m)) \mid_{\lambda'=\lambda} \frac{d\gamma}{\sin\gamma} \right\} \, d\lambda. \quad (11)$$

Again, the outer integral integrates along the source orbit. The inner integral, however, is a 1-D integral that integrates over a plane determined by λ, $\boldsymbol{x}$, θ_m and the integral parameter γ denotes the polar angle on this plane. Furthermore, $\boldsymbol{\alpha}$ denotes the unit vector in the direction of the projection ray, $\boldsymbol{x}-\Phi(\lambda)$, and $\boldsymbol{\alpha}^\perp$ is a unit vector perpendicular to $\boldsymbol{\alpha}$; the polar angle in the plane perpendicular to $\boldsymbol{\alpha}$ and through the origin is θ. At θ_m ($m = 1, 2, ...$), $\boldsymbol{\alpha}$ and $\boldsymbol{\alpha}^\perp$ are both lying on the integration plane which is a critical plane in the sense that it produces a jump in $c(\lambda,\boldsymbol{x})$, a weight function related to the number of intersections of a plane passing through $\boldsymbol{x}$ and $\Phi(\lambda)$ with the source orbit. Note, the jumps in $c(\lambda,\boldsymbol{x})$ occur only at finite number of θ_m's. To find these θ_m's and the corresponding critical planes, a set of nonlinear equations need to be solved. The critical plane contains either a tangent of $\Phi(\lambda)$ or an end point of $\Phi(\lambda)$. Interestingly, a large number of the integration planes thus selected correspond to the defective structure on the fiber bundle $\widehat{\mathbf{T}}$. This connection can be further addressed. See [10] for more detailed explanation of the inversion formula.

To carry out numerical implementation of Eqn. (10)-(11), it is important that the discretization step preserves the geometric relationship among the points, lines and planes hidden in the formulae. Fiber bundle geometry provides an ideal setting for such a discretization: discretizing the outer integral corresponds to discretizing the source orbit, the base space; discretizing the inner integral corresponds to discretizing the 2-D projective spaces of planes (Eqn. (10)) and lines (Eqn. (11)) which are the fibers. The second radial derivative in $R''f$ (Eqn. (10)) and the derivative of Df with respect to λ (Eqn. (11)), on the other hand, are performed over parallel planes and lines across projections. It is clear that appropriate coordinates are needed in each space encountered in order to facilitate the discretization.

3.2   A Discrete Approach: Reconstruction by Moving Frames

Yang and Katsevich's formulae share a common three-step procedure which is carried out repeatedly for a sequence of cone-beam projections. The three steps are: integration on the fiber space – it corresponds to the inner integral; differentiation across neighboring projections, *i.e.*, over parallel planes (Eqn. (10)) or parallel lines (Eqn. (11)); backprojection assigning results from the first two steps to points along each projection ray – it is also performed in the fiber space. There are extra steps in each formula need to be performed, such as evaluation of $R'f$ from Df via Fundamental Relation (for Eqn. (10)), and finding the critical planes by solving a set of nonlinear equations (for Eqn. (11)), etc. To save space, however, we will focus our discussion on the three-step process.

Consider the orthonormal moving frames $\left\{ \boldsymbol{\Phi}(\lambda); \boldsymbol{u}(\lambda), \boldsymbol{v}(\lambda), \boldsymbol{w}(\lambda) \right\}$ $(\lambda \in \Lambda)$ with the origin attached to the source orbit and the basis vectors determined by the local properties of $\boldsymbol{\Phi}(\lambda)$ (as discussed in Section 2.1). For some fixed λ, the local projective coordinates of lines and planes passing by $\boldsymbol{\Phi}(\lambda)$ can be obtained from the local Euclidean coordinates of points on the image plane. Thus, integration and differentiation on a fiber space present little challenge other than some irregularities in sampling. However, in order to perform differentiation over parallel lines or planes across projections, parallel lines or planes from neighboring projections need to be located. A coordinate that can flatly connect the set of parallel lines or planes, and can be transformed to and from the moving frame coordinates, is therefore needed. Such coordinate is identified in section 2.2 as the scan path parameter, λ, for lines and the radial distance, l, for planes. Displacement in λ or l indicates parallel translation if the direction of the line or the normal direction of the plane remains fixed. Consequently, differentiation can take place on the line bundle or the plane bundle which are curved manifolds.

Note that the pencil of lines and the pencil of planes growing out of a source point each forms a closed manifold. Each fiber space can be visualized by a unit sphere centered at the source position (see Fig. 3). A point on the sphere represents either a line or a plane passing through the source: the direction of the line or the normal of the plane coincides with the source-to-point line. In addition, for any two different source points, their corresponding fibers are disjoint. As λ smoothly varying along the source orbit, the disjoint fibers become connected to form a smooth and differentiable manifold. Now in the discrete approach, lines and planes from neighboring projections lie outside the closed fiber space of each other. Cross-projection differentiations is therefore an exterior differentiation. Differentiation inside the closed fiber space, for example, along the geodesics ζ and η (see Fig. 4), will *not* produce a *valid* exterior derivative.

To develop a discrete implementation of the exterior differentiation, parallel lines or planes from neighboring projections need to be aligned. This task is simpler in the case of lines, since two parallel lines have the same direction, *e.g.*, $\boldsymbol{\alpha}$, in the global Euclidean space, the rotating matrices representing the moving frames act on $\boldsymbol{\alpha}$ and generate orientations of the lines in the local frames. Thus, the intersections of the parallel lines with the corresponding image planes can be matched. To perform the geometric alignment for planes, we consider two

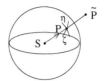

Fig. 3. *Fibers and connection.*   **Fig. 4.** *Exterior differentiation.*

consecutive projections and construct a set of planes in the second projection frame parallel to the set of planes in the first projection frame as follows.

Assume $(l_1, \boldsymbol{\beta})$ is the global coordinate of a plane from the first projection, with $l_1 = \boldsymbol{\Phi}(\lambda_1) \cdot \boldsymbol{\beta}$. In the second projection, the global coordinate of the plane passing through the source and parallel to $\boldsymbol{L}_{l_1, \boldsymbol{\beta}}$ is $(l_2, \boldsymbol{\beta})$ with $l_2 = \boldsymbol{\Phi}(\lambda_2) \cdot \boldsymbol{\beta}$. Denote by R the distance of the source from the rotational axis and D the distance of the source from the detector. Denote by (s, ϕ) the polar coordinate of the intersecting line between $\boldsymbol{L}_{l_2, \boldsymbol{\beta}}$ and the image plane (Fig.5). Let α be the angle between $\boldsymbol{L}_{l_2, \boldsymbol{\beta}}$ and the perpendicular from the source to the image plane. With the moving frames exemplified by Eqn. (4), the polar coordinate of the intersecting line between plane $\boldsymbol{L}_{l_2, \boldsymbol{\beta}}$ and the image plane can be expressed as

$$
\begin{cases}
s = D \dfrac{l_2}{\sqrt{R^2 - l_2^2}} \\
\phi = \arctan(\dfrac{\boldsymbol{\beta} \cdot \boldsymbol{v}}{\boldsymbol{\beta} \cdot \boldsymbol{u}})
\end{cases} ,
\tag{12}
$$

in which s is obtained by eliminating α from $\sin \alpha = l_2/R$ and $\tan \alpha = s/D$.

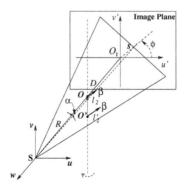

Fig. 5. *The second parallel plane intersecting the second image plane.*

With the moving frames exemplified by Eqn. (3), the perpendicular from the source to the image plane may not go through the origin. Instead, it meets the rotational axis at O' (see Fig. 5). In this case, the radial distance of the plane, l_2, in Eqn. (12) shall be offset by $OO' \cdot \boldsymbol{\beta}$.

It is clear that the moving frames provide a perfect vehicle for accurate alignment of parallel lines and planes. As a result, robust evaluation of the exterior derivatives is made possible.

The method of moving frames is one giant pillar among several in Cartan's geometry [1] which holds a prominent position in modern differential geometry. The first known application of moving frame technique to computerized tomography appeared in [7,8] for 2-D fan-beam reconstruction. In the field of computer vision, the method of moving frames has been used to treat differential invariance of curves and other geometric invariance in a multi-view geometric setting similar to the one seen in cone-beam CT [3].

4   Conclusions

In this paper, the intrinsic geometry underlying analytical cone-beam inverse is revealed, as well as the associated coordinate systems and coordinate transforms. We have shown that the method of moving frames allows exact cone-beam inversion formula to be discretized on the intrinsic cone-beam geometry; thus, sampling and interpolation errors can be minimized. In addition, the moving frame technique makes reconstruction applicable to a wide selection of source orbits and detector orientations.

References

1. É. Cartan "La Méthode du Repère Mobile, la Théorie des Groupes Continus et les Espaces Généralisés." *Exposés de Géométrie No. 5*, Hermann, Paris, 1935
2. R. Clack and M. Defrise "Cone-beam Reconstruction by the use of Radon Transform Intermediate Functions. " *J. of Opt. Soc. Am. A.*, Vol. 11, No. 2, 1994, pp. 580–585
3. O. Faugeras "Cartan's Moving Frame Method and its Application to the Geometry and Evolution of Curves in the Euclidean, Affine and Projective Planes." *Applications of Invariance in Computer Vision, Second Joint European - US Workshop*, Ponta Delgada, Azores, Portugal, J. L. Mundy, A. Zisserman, D. A. Forsyth (Eds.), October 9–14, 1993, pp. 11–46,
4. L.A. Feldkamp, L.C. David and J.W. Kress "Practical Cone-beam Algorithm." *J. Opt. Soc. Am. A.*, Vol. 1, No. 6, 1984, pp. 612–619
5. P. Grangeat "Mathematical Framework of Cone Beam 3-D Reconstruction via the First Derivative of the Radon Transform." *Mathematical methods in tomography, Lecture notes in mathematics 1497*, 1991. pp. 66–97
6. S. Helgason *The Radon Transform*, 2nd Edition, Birkhäuser, 1999
7. B.K.P. Horn "Density Reconstruction using Arbitrary Ray Sampling Schemes." *Proceedings of the IEEE*, Vol. 66, No. 5, May 1978, pp. 551–562.
8. B.K.P. Horn "Fan-beam Reconstruction Methods." *Proceedings of the IEEE*, Vol. 67, No. 12, December 1979, pp. 1616–1623.
9. A. Katsevich "Theoretically exact FBP-type Inversion Algorithm for Spiral CT." *SIAM J. of App. Math.*, Vol. 62, 2002, pp. 2012–2026

10. A. Katsevich "A General Scheme for Constructing Inversion Algorithms for Cone Beam CT." *Int. J. of Math. and Math. Sci.*, 2003:21, pp. 1305–1321
11. S. Kobayashi and K. Nomizu *Foundations of Differential Geometry*, John Wiley & Sons Inc., 1963
12. *Geometric Invariance in Computer Vision*, MIT Press, J. L. Mundy and A. Zisserman (Eds.), 1992
13. F. Natterer *The Mathematics of Computerized Tomography*, John Wiley & Sons Ltd. and B. G. Teubner, Stuttgart, 1986
14. B.D. Smith "Image Reconstruction from Cone-beam Projections: Necessary and Sufficient Conditions and reconstruction methods." *IEEE Trans. Med. Imag.*, Vol. 4, 1985, pp. 14–25
15. H.K. Tuy "An Inversion Formula for Cone-beam Reconstruction." *SIAM J. Appl. Math*, Vol. 43, 1983, pp. 546–552
16. X. Yang "Geometry of Cone-beam Reconstruction." *Ph.D. Thesis*, Massachusetts Institute of Technology, Dept. of Mathematics, Cambridge, MA, September 2001

AQUATICS Reconstruction Software: The Design of a Diagnostic Tool Based on Computer Vision Algorithms

Andrea Giachetti and Gianluigi Zanetti

CRS4 - Parco Scientifico e Tecnologico POLARIS,
Edificio 1, Loc. Pixina Manna, 09010 Pula (CA), Italy
{giach,zag}@crs4.it

Abstract. Computer vision methods can be applied to a variety of medical and surgical applications, and many techniques and algorithms are available that can be used to recover 3D shapes and information from images range and volume data. Complex practical applications, however, are rarely approachable with a single technique, and require detailed analysis on how they can be subdivided in subtasks that are computationally treatable and that, at the same time, allow for the appropriate level of user-interaction. In this paper we show an example of a complex application where, following criteria of efficiency, reliability and user friendliness, several computer vision techniques have been selected and customized to build a system able to support diagnosis and endovascular treatment of Abdominal Aortic Aneurysms. The system reconstructs the geometrical representation of four different structures related to the aorta (vessel lumen, thrombus, calcifications and skeleton) from CT angiography data. In this way it supports the three dimensional measurements required for a careful geometrical evaluation of the vessel, that is fundamental to decide if the treatment is necessary and to perform, in this case, its planning. The system has been realized within the European trial AQUATICS (IST-1999-20226 EUTIST-M WP 12), and it has been widely tested on clinical data.

1 Introduction

Computer vision (like computer graphics) provides many techniques and algorithms that can be used to recover 3D shapes and information from images range and volume data: pixel (voxel) classification techniques, isosurface extraction methods, etc. Some of them have been validated, even if only by using particular data under particular conditions, others are already used in industrial applications, while many others have only been proposed without the support of a large amount of experimental results. To choose the algorithm class that is best suited to a specific problem is indeed an important step in developing medical (as well as industrial) applications. Furthermore, a typical medical application may involve different sub-tasks, each with its own peculiarity, and often there is not a single reconstruction technique powerful enough to deal with all of them. The

M. Šonka et al. (Eds.): CVAMIA-MMBIA 2004, LNCS 3117, pp. 48–63, 2004.

application designer needs, therefore, to find specific solutions for each subtask and to combine these solutions in a, possibly, user friendly and effective software tool.

In the following sections we will show how we combined four different state-of-the art computer vision tools in a system that helps vascular surgeons and interventional radiologists in the pre–operative evaluation of the abdominal aorta. The system is capable of completely recover, with a fast and mostly automatic method, the geometrical structure of abdominal aorta from CT scans of the abdominal region, and to present clinicians with an interactive, measurable, 3D model of the vessel and ancillary structures.

The reconstruction of the aorta is very important for the evaluation of Abdominal Aortic Aneurysms (AAA): the precise measurement and evaluation of their geometrical parameters is fundamental to estimate rupture risk and to plan surgical or endovascular interventions, see [2,5,20,24,25].

Following the requirements coming from experts in vascular surgery, we developed specialized methods adapted to the different structures to be recovered, that is vessel lumen, vessel skeleton, plaques, thrombus. The result of our work are new flexible computer vision algorithms, and a user friendly software tool that includes all these algorithms and it can be used to obtain, in a fast and interactive way, a full vessel reconstruction.

2   Vessels Structures and CT

As an introduction and motivation to the following sections, we give here a brief description of the application context and image data features. As mentioned above, the goal of our work was to provide a tool for endovascular intervention planning capable of accurate pre–operative measurements based on a model of the vascular tree, of the arterial lumen, thrombus structures and calcified plaques obtained from the segmentation of CT images.

Arteries, e.g., the aorta, are vessels conducting the bulk of oxygenated blood flow to the body. The lumen of a vessel is the region where the blood flows; its volume is not perfectly constant in big elastic vessels due to pressure variation during the cardiac cycle, but it can be approximately considered constant for our application. Aneurysms are local dilation of the vessels greater than 150% of normal diameter. They are probably caused by atherosclerosis or cystic medial degeneration. If their diameter is larger than 55mm. the probability of their rupture – an event causing death in most cases – is extremely high and aneurysms of that size must be absolutely treated. In the aortic aneurysms the lumen is often separated from the vascular tissues by thrombus. Thrombus is an aggregation of blood factors, primarily platelets and fibrin with entrapment of cellular elements, frequently causing vascular obstruction at the point of its formation. Other structures often surrounding the aorta, and that it is necessary to localize in order to avoid problems during surgery or endovascular treatment, are calcified plaques i.e., fat, cholesterol and mineral deposits that can develop on the inside of arterial walls. Their presence may cause problems in fixing prostheses [20] or inserting catheters inside the vessel.

Segmentation is performed on acquired CT scans. CT angiography is the standard for pre operative aortic diagnosis. It creates a 3D set of X-ray absorption maps coded as gray levels with a resolution higher than any other 3D acquisition technique. The greatest limitations to CT angiography are partial volume effects, which result in gradual attenuation transitions between adjacent structures: models reconstructed must always be considered affected by an error at least equal to maximum between the slice thickness or the slice spacing of the CT acquisition. A typical slice thickness for these diagnostic protocols is between 1 and 2 mm.

It is not possible to discriminate vessel tissues from CT data, but it is possible to have a clear delineation of the lumen by injecting a contrast medium in the blood. By doing so, the gray level in the image, corresponding to a well defined Hounsfield value (the X-ray attenuation), becomes sufficiently distinguishable from the surrounding. Thrombus and calcified plaques have Hounsfield values very close to the level of other structures, but they can be usually identified, even though small calcifications cannot be located because they are typically masked by volume effects.

3   Surface Extraction Techniques

Our task involves the estimation of three different surfaces enclosing three different structures: vessel lumen, vessel walls with thrombus regions, calcified plaques. There are three main classes of algorithms in literature to recover surfaces from voxelized volume.

Contour based surface extraction: the volume of the CT data is cut with series of planes, possibly perpendicular to the vessel direction[1], and, on each plane, contours of the lumen intersection are evaluated using edge following, region growing or snake algorithms. Finally, contours are connected in tubes and tubes are connected in trees. This method gives an immediate estimation of the skeleton as connection of contour mass centers.

Iso-surface extraction with Marching Cubes: marching cubes [16] give a surface that separate voxels with gray value higher and lower than a defined threshold by defining look up table associating surface element to voxel neighborhoods. The extraction is done usually on classified or pre-processed data. The surfaces extracted are not connected, require post processing for mesh simplification and smoothing, even if a lot of work has been done to improve the quality of the extracted surfaces since the algorithm has been introduced;

Deformable models: surfaces in 3D can be defined with implicit or parametric functions and adapted locally to the images. Surveys of this class of methods can be found in [18,19]. Three dimensional snakes (inflatable balloons), and front propagation method [22] are examples of, respectively, a topology preserving / not preserving method in this class.

---

[1] This is not an easy task and so it is usually assumed, as a first approximation, that the vessel is oriented along one of the CT scan axis

Fig. 1. Steps in contour based lumen reconstruction: cutting planes are first selected, contour computed with a snake algorithm, triangulated tubes are generated and finally joined after finding their intersection.

We now proceed in the analysis of advantages and drawbacks of each of these methods when applied to our reconstruction tasks.

4   Lumen Reconstruction

4.1   Contour Based Surface Extraction

For the lumen reconstruction all the techniques could be applied, we therefore compared their results. We found, however, that is difficult to recover complete vessel lumen geometries using a 2D contour based approach, because vessels have foldings and irregularities along their length. We implemented for comparison sake a 2D contour based method with the contours defined on 2D images obtained by tri–linear interpolation on arbitrary, user selected, planes across the dataset. Starting from contours series we then build tubes and assemble them in a vessel tree structure using geometrical engines like GTS [12]. This approach was dropped because it requires strong user interaction to obtain reliable results on all data sets, especially in the reconstruction of arterial tree bifurcations and it is not generally applicable.

4.2   Iso-Surface Extraction with Marching Cubes

Given the difficulties encountered with 2D contour based methods, we moved to a fully 3D method, based on first binarizing the volume data between a connected vessel lumen region and the rest, and then extracting the vessel surface as an iso–surface. To binarize the data we used a region growing method based on front propagation, that was initialized with a point inside the region of interest and whose growth was continued until it encountered voxels with gray level differing from the reference value more than a threshold. Holes were then filled using a topological closing algorithm. After data binarization, we applied a standard marching cubes algorithm. The resulting surfaces needed then to be regularized and simplified with triangle decimation. This approach, however, did not give reliable results: surfaces are good only in the case of well contrasted lumen with negligible noise and artifacts.

4.3   Deformable Models

In literature, model based approach [15,1] based on an initial ridge extraction at different scales (hard in noisy and complex situation) or surface based approaches [17,11] are the methods proposed mainly for this task.

Among all the possible deformable model algorithms we selected an explicit method deforming a closed surface. The reasons for this choice are the following.

- Fast computation: the use of implicit methods, finite elements, etc. makes evolution slower.
- Topology preservation: it is assumed that the lumen is an unique surface not separable into isolated parts.
- Sensitivity to noise: elastic forces keep the contour smooth and are less influenced by local noise or artifacts.

We have implemented a deformable surface algorithm, called "fast simplex mesh balloon", specifically designed for this task. It is based on the Simplex Mesh geometry introduced in [9]. A generic Simplex Mesh is a N dimensional mesh with N+1 connectivity. The Simplex Mesh we use is therefore a closed surface mesh composed by nodes each connected with three neighbors. Nodes move under the influence of an inflating force directed along the surface normal vector, an elastic smoothing force described ("surface orientation continuity constraint") and two image forces. The first, a deflating force directed against the surface normal, compensates the inflating force when the local average of the gray level differs from the internal value more than a fixed threshold. The second, an edge attraction force, pushes nodes toward the maximum of the gray level gradient modulus in the neighborhood. To avoid a large variance in simplex sizes, the latter are controlled by a simplex merging/splitting algorithm that is invoked every so many iteration steps. Our simplex algorithm is adaptive and optimized for the extraction of tubular structures: the maximum face size is not a global value, but is proportional to the local curvature. To speed up the computation, nodes that have already reached the desired border (i.e., an edge with the gray level which differs more than a fixed thresholds from the internal value) are labeled as fixed. The algorithm generates surfaces well adapted to complex structures, and the computation is fast because at each step only the free "front" of the surface in the tubular structure is moved. The simplex mesh is composed by polygons that are not necessarily planar and cannot be easily rendered, and therefore the final simplex mesh is converted to its "Dual" form (i.e., a new triangulated mesh with nodes in the center of the faces and connections corresponding to the simplex edges) to have a smooth triangulation [9]. The surface is usually initialized as a small sphere inside the lumen and then undergo the evolution determined by the forces applied. The user can control the maximum number of iterations to be performed, force parameters and the maximum and minimum size of the polygons. Auto–intersections are prevented by an appropriate test.

Surface evolution can be automatically stopped when the nodes do not move relevantly, but in our application it is usually stopped manually in order to avoid the detection of structures that are not interesting for our application.

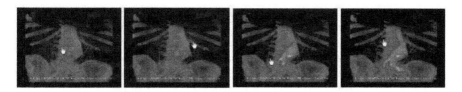

Fig. 2. Four successive steps of a balloon growth visualized over the corresponding volume-rendered CT data set.

The final procedure is described by the following lines of pseudo–code.

```
Initialize geometry as a sphere
While all the interested lumen is not recovered:
   Copy Simplex into BufferSimplex
   For ITER iterations:
      Foreach node n
         if not blocked(n)
            compute delta(n),
            verify delta(n),
      end
      For each node n
         if not blocked(n)
            move n in n + delta(n)
            update blocked(n)
      end
   end
   Foreach face f
      if surface(f) > THRESHOLD1 split f
      if surface(f) < THRESHOLD2 merge f
   end
   If auto_intersect(Simplex)
      copy BufferSimplex Simplex;
      return to user interaction;
end
```

This approach gave the more precise results requiring the minumum user interaction and was therefore chosen for the application.

5   Calcifications Reconstruction

The recovery of the calcium boundaries is an ideal application of isosurface extraction. For this task, in fact, it is simply required to extract boundaries of voxels with a well defined HU value. No topological properties or support for measurements are needed. We applied therefore the well known "marching cubes" algorithm [16] with a threshold chosen to represent the calcification boundaries. Even in this case, however, it is necessary to customize the procedure and to consider some peculiarities of the problem. This threshold cannot be set at the 120 HU suggested, for example, in [13], because this value is lower than the level of the contrast medium injected in the lumen. We put the threshold usually at about 320 HU, considered by many the lowest value in plaques [10].

We also limited the isosurface computation to a region defined by the user by selecting a bounding box.

Finally, if geometries must be exported or used for Internet applications or fast rendering there is the possibility of reducing the number of triangles with standard decimation routines provided by the GTS library [12].

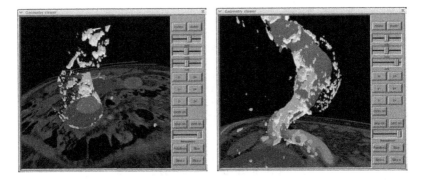

Fig. 3. Left: external surfaces of calcified regions extracted with marching cubes at 320 HU. Right: Lumen and calcium surfaces superimposed to the CT scan

6   Thrombus Reconstruction

It is difficult to automatically identify thrombus. Deformable surface methods are not useful since thrombus is not contrasted and its density, 20-50 HU, is too close to those of fat and of the non-contrasted vessels, and there are too many edges inside it due to calcifications. The best option seems, therefore, to use a 2D approach based on computing series of snakes or inflated balloons ([14,8]). 2D contours can be easily controlled, constrained and manually corrected by the user (see Fig.4.1). 3D tubular surfaces can, as seen before, recovered by joining contours with an algorithm finding point to point correspondences and, since ion this case the thrombotic regions are usually reasonably "straight", the approach provides reasonably good results. De Bruijne et al., [6], have recently proposed what amounts to the first specialize thrombotic vessels segmentation method. In their work they report a semi–automated procedure that uses contour based methods with model based constraints based on Active Shape Models. In our opinion, the use of model based constraint methods is limited by the great variability of physiological shapes and the limited training set generally used to build shape models. De Bruijne et al. considered also this fact and relaxed the constraints by adding synthetic covariance in the deformation model they built.

We completely dropped the statistical approach, using still a constrained contour based method. We introduced contour evolution constraints by using a simple Fourier snake, like those described in [23], with a weighted correction aiming at moving the contour close to the correct boundaries.

The algorithm works directly on CT slices. We know in advance the lumen geometry and its skeleton and thus we do not need to recover the vessel structure with other model based approaches as in [6]. The reference model used is therefore described by:

$$f_x(i, t) = a_0 + \sum_{k=1}^{n} a_k \sin(k2\pi i/N) \qquad (1)$$

$$f_y(i, t) = b_0 + \sum_{k=1}^{n} b_k \sin(k2\pi i/N)$$

where i, t, N, n are, respectively, the point label, the time step, the number of points defining the snake and is highest order in the Fourier expansion.

At each iteration, the snake points are driven by standard internal forces, a rejecting force depending on a threshold on the difference between local HU value and thrombus HU, and a specially designed edge force. The latter is a force directed along the derivatives of the image gradient that is active only if the edge shape is compatible with the border of a thrombotic region. This activation is done by computing a weight w for each border point as follows:

- Define a search space locally perpendicular to the curve (we use ±4 pixels)
- Count in the search space internal pixels in the range of thrombus values
- Count in the search space external pixels in the range outside thrombus values

if both counts are larger than 1, the edge is considered a possible thrombus limit and the value of w is set to 1 (0 otherwise). The final formula is

$$F_e(i) = -\alpha \cdot w \cdot \nabla |E(\boldsymbol{p}(i))| step(|\nabla E(\boldsymbol{p}(i))| - threshold) \qquad (2)$$

At each iteration step, we compute the displaced points $\boldsymbol{s}(i)$ by applying as finite differences the standard inflated balloon forces [8]. At each iteration of the point update, we then compute the truncated Fourier approximation of $\boldsymbol{s}(i, t)$, $\boldsymbol{f}(i, t)$, i.e., the constrained snake, and then obtain the final point position as a linear combination of the free and constrained displacement, using, for the free displacements, weights proportional to the previously computed "scores":

$$\boldsymbol{p}(i, t+1) = \gamma \cdot w\boldsymbol{s}(i, t+1) + (1 - \gamma \cdot w)\boldsymbol{f}(i, t+1) \qquad (3)$$

where γ is an estimate of the accuracy in the thrombus boundary delineation. The "filtering" step close to edges limiting the thrombotic region. We found this

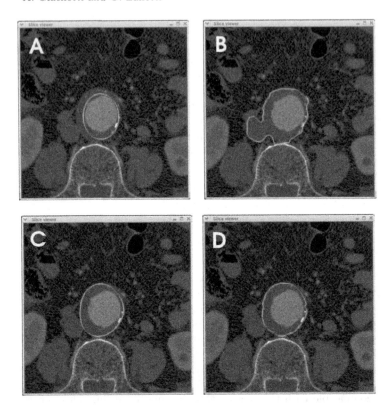

Fig. 4. Examples of thrombus segmentation. A: automatic initialization outside the lumen surface. B: unconstrained evolution: problems are created in regions lacking information. C: Fourier constrained evolution. D: filtered evolution: the border is well adapted to borders near the edges.

procedure sufficient in order to avoid some false detections due to the poor contrast between the thrombus HU and the environment.

In some cases image information is too poor and it is not possible to eliminate completely the possibility of a wrong contour placement. User interaction is thus required for correction. We, therefore, concentrated our efforts on finding a procedure with fast extraction capability but whose behavior could be easily controlled by user–interaction. The procedure works as follows:

- First contour is started automatically as an ellipse outside the lumen.
- Standard filtered evolution is launched.
- Result is visually inspected. If something is wrong the user can immediately correct the contour, both by changing segmentation parameters, and manually moving points.
- A simple menu allows the transition to the next image. Here the contour can be initialized by duplicating the previous one. If it is not considered

appropriate the user can either choose an ellipsoid outside the lumen or a contour can be easily drawn manually.

- Continuing the extraction of the following contours, the user can also see the 3D surface generated in an OpenGL window together with the other structures and textured planes representing coronal axial or sagittal sections.

When all the contours are computed, they are resampled with the same number of nodes and connected in a tubular geometry. If it is considered necessary, it is possible to extract several tubular parts and join them in bifurcated structures. The procedure described allows a sufficiently fast thrombus recovery, since the need of performing manual corrections of the contour is reduced at less than 5% of the CT images analyzed and it is extremely simple.

It is clear that the thrombus extraction remains the most difficult part of the complete reconstruction due to its poor contrast. Fig.4 shows a typical segmentation procedure on a single slice: Fig.4A shows the initialization as an ellipse outside the lumen, Fig.4B the result of a non-constrained evolution, Fig.4C the result of a completely constrained evolution, while Fig.4D the result of a "filtered" one. Fig. 5 shows a screen shot of the thrombus segmentation procedure. Fig 6 shows a complete thrombus segmentation superimposed to a CT section.

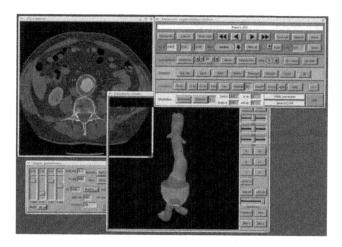

Fig. 5. Screenshot taken during the thrombus segmentation.

7   Skeletonization of the Lumen

Skeleton extraction is fundamental to capture the local direction of the "vessel tube" and the networked structure of the whole organ. In 3D things are much more complicated than in 2D, where skeletons can be easily extracted with a

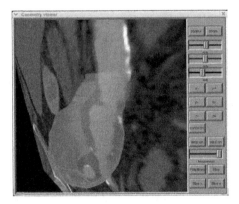

Fig. 6. An extracted thrombus superimposed to a sagittal section of the abdomen.

medial axis transform [4]. The "medial axis" in 3D is a surface. In 3D it is even difficult to give a definition of skeleton. For voxelized geometries it is usually defined as a set of one voxel thick lines with particular properties, i.e. they are centered, they are connected, they are smooth. Two main techniques have been proposed to extract this kind of lines from classified voxels (methods based on surfaces have been also proposed [26] but with less reliable results): topological thinning [21] or voxel coding based [27,7,3]. Considering advantages and drawbacks, we finally chosen and implemented an improved voxel coding method that uses a multi-scale approach and a snake-based regularization. Voxel coding algorithms have been recently introduced and seem the simplest and more general methods able to give fast and sufficiently accurate results. Considering that a distance map from the border (BSC,boundary seeded code) in the 3D case is not sufficient to extract one voxel thick skeletons as in the 2D case, the idea of these methods is to compute first paths inside the volume, and then center them using the distance map. To extract the paths another voxel coding is defined, called "Single Seeded Code" (SSC) or "Distance from Seed", measuring the distance of volume points from a seed voxel. Taking as starting points local maxima of the SSC with high values, paths are extracted searching for voxels with lower SSC in the neighborhood. When the voxel has been found, it is added to the centerline and then a new voxel with lower SSC is searched around it. The procedure is stopped when the seed is reached or when the line is close to a previously extracted one. The extracted lines are approximately "shortest" paths joining the starting point and the seed. Paths are depending on the metric used to compute the SSC and on the search strategy. The skeleton defined in this way have some nice properties: it is composed by lines, i.e. by lists of connected point, it capture the network structure of the vessel and its points are inside the volume. Two desired properties can be, however, still missing: centering and smoothness. The usual approach presented by authors to center the lines is derived by Zhou and Toga and consists of the following steps:

- For each point of the skeleton, find the cluster of voxels with the same SSC, connected with that point.
- Find the voxel of the cluster with maximum BSC
- Move the centerline point to the position of that voxel

Results are not always satisfactory. This procedure can give reasonable skeletons in the case, for example, of vascular structures with approximately constant radius, but are strongly dependent on the position of the seed and on the shape of the object to be skeletonized.

Fig. 7. Example of skeleton extraction. White line: Shortest path at high resolution. Black line: Final snake-based centerline extracted.

We have improved this algorithm by introducing a multi–scale snake based regularization, and it is now faster and less influenced by local structure. Our multi-scale snake based regularization is driven by the distance from border map. The latter is acting as an energy field and the resulting elastic forces makes the lines centered and smooth. With our method we obtain results compliant with our requirements: i.e., continuous curves connected in a tree structure and locally centered in the volume. The algorithm works as follows:

- Find the internal region on the full dataset by region growing inside the previously extracted surface.
- Create a low resolution binarized dataset labeling as internal all the voxel at the low resolution including an internal voxel at the high resolution. The user interaction is therefore only in the choice of the desired initial resolution and in the selection of the starting point.
- Compute the centerline at the low resolution, i.e. compute the BSC and the SSC at the low resolution, and find the tree structure.
- Compute the boundary seeded code map at the high resolution, called BSCH

- Move each skeleton point to the high resolution voxel location corresponding to the maximum of the BSCH inside the low resolution voxel.
- Resample and regularize the line with the snake algorithm.
- Go on finding the other branches, joining their last point to the closest point of the previous lines. Lines shorter than a fixed threshold are removed.

We found that in our application this revised method is extremely fast and reliable. Fig.7 shows an example of the procedure.

8   Validation

The reconstruction software described in the previous sections was used in the AQUATICS trial within the European Project IST EUTIST-M. The basic idea of AQUATICS was to build a prototype of a service for surgical centers able to provide in few hours after a CT scan and, using the web as delivery mechanism (see Fig. 9, 3D measurable models of the aorta in order to support the collaborative planning of endovascular treatment. The system evolved during the project and it is now complete, enabling the reconstruction of a complete model in about one hour. During the project two different technicians performed reconstructions using the tool and three clinical specialists used the models to measure a set of parameters necessary for endovascular procedure planning. More than 40 patient specific aortic models have been reconstructed and models of a synthetic phantom have been recovered from CT scans for validation. AQUATICS measurements are compatible with phantom's true data and patient data measurements done manually by radiologists using standard methods. The t-test showed a very good correlation between the measurements obtained on phantom with the Aquatics system and the true measurements of the phantom ($p < 0.0001$) demonstrating the reliability of the system. The correlation between observers was also tested with the Spearman rank test and again a statistical significant correlation was proved ($p < 0.0001$). Similar results were obtained on measurement performed on models reconstructed by different operators. Therefore the system proved to be reliable and its results reproducible.

9   Discussion

In order to achieve a complex diagnostic task, i.e. supporting a fully 3D geometrical quantitative evaluation of Abdominal Aortic Aneurysm, we selected and customized four computer vision techniques able to recover different parts of the model and used them as ingredients to build an integrated application with an user friendly interface, that can be used by trained radiologists in ordinary conditions. Experimental results show that the two main goals of the applications have been reached with this approach: in fact complete aortic reconstruction with all the four interesting structure can be reconstructed by a trained operator within a "reasonable time" (approx. 1 hour) the clinical evaluations performed on the

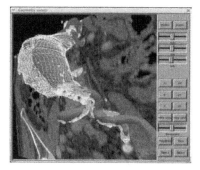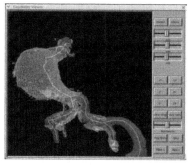

Fig. 8. Left: Reconstruction of the three different (lumen, thrombus, calcium) obtained with the different algorithms superimposed to the CT data. Right: Same model with the automatically extracted skeleton.

Fig. 9. Example of a completely reconstructed aneurysm viewed on a web interface allowing measurements.

model was found sufficiently precise compared with other methodologies during the validation trial.

The experience acquired during the system development suggested us that to the design of the complex application that can be effectively used in a clinical environment requires

- A good knowledge of the state of the art and a careful analysis of the users requirements, since many factors have an influence on how algorithms are chosen. Efficiency and precision are not the only factors to be considered, simplicity and easiness of use must be also taken into great account.
- The development of simple, but powerful user interfaces that allow the user to have immediate visual feedback for the result of all the algorithms applied. Not all the computer algorithms can give reliable results in all conditions

and this must be always known by the user that must have the possibility to check the results.

We believe that image processing and computer vision tools will be applied to many new tasks and become widely used in hospitals and clinical institutions if well designed applications will be developed and a correct information about the power and the limits of these techniques will be brought to the medical community.

Acknowledgments: We would like to thank Emanuele Neri, Irene Bargellini, (University of Pisa), Ammar Mallhoui (University of Innsbruck) and Massimiliano Tuveri for data selection and medical analysis. Enrico Bertolazzi and Gianmarco Manzini for providing their simplex library. Work was supported by the EUTIST-M EU funding (IST-1999-20226).

References

1. S.R. Aylward,"Initialization, Noise, Singularities and Scale in Height Ridge Traversal for Tubular Object Centerline Extraction" IEEE Trans. on Medical Imaging, 21,2 61–75 (2002)
2. K. M. Baskin et al., "Volumetric Analysis of Abdominal Aortic Aneurysm", Medical Imaging 1996: Physiology and Function from Multidimensional Images, Eric A. Hoffman, Editor, Proc. SPIE 2709, p. 323-337 (1996).
3. I. Bitter, A. Kaufman and M. Sato(2001) " Penalized-Distance Volumetric Skeleton Algorithm ," IEEE Transactions on Visualization and Computer Graphics, Vol. 7, No. 3, July-Sept. 2001, pp. 195-206
4. H. Blum, "A transformation for extracting new descriptors of shape," Proc. Symp. Models for the Perception of Speech and Visual Form, MIT Press, Cambridge, MA, pp. 362-380, 1967
5. Blankesteijn, J.D., "Imaging techniques for endovascular repair of abdominal aortic aneurysm". Medica Mundi 44/2 November 2000
6. M. de Bruijne et al, "Active shape model based segmentation of abdominal aortic aneurysms in CTA images". Medical Imaging 2002, Image Processing Proc. SPIE Vol 4684 pp. 463–474 (2002)
7. D. Chen et al, " A Novel Approach to Extract Colon Lumen from CT Images for Virtual Colonoscopy ," IEEE Transactions on Medical Imaging, Vol. 19, No. 12, December 2000, pp. 1220-1226.
8. L.D. Cohen and I. Cohen, "A finite element method applied to new active contour models and 3D reconstructions from cross-sections" Proc. of 3rd Int. Conf. on Comp. Vision, pp. 587–591 (1990).
9. H. Delingette, "Simplex meshes: a general representation for 3d shape reconstruction", *in CVPR94*, pp. 856–859, 1994.
10. P. Felkel, "Segmentation of Vessels in Peripheral CTA Datasets", VRVis Center Technical report TR-VRVis-2000-008, Vienna, Austria, 2000
11. A.F. Frangi et, al., "Quantitative Analysis of Vascular Morphology from 3D MR angiograms: in Vitro and In Vivo Results" Magn Res. in Med. 45,311-322 (2001)
12. S.Popinet, Project: The GNU Triangulated Surface Library
    http://sourceforge.net/projects/gts

13. I Isgrum et al., "Automatic detection of calcifications in the Aorta from abdominal CT scans", Excerpta Medica ICS1256, proc. CARS 2003, pp. 1037-1042 (2003)
14. A. Kass, A. Witkin and D. Terzopoulos, "Snakes: Active contour models," Int. J. of Comp. Vision 1, 321–331 (1988).
15. K. Krissian et al. "Model Based Multiscale Detection and Reconstruction of 3D vessels" INRIA Sophie Antipolis Report n.3442 (1998)
16. W.E. Lorensen and H. E. Cline, "Marching cubes: a high resolution 3D surface construction algorithm". In M.C. Stone ed., SIGGRAPH '87 Conference Proceedings, pp. 163–170 (1987).
17. D. Magee, A. Bulpitt, E. Berry, "3D Automated Segmentation and Structural Analysis of Vascular Trees Using Deformable Models" Proc. IEEE Workshop on Variational and Level Set Methods in Computer Vision, 2001.
18. T. Mc Inrey and D. Terzopulos, "Deformable models in medical image analysis, a survey" Medical Image Analysis, 1(2): 840–850, 1996
19. Montagnat, J, Delingette, H, and Ayache, N, "A review of deformable surfaces: topology, geometry and deformation," Image and Vision Computing, vol. 19, pp. 1023-1040, 2001.
20. J.C. Parodi, J.C. Palmaz, H.D. Barone, "Transfemoral intraluminal graft implantation for abdominal aortic aneurysms" Ann Vasc Surg 1991;5:491-499.
21. R.J.T. Sadleir and P.F. Whelan, "Colon Centerline Calculation for CT Colonography using Optimised 3D topological thinning" Proc. IEEE 3DPVT, pp.800-803 (2002)
22. J.A. Sethian, "Level Set Methods & Fast Marching Methods: Evolving Interfaces in Computational Geometry, Fluid Mechanics, Computer Vision & Materials Science, Cambridge University Press, 1996
23. L.H. Staib and J.S. Duncan, "Boundary Finding with Parametrically Deformable Models," IEEE Transactions on Pattern Analysis and Machine Intelligence, 14(11):1061-1075, 1992.
24. J.D. Santilli and S. M. Santilli, "Diagnosis and treatment of Abdominal Aortic Aneurysms" American Family Physician 56:4 (1997)
25. Tillich M, Hill BB, Paik DS, Petz K, Napel S, Zarins CK, Rubin GD., "Prediction of aortoiliac stent-graft length: comparison of measurement methods." Radiology 2001 Aug;220(2):475-83
26. Masayuki Hisada, Alexander G. Belyaev, Tosiyasu L. Kunii, 3D Voronoi-Based Skeleton and Associated Ninth Pacific Conference on Computer Graphics and Applications (PG'01) Surface Features
27. Y. Zhou and A. W. Toga, "Efficient skeletonization of volumetric objects", *TVCG*, vol. 5, 1999.

Towards Automatic Selection of the Regularization Parameters in Emission Tomgraphy by Fourier Synthesis

P. Maréchal[1], D. Mariano-Goulart[2], L. Giraud[3], and S. Gratton[3]

[1] Université de Montpellier 2, Dpt. des Sciences Mathématiques, Place Eugène Bataillon, 31 095 Montpellier Cedex 5, France
[2] Faculté de médecine de Montpellier, Service de médecine nucléaire, CHU Lapeyronie, 371 av. du Doyen Gaston Giraud, 34 295 Montpellier Cedex 5, France
[3] CERFACS, 42 av. Gaspard Coriolis, 31057 Toulouse Cedex, France

Abstract. The problem of image reconstruction in emission tomography in an ill-posed inverse problem. The methodology FRECT (Fourier regularized computed tomography) allows not only for *a priori* analysis of the stability of the reconstruction process but also for an exact definition of the resolution in the slices. Its natural regularization parameter, namely the cutoff frequency ν of the filter underlying the definition of the FRECT solution, can be calibrated by estimating the condition number for a range of values of ν. We first outline the methodology FRECT. We then discuss the numerical strategies which can be implemented in order to estimate the condition numbers of large matrices. Finally, we present a few results obtained in the context of SPECT reconstructions, and discuss the possibility to determine automatically the best possible cutoff frequency from the analysis of the stability.

1 Introduction

In the last decade, iterative methods such as EM (Expectation Maximization) have been extensively studied in single photon emission computed tomography (SPECT). This is mainly due their ability to incorporate corrections of artefacts that are common in nuclear medicine images, such as correction of the geometrical system response, of Compton scattering and of attenuation [7,33]. However, whatever the algorithm used, the reconstruction of slices consists in solving an ill-posed problem with an unstable solution. As a consequence, noise in the reconstructed image usually increases as iterations of the algorithm proceed. This noise is composed of a statistical noise which depends on the propagation of the noise from the emission projection data and a deterministic inaccuracy which depends on convergence properties of the algorithm, truncation, round-off errors and imperfection of the model [26]. Due to the noise in the projection data and to these deterministic innacuracies, frequency components of the reconstructed image above a certain frequency cannot be recovered, regardless of the iterative algorithm used [34] unless some *a priori* information or regularization is used.

M. Šonka et al. (Eds.): CVAMIA-MMBIA 2004, LNCS 3117, pp. 64–74, 2004.
© Springer-Verlag Berlin Heidelberg 2004

This has prompted most users to terminate the iteration process after only a few iterations [12], a strategy which is, in essence, equivalent to the Tikhonov regularization method [6]. However, the rate of convergence of iterative algorithms is complex. It depends on the frequencies in the expected slice as well as on the applied model. As a consequence, stopping the iterative process after a certain number of steps remains a speculative method with uncertain consequences in terms of noise and resolution of the reconstructed slices [34,4]. Thus, it has been proposed to control noise propagation in iterative reconstruction procedures thanks to a combination of the likelihood function and a penalty function [18,11,37,22,17,28,21]. These methods have been shown to have significant advantages in terms of noise performance, but these advantages are highly dependent on the choice of the penalty function and of the parameters [20,14]. This has been a serious hindrance to the clinical application of iterative reconstruction technique in routine clinical settings. There is an extensive literature studying the noise propagation with EM as well as with FBP [16,8,36,19,39,26,27,1,13,38,5]. On the other hand, the noise propagation in SPECT images reconstructed using other optimization procedures such as conjugate gradients or BFGS [2] are not well known, mainly because of the difficulties of formulating theoretical expressions describing the propagation of this noise from the emission projection data. The purpose of this paper is to describe how the convergence properties of an iterative reconstruction algorithm can be measured and controlled. The method proposed in this paper will be applied to the particular case of the methodology FRECT (Fourier Regularized Computed Tomgraphy), which has been recently developped in a previous paper [30]. We will show how this method leads to the definition of a range of cut-off frequencies which are compatible with a numerical convergence of iterative algorithms and with the reconstruction of slices without undesirable texture properties such as those observed when one is trying to minimize non-preconditionned likelihood functions [26,7].

2   Background

Inverse Problems and Ill-Posedness

Mathematically speaking, tomography takes the form of a linear inverse problem. The transformation of the unknown distribution into the instrumental data may be modeled by

(1) the action of some *Radon-type operator*;
(2) the sampling of the resulting function;
(3) the corruption of the samples by some noise.

Recovering the original distribution is always impossible in practice, because of the ill-posedness of the problem, which makes it necessary to reformulate the problem. The terminology *Radon-type operator* refers to the well-known Radon transformation. Recall that the Radon transform of a function f of the p-dimensional vector $\mathbf{x}$ is the function Rf defined on $Z := S^{p-1} \times \mathbb{R}$ by

$$(Rf)(\boldsymbol{\theta}, s) := \int f(\mathbf{x})\delta(s - \langle \boldsymbol{\theta}, \mathbf{x} \rangle) \, d\mathbf{x}. \tag{1}$$

As usual, we denote by S^{p-1} the unit sphere of $\mathbb{R}^p$. In medical imaging, of course, $p = 2$ or $p = 3$. The Radon transformation is an ideal version of the operator involved in Step (1). More realistic models must be considered, so as to account for the physics of the radiation propagation as well as the characteristics of the cameras. In their discrete version, they are subsequently referred to as *tomographic matrices*. In this paper, the tomographic matrix is designed so as to take into account the depth dependence response of the gamma-camera used, according to the model described in [7].

Survey of Reconstruction Methods

We focuse here on *regularized methods*, that is, methods for which the reconstructed object is defined to be the minimizer of some *regularized functional* of the form

$$F(\mathbf{f}) := \|\mathbf{g} - R\mathbf{f}\|^2 + \rho_\alpha(\mathbf{f}). \tag{2}$$

In the above equation, $\mathbf{g}$, R and $\mathbf{f}$ denote respectively the data vector, the tomographic matrix, and the unknown vector; α is some positive number called the *regularization parameter* and ρ_α may be called a *regularizer* or a *neg-entropy*. Classical examples of regularizers are the Tikhonov regularizer $(\rho_\alpha(\mathbf{f}) := \alpha \|\mathbf{f}\|^2)$, the generalized Tikhonov regularizer $(\rho_\alpha(\mathbf{f}) = \alpha \langle \mathbf{f}, Q\mathbf{f} \rangle / 2$ where Q is a symmetric positive semi-definite matrix such that $R^\star R + \alpha Q$ is invertible) and the Boltzmann-Shannon neg-entropy $(\rho_\alpha(\mathbf{f}) := \alpha \sum f_j \ln f_j)$. At all events, the second component of F should be designed in such a way that

(1) F has a *unique* minimizer $\bar{\mathbf{f}}(\mathbf{g})$ for every data vector $\mathbf{g}$;
(2) the dependence of $\bar{\mathbf{f}}$ on $\mathbf{g}$ is controllable and controlled (numerically);
(3) $\bar{\mathbf{f}}$ is physically relevant, that is, it is interpretable in the sense that part of the information of the real object can be retrieved from $\bar{\mathbf{f}}$.

Numerical convergence is required for the regularized methods, and the interruption of the algorithm is governed by some stopping criterion. This is why numerical analysis plays a leading role in the implementation of these methods.

A certain degree of subjectivity seems to enter in the choice of ρ_α. In fact, once a type of regularizer has been (subjectively) chosen, some objectivity can be introduced in the regularization parameter. Defining the reconstructed object as the minimizer of some suitably chosen functional allows, in principle, for quite a rigorous *error analysis* (see [31]). As a matter of fact, $\bar{\mathbf{f}}$ appears as an implicit function of $\mathbf{g}$, which makes it possible to analyse a *posteriori* the propagation of errors. Moreover, this a *posteriori* analysis can be performed a *priori* whenever the regularizer is of *Tikhonov type* since in this case $\bar{\mathbf{f}}$ depends linearly on $\mathbf{g}$. The estimation of the stability of the regularized problem can be used to select the regularization parameter, as we shall see in this paper. We focuse here on the methodology FRECT, which we now outline.

Fourier Regularization

A rather abstract problem appears to be central to various problems of image reconstruction: the problem of Fourier synthesis. It can be formulated as follows:

> Suppose f is an unknown function in $L^2(V)$, where V is a bounded subset of $\mathbb{R}^p$. Recover f from the knowledge of its Fourier transform on a bounded domain W.

If W contains an open subset, then f can be fully recovered, theoretically, as a consequence of the analyticity of its Fourier transform. Otherwise expressed, the operator

$$A\colon L^2(V) \longrightarrow L^2(W)$$
$$f \longmapsto Af := \mathbb{I}_W Uf, \tag{3}$$

where $\mathbb{I}$ denotes the characteristic function of W and U denotes the Fourier operator, is injective. However, the problem turns out to be *ill-posed*. More precisely:

(1) $A^{-1}\colon \operatorname{ran} A \to L^2(W)$ is not continuous;
(2) the set $\Lambda(A^\star A)$ of all eigen values of the compact hermitian operator $A^\star A$ (A is a Hilbert-Schmidt operator) is contained in $(0,1)$, has 0 as limit point, and the largest eigenvalue $\|A^\star A\|$ is (strictly) less than 1;
(3) the range of A is not closed, so that the domain of the pseudo-inverse A^+, $\mathcal{D}(A^+) = \operatorname{ran} A + \operatorname{ran} A^\perp$, is properly contained in $L^2(W)$; otherwise expressed, the least square solution does not always exist;
(4) the pseudo-inverse is not continuous:

$$\|A^+\| := \sup\left\{\|A^+g\| \mid g \in \mathcal{D}(A^+),\ \|g\| = 1\right\} = \infty. \tag{4}$$

One then needs to resort to an appropriate regularization theory, which accounts for the spectral properties of the *Fourier truncated operator*. At all events, the above elements show that it is necessary to give up reconstructing f. The problem must be reformulated. A possible approach consists in aiming at reconstructing a limited resolution version of f, that is, $f * \gamma$, where γ is some *convolution kernel*. If γ is suitably chosen, part of the information of the ideal object f is *readable* from $f * \gamma$. In practice, the level of resolution corresponding to a given convolution kernel can be characterized by some *cutoff frequency*. One can show that this amounts to reformulate the problem as one of *Fourier interpolation*, that is, a problem of Fourier synthesis in which W is such that its complementary W^c is bounded. Such an idea goes back to pioneering works by Lannes *et al* [25], where the well-posedness of the Fourier interpolation problem was established.

It was shown that tomography, which *a priori* involves the Radon transform rather than the Fourier transform, can also be regarded as a problem of Fourier synthesis [30]. We will show that reconstruction methods will benefit form this new way of approaching the problem. In the following subsection, we outline the main features of such an approach.

Overview of FRECT

The corner stone of the methodology FRECT is the Fourier slice theorem, which asserts that the Fourier transform of Rf with respect to its second argument and the p-dimensional Fourier transform of f are equal, up to a change of variable:

$$(U_s Rf)(\boldsymbol{\theta}, \sigma) = (Uf)(\sigma\boldsymbol{\theta}). \tag{5}$$

We have denoted by U_s the Fourier transformation with respect to the second argument, and by σ the variable dual to s. The above formula is valid for f in the Schwartz space and, by extension, in much richer spaces.

In tomography, Rf is (approximately) known on a finite sampling, that is, for $\boldsymbol{\theta} \in \{\boldsymbol{\theta}_i\}_{i\in I}$ and $s \in \{s_j\}_{j\in J}$, where I and J are finite. Let us forgets (temporarily) the sampling along s. The Fourier slice theorem then shows that the knowledge of Rf on $\{\boldsymbol{\theta}_i\}_{i\in I} \times \mathbb{R}$ is equivalent to the knowledge of Uf on $\mathbb{R}\{\boldsymbol{\theta}_i\}_{i\in I}$. In practice, of course, the limited resolution of the camera implies that this information on Uf is in fact limited to a bounded *star-shaped* domain of the form $[-\nu_e, \nu_e]\{\boldsymbol{\theta}_i\}_{i\in I}$. We may then aim at reconstructing $f * \gamma$, where γ is a suitably chosen convolution kernel. The Fourier transform $\hat{\gamma}$ of γ is a *filter*. A wide variety of filter shapes can be considered, but once a shape has been chosen, the *cutoff frequency* remains to be determined. Our central purpose is precisely, here, to select a suitable cutoff frequency.

Of course, since the objective of the reconstruction process is $f * \gamma$ rather than f, the data should be replaced, as much as possible, by data corresponding to $f * \gamma$, for obvious consistency purposes. It is a nice feature of Radon-type inverse problems that they allow for such a replacement. Here again, the Fourier slice Theorem provides the answer. As a matter of fact, it implies that

$$R(f * \gamma) = (Rf) \circledast (R\gamma), \tag{6}$$

where $\circledast$ denotes the convolution with respect to the second argument. The data corresponding to $f * \gamma$ can therefore be computed from the actual data by convolution with $R\gamma$. If an isotropic filter is chosen, that is, if $\hat{\gamma}(\boldsymbol{\xi}) = \varphi(\|\boldsymbol{\xi}\|)$, then

$$U_s R\gamma(\boldsymbol{\theta}, \sigma) = \hat{\gamma}(\sigma\boldsymbol{\theta}) = \varphi(\mod \sigma), \tag{7}$$

so that $g \circledast (R\gamma)$ is computed by taking the one-dimensional Fourier transform of g, multiplying the resulting function of $(\boldsymbol{\theta}, \sigma)$ by $\varphi(\mod \sigma)$, and taking the inverse Fourier transform. The regularized functional is then designed in such a way that the fit term penalizes the discrepancy between Rf and the *regularized data* $g \circledast (R\gamma)$, and the regularization term penalizes the frequencies which are above the cutoff frequency of the filter $\hat{\gamma}$. In its discrete formulation, the function to be minimized then takes the following form:

$$F(\mathbf{f}) := \left\| U_s^{-1} \Phi_\nu U_s \mathbf{g} - R\mathbf{f} \right\|^2 + \left\| \Psi_\nu U \mathbf{f} \right\|^2, \tag{8}$$

where U_s and U are the 1- and 2-dimensional discrete Fourier transform, and Φ_ν and Ψ_ν represent the multiplications by φ and $1 - \hat{\gamma}$, respectively. The subscript ν

recalls the dependence on the selected cutoff frequency. The regularization term can be regarded as the *energy* of the image in the high-frequency band. For the sake of conciseness, we shall write $L_\nu := U_s^{-1}\Phi_\nu U_s$ and $H_\nu := \Psi_\nu U$. Note that the usual weight α of the regularization term is here equal to 1. The natural regularization parameter is the cutoff frequency ν underlying the definition of γ. The function F can be minimized using various well-known algorithms, such as the *conjugate gradients*. Positivity constraints may be taken into account by using more sophisticated algorithms such as L-BFGS-B [2]. Finally, recall that the normal equation corresponding to the minimization of F takes the form $(R^\star R + H_\nu^\star H_\nu)\mathbf{f} = R^\star L_\nu \mathbf{g}$, where $\star$ denotes, as usual, the transpose of the (complex) conjugate. The linear system under consideration then takes the following form:

$$C\mathbf{f} = \mathbf{d}. \quad \text{with} \quad C := R^\star R + H_\nu^\star H_\nu \quad \text{and} \quad \mathbf{d} := R^\star L_\nu \mathbf{g}. \tag{9}$$

3   Numerical Challenge

The condition number of a rectangular matrix A is defined as the ratio $\kappa = \sigma_{\max}(A)/\sigma_{\min}(A)$ where $\sigma_{\max}(A)$ (resp. $\sigma_{\min}(A)$) is the largest (resp. smallest) singular value of A. If $\|\cdot\|$ denotes the spectral 2-norm, and A^+ is the More-Penrose inverse of A, an alternative expression for κ is given by $\kappa = \|A\|\cdot\|A^+\|$. The quantity κ plays an important role in numerical linear algebra. For instance, it is often used to quantify the sensitivity of the solution $\bar{\mathbf{f}}$ of a nonsingular square linear system $C\mathbf{f} = \mathbf{d}$ to the perturbation E of the matrix C. It is indeed possible to show that if $\kappa\|E\|/\|C\| < 1$ and $\kappa = \sigma_{\max}(C)/\sigma_{\min}(C)$, the solution $\mathbf{f}(E)$ of $(C + E)\mathbf{f}(E) = \mathbf{d}$ satisfies [35]

$$\frac{\|\mathbf{f}(E) - \bar{\mathbf{f}}\|}{\|\bar{\mathbf{f}}\|} \leq \frac{\kappa\|E\|/\|C\|}{1 - \kappa\|E\|/\|C\|}. \tag{10}$$

However the computation of the condition number remains a challenge in many applications. The main reason is related to the computational cost associated to this calculation. Since the singular values of A are the square roots of the nonzero eigenvalue of $C = A^\star A$, it is not surprising that the most robust numerical methods for this problem are based on the QR algorithm for computing the eigenvalues of a matrix. But a common characteristic of the best algorithms is that they work *only implicitly* on C, the main reason being that computing C in floating point arithmetic introduces a perturbation ΔC, and that the exact eigenvalues of $C + \Delta C$ may be very far from those of $A^\star A$ [10]. One of the most robust algorithms, called Golub-Reinsch SVD [9], starts with an Householder bidiagonalization, where two unitary matrices U and V are found so that

$$U^\star A V = \begin{bmatrix} B \\ 0 \end{bmatrix}, \tag{11}$$

and B is a bidiagonal matrix. Since the singular values of B are the singular values of A, the next step consists in computing the singular values of B using an implicit QR sweep [9]. In practice, the whole algorithm is reliable in the sense that the singular values obtained in floating point arithmetic are the exact singular value of a perturbed matrix $A + \delta A$, with $\|\delta A\| \leq \eta \|A\|$, and $\eta \ll 1$. In our experiments we have used the LAPACK routine ZGESVD which implements this idea. We denote by κ^{GR} the associated estimate of κ, which will serve as a reference, because of the above mentioned robustness of this SVD process. The quantity κ^{GR} will especially be very helpful to assess the numerical reliability of estimates "cheaply" computed by Krylov methods.

Indeed, an alternative algorithm for computing the singular value is the Lanczos method for computing the eigenvalues of the symmetric matrix C. In this case, an orthogonal basis $V_k = [\mathbf{v}_1, \ldots, \mathbf{v}_k]$ of the (Krylov) subspace spanned by $(\mathbf{v}_1, \ldots, A^{k-1}\mathbf{v}_1)$ is generated using the Lanczos recursion $CV_k = V_k T_k + \beta \mathbf{v}_{k+1} \mathbf{e}_k^\star$, where β is a scalar and $\mathbf{e}_k$ is the last vector of the canonical basis of $\mathbb{R}^k$. It is possible to show that the largest (resp. smallest) eigenvalue of the matrix T_k converges to the square of the largest (resp. smallest) singular values of A as k grows. This algorithm is an iterative process, and a natural stopping criterion for it is based on the so called *backward error*

$$\eta(\lambda, \mathbf{w}) = \frac{\|C\mathbf{w} - \lambda\mathbf{v}\|}{\|\mathbf{w}\| \|C\|}, \tag{12}$$

where $\mathbf{w} = V_k \mathbf{z}$, $\mathbf{z}$ being the eigenvector associated with the eigenvalue λ of T_k. The quantity $\eta(\lambda, \mathbf{w})$ satisfies [15]

$$\eta(\lambda, \mathbf{w}) = \min_{(C+\Delta C)\mathbf{w}=\lambda\mathbf{w}} \frac{\|\Delta C\|}{\|C\|}. \tag{13}$$

Thus, among the relative norms of the perturbations ΔC for which λ and $\mathbf{w}$ are exact eigenpairs of $C + \Delta C$, $\eta(\lambda, \mathbf{w})$ is the smallest. In practice, if at a certain step k of the Lanczos algorithm, $\eta(\lambda_k, \mathbf{w}_k)$ is close to the machine precision $\psi \sim 2 \ 10^{-16}$, the computed eigenpairs are the eigenpairs of a nearby perturbed matrix. The backward errors enables also to deal with uncertainties in the matrix C. Suppose that C is contaminated with an error matrix ΔC, resulting from a discretization or from the use of physical devices, and that $\|\Delta C\| < \delta \|C\|$, it is reasonable to stop the iterative algorithm as soon as $\eta(\lambda, \mathbf{w}) \leq \delta$.

Another important issue when implementing the Lanczos algorithm in floating point arithmetic is that after a relatively small number of steps, the matrix V_k is no longer an orthogonal matrix. Practical implications are that spurious eigenvalues appear and that the convergence of some eigenvalues may be delayed. A natural cure for this problem is to add a reorthogonalization process consisting in reorthogonalizing the newly computed $\mathbf{v}_k$ against its predecessors. A problem with this strategy may be its computational cost, but it turns out that for our problems the computational time is still reasonable, this is why we did not implement more sophisticated approaches such as the selective reorthogonalization [32]. Finally, in our experiments, we want to solve the linear system $C\mathbf{f} = \mathbf{d}$ and to compute the condition number of C. A naive approach would have consisted in running separately the conjugate gradient on the system and the Lanczos algorithm to compute the singular values. But as suggested in [10] we use the well-known equivalence between the quantities generated by the conjugate gradient and by Lanczos to obtain the singular value information directly from the conjugate gradient iterations. We denote by κ^K the estimate obtained using these conjugate gradient/Lanczos iterations.

4   Results

Emission projection data were acquired with a dual detector γ-camera equipped with low-energy high resolution collimators. One hundred and twenty-eight projections were recorded to reconstruct slices onto a 128×128 matrix corresponding to pixels of 3.4 mm. SPECT projections of a Jaszczak resolution phantom were acquired after filling this phantom with a ^{99m}Tc solution $(20\,mCi, 740\,MBq)$. Spatially variant collimator blurring was corrected by modelling the appropriate gaussian shape of the projections in the projection and backprojection subroutines used to compute the Radon matrix, according to the method proposed by Formiconi [7] and Passeri [33]. The extent of this Gaussian projection was limited to two projection bins around the central bin onto which the projection of a given pixel in the reconstructed slice is maximal. The evaluation of the condition number as well as the reconstructions were performed using FRECT, with a Butterworth filter of order 5. The iterative process was stopped when the backward error on the reconstructed slice fell below 10^{-7}.

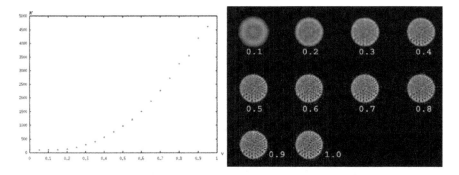

Fig. 1. Left: Condition number versus cutoff frequency. Right:FRECT Reconstructions of Jaszczak Phantom, for ν ranging linearly from 0.1 to 1.

Figure 1 shows the dependence of the condition number on the cutoff frequency, in the experimental setting described above, as well as the reconstructions obtained by FRECT for the same range of cutoff frequencies. The curve is increasing, convex, and the condition number becomes critical above the Nyquist frequency 0.4.

We can observe that the number of hypo-active patterns which can be detected from the reconstructed slice increases with the cutoff frequency up to a limit value of ν of approximately 0.4 to 0.5. Above this limit, spurious features appear and damage the image legibility. We emphasize that such a critical cutoff frequency depends on the tomographic matrix, which in turn depends on the projection model considered as well as on the experimental conditions. However, once the experimental protocol is set, the condition number is a function of ν only. A graph κ versus ν can then be computed once for ever, which will indicate an upper limit for the resolution of the reconstruction process.

References

1. H.H. BARRETT, D.W. WILSON and B.M.W. TSUI, *Noise properties of the EM algorithm:1-Theory 2- Monte Carlo simulations*, Phys. Med. Biol 39 (1994) 833-873.

2. R.H. BYRD, P. LU, J. NOCEDAL and C. ZHU, *A lilited memory algorithm for bound constrained optimization*, Technical Report NAM-08, Northwestern University (1994).

3. J. CULLUM, R. WILLOUGHBY and M. LAKE, *A Lanczos algorithm for computing singular values and vectors of large matrices*, SIAM J. Sci. Stat. Comput., 4 (2) (1983) 196-215.

4. C. FALCON, I. JUVELLS, J. PAVIA and D. ROS, *Evaluation of a cross-validation stopping rule in MLE SPECT reconstruction*, Phys. Med. Biol 43 (1998) 1271-1285.

5. J.A. FESSLER, *Mean and variance of implicitly defined biased estimator (such as penalized maximum likelihood): applications to tomography*, IEEE Trans. Image Processing 5 (1996) 493-506.

6. H.E. FLEMMING, *Equivalence of regularization and truncated iteration in the solution of ill-posed image reconstruction problems*, Linear Algebra and its applications 130 (1990) 133-150.

7. A.R. FORMICONI, A. PUPI and A. PASSERI, *Compensation of spatial system response in SPECT with conjugate gradient reconstruction technique*, Phys. Med. Biol. 34 (1989) 69-84.

8. G.J. GILLEN, *A simple method for the measurements of local statistical noise level in SPECT*, Phys. Med. Biol 37 (1992) 1573-1379.

9. G.H. GOLUB and C. REINSCH, *Singular value decomposition and least squares solution*, Numerische Mathematik, 14 (1970) 403–420.

10. G.H. GOLUB and C.F. VAN LOAN, *Matrix Computations*, Third Edition, Johns Hopkins University Press, Baltimore, MD, USA (1996).

11. P. GREEN, *Bayesian reconstructions from emission tomography using a modified EM algorithm*, IEEE Trans. Med. Imaging 9 (1990) 84-93.

12. T.J. HEBERT, *Statistical stopping criteria for iterative maximum likelihood reconstruction of emission images*, Phys. Med. Biol 35 (1990) 1221-1232.

13. G.T. HERMAN, *On the noise in images produced by computed tomography*, Computer Graphics and Image Processing 12 (1980) 271-285.

14. D.M. HIGDON, J.E. BOWSHER, V.E. JOHNSON, T.G. TURKINGTON, D.R. GILLAND and R.J. JASZCZAK, *Fully Bayesian estimation of Gibbs hyperparameters for emission computed tomography data*, IEEE Trans. Med. Imaging 16 (1997) 516-526.

15. N.J. HIGHAM, Accuracy and Stability of Numerical Algorithms, Society for Industrial and Applied Mathematics", Philadelphia, PA, USA, 2002.
16. R.H. HUESMAN, *The effects of a finite number of projection angles and finite lateral sampling of projections on the propagation of statistical errors in transverse section reconstructions*, Phys. Med. Biol 22 (1977) 511-521.
17. L. KAUFMAN and A. NEUMAIER, *PET regularization by enveloppe guided conjugate gradients*, IEEE Trans. Med. Imaging 15 (1993) 385-389.
18. S. KAWATA and O. NALCIOGLU, *Constrained iterative reconstruction by the conjugate gradient method*, IEEE Trans. Med. Imaging 4 (1985) 65-71.
19. H.J. KIM, B.R. ZEBERGand R.C. REBA, *Evaluation of reconstruction algorithms in SPECT neuroimaging: I-Comparison of statistical noise in SPECT neuroimages with 'naive' and 'realistic' predictions*, Phys. Med. Biol. 38 (1993) 863-881.
20. D.S. LALUSH and B.M.W. TSUI, *Simulation evaluation of Gibbs prior distributions for use in maximum a posteriori SPECT reconstructions*, IEEE Trans. Med. Imaging 11 (1992) 267-275.
21. D.S. LALUSH and B.M.W. TSUI, *A fast and stable weighted least squares MAP conjugate gradient algorithm for SPECT*, Proceedings of the 40th annual meeting, IEEE Trans. Med. Imaging 34 (1993) 101.
22. D.S. LALUSH and B.M.W. TSUI, *A fast and stable maximum a posteriori conjugate gradient reconstruction algorithm*, Med. Phys 22 (1995) 1273-1284.
23. A. LANNES, E. ANTERRIEU and K. BOUYOUCEF, *Fourier interpolation and reconstruction via Shannon-type techniques; part I: Regularization principle*, Journal of Modern Optics 41 8 (1994) 1537–1574.
24. A. LANNES, E. ANTERRIEU and P. MARÉCHAL, *Clean and Wipe*, Astronomy and Astrophysics, Suppl. Series, 123 (1997) 183-198.
25. A. LANNES, S. ROQUES and J. CASANOVE, *Stabilized reconstruction in signal and image processing; part I: Partial deconvolution and spectral extrapolation with limited field*, Journal of Modern Optics 34 2 (1987) 161–226.
26. S.C. LIEW, B.H. HASEGAWA, J.K. BROWN and T.F. LANG, *Noise propagation in SPECT images reconstructed using an iterative maximum likelihood algorithm*, Phys. Med. Biol 38 (1993) 1713-1727.
27. J.S. LIOW and S.C. STROTHER, *Noise and signal decoupling in maximum likehood reconstructions and Metz filters for PET brain images*, Phys. Med. Biol 39 (1994) 735-750.
28. P. LOBEL, L. BLANC-FÉRAUD, C. PICHOT and M. BARLAUD, *Conjugate gradient algorithm with edge-preserving regularization for microwave inverse scattering*, Processing PIERS'96, Innsbruck, Austria (1996).
29. P. MARÉCHAL and A. LANNES, *Unification of some deterministic and probabilistic methodologies for the solution of linear inverse problems via the principle of maximum entropy on the mean*, Inverse Problems, 13 (1997) 135-151.
30. P. MARÉCHAL, D. TOGANE and A. CELLER, *A new reconstruction methodology for Computerized Tomography: FRECT (Fourier Regularized Computed Tomography)*, IEEE, Transactions on Nuclear Science, 47 (2000) 1595-1601.
31. P. MARÉCHAL, D. TOGANE, A. CELLER and J.M. BORWEIN, *Computation and stability analysis for regularized tomographic reconstructions*, IEEE, Transactions on Nuclear Science, 46 (1999) 2177-2184.
32. B.N. PARLETT and D.S. SCOTT, The Lanczos algorithm with selective reorthogonalization, Math. Comp. 33 (1979) 217–238.
33. A. PASSERI, A.R. FORMICONI and U. MELDOLESI, *Physical modelling (geometrical system response, Compton scattering and attenuation) in brain SPECT using the conjugate gradient reconstruction method*, Phys. Med. Biol. 37 (1992) 1727-1744.

34. D.L. SNYDER, M.I. MILLER, L.J. THOMAS and D.G. POLITTE, *Noise and edge artifacts in Maximum-Likelihood Reconstructions for Emission Tomography*, IEEE Trans. Med. Imaging 6 (1987) 228-238.

35. G.W. STEWART, Afternotes on Numerical Analysis, Society for Industrial and Applied Mathematics, Philadelphia, PA, USA, 1996.

36. M.J. TAPIOVAARA and R.F. WAGNER, *SNR and Noise measurements for medical imaging: 1-A practical approach based on statistical decision theory*, Phys. Med. Biol 38 (1993) 71-93.

37. B.M.W. TSUI, X. ZHAO, E. FREY and G.T. GULLBERG, *Comparison between ML-EM and WLS-CG algorithms for SPECT reconstruction*, IEEE Trans. Nuclear. Sciences 6 (1991) 1766-1772.

38. W. WANG and G. GINDI, *Noise analysis of MAP-EM algorithms for emission tomography*, Phys. Med. Biol 42 (1997) 2215-2232.

39. D.W. WILSON and B.M.W. TSUI, *Noise properties of filtered-backprojection and ML-EM reconstructed emission tomographic images*, IEEE Trans. Nuclear. Sciences 40 (1993) 1198-1203.

Extraction of Myocardial Contractility Patterns from Short-Axes MR Images Using Independent Component Analysis

A. Suinesiaputra[1], A.F. Frangi[2], M. Üzümcü[1], J.H.C. Reiber[1], and
B.P.F. Lelieveldt[1]

[1] Division of Image Processing, Department of Radiology,
Leiden University Medical Center, Leiden, the Netherlands
[2] Computer Vision Group, Aragon Institute of Engineering,
University of Zaragoza, Zaragoza, Spain
a.suinesiaputra@lumc.nl

Abstract. Regional myocardial wall motion analysis has been used in clinical routine to assess myocardial disease, such as infarction and hypertrophy. These diseases can be distinguished from normals by looking at the local abnormality of cardiac motion. In this paper, we present a first result of a feature extraction experiment using the Independent Component Analysis (ICA), where abnormal patterns of myocardial contraction from patients are recognizable and distinguishable from normal subjects.

1 Introduction

Myocardial contractility is an important quantitative indicator for the diagnosis of myocardial diseases. This function can be visually examined and quantified by using a cine MRI sequence. Two most important phases for myocardial contraction are the *end-diastole* (ED), or the start of contraction, and the *end-systole* (ES), or the end of contraction.

Abnormal myocardial contraction is mainly caused by the occlusion of coronary arteries, particularly in the infarcted regions. Figure 1 shows two examples of MRI images from a healthy volunteer and an infarct patient, both at ES phase. Note that the inferior region (indicated by a white arrow) of the infarct patient does not contract. This region has a small wall thickness value.

Subspace analysis techniques have been used recently in many areas, such as appearance-based modeling and recognition. Principal Component Analysis (PCA) is the common subspace analysis for dimensionality reduction. Independent Component Analysis (ICA) is another subspace analysis, which seeks statistically independent components of the observed data. ICA is commonly used for blind source separation of an observed signal.

In machine learning, both PCA and ICA can be used for feature extraction [1, 2, 3]. There has been some literature showing a comparison between both methods with different results. Moghaddam [4] shows no statistical differences

M. Šonka et al. (Eds.): CVAMIA-MMBIA 2004, LNCS 3117, pp. 75–86, 2004.

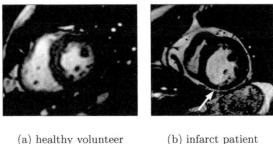

(a) healthy volunteer   (b) infarct patient

Fig. 1. MRI images of a healthy volunteer and an infarct patient at end-systole (the final contraction phase in the cardiac cycle). White arrow points to the infarcted tissue of the patient, where that myocardium region has a small contraction.

between PCA and ICA. Draper et al. [5] compared ICA and PCA for face recognition and reported that some ICA algorithms give better performance than PCA, but some do not.

Regardless of these comparisons, PCA and ICA are both linear generative models, because every training shape can be approximated by a linear combination of the components. An important difference between ICA and PCA lies in the shape variation. Independent components from ICA create local shape variation, while principal components from PCA give a global shape variation [6]. This indicates that ICA is more suitable for extracting local shape features, than PCA, which is desired in our study.

In this paper, we present an ICA-based local feature extraction method for the diagnosis of myocardial disease, especially for myocardial infarction. Section 2 describes our shape model, the ICA method and a new sorting method for ICA modes. Section 3 presents experimental results, followed by a discussion in Section 4 and some perspective on future work in Section 5.

2   Methodology

2.1   ICA Model

In this study, the observation data are left ventricular (LV) myocardial contours, manually drawn from short-axis cardiac MRI images at ED and ES phases. Samples for each observation are landmark points, defined by equal angular distance along each contour.

To model the contractility pattern between ED and ES, contours for each subject are combined serially into one *shape* vector. A shape $\mathbf{x} \in \mathbb{R}^{2m}$ is defined by m landmark points from 4 contours together in the following order: endocardium (inner) contour at ED, epicardium (outer) contour at ED, endocardium contour at ES and epicardium contour at ES. Thus the shape analysis is performed on all concatenated contours together, preserving the aspect ratio between ED and ES because of the contraction.

The shape vector $\mathbf{x}$ consists of m pairs of (x, y) coordinates of landmark points:

$$\mathbf{x} = (x_1, y_1, x_2, y_2, \ldots, x_m, y_m)^T \tag{1}$$

The mean shape $\bar{\mathbf{x}}$ from n shapes is defined by

$$\bar{\mathbf{x}} = \frac{1}{n} \sum_{i=1}^{n} \mathbf{x}_i \tag{2}$$

Each observed data (shape) $\mathbf{x}$ can be generated by a linear combination of the independent components $\Phi \in \mathbb{R}^{2m \times p}$. This linear generative model is formulated as follows

$$\mathbf{x} \approx \bar{\mathbf{x}} + \Phi \mathbf{b} \tag{3}$$

where $\bar{\mathbf{x}}$ is the mean shape and $\mathbf{b} \in \mathbb{R}^p$ is the component weighting vector.

In ICA, the basis of the subspace is sought to be statistically independent, with the main assumption of the non-gaussian distribution of the observed data [7]. The resulting subspace is non orthogonal and unordered. There is no closed form solution for ICA. Several numerical algorithms to estimate ICA are available (see [8] for the survey of ICA algorithms).

When applied to shape modeling, there is an important property of ICA in its *modes*. As the number of computed independent components increases, the component gives more localized shape variations. On the contrary, if the number of independent components is too small, then the component gives global shape variation, much like PCA modes. A shape variation in ICA has a general shape of a local bump, whereas the remainder of the shape is unaffected (see Fig. 2(a)). This is the difference between ICA and PCA: PCA modes give global shape variations, distributed over the entire contour (see Fig. 2(b)). Üzümcü et. al. [6] have presented the comparison between PCA and ICA in the modelling of cardiac shapes.

2.2   Geometry-Based Sorting for ICA Modes

In subspace analysis such as ICA or PCA, the number of selected components is less than the number of dimensions of the observed data. This allows a lower dimensional representation that still covers enough information of the observed data, either for description, detection or recognition.

Principal components are ordered from higher variance to the lowest, making it easy to select which and how many components to retain for further analysis; this is however not the case in ICA. There is no natural sorting criteria for independent components. One needs to define a sorting method for independent components that is suitable for a specific application. Since ICA components are local, we can however sort them based on their local position along the contour and this sorting criterion gives a more intuitive interpretation of local shape variations.

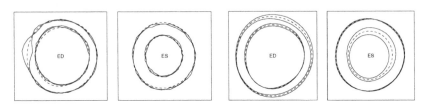

(a) ICA mode (variation is at ED-epi)   (b) The first PCA mode

Fig. 2. Examples of local shape variation from an ICA mode. As a comparison, the first PCA mode is given. The mean shape is shown with dashed lines. The solid lines are shape variations, i.e. $\bar{\mathbf{x}} \pm \Phi\mathbf{a}$ (see Eq. 4).

Let i-th mode $\hat{\mathbf{x}}_i$ be defined as the shape variation at the i-th column of Φ:

$$\hat{\mathbf{x}}_i = \bar{\mathbf{x}} + \Phi\mathbf{e_i} \tag{4}$$

where $1 \leq i \leq p$ and $\mathbf{e}_i \in \mathbb{R}^p$ is a vector that has element 1 at the i-th position whereas the rest are 0. Thus, $\hat{\mathbf{x}}_i$ describes the shape variation of the i-th component.

To locate the position of each $\hat{\mathbf{x}}_i$ along a contour, we use a bank of Gaussian filters and perform normalized cross-correlation of each of the filters with a *distance vector* of each mode $\hat{\mathbf{x}}_i$. The distance vector of the i-th mode, $\mathbf{d}_i \in \mathbb{R}^m_+$, is defined as the distance of each landmark point in the shape variation $\mathbf{x}_i$ to the mean shape. Each element j of the i-th distance vector is defined by

$$\mathbf{d}_i^{(j)} = \sqrt{\sum_{k=2j-1}^{2j} \left(\hat{\mathbf{x}}_i^{(k)} - \bar{\mathbf{x}}^{(k)}\right)^2} \tag{5}$$

where $j = 1, 2, \ldots, m$.

The cross-correlation is performed only on a particular contour, circularly. Thus there are four cross-correlation processes, because there are four contours for each shape.

The Gaussian filter giving the maximum cross-correlation for vector $\mathbf{d}_i$ is stored. The center of this filter defines the position of the i-th component; the width of the Gaussian filter represents the width of the component. Figure 3(a) shows an example of the cross-correlation response from a component.

There is an extra advantage of using the normalized cross-correlation for sorting ICA modes. Modes that consist of noise are automatically detected and thus can be eliminated. Noise modes have a global wrinkled shape variation along the whole contour, which correlates best with the widest Gaussian filter. Figure 3(b) shows an example of the cross-correlation response for a noise component.

After all modes have been cross-correlated, positions of all modes are determined. We sort ICA modes based on position along the contour.

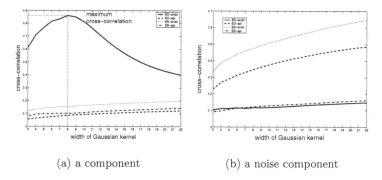

(a) a component   (b) a noise component

Fig. 3. Example of maximum cross-correlation results of two components.

2.3   Cluster Measurement Metrics

To evaluate the cluster formation between normal and patient subjects, a number of q components ($q \leq p$) are selected from the weighting coefficient matrix $\mathbf{b}$.

Let $\mathcal{D} = \sum_i^c \mathcal{D}_i \subset \mathbb{R}^q$ be a subset of the weighting coefficient matrix $\mathbf{b}$, after q components are selected. Let c be the number of classes. In this case, $c = 2$, because there are only two classes, i.e. normals and patients.

The first measurement is called *within-cluster scatter matrix*, which measures the compactness of a cluster. The within-cluster scatter matrix, $\mathbf{S}_W$, is defined as the sum of scatter matrices for each group:

$$\mathbf{S}_W = \sum_{i=1}^{c} \sum_{\mathbf{x} \in \mathcal{D}_i} (\mathbf{x} - \mathbf{m}_i)(\mathbf{x} - \mathbf{m}_i)^T \tag{6}$$

where $\mathbf{m}_i$ is the mean ("center of gravity") of the cluster i.

A scalar value representing the measurement of the compactness from this metric, is simply its trace. The trace of a scatter matrix accounts for the square of the scattering radius, because it is actually the sum of the variances in each coordinate direction. This scalar value is equal to the sum-of-squared error. Thus one seeks the minimum of this value to get the best representation of a cluster. The compactness measurement, J_W, is defined as

$$J_W = \mathrm{tr}[\mathbf{S}_W] \tag{7}$$

The second measurement is *between-cluster scatter matrix* measurement, $\mathbf{S}_B$, represents how far clusters are separated. It is defined as follows

$$\mathbf{S}_B = \sum_{i=1}^{c} n_i \, (\mathbf{m}_i - \mathbf{m})(\mathbf{m}_i - \mathbf{m})^T \tag{8}$$

where n_i is the number of subject in cluster i and $\mathbf{m}$ is the total mean:

$$\mathbf{m} = \frac{1}{n} \sum_{\mathbf{x} \in \mathcal{D}} \mathbf{x} \tag{9}$$

The scalar measurement value of the between-cluster scatter matrix is also its trace:

$$J_B = \text{tr}[\mathbf{S}_B] \tag{10}$$

The within-cluster and between-cluster scatter matrices are mostly used to design cluster validity indices for clustering methods [3]. In this study, we used these measurements to compare the quality of the cluster representation given by PCA and ICA components.

To visualize the cluster distribution, the Fisher discriminant line [3] is calculated and coefficient values from the selected components are projected to the Fisher line. Fisher linear discriminant accounts the ratio between the between-cluster and the within-cluster matrix measurements and it is given by:

$$\mathbf{w} = \mathbf{S}_W^{-1} (\mathbf{m}_1 + \mathbf{m}_2) \tag{11}$$

where $\mathbf{w}$ is a vector with the direction that maximizes the separation between two clusters.

3   Experimental Results

In this study, 42 normal subjects and 47 patients suffering from myocardial infarction were investigated. For each subject, endocardium and epicardium contours of the left ventricle myocardium at ED and ES phases from short-axis MRI were drawn manually by experts.

Contours were resampled to 40 landmarks defined by equi-angular sampling, starting from the intersection point between the lower right ventricular myocardium with the left ventricular myocardium. The total number of landmark points for each shape then becomes 160 points.

The calculation of ICA was performed using the JADE algorithm [9], implemented in Matlab. The number of ICA modes is selected carefully to 40 in this study, that gives enough local shape variations for each of the four contours. If the number is too small, then the shape variations become more global. If the number is too large, then too many local shape variations may occur, which look like noise components.

In the sorting of ICA modes, 20 Gaussian filters are used, ranging from width 3 to 22. Modes correlating with a Gaussian filter, which has width larger than 20 (half of a contour), were considered to be noise. From the original 40 ICA modes, the sorting method retains 35 modes, thus eliminating 5 noise modes.

3.1   Weighting Coefficient Matrix

Figure 4(a) shows the weighting matrix $\mathbf{b}$ of the ICA model that is constructed from shapes of normal subjects and infarct patients. The weighting coefficient matrix contains values that are needed to generate each training shape. These coefficient values are different for each subject. Thus the weighting matrix $\mathbf{b}$ is the most important value for classification purposes.

From Fig. 4(a), a clear difference can be seen distinguishing between the two groups in the endocardium at the ES phase. As a comparison, Figure 4(b) shows the PCA model from the same data. With PCA, the difference between the two groups is less pronounced, only clearly visible from the first component.

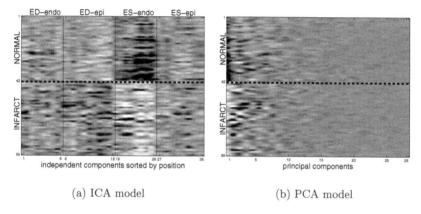

(a) ICA model   (b) PCA model

Fig. 4. The weighting coefficient between normal subjects and infarct patients.

3.2   Mean Cluster Distance

To enable the comparison between PCA and ICA, the weighting coefficient matrices for both models are normalized, such that $||\mathbf{b}|| = 1$. Hence weighting coefficient matrices for PCA and ICA are both in the same unit.

The distance between means of normal and patient subjects for each component is calculated using the *mean cluster distance* (MCD), as given by:

$$d_i = |\mathbf{m}_{n,i} - \mathbf{m}_{p,i}| \tag{12}$$

where i is an index of a component, $m_{n,i}$ and $m_{p,i}$ are the mean of the weighting coefficient values at the i-th component for normal and patient subjects respectively. Figure 5 shows the bar plot of the MCD of PCA and ICA for each mode.

A t-test experiment was conducted on each of independent and principal component to see whether the two means from normal and patient coefficient values come from two different clusters. The result is illustrated in Figure 5. From 35 selected independent components, there are 27 components with each has statistically significant difference of two means, while PCA only gives 1 component (the first principal component). The t-tests were performed with 95% confidence interval.

It is evident that independent components at ES-endo are among the highest
MCD value. Mean cluster distance of the first PCA mode is the highest among
others, even compared with ICA.

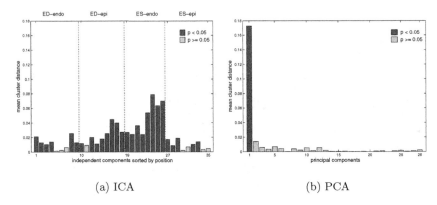

(a) ICA   (b) PCA

Fig. 5. Mean cluster distance of each component from ICA and PCA. The results
of t-test experiment on each component are shown as dark gray for $p < 0.05$ and
light gray bars for $p \geq 0.05$.

3.3   Cluster Analysis

In this study, we only present an analysis of cluster properties, but **not yet** a
classification result. Clusters are defined by selecting all independent components
from ICA and principal components that covers 95% of total variance from PCA.
This gives 35 ICA components and 16 PCA components.

Table 1 shows the measurement results using Eq. 7 for the cluster compactness and Eq. 10 for the cluster separation. Figure 6 shows result of the projected
coefficient values to their Fisher discriminant line.

Table 1. Cluster validity measurement results.

	compactness (J_W)	separation (J_B)
ICA	1.84	0.66
PCA	0.65	0.12

PCA gives better compactness than ICA, but less separable (see Tab. 1).
However the projection to the Fisher discriminant line favors ICA (see Fig. 6).
There is only one point of misclassification in ICA, if a threshold value is defined.

Fig. 6. Projection of independent components (above) and principal component (below) to their Fisher discriminant line.

However there are more overlaps in the projection of principal components to the Fisher discriminant line.

3.4   Separation Degree

The MCD in Eq. 12 can be used to map the cluster separation for each component onto the same information for each landmark points. This enables a more intuitive regional interpretation of the differences between the two groups.

From the sorting of independent components, location and width of each component are retrieved. Thus we can generate the corresponding Gaussian function for each component and multiply it with its MCD, resulting a Gaussian mixture for each landmark point. The sum of the Gaussian mixture is called *separation degree*. Figure 7(a) shows the separation degree of the ICA model from normal and patient subjects. Figure 7(b) also shows the same visualization, but a more intuitive way using the bullseye plot, where the color denotes the separation degree.

Figure 7(b) corresponds with Figure 4(a), where the most important feature to distinguish between normal and patient is the endocardium at ES phase. The least important features lie on the epicardium contour at ES phase, where there is a small separation degree.

4   Discussion

In this paper, we have investigated the potential of ICA in the computer-aided diagnosis of myocardial diseases, based on cardiac shapes. The first result indicates that the ICA method is a promising analysis tool to extract local shape deformations from observed data. The sorting method of independent components based on their position leads to an anatomically meaningful interpretation

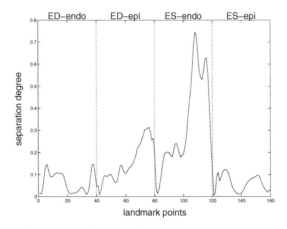

(a) Separation degree for each ICA mode

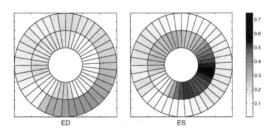

(b) Bullseye plot of the separation degree. The inner wall is endo-contour and the outer is epi-contour.

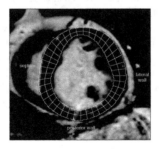

(c) An illustration of the bullseye plot interpretation in the short-axes MRI.

Fig. 7. The separation degree of the ICA model between normal subjects and infarct patients.

for classification purposes. We have shown that the weighting coefficient matrix from the ICA model can clearly distinguish between the two different groups in the endo-contour at ES.

From the cluster analysis, projection of independent components to the Fisher discriminant line gives better cluster representation than principal components. Given the ability to classify globally and to extract local features, ICA is a powerful tool to detect and to localize shape abnormalities, comparing favorably to PCA.

In our study, we found that most of the infarction area affects the endocardium in the infero-lateral wall, because our data contains most patients who have infarction in the lateral and inferior regions. A few patients have infarction in the septum area. From this study, the endocardium at end-systole phase is the most distinguishable feature, because this is the part of myocardium having the most deformation process due to contraction.

The reason why we do not perform any classification experiment in this study is that the problem of classifying a patient versus normal is a toy problem. In clinical routine, it is not interesting to determine a subject as a patient. It is more important to detect if there is an anomaly, to localize it and then to quantify the disease.

5   Future Work

The number of computed independent components is a free parameter to choose. The smaller the number is, the more global the independent components are for a shape variation. On the other hand, the shape variation becomes more localized if this parameter is increased. Thus a method to find an optimal number of independent components is needed. An analysis of how sensitive this parameter is to the diagnostic performance in this case will be helpful to define the optimal value.

The next important clinical question for the diagnosis of myocardial infarction is at which particular region of myocardium a patient has an infarction. This basically to localize the local abnormality and to quantify the severity of the disease. These are the topics of ongoing research.

Acknowledgement This work is supported by the Dutch Science Foundation (NWO), under the 2nd batch of the innovational research incentive grant, vernieuwingsimpuls 2001. A.F. Frangi is supported by a Ramón y Cajal Research Fellowship and grants TIC2002-04495-CO2 and ISCIII G03/185 from the Spanish Ministries of Science & Technology, and Health, respectively.

References

[1] Bartlett, M.S., Movellan, J.R., Sejnowski, T.J.: Face Recognition by Independent Component Analysis. IEEE Trans. on Neural Networks **13** (2002) 1450–1464

[2] Lee, T.W., Lewicki, M.S., Sejnowski, T.J.: ICA Mixture Models for Unsupervised Classification of Non-Gaussian Classes and Automatic Context Switching in Blind Signal Separation. IEEE Trans. on PAMI **22** (2000)

[3] Duda, R.O., Hart, P.E., Stork, D.G.: Pattern Classification. 2 edn. John Wiley & Sons, Inc. (2001)

[4] Moghaddam, B.: Principal Manifolds and Probabilistic Subspaces for Visual Recognition. IEEE Trans. on PAMI **24** (2002)

[5] Draper, B.A., Baek, K., Bartlett, M.S., Beveridge, J.R.: Recognizing Faces with PCA and ICA. Computer Vision and Image Understanding **91** (2003) 115–137

[6] Üzümcü, M., Frangi, A.F., Reiber, J.H., Lelieveldt, B.P.: Independent Component Analysis in Statistical Shape Models. In Sonka, M., Fitzpatrick, J.M., eds.: Proc. of SPIE. Volume 5032. (2003) 375–383

[7] Hyvärinen, A., Oja, E.: Independent Component Analysis: Algorithms and Applications. Neural Networks **13** (2000) 411–430

[8] Hyvärinen, A.: Survey on Independent Component Analysis. Neural Computing Surveys **2** (1999) 94–128

[9] Cardoso, J., Souloumiac, A.: Blind Beamforming for Non Gaussian Signals. IEEE Proceedings-F **140** (1993) 362–370

Principal Geodesic Analysis on Symmetric Spaces: Statistics of Diffusion Tensors

P. Thomas Fletcher and Sarang Joshi

Medical Image Display and Analysis Group,
University of North Carolina at Chapel Hill
fletcher@cs.unc.edu

Abstract. Diffusion tensor magnetic resonance imaging (DT-MRI) is emerging as an important tool in medical image analysis of the brain. However, relatively little work has been done on producing statistics of diffusion tensors. A main difficulty is that the space of diffusion tensors, i.e., the space of symmetric, positive-definite matrices, does not form a vector space. Therefore, standard linear statistical techniques do not apply. We show that the space of diffusion tensors is a type of curved manifold known as a Riemannian symmetric space. We then develop methods for producing statistics, namely averages and modes of variation, in this space. In our previous work we introduced principal geodesic analysis, a generalization of principal component analysis, to compute the modes of variation of data in Lie groups. In this work we expand the method of principal geodesic analysis to symmetric spaces and apply it to the computation of the variability of diffusion tensor data. We expect that these methods will be useful in the registration of diffusion tensor images, the production of statistical atlases from diffusion tensor data, and the quantification of the anatomical variability caused by disease.

1 Introduction

Diffusion tensor magnetic resonance imaging (DT-MRI) [2] produces a 3D diffusion tensor, i.e., a 3×3, symmetric, positive-definite matrix, at each voxel of an imaging volume. This tensor is the covariance in a Brownian motion model of the diffusion of water at that voxel. In brain imaging DT-MRI is used to track the white matter fibers, which demonstrate higher diffusivity of water in the direction of the fiber. The aim of this paper is to provide new methods for the statistical analysis of diffusion tensors.

Diffusion tensor imaging has shown promise in clinical studies of brain pathologies, such as multiple sclerosis and stroke, and in the study of brain connectivity [4]. Several authors have addressed the problem of estimation and smoothing within a DT image [6, 7, 14]. Further insights might be had from the use of diffusion tensor imaging in intersubject studies. Statistical brain atlases have been used in the case of scalar images to quantify anatomical variability across patients. However, relatively little work has been done towards constructing statistical brain atlases from diffusion tensor images. Alexander *et al.* [1] describe a method for the registration of multiple DT images into a common coordinate frame, however, they do not include a statistical analysis of the diffusion tensor data. Previous attempts [3, 12] at statistical analysis of diffusion

M. Šonka et al. (Eds.): CVAMIA-MMBIA 2004, LNCS 3117, pp. 87–98, 2004.
© Springer-Verlag Berlin Heidelberg 2004

tensors within a DT image are based on a Gaussian model of the linear tensor coefficients. In this paper we demonstrate that the space of diffusion tensors is more naturally described as a Riemannian symmetric space, rather than a linear space. In our previous work we introduced *principal geodesic analysis* (PGA) as an analog of principal component analysis for studying the statistical variability of Lie group data. Extending these ideas to symmetric spaces, we develop new methods for computing averages and describing the variability of diffusion tensor data. We show that these statistics preserve natural properties of the diffusion tensors, most importantly the positive-definiteness, that are not preserved by linear statistics. The framework presented in this paper thus provides the statistical methods needed for constructing statistical atlases of diffusion tensor images.

2   The Space of Diffusion Tensors

Recall that a real $n \times n$ matrix A is symmetric if $A = A^T$ and positive-definite if $x^T A x > 0$ for all nonzero $x \in \mathbb{R}^n$. We denote the space of all $n \times n$ symmetric, positive-definite matrices as $P(n)$. The tensors in DT-MRI are thus elements of $P(3)$. The space $P(n)$ forms a convex subset of $\mathbb{R}^{n^2}$. One can define a linear average of N positive-definite, symmetric matrices $A_1, \ldots, A_N$ as $\mu = \frac{1}{N} \sum_{i=1}^{N} A_i$. This definition minimizes the Euclidean metric on $\mathbb{R}^{n^2}$. Since $P(n)$ is convex, μ is lies within $P(n)$, however, linear averages do not interpolate natural properties. The linear average of matrices of the same determinant can result in a matrix with a larger determinant. Second order statistics are even more problematic. The standard principal component analysis is invalid because the straight lines defined by the modes of variation do not stay within the space $P(n)$. In other words, linear PCA does not preserve the positive-definiteness of diffusion tensors. The reason for such difficulties is that space $P(n)$, although a subset of a vector space, is not a vector space, e.g., the negation of a positive-definite matrix is not positive-definite.

In this paper we derive a more natural metric on the space of diffusion tensors, $P(n)$, by viewing it not simply as a subset of $\mathbb{R}^{n^2}$, but rather as a Riemannian symmetric space. Following Fréchet [9], we define the average as the minimum mean squared error estimator under this metric. We develop the method of principal geodesic analysis to describe the variability of diffusion tensor data. Principal geodesic analysis is the generalization of principal component analysis to manifolds. In this framework the modes of variation are represented as flows along geodesic curves, i.e., shortest paths under the Riemannian metric. These geodesic curves, unlike the straight lines of $\mathbb{R}^{n^2}$, are completely contained within $P(n)$, that is, they preserve the positive-definiteness. Principal component analysis generates lower-dimensional subspaces that maximize the projected variance of the data. Thus the development of principal geodesic analysis requires that we generalize the concepts of variance and projection onto lower-dimensional subspaces for data in symmetric spaces.

To illustrate these issues, consider the space $P(2)$, the 2×2 symmetric, positive-definite matrices. A matrix $A \in P(2)$ is of the form

$$A = \begin{pmatrix} a & b \\ b & c \end{pmatrix}, \quad ac - b^2 > 0, \quad a > 0.$$

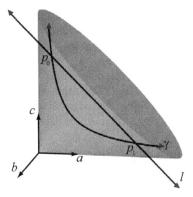

Fig. 1. The space $P(2)$, showing the geodesic γ and the straight line l between the two points p_0 and p_1.

If we consider the matrix A as a point $(a, b, c) \in \mathbb{R}^3$, then the above conditions describe the interior of a cone as shown in Fig. 1. The two labelled points are $p_0 = (1, 0, 7), p_1 = (7, 0, 1)$. The straight line l between the two points does not remain contained within the space $P(2)$. The curve γ is the geodesic between the two points when $P(2)$ is considered as a Riemannian symmetric space. This geodesic lies completely within $P(2)$. We chose $P(2)$ as an example since it can be easily visualized, but the same phenomenon occurs for general $P(n)$, i.e., $n > 2$.

3   The Geometry of $P(n)$

In this section we show that the space of diffusion tensors, $P(n)$, can be formulated as a Riemannian symmetric space. This leads to equations for computing geodesics that will be essential in defining the statistical methods for diffusion tensors. The differential geometry of diffusion tensors has also been used in [6], where the diffusion tensor smoothing was constrained along geodesic curves. A more thorough treatment of symmetric spaces can be found in [5, 10].

A *symmetric space* is a connected Riemannian manifold M such that for each $x \in M$ there is an isometry σ_x which (1) is involutive, i.e., $\sigma_x^2 = \text{id}$, and (2) has x as an isolated fixed point, that is, there is a neighborhood U of x where σ_x leaves only x fixed. It can be shown that σ_x is the map that reverses all geodesics through the point x. Riemannian symmetric spaces, and the methods for computing geodesics and distances on them, arise naturally from Lie group actions on manifolds.

3.1   Lie Group Actions

A *Lie group* is an algebraic group G that also forms a differentiable manifold, where the two group operations, multiplication and inversion, are smooth mappings. Many common geometric transformations of Euclidean space form Lie groups. For example, rotations, translations, and affine transformations of $\mathbb{R}^n$ all form Lie groups. More generally, Lie groups can be used to describe transformations of smooth manifolds.

Given a manifold M and a Lie group G, a *smooth group action* of G on M, or *smooth G-action* on M, is a smooth mapping $\phi : G \times M \rightarrow M$ such that for all $g, h \in G$, and all $x \in M$ we have $\phi(e, x) = x$, and $\phi(g, \phi(h, x)) = \phi(gh, x)$, where e is the identity element of G. Consider the Lie group of all $n \times n$ real matrices with positive determinant, denoted $GL^+(n)$. This group acts on $P(n)$ via

$$\phi : GL^+(n) \times P(n) \rightarrow P(n)$$
$$\phi(g, p) = gpg^T. \tag{1}$$

The *orbit* under ϕ of a point $x \in M$ is defined as $G(x) = \{\phi(g, x) : g \in G\}$. In the case that M consists of a single orbit, we call M a *homogeneous space* and say that the G-action is *transitive*. The space $P(n)$ is a homogeneous space, as is easy to derive from the fact that any matrix $p \in P(n)$ can be decomposed as $p = gg^T = \phi(g, I_n)$, where $g \in GL^+(n)$ and I_n is the $n \times n$ identity matrix. The *isotropy subgroup* of x is defined as $G_x = \{g \in G : \phi(g, x) = x\}$, i.e., G_x is the subgroup of G that leaves the point x fixed. For $P(n)$ the isotropy subgroup of I_n is $SO(n) = \{g \in GL^+(n) : \phi(g, I_n) = gg^T = I_n\}$, i.e., the space of $n \times n$ rotation matrices.

Let H be a closed Lie subgroup of the Lie group G. Then the *left coset* of an element $g \in G$ is defined as $gH = \{gh : h \in H\}$. The space of all such cosets is denoted G/H and is a smooth manifold. There is a natural bijection $G(x) \cong G/G_x$ given by the mapping $g \cdot x \mapsto gG_x$. Therefore, we can consider the space of diffusion tensors, $P(n)$, as the coset space $GL^+(n)/SO(n)$. An intuitive way to view this is to think of the polar decomposition, which decomposes a matrix $g \in GL^+(n)$ as $g = pu$, where $p \in P(n)$ and $u \in SO(n)$. Thus, the diffusion tensor space $P(n) \cong GL^+(n)/SO(n)$ comes from "dividing out" the rotational component in the polar decomposition of $GL^+(n)$.

3.2   Invariant Metrics

A *Riemannian metric* on a manifold M smoothly assigns to each point $x \in M$ an inner product $\langle \cdot, \cdot \rangle_x$ on $T_x M$, the tangent space to M at x. If ϕ is a smooth G-action on M, a metric on M is called *G-invariant* if for each $g \in G$ the map $\phi_g : x \mapsto \phi(g, x)$ is an isometry, i.e., ϕ_g preserves distances on M. The space of diffusion tensors, $P(n)$, has a metric that is invariant under the $GL^+(n)$ action, which follows from the fact that the isotropy subgroup $SO(n)$ is connected and compact (see [5], Theorem 9.1).

The tangent space of $P(n)$ at the identity matrix can be identified with the space of $n \times n$ symmetric matrices, $\mathrm{Sym}(n)$. Since the group action $\phi_g : s \mapsto gsg^T$ is linear, its derivative map, denoted $d\phi_g$, is given by $d\phi_g(X) = gXg^T$. If $X \in \mathrm{Sym}(n)$, it is easy to see that $d\phi_g(X)$ is again a symmetric matrix. Thus the tangent space at any point $p \in P(n)$ is also equivalent to $\mathrm{Sym}(n)$. If $X, Y \in \mathrm{Sym}(n)$ represent two tangent vectors at $p \in P(n)$, where $p = gg^T, g \in GL^+(n)$, then the Riemannian metric at p is given by the inner product

$$\langle X, Y \rangle_p = \mathrm{tr}(g^{-1} X p^{-1} Y (g^{-1})^T).$$

Finally, the mapping $\sigma_{I_n}(p) = p^{-1}$ is an isometry that reverses geodesics of $P(n)$ at the identity, and this turns $P(n)$ into a symmetric space.

3.3 Computing Geodesics

Geodesics on a symmetric space are easily derived via the group action (see [10] for details). Let p be a point on $P(n)$ and X a tangent vector at p. There is a unique geodesic, γ, with initial point $\gamma(0) = p$ and tangent vector $\gamma'(0) = X$. To derive an equation for such a geodesic, we begin with the special case where the initial point p is the $n \times n$ identity matrix, I_n, and the tangent vector X is diagonal. Then the geodesic is given by

$$\gamma(t) = \exp(tX),$$

where exp is the matrix exponential map given by the infinite series

$$\exp(X) = \sum_{k=0}^{\infty} \frac{1}{k!} X^k.$$

For the diagonal matrix X with entries x_i, the matrix exponential is simply the diagonal matrix with entries e^{x_i}.

Now for the general case consider the geodesic γ starting at an arbitrary point $p \in P(n)$ with arbitrary tangent vector $X \in \mathrm{Sym}(n)$. We will use the group action to map this configuration into the special case described above, i.e., with initial point at the identity and a diagonal tangent vector. Since the group action is an isometry, geodesics and distances are preserved. Let $p = gg^T$, where $g \in GL^+(n)$. Then the action $\phi_{g^{-1}}$ maps p to I_n. The tangent vector is mapped via the corresponding tangent map to $Y = d\phi_{g^{-1}}(X) = g^{-1}X(g^{-1})^T$. Now we may write $Y = v\Sigma v^T$, where v is a rotation matrix and Σ is diagonal. The group action $\phi_{v^{-1}}$ diagonalizes the tangent vector while leaving I_n fixed. We can now use the procedure above to compute the geodesic $\tilde{\gamma}$ with initial point $\tilde{\gamma}(0) = I_n$ and tangent vector $\tilde{\gamma}'(0) = \Sigma$. Finally, the result is mapped back to the original configuration by the inverse group action, ϕ_{gv}. That is,

$$\gamma(t) = \phi_{gv}(\tilde{\gamma}(t)) = (gv)\exp(t\Sigma)(gv)^T.$$

If we flow to $t = 1$ along the geodesic γ we get the Riemannian exponential map at p (denoted Exp_p, and not to be confused with the matrix exponential map), that is,

$$\mathrm{Exp}_p(X) = \gamma(1).$$

In summary we have

Algorithm 1 (Riemannian Exponential Map).
Input: Initial point $p \in P(n)$.
        Tangent vector $X \in \mathrm{Sym}(n)$.
Output: $\mathrm{Exp}_p(X)$
    Let $p = u\Lambda u^T$ ($u \in SO(n)$, Λ diagonal)
    $g = u\sqrt{\Lambda}$
    $Y = g^{-1}X(g^{-1})^T$
    Let $Y = v\Sigma v^T$ ($v \in SO(n)$, Σ diagonal)
    $\mathrm{Exp}_p(X) = (gv)\exp(\Sigma)(gv)^T$

An important property of the geodesics in $P(n)$ under this metric is that they are infinitely extendible, i.e., the geodesic $\gamma(t)$ is defined for $-\infty < t < \infty$. A manifold with this property is called *complete*. Again, Fig. 1 demonstrates that the symmetric space geodesic γ remains within $P(2)$ for all t. In contrast the straight line l quickly leaves the space $P(2)$.

The map Exp_p has an inverse, called the Riemannian log map and denoted Log_p. It maps a point $x \in P(n)$ to the unique tangent vector at p that is the initial velocity of the unique geodesic γ with $\gamma(0) = p$ and $\gamma(1) = x$. Using a similar diagonalization procedure, the log map is computed by

---

Algorithm 2 (Riemannian Log Map).
Input: Initial point $p \in P(n)$.
      End point $x \in P(n)$.
Output: $\mathrm{Log}_p(x)$
    Let $p = u\Lambda u^T$ ($u \in SO(n)$, Λ diagonal)
    $g = u\sqrt{\Lambda}$
    $y = g^{-1}x(g^{-1})^T$
    Let $y = v\Sigma v^T$ ($v \in SO(n)$, Σ diagonal)
    $\mathrm{Log}_p(x) = (gv)\log(\Sigma)(gv)^T$

Using the notation of Algorithm 2, geodesic distance between the diffusion tensors $p, x \in P(n)$ is computed by $d(p, x) = \| \mathrm{Log}_p(x) \|_p = \mathrm{tr}(\log(\Sigma)^2)$.

4 Statistics of Diffusion Tensors

Having formulated the geometry of diffusion tensors as a symmetric space, we now develop methods for computing statistics in this nonlinear space.

4.1 Averages of Diffusion Tensors

To define an average of diffusion tensors we follow Fréchet [9], who defines the mean of a random variable in an arbitrary metric space as the point that minimizes the expected value of the sum-of-squared distance function. Consider a set of points $A = \{x_1, \ldots, x_N\}$ on a Riemannian manifold M. Then we will be concerned with the sum-of-squared distance function

$$\rho_A(x) = \frac{1}{2N} \sum_{i=1}^{N} d(\mu, x_i)^2,$$

where d is geodesic distance on M. The *intrinsic mean* of the points in A is defined as a minimum of ρ_A, that is,

$$\mu = \arg \min_{x \in M} \rho_A(x). \tag{2}$$

The properties of the intrinsic mean have been studied by Karcher [11], and Pennec [13] describes a gradient descent algorithm to compute the mean. Since the mean is given by the minimization problem (2), we must verify that such a minimum exists and is unique. Karcher shows that for a manifold with non-positive sectional curvature the mean is uniquely defined. In fact, the space $P(n)$ does have non-positive sectional curvature, and, thus, the mean is uniquely defined. Also, the gradient of ρ_A is given by

$$\nabla \rho_A(x) = -\frac{1}{N} \sum_{i=1}^{N} \text{Log}_x(x_i)$$

Thus the intrinsic mean of a collection of diffusion tensors is computed by the following gradient descent algorithm:

Algorithm 3 (Intrinsic Mean of Diffusion Tensors).
Input: $p_1, \ldots, p_N \in P(n)$
Output: $\mu \in P(n)$, the intrinsic mean
  $\mu_0 = I$
  Do
    $X_i = \frac{1}{N} \sum_{k=1}^{N} \text{Log}_{\mu_i}(p_k)$
    $\mu_{i+1} = \text{Exp}_{\mu_i}(X_i)$
  While $||X_i|| > \epsilon$.

4.2 Principal Geodesic Analysis

Principal component analysis (PCA) is a useful method for describing the variability of Euclidean data. In our previous work [8] we introduced *principal geodesic analysis* (PGA) as a generalization of PCA to study the variability of data in a Lie group. In this section we review the method of principal geodesic analysis and apply it to the symmetric space of diffusion tensors. We begin with a review of PCA in Euclidean space. Consider a set of points $x_1, \ldots, x_N \in \mathbb{R}^d$ with zero mean. Principal component analysis seeks a sequence of linear subspaces that best represent the variability of the data. To be more precise, the intent is to find a orthonormal basis $\{v_1, \ldots, v_d\}$ of $\mathbb{R}^d$, which satisfies the recursive relationship

$$v_1 = \arg\max_{||v||=1} \sum_{i=1}^{N} \langle v, x_i \rangle^2, \tag{3}$$

$$v_k = \arg\max_{||v||=1} \sum_{i=1}^{N} \sum_{j=1}^{k-1} \langle v_j, x_i \rangle^2 + \langle v, x_i \rangle^2. \tag{4}$$

In other words, the subspace $V_k = \text{span}(\{v_1, \ldots, v_k\})$ is the k-dimensional subspace that maximizes the variance of the data projected to that subspace. The basis $\{v_k\}$ is computed as the set of eigenvectors of the sample covariance matrix of the data.

Now turning to manifolds, consider a set of points $p_1, \ldots, p_N$ on a Riemannian manifold M. Our goal is to describe the variability of the p_i in a way that is analogous to PCA. Thus we will project the data onto lower-dimensional subspaces that best represent the variability of the data. This requires first extending three important concepts of PCA into the manifold setting:

- **Variance.** Following the work of Fréchet, we define the sample variance of the data as the expected value of the squared Riemannian distance from the mean.
- **Geodesic subspaces.** The lower-dimensional subspaces in PCA are linear subspaces. For manifolds we extend the concept of a linear subspace to that of a *geodesic submanifold*.
- **Projection.** In PCA the data is projected onto linear subspaces. We define a projection operator for geodesic submanifolds, and show how it may be efficiently approximated.

We now develop each of these concepts in detail.

Variance The variance σ^2 of a real-valued random variable x with mean μ is given by the formula $\sigma^2 = \mathcal{E}[(x - \mu)^2]$, where $\mathcal{E}$ denotes expectation. It measures the expected localization of the variable x about the mean. The definition of variance we use comes from Fréchet [9], who defines the variance of a random variable in a metric space as the expected value of the squared distance from the mean. That is, for a random variable x in a metric space with intrinsic mean μ, the variance is given by

$$\sigma^2 = \mathcal{E}[d(\mu, x)^2].$$

Thus in the manifold case, given data points $p_1, \ldots, p_N \in M$ with mean μ, we define the sample variance of the data as

$$\sigma^2 = \sum_{i=1}^{N} d(\mu, p_i)^2 = \sum_{i=1}^{N} \| \operatorname{Log}_\mu(p_i) \|^2. \tag{5}$$

Notice that if M is $\mathbb{R}^n$, then the variance definition in (5) is given by the trace of the sample covariance matrix, i.e., the sum of its eigenvalues. It is in this sense that this definition captures the total variation of the data.

Geodesic Submanifolds The next step in generalizing PCA to manifolds is to generalize the notion of a linear subspace. A geodesic is a curve that is locally the shortest path between points. In this way a geodesic is the generalization of a straight line. Thus it is natural to use a geodesic curve as the one-dimensional subspace, i.e., the analog of the first principal direction in PCA.

In general if N is a submanifold of a manifold M, geodesics of N are not necessarily geodesics of M. For instance the sphere S^2 is a submanifold of $\mathbb{R}^3$, but its geodesics are great circles, while geodesics of $\mathbb{R}^3$ are straight lines. A submanifold H of M is said to be *geodesic at* $x \in H$ if all geodesics of H passing through x are also geodesics of M. For example, a linear subspace of $\mathbb{R}^d$ is a submanifold geodesic at 0. Submanifolds geodesic at x preserve distances to x. This is an essential property for PGA because variance is defined by squared distance to the mean. Thus submanifolds geodesic at the mean will be the generalization of the linear subspaces of PCA.

Projection The projection of a point $x \in M$ onto a geodesic submanifold H of M is defined as the point on H that is nearest to x in Riemannian distance. Thus we define the projection operator $\pi_H : M \to H$ as

$$\pi_H(x) = \arg\min_{y \in H} d(x, y)^2.$$

Since projection is defined by a minimization, there is no guarantee that the projection of a point exists or that it is unique. However, because $P(n)$ has non-positive curvature and no conjugate points, projection onto geodesic submanifolds is unique in this case.

Projection onto a geodesic submanifold at μ can be approximated in the tangent space to the mean, $T_\mu M$. If $v_1, \ldots, v_k$ is an orthonormal basis for $T_\mu H$, then the projection operator can be approximated by the formula

$$\mathrm{Log}_\mu\left(\pi_H(x)\right) \approx \sum_{i=1}^{k} \langle v_i, \mathrm{Log}_\mu(x) \rangle_\mu. \tag{6}$$

4.3 Computing Principal Geodesic Analysis

We are now ready to define principal geodesic analysis for data $p_1, \ldots, p_N$ on a connected Riemannian manifold M. Our goal, analogous to PCA, is to find a sequence of nested geodesic submanifolds that maximize the projected variance of the data. These submanifolds are called the *principal geodesic submanifolds*.

The principal geodesic submanifolds are defined by first constructing an orthonormal basis of tangent vectors $v_1, \ldots, v_d$ that span the tangent space $T_\mu M$. These vectors are then used to form a sequence of nested subspaces $V_k = \mathrm{span}(\{v_1, \ldots, v_k\})$. The principal geodesic submanifolds are the images of the V_k under the exponential map: $H_k = \mathrm{Exp}_\mu(V_k)$. The first principal direction is chosen to maximize the projected variance along the corresponding geodesic:

$$v_1 = \arg\max_{||v||=1} \sum_{i=1}^{N} || \mathrm{Log}_\mu(\pi_H(p_i)) ||^2, \tag{7}$$

$$\text{where} \quad H = \exp(\mathrm{span}(\{v\})).$$

The remaining principal directions are then defined recursively as

$$v_k = \arg\max_{||v||=1} \sum_{i=1}^{N} || \mathrm{Log}_\mu(\pi_H(p_i)) ||^2, \tag{8}$$

$$\text{where} \quad H = \exp(\mathrm{span}(\{v_1, \ldots, v_{k-1}, v\})).$$

If we use (6) to approximate the projection operator π_H in (7) and (8), we get

$$v_1 \approx \arg\max_{||v||=1} \sum_{i=1}^{N} \langle v, \mathrm{Log}_\mu(p_i) \rangle_\mu^2,$$

$$v_k \approx \arg\max_{||v||=1} \sum_{i=1}^{N} \sum_{j=1}^{k-1} \langle v_j, \mathrm{Log}_\mu(p_i) \rangle_\mu^2 + \langle v, \mathrm{Log}_\mu(p_i) \rangle_\mu^2.$$

The above minimization problem is simply the standard principal component analysis in $T_\mu M$ of the vectors $\mathrm{Log}_\mu(p_i)$, which can be seen by comparing the approximations above to the PCA equations, (3) and (4). Applying these ideas to $P(n)$, we have the following algorithm for approximating the PGA of diffusion tensor data:

Algorithm 4 (PGA of Diffusion Tensors).

Input: $p_1, \ldots, p_N \in P(n)$

Output: Principal directions, $v_k \in \mathrm{Sym}(n)$

       Variances, $\lambda_k \in \mathbb{R}$

  $\mu = $ intrinsic mean of $\{p_i\}$ (Algorithm 3)

  $x_i = \mathrm{Log}_\mu(p_i)$

  $\mathbf{S} = \frac{1}{N}\sum_{i=1}^{N} x_i x_i^T$ (treating the x_i as column vectors)

  $\{v_k, \lambda_k\}$ = eigenvectors/eigenvalues of $\mathbf{S}$.

A new diffusion tensor p can now be generated from the PGA by the formula $p = \mathrm{Exp}_\mu\left(\sum_{k=1}^{d}\alpha_k v_k\right)$, where the $\alpha_k \in \mathbb{R}$ are the coefficients of the modes of variation.

5   Properties of PGA on $P(n)$

We now demonstrate that PGA on the symmetric space $P(n)$ preserves certain important properties of the diffusion tensor data, namely the properties of positive-definiteness, determinant, and orientation. This makes the symmetric space formulation an attractive approach for the statistical analysis of diffusion tensor images. We have already mentioned that, in contrast to linear PCA, symmetric space PGA preserves positive-definiteness. That is, the principal geodesics are completely contained within $P(n)$, and any matrix generated by the principal geodesics will be positive-definite.

The next two properties we consider are the determinant and orientation. Consider a collection of diffusion tensors that all have the same determinant D. We wish to show that the resulting average and any tensor generated by the principal geodesic analysis will also have determinant D. To show this we first look at the subset of $P(n)$ of matrices with determinant D, that is, the subset $P_D = \{p \in P(n) : \det(p) = D\}$. This subset is a *totally geodesic submanifold*, meaning that any geodesic within P_D is a geodesic of the full space $P(n)$. Notice the difference from the definition of a submanifold geodesic at a point; totally geodesic submanifolds are geodesic at *every* point. Now, the fact that P_D is totally geodesic implies that the averaging process in Algorithm 3 will remain in P_D if all the data lies in P_D. Also, the principal directions v_k in the PGA will lie in the tangent subspace $T_\mu P_D$. Thus any diffusion tensor generated by the principal geodesics will remain in the space P_D.

The same argument may be applied to show that symmetric space averaging and PGA preserve the orientation of diffusion tensors. In fact, the subset of all diffusion tensors having the same orientation is also a totally geodesic submanifold, and the same reasoning applies. Unlike the positive-definiteness and determinant, orientations are also preserved by linear averaging and PCA.

To demonstrate these properties, we simulated random 3D diffusion tensors and computed both their linear and symmetric space statistics. We first tested the determinant preservation by generating 100 random 3D diffusion tensors with determinant 1.

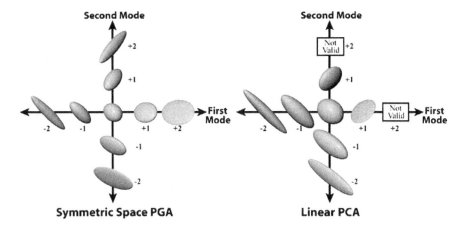

Fig. 2. The first two modes of variation of the simulated data: (left) using the symmetric space PGA, and (right) using linear PCA. Units are in standard deviations. The boxes labelled "Not Valid" indicate that the tensor was not positive-definite, i.e., it had negative eigenvalues.

To do this we first generated 100 random 3×3 symmetric matrices, with entries distributed according to a normal distribution, $N(0, \frac{1}{2})$. Then, we took the matrix exponential of these random symmetric matrices, thus making them positive-definite diffusion tensors. Finally, we normalized the random diffusion tensors to have determinant 1 by dividing each tensor by the cube root of its determinant. We then computed the linear average and PCA and symmetric space average and PGA of the simulated tensors. The results are shown in Fig. 2 as the diffusion tensors generated by the first two modes of variation. The linear PCA generated invalid diffusion tensors, i.e., tensors with negative eigenvalues, at $+2$ standard deviations in both the first and second modes. All of the diffusion tensors generated by the symmetric space PGA have determinant 1. The linear mean demonstrates the "swelling" effect of linear averaging. It has determinant 2.70, and the linear PCA tensors within ± 2 standard deviations have determinants ranging from -2.80 to 2.82. The negative determinants came from the tensors that were not positive-definite. Therefore, we see that the symmetric space PGA has preserved the positive-definiteness and the determinant, while the linear PCA has preserved neither.

Next we tested the orientation preservation by generating 100 random, axis-aligned, 3D diffusion tensors. This was done by generating 3 random eigenvalues for each matrix, corresponding to the x, y, and z axes. The eigenvalues were chosen from a lognormal distribution with log mean 0 and log standard deviation 0.5. Next we generated a random orientation $u \in SO(3)$ and applied it to all of the axis-aligned matrices by the map $p \mapsto upu^T$. Thus each of the diffusion tensors in our test set had eigenvectors equal to the columns of the rotation matrix u. We computed both the symmetric space and linear statistics of the data. As was expected, both methods preserved the orientations. However, the linear PCA again generated tensors that were not positive-definite.

6 Conclusion

We have presented a framework for the statistical analysis of diffusion tensor images. The methods rely on regarding the space of diffusion tensors as a Riemannian symmetric space. We developed algorithms for computing averages and modes of variation of diffusion tensor data by extending statistical methods to the symmetric space setting. The methods presented in this paper lay the groundwork for statistical studies of the variability of diffusion tensor images across patients.

7 Acknowledgements

We would like to thank Dr. Guido Gerig and Dr. Stephen Pizer for useful discussions and suggestions. This work was done with support from NIH grants P01 CA47982 and EB02779.

References

[1] D. C. Alexander, C. Pierpaoli, P.J. Basser, and J.C. Gee. Spatial transformations of diffusion tensor MR images. *IEEE Transactions on Medical Imaging*, 20(11):1131–1139, 2001.

[2] P. J. Basser, J. Mattiello, and D. Le Bihan. MR diffusion tensor spectroscopy and imaging. *Biophysics Journal*, 66:259–267, 1994.

[3] P. J. Basser and S. Pajevic. A normal distribution for tensor-valued random variables: applications to diffusion tensor MRI. *IEEE Transactions on Medical Imaging*, 22(7):785–794, 2003.

[4] D. Le Bihan, J.-F. Mangin, C. Poupon, C. A. Clark, S. Pappata, N. Molko, and H. Chabriat. Diffusion tensor imaging: concepts and applications. *Journal of Magnetic Resonance Imaging*, 13:534–546, 2001.

[5] W. M. Boothby. *An Introduction to Differentiable Manifolds and Riemannian Geometry.* Academic Press, 2nd edition, 1986.

[6] C. Chefd'hotel, D. Tschumperlé, R. Deriche, and O. Faugeras. Constrained flows of matrix-valued functions: Application to diffusion tensor regularization. In *European Conference on Computer Vision*, pages 251–265, 2002.

[7] O. Coulon, D. C. Alexander, and S. Arridge. Diffusion tensor magnetic resonance image regularization. *Medical Image Analysis*, 8(1):47–68, 2004.

[8] P. T. Fletcher, C. Lu, and S. Joshi. Statistics of shape via principal geodesic analysis on Lie groups. In *IEEE Conf. on Computer Vision and Pattern Recognition*, pages 95–101, 2003.

[9] M. Fréchet. Les éléments aléatoires de nature quelconque dans un espace distancié. *Ann. Inst. H. Poincaré*, (10):215–310, 1948.

[10] S. Helgason. *Differential Geometry, Lie Groups, and Symmetric Spaces.* Academic Press, 1978.

[11] H. Karcher. Riemannian center of mass and mollifier smoothing. *Communications on Pure and Applied Mathematics*, 30(5):509–541, 1977.

[12] S. Pajevic and P. J. Basser. Parametric and non-parametric statistical analysis of DT-MRI. *Journal of Magnetic Resonance*, 161(1):1–14, 2003.

[13] X. Pennec. Probabilities and statistics on Riemannian manifolds: basic tools for geometric measurements. In *IEEE Workshop on Nonlinear Signal and Image Processing*, 1999.

[14] Z. Wang, B. C. Vemuri, Y. Chen, and T. Mareci. A constrained variational principle for direct estimation and smoothing of the diffusion tensor field from DWI. In *Information Processing in Medical Imaging*, pages 660–671, 2003.

Symmetric Geodesic Shape Averaging and Shape Interpolation

Brian Avants and James Gee

University of Pennsylvania
Philadelphia, PA, USA 19104-2644
{avants,gee}@grasp.cis.upenn.edu

Abstract. Structural image registration is often achieved through diffeomorphic transformations. The formalism associated with the diffeomorphic framework allows one to define curved distances which are often more appropriate for morphological comparisons of anatomy. However, the correspondence problem as well as the metric distances across the database depend upon the chosen reference anatomy, requiring average transformations to be estimated. The goal of this paper is to develop an algorithm which, given a database of images, estimates an average shape based on the geodesic distances of curved, time-dependent transformations. Specifically, this paper will develop direct, efficient, symmetric methods for generating average anatomical shapes from diffeomorphic registration algorithms. The need for these types of averages is illustrated with synthetic examples and the novel algorithm is compared to the usual approach of averaging linear transformations. Furthermore, the same algorithm will be used for shape interpolation that is independent of the multi-scale framework used.

1 Introduction

An atlas may be used as an instance of anatomy upon which teaching or surgical planning is based [1], a reference frame for understanding the normal variation of anatomy [2], a coordinate system for functional localization studies [3], and as a probabilistic space into which functional or structural features are mapped [4]. Least biased examples are desirable for teaching, as well as for creating coordinate systems that are near the centroid of a population distribution. Performance of algorithms based on manipulating canonical information, such as active shape, should also improve when using an average model.

Computerized atlases based on MRI images may capture either average shape [4], average intensity or both [5] within a single image. Deviations from the mean shape or intensity may be stored separately by statistical models such as principal components [4]. Average intensities are found by first computing transformations from a given anatomical instance to a population dataset. These transformations give intensity correspondence, allowing subsequent averaging. Average shapes are gained by estimating the average of these transformations,

M. Šonka et al. (Eds.): CVAMIA-MMBIA 2004, LNCS 3117, pp. 99–110, 2004.

which take a given member of population to the remainder of the data. This average transformation must then be inverted to gain the average shape [5].

One difficulty with this approach is that the process of averaging transformations may destroy the physical and optimal properties of the individual transformations. For example, the average of large deformation elastic displacement fields, each of which satisfy the minimization of a well-defined variational energy, may no longer be an optimizing elastic displacement field. Another example is given by time-parameterized mappings. The flows defining these transformations at each time satisfy the fluid equations, allowing the maps to be interpreted as members of the diffeomorphism group [6]. This invites group theoretical population studies where one bases structural comparisons on the geodesic distances of the group. Thus, it is important to be able to compute atlases which are least-biased within this theoretical framework, as in the small deformation case. This work provides a general algorithm for allowing shape averaging that enables properties of the physical model used in the registration to persist in the average shape transformation. The distances given by the diffeomorphism group are used to illustrate the techniques.

2   Population Shape Averaging

Consider a set of anatomical images defined on bounded domain Ω, each of which contains identical topology initially at positions $\{\mathbf{x}_i\}$. Shape normalization requires a reparameterization of this population dataset, $P = \{\mathbf{x}_i\}$, into a common coordinate space. Each coordinate $\bar{\mathbf{x}}$ then identifies the same anatomical position in each example. Formally, this requires a mapping set $\{\boldsymbol{g}_i : \bar{\mathbf{x}} \rightarrow \mathbf{x_i}\}$ that gives,

$$\boldsymbol{g}_1^{-1}\mathbf{x_1} = \bar{\mathbf{x}},$$

$$\cdots$$

$$\boldsymbol{g}_n^{-1}\mathbf{x_n} = \bar{\mathbf{x}}. \tag{1}$$

Each mapping gives the coordinate transformation between the canonical configuration $\bar{\mathbf{x}}$ and $\mathbf{x_i}$, such that $\boldsymbol{g}_i = \mathbf{Id} + \mathbf{u}$, where $\mathbf{Id}$ is the identity. This gives $\boldsymbol{g}_i(\bar{\mathbf{x}}) = \bar{\mathbf{x}} + \mathbf{u}(\bar{\mathbf{x}}) = \mathbf{x_i}$. If $\boldsymbol{g}_i$ is time-parameterized in interval $[0, 1]$, its value is taken at $\boldsymbol{g}_i(1)$, the final state.

The individual mappings, $\boldsymbol{g}_i$, may be found by using non-rigid image registration algorithms [4, 3, 7]. In general, these methods return a displacement field, $\mathbf{u}$, that models the motion of a continuum deforming under external forces. Solutions of this kind minimize a balance of regularization and similarity terms. The displacement field is found in either the Lagrangian reference frame, where the reference configuration $\mathbf{x}$ is fixed, or in the Eulerian frame, where the configuration is a function of time, $\mathbf{x}(t)$. The distinction here is that the Eulerian frame tracks the flow in time, giving the displacement as the time-integration of a velocity field, $\frac{D\boldsymbol{g}}{dt} = \boldsymbol{v}(t)$, where the material derivative is used. Given a value for $\mathbf{u}$, the solution will transform the moving image $J(\mathbf{x}_i)$ to the fixed domain $I(\bar{\mathbf{x}})$ such that $J'(\bar{\mathbf{x}}) = J(\mathbf{Id} + \mathbf{u}_i^{-1})(\mathbf{x}_i) = J \circ g_i^{-1} \circ \mathbf{x_i}$.

2.1   Shape Average from Mean Deformation: Linear Averaging

Here, we assume a registration algorithm has provided a correspondence field. Given the ability to gain this solution, average shapes are found by choosing an arbitrary instance as the reference configuration, $\mathbf{x_o} = \mathbf{x_j}$, and then computing $\{g_i\}$ with respect to this configuration. The resulting average displacement field from $\mathbf{x_o}$ to $\{\mathbf{x_i}\}$ is,

$$\bar{\mathbf{u}}(\mathbf{x_o}) = (N)^{-1} \sum_{i=1}^{N} \mathbf{u}_i. \tag{2}$$

This mean deformation minimizes the energy,

$$\bar{\mathbf{u}}(\mathbf{x_o}) = \underset{\mathbf{u}}{\operatorname{argmin}} \frac{1}{2} \sum_{i=1}^{N} |\mathbf{u}_i - \mathbf{u}|^2 \tag{3}$$

Note that, as the total displacement fields are used, all scales of information are treated equally. The average configuration is then computed as $\bar{\mathbf{x}} = \bar{g}^{-1}\mathbf{x_o}$, where an inversion of the mean deformation field is required. Averaging of vector fields does not necessarily preserve the large deformation continuum model, nor does it satisfy the correct optimization model, as illustrated in figure 1.

3   Curved Case: The Diffeomorphism Group and Its Distances

3.1   Definitions and Group Properties

The set of one to one and onto differentiable maps with differentiable inverse gives the diffeomorphism group, $\mathcal{G}$. Elements of the group may be composed with each other and distances between them measured by (in the case of image registration),

$$D(I, J) = \inf_{v \in \mathcal{G}} \{ \int_0^1 \|v(t)\|_L dt \mid J \circ g^{-1}(0) = J \wedge J \circ g^{-1}(1) = I \}. \tag{4}$$

The differential Sobolev norm on v is determined by the associated linear (e.g. Cauchy-Navier) operator L. This is a true distance in that it is positive, symmetric and satisfies the triangle inequality [8]. The incremental integration of the velocity field is what gives this property (consider that the flow along the velocity field is, in the infinisimial limit, piece-wise linear with equivalent norm forward and backward in time). In contrast, deformation-based norms taken from continuum mechanics are also positive and equal zero at the identity, but may not be symmetric.

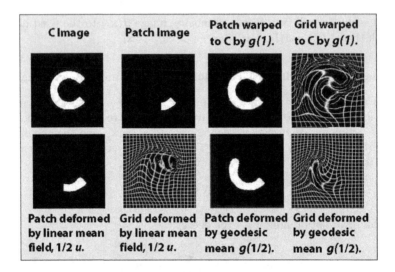

Fig. 1. The "C" and "C patch" images (first and second in the top row) are registered with the large deformation diffeomorphic method in the top row, giving transformation $g(t)$. The result of linearly averaging the vector field u at $g(1)$ with **Id** is shown in the bottom row left and left middle. The averaging given by geodesic distances, at bottom row right, is more natural. Deformed grid images are also shown for the geodesic average. The jacobian of the C to C patch map is strictly positive with minimum value 0.14.

3.2 The Diffeomorphic Registration Algorithm

The optimization problem for the registration is to compute the mapping, $\boldsymbol{g}$, such that,

$$\boldsymbol{g}^{\star} = \mathop{\mathrm{argmin}}_{\boldsymbol{v}(t)} \; \Big\{ \; \int_0^1 \; \|\boldsymbol{v}\|_L^2 + \|I\boldsymbol{g}^{-1} - J\| \; dt \; \Big\}, \tag{5}$$

is minimized where the brightness constancy assumption is used as the driving force [9]. Additionally, the maps are fixed to the identity at the boundary of the domain, $d\Omega$.

The Euler-Lagrange (E-L) equations for this problem were recently derived [8]. Rather than using the local E-L equations, we solve the variational problem in the integral form by using the Galerkin finite element (FE) method [10]. This method finds an optimal finite dimensional estimate to the infinite-dimensional solution. Using this method we compute the instantaneously optimal velocity field as,

$$\boldsymbol{v}(\cdot, t) = \mathop{\mathrm{argmin}}_{\boldsymbol{v} \in \mathcal{G}} \; \{ \; w_1\|I\boldsymbol{g}^{-1} - J\| + w_2\|\boldsymbol{v}\|_L^2 \; \}, \tag{6}$$

which gives the optimal gradient in the space of diffeomorphic flows. The optimal estimate to the time-integrated map is approximated by using finite differences.

This requires parameterization of g by arc length, the unique and natural choice for (even infinite-dimensional) curves.

The time dependent integral for g is estimated with finite differences in time via the trapezoidal rule. Because the optimization process is not locally smooth in time, we measure the arc length at a step-size, h, that is larger than that of the optimization step-size $\|\delta v\|$, with δ a small scalar. This is illustrated for a one dimensional map in figure 2 (the ratio is typically near 0.1). The incremental velocities are accumulated via gradient descent such that $v^\star(t) \approx \mathbf{Id} + \sum_{i=0}^{i=n} \delta v_i$. The total map $g(t)$ is then integrated to $g(t+h)$ using $v^\star(t)$ when $\|v^\star(t)\|$ reaches the desired constant value, h. If the arc length oversteps h, a local line search on δv_n corrects the size of $\|v^\star\|$. The trapezoidal rule then gives the optimal in time approximation to the length as,

$$\int_{t_a}^{t_b} \|v(t)\|_L \, dt \approx \sum_{i=1}^{i=n} \frac{h}{2}(\|v(t_i + (i-1)h)\|_L + \|v(t_i + ih)\|_L). \tag{7}$$

This gives a more robust estimate of the geodesic distance and is also beneficial for the shape averaging application (we have found the distances estimated by the greedy method in [7] are too noisy).

To summarize, the following steps are needed in the algorithm for computing geodesics:

1. Solve for the instantaneous regularized velocity field using the FE method.
2. Use the FE solution for gradient descent, accumulating δv until the arc length reaches h.
3. Integrate v to augment g in time and to compute a robust estimate of the geodesic distance.

Note the advantage that the velocity field is only needed at two time points, although an optimal in time solution is computed. Regridding is also performed, as in [7].

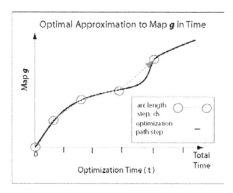

Fig. 2. The computation of the optimal g in time is performed using the trapezoidal rule, requiring constant arc length parameterization.

4   The Variational Problem for Diffeomorphic Averaging

We recover the average-shape image from an image dataset by solving an inverse problem involving the geodesic distances between the images and a boundary value constraint on the transformed image appearances. Find $\{g_i\}$ such that,

$$\begin{cases} \forall j \ \ I_j \circ g_j^{-1} = I_j g_j^{-1} = \ \bar{I} \\ E(\{g_j\}) \qquad\qquad \text{is minimal.} \end{cases} \tag{8}$$

The existence of geodesic paths on the diffeomorphism manifold as well as the symmetry of the distances given by those paths are important facts for this algorithm. Furthermore, these paths, as mentioned above, are also parameterized with constant arc length.

The simplest non-trivial case of this inverse problem is given by a single pair of images. First, consider the naive algorithm for minimization.

1. Register images I and J while measuring the distance, $D(I, J)(t)$, between them.
2. Repeat the registration stopping at $t_{\frac{1}{2}}$, where $D(I, J)(t_{\frac{1}{2}}) = \frac{1}{2}D(I, J)(t = 1)$.

This numerical minimization can be achieved successfully and was used to generate the results of figure 1. However, considering that, in practice, the optimization process continues in a coarse to fine fashion, one observes that coarse scale corrections will occur first in time. This is an undesirable bias that makes the averages appear visually incorrect when features exist at multiple scales, such as in anatomical images, as in figure 3. This caveat also makes the naive approach highly asymmetric.

The solution used is to solve the variational problem given in 8 explicitly. The variational problem for averaging pairs of images is then,

$$g_1^{\star}, g_2^{\star} = \operatorname*{argmin}_{v_1(t)} \operatorname*{argmin}_{v_2(t)} \ \{ \ \int_0^1 \|v_1\|_L^2 + \|v_2\|_L^2 + \|Ig_1^{-1} - \bar{I}\| \ dt \ \} + \|Jg_2^{-1} - \bar{I}\| \ dt \ \}.$$

Rearranging terms using the equality constraints given in the original problem gives,

$$g_1^{\star}, g_2^{\star} = \operatorname*{argmin}_{v_1(t)} \operatorname*{argmin}_{v_2(t)} \ \{ \ \int_0^1 \ \|v_1\|_L^2 + \|v_2\|_L^2 + \|Ig_1^{-1} - Jg_2^{-1}\| \ dt \ \}. \tag{9}$$

Solving this problem, via alternating minimization with respect to g_i and all h_i constant, provides average deformations that are optimized *symmetrically* using information at all scales. The geodesic averaging constraint $E(g_1) = E(g_2)$ is upheld by construction and the configurations Ig_1^{-1} and Jg_2^{-1} are both in average position. Note also that the transformation from I to J is given by $g_1^{-1} \circ g_2$. We will denote the output of this algorithm as $\mathcal{A}(\cdot, \cdot)$ where the input is a pair of images. Intuitively, the algorithm lets the images I and J "meet" at the mean configuration. A similar idea was introduced recently in [11], in which intensity averaging was incorporated.

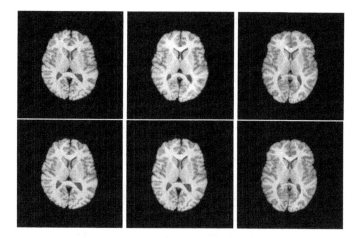

Fig. 3. The top row shows, in the center, the geodesic shape average of the image on the left and the image on the far right. For comparison, the bottom row shows, in the center, the naive geodesic shape average, which is biased towards coarse-scale corrections. Note that the outline of the naive average is similar to the image on the right, but the ventricles are similar to the image on the left. The geodesic average improves upon this bias.

4.1 Recursive Algorithm for Diffeomorphic Averaging and Diffeomorphic Shape Interpolation

The constraints given above allow one to recursively compute either the minimal energy configuration over a dataset or, alternatively, the full-scale time-dependent shape interpolation between a pair of images. The latter application is a practical way to resolve the fact that measuring physical energies within a multiple-scale optimization process introduces a significant bias in the resulting computed intermediate mappings. That is, deformations near the zero time-point will accomodate coarse scale differences, while transformation adjustments occurring later in time will be at a fine scale.

The full-scale minimization of (8) is achieved as a recursive least squares estimation problem. That is, given A, B, C, D, averages may be computed as,

$$\mathcal{A}(A, B, C, D) = \mathcal{A}(\mathcal{A}(A, B), \mathcal{A}(C, D)), \tag{10}$$

where $\mathcal{A}$ is the averaging function. The symmetric diffeomorphic approach used here avoids exclusive dependence on the (possibly individual specific) topology of a specific template anatomy I_i, as in deformation field averaging. Furthermore, the group theoretical framework and geodesics used by our algorithm and those described in [6] will ensure the g_i are in $\mathcal{G}$ after composition. An average transport o.d.e. may also be used to minimize the energy, as in [12].

Pseudocode is given in algorithm 1. One is guaranteed that the final mean configuration is derived from the composition of diffeomorphic transformations, insuring that topology of the mean anatomy is preserved and that the mean transformation exists in the shape space provided by the continuum model. This may be proven inductively by using the fact that if $g, h \in \mathcal{G}$ then $f = g \circ h \in \mathcal{G}$, that is, the composition of a geodesic diffeomorphic (g.d.) transformation with another g.d. transformation is within $\mathcal{G}$ and g.d. Note also that the set of transformations $\{g_i\}$ may be recovered after the end of the algorithm. For simplicity, we assume here that the size of the database is dyadic, though this is not a necessary condition. An illustration of a non-dyadic case is shown in figure 4.

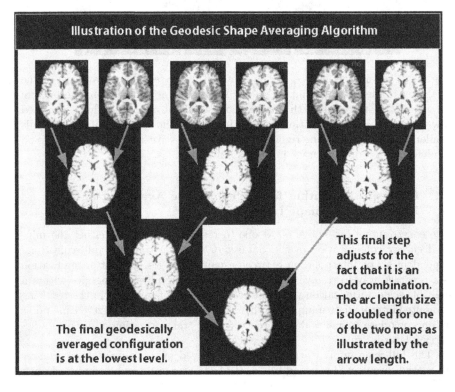

Fig. 4. The progress of the recursive averaging algorithm is shown above. Note the adjustment made for the uneven number of averages performed.

A similar algorithm may be used for geodesic shape interpolation, an example of which is shown in figure 5.

Algorithm 1 : Diffeomorphic Shape Averaging

Divide the database of images into unique pairs, $\mathcal{P} = \{\mathcal{P}_i = (I_i, I_j)|i \neq j\}$. Set $i = 1$.
Denote the cardinality of $\mathcal{P}$ as $\sharp \mathcal{P}$.
while $i < \sharp \mathcal{P}$ **do**
    $\mathcal{P} \cup (\mathcal{A}(\mathcal{P}_i), \mathcal{A}(\mathcal{P}_{i+1}))$.
    $i = i + 2$.
end while
$\bar{I} = \mathcal{A}(\mathcal{P}_{\sharp \mathcal{P}})$.

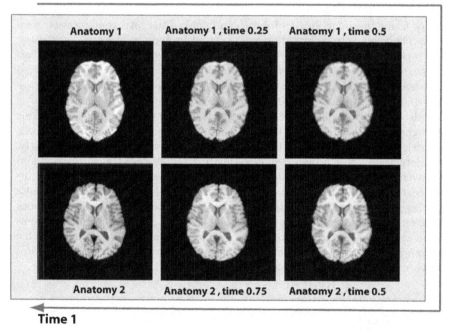

Full-Scale Anatomical Shape Interpolation

Time 0

Time 1

Fig. 5. Three time-points of scale consistent shape interpolation are generated from a pair of anatomical instances. The pair-wise symmetric registration method was used to generate the results here and to insure that the interpolated anatomy is consistent for all scales of information. The original images are at top left and bottom left respectively. This anatomical pair is in correspondence at time 0.5, which is the average of the anatomy at time 0 with the anatomy at time 1. Note that here we have used the topology of the closest anatomy at all points. It would also be natural to use an intensity average where the relative weights are determined by the time values.

5   Experiments

As was shown in figure 1, figure 3 and figure 5, the symmetric geodesic averaging algorithm is essential in some cases. We now investigate the effect of diffeomorphic averaging on normal anatomical images. A dataset of 6 normal female human cortices were manually segmented from volumetric MRI. The cortices were initially aligned by similarity transformation to an arbitrarily chosen reference. The current experiments are in two dimensions, although the implementation is equally functional in three dimensions.

5.1   Comparison of Geodesic and Linear Averaging

Linear Average. The diffeomorphic fluid algorithm was used to register an arbitrarily chosen reference topology to the dataset. The deformation fields provided by the non-rigid registration were then averaged in the Lagrangian reference frame, meaning vectors from the original to the final configuration were used. The average transformation was inverted to find the average shape atlas. The registration was repeated and the root mean square distance from the average shape atlas to the dataset was computed. A second reference image was also chosen and the study was repeated. The overlap ratio between the pair of average shape cortices is also computed. The results are summarized in figure 6(c,d).

Geodesic Average. The same registration algorithm was used with the geodesic averaging procedure of algorithm 1. The computational cost of this study is a logarithmic factor larger than the linear averaging, but without the (not costly, but potentially error prone) step of estimating the average transformation and its inverse. Because the algorithm moves from dataset instance to dataset instance, the order of the dataset was randomized and the study repeated. Results for these studies are summarized in figure 6(a,b). The similarity in appearance between the curved and linear averages suggest that the transformations computed are not highly curved, in contrast to those shown in figure 1. Finally, Table 1 shows a summary of metrics computed from the atlases to the dataset and also between the two instances of the atlases.

Algorithm	Overlap between 1 and 2	Intensity Squared Difference (SSD)
Geodesic	0.989	0.478
Linear	0.990	0.503

Table 1. Summary of Algorithm Dependency on Dataset. The overlap and sum of squared differences in intensity (SSD) are measured between the atlases generated by the same method but with a different dataset ordering and/or reference anatomy.

6   Conclusion

We have described an algorithm for geodesic shape averaging and interpolation, argued its correctness and illustrated its results. Furthermore, a finite element

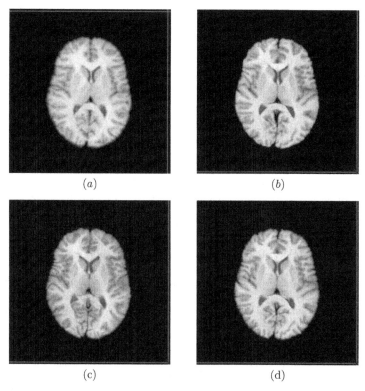

(a) (b)

(c) (d)

Fig. 6. The geodesic and linear approach to shape averaging are compared. The template anatomy for the first geodesic average example is the same as that of the first linear example. The second examples also share the same topology. One may note that, qualitatively, the geodesic results appear to be more plausible shapes, as the anatomy is deformed more smoothly. (a) Geodesic shape average one. (b) Geodesic shape average two. (c) Linear shape average one. (d) Linear shape average two.

method algorithm for estimating geodesic distances between images was given. This algorithm is symmetric with respect to an image pair without the need for explicit penalization of the difference between the forward and inverse transformations. It also has the property that it divides the deformation needed for correct registration evenly between each image, as is guaranteed by robust measures of the geodesic distance. Future work will investigate improvements to the current geodesic estimation scheme as well as its properties as an image registration algorithm on its own. We also intend to investigate solving problem (8) in parallel. This method will combine an initial estimate to $\bar{I}$ with the symmetric image registration algorithm given here. The solution will then be a piecewise linear estimate to the average curved transformation which can be compared with linear averaging and the recursive estimation in this work.

References

[1] R. Kikinis, M. E. Shenton, D. V. Iosifescu, R. W. McCarley, P. Saiviroonporn, H. H. Hokama, A. Robatino, D. Metcalf, C. G. Wible, C. M. Portas, R. M. Donnino, and F. A. Jolesz, "A digital brain atlas for surgical planning, model-driven segmentation, and teaching," *IEEE Trans. Visualization and Comp. Graph.*, vol. 2, pp. 232–241, 1996.

[2] J. Talairach and P. Tournoux, *Coplanar stereotaxic axis of the human brain*, Thieme, New York, 1988.

[3] J. Ashburner and K. Friston, "Fully three-dimensional nonlinear spatial normalization: A new approach," in *2nd Int. Conf. Functional Mapping of the Hum. Brain*, A. W. Toga, R. S. J. Frackowiak, and J. C. Mazziotta, Eds., 1996, vol. 3, p. S111.

[4] L. Le Briquer and J. C. Gee, "Design of a statistical model of brain shape," in *Information Processing in Medical Imaging*, J. S. Duncan and G. Gindi, Eds., pp. 477–482. Springer-Verlag, Heidelberg, 1997.

[5] A. Guimond, J. Meunier, and J.-P. Thirion, "Average brain models: A convergence study," *Computer Vision and Image Understanding*, vol. 77, no. 2, pp. 192–210, 2000.

[6] M. I. Miller and L. Younes, "Group actions, homeomorphisms and matching: a general framework," *Int. J. Computer Vision*, vol. 41, pp. 61–84, 2001.

[7] G. E. Christensen, R. D. Rabbitt, and M. I. Miller, "A deformable neuroanatomy textbook based on viscous fluid mechanics," in *27th Annual COnference on Information and Systems*, J. L. Prince and T. Runolfsson, Eds., Baltimore, MD, 1993, pp. 211–216.

[8] M. Miller, A. Trouve, and L. Younes, "On the metrics and euler-lagrange equations of computational anatomy," *Annu. Rev. Biomed. Eng.*, vol. 4, pp. 375–405, 2002.

[9] P. Dupuis, U. Grenander, and M. I. Miller, "Variational problems on flows of diffeomorphisms for image matching," *Quarterly of Applied Mathematics*, vol. 56, no. 3, pp. 587–600, 1998.

[10] O. C. Zienkiewicz, *The Finite Element Method in Engineering Science*, McGraw-Hill, New York, 1971.

[11] B. Davis, P. Davies, and S. Joshi, "Large deformation minimum mean squared error template estimation for computational anatomy," *IEEE International Symposium on Biomedical Imaging*, 2004.

[12] B. Avants and J.C. Gee, "Shape averaging with diffeomorphic flows for atlas creation," *IEEE International Symposium on Biomedical Imaging*, 2004.

Smoothing Impulsive Noise Using Nonlinear Diffusion Filtering

Omer Demirkaya

Department of Biostatistics, Epidemiology, and Scientific Computing
King Faisal Specialist Hospital and Research Center, Riyadh, 11211, Saudi Arabia
demirkaya@ieee.org

Abstract. A new anisotropic diffusion-filtering scheme to smooth images with heavy-tailed or binary noise types similar to salt&pepper noise is presented. The proposed scheme estimates edge gradient from an image that is smoothed or "regularized" with a median filter. Its performance was demonstrated on synthetic images that were corrupted by Gaussian, salt&pepper and Weibull noises, and actual medical images. The visual and quantitative evaluation of the scheme demonstrated comparable or better performance.

1   Introduction

Preprocessing of medical images may be necessary to improve the performance of the subsequent processing stages (e.g., segmentation and feature extraction). Depending on the noise type, different filtering methods can be used for denoising images. Anisotropic diffusion filtering has recently received a great deal of attention because of its impressive performance in preserving edge sharpness and suppressing noise. A special issue of *IEEE Trans. on Image Processing* (vol.7, No.3, 1998) was dedicated to this topic (See [1] for other approaches on anisotropic diffusion filtering). Several of its applications in biological as well as medical images have been reported [2]. The anisotropic diffusion filtering schemes perform well on images with Gaussian or Poisson noise. However, their performances decline substantially when the noise is impulsive such as salt&pepper noise. In this study, we propose a new scheme which uses median regularization instead of Gaussian regularization. In other words, it estimates the edge gradient from the image that is smoothed or "regularized" with a median filter. An impulsive noise type follows a rather long-tailed (or skewed) distribution as the observations containing outliers often skew the distribution. Thus in the validation of the proposed scheme, the noiseless images were also corrupted by the noise following a Weibull distribution, which exhibits impulsive characteristics. The following two sections briefly summarize the two anisotropic diffusion-filtering schemes that have been frequently referred to in literature and that are relevant to the proposed method here.

M. Šonka et al. (Eds.): CVAMIA-MMBIA 2004, LNCS 3117, pp. 111–122, 2004.
© Springer-Verlag Berlin Heidelberg 2004

1.1   Perona-Malik Scheme

Anisotropic diffusion filtering was first proposed by Perona&Malik for multiscale description, enhancement and segmentation (edge detection) of images [3]. Let a gray-scale and 2D (scalar-valued) image u be represented by a real-valued mapping u: $R^2 \rightarrow R$. In Perona-Malik (PM) diffusion, the initial image u_o is modified using the anisotropic diffusion equation

$$\partial u_t = div(g(\|\nabla u\|)\nabla u) \quad u(0) = u_0 \tag{1}$$

where div denotes the divergence operator, u is the smoothed image at time step t, $\|\nabla u\|$ is the gradient magnitude of u and $g(\|\nabla u\|)$ is the diffusivity function. $g(.)$ should be a nonnegative and monotonically decreasing function ($g(0)=1$ and $g(0) \geq 0$), and approaching zero at infinity so that the diffusion process will take place only in the interior of regions and will not affect edges where the gradient magnitude is sufficiently large. Some diffusivity functions that were suggested by Perona and Malik and the others are shown in Table 1. If the diffusivity is constant for the entire image domain, i.e., not a function of the differential structure, then this diffusion is sometimes called isotropic nonlinear diffusion. In this paper, only scalar-valued diffusivities are considered. The PM diffusion can enhance (i.e., backward diffusion) the edges with gradients whose absolute value is larger than δ, the noise threshold and smooth edges with gradients whose absolute value is less than δ.

An extensive analysis of the behavior of the various anisotropic filtering techniques can be found in [4]. The PM diffusion has been studied and shown to be ill-posed in the sense that the images close to each other (stereo images, for instance) may diverge as the diffusion process evolves [4]. The stability issue was addressed in [5] by biasing the algorithm toward the original image with the additional term u_t-u_0. It was also observed [6] that the PM diffusion might produce false step edges. More importantly, the PM diffusion cannot distinguish high gradient oscillations of the noise from the real edges. Therefore, high-gradient spurious edges will be preserved in the final image.

1.2   Catte's Scheme

Catte's scheme [7] is a slightly modified version of the PM algorithm. Similarly, the smooth image is the solution of the same diffusion equation $\partial u_t = div(g(\|\nabla u_\sigma\|)\nabla u)$ except for ∇u_σ term. This term denotes the gradient of the filtered version of the image u, and is obtained by convolving the image u with a Gaussian kernel of standard deviation σ

$$\nabla u_\sigma = \nabla(G_\sigma * u) \tag{2}$$

Catte's method is expected to maintain stability during the iteration process since it obtains its edge estimate from the smoothed image. The existence and uniqueness of the scheme has been discussed in detail [7].

The anisotropic diffusion filtering scheme proposed in this paper suggests that, instead of smoothing with a Gaussian function, the edge estimation is calculated from an image that is smoothed with a median filter. Median filtering is more appropriate if the underlying noise is impulsive or binary. Here although these two schemes are compared, they may be viewed as alternative schemes depending on the underlying noise.

The method section discusses the proposed anisotropic diffusion-filtering scheme, its numerical implementation, the selection of the parameters, and the images used to evaluate the schemes. The results were presented in the results section, while the discussion of the results and the conclusions can be found in the discussion section.

2   Method

2.1   Numerical Implementation

To solve Eq.1 a finite-difference based approach is used as it is relatively easy to implement on digital images; see [8] for the details of this implementation. Let us set pixel centers and the diffusion time as $x_i := (i-1/2)h_1$, $y_j := (i-1/2)h_2$ and $t_k := k\tau$, respectively. h_1 and h_2 denote the pixel sizes; the pixels are assumed to have unit length and unit aspect ratio. The approximation of the smooth image $u(x_i, y_j, t_k)$ at time t_k is denoted by $I_{i,j}^k$. Eq.1 was then approximated using an explicit time-differencing scheme as follows

$$
\begin{aligned}
\frac{2h^2 \left(I_{i,j}^{k+1} - I_{i,j}^k \right)}{\tau} &= \left[\left(g_{i+1,j} + g_{i,j} \right) \cdot \left(I_{i+1,j}^k - I_{i,j}^k \right) \right] \\
&- \left[\left(g_{i,j} + g_{i-1,j} \right) \cdot \left(I_{i,j}^k - I_{i-1,j}^k \right) \right] \\
&+ \left[\left(g_{i,j+1} + g_{i,j} \right) \cdot \left(I_{i,j+1}^k - I_{i,j}^k \right) \right] \\
&- \left[\left(g_{i,j-1} + g_{i,j} \right) \cdot \left(I_{i,j-1}^k - I_{i,j}^k \right) \right]
\end{aligned}
\tag{3}
$$

where the diffusivities were computed as $g_{i,j} = g\left(\|\nabla V\|_{i,j} \right)$, and the image gradients were computed using the central differencing scheme:

$$
\|\nabla V\|_{i,j} = \frac{1}{2h} \sqrt{\left| V_{i+1,j}^k - V_{i-1,j}^k \right|^2 + \left| V_{i,j+1}^k - V_{i,j-1}^k \right|^2}
\tag{4}
$$

where $V_{i,j}^k$ is the filtered version of the image $I_{i,j}^k$ at time t_k. In Catte's scheme $V_{i,j}^k$ is the Guassian-filtered version of $I_{i,j}^k$. In the proposed scheme, however, $V_{i,j}^k$ is obtained by median filtering $I_{i,j}^k$; that is $V_{i,j} = \text{Median}(I_{i-r,j-s})$, $(r, s) \in W$. The neighborhood W is commonly defined as an $N \times N$ (where N is odd), square window chosen around the center pixel (i, j). If $\{x_{(m)}\}$ is the sequence representing the ordered pixels of the neighborhood W around pixel (i, j) such that $x_{(1)} \leq x_{(2)} \leq \cdots \leq x_{(M)}$, then $V_{i,j} = x_{(M+1)/2}$. As the window size increases, the level of smoothing also increases. During median filtering the objects smaller than $M/2$ will disappear. Therefore, it is essential to find a window size that is a good compromise between noise suppression and the smallest object to be preserved. The only limitation of this explicit discretization scheme is the stability requirement which limits the time step size τ by $1/2m$ [9], where m denotes the number of dimensions along which the gradients were calculated. This limitation affects the efficiency, especially for higher dimensions, but not the accuracy of the scheme as discussed in [9]. Unlike Gaussian filtering, median filtering is a nonlinear transformation of the input image. Median filtering is particularly effective if the noise is heavy-tailed or binary such as salt&pepper noise.

2.2   Noise Modeling and Quantitative Evaluation

To evaluate the performance of the proposed scheme, the synthetic images of a hexagon with ideal step edges were corrupted by additive Gaussian and salt&pepper noise types as follows

$$I_n = I_o + \eta \qquad (5)$$

where I_n, I_o and η are noisy image, original (noiseless) image and the additive noise, respectively. The proposed scheme was also validated on images corrupted by the Weibull noise whose density function is defined by [10]

$$f(x,a,b) = abx^{b-1} \exp(-ax^b) \quad 0 \leq x \leq \infty \qquad (6)$$

where a is the scale and b is the shape parameter. The expected value of a random variable that has a Weibull distribution is $a^{-1/b}\Gamma(b^{-1}+1)$, where $\Gamma(s)=(s-1)!$ is the gamma function. The median of the distribution is $[a^{-1}log(2)]^{1/b}$. The right-hand tail of the distribution is heavier than the left-hand one; therefore, the distribution is positively skewed. One can adjust the amount of skewness by changing the shape parameter. As b gets smaller the tail of the distribution gets heavier, and therefore the distribution presents an impulsive behavior. For $b=1$ the Weibull distribution becomes an exponential distribution. To draw random samples from the Weibull distribution, the *weibrnd* function in Matlab™ (The Mathworks, Inc., Natic, MA.) was used. The two-dimensional random matrix whose elements were drawn from the Weibull distribution was added to the noiseless images.

For quantitative comparison, the Normalized Mean Square Error (NMSE) was used. NMSE is given by

$$NMSE = \sum_{i,j}\left(I_f(i,j) - I_o(i,j)\right)^2 \Big/ \sum_{i,j}\left(I_n(i,j) - I_o(i,j)\right)^2 \qquad (7)$$

where I_f is filtered image. The NMSE was computed following each iteration step and plotted against the number of iteration.

2.3   Parameter Selection

The time step τ affects the efficiency and stability of the filter and can assume a value
in the range $0 < \tau \leq 0.25$. Since τ is a stabilization factor, no optimization was
required; one can chose a value as high as 0.25. The contrast parameter δ was
computed for the entire image using the noise estimator described by Canny [11] and
used by [3]. It computes the histogram of the absolute value of the gradient for the
entire image and then sets the δ equal to the Kth quantile of the cumulative
distribution at every iteration. The smaller the quantile the slower the diffusion. In this
study, the quantile was adjusted to the problem at hand, and the same contrast
parameter was used for all the schemes. The L_1-norm measure $\|I^k - I^{k-1}\| / \|I^{k-1}\|$ was used
to measure the change between consecutive iteration steps. $\|I\|$ is a matrix norm
known as maximum absolute column sum. A value of 0.0001 was used as a threshold
for the change between successive iterations. The kernel size of the Gaussian filter
was approximated by 8.48σ. The optimal values of the σ and the median kernel size N
were obtained separately. Catte's scheme and the proposed algorithm were iterated 50
times for different values of the σ and the N, resepctively on the symthetic images of
the hexagon corrupted with Weibull noise. The values ($\sigma = 1.3$ and $N=5$) that
minimized the NMSE were used as optimal values for both parameters. The same
experiment was repeated for different shape parameters of the Weibull, and the σ and
N were found to be the same. The performances of the proposed filter for $N = 3$ and 5
were very close. However, for the actual images it was difficult to find the optimal
values quantitatively due to the lack of the ground truth.

2.4   Synthetic and Medical Images

Synthetic image of a hexagon with ideal step edges was created on a 64×64 grid. The
background pixels were assigned a value of 5 while 10 was assigned to the pixels of
the hexagon. The images of the hexagon were then corrupted by Gaussian of standard
deviation 1.41, salt&pepper with a density (the percentage of the image pixels that are
turned black or white) of 0.08 and a heavy-tailed Weibull ($a = 2$, $b = 1$) noise types.
    The tomographic slices of the attenuation map of the human body at the chest
level was acquired by the positron emission tomograhy (PET) scanner Siemens-CTI
ECAT EXACT (Model 921), CTI, Inc., Knoxville, TN USA. The natural logarithm of
the ratio of a standard 60-min blank image to a 10-min transmission scan was
computed. The tomographic attenuation maps were then reconstructed into a 128×128
image using ordered subset expectation-maximization (OSEM). These attenuation
maps are used to correct for the loss in emission due to the attenuation of the gamma
photons.
    The tomographic slices of PET emission images of a cylinder water (mixed with
^{18}F) phantom containing small cylinder inserts filled with higher (than the activity in
the water) concentration of ^{18}F; the concentration ratio was 10 to 1. The 256×256
image with a pixel size of 0.171×0.171 cm was reconstructed using the filtered
backprojection algorithm (with Hanning window with a FWHM of 4.5 mm) within
the ECAT 7.2 software (CTI, Inc., Knoxville, TN). In PET, one can always use a
higher cutoff frequency to preserve edge sharpness and then post-smooth the

tomographic slices. Using higher cutoff frequency results in sharper images, albeit noisier, with less profound correlated noise.

Table 1. Some diffusivity functions suggested in the literature. The parameter δ is a constant.

Diffusivities	Suggested by
$g_1(x) = 1/\left(1 + x^2/\delta^2\right)$, $g_2(x) = \exp(-x^2/\delta^2)$	[3]
$g_3(x) = \begin{cases} 1 - \exp\left(-3.15/(x/\delta)^4\right) & x \leq 0 \\ & x > 0 \end{cases}$	[12]

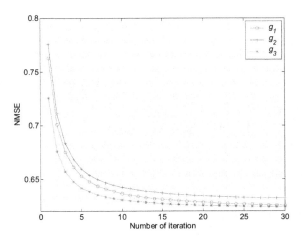

Fig. 1. NMSE plots were computed for thirty successive iterations. The original hexagon image was corrupted by Weibull noise (a=1.2, b=1.3). The filter parameters were: $\tau = 0.15$, $K = 0.88$.

3   Results

The noise-smoothing abilities of the diffusivities that are given in Table 1 were tested on the synthetic hexagon images corrupted with additive Weibull noise. Fig. 1 shows the NMSE plots computed for thirty successive iterations following every iteration step. Based on the NMSE measurements, among the diffusivities tested, g_2 performed worst while g_3 performed best. Hence, all the results reported in this paper were obtained using the g_3. In the NMSE plots, "No filter" refers to the regular PM algorithm; the proposed scheme was referred to as "Proposed"; and "Gaussian" refers to Catte's algorithm. Fig. 2 shows the performance of the three schemes on images containing Weibull noise only. The performance of the PM scheme was worst. The performance of the Catte's scheme was similar to the proposed method except at the edges. The NMSE plot also shows the differences in performances. Fig. 3 shows the original and filtered images corrupted by Gaussian and salt&pepper noise. The proposed scheme removed the salt&pepper noise and preserved edges better than the other two schemes. Note again the relatively poor performance of Catte's scheme around edges. The images in Fig. 4 show the original and filtered tomographic slices of the attenuation map of the human body at chest level acquired by the PET scanner. When observed carefully, one can see that small structures within the lungs were preserved better by the proposed and PM schemes. However, the three schemes performed identical in smoothing and preserving large structures. To study the effect of post-reconstruction smoothing of the PET emission images, the phantom image was filtered using the three schemes as shown in Fig. 5. Catte's and the proposed scheme exhibited similar performance. In Fig. 6, the original and filtered images of a Gaussian function are shown to demonstrate the rotational invariance of the three schemes.

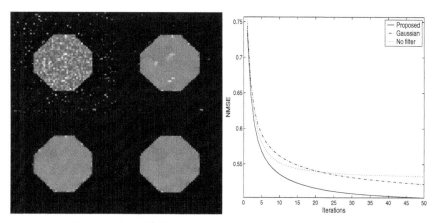

Fig. 2. Original corrupted by Weibull noise (a=2,b=1) and filtered images of hexagon. The parameters of the filters were: $\tau = 0.1$, $K = 0.7$, $k = 50$, $N = 5$, $\sigma = 1.3$. Original (top left). PM (top right). Catte's scheme (bottom left). Proposed scheme (bottom right). The graph on the right shows NMSEs as a function of number of iteration.

4   Discussion

The proposed diffusion scheme was able to handle Gaussian, binary and heavy-tailed Weibull noise types successfully. It preserved edge sharpness and contour better in general, owing to the innate edge-preserving ability of the median filter. Unlike Gaussian filtering, median filtering is a nonlinear filtering method, thereby more related in spirit to the nonlinear anisotropic diffusion filtering. The quantitative evaluation on synthetic images degraded by the introduction of Gaussian or Weibull noise showed that the rate of reduction of the NMSE was slightly faster in general for the proposed scheme than for the PM and Catte's schemes. Thus, the proposed scheme required relatively fewer iteration steps to achieve identical noise suppression. There was also a difference between the minimum achievable NMSE of the proposed scheme and that of the other two. In the case of Weibull noise, the Catte's scheme performed better than the PM scheme.

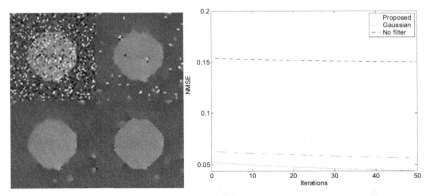

Fig. 3. Original (corrupted by Gaussian and salt&pepper noise) and filtered images of the hexagon. The parameters: $\tau = 0.1$, $k = 30$, $K = 0.7$, $N = 5$, $\sigma = 1.3$. Original (top left). PM (top right). Catte's scheme (bottom left). Proposed scheme (bottom right). The plot on the right shows the corresponding NMSEs.

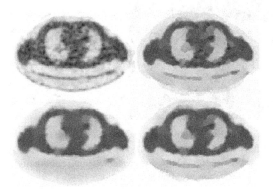

Fig. 4. Original and filtered attenuation maps of PET at torso level. Original image (top left). PM (top right). Catte's scheme (bottom left). Proposed scheme (bottom right). The parameters were: $\tau = 0.2$, $K = 0.85$, $m = 5$, $k = 30$, $\sigma = 1.3$.

The results in general indicate that the proposed scheme performs better in suppressing noise at edges due to the superior performance of median filter in estimating the true edge values, especially when the underlying neighborhood trend is flat and the noise distribution has heavy tails [13]. The relatively poor performance of Catte's scheme around edges was also reported earlier [12]. The noise around edges can be reduced using the nonlinear anisotropic filtering as proposed in [12], but, due to the permitted smoothing along edges, the corners may be rounded.

Gaussian smoothing, especially of large standard deviations, has two important limitations. It dislocates edges resulting in inaccurate estimation of edge location, and blurs edges causing the underestimation of edge gradient. The former one may render Catte's scheme ineffective to the noise near edges when Gaussian filter shifts edges toward regions where noise exists. It was also observed that the region around an edge affected by this phenomenon gets larger with increasing σ (Fig. 7). However, in the proposed scheme the effect is not as profound as that of Catte's (Fig. 7). The latter limitation of Gaussian filtering limits the edge-enhancing and -preserving ability of Catte's scheme.

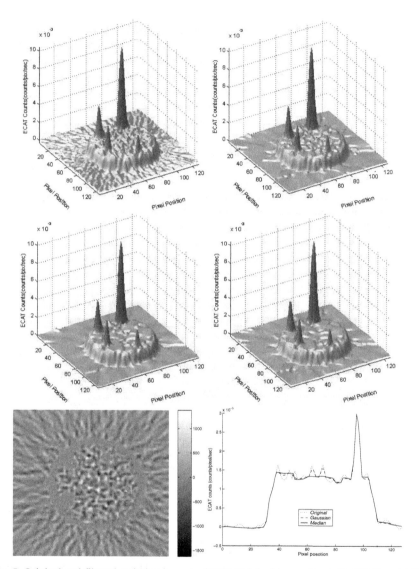

Fig. 5. Original and filtered emission images of PET. Original image (top left). PM (top right). Catte's scheme (middle left). Proposed scheme (middle right). The difference of the original and the proposed (Median) (bottom left). The intensity profile across the smallest hot cylinder insert (bottom right). The parameters of the filters were: $N = 7$, $k = 50$, $\sigma = 1$, $\tau = 0.2$, $K = 0.65$.

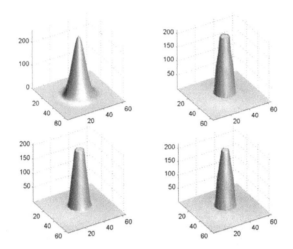

Fig. 6. Original and filtered images of a Gaussian function. Original Gaussian function image (top left). PM (top right). Catte's scheme (bottom left). Proposed scheme (bottom right). The filter parameters were: $N = 5$, $k = 300$, $\sigma = 1$, $\tau = 0.25$, $K = 0.9$.

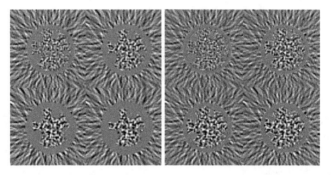

Fig. 7. Difference (original – filtered) PET emission images. Images on the left were filtered with Catte's scheme with $\sigma = 0.8$ (top-left), 1.6 (top-right), 2.4 (bottom-left), 3.2 (bottom-right). Images on the right were filtered using the proposed scheme with $N = 3$ (top-left), 5 (top-right), 7 (bottom-left), 9 (bottom-right). The parameters of the filters were: $K = 0.6$, $k = 50$, $\tau = 0.25$.

The noise in PET images is correlated and found to be difficult to remove using post-reconstruction filtering methods as discussed in [14]. This can be true for both emission and transmission images. The proposed nonlinear diffusion scheme has performed well in smoothing such correlated noise in both transmission and emission images (Fig. 4, 5). In PET, the attenuation maps are used to correct for the attenuation of the emission photons. To alleviate noise problem in attenuation images, the segmented attenuation correction (SAC) is the most common method used to produce approximate attenuation maps, which are obtained by segmenting the regions and assigning average gray-level intensity to the pixels of each segmented region [15].

The accurate segmentation of the noisy attenuation maps is therefore critical. The author suggested a new attenuation correction method based on the filtration of the measured attenuation maps using nonlinear diffusion filtering [16]. Moreover, the smoothed attenuation maps using anisotropic diffusion filtering, if used in SAC method to identify the regions, may also help improve the performance of SAC methods.

Although a global K value was applied to the medical images in this paper, the K can also be estimated locally, if the magnitude of the noise varies with position over an image domain. In fact, this can be true for PET images. Consider, for instance, the emission image of a radioactive, absorbing cylinder positioned axially in the center of the detector ring. The magnitude of the noise within the cylinder decreases radially with increasing radius due to the absorption of the photon [17]. In this case applying a different K value to each different radial region may be a more effective strategy to reduce the spatially varying noise. Here the schemes were tested for the same K values, but K value ought to be adjusted to a problem at hand. The proposed scheme was able to preserve edge sharpness better for a relatively large structure with weak edge strength.

Median filtering may result in corner clipping when the object embedded in the noisy background has sharp corners, but this rarely occurs in medical images. It has also been reported that median filtering might produce other undesired artifacts such as streaking, blotching, or false contouring [18]. Another disadvantage of the proposed filter is the smallest object one can preserve. When the number of object pixels is less than half the window size, the object may disappear. Similarly, the proposed scheme does not remove impulsive noise if the number of noise pixels within the window is greater than $M/2$.

It was also observed that the proposed scheme performed better, in preserving edge sharpness and removing noise, than the repeated application of the underlying median filter itself. Although median filtering is computationally more involved than Gaussian filtering, the computational cost was not prohibitive even though no attempt was made to implement the algorithms in an efficient manner.

The proposed scheme here suggests incorporating an order-statistics based filtering technique, namely median filter that is discrete in nature, into the continuous process of nonlinear diffusion. This fact and the highly nonlinear nature of median filtering process make the theoretical analysis (e.g., stability and convergence) of the proposed scheme very difficult, if not impossible. In regard to the convergence of median filter itself, it was showed [19] that the repeated application of a median filter to a one-dimensional signal produces a signal that is unmodified by further median filtering. It would however be possible to replace median filter with the mean curvature motion, which can be regarded as the analog equivalent of median filter [20]. This would require iterating the mean curvature motion process a number of times at each iteration step of the anisotropic scheme to obtain a median-filtered equivalent.

References

1. Carmona, R.A. and Zhong, S. Adaptive smoothing respecting feature directions. IEEE Trans. on Image Processing. 7 (1998) 353-358

2. Der-Shan, L., King, M.A. and Glick, S. Local Geometry variable conductance diffusion for post-reconstruction filtering. IEEE Trans on Nuclear Science. 41 (1994) 2800-2806
3. Perona, P. and Malik, J. Scale-space and edge detection using anisotropic diffusion. IEEE Trans. on Pattern Analysis and Machine Intelligence. 12 (1990) 629-639
4. You, Y., Xu, W., Tannenbaum, A. and Kaveh, M. Behavioral analysis of anisotropic diffusion in image processing. IEEE Trans. on Image Processing. 5 (1996) 1539-1552
5. Nordstrom, K.N. Biased anisotropic diffusion: a unified regularization and diffusion approach to edge detection. *Image and Vision Computing.* 8 (1990) 318-327
6. Whitaker, R.T. and Gerig, G. A multiscale approach to nonuniform diffusion. *CVIP: Image Understanding.* 57 (1993) 99-110
7. Catte, F., Lions, P.L., Morel, J.M. and Coll, T. Image selective smoothing and edge detection by nonlinear diffusion. SIAM J. Numer. Anal. 29 (1992) 182-193
8. Weickert, J.: Nonlinear diffusion filtering, Handbook of Computer Vision and Application. B. Johneet al. Academic Press, 2 (1999) 423-450
9. Weickert, J., Romeny, B.M.t.H. and Viergever, M.A. Efficient and reliable schemes for nonlinear diffusion filtering. IEEE Trans. on Image Processing. 7 (1998) 398-410
10. Collett, D.: Modeling Survival Data in Medical Research. Chapman&Hall, London (1994)
11. Canny, J. A computational approach to edge detection. IEEE Trans. on Pattern Analysis and Machine Intelligence. PAMI-8 (1986) 679-698
12. Weickert, J.: Anisotropic Diffusion in Image Processing. B. G. Teubner Stuttgart, Stuttgart (1998)
13. Haralick, R.M. and Shapiro, L.G.: Computer and Robot Vision. Addison-Wesley Publishing Company, Inc., (1992)
14. Ollinger, J.M. and Fessler, J.A. Positron Emission Tomography. IEEE Sig. Proc. Mag. 14 (1997) 43-55
15. Xu, M., Luk, W.K., Cuttler, P.D. and Digby, W.M. Local threshold segmented attenuation correction of PET imaging of the thorax. IEEE Trans on Nuclear Science. 41 (1994) 1532-1537
16. Demirkaya, O. and Mazrou, R.Y.A. Filtered Attenuation correction in Positron Emission Tomography. European Journal of Nuclear Medicine. 28 (2001) OS_32(968)
17. Alpert, N.M., Chesler, D.A., et al. Estimation of the local statistical noise in emission computed tomography. IEEE Trans. on Medical Imaging. 1 (1982) 142-136
18. Bovik, A.C. Streaking in median filtered images. IEEE Trans. Acout. Speech, Signal Process. ASSP-35 (1987) 493-503
19. Gallagher, N.C. and Wise, G.L. A theoretical analysis of the properties of median filters. IEEE Trans. Acoust., Speech, Signal Process. ASSP-29 (1981)
20. Guichard, F. and Morel, J.-M.: Partial differential equations and image iterative filtering. The state of the art in numerical analysis. Clarendon Press, Duff IS,Watson GA. Oxford (1997)

Level Set and Region Based Surface Propagation for Diffusion Tensor MRI Segmentation

Mikaël Rousson, Christophe Lenglet, and Rachid Deriche

I.N.R.I.A.
B.P. 93, 2004 Route des Lucioles,
06902 Sophia Antipolis Cedex, France
{Mikael.Rousson,Christophe.Lenglet,Rachid.Deriche}@sophia.inria.fr

Abstract. Diffusion Tensor Imaging (DTI) is a relatively new modality for human brain imaging. During the last years, this modality has become widely used in medical studies. Tractography is currently the favorite technique to characterize and analyse the structure of the brain white matter. Only a few studies have been proposed to group data of particular interest. Rather than working on extracted fibers or on an estimated scalar value accounting for anisotropy as done in other approaches, we propose to extend classical segmentation techniques based on surface evolution by considering region statistics defined on the full diffusion tensor field itself. A multivariate Gaussian is used to approximate the density of the components of diffusion tensor for each sub-region of the volume. We validate our approach on synthetical data and we show promising results on the extraction of the corpus callosum from a real dataset.

1 Introduction

Diffusion imaging is a magnetic resonance imaging technique introduced in the mid 1980s [6], [18] which provides a very sensitive probe of biological tissues architecture. Regular MRI techniques enable us to easily and automatically distinguish and classify gray matter, white matter and cephalo-spinal fluid. However, white matter does retain an homogeneous aspect, preventing any observation of neural fibers and thus of neuronal connectivity. Diffusion imaging offers the great possibility to non-invasively probe and quantify the anisotropic diffusion of water molecules in biological tissues like brain and muscles (in particular the heart). Some of the first images of anisotropic diffusion obtained *in vivo* were introduced by Moseley [22] in 1990. In 1994, Basser [4], [3] proposed the model now widely used of the diffusion tensor featuring an analytic and systematic means to precisely describe and quantify multidimensional anisotropy of tissues. The volumic image produced in Diffusion Tensor Imaging (DTI) contains, at each voxel, a 3×3 tensor. The estimation of this tensor at each location requires the acquisition of diffusion weighted data associated to different sampling directions of the diffusion process and different mean distance displacements. In order to visualize these tensor fields, we will establish, as in [40], a geometrical mapping

M. Šonka et al. (Eds.): CVAMIA-MMBIA 2004, LNCS 3117, pp. 123–134, 2004.

onto ellipsoids whose 3 main axis describe a local orthogonal coordinate system. The directions and norms of these axis respectively represent the eigenvectors and eigenvalues of each tensor.

One of the most successful clinical applications of diffusion MRI since the early 1990s has been acute brain ischemia detection [1], [2], [31], but many other potential applications like stroke, Alzheimer disease... etc can be foreseen. In the context of brain surgery, for instance, which may cause irreversible alterations to important fiber bundles, knowledge of their extension could minimize functional damage to the patient [33]. The information provided by this new modality is of great help to recover the neural connectivity in the human brain, leading to a better understanding of how brain areas communicate as part of a distributed network [35], [36].

Several different approaches for DTI-based fibers tracking have been proposed in the last decade (see [16] for a short survey). Recent research works have concentrated on the analysis of the properties of groups of fibers extracted by tractography algorithms. Registration or statistical analysis of diffusion properties require to identify some sort of coherence among the fibers in order to recover anatomical structures such as the corpus callosum, the corona radiata ...etc and relate them, for example, to functional activities. In [11], the authors address the issue of fibers clustering into well defined tracts through the definition of a distance between fibers.

In the following, we will address the direct segmentation of cerebral structures on the basis of statistics over the field of diffusion tensors. Wiegell et al. [41] proposed a method relying on the k-means algorithm for the parcellation of the thalamus by DTI. They use a simple distance between between tensors with a spatial coherence term that yielded impressive results. The thalamic nuclei are indeed compact, spherical and homogeneous structures that verify the restrictive hypothesis of the algorithm (isotropic distribution in the space of the data and low-curvature shape of the clusters). This is not the case for most of the brain structures. Zhukov et al. [43] segmented strongly anisotropic regions of the brain through a level set-based surface evolution controlled by scalar and invariant anisotropy measures. In [12], Feddern et al. proposed an extension of classical geodesic active contours to DTI. This approach is based on the propagation of a contour with a stopping function defined from image gradient. In [12], this stopping function was replaced by a scalar measure of discontinuities between tensors. Finally, the most closely related work can be found in [38] where Wang et al. used the Frobenius norm to define a distance between tensors. Note however that only the 2D case is illustrated in this nice contribution.

In the following, we will derive a novel 3D method for the segmentation of DTI data by exploiting the entire information encapsulated by the diffusion tensor. Moreover, based on our previous work [29,30], we will aim to take advantage of the statistical information like the covariance of the tensors components to refine the segmentation process and hence recover irregular anatomical structures such as the minor and major forceps of the corpus callosum.

2   From Diffusion Weighted MRI to Fiber Tracking

In the following, we describe the method used for the acquisition of our data and the robust estimation of the diffusion tensor. We briefly review classical tractography algorithms since we will use their result to illustrate in Fig.5 the accuracy of our segmentation algorithm.

2.1   Data Acquisition, DTI

Our dataset consists of 30 diffusion weighted images $S_k : \Omega \to \mathbb{R}, \ k = 1, ..., 30$ as well as 1 image S_0 corresponding to the signal intensity in the absence of a diffusion-sensitizing field gradient (ie. $b = 0$ in equation 1). They were obtained on a GE 1.5 T Signa Echospeed with standard 22 mT/m gradient field. The echoplanar images were acquired on 56 evenly spaced axial planes with a 128 × 128 pixels in each slice. Voxel size is 1.875 mm × 1.875 mm × 2.8 mm. 6 gradient directions $\mathbf{g}_k$, each with 5 different b-factors and 4 repetitions were used. Imaging parameters were: b values between 0 and 1000 $s.mm^{-2}$, $TR = 2.5 \ s$, $TE = 84.4 \ ms$ and a square field of view of 24 cm [28]. Those data are courtesy of CEA-SHFJ/Orsay, France[1]. We recall that the estimation of a field of 3 × 3 symmetric positive definite tensors $\mathbf{T}$ is done by using the Stejskal-Tanner equation [32] for anisotropic diffusion 1 at each voxel x.

$$S_k(x) = S_0(x)e^{-b\mathbf{g}_k^T \mathbf{T}(x)\mathbf{g}_k} \quad \forall x \in \Omega \tag{1}$$

where $\mathbf{g}_k$ are the normalized non-collinear sensitizing gradient and b the diffusion weighting factor. Various methods have been proposed for the estimation of the 6 elements of $\mathbf{T}(x)$ by using equation 1 (see figure 1). A survey of these approaches and a variational framework for the estimation and the regularization of of DTI data can be found in [34]. This last method provides a convenient mean to impose important constraints on the sought solution such as tensor positivity, orthonormality of the eigenvectors or some degree of smoothness of the result. This is performed by minimizing the following energy on the manifold of positive definite tensors $P(3)$:

$$\underset{\mathbf{T} \in P(3)}{\mathrm{Arg\,min}} \int_{\Omega} \sum_{k=1}^{n} \psi(\| \ln(S_0/S_k) - b\mathbf{g}_k^T \mathbf{T}\mathbf{g}_k\|) + \alpha\rho(\|\nabla\mathbf{T}\|)d\Omega \tag{2}$$

2.2   Fiber Tracking

The main idea on which relies classical tractography [20], [19], [28], [42] is that, despite the potentially multi-directional environment within a voxel, water diffusion in many regions of the white matter is highly anisotropic and consequently

---

[1] The authors would like to thank J.F. Mangin and J.B Poline for providing us with the data

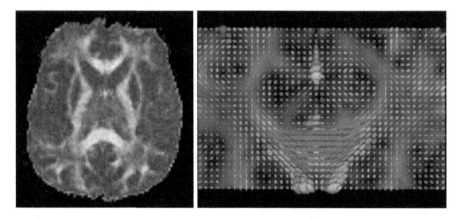

Fig. 1. [left] Fractional Anisotropy [right] Tensors in the genu of the corpus callosum

the orientation of the largest tensor eigenvector aligns with predominant axonal orientation [21]. It should be safe to say that, accepting this restrictive assumption will enable us to identify macroscopical 3D architectures of the white matter. This gives rise to the line propagation technique that we have implemented and tested with various possible approaches. However, these local methods incorporate strong limitations and refinements have been proposed [5], [14], [15], [17], [35], [39], [8], [37]. More global algorithms [16], [23], [25], [27], [10], stochastic modeling [7], [26], [13] or new acquisition methods were also introduced to try to overcome that restriction.

3   Tensor Field Segmentation

As shown in the previous section, the diffusion tensor is directly related to tissue properties. Then, classical segmentation techniques can be applied on this type of images for the extraction of structures of particular interest. The level set representation is a well-suited framework for curve/surface evolution. Let $\mathcal{S}$ be the surface between the 3D object to extract and the 3D background, we introduce the level set function $\phi : \Omega \to \mathcal{R}^3$, defined as follow:

$$\begin{cases} \phi(\mathbf{x}) = 0, & \text{if } \mathbf{x} \in \mathcal{S} \\ \phi(\mathbf{x}) = \mathcal{D}(\mathbf{x}, \mathcal{S}), & \text{if } \mathbf{x} \in \mathcal{S}_{in} \\ \phi(\mathbf{x}) = -\mathcal{D}(\mathbf{x}, \mathcal{S}), & \text{if } \mathbf{x} \in \mathcal{S}_{out} \end{cases} \tag{3}$$

where $\mathcal{D}(\mathbf{x}, \mathcal{S})$ stands for the Euclidean distance between $\mathbf{x}$ and $\mathcal{S}$. Furthermore, let $H_\epsilon(z)$ and $\delta_\epsilon(z)$ be regularized versions of the Heaviside and Dirac functions as defined in [9].

Let $p_{\mathcal{S}_{in}}$ and $p_{\mathcal{S}_{out}}$ be the probability density functions of the diffusion tensor inside and outside $\mathcal{S}$. Then, according to the Geodesic Active Regions model [24], the object can be recovered by minimizing:

$$E(\phi) = - \int_{\Omega} \left(H_\epsilon(\phi) \log p_{\mathcal{S}_{in}} T(\mathbf{x}) + (1 - H_\epsilon(\phi)) \log p_{\mathcal{S}_{out}} T(\mathbf{x}) \right) d\mathbf{x} \qquad (4)$$

The direct definition of a probability density function in the space of symmetric positive definite matrix is a difficult problem and thus, we will rather consider vector representations of the tensors in $\mathbb{R}^6$. By analogy to the information geometry approach, we consider a statistical distribution on linear spaces which overcome the hypothesis of isotropic distribution. Hence, as done in [30] for texture images with the structure tensor, we consider a parametric approximation with a 6D Gaussian. Let u be the vector representation of a tensor T, the likelihood of u in the region X is given by:

$$p_X(u|\mu_X, \Sigma_X) = \frac{1}{(2\pi)^3 |\Sigma_X|^{1/2}} e^{-\frac{1}{2}(u-\mu_X)^T \Sigma_X^{-1}(u-\mu_X)} \qquad (5)$$

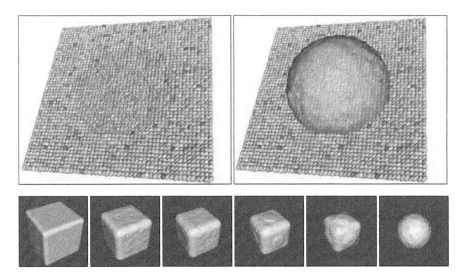

Fig. 2. Segmentation of a noisy tensor field composed by two regions with same orientation but different scale (TOP LEFT: 2D-cut of the tensor field, TOP RIGHT: same with final segmentation, BOTTOM: surface evolution).

By construction, the diagonal and non-diagonal components of a diffusion tensor are highly correlated and so, a full covariance must be considered in the density of its vector representation u. Then, the vector means and the covariances of these densities are also supposed unknown. However, these parameters can be introduced as unknown in (4). If we also add a regularity constraint on the interface, we obtain the final objective function:

$$E(\phi, \{\mu_X, \Sigma_X\}) = \nu \int_\Omega |\nabla H_\epsilon(\phi)| d\mathbf{x}$$
$$- \int_\Omega H_\epsilon(\phi) \log p_{S_{in}}(u(\mathbf{x})|\mu_{S_{in}}, \Sigma_{S_{in}}) d\mathbf{x} \qquad (6)$$
$$- \int_\Omega (1 - H_\epsilon(\phi)) \log p_{S_{out}}(u(\mathbf{x})|\mu_{S_{out}}, \Sigma_{S_{out}}) d\mathbf{x}$$

This type of energy was studied in [29], the Euler Lagrange equation for ϕ furnish the following evolution equation for the Level Set function:

$$\phi_t(\mathbf{x}) = \delta_\epsilon(\phi(\mathbf{x})) \left(\nu \operatorname{div} \frac{\nabla \phi}{|\nabla \phi|} + \frac{1}{2} \log \frac{|\Sigma_{S_{out}}|}{|\Sigma_{S_{in}}|} \right.$$
$$- \frac{1}{2}(u(\mathbf{x}) - \mu_{S_{in}})^T \Sigma_{S_{in}}^{-1}(u(\mathbf{x}) - \mu_{S_{in}})$$
$$\left. + \frac{1}{2}(u(\mathbf{x}) - \mu_{S_{out}})^T \Sigma_{S_{out}}^{-1}(u(\mathbf{x}) - \mu_{S_{out}}) \right) \quad \forall \mathbf{x} \in \mathbb{R}^3$$
$$(7)$$

while the statistical parameters are updated with:

$$\mu_{S_{in}}(\phi) = \frac{\int_\Omega u(\mathbf{x}) H_\epsilon(\phi) d\mathbf{x}}{\int_\Omega H_\epsilon(\phi) d\mathbf{x}}$$
$$\mu_{S_{out}}(\phi) = \frac{\int_\Omega u(\mathbf{x})(1 - H_\epsilon(\phi)) d\mathbf{x}}{\int_\Omega (1 - H_\epsilon(\phi)) d\mathbf{x}}$$
$$\Sigma_{S_{in}}(\phi) = \frac{\int_\Omega (\mu_{S_{in}} - u(\mathbf{x}))(\mu_{S_{in}} - u(\mathbf{x}))^T H_\epsilon(\phi) d\mathbf{x}}{\int_\Omega H_\epsilon(\phi) d\mathbf{x}} \qquad (8)$$
$$\Sigma_{S_{out}}(\phi) = \frac{\int_\Omega (\mu_{S_{out}} - u(\mathbf{x}))(\mu_{S_{out}} - u(\mathbf{x}))^T (1 - H_\epsilon(\phi)) d\mathbf{x}}{\int_\Omega (1 - H_\epsilon(\phi)) d\mathbf{x}}$$

Adequate implementation schemes for this type of optimization can be found in [9]. Two important details must be noted: (i) the explicit scheme is not stable for any time step because of regularization term, (ii) the level set function is reinitialized to the distance function at each iteration.

If we restrict the covariance matrix to the identity matrix, these equations simplify and the log-likelihoods in Eq.(4) become simply the Euclidean distance between the vectors u and μ_X, which is equivalent to the Frobenius norm of the difference between the corresponding tensors. With this simplification we obtain the same evolution equation as the one proposed in [38] where the authors also considered the full diffusion tensors for segmentation but without statistical modeling.

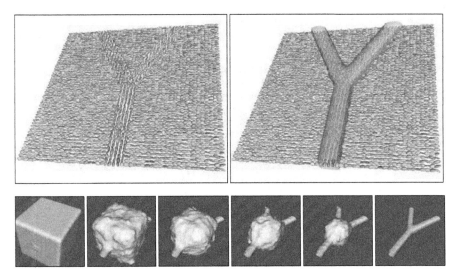

Fig. 3. Segmentation of a noisy tensor field composed by two regions with same scale but different orientations (TOP LEFT: 2D-cut of the tensor field, TOP RIGHT: same with final segmentation, BOTTOM: surface evolution).

4   Experimental Results

4.1   Synthetical Tensor Images

In a first time, we present several results on synthetical tensor field data. In diffusion tensor images, the tensor stands for the covariance matrix of the displacement of water molecules. Then, the principal eigenvector of the diffusion tensor will represent the most likely displacement direction and the corresponding eigenvalue will be its probable intensity. Thus, we consider the spectral decomposition of a tensor to generate appropriate synthetical data.

First, let the eigenvectors be identical for the two regions while the eigenvalues are slightly different. With some Gaussian noise on each component of the tensors, we generate the *sphere* 3D image shown in Fig.2. In Fig.3, we show a second synthetic case where only the orientation of the tensors differ for one region to an other. Three slightly different orientations are used inside the Y shape. The good result obtained for such a case show the ability of our approach to capture regions with varying tensor characteristics.

4.2   Human Brain Diffusion Tensor Images

We finally show a result on a real diffusion tensor image. As we assume a bi-partitioning of the 3D image domain, we first restrict the image domain around

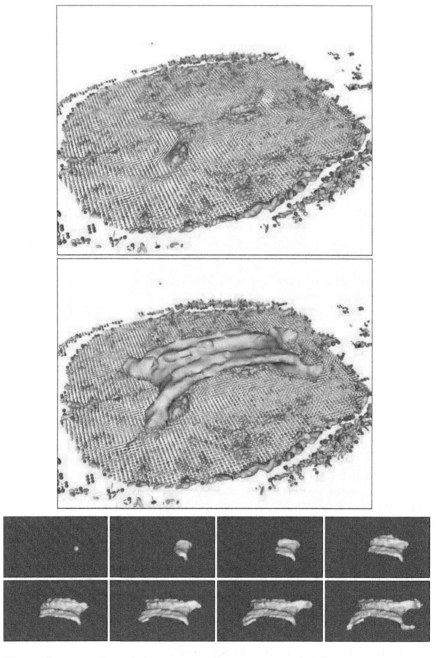

Fig. 4. Segmentation of the corpus callosum in a real diffusion tensor image (TOP: 2D-cut of the tensor field, MIDDLE: same with final segmentation, BOTTOM: surface evolution).

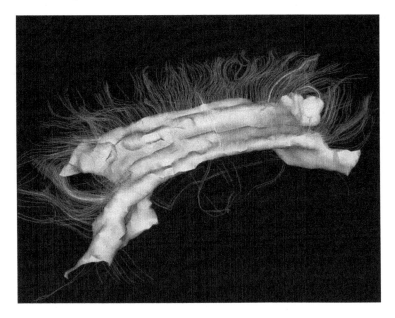

Fig. 5. Fusion of commissural fibers of the corpus callosum with their 3D segmentation (posterior-anterior: left to right).

the object of interest which is the corpus callosum in our example. Then, we initialize the interface with a small sphere inside the object. Outside initializations like the ones used for synthetic data would lead to a mixed segmentation of the corpus callosum and the lateral brain ventricles. Input image, surface evolution and final segmentation are shown in Fig.4. The segmentation is globally in accordance with what is expected and is quite good given the poor resolution of diffusion tensor images and despite the high variation in orientation and scale of the diffusion tensor inside the object.

However, the evolving surface does not capture entirely all the irregularities of the corpus callosum. This behavior is not surprising considering the statistical approximation used. Diffusion tensors at the irregularities get orientations rather different from the global region properties. Higher order or mixture models should be studied and could be used within the same framework so as to tackle this problem.

One important point to be mentioned on these experiments is the absence of painfull parameters to be set, only the regularization weight μ has to be chosen. Actually, this weight can be generally set to 1, lower weights will increase the accuracy while higher ones will give very smooth surfaces.

5   Conclusion

We have shown in this paper an extension of well-known region-based segmentation techniques to diffusion tensor images. Only a few segmentation approaches have been proposed for this modality. The introduction of region statistics using all the information brought by the DTI data is the main novelty of our approach. Promising results show the interest of considering the whole diffusion tensors instead of a given measure of anisotropy. Future works will consist in the validation of these very new results for this modality and the study of geometrical properties of the diffusion tensors to define more relevant region statistics.

References

1. G.W. Albers, M.G. Lansberg, A.M. Norbash, D.C. Tong, M.W. O'Brien, A.R. Woolfenden, M.P. Marks, and M.E. Moseley. Yield of diffusion-weighted MRI for detection of potentially relevant findings in stroke patients. *Neurology*, 54:1562–1567, 2000.
2. A.E. Baird and S.Warach. Magnetic resonance imaging of acute stroke. *J. Cerebral Blood Flow Metabolism*, 18:582–609, 1998.
3. P.J. Basser, J. Mattiello, and D. LeBihan. Estimation of the effective self-diffusion tensor from the NMR spin echo. *Journal of Magnetic Resonance*, B(103):247–254, 1994.
4. P.j. Basser, J. Mattiello, and D. LeBihan. MR diffusion tensor spectroscopy and imaging. *Biophysica*, (66):259–267, 1994.
5. P.J. Basser, S. Pajevic, C. Pierpaoli, J. Duda, and A. Aldroubi. In vivo fiber tractography using DT-MRI data. *Magn. Res. Med.*, 44:625–632, 2000.
6. D. Le Bihan, E. Breton, D. Lallemand, P. Grenier, E. Cabanis, and M. Laval-Jeantet. MR imaging of intravoxel incoherent motions: Application to diffusion and perfusion in neurologic disorders. *Radiology*, pages 401–407, 1986.
7. M. Bjornemo, A. Brun, R. Kikinis, and C.F. Westin. Regularized stochastic white matter tractography using diffusion tensor MRI. In *MICCAI*, pages 435–442, 2002.
8. J.S.W. Campbell, K. Siddiqi, B.C. Vemuri, and G.B Pike. A geometric flow for white matter fibre tract reconstruction. In *IEEE International Symposium on Biomedical Imaging Conference Proceedings*, pages 505–508, July 2002.
9. T. Chan and L. Vese. An active contour model without edges. In *Scale-Space Theories in Computer Vision*, volume 1682 of *Lecture Notes in Computer Science*, pages 141–151. Springer–Verlag, 1999.
10. O. Cicarelli, A.T. Toosy, G.J.M. Parker, C.A.M Wheeler-Kingshott, G.J. Barker, D.H. Miller, and A.J. Thompson. Diffusion tractography based group mapping of major white matter pathways in the human brain. *NeuroImage*, 19:1545–1555, 2003.
11. Z. Ding, J.C. Gore, and A.W. Anderson. Classification and quantification of neuronal fiber pathways using diffusion tensor MRI. *Magn. Res. Med.*, 49:716–721, 2003.
12. C. Feddern, J. Weickert, and B. Burgeth. Level-set methods for tensor-valued images. In *Proc. Second IEEE Workshop on Variational, Geometric and Level Set Methods in Computer Vision*, pages 65–72, Nice, France, 2003.

13. P. Hagmann, J.P. Thiran, L. Jonasson, P. Vandergheynst, S. Clarke, P. Maeder, and R. Meuli. DTI mapping of human brain connectivity: Statistical fiber tracking and virtual dissection. *NeuroImage*, 19:545–554, 2003.

14. M. Lazar, D. Weinstein, K. Hasan, and A.L. Alexander. Axon tractography with tensorlines. In *Proceedings of International Society of Magnetic Resonance in Medicine*, volume 482, 2000.

15. M. Lazar, D.M. Weinstein, J.S. Tsuruda, K.M. Hasan, K. Arfanakis, M.E. Meyerand, B. Badie, H.A. Rowley, V.Haughton, A. Field, and A.L. Alexander. White matter tractography using diffusion tensor deflection. In *Human Brain Mapping*, volume 18, pages 306–321, 2003.

16. C. Lenglet, R. Deriche, and O. Faugeras. Inferring white matter geometry from diffusion tensor MRI: Application to connectivity mapping. In T. Pajdla and J. Matas, editors, *Proceedings of the 8th European Conference on Computer Vision*, Prague, Czech Republic, May 2004. Springer–Verlag.

17. T.E. McGraw. Neuronal fiber tracking in DT-MRI. Master's thesis, University of Florida, 2002.

18. K.D. Merboldt, W. Hanicke, and J. Frahm. Self-diffusion NMR imaging using stimulated echoes. *J. Magn. Reson.*, 64:479–486, 1985.

19. S. Mori, B.J. Crain, V.P. Chacko, and P.C.M. Van Zijl. Three-dimensional tracking of axonal projections in the brain by magnetic resonance imaging. *Annals of Neurology*, 45(2):265–269, February 1999.

20. S. Mori, B.J. Crain, and P.C. van Zijl. 3d brain fiber reconstruction from diffusion MRI. In *Proceedings of the International Conference on Functional Mapping of the Human Brain*, 1998.

21. M.E. Moseley, Y. Cohen, J. Kucharczyk, J. Mintorovitch, H.S. Asgari, M.F. Wendland, J. Tsuruda, and D. Norman. Diffusion-weighted MR imaging of anisotropic water diffusion in cat central nervous system. *Radiology*, 176:439–445, 1999.

22. M.E. Moseley, Y. Cohen, J. Mintorovitch, J. Kucharczyk, J. Tsuruda, P. Weinstein, and D. Norman. Evidence of anisotropic self-diffusion. *Radiology*, 176:439–445, 1990.

23. L. O'Donnell, S. Haker, and C.F. Westin. New approaches to estimation of white matter connectivity in diffusion tensor MRI: Elliptic pdes and geodesics in a tensor-warped space. In *MICCAI*, 2002. 459–466.

24. N. Paragios and R. Deriche. Geodesic active regions and level set methods for supervised texture segmentation. *The International Journal of Computer Vision*, 46(3):223, 2002.

25. G.J.M. Parker. Tracing fibers tracts using fast marching. In *Proceedings of the International Society of Magnetic Resonance*, volume 85, 2000.

26. G.J.M. Parker and D.C Alexander. Probabilistic monte carlo based mapping of cerebral connections utilising whole-brain crossing fibre information. In *IPMI*, pages 684–695, 2003.

27. G.J.M. Parker, C.A.M. Wheeler-Kingshott, and G.J. Barker. Estimating distributed anatomical connectivity using fast marching methods and diffusion tensor imaging. *Trans. Med. Imaging*, 21(5):505–512, 2002.

28. C. Poupon. *Dtection des faisceaux de fibres de la substance blanche pour l'tude de la connectivit anatomique crbrale.* PhD thesis, Ecole Nationale Suprieure des Tlcommunications, December 1999.

29. M. Rousson and R. Deriche. A variational framework for active and adaptative segmentation of vector valued images. In *Proc. IEEE Workshop on Motion and Video Computing*, pages 56–62, Orlando, Florida, December 2002.

30. M. Rousson, Thomas Brox, and Rachid Deriche. Active unsupervised texture segmentation on a diffusion based space. In *IEEE Conference on Computer Vision and Pattern Recognition*, volume 2, pages 699–704, Madison, Wisconsin, USA, June 2003.
31. C. Sotak. The role of diffusion tensor imaging (DTI) in the evaluation of ischemic brain injury. *NMR Biomed.*, 15:561–569, 2002.
32. E.O. Stejskal and J.E. Tanner. Spin diffusion measurements: spin echoes in the presence of a time-dependent field gradient. *Journal of Chemical Physics*, 42:288–292, 1965.
33. I-F Talos, L. O'Donnell, C-F Westin, S. Warfield, W. Wells III, S-S Yoo, L. Panych, A. Golby, H. Mamata, S. Maier, P. Ratiu, C. Guttmann, P. Black, F. Jolesz, and R. Kikinis. Diffusion tensor and functional MRI fusion with anatomical MRI for image-guided neurosurgery. In *MICCAI*, 2003. 407-415.
34. D. Tschumperl and R. Deriche. Variational frameworks for DT-MRI estimation, regularization and visualization. In *Proceedings of the 9th International Conference on Computer Vision*, Nice, France, 2003. IEEE Computer Society, IEEE Computer Society Press.
35. D.S. Tuch. Mapping cortical connectivity with diffusion MRI. In *ISBI*, pages 392–394, 2002.
36. D.S. Tuch, T.G. Reese, M.R. Wiegell, N.G. Makris, J.W. Belliveau, and V.J. Wedeen. High angular resolution diffusion imaging reveals intravoxel white matter fiber heterogeneity. *Magn. Res. Med.*, 48:577–582, 2002.
37. B. Vemuri, Y. Chen, M. Rao, T. McGraw, T. Mareci, and Z. Wang. Fiber tract mapping from diffusion tensor MRI. In *1st IEEE Workshop on Variational and Level Set Methods in Computer Vision (VLSM'01)*, July 2001.
38. Z. Wang and B.C. Vemuri. Tensor field segmentation using region based active contour model. In *Proc. The 8th European Conference on Computer Vision*, Prague, Czech Republic, May 2004.
39. D.M. Weinstein, G.L. Kindlmann, and E.C. Lundberg. Tensorlines: Advection-diffusion based propagation through tensor fields. In *IEEE Visualization*, pages 249–253, 1999.
40. C.F Westin, S.E Maier, H. Mamata, A. Nabavi, F.A. Jolesz, and R. Kikinis. Processing and visualization for diffusion tensor MRI. In *In proceedings of Medical Image Analysis*, volume 6(2), pages 93–108, 2002.
41. M.R. Wiegell, D.S. Tuch, H.W.B. Larson, and V.J. Wedeen. Automatic segmentation of thalamic nuclei from diffusion tensor magnetic resonance imaging. *NeuroImage*, 19:391–402, 2003.
42. L. Zhukov and A.H. Barr. Oriented tensor reconstruction: Tracing neural pathways from diffusion tensor MRI. In *Proceedings of the conference on Visualization '02*, pages 387–394, 2002.
43. L. Zhukov, K. Museth, D. Breen, R. Whitaker, and A.H. Barr. Level set segmentation and modeling of DT-MRI human brain data. *Journal of Electronic Imaging*, 2003.

The Beltrami Flow over Triangulated Manifolds

Lucero Lopez-Perez[1], Rachid Deriche[1], and Nir Sochen[2]

[1] Odyssee Project, INRIA,
06902 Sophia Antipolis, France
{Lucero.Lopez_Perez, Rachid.Deriche}@inria.fr
http://www-sop.inria.fr/odyssee
[2] Department of Applied Mathematics,
University of Tel-Aviv,
Tel-Aviv 69978, Israel
sochen@math.tau.ac.il
http://www.math.tau.ac.il/~sochen/index.html

Abstract. In several image processing applications one has to deal with noisy images defined on surfaces, like electric impulsions or diffusion tensors on the cortex. We propose a new regularization technique for data defined on triangulated surfaces: the Beltrami flow over intrinsic manifolds. This technique overcomes the over - smoothing of the L_2 and the stair-casing effects of the L_1 flow for strongly noised images. To do so, we locally estimate the differential operators and then perform temporal finite differences. We present the implementation for scalar images defined in 2 dimensional manifolds and experimental results.

1 Introduction

To regularize data on manifolds, differential geometry and calculus of variation are frequently used in two principal ways: *The Polyakov action* [8,9,10,3,4], which uses an intrinsic-parametric description of the manifold and an explicit form of the metric; and *The Harmonic maps* [1,13,14,2,17], which uses an implicit representation of the manifolds. The relation between these two approaches is explained in [18,19,20], in which is introduced a new approach to perform regularization on manifolds: The Beltrami Flow.

It has been shown that the Beltrami flow interpolates between the L_2 norm flow and the L_1 norm flow, for flat gray-value images [9,11], and for general non-flat surfaces [18,19,20]. In [19] is shown its implementation for the case of a manifold represented by a level set surface, but this has not be done for the case of intrinsically represented manifolds, often used in image processing.

Even though the level set approach is easier to implement, for certain applications it is better to handle triangulated-based techniques rather than implicit ones. For example when the regularization is an intermediate step in the process to achieve a further goal, and the same triangulation is needed for the input and output of the step.

M. Šonka et al. (Eds.): CVAMIA-MMBIA 2004, LNCS 3117, pp. 135–144, 2004.

To compute the Beltrami Flow, we propose a finite differences scheme for the time discretization and a spatial average of the differential operator on the vertex of the triangulation.

This article is organized as follows: Section 2 reviews the intrinsic formulation of the problem for the case of a 2D surface with scalar data, Section 3 shows how to estimate the differential operator. Section 4 presents the implementation details to compute the flow and some examples and results and we conclude in Section 5.

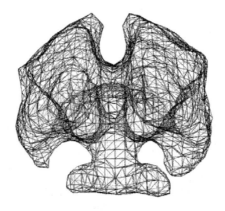

Fig. 1. Triangulated cortex

2   Intrinsic Formulation

Let S be a 2-dimensional manifold described by an arbitrary parameterization with coordinates u, v, that induce a metric $(\tilde{g}_{ij})$. It is given a scalar function $I : S \to \mathbb{R}$, the data function.

As it is explained in [20], we introduce the manifold Σ that describes $I(u, v)$ as a surface embedded in the 3D fiber bundle $\mathcal{M} = S \times \mathbb{R}$ Assuming an isometric embedding i.e. $ds_\Sigma = ds_\mathcal{M}$, the metric $g_{i,j}$ induced on the section Σ is:

$$ds_\Sigma = \tilde{g}_{11}du^2 + 2\tilde{g}_{12}dudv + \tilde{g}_{22}dv^2 + \beta^2 \left(I_u du^2 + 2I_u I_v dudv + I_v^2 dv^2 \right) ,$$

where β^2 takes into account the differences in dimensions between the spatial directions and the intensity. This metric can be used to calculate the Laplace Beltrami Operator

$$\Delta_g I = \frac{1}{\sqrt{g}} \text{Div} \left(\sqrt{g} G^{-1} \nabla I \right) . \tag{1}$$

where G is the matrix whose elements are g_{ij}, and $g = det(G)$. The equation of motion that results from the Polyakov action [5] is: $I_t = \Delta_g I$ It is shown in [20] that this flow becomes the L_2 flow if we take the limit when $\beta \to 0$ and it becomes the L_1 flow if we take the limit when $\beta \to \infty$

3   Estimating the Differential Operators

Let S be a surface parametrized by

$$P(\mathbf{u}) = \{x(\mathbf{u}), y(\mathbf{u}), z(\mathbf{u}) : \mathbf{u} = (u^1, u^2) = (u, v) \in D\}$$

Let $G = (G_{i,j})$, $G_{i,j} = \langle P_i, P_j \rangle$ be the Riemannian metric tensor for this parametrization.

Then, for a function $I : S \to R$

$$\nabla_P I(x) = \nabla_{u,v} I(x) = \sum_{i,j=1}^{2} G^{i,j} \frac{\partial I}{\partial u^i} P_i$$

where $(G^{i,j}) = G^{-1}$ We will use the (u, v)-space, with the metric induced by the local parameterization so that (1) can be expressed as:

$$I_t = \Delta_g I = \frac{1}{\sqrt{1 + \beta |\nabla_{u,v} I|^2}} \operatorname{Div}\left(\sqrt{1 + \beta |\nabla_{u,v} I|^2}\, \nabla_{u,v} I\right),$$

Let us call $\nabla_S I(x) = \nabla_{u,v} I(x)$ for $x \in S$, and

$$\phi(|\nabla_S(I(x))|) = \frac{1}{\sqrt{1 + \beta |\nabla_{u,v} I(x)|^2}} \tag{2}$$

We look for a local approximation $\widehat{\Delta_g I}$ on the nodes of S . p being a node of the triangulated surface, and ϕ a function $\phi : \mathbb{R} \to \mathbb{R}$.

Following the ideas in [22] , we take the spatial mean of this quantity in the area A defined by the triangles inmediatly surrounding p (see fig 2)

$$\nabla_S \cdot (\phi(|\nabla_S I(p)|)\nabla_S I(p)) \approx \frac{1}{A} \int_A \nabla_S \cdot (\phi(|\nabla_S I(x)|)\nabla_S I(x)) dx$$

By the Gauss Theorem and because F is linear on each triangle (and so $\nabla \phi(|\nabla I(x)|)$ is constant),

$$\frac{1}{A} \int_A \nabla_S \cdot (\phi(|\nabla_S I(x)|)\nabla_S I(x)) dx = \frac{1}{A} \int_{\partial A} \phi(|\nabla_S I(x)|)\nabla_S I(x) \cdot \mathbf{n}_{u,v} dl$$

$$= \frac{1}{A} \sum_{T_i \in A} \int_{\partial A \cap T} \phi(|\nabla_S I(x)|)\nabla_S I(x) \cdot \mathbf{n}_{u,v} dl$$

$$= \frac{1}{A} \sum_{T_i \in A} \phi(|\nabla_S I(x)|)\nabla_S I(x) \cdot [X_i - X_{i+1}]^\perp \mathcal{I}_{\partial A \cap T_i}(x)$$

where the triangle T_i has p, p_i, p_{i+1} as vertex; X, X_i, X_{i+1} are the correspondences of the vertex in the (u, v) space; and $\mathcal{I}_{\partial A \cap T_i}(x)$ stands for the indicating function over the set $\partial A \cap T_i$.

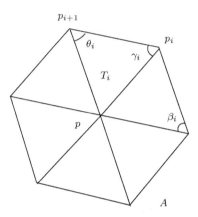

Fig. 2.

Let us now take a fixed triangle T_i. Let B_l, $l = 1, 2, 3$ be the linear basis functions over the triangle T_i. Because of $(B_1 + B_2 + B_3)(u, v) = 1$,

$$\nabla_S I(x) = I(p)\nabla_S B_1 + I(p_i)\nabla_S B_2 + I(p_{i+1})\nabla_S B_3$$
$$= (I(p_i) - I(p))\nabla_S B_2(u, v) + (I(p_{i+1}) - I(p))\nabla_S B_3(u, v)$$
$$= \frac{1}{2A_{T_i}}[(I(p_i) - I(p))(X - X_{i+1})^\perp$$
$$+ (I(p_{i+1}) - I(p))(X_i - X)^\perp)]$$

and we found

$$\nabla B_2(u, v) = \frac{1}{2A_{T_i}}(X - X_{i+1})^\perp$$
$$\nabla B_3(u, v) = \frac{1}{2A_{T_i}}(X_i - X)^\perp$$

where A_{T_i} is the area of the triangle T_i. Using the fact that A_{T_i} is proportional to the sine of any angle of the triangle,

$$\nabla_S I(x) \cdot [X_i - X_{i+1}]^\perp = [cot(p_{i+1})(I(p_i) - I(p)) + cot(p_i)(I(p_{i+1}) - I(p))]$$

So we get

$$\widehat{\Delta_g I(p)} = \frac{\phi(|\widehat{\nabla_S I(p)}|)}{A} \sum_{T_i \in A} \{ \phi(|\widehat{\nabla_S I(p)}|) \cdot$$
$$[cot\, \theta_i(I(p_i) - I(p)) + cot\, \gamma_i(I(p_{i+1}) - I(p))] \}$$

for x in the triangle T_i, where θ_i is the internal angle of the node p_{i+1} and γ_i is the internal angle of the node p_i, and

$$|\widehat{\nabla_S I(p)}| = \frac{1}{2A_T} \sum_{T_i \in A} |(I(p_i) - I(p))(p - p_{i+1}) + (I(p_{i+1}) - I(p))(p_i - p)|$$

Note that the approximation is independent from the parameterization chosen, and it can be used to approximate other differential operators of the form

$$\nabla_S \cdot (\phi(|\nabla_S I(p)|)\nabla_S I(p)) \tag{3}$$

for ϕ being a function $\phi : \mathbb{R} \to \mathbb{R}$.

Remark that if we take $\beta \to 0$, we recover the expression of [21] which approximates the Laplace Beltrami operator in order to perform isotropic smoothing:

$$\lim_{\beta \to 0} \widehat{\Delta_g I(p)} = \lim_{\beta \to 0} \frac{1}{A\sqrt{1 + \beta|\nabla_{u,v}I(x)|^2}} \sum_{T_i \in A} \left\{ \frac{1}{\sqrt{1 + \beta|\nabla_{u,v}I(x)|^2}} [\cot\theta_i(I(p_i) \right.$$
$$\left. - I(p)) + \cot\gamma_i(I(p_{i+1}) - I(p))] \right\}$$
$$= \frac{1}{A} \sum_{T_i \in A} [\cot\theta_i(I(p_i) - I(p)) + \cot\gamma_i(I(p_{i+1}) - I(p))]$$

which is the expression found in [21] as $\widehat{\Delta_{u,v}I(p)}$, that can be written as

$$\widehat{\Delta_{u,v}I(p)} = \sum_{T_i \in A} w_i(I(p_i) - I(p))$$

$$\text{with} \quad w_i = \frac{\cot\theta_i + \cot\beta_i}{A_{T_i}}$$

using some common trigonometric identities.

4   Examples and Results

4.1   Implementation Details

The implementation was done using the 3D visualization package developed at (Hidden for anonymous review). We compute the value of I_p^n, the value of I on the vertex p of Σ at the nth iteration based on the values of $I_{p_i}^{n-1}$, $p_i, .., p_{nb\_of\_neigh}$ being the vertex neighboring p.

First, we compute the $\cot\theta_i, \cot\gamma$, and A_{T_i} for each node p only once. Then, for each iteration n, we actualize the flow in this manner:

$$I_p^n = I_p^{n-1} + dt\widehat{\Delta_g I(p)}$$

$$\widehat{\Delta_g I(p)} = \frac{\phi(|\widehat{\nabla_S I(p)}|)}{A} \sum_{T_i \in A} \left\{ \phi(|\widehat{\nabla_S I(p)}|) \cot\theta_i(I(p_i) - I(p)) \right.$$
$$\left. + \cot\gamma_i(I(p_{i+1}) - I(p)) \right\}$$

4.2   Examples

For the first example (fig. 3) we use a triangulation from the Stanford's surface data base with the Japanese word for *peace* as the data function, and we added a gaussian noise with $\sigma = 40$. The first stage of the algorithm takes about 2 minutes to be computed, and the iterations a few more minutes, (from 1 to 5 depending on the value of β).

For the second example example (fig. 5) a slice of cortex is taken from our database. The scalar data is a variable that needs to be regularized as an intermediate step to obtain a map of the visual areas on the cortex.

The scalar data is naturally noisy because of the measurement errors. We already have from the beginning a stair-casing effect due to the differences of resolution between the anatomic and functional brain images.

Even though we have no access to the original non-noisy image, we can select a region where we know that the original image has null variance. We can do this because we know that there should be no electric impulses outside a certain region of the cortex. To compare the performance with different values of β, we applied the flow until the variance measurement in the selected region reaches a fixed threshold. Then we observed how different values of β act on discontinuities on the image for the same amount of noise reduction on the selected region.

5   Conclusions

We have shown a method to compute the Beltrami flow for scalar functions defined on triangulated manifolds using a local approximation of the operator. This procedure can be extended to any operator of the form (3). We have also illustrated the utility of this approach showing synthetic and real examples.

References

1. M. Bertalmío, L. T. Cheng, S. Osher and G. Sapiro, "Variational Problems and Partial Differential Equations on Implicit Surfaces", Journal of Computational Physics 174 (2001) 759-780.
2. T. Chan and J. Shen, "Variational restoration of non-flat image features: Models and algorithms", SIAM J. Appl. Math., 61 (2000) 1338-1361.
3. R. Kimmel and R. Malladi and N. Sochen, "Images as Embedding Maps and Minimal Surfaces: Movies, Color, Texture, and Volumetric Medical Images", International Journal of Computer Vision 39(2) (2000) 111-129.
4. N. Sochen and R. Kimmel, "Stereographic Orientation Diffusion", in proceedings of the 4th Int. Conf. on Scale-Space, Vancouver Canada, October 2001.
5. A. M. Polyakov, "Quantum geometry of bosonic strings", *Physics Letters*, **103B** (1981) 207-210.

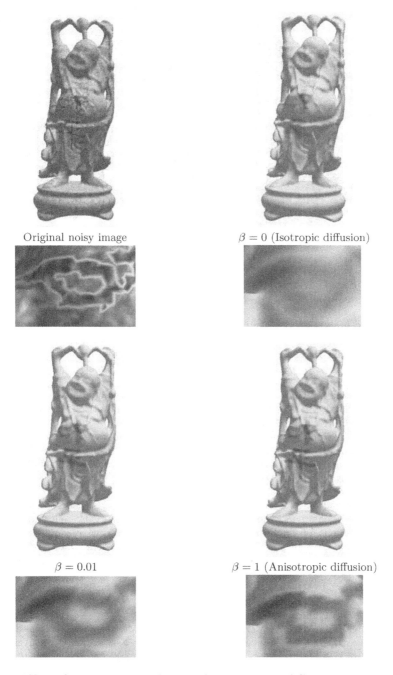

Original noisy image $\beta = 0$ (Isotropic diffusion)

$\beta = 0.01$ $\beta = 1$ (Anisotropic diffusion)

Fig. 3. Note the stair-casing effect on the anisotropic diffusion regularization and the blurry image obtained with the isotropic one

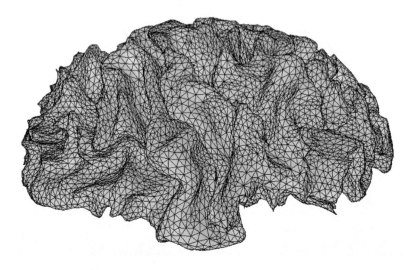

Fig. 4. Triangulation used: 18979 vertex, 37954 triangles

6. L. Rudin, S. Osher and E. Fatemi, " Non Linear Total Variation Based Noise Removal Algorithms", *Physica D 60 (1992) 259-268.*

7. N. Sochen and R. Kimmel and A. M. Bruckstein, "Diffusions and confusions in signal and image processing", accepted to *Journal of Mathematical Imaging and Vision.*

8. N. Sochen and R. Kimmel and R. Malladi, "From high energy physics to low level vision", Report, LBNL, UC Berkeley, LBNL 39243, August, Presented in ONR workshop, UCLA, Sept. 5 1996.

9. N. Sochen and R. Kimmel and R. Malladi, "A general framework for low level vision", *IEEE Trans. on Image Processing,* 7 (1998) 310-318.

10. N. Sochen and Y. Y. Zeevi, "Representation of colored images by manifolds embedded in higher dimensional non-Euclidean space", Proc. IEEE ICIP'98, Chicago, 1998.

11. N. Sochen and Y. Y. Zeevi, "Representation of images by surfaces embedded in higher dimensional non-Euclidean space", 4th International Conference on Mathematical Methods for Curves and Surfaces, Lillehamer, Norway, July 1997.

12. B. Tang and G. Sapiro and V. Caselles, "Diffusion of General Data on Non-Flat Manifold via Harmonic Map Theory: The Direction Diffusion Case", *International Journal on Computer Vision* 36(2) 149-161, 2000.

13. F. Memoli and G. Sapiro and S. Osher, "Solving Variational Problems and Partial Differential Equations, Mapping into General Target Manifolds", January 2002 UCLA CAM Technical Report (02-04).

14. L. Cheng, P. Burchard, B. Merriman and S. Osher, "Motion of Curves Constrained on Surfaces Using a Level Set Approach", September 2000 UCLA CAM Technical Report (00-32).

15. M. Clerc, O. Faugeras, R. Keriven, J. Kybic, T. Papadopoulo, "A level set method for the inverse EEG/MEG problem", Poster No.: 10133, NeuroImage Human Brain Mapping 2002 Meeting

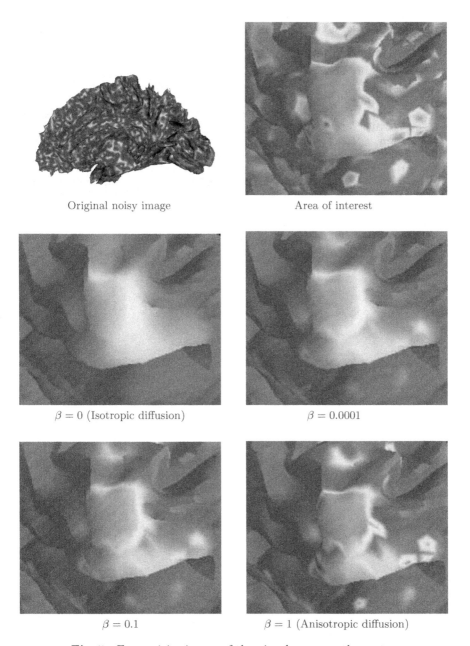

Original noisy image   Area of interest

$\beta = 0$ (Isotropic diffusion) $\beta = 0.0001$

$\beta = 0.1$ $\beta = 1$ (Anisotropic diffusion)

Fig. 5. Eccentricity image of the visual areas on the cortex

16. P. Kornprobst, R. Deriche, and G. Aubert. "Nonlinear operators in image restoration". In Proceedings of the International Conference on Computer Vision and Pattern Recognition - pages 325-331.IEEE Computer Society. San Juan, Puerto Rico, June 1997.
17. G. Sapiro, "Geometric Partial Differential Equations and Image Analysis", Cambridge University Press, January 2001.
18. N. Sochen, R. Deriche, and L. Lopez-Perez, "Variational Beltrami Flows Over Manifolds", IEEE ICIP 2003, Barcelone 2003.
19. N. Sochen, R. Deriche, and L. Lopez-Perez, "The Beltrami Flow over Implicit Manifolds", ICCV 2003.
20. N. Sochen, R. Deriche, and L. Lopez-Perez, "Variational Beltrami Flows Over Manifolds", INRIA Resarch Report 4897, June 2003.
21. Moo K. Chung, Keith J. Worsley, Jonathan Taylor, Jim Ramsay, Steve Robbins, Alan C. Evans, "Diffusion Smoothing on the Cortical Surface", Human Brain Mapping 2001 Conference.
22. M. Meyer, M. Desbrun, P. Schröder, and A. H. Barr, Discrete differential-geometry operators for triangulated 2-manifolds. In Hans-Christian Hege and Konrad Polthier, editors, Visualisation and Mathematics III, pages 35-57. Springer-Verlag, Heidelberg, 2003.

Hierarchical Analysis of Low-Contrast Temporal Images with Linear Scale Space

Tomoya Sakai and Atsushi Imiya

Institute of Media and Information Technology, Chiba University
Yayoi-cho 1-33, Inage-ku, 263-8522, Chiba, Japan
{tsakai, imiya}@faculty.chiba-u.jp

Abstract. This paper focuses on the spatio-temporal analysis to the topology of topography of temporal gray-value images. We extract a sequence of trees which expresses the hierarchical structure of a temporal gray-value image using the linear scale space analysis. This hierarchical features of temporal images provide topological and geometrical information for the global understanding of temporal images.

1 Introduction

This paper focuses on the spatio-temporal analysis to the topology of topography of temporal gray-value images. Zhao and Iijima [2,3,4,9,10] proposed a unique hierarchical expression of a gray-valued image using stationary points on the stationary-curves, which are sometimes called fingerprints for one dimensional real signals, in the linear scale space [1,11], in the linear scale space. Extending their results to temporal images, we extract a sequence of trees which expresses the hierarchical structure of a temporal gray-value image.

Discrete-Signal-Processing base method [6] achieves a fast extraction of these hierarchical structures proposed by Zhao and Iijima[2,3,4]. This fast computation allows applications of the method to the hierarchical analysis of temporal image. In this paper, we show a result of the application of Zhao and Iijima 's idea to temporal analysis of medical image.

Extracted features from temporal images allow us the symbolic analysis of temporal image sequences. For the symbolic analysis of temporal changes on hierarchical structure, we introduce a fast algorithm for the computation of distance among tree structures [5,8]. Since our trees correspond to the hierarchical structures of images, the algorithm detects temporal transition of hierarchical structure of images. As an application, this tree based analysis enables us the detection of the topological transition in the sequence of of low-contrast images such as medical ultrasonic image-sequences.

2 Stationary-Curves and Tree in Linear Scale Space

In the two-dimensional Euclidean space $\mathbf{R}^2$, for an orthogonal coordinate system x-y defined in $\mathbf{R}^2$, a vector in $\mathbf{R}^2$ is expressed by $\boldsymbol{x} = (x, y)^\top$ where $\cdot^\top$ is the

M. Šonka et al. (Eds.): CVAMIA-MMBIA 2004, LNCS 3117, pp. 145–156, 2004.

transpose of a vector. Setting $|\boldsymbol{x}|$ to be the length of $\boldsymbol{x}$, the linear scale-space transform for function $f(\boldsymbol{x})$, such that

$$f(\boldsymbol{x}, \tau) = \frac{1}{(\sqrt{4\pi\tau})^2} \int_{\mathbf{R}^2} f(\boldsymbol{y}) \exp(-\frac{|\boldsymbol{x} - \boldsymbol{y}|^2}{\tau}) d\boldsymbol{y}, \tag{1}$$

defines the general image of function $f(\boldsymbol{x})$. Therefore, function $f(\boldsymbol{x}, \tau)$ is defined in $\mathbf{R}^2 \times \mathbf{R}_+$ [1]. The function $f(\boldsymbol{x}, \tau)$ is the solution of the linear diffusion equation

$$\frac{\partial}{\partial \tau} f(\boldsymbol{x}, \tau) = \Delta f(\boldsymbol{x}, \tau), \ \tau > 0, \ f(\boldsymbol{x}, 0) = f(\boldsymbol{x}). \tag{2}$$

The solution of eq. (2) is formally expressed

$$f(\boldsymbol{x}, \tau) = \exp(\Delta \tau) f(\boldsymbol{x}) \tag{3}$$

using the theory of Lie group [13].

Stationary points for the topographical maps in the scale space [1,2] are defined as the solutions of the equation $\nabla f(\boldsymbol{x}, \tau) = 0$. The stationary-curves in the scale space are the collections of the stationary points. We denote the trajectories of the stationary points as $\boldsymbol{x}(\tau)$. Setting $\boldsymbol{H}$ to be the Hessian matrix of $f(\boldsymbol{x}, \tau)$, Zhao and Iijima [2] showed that the stationary-curves for a two-dimensional image $f(\boldsymbol{x})$ are the solution of,

$$\boldsymbol{H} \frac{d\boldsymbol{x}(\tau)}{d\tau} = -\nabla \Delta f(\boldsymbol{x}(\tau), \tau) \tag{4}$$

and clarified topological properties of the stationary-curves for two-dimensional patterns.

Since the Hessian matrix is always singular for singular points, this equation is valid for nonsingular points. Their definitions are formally valid to functions defined in $\mathbf{R}^n$ for $n \geq 3$.

Using the second derivations of $f(\boldsymbol{x}, \tau)$, we classify the topological properties of the stationary points on the topographical maps. Since the second directional derivation of $f(\boldsymbol{x}, \tau)$ for point $\boldsymbol{x}$ is defined as

$$D_{\boldsymbol{x}}^2(\theta) = \frac{d^2}{dn^2} f(\boldsymbol{x}, \tau), \tag{5}$$

where $\boldsymbol{n}(\theta) = \boldsymbol{\omega} - \boldsymbol{x}$ for $\boldsymbol{\omega} = (\cos\theta, \sin\theta)^\top$, $0 \leq \theta \leq 2\pi$. In the neighbourhood of the point $\boldsymbol{x}$ which satisfies the relation $\nabla f(\boldsymbol{x}, \tau) = 0$, we have the equation

$$\frac{d^2 f}{dn^2} = \boldsymbol{n} \cdot \nabla(\boldsymbol{n} \cdot \nabla f) = \boldsymbol{n}^\top \boldsymbol{H} \boldsymbol{n}. \tag{6}$$

Equation (6) means that the eigenvectors of Hessian matrix of $f(\boldsymbol{x}, \tau)$ gives the extremal of D^2 and that the extremal are achieved by the eigenvalues of the Hessian of $f(\boldsymbol{x}, \tau)$, since $\alpha_1 \geq \boldsymbol{n}^\top \boldsymbol{H} \boldsymbol{n} \geq \alpha_2$ for $|\boldsymbol{n}| = 1$, where $\alpha_1 \geq \alpha_2$ are eigenvalues of the Hessian matrix. Therefore, we have $\max(D_{\boldsymbol{x}}^2) = \alpha_1$ and $\min(D_{\boldsymbol{x}}^2) = \alpha_2$.

Denoting the signs of the eigenvalues of the minus of the Hessian matrix as $(+,+)$, $(+,-)$ and $(-,-)$ in the linear scale space, these labels of points correspond to the local maximum points, the saddle points, and the local minimum points, respectively. In [2,3], they payed attention to the maximum and minimum points.

The saddle points in the scale space appear on walls and valley which connect maximum points and minimum points, respectively, The motion of the saddle points in the scale space corresponds to the changes of the topology of gray-value images in the scale space.

According to the second directional derivation, we can define three types of stationary-curves: maximum curves, minimum curves, and saddle curves. Furthermore, since the stationary-curves consist of many curves for $\tau > 0$, we call each curve a branch curve. The point $\boldsymbol{x}_\infty$ for

$$\lim_{\tau \to \infty} \boldsymbol{x}(\tau) = \boldsymbol{x}_\infty \tag{7}$$

is uniquely determined for any image. We call a curve on which point $\boldsymbol{x}_\infty$ lies and a curve which is open to the direction of $-\tau$ the trunk and branch, respectively. On the top of each branch, a singular point exists. Therefore, for the construction of a unique hierarchical expression of stationary points, Zhao and Iijima [2,3,4] proposed the following rules.

Rules 1

1. The sub-root of a branch is the singular point, such that $\nabla f = 0$, of the top of the branch curve.
2. The a sub-root is connected to the trunk by a line segment $\tau = constant$.

These rules yield a monotonically branching curves from the infinity to zero along τ-axis in the linear scale space.

For $S(\boldsymbol{x}, \tau) = |\frac{d\boldsymbol{x}(\tau)}{d\tau}|$, Zhao and Iijima [2,3] defined the stationary points on the stationary-curves which satisfy $S(\boldsymbol{x}, \tau) = 0$ or isolated points with the conditions

$$\frac{d}{d\tau} S(\boldsymbol{x}, \tau) = 0, \quad \frac{d^2}{d^2\tau} S(\boldsymbol{x}, \tau) = 0. \tag{8}$$

They also developed an algorithm to define a unique tree whose nodes are the stationary points on the stationary-curves, and introduced a unique hierarchical expression of an image using this tree.

Definition 1. *For the stationary points on the stationary-curves which are merged using rules 1, the order of the stationary points is defined as*

$$\boldsymbol{x}(\tau) \succ \boldsymbol{x}(\tau') \ if \ \tau > \tau' \ on \ a \ branch.$$

Denoting a stationary point on the stationary-curves as $(\boldsymbol{x}_i, \tau_i)$, $\boldsymbol{x}_i$ and τ_i are called the stable view-point and the field of vision, and that

$$f(\boldsymbol{x}, \boldsymbol{x}_i, \tau_i) = \exp(-\frac{|\boldsymbol{x} - \boldsymbol{x}_i|^2}{\tau_i})f(\boldsymbol{x}) \tag{9}$$

is called a view-controlled image of the original image, since $f(\boldsymbol{x}, \boldsymbol{x}_i, \tau_i)$ approximates an image in the region of interest $\boldsymbol{R}(\boldsymbol{x}_i, \tau_i)$,

$$\boldsymbol{R}(\boldsymbol{x}_i, \tau_i) = \{\boldsymbol{x} \,|\, |\boldsymbol{x} - \boldsymbol{x}_i| < \tau_i\}, \tag{10}$$

observed by a vision system which has mechanisms similar to those of the view-controlling system of human beings [1].

Using the radii of the fields of views for the stationary points, in this paper, we reformulate the order of points along the stationary-curves.

Rules 2

1. *On the trunk, if $\tau > \tau'$, we define the order of the stationary points as $\boldsymbol{x}(\tau) \succ \boldsymbol{x}(\tau')$.*
2. *On each branch $\boldsymbol{x}_i(\tau)$, we express the stationary point $\boldsymbol{x}_i(\tau_{i(j)})$. Assuming that the maximum scale parameter on this branch is $\tau_{i(0)}$, we set $\boldsymbol{x}_{i(j)} = (x_{ij}, y_{ij})^\top$ for point $\boldsymbol{x}_i(\tau_j)$ in the scale space.*
3. *We define the order of the stationary points on each branch using the fields of views.*
4. *On each branch curve, for $\tau_{i(m)} > \tau_{i(n)}$, if the relation*

$$|\boldsymbol{x}_{i(m)} - \boldsymbol{x}_{i(n)}| \leq \sqrt{2\tau_{i(m)}}$$

   is satisfied, then we define $\boldsymbol{x}_{i(m)} \succ \boldsymbol{x}_{i(n)}$.
5. *For a pair of branch curves $\boldsymbol{x}_i(\tau)$ and $\boldsymbol{x}_j(\tau)$ and a pair of fixed scales $\tau_{i(m)}$ and $\tau_{j(0)}$, if the relation*

$$|\boldsymbol{x}_{i(m)} - \boldsymbol{x}_{j(0)}| \leq \sqrt{2\tau_{i(m)}}$$

   is satisfied, then we define $\boldsymbol{x}_{i(m)} \succ \boldsymbol{x}_{j(0)}$.

The order based on fifth rule permits to merge stationary points among branches and the trunk. Therefore, these rules for the order of the stationary points along the stationary-curves defines the hierarchical tree of the stationary points for an image. We call this tree the structure tree of an image. For example, if the orders of the stationary points are

$$\boldsymbol{x}_\infty \succ \boldsymbol{x}(\tau_1), \boldsymbol{x}(\tau_1) \succ \boldsymbol{x}_2(\tau_{2(0)}), \boldsymbol{x}_2(\tau_{2(0)}) \succ \boldsymbol{x}_2(\tau_{2(1)}), \ \boldsymbol{x}_2(\tau_{2(0)}) \succ \boldsymbol{x}_2(\tau_{2(2)}), \tag{11}$$

we obtain the tree for the stationary points as

$$T = \langle \boldsymbol{x}_\infty \langle \boldsymbol{x}(\tau_1), \langle \boldsymbol{x}_2(\tau_{2(0)}), \langle \boldsymbol{x}_2(\tau_{2(1)}), \boldsymbol{x}_2(\tau_{2(2)}) \rangle \rangle \rangle \rangle, \tag{12}$$

where $T = \langle r, \langle T_1, T_2 \rangle \rangle$ means that the root of tree T is r and T_1 and T_2 are both subtrees whose roots are r.

Figure 1 shows scale space analysis of a practical hand-image. (a) is the original image, and (b) shows the field of view of the stationary points projected to the plane $\tau = 0$. (c) shows the field of view of the stationary points, and (d) shows the stationary points along the stationary curve and the tree in the scale space.

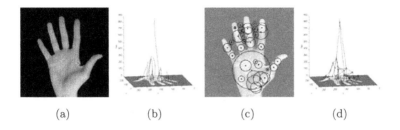

     (a)   (b)   (c)   (d)

Fig. 1. Scale space analysis of an image. (a) is the original image, (b) shows the stationary curve. (c) shows the field of view of the stationary points. (d) shows the stationary points along the stationary curve in the scale space.

3 Temporal Structure Tree

In this section, we define the structure forest for a time-varying image $f(x, y, t)$. For the sampled sequence $f(x, y, 1)$, $f(x, y, 2)$, $\cdots$, $f(x, y, t)$, $f(x, y, t + 1)$, $\cdots$, we construct the structure tree $T(t)$ for each image in this sequence.

For the generation of a temporal tree sequence, we adopt the following rules.
Rules 3

1. *If each of pair of successive trees $T(t)$ and $T(t+1)$ are topologically different, we affix new labels for nodes, excepting the root.*
2. *For topologically equivalent trees $T(t)$ and $T(t + 1)$, if stationary points of $T(t + 1)$ do not remain in the field of view of each node, we consider these two trees to be different and $T(t + 1)$ produces new nodes.*
3. *We eliminate old symbols of nodes in $T(t)$ and affix new symbols to new nodes in $T(t + 1)$.*

Using these operations, which are expressed as

$$\Theta\left(\frac{\partial}{\partial \tau} f(\boldsymbol{x}, \tau, t) = \Delta f(\boldsymbol{x}, \tau, t))\right) = T(t), \tag{13}$$

we can extract the motion of stationary points and the change of the field of views on the image plane $\tau = 0$.

This process detects dominant motion in a sequence of images.

Figure 2 illustrates the changing of trees of a model hand-image. This synthetic image sequence expresses the motion of the first finger.

4 Tree Distance and Fast Computation

For quantitative analysis of time-varying image with temporal trees extracted in the linear scale space, we introduce the distance between trees based on the

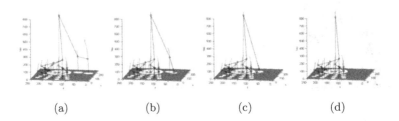

(a)　　　　　　　(b)　　　　　　　(c)　　　　　　　(d)

Fig. 2. Temporal scale structure. (a), (b), (c), and (d) show a sequence of temporal trees of a sequence of images.

editing of the tree structure. Since it is possible to transform irregular trees to regular trees by adding special nodes (∗) on trees, we assume that our trees are regular. Furthermore, since our trees extracted using scale space analysis are rooted tree, we develop a fast computation method for rooted trees which is applicable to time-varying image sequence analysis [7]. Therefore, we assume that trees are m-regular, for $m \geq 2$.

Setting α to be k-digit number, whose each digit is from 0 to $k - 1$, the subtree of the node α is expressed as

$$n_\alpha(T) = t_\alpha[T_{\alpha 1}, T_{\alpha 2}, \cdots, T_{\alpha m}], \tag{14}$$

where t_α is the label of node n_α. For $\alpha = 0$, equation (14) expresses the tree and n_0 is the label of the root. Therefore, the number of digits of α expresses the depth of a subtree.

The operations to a tree are the transform of node-label, the permutation of subtrees, the insertion of a subtree to ∗, and the elimination of subtree which are mathematically expressed as

$$E_t : t_\alpha[T_{\alpha 1}, \cdots, T_{\alpha m}] = x_\alpha[T_{\alpha 1}, \cdots, T_{\alpha m}], \tag{15}$$

$$E_p : t_\alpha[T_{\alpha 1}, \cdots, T_{\alpha i} \cdots T_{\alpha j} \cdots T_{\alpha m}] = t_\alpha[T_{\alpha 1}, \cdots, T_{\alpha j} \cdots T_{\alpha i} \cdots T_{\alpha m}], \tag{16}$$

$$E_i(S) : t_\alpha[T_{\alpha 1} \cdots * \cdots T_{\alpha m}] = t_\alpha[T_{\alpha 1} \cdots S \cdots T_{\alpha m}], \tag{17}$$

$$E_i(T_{\alpha k}) : t_\alpha[T_{\alpha 1} \cdots T_{\alpha k} \cdots T_{\alpha m}] = t_\alpha[T_{\alpha 1} \cdots * \cdots T_{\alpha m}]. \tag{18}$$

Furthermore, a successive application of E_n derives the transformation of subtree such as

$$E_t(T_{\alpha,k}, S) : t_\alpha[T_{\alpha 1}, \cdots, T_{\alpha k} \cdots, T_{\alpha m}] = x_\alpha[T_{\alpha 1}, \cdots, S, \cdots, T_{\alpha m}]. \tag{19}$$

For these operations, we define the lengths of operations as

$$d(s_\alpha) = \frac{1}{1 + l_k}|s_\alpha| \tag{20}$$

where

$$l_\alpha = \begin{cases} \text{the number of digits of } \alpha, & \text{if } \alpha \neq 0, \\ 0, & \text{otherwise,} \end{cases} \tag{21}$$

and

$$|s_\alpha| = \begin{cases} 1, & \text{if } s_\alpha \text{ is the node-label transform,} \\ |S|, & \text{if } s_\alpha \text{ is the insertion,} \\ |S|, & \text{if } s_\alpha \text{ is the elimination,} \\ \text{the number of permutation,} & \text{if } s_\alpha \text{ is the permutation.} \end{cases} \tag{22}$$

Using these lengths, we define the distance between trees as

$$D(T, T') = \sum_{\alpha=1}^{n} d(s_\alpha) \tag{23}$$

for the sequence of operation $\{s_1, s_2, \cdots, s_n\}$ which transforms T to T'. This tree distance satisfies the following lemma.

Lemma 1 *For trees with almost same order, the distance in eq. (23) is metric, that is, it satisfies the conditions of distance.*

(*Proof*) It is obvious that $D(T, T) = 0$ and that $D(T, T') = D(T', T)$. Setting $\{s_1, s_2, \cdots, s_n\}$, $\{t_1, t_2, \cdots, t_n\}$, and $\{u_1, u_2, \cdots, u_n\}$ to be sequences of transformation from T to T' and T' to T'', for a triplet of almost same size trees, we have the relation $|s_k| + |t_k| \geq |u_k|$ with considering non-operation which satisfies $|\text{operation}| = 0$. This relation derives the relation $D(T, T') + D(T', T'') \geq D(T, T'')$.   (Q.E.D.)

Figure 3 shows 1,6,7,8,11,12,13,31,32,33,38 frames from 1 to 38 frames of beating heart sequence [14]. Figure 4 shows stationary-curves of these frames from beating heart. The temporal tree analysis found that from 6 to 7, from 7 to 8, from 11 to 12, from 12 to 13, from 31 to 32, and from 32 and 33, gray-values of images are topologically different and that from 1 to 6, from 8 to 11, from 13 to 31, and from 33 to 38, gray-values of images are topologically equivalent. These topological transitions extracted using the tree metric for trees shown in Figure 5. The distances among trees which topologically different are

$$D(T^{(6)}, T^{(7)}) = 1.5, \quad D(T^{(7)}, T^{(8)}) = 3, \quad D(T^{(11)}, T^{(12)}) = 3,$$
$$D(T^{(12)}, T^{(13)}) = 1.5, \quad D(T^{(31)}, T^{(32)}) = 1.5, \quad D(T^{(32)}, T^{(33)}) = 1.5.$$

Since this sequence of beating heart is low-contrast, it is not easy to follow topological changes of images in a sequence. The temporal scale space analysis achieves the detection of topological changes of beating heart. This results indicates that our temporal scale space analysis based on tree-construction in the scale space is feasible to the sequential analysis of low-contrast medical images as this example from [14].

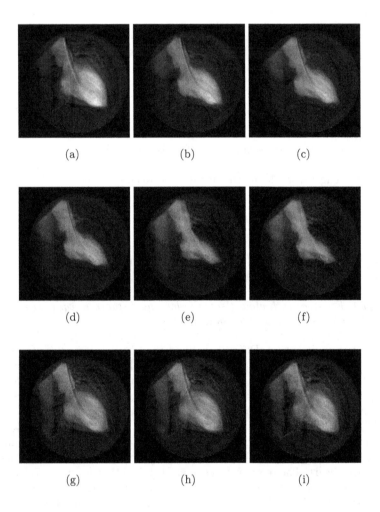

Fig. 3. Sequence of beating heart. 1,6,7,8,11,12,13,31,32,33,38 frames from 1 to 38 frames. From 6 to 7, from 7 to 8, from 11 to 12, from 12 to 13, and from 31 to 32, there is topological changes. From 1 to 6, from 8 to 11, from 13 to 31, and from 33 to 38, there is no topological changes. These changes extracted using tree analysis.

5   Discussion and Concluding Remarks

As an application of the scale space analysis for time-varying images, we developed a method for the extraction of dominant motion from a sequences of images. The method does not assume the scale-space transformation with respect to the time variable. Computational examples show that our method is suitable for the spatiotemporal analysis of sequences of low-contrast images.

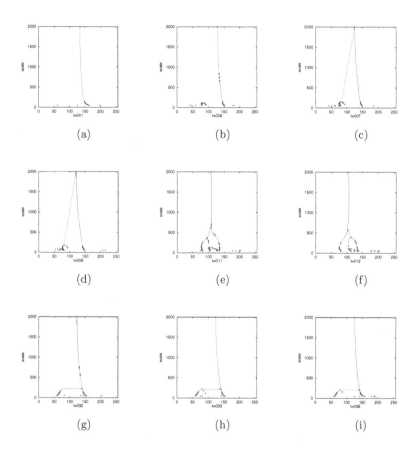

Fig. 4. Sequence of stationary-curves of beating heart. 1,6,7,8,11,12,13,31,32, 33,38 frames from 1 to 38 frames. Points on the curves illustrate the stationary points on the curves.

Setting τ_α to be an arbitral large scale, for $\tau > \tau_\alpha$, equation (9) allows to approximate the topographical maps in the scale space by the function

$$\hat{f}(\boldsymbol{x}) = \sum_{n=1}^{n(\tau_\alpha)} f_n \exp(-\frac{|\boldsymbol{x} - \boldsymbol{p}_n|^2}{\sigma_n}). \tag{24}$$

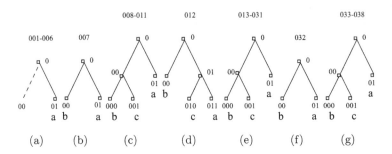

Fig. 5. Temporal trees of a sequence of images. (a) Tree of from 1 to 6. (b) Tree of 7. (c) Tree of from 8 to 11. (d) Tree of 12. (e) Tree of from 13 to 31. (f) Tree of 32. (g) Tree of from 33 to 38.

Setting $w_n = \ln f_n$, from eq. (24), we have the generalized Voronoi distance

$$d(\boldsymbol{x}, \boldsymbol{p}_n) = \exp(-\frac{|\boldsymbol{x} - \boldsymbol{p}_n|^2}{\sigma_n} + w_n) \tag{25}$$

with respect to the generators $\{\boldsymbol{p}_n\}_{n=1}^{n(\tau_\alpha)}$ [15]. The generators, Voronoi vertices, and Voronoi edges correspond to the local maximum, saddle, and local minimum points, respectively. Therefore, if we have function $\hat{f}(\boldsymbol{x}, \tau)$ such that

$$\int_{\mathbf{R}^2} |\hat{f}(\boldsymbol{x}, \tau) - f(\boldsymbol{x}, \tau)| d\boldsymbol{x} \le \epsilon, \tag{26}$$

for a small positive constant ϵ, we can estimate the topological configuration of stationary points using combinatorial optimization.

Figure 6 shows scale space analysis of a simple image. (a) is the original image, (b) shows the field of views of the saddle points in the linear scale space. (c) shows the field of views of all stationary points in the scale space. (d) shows the field of view of the point whose scale parameter is infinity. As shown in this example, the motion of the saddle points describes the topological structure of images. This analysis shows the validity of the combinatorial analysis to simple images for a large scale parameters.

The structure tree of triangles is

$$T_{triangle} = \langle(+,+) \succ \langle(-,-),(+,+),(+,-),(+,+),(+,-),(+,+),(+,-)\rangle\rangle, \tag{27}$$

since, in the scale space, a triangle is approximated three Gaussian whose centers are located at the vertices. If a vertex moves to the center of the opposite edge, we have three Gaussians on a line segment. This motion of Gaussian yields the transition of structure tree to

$$T_{line-segment} = \langle(+,+) \succ \langle(+,+),(+,-),(+,+),(+,-),(+,+)\rangle\rangle. \tag{28}$$

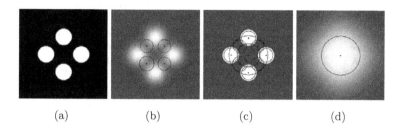

(a)   (b)   (c)   (d)

Fig. 6. Scale space analysis of an image. (a) is the original image, (b) shows the field of views of the saddle points in the linear scale space. (c) shows the field of views of all stationary points in the scale space. (d) shows the field of view of the point whose scale parameter is infinity.

This combinatorial observation suggests that our motion analysis method detects the motion of meaning parts using the transition of the distribution of singular points in scale space. Although, for both cases, functions are expressed as

$$\hat{f}(\boldsymbol{x}) = \sum_{n=1}^{3} f_n \exp(-\frac{|\boldsymbol{x} - \boldsymbol{p}_n|^2}{\sigma_n}), \tag{29}$$

for the first and second cases three vectors $\{\boldsymbol{p}_1, \boldsymbol{p}_2, \boldsymbol{p}_3\}$, which are peaks of three Gaussians, lie in the general position and on a line, respectively, on a plane. This property shows that the structure-tree analysis extracts these topological differences of functions on a plane detecting spatiotemporal trajectory of view-fields of images, which is first introduced by Iijima [1], to the automatic selection of the best scale-parameters [12].

References

1. Iijima, T., *Pattern Recognition,* Corona-sha, Tokyo, 1974 (in Japanese).
2. Zhao, N.-Y., Iijima, T., Theory on the method of determination of view-point and field of vision during observation and measurement of figure IECE Japan, Trans. D., **J68-D**, 508-514, 1985 (in Japanese).
3. Zhao, N.-Y., Iijima, T., A theory of feature extraction by the tree of stable view-points. IECE Japan, Trans. D., **J68-D**, 1125-1135, 1985 (in Japanese).
4. Zhao, N.-Y., *A Study of Feature Extraction by the Tree of Stable View-Points,* Dissertation to Doctor of Engineering, Tokyo Institute of Technology, 1985 (in Japanese).
5. Zhang, K., A constrained edit distance between unordered labeled trees. Algorithmica **15**, 205-222, 1996.
6. Imiya, A., Sugiura, T., Sakai, T, Kato, Y., Temporal structure tree in digital linear scale space, LNCS, **2695**, 356-371, 2003.

7. Kawashima, T., Imiya, A., Nishida, F., Approximate tree distance, Technical Report of IEICE, PRMU96-36, 81-87, 1996.
8. Pelillo, M., Siddiqi, K., Zucker, S.W., Matching hierarchical structures using Association graphs, IEEE, Trans, PAMI **21**, 1105-1120, 1999.
9. Witkin, A.P., Scale space filtering, Pros. of 8th IJCAI, 1019-1022, 1993.
10. Yuille, A. L., Poggio, T., Scale space theory for zero crossings, IEEE PAMI, **8**, 15-25, 1986.
11. Lindeberg, T., *Scale-Space Theory in Computer Vision,* Kluwer, Boston 1994.
12. Lindeberg, T. Feature detection with automatic selection, International Journal of Computer Vision, **30**, 79-116, 1998.
13. Otsu, N., *Mathematical Studies on Feature Extraction in Pattern Recognition,* Researches of The Electrotechnical Laboratory, **818**, 1981 (in Japanese).
14. http://sampl.eng.ohio-state.edu/ sampl/data/motion/Heart/index.htm
15. Okabe, A., Boots, B., Sugihara, K., *Spatial Tessellations: Concepts and Applications of Voronoi Diagrams,* John Wiley & Sons, Chichester, 1992.

Segmentation of Medical Images with a Shape and Motion Model: A Bayesian Perspective

Julien Sénégas[1], Thomas Netsch[1], Chris A. Cocosco[1], Gunnar Lund[2], and Alexander Stork[2]

[1] Philips Research Laboratories, Röntgenstr. 24, 22335 Hamburg, Germany
[2] Universitätsklinikum Eppendorf, Martinistr. 52, 20246 Hamburg, Germany

Abstract. This paper describes a Bayesian framework for the segmentation of a temporal sequence of medical images, where both shape and motion prior information are integrated into a stochastic model. With this approach, we aim to take into account all the information available to compute an optimum solution, thus increasing the robustness and accuracy of the shape and motion reconstruction. The segmentation algorithm we develop is based on sequential Monte Carlo sampling methods previously applied in tracking applications. Moreover, we show how stochastic shape models can be constructed using a global shape description based on orthonormal functions. This makes our approach independent of the dimension of the object (2D or 3D) and on the particular shape parameterization used. Results of the segmentation method applied to cardiac cine MR images are presented.

1 Introduction

We address the problem of estimating the shape of an organ in a temporal sequence of medical images (2D or 3D). The target application is the segmentation of the heart in Magnetic Resonance Imaging (MRI) scans, but the methods we present are not restricted to a particular image modality or organ.

While much work has been devoted to the extraction of organ shapes, the temporal aspect raised by image sequences is receiving more and more attention [1, 2]. For cardiac applications for instance, the most relevant clinical information for the diagnosis is contained in the motion pattern. Hence, dedicated techniques for the detailed reconstruction of shape and motion need to be applied. If, for example, each imaged volume is processed individually, the reconstructed motion patterns contain artefacts due to over-fitting of the shape at the indivual time steps. To avoid this, a global optimum for the whole sequence needs to be computed. Techniques based on shape models have proven successful to segment organs while preserving their spatial structure [3]. This approach can be naturally extended to the temporal dimension by incorporating prior information about the motion. For this, we propose a general Bayesian framework that explicitly addresses the spatio-temporal dimension of the problem. The idea is to decompose the Bayesian posterior and to use a stochastic motion model to sequentially propagate the shape in time. The segmentation solution can then be

M. Šonka et al. (Eds.): CVAMIA-MMBIA 2004, LNCS 3117, pp. 157–168, 2004.

efficiently computed by sequential Monte Carlo algorithms [4]. This approach has been already applied successfully in tracking systems [5], but to our knowledge its application to segmentation of sequences of medical images is new. In this work, we propose a modified bootstrap filter algorithm: a gradient descent step is added to the propagation step in order to directly integrate data information in the sampling and to avoid the degeneration of the sample set.

The application of Bayesian methods requires the construction of adequate models for the likelihood (image model) and for the prior (shape and motion model). In most segmentation applications, the image model is based on intensity gradients, likely to indicate the position of the contours [6, 7]. However, this uses only a fraction of the image information: the grey values inside the contours for example are not considered. Moreover, the gradient information is not always reliable because of unexpected features, like the presence of fat in the vicinity of organs. The model we propose, based on grey value distributions within the segmented regions, provides a more robust description of image features. Such a model can be seen as a discrete statistical version of the data term in the Mumford-Shah functional, used in the level set formulation of segmentation [8].

Many approaches to shape modeling describe one organ by means of anatomical landmarks [9] or meshes [10] and possibly use a Principal Component Analysis (PCA) to reduce the number of variables; one popular example is the active shape model presented in [11]. We follow here a different approach, which consists in finding a suitable parameterization of the contour or the surface and in decomposing it using some basis functions. In comparison to descriptions relying on meshes, this offers a compact, yet accurate description of shape, while implicitly ensuring the smoothness of the boundaries. We are inspired here by methods proposed in [6, 12, 13], which extend the application of Fourier descriptors to higher dimensions. In this paper, we develop a general method to build a stochastic shape model based on the definition of an inner-product and a set of orthonormal functions.

2   A Bayesian Framework for Segmentation

We denote z the shape of the organ and y the information provided by the images (i.e. the grey values). For the moment, we do not impose any mathematical representation for z. It may be as set of anatomical landmarks, of discrete points in a mesh representation, or of elementary volumes in a finite element approach. Similarly, y may consist of a set of slices of any spatial resolution.

One approach to the segmentation problem is to consider the conditional probability density (or posterior) of the shape z given the images y, denoted $\pi(z|y)$. According to Bayes' rule, we have $\pi(z|y) = \frac{\pi(y|z)\pi(z)}{\pi(y)}$, where $\pi(z)$ is the a priori probability distribution of the shape z and $\pi(y|z)$ is the likelihood of the image y given the shape z.

Let us consider a temporal sequence of images. We adopt the following notations: z_u denotes the shape at time u and $z_{u:v} = (z_u, z_{u+1}, ..., z_v)$. Similarly, y_u denotes the image information available at time u and $y_{u:v} = (y_u, y_{u+1}, ..., y_v)$.

We are now interested in the conditional density $\pi(z_{0:t}|y_{0:t})$, where $t+1$ is the total number of time steps available in the sequence. We make the usual assumption [4] that the images are conditionally independent, i.e. $\pi(y_{0:u}|z_{0:u}) = \prod_v \pi(y_v|z_v)$. Simple Bayesian calculations lead to the following relation [4, 14]:

$$\pi(z_{0:t}|y_{0:t}) = \frac{\pi(y_0|z_0)\pi(z_0)}{\pi(y_0)} \prod_{u=1}^{t} \frac{\pi(y_u|z_u)\pi(z_u|z_{0:u-1})}{\pi(y_u|y_{0:u-1})} . \tag{1}$$

This equation describes the Bayesian model we propose to apply for the segmentation. It is a made of a series of likelihood terms $\pi(y_u|z_u)$ and stochastic priors $\pi(z_u|z_{0:u-1})$. The likelihood describes the expected structure of the image for a known shape, while the prior describes the shape of the myocardium at time u given the previous shapes $z_{0:u-1}$ and therefore embeds shape and motion information. Equation 1 nicely shows how the segmentation of a time series can be interpreted as a sequential segmentation task and will be used in section 4 to derive the segmentation algorithm.

3   Derivation of the Stochastic Model

In this section, we present explicit expressions for the likelihood term and prior densities of the Bayesian model of equation 1.

3.1   A General Likelihood Model

Our approach to construct a likelihood model, which is presented in more details in [14], is to describe the image structure y_u once the shape z_u is known. The segmentation of the organ defines a partition of the image. We make the assumption that the regions of this partition have homogeneous grey values. Specifically, we assume that each region can be characterized by a Gaussian distribution, with the further simplification that within the regions the intensity values are spatially independent. If one region is made of different tissues with different intensity properties that cannot be individually modeled, a Gaussian mixture can be used to model the heterogeneities. For our cardiac application for example, we model the intensity values of the blood pool with a Gaussian mixture to take into account the presence of dark patches due to the papillary muscles (see section 5).

We denote $\Omega_1(z_u), ..., \Omega_l(z_u)$ the l regions defined by the shape z_u. In the simplest case, there are only two regions (the interior and the exterior of the organ), but the vector z_u may also describe several distinct parts of one organ. At each time step u, the likelihood model is

$$\pi(y_u|z_u) = \prod_{a=1}^{l} \prod_{\mathbf{x} \in \Omega_a(z_u)} \frac{1}{\sqrt{2\pi}\sigma_a} \exp\left(-\frac{(y_u(\mathbf{x}) - m_a)^2}{2\sigma_a^2}\right) . \tag{2}$$

The parameters of the model are the mean value m_a and the standard deviation σ_a of the regions $\Omega_a(z_u)$. Note that we could also let them vary in time. In practice, estimates of these parameters are needed. For MRI applications, grey values of the same organ may vary significantly from acquisition to acquisition, so that automatic estimation algorithms are required. In this work, we use the stochastic EM algorithm of [15]; details about the implementation are given in [14].

3.2   Prior Shape Model

The shape model may consist of closed contours in a 2D setting or closed surfaces in a 3D setting. Here, we assume that the shape of the organ (or at least of its individual components) can be uniquely parameterized in an appropriate coordinate system (e.g. spherical, cylindrical or spheroidal). In some cases, this may be a limitation: for example, in a spherical coordinate system, this requires the object to be star-shaped. However, advanced re-parameterization techniques [13] allow to use a spherical parameterization for general objects. Once the parameterization system is chosen, the shape of the organ can be described as a function $z(\phi)$ of the parameterization variables $\phi \in \Phi$ (for example the latitude and longitude in a spherical coordinate system).

On the shape space an inner-product between two shapes z and z' can be defined by taking the integral over the domain Φ of the product $z(\phi)z'(\phi)$:

$$< z, z' >= \frac{1}{|\Phi|} \int_\Phi z(\phi)z'(\phi)d\phi , \tag{3}$$

where $|\Phi|$ denotes the size of Φ. This inner-product induces a norm and a distance

$$||z|| = \sqrt{< z, z >}, \quad d(z, z') = ||z - z'|| . \tag{4}$$

The latter can be interpreted as the root mean square distance between the two shapes along the domain Φ.

Our idea is to use this distance to construct a stochastic model of shape. Consider a reference shape $\bar{z}$ of the organ to be modeled; we propose to describe the shape variations with respect to $\bar{z}$ by the following probability density

$$\pi(z) \propto \exp\left(-\frac{1}{2\kappa^2}d^2(z, \bar{z}) \right) , \tag{5}$$

where the parameter κ can be interpreted as a standard deviation.

The interest of defining the shape model with a distance measure lies in the possibility of using a set of orthonormal functions to represent the shape. More precisely, suppose that the functions $\{\chi_i(\phi), i \leq L\}$ are orthonormal for the inner-product of equation 3. If we restrict the set of parameterized shapes to the set of finite linear combinations of the functions $\chi_i(\phi)$, we obtain the following expression for z

$$z(\phi) = \sum_{i=1}^{L} p_i\chi_i(\phi) , \tag{6}$$

where $p = (p_1, \ldots, p_L)$ are the shape parameters. Since $< \chi_i, \chi_j >= \delta_i^j$, the stochastic shape model of equation 5 takes the form of a Gaussian density on the shape parameters

$$\pi(p) = \frac{1}{(\sqrt{2\pi}\kappa)^L} \exp\left(-\frac{1}{2\kappa^2}\sum_{i=1}^{L}(p_i - \bar{p}_i)^2\right). \tag{7}$$

Note that this model is directly constructed on the linear space defined by the functions $\chi_i(\phi)$; we do not assume at this stage that we approximate a given shape with some basis functions.

Significant differences in organ size from patient to patient may occur. In that case, we propose to explicity model the global size of the organ with a parameter s. To ensure the uniqueness of the solution, the norm of the reference shape needs to be imposed, for example $||\bar{z}|| = \sum_{i=1}^{L} \bar{p}_i^2 = 1$. The preceding shape model can then be used conditionally upon the size s:

$$\pi(p, s) = \pi(p|s)\pi(s) = \frac{1}{(\sqrt{2\pi}s\kappa)^L} \exp\left(-\frac{1}{2s^2\kappa^2}\sum_{i=1}^{L}(p_i - s\bar{p}_i)^2\right)\pi(s). \tag{8}$$

For the size prior, a uniform distribution over an interval $[s_{\min}, s_{\max}]$ can be postulated, where $s_{\min}$ and $s_{\max}$ are respectively the minimum and maximum size factors.

One example of orthonormal functions with respect to the inner-product of equation 3 are the surface harmonics, which can be defined as the solution to Laplace's equation in different coordinate systems [12]. For example, for a polar coordinate system in 2D, these are the conventional Fourier descriptors, and for a spherical coordinate system in 3D they correspond to the spherical harmonics. They are attractive for the possibility of accurately representing shapes with arbitrary fine details by increasing the number of harmonic coefficients. An example of their use to construct a stochastic shape model similar to that of equation 7 is given in [6].

3.3   Motion Model

The motion model is embedded in the stochastic distribution $\pi(z_u|z_{0:u-1})$. We here assume that the motion of the organ can be described by an analytical model F predicting the shape of the organ at time u given the previous shapes. Using a similar approach as in section 3.2, the motion prior can be expressed as

$$\pi(z_u|z_{0:u-1}) \propto \exp\left(-\frac{1}{2\kappa^2}d^2(z_u, F(z_{0:u-1}))\right). \tag{9}$$

When the shape is decomposed using a set of orthonormal functions, F is a function of the shape parameters $p_{0:u-1}$. The mean parameter vector for the time step u is $\bar{p}_u = F(p_{0:u-1})$ and the motion prior takes the same expression as in equation 7.

In practice, F depends on motion parameters, such as scaling factors or rotation angles. Since these parameters are usually known up to a given approximation, it is very convenient to treat them as random variables and to estimate them together with the shape.

3.4   Estimation of Model Parameters and Shape Alignement

In practice, the mean shape $\bar{z}$ and the standard deviation κ need to be estimated from a data base. This data base should contain various instances of the organ shape (e.g. in the form of manually segmented images) and cover as much as possible of the expected variability. The first step consists in fitting the model of equation 6 to the segmented object. This fitting problem can be efficiently solved using least-square techniques involving the inversion of a linear system (see [12] in the case of surface harmonics). At this stage, it is necessary to analyze the number of shape parameters required to achieve the desired accuracy. The second step consists in aligning the fitted shapes. In the case of a shape description based on surface harmonics, we adopted the following method: first, the center of the local coordinate system is determined using a circular fit (in 2D) or a spherical fit (in 3D). This filters out the global translation. Then, the global rotation is estimated directly on the harmonic coefficients by minimizing the distance $d(z, z') = \sum_{i=1}^{L}(p_i - p_i')^2$ where z' is some reference configuration.

The fitting step yields n shape parameters $p^j = (p_1^j, \ldots, p_L^j), j = 1, n$, where n is the size of the data base. The shape parameters $\bar{p}$ and the standard deviation κ can then be estimated, using a maximum likelihood criterion, involving the maximization of the density of equation 7 and yielding the usual estimates for mean and standard deviation in a Gaussian framework. When a size coefficient s is used in the prior model, the estimation of the model parameters is more complex because the sizes of the shapes are unknown variables. To circumvent this problem, we propose to simultaneously estimate prior parameters and size coefficients, using a maximum likelihood criterion. We solve for parameters $\bar{p}$, κ and $s_j, j = 1, n$ which maximize the density of equation 8 under the constraint $\sum_{i=1}^{L} \bar{p}_i^2 = 1$. We use the method of Lagrange multipliers and the iterative method of Newton-Raphson to compute the solution [16].

4   Model-Based Segmentation

To compute a solution of the segmentation problem based on the posterior distribution given in equation 1, we propose to use a modified version of the so-called bootstrap particle filter [4], also known to the computer vision community as the condensation algorithm [5]. The idea is to generate a sample set for the initial time step and to propagate in time the samples using the stochastic motion model $\pi(z_u|z_{0:u-1})$. At each time step, the samples z_u^k are weighted proportionally to the likelihood term $\pi(y_u|z_u^k)$. Then, a resampling step is performed, so to keep only those samples which have a significant weight, while the other ones are discarded.

However, one well-known problem with standard particle filtering algorithms is the degeneration of the sample set after a few iterations, because the available data (the images) are used only for weighting the samples. Resampling, as done in the condensation algorithm, can only partially limit this effect. As underlined in [4] an increased stability can be reached through Markov chain sampling techniques. The algorithm we propose is inspired by Markov chains based on Langevin Diffusions [17], for which a combination of a gradient descent step and a sampling step is used. With the gradient descent, knowledge on the available data is directly integrated in the propagation step, not only in the weighting.

We denote Δz the amplitude of the gradient descent, and G_i the partial derivative of the log-likelihood term with respect to the parameters p_i:

$$G_i = \frac{\partial}{\partial p_i} \left(\sum_{a=1}^{l} \sum_{\mathbf{x} \in \Omega_a(p)} \frac{(y(\mathbf{x}) - m_a)^2}{2\sigma_a^2} + \log \sigma_a \right), \quad i = 1, L . \tag{10}$$

The computation of G_i is not straightforward because the summation regions Ω_a depend on the parameter p_i. We give in the appendix a general expression that allows for efficient computation by only using values located at the boundary of the region Ω_a and derive explicit equations in one particular case. The segmentation algorithm is then as follows:

1. Generate a sample set $\{z_0^1, ..., z_0^n\}$ according to $\pi(z_0|y_0)$, and set $u = 1$.
2. Propagate each sample using the motion model F and set $z_u^k = F(z_{0:u-1}^k)$.
3. Compute the gradient G, and sample $\tilde{z}_u^k$ from a Gaussian distribution with mean $z_u^k - G.\Delta z$ and standard deviation Δz, whose density we denote ϕ, and set $\tilde{z}_{0:u-1}^k = z_{0:u-1}^k$.
4. For each sample, evaluate the importance weights

$$w_u^k = \pi(y_u|\tilde{z}_u^k) \frac{\pi(\tilde{z}_u^k|z_{0:u-1}^k)}{\phi(\tilde{z}_u^k)} . \tag{11}$$

5. Normalize the importance weights and resample with replacement the n samples $z_{0:u}^k$ from the n samples $\tilde{z}_{0:u}^k$ according to the weights w_u^k.
6. Set $u \leftarrow u + 1$ and go to step 2, until $u = t$.

The expression of the importance weights is slighlty different to the one used in the condensation algorithm, because it is necessary to correct for the statistical bias introduced by the gradient descent step. Note that the motion parameters that are treated as random variables are sampled together with the shape parameters during step 2. This possibility of straightforwardly incorporating uncertainty about the parameters of the model is a powerful feature of the Monte Carlo approach.

5   Application to Cardiac Segmentation of Cine MRI

We propose to apply the stochastic model described in section 3 together with the segmentation algorithm of section 4 to the analysis of cardiac cine MRI.

Such data consist of a sequence of imaged cardiac volumes, covering an entire heart cycle. The cardiac motion can be roughly decomposed into two phases: the systole, where the heart contracts and pumps blood out of the ventricles, and the diastole, where the ventricles fill with blood. With cardiac cine MRI, it is possible to assess the cardiac function by computing parameters such as the end-diastolic and end-systolic volumes of the left ventricle. A more advanced analysis is the detailed reconstruction of the local wall motion, which for example allows to precisely localize an ischemic or infarcted area. However, these computations require to first extract the myocardium shape from the image sequence. Since a complete anatomic coverage of the left ventricle over the entire heart cycle can result in the acquisition of several hundred slices, automatic segmentation algorithms are required.

5.1   A 2D+time Model

As a proof of concepts, we implemented a 2D+time approach: we considered each slice independently and tracked the 2D cardiac contour along time. Of course, a robust, comprehensive analysis of cardiac cine MRI requires a full 3D+time approach, which will be addressed in future work. However, as stated previously, our approach is not dependent on the dimension and for validation purposes working with 2D contours is sufficient and easy to visualize.

The shape model we use is made of the inner and outer contours for the left ventricle (the endocardium and the epicardium) and one contour for the blood pool of the right ventricle (the thickness of the corresponding wall cannot be resolved using standard cine MRI). For each contour, we use a polar coordinate system: given the position of the center, the contour is described by expressing the radius r as a function of the polar angle ϕ. Then, following the approach described in section 3.2, a Fourier decomposition is used, yielding the expression

$$r(\phi) = p_1 + \sum_{i=1}^{L} p_{2i} \cos(i\phi) + p_{2i+1} \sin(i\phi) . \tag{12}$$

With this representation, the shape vector z is made of the Fourier coefficients p_i, $i = 1, \ldots, 2L + 1$.

Using 30 manually segmented cine cardiac MRI data sets (only the end-diastolic and end-systolic phases), we first experimentally estimated the required dimension for the Fourier decomposition. We found that with $L = 5$ (i.e. 11 harmonic coefficients) the mean distance between the original contours and the reconstructed Fourier estimators was below 0.5 mm, with no significant improvement for higher dimensions. The fitted contours were subsequently used to compute a mean for end-diastole (ED) and end-systole (ES), denoted respectively $\bar{p}_{ED}$ and $\bar{p}_{ES}$, as well as standard deviations.

The motion model we use is based on a linear approximation of the cardiac motion between ED and ES. However, significant deviations from this motion model are expected. The major reason is that in medical practice data with clinical pathologies are analyzed. For example, the myocardium of infarcted patients is much less contracting than that of healthy patients, and the motion pattern is not homogenous, with the infarcted areas almost not contracting. Therefore, we introduce a correction factor c_u, which is time dependent. The stochastic motion model F takes the expression

$$F(p_{0:u-1}) = p_{u-1} + \frac{c_u \Delta t}{t_{ES} - t_{ED}} (\bar{p}_{ES} - \bar{p}_{ED}) , \quad c_u = c_{u-1}(1 + \epsilon_u) , \quad (13)$$

where Δt is the time difference between two images and ϵ_u is a perturbation factor. The constraint imposed in the second equation aims to avoid too strong deviations from the linear model.

5.2   Segmentation Results

We tested the segmentation algorithm with 10 cine cardiac MRI data sets of infarcted patients. Note that these data were not used to build the statistical model. The size of the image volumes is $256 \times 256 \times 11$ voxels (in-plane pixel size: $1.36 \times 1.36 \, \text{mm}^2$, slice thickness: 8 mm, with 2 mm gap between two slices). Each cine data set consists of 18 heart phases.

Initialization of the algorithm is made by manually positioning the mean model and then exhaustively searching for the optimal size parameter. Then, the sequential Monte Carlo segmentation algorithm is started, using $n = 500$ samples. The analysis of a whole heart cycle for one slice took approximatively 4 min on a PC with 2.4 GHz Intel processor (for comparison, the acquisition time of a cardiac cine MRI may take up to 30 minutes). Most of the computation time is spent for evaluating the likelihood term given by equation 2; optimizing this computation would speed up significantly the method. Note that the computation time is linear in the number of model parameters, samples, and slices analyzed, which is an important feature of the Monte Carlo approach.

Examples of segmentation results for two different MRI data sets are shown in figure 1. The advantages of a parametric description of shape based on harmonic surfaces can clearly be seen: the model adapts well to the shape of the myocardium while reminding smooth. MR images typically show good contrast between blood and muscle; however, as it can be seen in figure 1, the presence of fat (which appears also bright) next to the heart, the poor contrast between the muscle and the lung (both are dark), and the presence of the papillary muscles (dark patches inside the blood pool) pose a challenge. Despite these problems, the segmentation algorithm produced robust and qualitatively satisfying results on the 10 different data sets it was tested on. In particular, the likelihood model we use, based on statistics computed over the grey values of the segmented regions, allows to efficiently distinguish between the different components of the heart and the background. Note that we have explicitly modeled the presence of the papillary muscles inside the blood pool with a mixture of two Gaussian distributions.

The segmentation results of figure 1 also demonstrate the capability of the sequential Monte Carlo algorithm to precisely follow the cardiac motion, with

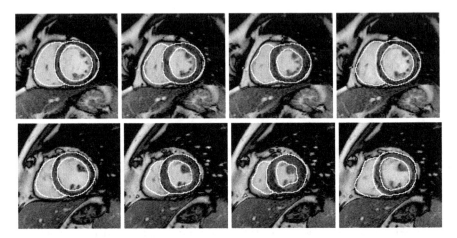

Fig. 1. Automatic segmentation of the myocardium over an entire heart cycle (every fourth frame is displayed) for two different patients (top and down) - Contours of the segmented shape are shown in white.

the global deformation (contraction of the endocardium) as well as the local deformations well reproduced, see the enclosed file `cardiac_smc.avi` for an animated view of the segmented sequence. The prior information about the motion is used at two levels: to predict the position of the contours at the consecutive time steps, and to constrain temporally the solution of the segmentation problem. For comparison, we computed a solution using a sequential optimization algorithm based on gradient descent: at each time step, the marginal distribution of the current heart phase is optimized. One obtains a sequence with good segmentation results when one looks at the heart phases individually, but a poor, jaggy reconstruction of the cardiac motion (see enclosed file `cardiac_opt.avi`). Comparatively, the sequential Monte Carlo algorithm makes full use of the whole posterior, thus yields a nice smoothed estimation of the cardiac motion, where artefacts due to individual heart phases are filtered out. This is in our opinion the most attractive feature of the Monte Carlo approach.

6   Conclusion

In this paper we pointed out the necessity of developing a spatio-temporal framework for the segmentation of temporal sequences of medical images. We think that the Bayesian framework we proposed is appropriate for this segmentation task because it explicitly integrates prior knowledge about the shape and the motion of organs. To compute a solution that integrates the full prior and image information we proposed to use sequential Monte Carlo sampling techniques. Using a sample set to represent a posterior distribution has the advantage that a wide range of solutions are considered, which increases the robustness of the algorithm against attraction to spurious image features. The modification we proposed, which consists in performing a gradient descent step after each propagation step of the condensation algorithm, enables to explicitly integrate image information into the tracking.

For the shape description, we developed a general stochastic model based on the definition of an inner-product and the choice of orthonormal functions. With the same approach one can model contours in a two-dimensional setting as well as surfaces in a three-dimensional problem, with different parameterization choices possible: only the basis functions need to be adapted. Another advantage lies in the compact expression of this model: only a reference shape and a standard deviation need to be estimated. These parameters have an appealing meaning (mean shape, mean square distance between two shapes) for clinicians, which increases their practical interest.

We presented here some promising results for the segmentation of cardiac cine MRI. This work will be completed by the setting of a 3D myocardium shape and motion model based on surface harmonics. Most importantly, future work will include a thorough clinical validation of the automatic segmentation method based on manual reference segmentations. This validation should not only consider the accuracy of the algorithm to reconstruct the myocardial surfaces but also its adequacy for computing the relevant clinical cardiac parameters such as ejection fraction or wall motion.

Appendix

In the following, we give the expression of the gradient of the log-likelihood term. More generally, let us consider the integral of a measurable function $I(\mathbf{x}), \mathbf{x} \in \mathbb{R}^d$ over a region $\Omega(p) \subset \mathbb{R}^d$, depending on some parameter p. The closed boundary of $\Omega(p)$ is denoted $\mathcal{C}(p)$. The outer normal of the boundary $\mathcal{C}(p)$ is denoted $\mathbf{n}$. For any $\mathbf{x} \in \mathcal{C}(p)$, the velocity vector is defined as $\mathbf{v} = \frac{\partial \mathbf{x}}{\partial p}$. Since I does not explicity depend on p, Theorem 1 of [18] gives

$$\frac{\partial}{\partial p} \int_{\Omega(p)} I(\mathbf{x}) d\mathbf{x} = \int_{\mathcal{C}(p)} I(\mathbf{x})(\mathbf{n} \cdot \mathbf{v}) d\mathbf{x} . \tag{14}$$

As an illustation, let us apply this relation in a two-dimensional case: the curve $\mathcal{C}(p)$ is parametrized in a polar coordinate system as the radius r depending on some parameters p_i (e.g. Fourier coefficients). Denoting $a = 0$ and $a = 1$ the inner and outer regions of the curve $\mathcal{C}(p)$, the gradient of the log-likelihood becomes

$$G_i = \sum_{\mathbf{x} \in \mathcal{C}(p)} \left(\frac{(y(\mathbf{x}) - m_0)^2}{2\sigma_0^2} - \frac{(y(\mathbf{x}) - m_1)^2}{2\sigma_1^2} + \log \frac{\sigma_0}{\sigma_1} \right) r(\mathbf{x}) \frac{\partial r}{\partial p_i}(\mathbf{x}) . \tag{15}$$

Acknowledgment: This research has been supported by a Marie Curie Fellowship of the European Community programme "Creating a User-Friendly Information Society" IST-00-7-2B under contract number IST-2001-82936.

References

[1] Lelieveldt, B., Mitchell, S., Bosch, J., van der Geest, R., Sonka, M., Reiber, J.: Time-continuous segmentation of cardiac image sequences using active appearance motion models. In Insana, M., Leahy, R., eds.: IPMI 2001, LNCS 2082. (2001) 446–452

[2] Paragios, N.: A level set approach for shape-driven segmentation and tracking of the left ventricle. IEEE Transactions on Medical Imaging **22** (2003) 773–776

[3] McInerney, T., Terzopoulos, D.: Deformable models in medical image analysis: a survey. Medical Image Analysis **1** (1996) 91–108

[4] Doucet, A., de Freitas, N., Gordon, N.: Sequential Monte Carlo Methods in Practice. Springer-Verlag, New York (2001)

[5] Isard, M., Blake, A.: CONDENSATION - Conditional density propagation for visual tracking. International Journal of Computer Vision **29** (1998) 5–28

[6] Staib, L., Duncan, J.: Model-based deformable surface finding for medical images. IEEE Transactions on Medical Imaging **15** (1996) 720–731

[7] Székely, G., Kelemen, A., Brechbühler, C., Gerig, G.: Segmentation of 2-D and 3-D objects from MRI volume data using constrained elastic deformations of flexible Fourier contour and surface models. Medical Image Analysis **1** (1996) 19–34

[8] Cremers, D., Tischhäuser, F., Weickert, J., Schnörr, C.: Diffusion Snakes: Introducing statistical shape knowledge into the mumford-shah functional. International Journal of Computer Vision **50** (2002) 295–313

[9] Dryden, I., Mardia, K.: Statistical Shape Analysis. John Wileys & Sons, Chichester (1998)

[10] Delingette, H.: General object reconstruction based on simplex meshes. International Journal of Computer Vision **32** (1999) 111–142

[11] Cootes, T., Taylor, C., Cooper, D., Graham, J.: Active shape models - their training and application. Computer Vision and Image understanding **61** (1995) 38–59

[12] Matheny, A., Goldgof, D.: The use of three- and four-dimensional surface harmonics for rigid and nonrigid shape recovery and representation. IEEE Transactions on Pattern Analysis and Machine Intelligence **17** (1992) 967–981

[13] Brechbühler, C., Gerig, G., Kübler, O.: Parametrization of closed surfaces for 3-D shape description. Computer Vision and Image Understanding **61** (1995) 154–170

[14] Sénégas, J., Cocosco, C., Netsch, T.: Model-based segmentation of cardiac MRI cine sequences: A Bayesian formulation. In: Proceedings of SPIE Medical Imaging, San Diego, California, USA. (2004) To appear.

[15] Celeux, G., Diebolt, J.: The SEM algorithm: a probabilistic teacher algorithm derived from the EM algorithm for the mixture problem. Comput. Statist. Quater. **2** (1985) 73–82

[16] Itô, K.: Encyclopedic Dictionary of Mathematics - Second Edition. The MIT Press, Cambridge (1993)

[17] Gilks, W., Richardson, S., Spiegelhalter, D.: Markov Chain Monte Carlo in Practice. Chapman and Hall, London (1996)

[18] Jehan-Besson, S., Barlaud, M.: DREAM^{2}S: Deformable regions driven by an Eulerian accurate minimization method for image and video segmentation. International Journal of Computer Vision **53** (2003) 45–70

A Multi-scale Geometric Flow for Segmenting Vasculature in MRI

Maxime Descoteaux[1], Louis Collins[2], and Kaleem Siddiqi[1]

McGill University
Montréal, QC, Canada
[1]School of Computer Science & Centre For Intelligent Machines
{mdesco,siddiqi}@cim.mcgill.ca
[2]McConnell Brain Imaging Centre, Montréal Neurological institute
{louis}@bic.mni.mcgill.ca

Abstract. Often in neurosurgical planning a dual echo acquisition is performed that yields proton density (PD) and T2-weighted images to evaluate edema near a tumour or lesion. The development of vessel segmentation algorithms for PD images is of general interest since this type of acquisition is widespread and is entirely noninvasive. Whereas vessels are signaled by black blood contrast in such images, extracting them is a challenge because other anatomical structures also yield similar contrasts at their boundaries. In this paper we present a novel multi-scale geometric flow for segmenting vasculature from PD images which can also be applied to the easier cases of computed tomography (CT) angiography data or Gadolinium enhanced MRI. The key idea is to first apply Frangi's vesselness measure [4] to find putative centerlines of tubular structures along with their estimated radii. This multi-scale measure is then distributed to create a vector field which is orthogonal to vessel boundaries so that the flux maximizing flow algorithm of [17] can be applied to recover them. We validate the approach qualitatively with PD, angiography and Gadolinium enhanced MRI volumes.

1 Introduction

A three-dimensional (3D) representation of vasculature can be extremely important in image-guided neurosurgery, pre-surgical planning and clinical analysis. It is unfortunately often the case that in order to obtain such representations from an MRI volume an expert has to interact with it manually slice by slice while colouring regions of interest and connecting them using image processing operations. This process is extremely laborious, is prone to human error and makes large scale clinical studies of vasculature infeasible. In computer vision there has been a significant amount of work towards automating the extraction of vessels or vessel centerlines. Whereas an exhaustive review of this literature is beyond the scope of this article, typical examples include: 1) active contours or surfaces for angiography data [13], 2) multi-scale methods for model-based segmentation of tubular structures [9], 3) statistical methods which use mixture models [18], and 4) methods based on intensity ridge detection and traversal [8, 3]. It should be pointed out that most of these methods have been demonstrated for 2D projection angiography, 3D CT angiography or Gadolinium enhanced MRI, and these modalities can

M. Šonka et al. (Eds.): CVAMIA-MMBIA 2004, LNCS 3117, pp. 169–180, 2004.
© Springer-Verlag Berlin Heidelberg 2004

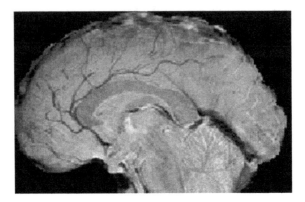

Fig. 1. A sagittal view of a proton density (PD) weighted MRI volume acquired at the Montreal Neurological Institute. The spaghetti-like structures correspond to vasculature.

require the injection of contrast agents. To our knowledge no method currently exists for the automatic extraction of vessel boundaries in standard MRI volumes such as the PD image shown in Figure 1. Here it is clear that a signal decrease is present in the vascular regions (the spaghetti-like structures), but the contrast between blood vessel and surrounding tissue is not as great when compared to the angiographic sequences. Hence, the problem of recovering vessels from image intensity contrast alone on PD-weighted images is a challenge and requires shape information to constrain the segmentation. If successful, such a procedure could result in a vascular model that could be used in surgical planning while eliminating the need for an additional scan thus saving time during image acquisition and easing the burden on the patient.

In this paper we introduce a novel algorithm for vessel segmentation which is designed for the PD images, but can be applied as well to angiographic data or Gadolinium enhanced MRI volumes. The algorithm is motivated in part by the approach in [15] where Frangi's vesselness measure [4] is thresholded to find centerlines. Tubular fits to vessel boundaries are then obtained using a form of connected component analysis and a generalized cylinder model. This latter step typically yields results that are disconnected. In our approach the vesselness measure is extended to yield a vector field which is locally normal to putative vessel boundaries. This in turn allows the flux maximizing geometric flow of [17] to be applied, which has a formal motivation, is topologically adaptive due to its implementation using level set methods, and finally is computationally efficient. We illustrate the power of this geometric-flow based framework with segmentation results on PD data, and also illustrate its applicability to Gadolinium enhanced MRI volumes and angiography data.

The paper is outlined as follows. In Section 2 we review relevant background material on geometric flows for vessel segmentation and on the use of the Hessian matrix to model tubular structures. We then develop our multi-scale geometric flow by incorporating Frangi's vesselness measure [4] in the flux maximizing flow algorithm of [17] in

Section 3. We present several reconstruction results to validate the algorithm in Section 4 and conclude by discussing ongoing work in Section 5.

2 Background

2.1 Geometric Flows

In the context of geometric flows for segmenting vasculature, there are two recent approaches which are relevant to the development here. First, Lorigo et al. propose a regularization of a geometric flow in 3D using the curvature of a 3D curve [12]. This approach is grounded in the recent level set theory developed for mean curvature flows in arbitrary co-dimension [2]. It yields a flow which is designed to recover vessel boundaries signaled by the gradient in angiography data, while under the influence of a smoothing term driven by the mean curvature of an implied centerline. Second, Vasilevskiy and Siddiqi derive the gradient flow which evolves a curve (2D) or a surface (3D) so as to increase the inward flux of a fixed (static) vector field through its boundary as fast as possible [17]. With S an evolving surface and $\overrightarrow{V}$ the vector field, this flow is given by

$$S_t = div(\overrightarrow{V})\overrightarrow{\mathcal{N}} \tag{1}$$

where $\overrightarrow{\mathcal{N}}$ is the unit inward normal to each point on S. This flow evolves a surface to a configuration where its normals are aligned with the vector field. In the context of segmenting vasculature in angiographic images, $\overrightarrow{V}$ can be selected to be the gradient of the intensity image which is expected to be orthogonal to vessel boundaries.

A limitation of both the above approaches is that they are designed specifically for angiographic data and hence require restrictive assumptions to hold:

1. Both methods are initialized essentially by thresholding such data, and thus would fail when vessel boundaries cannot be identified from contrast alone.
2. Neither approach has an explicit term to model tubular structures. Rather, each flow relies on the assumption that the gradient of the intensity image yields a quantity that is significant *only* at vessel boundaries.
3. Neither of these methods takes into account explicitly the multi-scale nature of vessels boundaries as they appear in all modalities.

In this paper we overcome several of these limitations by incorporating a measure of "vesselness" based on the Hessian matrix.

2.2 Modeling Vasculature Using the Hessian

Several multi-scale approaches to modeling tubular structures in intensity images have been based on properties of the Eigen values of the Hessian matrix $\mathbf{H}$ [11, 16, 4]. These methods exploit the fact that at locations centered within tubular structures the smallest Eigen value of $\mathbf{H}$ is close to zero (reflecting the low curvature along the direction of the vessel) and the two other Eigen values are high and are close to being equal, reflecting the fact that the cross-section of the vessel is approximately circular. The corresponding

Eigen vectors span the vessel direction and the cross-sectional plane. The Eigen value analysis can be pushed further to differentiate *tube-like*, *blob-like*, *sheet-like*, and *noise-like* structures from one another as summarized in Table 1.

Eigen value conditions	local structure	examples
$\lambda_1 \approx 0$, $\lambda_2 \approx \lambda_3 >> 0$	tube-like	vessel, bronchus
$\lambda_1 \approx \lambda_2 \approx 0$, $\lambda_3 >> 0$	sheet-like	cortex, skin
$\lambda_1 \approx \lambda_2 \approx \lambda_3 >> 0$	blob-like	nodule
$\lambda_1 \approx \lambda_2 \approx \lambda_3 \approx 0$	noise-like	noise

Table 1. A classification of local structures based on the Eigen values of the Hessian matrix. Here, we assume that $|\lambda_1| \leq |\lambda_2| \leq |\lambda_3|$. The sign of the highest Eigen values generally indicate whether the local structure is dark on a bright background or bright on a dark background. A positive sign corresponds to a dark structure on a bright background which is the case for PD weighted MRI volumes.

We choose to focus here on Frangi's vesselness measure [4] because it incorporates information from all three Eigen values. Three quantities are defined to differentiate blood vessels from other structures:

$$R_B = \frac{|\lambda_1|}{\sqrt{|\lambda_2 \lambda_3|}}, \quad R_A = \frac{|\lambda_2|}{|\lambda_3|}, \quad S = \sqrt{\lambda_1^2 + \lambda_2^2 + \lambda_3^2}.$$

From Table 1, it can be seen that R_B distinguishes blob-like structures from other patterns. The R_A ratio differentiates sheet-like from tube-like structures. Finally, S, the Frobenius norm, is used to ensure that random noise effects are suppressed from the response. For a particular scale σ the intensity image is first convolved by a Gaussian at that scale, $G(\sigma)$ following which the vesselness measure is defined by [1].

$$V(\sigma) = \begin{cases} 0 & \text{if } \lambda_2 < 0 \text{ or } \lambda_3 < 0 \\ (1 - \exp\left(-\frac{R_A^2}{2\alpha^2}\right))\exp\left(-\frac{R_B^2}{2\beta^2}\right)(1 - \exp\left(-\frac{S^2}{2c^2}\right)) & \end{cases}$$

(2)

This measure is designed to be maximum along the centerlines of tubular structures and close to zero outside vessel-like regions. In our implementation we set the parameters α, β and c to 0.5, 0.5 and half the maximum Frobenuis norm, respectively, as suggested in [4, 15]. At each voxel we compute vesselness responses using ten log scale increments between $\sigma = 0.2$ and $\sigma = 2.0$ (in our data the maximum radius of a vessel is 2 voxels) and select the maximum vesselness response along with its scale. The chosen scale gives the estimated radius of the vessel and the Eigen vector associated with the smallest Eigen value its local orientation.

---

[1] In practice we directly compute the entries which comprise the Hessian matrix by using derivatives of Lindeberg's γ-parametrized normalized Gaussian kernels [10], which allows us to compare responses at different scales.

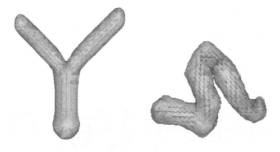

Fig. 2. A synthetic Y-shaped structure and a synthetic helix. For each structure the red vectors indicate the estimated vessel orientation at locations where the multi-scale vesselness measure (Eq. 2) is high.

This process is illustrated in Figure 2 for a synthetic Y-shaped structure and a synthetic helix. The grey surface coincides with a particular level set of the vesselness measure (which quickly drops to zero away from centerline locations). Within this surface locations of high vesselness are indicated by overlaying the Eigen vectors which correspond to the estimated vessel orientation. Observe that locations of high vesselness are close to vessel centerlines, and that the estimated vessel orientation at these locations is accurate. This information along with the estimated radius of associated vessels can be used to construct an appropriate vector field to drive the flux maximizing geometric flow, as we shall see in the following section.

3   A Multi-scale Geometric Flow for Segmenting Vasculature

Our goal now is to extend the flux maximizing flow algorithm of [17] so that the vector field which drives it lies along the surface of putative vessel boundaries. This allows us to lift many of the restrictions on the flow pointed out in Section 2, because an explicit model of a tubular structure is now incorporated along with an appropriate notion of scale.

3.1   Construction of the Vector Field

The key idea is to distribute the vesselness measure, which is concentrated at centerlines, to the vessel boundaries which are implied. At each voxel (x, y, z) where the vesselness measure is a local maximum in a 3x3x3 neighborhood we consider an ellipsoid with its major axis aligned with the estimated orientation and its two semi-minor axes equal to the estimated radius. In our implementation the semi-major axis length is chosen to be twice that of the semi-minor axes. The vesselness measure is then distributed over every voxel (x_e, y_e, z_e) on the boundary of the ellipsoid by scaling it by the projection of the vector from (x, y, z) to (x_e, y_e, z_e) onto the cross-sectional

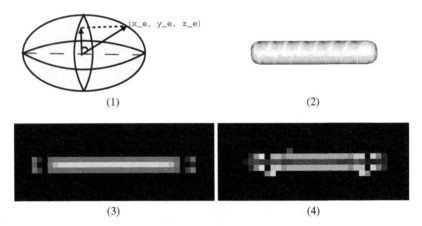

Fig. 3. Distributing the vesselness measure to the implied boundaries. (1) The vector from the center of the ellipsoid to the surface voxel (x_e, y_e, z_e), as well as its projection onto the cross-sectional plane, taken to be the xy plane. We distribute the vesselness measure to all (x_e, y_e, z_e) on the ellipsoid by scaling it by the magnitude of this projection. (2) A synthetic tube of radius 2. (3) A view of the vesselness measure in a slice. Brighter regions indicate stronger vesselness. (4) A view of the ϕ distribution in the same slice. As expected, we have local maxima of the vesselness measure on the centerline in (3) and local maxima at the boundaries of the tube on the ϕ distribution in (4).

plane, as illustrated in Figure 3. If (x, y, z) is taken to be the origin $(0, 0, 0)$ and the xy plane is taken to coincide with the cross-sectional plane this scale factor works out to be $\left\langle (x_e, y_e, z_e), \frac{(x_e, y_e, 0)}{\sqrt{x_e^2 + y_e^2}} \right\rangle = \sqrt{x_e^2 + y_e^2}$. This process of distributing the vesselness measure to the implied boundaries clearly favours voxels in the cross-sectional plane. We define the addition of the extensions carried out independently at all voxels to be the ϕ distribution. The extended vector field is now defined as the product of the normalized gradient of the original image with the above ϕ distribution

$$\vec{\mathcal{V}} = \phi \frac{\nabla \mathcal{I}}{|\nabla \mathcal{I}|}$$

This vector field embodies two important constraints. First, the magnitude of ϕ is maximum on vessel boundaries and the ellipsoidal extension performs a type of local integration [2]. Second, $\frac{\nabla \mathcal{I}}{|\nabla \mathcal{I}|}$ captures the direction information of the gradient, which is expected to be high at boundaries of vessels as well as orthogonal to them, which is the basic motivation for the flux maximizing geometric flow. It is important to normalize the gradient of the image so that its magnitude does not dominate the measure in

---

[2] This follows because the local maximum vesselness criterion enforces the condition that the extension is carried out only from locations as close as possible to vessel centrelines.

regions of very low vesselness. For example, structures such as white and gray matter boundaries could then get significant unwanted contributions.

3.2   The Multi-scale Geometric Flow

The extended vector field explicitly models the scale at which vessel boundaries occur, due to the multi-scale nature of the vesselness measure $V(\sigma)$ (Eq. 2) as well as the expected gradient in the direction normal to vessel boundaries. Thus, it is an ideal candidate for the static vector field in the flux maximizing geometric flow (Eq. 1). The surface evolution equation then works out to be

$$\begin{aligned} S_t &= div(\vec{V})\vec{N} \\ &= \left[\left\langle \nabla\phi, \tfrac{\nabla\mathcal{I}}{|\nabla\mathcal{I}|} \right\rangle + \phi div\left(\tfrac{\nabla\mathcal{I}}{|\nabla\mathcal{I}|} \right) \right] \vec{N} \\ &= \left[\left\langle \nabla\phi, \tfrac{\nabla\mathcal{I}}{|\nabla\mathcal{I}|} \right\rangle + \phi\kappa_{\mathcal{I}} \right] \vec{N} \end{aligned} \tag{3}$$

where $\kappa_{\mathcal{I}}$ is the Euclidean mean curvature of the iso-intensity level set of the image. Note that this is a hyperbolic partial differential equation since all terms depend solely on the vector field and not on the evolving surface. We now enumerate several properties of this geometric flow.

1. The first term $\left\langle \nabla\phi, \tfrac{\nabla\mathcal{I}}{|\nabla\mathcal{I}|} \right\rangle$ acts like a doublet. $\nabla\phi$ has a zero-crossing at vessel boundaries and $\nabla\mathcal{I}$ does not change sign. Hence, when the evolving surface overshoots the boundary slightly, this term acts to push it back towards the boundary.
2. The second term behaves like a geometric heat equation since $\kappa_{\mathcal{I}}$ is the mean curvature of the iso-intensity level set of the original intensity image. This equation has been extensively studied in the mathematics literature and has been shown to have remarkable smoothing properties [5, 6]. It is also the basis for several nonlinear geometric scale-spaces such as those studied in [1, 7].
3. Combining both terms, it is clear that the flow cannot leak in regions outside vessels since both ϕ and $\nabla\phi$ are zero there. Hence, when seeds are placed at locations where the vesselness measure $V(\sigma)$ is high the flow given by Eq. 3 will smoothly evolve toward zero level set of the divergence of the vector field $\vec{V}$.

3.3   Implementation Details

Below we review some of the details of the implementation of our multi-scale geometric flow (Eq. 3), which is based on level set methods [14].

1. We run five iterations of mean curvature type smoothing on the original image, which is a standard method to remove artifacts such as speckle noise since it smooths along iso-intensity level sets but not across them.
2. We compute the Hessian operator over 10 log scales and select the maximum vesselness response as described in Section 2. We use Jacobi's method for symmetric matrices to find Eigen values of the Hessian.

3. The ϕ distribution in Section 3.1 is carried out from voxels at vessel centerlines since at such locations one has strong confidence in the scale and orientation estimate from Frangi's vesselness measure [4]. This is done using the following procedure

$$\text{if } (V(\sigma) > \text{threshold \&\& } \tfrac{V(\sigma)}{\text{local\_max}} > \text{percentile})$$
$$\text{Distribute vesselness over ellipsoid}$$

For all examples we use a vesselness threshold of 0.01 and a percentile of 0.75 and local_max is the maximum vesselness response in a 3x3x3 neighborhood of the voxel.

4. The doublet term $\left\langle \nabla\phi, \frac{\nabla I}{|\nabla I|} \right\rangle$ is computed using central differences for the first term and a second-order essentially non-oscillatory (ENO) scheme for the second.

5. κ_I, the mean curvature of each intensity iso-surface is computed using a 3-neighbor central difference scheme for all derivatives:

$$\kappa_I = \frac{(I_{yy}+I_{zz})I_x^2 + (I_{xx}+I_{zz})I_y^2 + (I_{xx}+I_{yy})I_z^2 - 2(I_x I_y I_{xy} + I_x I_z I_{xz} + I_y I_z I_{yz})}{(I_x^2 + I_y^2 + I_z^2)^{\frac{3}{2}}} \quad (4)$$

6. A first-order in time discretized form of the level-set version of the evolution equation is given by

$$\Psi_n = \Psi_{n-1} + \Delta t * \mathcal{F} * ||\nabla \Psi_{n-1}||$$

where $\mathcal{F} = \left\langle \nabla\phi, \frac{\nabla I}{|\nabla I|} \right\rangle + \phi \, div\left(\frac{\nabla I}{|\nabla I|}\right)$, Ψ is the embedding hypersurface and Δt is the step size. This is now a standard numerical approach for solving partial differential equations of this type since it allows topological changes to occur without any additional computational complexity and can be made efficient using a narrow band implementation. The evolving surface S is obtained as the zero level set of the Ψ function. The numerical derivatives used to estimate $||\nabla \Psi||$ must be computed with up-winding in the proper direction as described in [14].

4   Examples

We illustrate our multi-scale geometric flow for segmenting vasculature on three different modalities: MRA, Gadolinium enhanced MRI and PD. The same parameters were used throughout as described in Section 3.3 with the exception that for the PD data the vesselness threshold was lowered to 0.005 and the numerical time step was lowered to 0.5 in order to capture smaller structures. We should point out that whereas prior geometric flow based methods [12, 17] could be applied to the angiography data set, they would fail entirely on the latter two modalities where high contrast regions are not limited to vessel boundaries.

Figure 4 shows iterations of the flow using three single voxel seeds on an MRA data set obtained from the Montreal Neurological Institute (MNI). The flow is able to pick up the main vessels automatically. Several of the finer vessels are less than one voxel wide and hence a super-sampling strategy would have to be applied in a preprocessing step to the data in order to recover them.

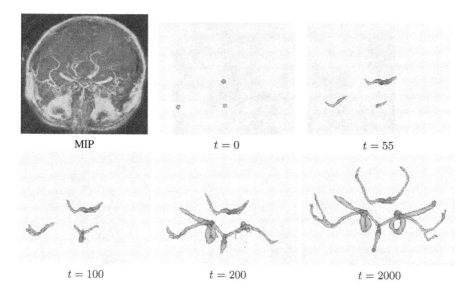

MIP $t = 0$ $t = 55$

$t = 100$ $t = 200$ $t = 2000$

Fig. 4. An illustration of the multi-scale geometric flow on a 68 x 256 x 256 MRA image. An MIP of the data is shown at the top left and the other images depict different stages of the evolution from three seeds.

Figure 5 depicts a 40mm x 53mm x 91mm region centered on the corpus callosum from a Gadolinium enhanced MRI volume obtained at the MNI. The 1mm isotropic data was super-sampled to 0.33mm using a tricubic interpolation kernel, because several vessels in the original data set were less than one voxel wide. In the image one can see the callosal and supra-callosal arteries (the long arching vessels running from left to right). We show an MIP of a sagittal and a transverse view in the top row. A segmentation obtained by thresholding the vesselness map, as carried out in [15], is shown in the second row. This results in many disconnected vessels as well as artifacts. Our segmentation is shown in the third row and results in the reconstruction of well connected tubular structures.

Finally, Figure 6 depicts the segmentation of the full proton density MRI volume shown in Figure 1, which is clearly a challenge for most vessel segmentation algorithms. The PD data is acquired with 2mm transverse slices with 1mm x 1mm in-plane voxels. For this data set an MIP of the original data would not correspond to vasculature. Hence we choose to show MIPs of a sagittal and a transverse view of the vesselness measure in the top row. We then show the corresponding reconstructions obtained by our flow in the second row. A movie animating these segmentation results is available from the authors' research pages. To our knowledge, this is the first segmentation of a PD weighted MRI performed by a geometric flow in the literature. The reconstruction does not recover some of the finer vessels located near the surface of the brain, but these could be recovered using a finer placement of seeds along with an adaptive lowering of the vesselness threshold in those regions.

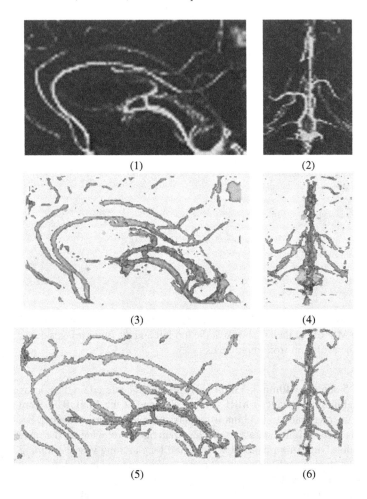

(1)   (2)

(3)   (4)

(5)   (6)

Fig. 5. An illustration of the flow on a 40 mm x 53 mm x 91 mm cropped region of a Gadolinium enhanced MRI. An MIP of the sagittal and transverse views of the data is shown in (1) and (2). Reconstructions obtained by simple thresholding for the same views are shown in (3) and (4). These are clearly sensitive to noise and result in disconnected or missing vessels. The results obtained by the multi-scale geometric flow are shown in (5) and (6). Observe that the flow has connected a section of the callosal arteries which is barely visible in the MIP (see (1),(3),(5)).

5   Conclusions

We have presented what to our knowledge is the first multi-scale geometric flow that can be applied for segmenting vasculature in PD weighted MRI volumes. The key idea is to incorporate a multi-scale vesselness measure in the construction of an appropriate

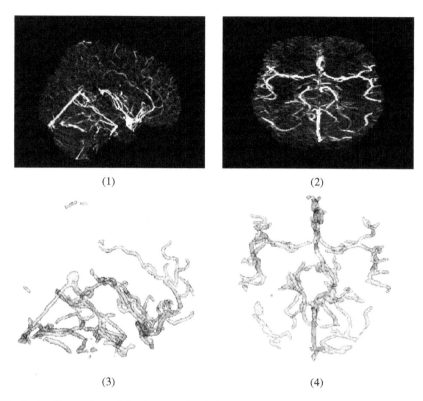

(1)   (2)

(3)   (4)

Fig. 6. An illustration of the flow on the full 181 x 217 x 181 proton density weighted MRI volume of Figure 1. We show MIPs of the vesselness measure $V(\sigma)$ for sagittal and transverse views in (1) and (2), where we have masked the outside skull and the skin. The reconstructions obtained using our geometric flow with 10 manually placed seeds are shown in the bottom row. A movie illustrating this segmentation is included with this submission

vector field for a geometric flow. We have validated the flow qualitatively on several modalities. In particular, we have shown that a significant amount of vasculature can be recovered by initializing the flow using a few isolated seeds. In our experience we have also found that finer vessels can also be recovered by the manual placement of seeds by a user along with an adaptive lowering of the vesselness threshold used in the construction of the extended vector field $\overrightarrow{\mathcal{V}}$.

In ongoing work we are carrying out a careful quantitative validation of the approach by acquiring data using different modalities on the same subject. This will allow us to evaluate the algorithm by using the results obtained on angiographic data as the ground truth. Once we have been able to fine tune its performance it is our hope that our implementation of this flow will become a basic image analysis tool for segmenting vasculature in clinical studies.

Acknowledgements This work was supported by grants from NSERC, FQRNT, CFI and CIHR. We are grateful to the reviewers for their helpful comments.

References

[1] L. Alvarez, F. Guichard, P. L. Lions, and J. M. Morel. Axiomes et équations fondamentales du traitement d'images. *C. R. Acad. Sci. Paris*, 315:135–138, 1992.

[2] L. Ambrosio and H. M. Soner. Level set approach to mean curvature flow in arbitrary codimension. *Journal of Differential Geometry*, 43:693–737, 1996.

[3] S. R. Aylward and E. Bullitt. Initialization, noise, singularities, and scale in height ridge traversal for tubular object centerline extraction. *IEEE Transactions On Medical Imaging*, 21(2):61–75, 2002.

[4] A. Frangi, W. Niessen, K. L. Vincken, and M. A. Viergever. Multiscale vessel enhancement filtering. In *MICCAI'98*, pages 130–137, 1998.

[5] M. Gage and R. Hamilton. The heat equation shrinking convex plane curves. *Journal of Differential Geometry*, 23:69–96, 1986.

[6] M. Grayson. The heat equation shrinks embedded plane curves to round points. *Journal of Differential Geometry*, 26:285–314, 1987.

[7] B. B. Kimia, A. Tannenbaum, and S. W. Zucker. Shape, shocks, and deformations I: The components of two-dimensional shape and the reaction-diffusion space. *International Journal of Computer Vision*, 15:189–224, 1995.

[8] T. M. Koller, G. Gerig, G. Székely, and D. Dettwiler. Multiscale detection of curvilinear structures in 2-d and 3-d image data. In *International Conference On Computer Vision*, pages 864–869, 1995.

[9] K. Krissian, G. Malandain, and N. Ayache. Model-based detection of tubular structures in 3d images. *Computer Vision and Image Understanding*, 80(2):130–171, November 2000.

[10] T. Lindeberg. Edge detection and ridge detection with automatic scale selection. *International Journal of Computer Vision*, 30(2):77–116, 1998.

[11] C. Lorenz, I. Carlsen, T. Buzug, C. Fassnacht, and J. Weese. Multi-scale line segmentation with automatic estimation of width, contrast and tangential direction in 2d and 3d medical images. In *CVRMED-MRCAS'97, Lecture Notes in Computer Science*, volume 1205, pages 233–242, 1997.

[12] L. M. Lorigo, O. D. Faugeras, E. L. Grimson, R. Keriven, R. Kikinis, A. Nabavi, and C.-F. Westin. Curves: Curve evolution for vessel segmentation. *Medical Image Analysis*, 5:195–206, 2001.

[13] T. McInerney and D. Terzopoulos. T-snakes: Topology adaptive snakes. *Medical Image Analysis*, 4:73–91, 2000.

[14] S. J. Osher and J. A. Sethian. Fronts propagating with curvature dependent speed: Algorithms based on hamilton-jacobi formulations. *Journal of Computational Physics*, 79:12–49, 1988.

[15] L. Ostergaard, O. Larsen, G. Goualher, A. Evans, and D. Collins. Extraction of cerebral vasculature from mri. In *9th Danish Conference on Pattern Recognition and Image Analysis*, August 2000.

[16] Y. Sato, S. Nakajima, N. Shiraga, H. Atsumi, S. Yoshida, T. Koller, G. Gerig, and R. Kikinis. 3d multi-scale line filter for segmentation and visualization of curvilinear structures in medical images. *Medical Image Analysis*, 2(2):143–168, 1998.

[17] A. Vasilevskyi and K. Siddiqi. Flux maximizing geometric flows. *IEEE Transactions on Pattern Analysis and Machine Intelligence*, 24(12):1–14, 2002.

[18] D. L. Wilson and A. Noble. Segmentation of cerebral vessels and aneurysms from mr aniography data. In *Information Processing in Medical Imaging*, pages 423–428, 1997.

A 2D Fourier Approach to Deformable Model Segmentation of 3D Medical Images

Eric Berg [1], Mohamed Mahfouz [2, 3], Christian Debrunner [1], William Hoff [1]

[1] Colorado School of Mines, Golden, Colorado
[2] University of Tennessee, Knoxville, Tennessee
[3] Oak Ridge National Laboratory, Oak Ridge, Tennessee

Abstract. Anatomical shapes present a unique problem in terms of accurate representation and medical image segmentation. Three-dimensional statistical shape models have been extensively researched as a means of autonomously segmenting and representing models. We present a segmentation method driven by a statistical shape model based on *a priori* shape information from manually segmented training image sets. Our model is comprised of a stack of two-dimensional Fourier descriptors computed from the perimeters of the segmented training image sets after a transformation into a canonical coordinate frame. We apply our shape model to the segmentation of CT and MRI images of the distal femur via an original iterative method based on active contours. The results from the application of our novel method demonstrate its ability to accurately capture anatomical shape variations and guide segmentation. Our quantitative results are unique in that most similar previous work presents only qualitative results.

1 Introduction

Current methods in three-dimensional image segmentation typically employ statistical shape models, first developed by Cootes and Taylor [1] as a means to incorporate *a priori* shape information. A statistical shape model is trained by a considering the canonical parameterization of a set of similar shape instances, or training shapes. Performing a principal components analysis (PCA) on the parameterized shapes highlights the statistical modes of variation in the shape, allowing for a possible reduction in the dimension of the model shape space, discussed in more detail in section 2.3. A well-constructed statistical model will provide a shape constraint on subsequent segmentations of new images.

The primary original contribution of this work is in our segmentation algorithm, consisting of two key steps: Development of a shape parameterization for a set of training instances and; autonomous segmentation of similar shapes in three-dimensional (3D) medical images, guided by the statistical shape model. For the purpose of developing and testing our method, we modeled the human distal femur from 19 sets of 3D images generated by both CT and MRI image modalities (15 CT, 4 MRI); the datasets include both left and right femurs, so we mirrored the left femur across the midsagittal plane as was done in [2, 3], creating additional samples of the right femur.

M. Šonka et al. (Eds.): CVAMIA-MMBIA 2004, LNCS 3117, pp. 181–192, 2004.

A particular instance of the distal femur is constructed as a stack of closed two-dimensional (2D) contours representing the outer surface of the bone on each slice. Each contour is parameterized by a Fourier descriptor (FD) decomposition after the stack of contours is transformed into a canonical coordinate frame. A bone instance is then represented as a single vector whose components are the FDs from all the slices comprising the instance, ordered identically from one bone instance to the next. The statistical 3D model of a class of bones (e.g., distal femurs) is captured by a PCA of such vectors from many bone instances, forming a model shape space.

Our segmentation algorithm employs an iterative process of 1) independently adjusting each boundary contour via a traditional active contours technique [4], followed by 2) a projection into the shape space defined by the statistical model. As we will show, this iterative process provides for local deformations of the shape model during segmentation, while partially constraining the global shape to be consistent with the prior shapes. Prior methods (see e.g., [5]) have explored combined optimization functions that include terms for both the local (image) constraints and the global (statistical model) constraints. The advantage of this combined optimization function is its ability to optimize a model's shape and its relation to the images simultaneously during segmentation. The inability of the combined function to capture shapes outside of the model shape space limits solutions to be fully within the shape space. Our segmentation technique is geared toward solving this problem. As we will explain in section 2.4, by separating the local and global optimizations, we allow for objects slightly outside of the shape space to be segmented, thus permitting the use of these new shapes as training instances to further refine future PCA results.

The iterative segmentation procedure yields a stack of 2D contours, each of which is simply a permutation of the contours initialized on each slice; the contours are then stacked to allow formation of a 3D surface model. Our results will demonstrate the ability of our method to accurately segment new datasets.

2   Approach

The statistical shape model consists of the average of the training shapes in addition to the primary modes of variation among the training shapes as determined by PCA. Model-guided segmentation produces a new model whose shape will conform globally to the training shapes used to form the statistical model, and locally to the images being segmented. In this section, we discuss the development of the statistical model from images and its application to our segmentation approach.

2.1   Image Preprocessing

Each 3D image volume to be used as a training set is manually segmented to extract the distal section of the femur. The binary (black and white) images resulting from the segmentation are rigidly registered to a coordinate system as shown in Fig. 1. The z-axis passes approximately through the center of the condyles and intersects the center of the shaft. We define the center of the condyles as the centroid of the segmented region in the image containing the proximal end of the intercondyloid fossa, the junction of the medial and lateral condyles. The center of the shaft is defined as the centroid of the segmented region in the image approximately 120 mm above the tip of the medial condyle. The x-axis coincides with a line drawn between the center of the medial and lateral condyles and intersects the distal end of the z-axis. The y-axis is positive in the posterior direction. Due to potentially large initial misalignment with the coordinate frame, new training image sets may be iteratively registered to ensure that proper alignment is achieved. We leave a detailed analysis of this registration process as future work.

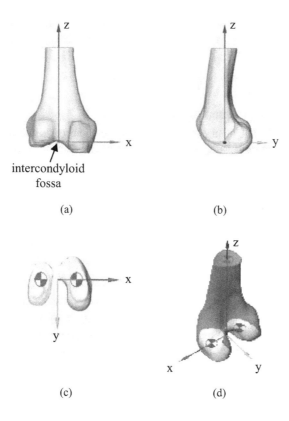

Fig. 1. Coordinate frame definition showing (a) coronal view, (b) sagittal view, (c) axial view, and (d) isometric view

2.2   Fourier Descriptors

The binary images resulting from the manual segmentations each contain at least one region representing the bone cross-section; in the case of images intersecting the condyles, two distinct regions may be present. The regions on each slice can be reduced to closed contours, allowing for a FD representation to be computed. FDs were originally developed by [6] for use in shape discrimination and identification as in [7]. A more recent application of FDs involves medical image segmentation [5], where the combined optimization approach discussed in the introduction is used.

Each contour is defined by a set of N perimeter pixels, whose indices, after multiplication by the pixel size in millimeters, represent x and y coordinates. Conversion to FDs normalizes contours of unequal length and shape and reduces the amount of data required to store each model. The pixel locations are represented as a vector of the form,

$$s = (s_1 \quad s_2 \quad \ldots \quad s_N)^T , \tag{1}$$

where $s_i = x_i + jy_i$ and j is $\sqrt{-1}$. The 2D FDs are computed via the discrete Fourier transform (DFT) as follows:

$$a_k = \frac{1}{N} \sum_{q=0}^{N-1} s_q \exp(\frac{-j2\pi qk}{N}) , \tag{2}$$

where the values of k are the indices $0, 1, \ldots, N-1$.

The most significant features of the contour are captured in the lower frequency terms of the Fourier transform, so we can produce a more concise description of the contour by eliminating the high-frequency terms. Due to the periodicity of the DFT, the low-frequency terms are located at the ends of the coefficient sequence, so we remove coefficients from the middle of the sequence. We found through experiments that the 32 lowest frequency coefficients sufficiently describe the shape of all distal femur cross-sections. To reconstruct a contour with N' points from this reduced form, the FD vector a' must be constructed as follows,

$$a' = (a_1 \quad \ldots \quad a_{16} \quad 0 \quad \ldots \quad 0 \quad a_{N'-15} \quad \ldots \quad a_{N'})^T , \tag{3}$$

where the number of zeros to be inserted is $N' - 32$, assuming $N > 32$. The vector is padded with zeros to create a vector of length N', while maintaining the exact shape of the contour as described by the 32 coefficients. The effect of the additional terms in a' is to increase the number of points to be reconstructed from the FDs. The reconstruction of the contour points is achieved through the inverse discrete Fourier transform (IDFT),

$$s_q = N' \sum_{k=0}^{N'-1} a_k' \exp(\frac{j2\pi kq}{N'}) . \tag{4}$$

After rounding the reconstructed coordinates to the nearest pixel, it is important to note that if $N' > N$, s_q will occasionally have repeated values representing the same pixel location. If the goal is to reconstruct images from the FDs, then this is not a problem; however, if the points are to be processed by an algorithm that assigns weights to each point, such as iterative closest point (ICP), the duplicated points should be removed to avoid improper bias. In our case, we are reconstructing images, so we assign a large value to N', ensuring that no gaps occur in the reconstructed contour.

2.3   Shape Model Representation and Construction

Each femur model is composed of M contour slices parallel to the axial plane and stacked in the z-direction (Fig. 2), where the previously defined z-axis is normal to the axial plane. Each of the M contours is described by Q FDs (in our case, $Q = 32$), which are complex pairs as prescribed by equations 1 and 2. A contour is represented by a single vector formed by concatenating the real and imaginary parts of the Q FD coefficients that represent it. The model vector m is then formed by concatenating the M contour vectors to form a vector of length $n = 2QM$. The multiple of 2 is due to the real and imaginary part of each FD. The vector formation is illustrated in Fig. 3.

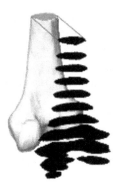

Fig. 2. Model of the distal femur demonstrating the slice structure. Note that the slices shown are a select few of the total number of slices

For a set of T models, $m_1, m_2, \ldots, m_T$, the $n \times 1$ mean vector, $\overline{m}$, is calculated by,

$$\overline{m} = \frac{1}{T}\sum_{i=1}^{T} m_i \cdot \tag{5}$$

The modes of variation among the training models are determined by a PCA. First, the mean model vector, $\overline{m}$, is subtracted from each m_i, forming a deviation matrix whose columns are the deviation vectors,

$$dm_i = m_i - \overline{m} \cdot \tag{6}$$

The PCA is computed using an eigendecomposition of the $n \times n$ covariance matrix formed from the deviation matrix, dm. The resulting orthonormal eigenvectors, p_k, correspond to eigenvalues, λ_k. Arranging the eigenvalues in descending order and reordering the eigenvectors accordingly, we can determine the eigenvectors that account for the most significant variance.

Any shape instance in the training set can be represented by the mean model and a linear combination of the eigenvectors [8]. Typically, a model can be accurately described by $t < T$ eigenvectors, or principal components (PCs), corresponding to the t largest eigenvalues. As Cootes *et al.* [9] and Hutton *et al.* [10] point out, the PCs

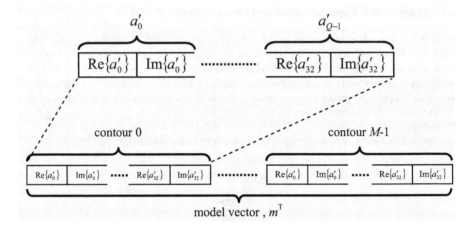

Fig. 3. Model vector formation. The upper vector shows a single image represented as Q FDs; the lower vector represents a single model, m as M sets of FDs. Note that m is shown transposed

representing 98% of the variance should be sufficient to capture the shape of anatomical models, while the remaining 2% is considered noise. A model is then approximated as,

$$m = \overline{m} + \sum_{i=1}^{t} b_i p_i ,$$ (7)

where b_i is the coefficient multiplying the ith PC. The orthonormal column vectors, p_i form the principal basis, or shape space of the model. Thus, our representation of the statistical model consists of the mean model vector and the vectors corresponding to the first t PCs. Section 3 will provide more insight into the effects of model reduction.

2.4   3D Image Segmentation

A 3D image volume that is not included in the training set can be segmented by iteratively deforming the FD statistical model until it closely matches the correct features in the 3D image set. The statistical model ensures a segmentation consistent with the training models. Prior to segmentation, the new image set must be registered to the coordinate frame described in section 2.1. Note that only three points must be manually selected for registration; the Fourier descriptor representation provides the feature correspondences required for the PCA. A search for the optimal solution occurs as separate local and global optimizations; a local search (unconstrained by the statistical model) is performed independently on each image using an active contours algorithm, and a global search takes the form of a projection of the active contours solution onto the principal basis of the statistical model. Since the two searches are forced to intersect occasionally, the constraints from both optimization functions are imposed. The approach is outlined in Algorithm 1.

Most previous work in this area involves minimizing a global objective function that combines terms driven by the image data and terms driven by the prior shape information. This approach will often result in a solution that is not the true global minimum, but a spurious local minimum. Our algorithm also accounts for the case where the optimal solution may not actually occur at a minimum, either local or global. For instance, if a dataset outside of the training set is segmented, the optimal solution will most likely fall slightly beyond the shape space defined by the PCs. By separating the search spaces, we can find solutions that the combined optimization cannot find.

Algorithm 1. Segmentation procedure

1) Initialize active contours (see *Local Search*) based on the mean model, $\overline{m}$
2) Allow active contours to deform independently on each image for h iterations
3) Convert active contours to Fourier descriptors
4) Project FDs onto principal basis
5) Form a new model from projected FDs
6) Check equation 8 for convergence (see below)
   a) if Δ < threshold, repeat steps 2 and 3 only
   b) if Δ > threshold, repeat steps 2-6 with new model in step 5 as new initialization for active contours

The alternating process of active contour deformation and shape space projection continues until the following convergence function reaches some empirical threshold,

$$\Delta = \sum_{i=1}^{t} \left(b_{ni} - b_{(n-1)i} \right)^2 \qquad \text{for n} > 1, \tag{8}$$

where Δ represents the change in the model parameters from one iteration to the next. When this squared sum is less than the specified threshold, the model is assumed to have converged on a shape space solution. An additional optimization of the active contours is performed after this convergence.

Local Search

The local search for a solution occurs in the individual 2D image spaces in the form of active contours, or snakes. Active contours, originally developed by Kass *et al.* [4] employ an energy minimization approach to detect features in images such as lines and edges. The technique typically works best with images that have clearly defined edges with minimal noise; otherwise a good initialization is required for an active contour to converge on an acceptable solution. In the case of shape modeling, we have a good initialization provided by the model information from the previous iteration, provided by steps 1 or 6b in Algorithm 1. The active contour is constructed as a spline, parametrically defined as $\mathbf{v}(r) = [x(r), y(r)]$, where $x(r)$ and $y(r)$ are the x and y positions, in pixel coordinates, of the nodes of the contour to be optimized. As in [4, 11], the energy of the spline can be represented as,

$$E_s = \int_0^1 \left[E_i(\mathbf{v}(r)) + E_e(\mathbf{v}(r)) \right] ds, \tag{9}$$

where E_i and E_e are the internal and external spline energies respectively. E_i can be expanded as,

$$E_i = \frac{1}{2} \left[\alpha |\mathbf{v}'(r)|^2 + \beta |\mathbf{v}''(r)|^2 \right], \tag{10}$$

where the first order term is analogous to elasticity between the nodes and the second order term controls rigidity of the spline. The coefficients α and β are used to control the extent to which each term constrains the deformation of the contour. E_e represents the effect on the energy functional of the image gradient, computed as,

$$E_e = -|\nabla I(x, y)|^2, \tag{11}$$

where ∇I is the image gradient computed via a Sobel operator. The combined internal and external energies tend to drive the contour toward the image gradients, while maintaining control over the shape of the contour.

Global Search

The global search for a solution occurs in the principal space by computing the parameters b_i in equation 7 by projecting the FDs from step 3 in Algorithm 1 onto the principal basis. This has the effect of constraining the active contours solution to be in the shape space, thus from one iteration to the next, the local solution is projected into shape space to find a global solution. After several iterations, the parameters b_i will vary negligibly, indicating that a global solution has been found. As previously discussed, this may not represent the optimal solution since the actual solution likely falls slightly beyond the shape space. With this optimal global solution as an initialization for one final local optimization, ie. an additional active contours adjustment, a solution that is close to the shape space, but optimized to fit the 3D image information can be found.

3   Results

In order to verify the ability of our modeling and segmentation techniques to extract anatomical features from medical images, we performed experiments with the 19 CT and MRI datasets. The datasets are each segmented manually and the resulting binary images are transformed and resampled as described in section 2.1. For testing purposes we sample the image volumes to a voxel size of 0.75 x 0.75 x 3.00 mm, resulting in 40 images spanning the distal 120 mm of the femur. The original grayscale images are transformed and resampled by the same transformation as the binary images so that subsequent model-based segmentations will be performed in the model domain.

Each of the 19 image sets is autonomously segmented according to Algorithm 1 with a model defined via a leave-one-out approach (see e.g., [12]), where the remaining 18 manual segmentations are used as training shapes. To illustrate the effect of the number of principal components on model-based segmentation, each of the 19 image sets is segmented multiple times, each time with a shape model defined by the remaining 18 datasets with a varying number of PCs ($t = 1, 2, \ldots , 18$). This results in $19*18 = 342$ total segmentations of the 19 datasets.

We compare the autonomous model-based segmentation results (actual results) to the manual segmentation results (expected results) to obtain a measure of the quality of the segmentation. This comparison is performed in the 3D image domain by computing the shortest 3D Euclidean distance between the two voxel "surfaces" for each voxel on the autonomously segmented set. For each of the 342 segmentations, we obtain a mean separation distance and a maximum, or worst case, distance. Ideally, these distances are zero for a perfect fit, assuming that the solution we seek is the same as the manual segmentation.

Two experiments are performed to verify that the iterative optimization with a final local optimization provides a better final result than a solution constrained to be fully within the shape space. Figs. 4 and 5 show, respectively, the mean and maximum distance averaged over all segmentations as a function of the number of PCs in the statistical model. The two curves in each plot represent the different final optimizations, one for the locally optimized solution and one for the shape space constrained solution.

In section 2.3, we noted that a model should capture approximately 98% of the variance in the training model data. Fig. 6 shows the cumulative variance as a function of the number of PCs for a typical model. The cumulative variance for the distal femur model approaches 98% at approximately 11 PCs.

The mean separation distance graphically shown in Fig. 4 demonstrates that an increase in the number of PCs yields an autonomous segmentation solution closer to the manual segmentation. Additionally, the final active contours adjustment pushes the mean distance between the expected surface and the actual surface to approximately half of the mean distance found by constraining the solution to be fully within the shape space. We can see the same trend for the maximum separation. Note that the mean distance levels off between 11 and 12 PCs, indicating that an increase in the number of PCs beyond 11 or 12 may not improve the segmentation.

Our best mean and maximum distance measures compare well to the best values presented in [3] and are summarized in Table 1. In fact, our best mean value is five times less than the best reported value by Kaus *et al.* [3]. We must note that [3] does not solve a segmentation problem, rather they are fitting a triangular mesh to manually segmented noiseless binary 3D images to form a unique surface model. Our method is applied to segment noisy 3D medical images and compare the results to a manual segmentation of the same sets. Their measure of deviation between the autonomously adjusted mesh (vertices) and the manually segmented binary 3D images (voxels) is similar to our measure of deviation between the autonomously and manually segmented 3D images (voxel to voxel), thus a comparison to their results is valid.

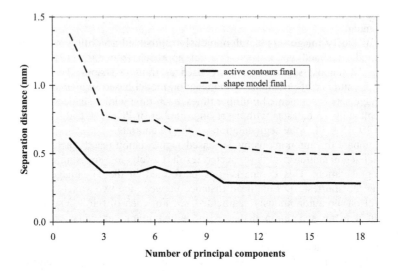

Fig. 4. Mean separation distance between autonomously segmented 3D image volumes and corresponding manually segmented volume. The solid line represents the solution where the active contours are adjusted after the final shape space projection; the dashed line is the solution resulting from the final shape space projection

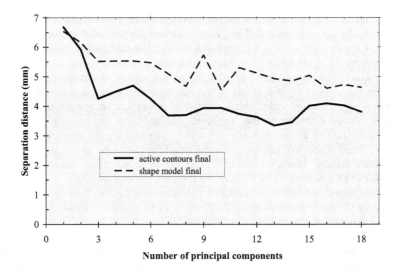

Fig. 5. Maximum separation distance between autonomously segmented 3D image volumes and corresponding manually segmented volume. The solid line represents the solution where the active contours are adjusted after the final shape space projection; the dashed line is the solution resulting from the final shape space projection

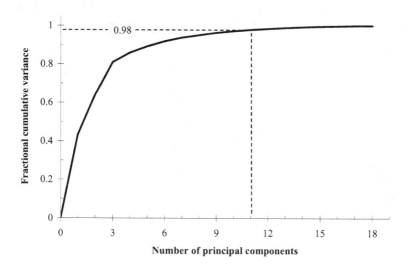

Fig. 6. Average cumulative variance as a function of the number of principal components

Table 1. Comparison of results with Kaus *et al.* Value in parenthesis is the lowest number of PCs at which the value occurs

	max Euclidean distance (mm)	mean Euclidean distance (mm)
Our results	3.35 (13)	0.28 (12)
Kaus *et al.*	~ 4.50 (20)	~ 1.40 (20)

4 Conclusion and Future Work

The described experiments have demonstrated that our model building method accurately and compactly captures the shape of the distal femur and our segmentation procedure successfully segments new datasets (Fig. 7). A comparison of our results to previously published values indicates that our segmentation method is accurate. With only 12 PCs we were able to segment a 3D image volume with an average deviation of only 0.28 mm, a deviation of less than a voxel in most 3D medical images.

Future work in this area will involve extending the size of the training set for more thorough testing and to explore a potential correlation between the number of training models and the number of PCs required to capture the statistics of the distal femur. Additional work will also include modeling more complex structures, including soft tissue.

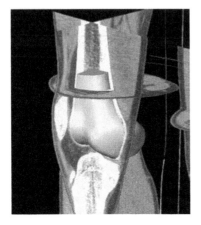 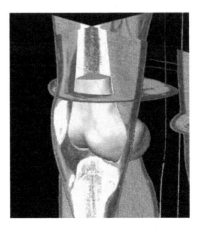

Fig. 7. Segmentation result. Initial mean model (left) and final, autonomously segmented model (right)

References

1. T. Cootes and C. Taylor, "Active shape models—'Smart snakes'," Proc. British Mach. Vision Conf., pp. 266-275, 1992.
2. C. Taylor, T. Cootes, A. Hill, and J. Haslam, "Medical Image Segmentation Using Active Shape Models," Proc. Medical Imaging Workshop, Brusseles, Belgium, pp. 121-143, 1995.
3. M. Kaus, V. Pekar, C. Lorenz, R. Truyen, S. Lobregt, and J. Weese, "Automated 3-D PDM Construction from Segmented Images Using Deformable Models," IEEE Transactions on Medical Imaging, Vol. 22, No. 8, pp. 1005-1013, Aug 2003.
4. M. Kass, A. Witkin, and D. Terzopoulos, "Snakes: Active contour models," Int. J. Comput. Vis., Vol. 1, pp. 321–331, 1987.
5. L. Staib and J. Duncan, "Boundary Finding with Parametrically Deformable Models," IEEE PAMI, Vol. 14, No. 11, pp. 1061-1075, Nov 1992.
6. C. Zahn and R. Roskies, "Fourier Descriptors for Plane Closed Curves," IEEE Transactions on Computers, Vol. 21, No. 3, pp. 269-281, Mar 1972.
7. E. Persoon and K. Fu, "Shape Discrimination Using Fourier Descriptors," IEEE Trans. on Sys.,Man, and Cyber., Vol. SMC-7, No. 3, pp. 629-639, Mar 1977.
8. T. Cootes, A. Hill, C. Taylor, and J. Haslam, "The Use of Active Shape Models for Locating Structures in Medical Images," Image and Vision Computing, Vol. 12, No. 6, pp. 355-365, Jul 1994.
9. T. Cootes, G. Edwards, and C. Taylor, "Active appearance models," in Proc. Eur. Conf. Computer Vision, Vol. 2, H. Burkhardt and B. Neumann, Eds., pp. 484–498, 1998.
10. T. Hutton , B. Buxton, P. Hammond, and H. Potts, "Estimating Average Growth trajectories in Shape-Space Using Kernel Smoothing," IEEE Transactions on Medical Imaging, Vol. 22, No. 6, pp. 747-753, Jun 2003.
11. C. Xu and J. Prince, "Gradient vector flow: A new external force for snakes," in IEEE Proc. Conf. on Computer Vision and Pattern Recognition, pp. 66–71, 1997.
12. A. Kelemen, G. Székely, and G. Gerig, "Elastic Model-Based Segmentation of 3-D Neuroradiological Data Sets," IEEE Transactions on Medical Imaging, Vol. 18, No. 10, pp. 828-839, Oct 1999.

Automatic Rib Segmentation in CT Data

Joes Staal, Bram van Ginneken, and Max A. Viergever

Image Sciences Institute, University Medical Center Utrecht, Heidelberglaan 100,
E.01.335, 3584 CX Utrecht, The Netherlands
`joes@isi.uu.nl`

Abstract. A supervised method is presented for the detection and segmentation of ribs in computed tomography (CT) data. In a first stage primitives are extracted that represent parts of the centerlines of elongated structures. Each primitive is characterized by a number of features computed from local image structure. For a number of training cases, the primitives are labeled by a human observer into two classes (rib vs. non-rib). This data is used to train a classifier. Now, primitives obtained from any image can be labeled automatically. In a final stage the primitives classified as ribs are used to initialize a seeded region growing process to obtain the complete rib cage.

The method has been tested on 20 images. Of the primitives, 96.9% is classified correctly. The results of the final segmentation are satisfactory.

1 Introduction

The latest generation of CT-scanners produces data with slice thickness and slice gaps of size similar to the in plane resolution. As a consequence, radiologists are at risk of being overwhelmed by the amount of data they have to examine. To overcome this problem computerized postprocessing methods are being developed. In [1] numerous examples are given, of which automated rib segmentation is one. The ribs are always depicted in chest CT, so they should be reported on. In practice, rib anomalies and fractures are frequently missed [2]. Therefore, we focus in this paper on the segmentation of ribs in CT-images of the thorax. Automated rib segmentation can be used for effective visualizations of the rib cage. It is also a first step for computerized detection of bone abnormalities. And, the segmented ribs can act as reference objects to segment other structures.

The method consists of the following steps. First, as ribs appear as bright elongated structures in CT-images, a technique is developed to extract 1D ridges (centerlines) in 3D data. Then, the ridge pixels are grouped together based on similarity measures to form straight line elements. The straight line elements form primitives on which the supervised part of the algorithm is based. For every primitive a set of features is computed, based on the local image structure around the primitive.

To construct a training set, a human observer divided the primitives of twenty images into ribs and non-ribs, so that every feature vector can be labeled according to its corresponding class. With the training set a kNN-classifier is trained,

M. Šonka et al. (Eds.): CVAMIA-MMBIA 2004, LNCS 3117, pp. 193–204, 2004.

that is used to classify the primitives obtained from other images. Finally, the primitives classified as rib are used as initialization for a seeded region growing process in the image to segment the rib cage.

Several methods have been implemented that can be used to segment the rib cage, or, more generally, segment elongated structures in CT data. None of these methods is completely automatic. In [3,4] centerlines are extracted from which the widths of the objects are estimated. In [5] a tracking algorithm is described, that proceeds from one 2D slice to the next. The method uses seeded region growing, for which the seeds must be supplied manually. The work in [6] is based on 3D region growing using locally adaptive thresholds. Segmentation based on watersheds [7] is another interesting approach.

This paper is organized as follows. In Section 2 our method is described in detail. Section 3 discusses the images that are used. Results are presented in Section 4. The paper ends with a discussion in Section 5.

2   Method

Because ribs are elongated structures, we develop a method to extract their centerlines. The intensity values of CT data are related to the density of the imaged tissue. Therefore, as a first step, the image is thresholded to obtain the bone structures. Next the thresholded (and now binary) image is blurred with a Gaussian kernel. As a result, there will be a local maximum at the centerline in the plane perpendicular to the rib, see Fig. 1. In the blurred image the centerlines are extracted as described in the following subsection.

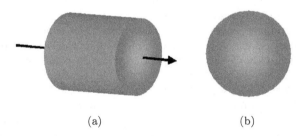

(a)   (b)

Fig. 1. (a) An elongated structure in 3D. Along the planes perpendicular to its centerline (subdimensional) maxima are found. (b) Image intensities in a plane perpendicular to the centerline.

2.1   Ridge Detection in 3D

To detect the local maximum in the (2D) plane perpendicular to the centerline, we must first estimate the direction of the plane at every voxel. For this purpose the eigenvectors $\mathbf{v}_i$, $i \in \{1, 2, 3\}$ of the Hessian matrix $\mathbf{H}$ can be used. The Hessian matrix is given by

$$\mathbf{H} = \begin{pmatrix} I_{xx} & I_{xy} & I_{xz} \\ I_{yx} & I_{yy} & I_{yz} \\ I_{zx} & I_{zy} & I_{zz} \end{pmatrix} , \tag{1}$$

where I_{ij}, $i, j \in \{x, y, z\}$ represents the second order derivative of the intensity with respect to the coordinates. The derivatives are taken in the scale space sense, i.e.

$$I_{ij} = I_{ij}(\mathbf{x}; \sigma) = \int_{\mathbb{R}^3} I(\mathbf{x}) G_{ij}(\mathbf{x} - \mathbf{x}'; \sigma) d\mathbf{x}' , \tag{2}$$

with $\mathbf{x} = (x, y, z)^T$, σ the scale and

$$G(\mathbf{x}; \sigma) = \frac{1}{(2\pi\sigma)^{\frac{3}{2}}} \exp\left(-\frac{\mathbf{x} \cdot \mathbf{x}}{2\sigma^2}\right)$$

the Gaussian kernel. For more information on scale space the reader is referred to [8] and references therein.

It is assumed that the $\mathbf{v}_i$ are ordered in decreasing magnitude of their corresponding eigenvalues λ_i, i.e. $|\lambda_1| \geq |\lambda_2| \geq |\lambda_3|$. The eigenvectors point in the principal directions of the intensity curvature, i.e. $\mathbf{v}_1$ points in the direction of largest curvature and $\mathbf{v}_3$ in the direction of smallest curvature. The vector $\mathbf{v}_2$ is perpendicular to the other two vectors. The plane we are looking for is defined by the first two eigenvectors of $\mathbf{H}$. Now, the detection of the 1D ridges boils down to checking at every voxel whether there is a local maximum of the intensity in the plane defined by $\mathbf{v}_1$ and $\mathbf{v}_2$. Note that the vector $\mathbf{v}_3$ is tangential to the ridge.

The detection of the maximum in the 2D plane is done as follows. Around the voxel $\mathbf{x}$, the circle

$$\mathbf{c}(\theta) = \mathbf{x} + \rho(\mathbf{v}_1 \cos\theta + \mathbf{v}_2 \sin\theta) , \quad \theta \in [0, 2\pi) ,$$

is defined, with ρ the radius of the circle. The image has a point on a 1D ridge if

$$I(\mathbf{x}) - I(\mathbf{c}(\theta)) > 0 , \text{ for all } \theta .$$

Of course, in the mathematical continuous world, the limit of ρ towards zero would be taken. On the discrete image lattice, a choice of $\rho = 1.0$ voxel seems natural. Furthermore, the polar angle θ must be discretized. In this paper we have chosen to use 8 different angles, corresponding to an eight-connected neighborhood in 2D images. Finally, note that in general $\mathbf{c}(\theta)$ will fall in between gridpoints. To evaluate I at those points, linear interpolation has been used.

2.2 Convex Sets

The next step is the construction of line elements from the set of 1D ridges. A local grouping process is used that takes into account the local orientation of the

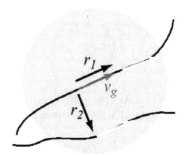

Fig. 2. The dark curved lines are two ridges. The diameter of the disk is ϵ_c. $\mathbf{v}_g$ is the eigenvector belonging to a grouped pixel, $\mathbf{v}_1$ and $\mathbf{v}_2$ are the eigenvectors of still ungrouped pixels. The vectors $\mathbf{r}_1$ and $\mathbf{r}_2$ are unit vectors pointing from the grouped pixels to the ungrouped pixels. The pixel that belongs to the same ridge will be added to the group, because it satisfies the conditions in (3)-(5). The pixel on the parallel ridge does not satisfy condition (5) and will not be grouped.

ridge. The idea is to investigate the local neighborhood around a ridge voxel and to add those ridge voxels in the neighborhood that adhere to some conditions. The first condition is that the candidate ridge voxel at $\mathbf{x}_c$ is in the neighborhood of the seed voxel $\mathbf{x}_s$

$$\|\mathbf{x}_c - \mathbf{x}_s\| \leq \epsilon_c , \qquad (3)$$

where $\epsilon_c \in [0, \infty)$ is the connectivity radius. The size of the radius determines the size of small gaps that can be closed. A second test investigates the similarity of the local orientation

$$|\mathbf{v}_{3,c} \cdot \mathbf{v}_{3,s}| \geq \epsilon_o , \qquad (4)$$

with $\epsilon_o \in [0, 1]$ a threshold that determines the orientation sensitivity. A higher threshold means stricter selectivity. Finally, it could happen that a candidate ridge voxel obeys the connectivity and orientation demands, but that it is located on a parallel ridge (see Fig. 2 as well). To prevent this, a final test is applied. The unit vector $\hat{\mathbf{r}}$ that points from $\mathbf{x}_c$ to $\mathbf{x}_s$ is compared to the local orientation vector at the seed

$$|\hat{\mathbf{r}} \cdot \mathbf{v}_{3,s}| \geq \epsilon_p . \qquad (5)$$

The threshold $\epsilon_p \in [0, 1]$ sets the parallellity sensitivity. Again, higher threshold means stricter selectivity. The sets that are found with these constraints are coined *(affine) convex sets.* Convex, because they approximate straight lines (the only 1D convex sets in 3D) and affine because Euclidean distance is replaced with geodesic distance (i.e. distance along the set).

In this work, $\epsilon_c = 5.0$, $\epsilon_o = 0.9$ and $\epsilon_p = 0.9$ have been used. Furthermore, a threshold can be set on the maximum size of a convex set; here a maximum of

$\epsilon_m = 20$ voxels is used. Figure 3 shows a visualization of the convex sets of one of the test datasets.

2.3   Feature Extraction, Feature Selection, and Rib Classification

From Fig. 3 it is clear that the convex sets that belong to the ribs are a subset of all the detected convex sets. In this subsection it is shown how a kNN-classifier can be used to divide the rib convex sets from the non-rib convex sets.

A classifier maps a feature vector extracted from the subject under investigation to class numbers or to a vector of probabilities, where each element in the vector represents a class. The mapping must be learned from example data. The learning for a kNN-classifier is trivial, because a kNN-classifier just stores its training samples. A sample that must be classified is compared to the k nearest neighbors in feature space and the probability that the sample belongs to class i is approximated by [9]

$$p_i = \frac{n_i}{k} \; , \tag{6}$$

where n_i is the number of neighbors that have class number equal to i. There exist optimized implementations for kNN-classifiers and the one used in this paper can be found in [10].

In our case the input for the classifier is a vector with representative features of a convex set and its output the chance that the input belongs to the class rib. The feature vector has been built from information on the local image structure around every convex set. For every voxel belonging to a convex set, the image derivatives upto and including second order have been computed at various scales, using Gaussian derivatives (cf. eq. (2)). The feature vector of a convex set consists of the mean of the feature vectors for every voxel in that convex set. We used 4 scales ($\sigma = 1.0, 2.0, 4.0$ and 8.0 voxels), resulting in $4 \times (1 + 3 + 6) = 40$ features. Furthermore, because kNN-classifiers are sensitive to scaling of the features, each feature has been linearly transformed to zero mean and unit variance. This transformation is deduced from the training data.

Beforehand, it is unknown which features produce good results and which features deteriorate the classification process. A means to determine the appropriate features is to conduct feature selection [9]. But before feature selection is discussed, a measure for good results must be defined.

Because the kNN-classifier can give as output a posterior probability, we have chosen to quantify the results of the classification process with ROC-curves [11]. An ROC-curve plots the fraction of pixels that is falsely classified as vessel against the fraction that is correctly classified as vessel. The fractions are determined by setting a threshold t_p on the posterior probability. The closer a curve approaches the top left corner, the better the performance of the system. A single measure to quantify this behavior is the area under the curve, A_z, which is 1 for a perfect system. A system that makes random classifications has an ROC-curve that is a straight line through the origin with slope 1 and $A_z = 0.5$.

The feature selection method that has been applied is sequential forward selection [12]. This algorithm starts with a null feature set and, for each step,

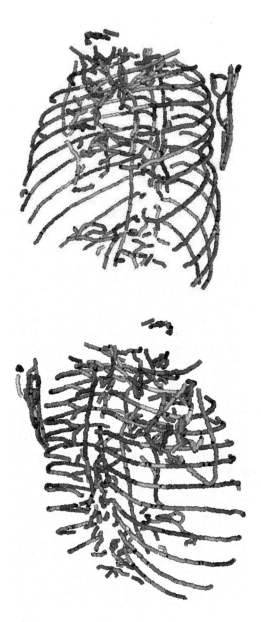

Fig. 3. Two views of the convex sets of a CT-scan of the thorax. Every set has its own color. Not only the centerlines of the ribs are detected, but also parts of the aorta, some other vessels, the spine, the shoulder blades, the lower jaw and some other bone structure. The vessel structure is detected because in this particular scan the patient was administered an intravenous contrast agent.

the best feature according to some criterion function is included with the current feature set. In this work, A_z is taken as the criterion function. If a feature is included, the performance of the current set of features is stored. After all features have been included, the subset that gives the best overall performance is chosen.

After training and feature selection, new data can be classified. However, since the output of the classifier is a probability, we must set a threshold to get a hard classification in rib and non-rib. In the ideal situation, the choice would be $t_p = 0.5$, however, it is observed from our experiments that another threshold might give higher accuracy, where the accuracy is defined as the ratio of the number of correctly classified convex sets (both rib and non-rib) divided by the total number of convex sets. For every t_p that is set for producing the ROC-curve, the accuracy can also be computed. Therefore, we have chosen to estimate the optimal threshold $t_{p,opt}$ from the training set.

2.4 Seeded Region Growing

After classification of the convex sets, the centerlines of the ribs have been estimated, and as a final step they are used to start a seeded region growing algorithm as described in [13]. At the start of the algorithm, the mean gray values of the image per convex set are computed. Then a list is initialized to which all the neighboring voxels of all convex sets are added. The voxel in this list that has the smallest difference in gray value as compared to the mean of its neighboring convex set is removed from the list and added to the convex set. Next, the mean of the convex set is updated and the neighbors of the added voxel, if not already present, are added to the list of boundary voxels. The algorithm continues until the list of boundary voxels is empty. To circumvent leaking in non bone structures, only voxels above a gray level threshold t_b and and closer than a distance d_{max} to the centerline are added to the boundary list.

The ribs may leak into bone structures that are not rib. For that reason the region growing is done on all convex sets, including the non-rib sets.

3   Material

In this study, 40 CT-scans of the thorax of different patients were used. The set contained both normal cases and pathology. The scans were randomly divided in two sets of 20 images so that a training set and a test set could be formed. The image sizes range from $512 \times 512 \times 407$ to $512 \times 512 \times 706$ voxels. Such high resolution is not needed for the detection of the centerlines of the ribs. Therefore, all images were downsampled with a factor 2 in all directions, resulting in sizes of $256 \times 256 \times 203$ to $256 \times 256 \times 353$ voxels.

The images are thresholded at a Hounsfield unit of 1100 and blurred with a Gaussian of $\sigma = 2.0$ voxels. The blurred images are used for the ridge detection, followed by the convex sets formation. In the training set 9,455 convex sets were found, in the test set 10,016. Manual labeling was done by clicking in a 3D

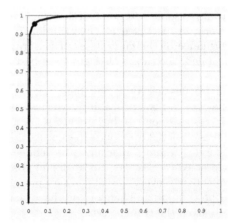

Fig. 4. The ROC-curve for the test set. $A_z = 0.988$ and the accuracy for $t_{p,opt} = 0.6$ is 0.961. The point at the ROC-curve for this threshold is marked with a dot.

visualization like the one in Fig. 3. The observer had the opportunity to view slices of the original CT-scan together with the convex set. In the training set 3,290 convex sets were labeled as rib (35%), in the test set this number is 3,208 (32%).

The final seeded region growing has been applied on the full size images.

Table 1. Confusion matrix for the convex sets in the test set consisting of 20 scans for $t_{p,opt} = 0.6$.

		gold standard		total
		rib	non-rib	
computer	rib	3061 (30.6%)	248 (2.4%)	3309 (33.0%)
	non-rib	147 (1.5%)	6560 (65.5%)	6707 (67.0%)
	total	3208 (32.1%)	6808 (67.9%)	10016

4 Results

4.1 Feature Selection

For the feature selection the training set is divided in two sets, one for training the classifier, the other for measuring the performance. Optimal classification was found for a feature set consisting of 25 features. The kNN-classifier was used with $k = 21$ nearest neighbors. The value of A_z for the determined set of features is 0.996. The optimal threshold is $t_{p,opt} = 0.6$, at which the accuracy is 0.969.

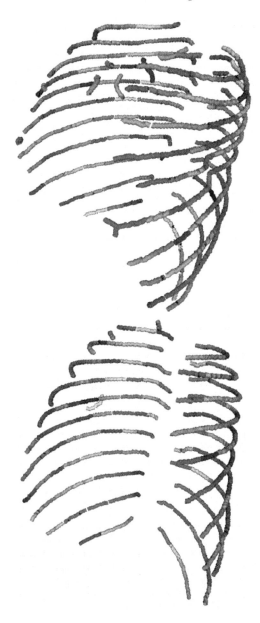

Fig. 5. The convex sets that are classified as rib for two datasets. The upper image contains the classified ribs of Fig. 3. Note that a few errors are made in the upper image. Some convex sets that are part of the sternum have been incorrectly classified. Note also the abnormalities in the 6th and 7th left rib (rib number 1 is not present in the scan). In the lower image one convex set that is near the throat and one that belongs to the shoulder blade have been incorrectly classified.

4.2   Classification

The results of the feature selection are biased, because the optimal features were determined for the subdivided training set. An independent classification was performed with the selected features on the convex sets of the test set with a kNN-classifier trained on the training set. The ROC-curve is shown in Fig. 4. The area under the curve is $A_z = 0.988$, the accuracy at $t_{p,opt}$ is 0.961. Figure 5 shows two example cases. In Table 1 the confusion matrix is given.

4.3   Seeded Region Growing

The final step in the segmentation algorithm is the seeded region growing. As a lower threshold a value of $t_b = 1100$ Hounsfield units is used. The maximum distance a voxel is allowed to be away from a convex set is set to $d_{max} = 40$ voxels. In Fig. 6 the surface renderings of the ribs from Fig. 5 are shown.

5   Discussion

In this paper a method has been presented for the segmentation of ribs based on classification of properly chosen image primitives. The primitives give a more global description of the data than the voxels do. For example, the CT-scans in this paper contain about 10^7 voxels, opposed to 500 convex sets on average. As a consequence, the size of the problem is reduced enormously.

Another advantage of the convex sets is that the construction of a large training set is possible, on average 160 convex sets had to be clicked per image. Manually labeling the convex set of one image takes about 5 minutes.

We have fixed the maximum size of the convex sets to be $\epsilon_m = 20$ voxels. If ϵ_m is made smaller the number of convex sets that has to be classified increases. If it is made larger, centerlines which belong to rib and other structures will merge. So, clearly there is a tradeoff.

In certain images, the centerlines of some of the vessels are detected by the convex sets because the patient was administered an intravenous contrast agent. However, the use of a classifier enables the discrimination between vessels and ribs.

The method's computation time is in the order of a few minutes. Computing the features for an image takes about 1 minute, the detection and classification of the convex sets about 2.5 minutes and the region growing about 3 minutes. All computations were done on a PC with an AMD Athlon XP 1800+ processor and 1 GB memory. The code used for this algorithm has not been optimized.

Despite small errors, the results are satisfying. Some of the errors are at the end of the ribs, as can be observed from Figs. 5 and 6, where the region growing leaks sometimes into the sternum or into the spine. A postprocessing step will be able to improve the results. Also, some convex sets are disconnected from the rib case and incorrectly classified as rib. A connectivity test should be able to remove those parts that are not connected.

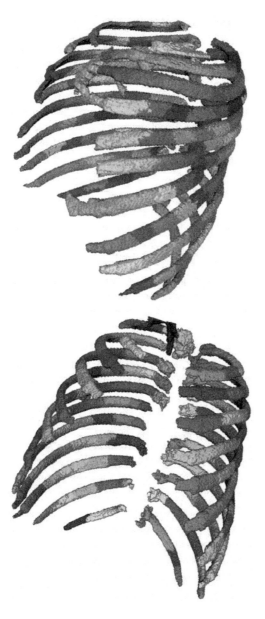

Fig. 6. Result of the seeded region growing on the convex sets of Fig. 5. In the upper image a few sets have grown into the sternum. Near the second left rib a part of the first rib (that is not completely scanned) has been found. The third and fourth rib have been connected via the sternum. In the lower image a convex set has grown into the spine. Another convex set near the throat was incorrectly classified.

At this moment an evaluation of the quality of the final segmentation is lacking. Manual segmentation of the complete rib cage in all the datasets seems not feasible in a fair amount of time. One option is to ask radiologists to qualitively rate the results, another is to compare the automatic segmentation with an interactive segmentation result. The methods described in [6] and [7] could be used for this purpose.

A further segmentation of the convex sets into labeled ribs (i.e. all convex sets belonging to a specific rib number) is currently under investigation. It is expected that such a scheme can reduce the number of false positives and false negatives as well.

References

1. R. M. Summers, "Road maps for advancement of radiologic computer-aided detection in the 21st century," *Radiology*, vol. 229, no. 1, pp. 11–13, 2003.
2. M. Prokop and M. Galanski, Eds., *Spiral and multislice computed tomography of the body.* Stuttgart: Thieme, 2003.
3. S. R. Aylward, E. Bullitt, S. Pizer, and D. Eberly, "Intensity ridge and widths for tubular object segmentation and description," in *Proceedings of the Workshop on Mathematical Methods in Biomedical Image Analysis*, 1996, pp. 131–138.
4. S. R. Aylward and E. Bullit, "Initialization, noise, singularities, and scale in height ridge traversal for tubular object centerline extraction," *IEEE Trans. Med. Imag.*, vol. 21, no. 2, pp. 61–75, 2002.
5. D. Kim, H. Kim, and H. S. Kang, "An object-tracking segmentation method: vertebra and rib segmentation in CT images," in *SPIE Proceedings: Medical Imaging 2002*, vol. 4684, 2002, pp. 1662–1671.
6. Y. Kang, K. Engelke, and W. A. Kalender, "A new accurate and precise 3-D segmentation method for skeletal structures in volumetric CT data," *IEEE Trans. Med. Imag.*, vol. 22, no. 5, pp. 586–598, 2003.
7. E. B. Dam and M. Nielsen, "Non-linear diffusion for interactive multi-scale watershed segmentation," in *Proc. MICCAI 2000.* Springer, 2000, pp. 216–225.
8. L. M. J. Florack, *Image structure.* Dordrecht: Kluwer Academic Press, 1997.
9. R. O. Duda, P. E. Hart, and H. G. Stork, *Pattern classification*, 2nd ed. New York: Wiley-Interscience, 2001.
10. S. Arya, D. M. Mount, N. S. Netanyahu, R. Silverman, and A. Y. Wu, "An optimal algorithm for approximate nearest neighbor searching in fixed dimensions," *J. ACM*, vol. 45, no. 6, pp. 891–923, 1998.
11. C. E. Metz, "Basic principles of ROC analysis," *Seminars in Nucl. Med.*, vol. 8, no. 4, pp. 283–298, 1978.
12. A. W. Whitney, "A direct method of non parametric measurement selection," *IEEE Trans. Comput.*, vol. 20, no. 9, pp. 1100–1103, 1971.
13. R. Adams and L. Bischof, "Seeded region growing," *IEEE Trans. Pattern Anal. Machine Intell.*, vol. 6, no. 16, pp. 641–647, 1994.

Efficient Initialization for Constrained Active Surfaces, Applications in 3D Medical Images

Roberto Ardon[1,2] and Laurent D. Cohen[2]

[1] MEDISYS-Philips France,
51, rue Carnot, 92156 Suresnes, France
[2] CEREMADE-Université Paris Dauphine,
Place du Maréchal de Lattre, 75016 Paris, France
roberto.ardon@philips.com

Abstract. A novel method allowing simplified and efficient active surface initialization for 3D images segmentation is presented. Our method
allows to initialize an active surface through simple objects like points
and curves and ensures that the further evolution of the active object
will not be trapped by unwanted local minima. Our approach is based
on minimal paths that integrate the information coming from the user
given curves and from the image volume. The minimal paths build a
network representing a first approximation of the initialization surface.
An interpolation method is then used to build a mesh or an implicit
representation based on the information retrieved from the network of
paths. From this initialization, an active surface converges quickly to the
expected solution. Our paper describes a fast construction obtained by
exploiting the Fast Marching algorithm. The algorithm has been successfully applied to synthetic images and 3D medical images.

1 Introduction

Since their introduction by Kass *et al.* in [7], deformable models have been
extensively used to find single and multiple objects in 2D and 3D images. The
common use of these models consists in introducing an initial object in the image
and transforming it until it reaches a wanted target. In most applications, the
evolution of the object is done in order to minimize an energy attached to the
image data until a steady state is reached. One of the main drawbacks of this
approach is that it suffers from local minima 'traps'. This happens when the
steady state reached by the active object does not correspond with the target
but with another local minimum. This is why, when considering the problem of
a single object segmentation in real 3D images, the initialization of the active
object is a major issue: if the initial position of the active object is too far from
the target, local minima can block the evolution, hence missing the objective.
Since the publication of [7], much work has been done in order to free the model
from this initialization dependency. A balloon force was early proposed in [5]
to cope with the shrinking problem of the first model, but this force supposed
a known direction in the evolution. Geodesic active objects [2, 3] were then

M. Šonka et al. (Eds.): CVAMIA-MMBIA 2004, LNCS 3117, pp. 205–217, 2004.
© Springer-Verlag Berlin Heidelberg 2004

a major step toward the improvement of the energy term, but still did not guarantee the uniqueness of a minimum in the general case. The introduction of region dependent energies [11] and the use of the level set technique [10, 9] that allows topological changes of the active model, contributed to create a more robust framework. Nonetheless, when dealing with 3D images and when looking for a precise object (like the left ventricle in 3D ultrasound images) the initialization of the model still is a fundamental step that is often made by simple geometric objects (spheres, cylinders) too far from the objective, or by tedious hand drawing.

The main contribution of our work is to provide an initialization surface that will allow the active object to avoid unwanted local minima and increase its convergence speed. This surface will be obtained through the interpolation of a network of 3D global minimal paths that will be generated between simple objects like points or curves introduced by the user and known to belong to the object of interest.

Our paper outline is as follows: we begin in section 2 by recalling the principles of geodesic active contours and surfaces as well as the global minimal paths framework. In section 3 we explain how minimal paths can be used to build a network of paths that is not concerned by the problem of local minima traps. In section 4 we present an improvement of the network construction where we project the minimal paths into suitable subspaces. In section 5 we give the final step of our algorithm which is the generation of the initialization surface from the network of paths. At last, in section 6 we show some examples on synthetic images and real medical images.

2   Active Surfaces and Minimal Paths

Active surfaces as well as minimal paths derived from deformable models introduced with the snake model [7]. This model consists in introducing a curve $\mathcal{C}$ into the image and make it evolve in order to minimize the energy,

$$E(\mathcal{C}) = \int \{\alpha.\,\|\mathcal{C}'(s)\| + \beta.\,\|\mathcal{C}''(s)\|\,ds\} + \int \mathcal{P}(\mathcal{C}(s))ds. \qquad (1)$$

The two first terms maintain the regularity of the curve and the last one is the data attachment. $\mathcal{P}$ represents an edge detector that has lower values on edges, for example if I is the image, a choice can be $\mathcal{P} = (1 + |\nabla I|^2)^{-1}$.

Caselles *et al* improved the energy formulation in [2, 3] by introducing the geodesic active contour model and its surface extension. In their approach the evolution of the initial curve $\mathcal{C}_0$ or surface $\mathcal{S}_0$ was driven by the minimization of the geodesic energy

$$E(\mathcal{C}) = \int \mathcal{P}(\mathcal{C}(s))\,\|\mathcal{C}'(s)\|\,ds, \qquad (2)$$

$$E(\mathcal{S}) = \int \int \mathcal{P}(\mathcal{S}(u,v))\,\|\mathcal{S}_u \times \mathcal{S}_v\|\,dudv \qquad (3)$$

Even though these models are only edge-driven most of the current approaches that integrates other informations (region, texture, a priori) are actually extensions. This is why in this paper we will concentrate on this models.

The most popular approach for solving the minimization problem is to consider the Euler-Lagrange equations for (2) and (3)(first variation of the energy) and derive from it the corresponding gradient descent schemes that will drive the model in the direction of steepest descent :

$$\frac{\partial \mathcal{C}}{\partial t} = (\mathcal{P}\kappa - \nabla \mathcal{P}.\boldsymbol{n})\,\boldsymbol{n} \text{ with } \mathcal{C}(.,0) = \mathcal{C}_0, \tag{4}$$

$$\frac{\partial \mathcal{S}}{\partial t} = (\mathcal{P}H - \nabla \mathcal{P}.\boldsymbol{N})\,\boldsymbol{N} \text{ with } \mathcal{S}(.,.,0) = \mathcal{S}_0, \tag{5}$$

where H and κ are respectively the mean curvature of the surface and the curvature of the curve. $\boldsymbol{N}$ and $\boldsymbol{n}$ are their outward normals.

However, in next section we recall a method introduced in [6] that allows to find the global minimum for the contour energy (2) when imposing the two end points and that does not use the evolution equation 4. Unfortunately such a method is not available for surfaces, we thus have to deal with the steepest gradient descent. The choice of $\mathcal{S}_0$ will then have a major impact on how well and how fast the model will recover the expected surface. In our approach to build a convenient $\mathcal{S}_0$ we made extensive use of the possibility to find the global minimum of the geodesic energy for curves.

2.1   Global Minimal Paths Between Two End Points

It was established in [8] that the global minimal path connecting p_0 and p_1 is the curve obtained by following the opposite gradient direction on a map $\mathcal{U}_{p_0}$ starting from p_1 until p_0 is reached, thus solving the problem:

$$\frac{d\mathcal{C}}{ds}(s) = -\nabla \mathcal{U}_{p_0}, \text{with } \mathcal{C}(0) = p_1 \text{ and } \mathcal{C}(L) = p_0. \tag{6}$$

It was also shown in [8] that the map $\mathcal{U}_{p_0}$ is the solution of the Eikonal equation

$$\|\nabla \mathcal{U}_{p_0}\| = \mathcal{P} \text{ and } \mathcal{U}_{p_0}(p_0) = 0. \tag{7}$$

Equation 6 can be numerically solved by simple ordinary differential equations techniques like Newton's or Runge-Kutta's. Hence, the fundamental point is the computation of the minimal action map $\mathcal{U}_{p_0}$. To solve equation 7 numerically, classic finite differences schemes tend to be unstable. In [14] Tsitsiklis introduced a new method that was independently reformulated by Sethian in [12] that relies on a one-sided derivative looking in the up-wind direction of the front, and giving the correct viscosity solution. This algorithm is known as the Fast Marching algorithm and is now widely used and understood, details can be found in [13]. Nevertheless it is important to highlight the major interest of this algorithm. After a simple initialization of $\mathcal{U}_{p_0}$ over the grid domain, setting $\mathcal{U}_{p_0}(p_0) = 0$ and

$\mathcal{U}_{p_0}(p) = \infty$ for any other point p, only one grid pass is needed, and by using min-heap data structure, an $O(N\log(N))$ complexity can be ensured on a grid of N nodes for the computation of $\mathcal{U}_{p_0}$.

To summarize, we are able, by imposing the two end points, to build a 3D global minimum path for the geodesic energy. On the other hand, an active surface's goal is to locate a local minimum of energy (3) that agrees with some user's criteria. The problem is that during the evolution process the surface can be trapped by other local minima.

In our work we have used the global minimum property of the paths to generate an initial surface $\mathcal{S}_0$ from points and/or curves drawn by the user.

3   First Approximation of the Initial Surface $\mathcal{S}_0$

In order to determine a first approximation of $\mathcal{S}_0$ we propose to build a network of global minimal paths between a curve (henceforth noted $\mathcal{C}_1$) and a point (henceforth noted p) or other curves (henceforth noted $\mathcal{C}_2$, $\mathcal{C}_3$ and so on). Clearly, when building a minimal path network between $\mathcal{C}_1$ and p, one will compute only one action map (noted $\mathcal{U}_p$ as in previous section) centered in p and the network will be built by gradient descents from the points of a discretized version of $\mathcal{C}_1$. Which yields in this way a very numerically efficient algorithm. Figure 1.a and

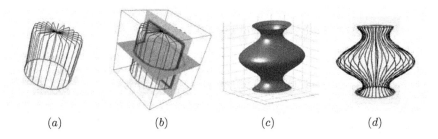

(a) (b) (c) (d)

Fig. 1. (a) Set of Minimal Paths between a point and a curve lying on a cylinder. (b) The paths are minimal with respect to a potential that takes small values on the boundaries of the cylinder.(c) is the original vase surface, (d) is the set of Minimal Paths between two curves lying on a synthetic image of this vase. The paths are minimal with respect to a potential that takes small values on the vase's boundaries.

1.b give an example of this construction. From a closed cylinder synthetic image, we generated minimal paths between a point in the upper part of the cylinder and a circle drawn on the opposite side.

When it comes to building a set of minimal paths between two curves, an extension of this approach has to be considered. In the general situation we do not want to associate all the points of $\mathcal{C}_1$ with all the points of $\mathcal{C}_2$, first because this would be too computationally expensive (at least N actions maps to build and $N \times N$ gradient descents, if N is the number of points of the discretized versions of $\mathcal{C}_1$ and $\mathcal{C}_2$), and second because we are only interested in the most relevant associations. This is why we introduced in [1] a way to compute the optimal path between a curve and a single point. In [1] we showed that this problem can also be solved by applying the Fast Marching algorithm to solve the equation $\|\nabla \mathcal{U}_{\mathcal{C}_1}\| = \mathcal{P}$ initializing $\mathcal{U}_{\mathcal{C}_1}$ by $\mathcal{U}_{\mathcal{C}_1}(q) = 0$ if $q \in \mathcal{C}_1$ and $\mathcal{U}_{\mathcal{C}_1}(q) = \infty$ otherwise. And the minimal path is obtained by a gradient descent initialized on p, just like in equation (6).

Consider now a discretized version of $\mathcal{C}_2$ containing n_2 points $\{q_i\}_{i=1...n_2}$. For each and every point q_i, we build the minimal path between this point and $\mathcal{C}_1$, thus generating a set of minimal paths from $\mathcal{C}_1$ to $\mathcal{C}_2$, $\left\{\mathcal{G}_i^{\mathcal{C}_1}\right\}_{i=1...n_2}$.

An illustration of this construction is given in figure 1.d, a potential adapted to finding the surface of a vase is used and the network is built between two curves drawn on it.

It is important to see that the construction of the network of paths is not symmetric. The set of paths $\left\{\mathcal{G}_i^{\mathcal{C}_1}\right\}_{i=1...n_2}$ is different from its homologue the set $\left\{\mathcal{G}_i^{\mathcal{C}_2}\right\}_{i=1...n_1}$. One can use this feature to generate a more dense set of paths and thus contributing to the generation of an interpolated surface $\mathcal{S}_0$.

In practice, this scheme produces well-behaved paths which provide enough information for the construction of an interpolated surface $\mathcal{S}_0$ (Figures 1.a, 1.c and 3.a). Unfortunately in some particular situations it is not the case. In fact, even though the number of paths can be controlled by the number of discretization points on each curve, in some images, this will not improve the information one can extract from the network because minimal paths tend to merge (see Figure 2.b). This not only further complicates the problem of interpolation but if a surface is generated it is usually not the surface expected.

In order to cope with this problem we propose a simple method to constrain the paths between $\mathcal{C}_1$ and $\mathcal{C}_2$ and thus produce a better distributed network around the surface we are looking for.

4   Constraining the Minimal Path

Figure 2 illustrates a simple situation where the set of paths described in the previous section is not distributed in a satisfactory manner. The potential is minimal and constant on a surface which is the blending of a plane and half a sphere. Minimal paths will cut around the sphere rather than 'climbing' on it because the potential has no influence (being constant on the surface) and the length of the paths becomes the predominant factor.

We propose a simple but effective method to obtain a network of paths that will be better distributed. We shall constrain the network to different planes.

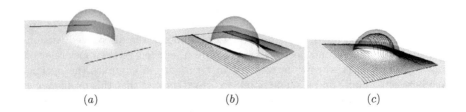

(a)   (b)   (c)

Fig. 2. (a) represents a half-sphere blended on a plane (transparent visualization) and $\mathcal{C}_1$ and $\mathcal{C}_2$ (black segments). b) Result without constraints:set of paths $\left\{ \mathcal{G}_i^{\mathcal{C}_1} \right\}_{i=1\ldots n_2}$ missing the half-sphere. c) Result with constrains.

First introduced in [1] this approach now relies on a sounder theoretical ground which is presented in more details in the appendix. Here we show why this restriction provides suitable paths for our purpose.

Indeed, in the appendix to this article (section 8) we have derived a local necessary condition a curve $\mathcal{C}$ traced on a surface $\mathcal{S}$ must satisfy in order to be a local minimum of energy (2). $\mathcal{C}$ must satisfy

$$\nabla P(\mathcal{C}).\boldsymbol{B} - P(\mathcal{C})\kappa(\boldsymbol{n}.\boldsymbol{B}) = 0, \tag{8}$$

where $\boldsymbol{B} = \boldsymbol{T} \wedge \boldsymbol{N}$, $\boldsymbol{N}$ is the Gauss map of $\mathcal{S}$, $\boldsymbol{T}$ is the tangent vector of $\mathcal{C}$, and n is the normal vector to the curve. Now, if the constraining surface $\mathcal{S}$ is a plane, the normal $\boldsymbol{n}$ to the curve is contained in this same plane. Therefore $\boldsymbol{T} \wedge \boldsymbol{N} = \boldsymbol{n}$ since by definition, $\boldsymbol{n}$ is normal to $\boldsymbol{T}$ and $\boldsymbol{N}$ is normal to both. Equation (8) boils down to

$$\nabla P(\mathcal{C}).\boldsymbol{n} - P(\mathcal{C})\kappa = 0,$$

which is exactly the Euler-Lagrange equation of the geodesic energy (2) in two dimensions.

In practice we geometrically restrict the back-propagation procedure that builds the minimal paths (equation 6), considering the construction of $\left\{ \mathcal{G}_i^{\mathcal{C}_1} \right\}_{i=1\ldots n_2}$, for a point p_i of the discretized version of $\in \mathcal{C}_2$ we choose a plane Π_{p_i} containing p_i and having $\overrightarrow{n_{p_i}}$ as its normal vector. We build path $\mathcal{G}_i^{\mathcal{C}_1}$ by solving the projected equation on Π_{p_i}:

$$\frac{d\mathcal{C}}{ds}(s) = -\nabla \mathcal{U}(\mathcal{C}) + \left(\nabla \mathcal{U}(\mathcal{C}). \overrightarrow{n_{p_i}} \right).\overrightarrow{n_{p_i}} . \tag{9}$$

Figure 2.c illustrates this construction, the network is obtained through the restriction of the paths to parallel planes which are orthogonal to $\mathcal{C}_1$ and $\mathcal{C}_2$ (n_{p_i} does not depend on p_i). In a more general case, for each point p_i, one can define plane Π_{p_i} by three points: G_1, center of mass of $\mathcal{C}_1$, G_2 center of mass of $\mathcal{C}_2$ and p_i, and thus

$$\overset{\square}{n}_{p_i} = \frac{\overset{\square}{G_1 G_2} \wedge \overset{\square}{G_1 p_i}}{\left\| \overset{\square}{G_1 G_2} \wedge \overset{\square}{G_1 p_i} \right\|}.$$

As the point p_i varies along C_2, the plane Π_{p_i} will "rotate" around the principal axis $G_1 G_2$.

5   Generating the Initialization Surface $\mathcal{S}_0$

The final step for the generation of $\mathcal{S}_0$ is its effective construction through the interpolation of the information given by the network of paths. We have chosen two different approaches to generate $\mathcal{S}_0$.

The first one assumes that we have enough information with only one of the unconstrained sets $\left\{ \mathcal{G}_i^{\mathcal{C}_j} \right\}_{i=1\dots n_j, j=1,2}$, which means that the paths will cross only if they merge and that the network is simple enough to use an analytical interpolation. In [1] we proposed an analytical method inspired by splines, that integrates information coming from both the network of paths and the curves C_1 and C_2, and produces a smooth mesh. An example of this construction is given in Figure 3.b, we have interpolated a network of paths obtained from an ultrasound image of the left ventricle. This first method produces a mesh representation,

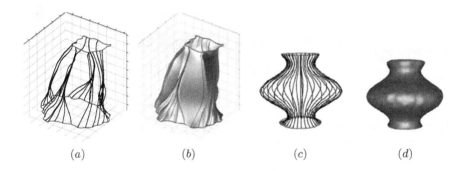

(a)   (b)   (c)   (d)

Fig. 3. (a) is the network of minimal paths obtained from an ultrasound image of the left ventricle. The user initialized the model by drawing the upper and lower closed curves. (b) is the analytically interpolated surface. (c) is the network obtained from our synthetic vase image, (d) it the variational scattered data points interpolation.

and is thus adapted to the use of active meshes. Nonetheless, if needed one can produce a Level set representation using the Fast Marching method initialized with the mesh and with a constant potential of value 1.

In spite of its great speed and good results, this method is only applicable under the conditions we stated. When considering the symmetrical network construction or when constraining the paths, the numerous crossings makes it very difficult to exploit the fact that we are interpolating curves and a scattered points approach is better suited.

The second interpolation method we have used is thus the one proposed by Zhao et al. in [15] where a variational approach is considered for the interpolation. Figure 3.d gives an example on the vase.

6   Application to Synthetic and Medical Images

It is a common practice in 3D medical images to perform, as a first step, 2D segmentation on a slice. When images are of very low quality the practitioner does the segmentation by hand. Our algorithm allows to rapidly build a good initialization and by so a 3D model. Figure 4 shows the result of the segmentation of a 3D ultra sound image of the left ventricle. As can be seen in Figure 4.b the restricted set of paths has already rebuilt perceptually the ventricle. Figure 4.c represents the interpolated surface with the variational method. We then applied a classical level set method evolution to refine the segmentation (Figure 4.d and 4.e).

In figure 5 we have given an other application of our method. We have considered the segmentation of a 3D magnetic resonance image representing an aneurysm.

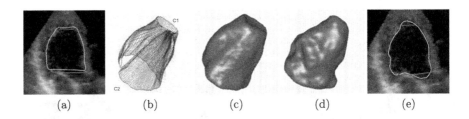

| (a) | (b) | (c) | (d) | (e) |

Fig. 4. (a) A slice of the 3D ultrasound image, we also have drawn the projection of the user given curves and the intersection of our interpolated surface with this plane. (b) Set of paths. (c) Interpolated surface. (d) final segmentation after a few iterations of the level set, (e) Planar view of the same slice, intersection with the model evolved as a level set.

In figure 6 we compare our method to a classical active surface. Figure 6.a is a difficult to segment image, it was generated from three 'S' shaped tubes placed one inside the other. The difficulty resides in the extraction of the middle one. Without a good initialization, a gradient descent will fail to recover the surface because of the presence of many local minima. Our method manages to generate a suitable initialization (figure 6.c) with the only information of two curves lying on it. An active surface, initialized with a cylinder containing the initialization curves (Figure 6.e and 6.f), will fail to recover the middle tube (Figure 6.g and 6.h).

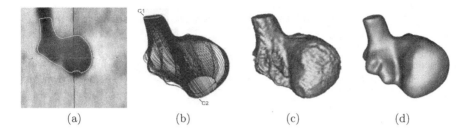

(a)   (b)   (c)   (d)

Fig. 5. (a) Intersection of our interpolated surface with a slice of a 3D MR image. (b) Set of paths. (c) Interpolated surface. (d) final segmentation after a few iterations of a level set.

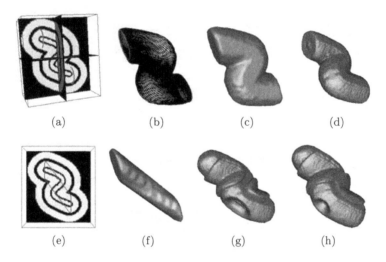

Fig. 6. (a) View of different intersecting planes of a 3D volume with the two constraining curves drawn on it. (b) Network of paths obtained with our method. (c) Interpolated surface. (d) Surface after few iterations of a level set. (e) and (f) Simple initialization of an active object. (g) surface after 150 iterations and (h) after 500 iterations.

7 Conclusion

In this paper we have presented a method that allows to greatly simplify the initialization process of active surfaces. The model can be initialized by simple objects like curves and points instead of volumes. Our approach is also capable of taking a maximum advantage of the information given by the user through the initialization curves, since the surface it generates is constrained to include those curves. Our method uses globally minimal paths to generate a surface which is the initialization of an active surface model. Hence, the final surface is not concerned by the problem of the local minima traps as all other active objects approach are. It is particularly well suited for medical image segmentation, in particular for ultrasound images segmentation. In cases where the image quality is very poor, our approach handles the introduction of additional information coming from the practitioner in a very natural manner. A few 2D segmentations can be enough to generate a coherent complete surface.

8   Appendix

In this appendix, inspired by the methods used in [4], we give a proof of the necessary condition a curve $\mathcal{C}$, traced on a surface $\mathcal{S}$, should satisfy in order to be a local minimum of the geodesic energy (3). We should note Ψ the signed distance function to $\mathcal{S}$, $\boldsymbol{T} = \frac{\mathcal{C}_t}{|\mathcal{C}_t|}$ the tangent vector along the curve, $\boldsymbol{N}(\alpha)$ the normal vector to $\mathcal{S}$ on α, $\boldsymbol{n}$ the normal vector to $\mathcal{C}$, and $\boldsymbol{B} = \boldsymbol{T} \wedge \boldsymbol{N}$ (figure 7).

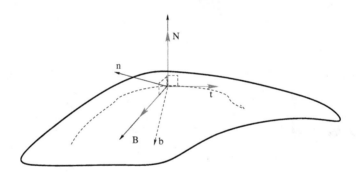

Fig. 7. Illustration showing the notation we use.

Let U_δ ($\delta \geq 0$) be a neighborhood of $\mathcal{S}$ defined by $U_\delta = \{\alpha|\Psi(\alpha) \leq \delta\}$. It can be shown that if δ is small enough, we have $\forall \alpha \in U_\delta$ $\nabla\Psi(\alpha) = \boldsymbol{N}(\alpha_\mathcal{S})$, where $\alpha_\mathcal{S}$ is the closest point to α on $\mathcal{S}$. And, since Ψ is the distance function to $\mathcal{S}$, we have that, in that case $\alpha_\mathcal{S} = \alpha - \Psi(\alpha)\nabla\Psi(\alpha)$. We then define the the operator $\Pi(\alpha) = \alpha - \Psi(\alpha)\nabla\Psi(\alpha)$ on U_δ, with δ small enough. Let $\mathcal{C}_\lambda$ be a variation of $\mathcal{C}$, $\mathcal{C}_\lambda = \mathcal{C} + \lambda\eta$, where η is a function which has the suitable regularity properties and boundary conditions, $\lambda \in \mathbb{R}$. This variation of $\mathcal{C}$ is not correct in our case, since $\mathcal{C}_\lambda$ is not necessarily traced on $\mathcal{S}$. Hence we will consider $\Pi(\mathcal{C}_\lambda) = \mathcal{C}_\lambda + \Psi(\mathcal{C}_\lambda)\nabla\Psi(\mathcal{C}_\lambda)$ instead and will be interested in the value of the derivative of

$$E(\lambda) = \int \mathcal{P}(\Pi(\mathcal{C}_\lambda)) \left| \Pi(\mathcal{C}_\lambda)_t \right| dt \text{ at } \lambda = 0, \tag{10}$$

$$\left. \frac{dE}{d\lambda} \right|_{\lambda=0} = \underbrace{\left. \int \frac{d}{d\lambda} \{\mathcal{P}(\Pi(\mathcal{C}_\lambda))\} \cdot \left| \Pi(\mathcal{C}_\lambda)_t \right| dt \right|_{\lambda=0}}_{I_1} + \underbrace{\left. \int \mathcal{P}(\Pi(\mathcal{C}_\lambda)) \cdot \frac{d}{d\lambda} \{|\Pi(\mathcal{C}_\lambda)_t|\} \, dt \right|_{\lambda=0}}_{I_2}$$

If curve $\mathcal{C}$ is a minimum of E this derivative should be zero.
Note that $\mathcal{C}$ being traced on $\mathcal{S}$, $\Psi(\mathcal{C}) = 0$ and $\nabla\Psi(\mathcal{C}).\mathcal{C}_t = N(\mathcal{C}).T(\mathcal{C}) = 0$. Thus

$$\begin{aligned}
\left. \frac{d}{d\lambda} \{\mathcal{P}(\Pi(\mathcal{C}_\lambda))\} \right|_{\lambda=0} &= \nabla\mathcal{P}(\mathcal{C}). \left(\eta - \nabla\Psi(\mathcal{C}).\eta\nabla\Psi(\mathcal{C}) - \underbrace{\Psi(\mathcal{C})(...)}_{=0} \right) \\
&= \left(\nabla\mathcal{P}(\mathcal{C}) - (N(\mathcal{C}).\nabla\mathcal{P}(\mathcal{C}))N(\mathcal{C}) \right).\eta
\end{aligned} \tag{11}$$

and

$$\Pi(\mathcal{C}_\lambda)_t|_{\lambda=0} = \mathcal{C}_t - \underbrace{(\nabla\Psi(\mathcal{C}).\mathcal{C}_t)}_{=0} \nabla\Psi(\mathcal{C}) - \underbrace{\Psi(\mathcal{C})(...)}_{=0} = \mathcal{C}_t \tag{12}$$

Using this relations we obtain:

$$I1 = \int \left(\nabla\mathcal{P}(\mathcal{C}) - (\nabla\Psi(\mathcal{C}).\nabla\mathcal{P}(\mathcal{C}))\nabla\Psi(\mathcal{C}).\eta \right) |\mathcal{C}_t| \, dt \tag{13}$$

Now concerning I_2, from (12) its second factor can be written as

$$\left. \frac{d}{d\lambda} \{|\Pi(\mathcal{C}_\lambda)_t|\} \right|_{\lambda=0} = \frac{\mathcal{C}_t}{|\mathcal{C}_t|} \cdot \left. \frac{d}{d\lambda} \{\Pi(\mathcal{C}_\lambda)_t\} \right|_{\lambda=0} = T. \left. \frac{d}{d\lambda} \{\Pi(\mathcal{C}_\lambda)_t\} \right|_{\lambda=0} \tag{14}$$

And

$$\left. \frac{d}{d\lambda} \{\Pi(\mathcal{C}_\lambda)_t\} \right|_{\lambda=0} = \frac{d}{dt} \left\{ \left. \frac{d}{d\lambda} \{\Pi(\mathcal{C}_\lambda)\} \right|_{\lambda=0} \right\} = \frac{d}{dt} \{\eta - (\nabla\Psi(\mathcal{C}).\eta)\nabla\Psi(\mathcal{C})\}$$

$$= \eta_t - \frac{d}{dt} \{(N(\mathcal{C}).\eta)\} N(\mathcal{C}) - (N(\mathcal{C}).\eta)H_\Psi(\mathcal{C})\mathcal{C}_t$$

H_Ψ being the Hessian of Ψ. And going back to 14, noticing that $N(\mathcal{C}).T = 0$,

$$T. \left. \frac{d}{d\lambda} \{\Pi(\mathcal{C}_\lambda)_t\} \right|_{\lambda=0} = T.\eta_t - (N(\mathcal{C}).\eta)(T.H_\Psi(\mathcal{C})\mathcal{C}_t)$$

following that

$$\begin{aligned}
I_2 &= \int \mathcal{P}(\mathcal{C})(T.\eta_t) \, dt - \int \mathcal{P}(\mathcal{C})(\nabla\Psi(\mathcal{C}).\eta)(T.H_\Psi(\mathcal{C})T) |\mathcal{C}_t| \, dt \\
&= -\int \left((\nabla\mathcal{P}.T)T + \mathcal{P}\kappa n + \mathcal{P}(T.H_\Psi(\mathcal{C})T)N(\mathcal{C}) \right) . \eta \, |\mathcal{C}_t| \, dt,
\end{aligned}$$

thanks to an integration by parts, and where κ is the curvature of $\mathcal{C}$. Combining I_1 and I_2 we get

$$\left. \frac{dE}{d\lambda} \right|_{\lambda=0} = \int \left(\nabla\mathcal{P} - (N.\nabla\mathcal{P})N - (\nabla\mathcal{P}.T)T - \mathcal{P}(\kappa n + (T.H_\Psi(\mathcal{C})T)N) \right) . \eta \, |\mathcal{C}_t| \, dt.$$

Finally, taking the following relations into account

$$\nabla \mathcal{P} - (\mathbf{N}.\nabla \mathcal{P})\mathbf{N} - (\nabla \mathcal{P}.\mathbf{T})\mathbf{T} = (\nabla \mathcal{P}.\mathbf{B})\mathbf{B},$$
$$\kappa \mathbf{n} + (\mathbf{T}.H_\Psi(\mathcal{C})\mathbf{T})\mathbf{N} = \kappa \mathbf{n} - (\mathbf{n}.\nabla \Psi)\kappa \mathbf{N} = \kappa(\mathbf{n} - (\mathbf{n}.\mathbf{N})\mathbf{N}) = (\mathbf{n}.\mathbf{B})\kappa \mathbf{B}$$

we get

$$\left.\frac{dE}{d\lambda}\right|_{\lambda=0} = \int \left((\nabla \mathcal{P} - \mathcal{P}\kappa \mathbf{n}) . \mathbf{B}\right)(\mathbf{B}. \eta)|\mathcal{C}_t| \, dt$$

Since this integral is equal to zero for every function η, we get that for every t of the parameterization domain of $\mathcal{C}$

$$\nabla \mathcal{P}(\mathcal{C}).\mathbf{B}(\mathcal{C}) - \mathcal{P}(\mathcal{C})\kappa(\mathbf{n}.\mathbf{B}) = 0$$

References

[1] R. Ardon and L.D. Cohen. Fast Constrained surface extracion by minimal paths. *2nd IEEE Workshop on Variational, Geometric and Level Set Methods in Computer Vision*, pages 233–244, October 2003.

[2] V. Caselles, R. Kimmel, and G. Sapiro. Geodesic active contours. *International Journal of Computer Vision*, 22(1):61–79, 1997.

[3] V. Caselles, R. Kimmel, G. Sapiro, and C. Sbert. Minimal-surfaces based object segmentation. *IEEE Transactions On Pattern Analysis and Machine Intelligence*, 19(4):394–398, April 1997.

[4] Li-Tien Cheng. *The Level Set Method Applied to Geometrically Based Motion, Materials Science, and Image Processing*. PhD thesis, University of California, Los Angeles, 2000.

[5] L.D. Cohen. On active contour models and balloons. *Computer Vision, Graphics, and Image Processing: Image Understanding*, 53(2):211–218, 1991.

[6] L.D. Cohen and R. Kimmel. Global minimum for active contour models: A minimal path approach. *International Journal of Computer Vision*, 24(1):57–78, August 1997.

[7] M. Kass, A. Witkin, and D. Terzopoulos. Snakes: Active contour models. *International Journal of Computer Vision*, 1(4):321–331, 1988.

[8] R. Kimmel and J.A. Sethian. Optimal algorithm for shape from shading and path planning. *Journal of Mathematical Imaging and Vision*, 14(3):237–244, 2001.

[9] R. Malladi, J.A. Sethian, and B.C. Vemuri. Shape modelling with front propagation: A level set approach. *IEEE Transactions On Pattern Analysis and Machine Intelligence*, 17(2):158–175, February 1995.

[10] S. Osher and J.A. Sethian. Fronts propagating with curvature dependent speed: algorithms based on the hamilton-jacobi formulation. *Journal of Computational Physics*, 79:12–49, 1988.

[11] N. Paragios and R. Deriche. A pde-based level-set approach for detection and tracking of moving objects. Technical Report 3173, ROBOTVIS Project, INRIA Sophia-Antipolis, May 1997.

[12] J.A. Sethian. A fast marching level set method for monotonically advancing fronts. *Proceedings of the Natural Academy of Sciences*, 93(4):1591–1595, February 1996.

[13] J.A. Sethian. *Level set methods: Evolving Interfaces in Geometry, Fluid Mechanics, Computer Vision and Materials Sciences*. Cambridge University Press, University of California, Berkeley, 2nd edition, 1999.

[14] J. N. Tsitsiklis. Efficient algorithms for globally optimal trajectories. *IEEE Transactions on Automatic Control*, 40(9):1528–1538, Septembe 1995.

[15] H. Zhao, S. Osher, and R. Fedkiw. Fast surface reconstruction using the level set method. *Worksohp on Variational and Level Set Methods In Computer Vision*, pages 194–201, July 2001.

An Information Fusion Method for the Automatic Delineation of the Bone-Soft Tissues Interface in Ultrasound Images

Vincent Daanen[1] Ph.D, Jerome Tonetti[2] M.D, Ph.D, and Jocelyne Troccaz[1]Ph.D

[1] Joseph Fourier University,
TIMC Laboratory, GMCAO Department
Institut d'Ingénierie de l'Information de Santé (IN3S)
Faculty of Medecine - 38706 La Tronche cedex - France
[2] University Hospital
Orthopaedic Surgery Department
CHU A Michallon, BP217
38043 Grenoble

Abstract. We present a new method for delineating the osseous interface in ultrasound images. Automatic segmentation of the bone-soft tissues interface is achieved by mimicking the reasoning of the expert in charge of the manual segmentation. Information are modeled and fused by the use of fuzzy logic and the accurate delineation is then performed by using general a priori knowledge about osseous interface and ultrasound imaging physics. Results of the automatic segmentation are compared with the manual segmentation of an expert.

1 Introduction

In computer-aided orthopedic surgery (CAOS), the knowledge of the bone volume position and geometry in the operative room is essential. The usual way to acquire it is to register pre-operative data, which were accurately acquired, to intra-operative data. A recent way for acquire intra-operative data consists in the use of ultrasound imaging as intra-operative imaging [1, 2, 3] because this imaging modality is inexpensive, riskless and using a 6D localized ultrasound probe makes it possible to reconstruct the 3D shape of a structure after its delineation. The accurate delineation of structures in ultrasound images is still a very difficult task because of their very poor quality, i.e. low contrast, low signal-to-noise ration and speckle noise. Therefore, extraction of features can be :

- manual but manual segmentation is known to be operator-dependent and ultrasound images segmentation is difficult. This gives rise to uncertainty and inaccuracy of the segmentation and errors may reflect on registration results.
- semi-automatic : several methods based on the successive use of usual image processing methods such as contrast-enhancement, smoothing, edge-detection, morphological operations [4, 5] have been proposed but such methods often fail because of the poor quality of ultrasound images and therefore an user-interaction is required either to initialize the process or make the final choice.

M. Šonka et al. (Eds.): CVAMIA-MMBIA 2004, LNCS 3117, pp. 218–229, 2004.
© Springer-Verlag Berlin Heidelberg 2004

- automatic: automatic methods are either based on active contours for the delineation of endocardial and epicardial boundaries of the heart ([6, 7]) or bone segmentation ([8, 9]) ; or are based on the multimodal registration of ultrasound datasets within more discriminant modalities such as CT [10] or MRI [11]. Compared with bone segmentation in ultrasound images,[2, 3, 12] belong to this last category of method. Moreover, in regards to orthopaedic CAS, the methods proposed in the literature are specific to a part of the human body : vertebrae [3], pelvis [12].

We propose a fully automated method designed for the delineation of the bone-soft tissues interface in ultrasound images based on information fusion. Data available in images are modeled and fused relatively to knowledge about the physics of ultrasound imaging. Expert's reasoning process is then mimicked in order to accurately delineate the osseous interface.

2   Material

Ultrasound imaging is achieved using a linear US probe, 25 mm large, working at a frequency of 7.5 MHz. The probe is localized in 3D space by an optical localizer. The US probe is calibrated according to the technique described in [13] (the pixel size is about 0.1mm/pixel). The position of an image pixel is known in 3D space with a precision in the range of the optical localizer (i.e. 1mm) (see [14] for details on the reconstruction of 3D shape from localized ultrasound images). Image size is 640×480 pixels and a subimage (214×422) is extracted before processing.

3   Method

In this section, we introduce the expert's reasoning and the way we mimic it in order to achieve the segmentation of the osseous interface.

3.1   Expert's Reasoning

Several information, based on the physics of the ultrasound imaging and on anatomy, can be used to delineate the osseous interface in ultrasound images :

1. bones appear to be hyper-echoic,
   the amplitudes of the US echoes are proportional to the difference between acoustical impedances caused by successive tissue layers and in the case of bone imaging, the great difference of acoustical impedance between bones ($Z_{bone} \approx [3.65 - 7.09] \times 10^6$ kg/m^2/s) and the surrounding soft tissues ($Z_{soft\,tissues} \approx 1.63 \times 10^6$ kg/m^2/s) generates an important echo.
2. bones are said to 'stop' ultrasound waves,
   this is due to the high absorption rate of bones which is about 10 dB/cm/MHz whereas the absorption rate for soft tissues is less than 2 dB/cm/MHz.
3. the reflection is almost completely specular,
   only interfaces perpendicular to the direction of the ultrasound beam will reflect so features of interest appear to be composed of horizontal (or near horizontal) parts.

4. bone surfaces do not present major discontinuities
   and therefore the found osseous interface should be as smooth as possible.
5. among an osseous interface, the contrast appears to be homogeneous.

The proposed method achieves the fusion of these information in 3 stages :

- first, an image processing step aims at modeling the information available in the images and then concentrate them into one image representing the membership of the pixel to a given property. This step models and fuses points 1,2 and 3 cited above.
- Then the computation of the continuousness cost function which purpose is to extract continuous osseous interfaces from the fuzzy image.
- Finally, we compute the optimal osseous interface from the candidates found at the previous step by choosing the one that ensures an osseous interface among which the contrast is maximum and homogeneous.

3.2   Image Processing Step

The image processing aims, in a first step, at modeling the information available in the image. Then the data fusion step concentrates the information in order to produce an image whom the value of a pixel represents the membership of the pixel to a property.

Fuzzy Intensity Image This stage attempts to model the first information listed above : bones appear to be hyper-echoic i.e. *bright* pixels constitute an indication of the location of the osseous interface, but is not an absolute criteria and consequently, the fuzzification function have to give an important (resp. low) membership value to *bright* (resp. *dark*) pixels.

In a previous development [15], we pointed out that binarizing the initial ultrasound image using the Otsu's threshold (T_{Otsu}) gives a good approximation of the echogenic area and so, of the position of the osseous interface.

We make use of this information to build the fuzzification function μ_{Int} : the criterion (we call V_{Otsu} : Fig.1-b, *solid curve*), needed to compute T_{Otsu}, is used as follows : first, V_{Otsu} is normalized and cumulated (Fig.1-b, *dotted curve*) and it is then shifted in order to force the membership function value : $\mu_{Int}(T_{Otsu}) = 0.5$.

Processing this way, the fuzzification function (Fig.1-b, *dashed curve*) is closed to the well-known S-function [16]. Finally, we apply the described fuzzification function over the gray-level image in order to construct the fuzzy intensity image[1] $FII(p)$ (Fig 1-c) which gives for a pixel p of the intensity image its membership degree to the echogenic area.

Fuzzy Gradient Image The transition from soft tissues to bone suggests to search for highly contrasted areas and so the fuzzy gradient image $FGI(p)$ is of great interest.

The computation of the gradient image is a way to model informations 2 and 3 because it allows us :

---

[1]Illustrating images have been cropped to half their length since the other half is a dark area and brings no information (the whole image is processed)

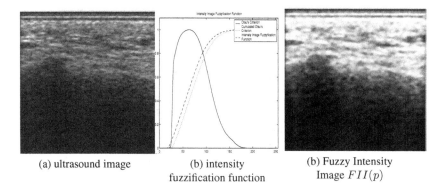

| (a) ultrasound image | (b) intensity fuzzification function | (b) Fuzzy Intensity Image $FII(p)$ |

Fig. 1. Computation of Fuzzy Intensity Image (FII) from the original ultrasound image

- to detect features which have a particular direction by using a directional edge detector,

- and to get an information about the gray-level transition.

We use a 5x5 'horizontal-direction' MDIF edge detector which is first-order derivative filter obtained by the convolution of the 4-connexity 3×3 mean lowpass filter with the Prewitt's derivative kernels. It allows us to select areas presenting horizontal (or near) contrast. Thresholding this image allows us to keep only areas where the transition occurs from bright-to-dark pixels (Fig. 2-a).

Finally, we use the S-shape function to perform the *fuzzification* of the gradient image and obtain the *Fuzzy Image Gradient* $FGI(p)$ (Fig. 2-b). The parameters of the S-shape function are computed such that $S(x)$ is the closest s-shape function to the normalized cumulative histogram.

Data Fusion The data fusion step aims at concentrating all the information in order to produce a single membership value for each pixel of the analyzed image to the osseous interface. For our purpose, a pixel may belong to the osseous interface if both its gray-level and gradient are 'high'. This combination is naturally achieved by a 'conjunctive-type' combination operator *min* ; therefore the membership of a pixel to the osseous interface is given by :

$$FI(p) = min(FII(p), FGI(p)) \qquad (1)$$

$FI(p)$ denotes the global degree of membership of a pixel to an echogenic and highly contrasted area.

3.3   Determination of the Osseous Interface

According to the expert's reasoning, the optimal threshold described a continuous interface where the local contrast is maximum and homogeneous. For each membership

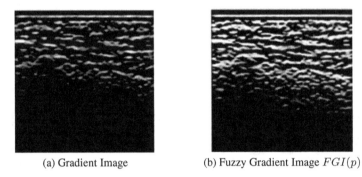

(a) Gradient Image   (b) Fuzzy Gradient Image $FGI(p)$

Fig. 2. Gradient image and Fuzzy Gradient Image of the ultrasound image shown in Fig 1-a

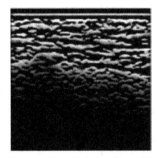

Fig. 3. Fusion Image

degree $0 < \mu < 1$ (μ space is discretized with a step $\delta_\mu = 0.005$), the defuzzification of $FI(p)$ is performed and the continuousness of the profile is evaluated. We then choose the membership degree which maximizes the local contrast and its homogeneity, and also ensures a local maximum continuity of the profile.

In this section, we present the defuzzification process which aims at extracting from the fuzzy image $FI(p)$ the osseous interface related to a membership degree μ_{ref}. We then explain the way we measure the continuity of a given osseous interface and finally we explain the way we compute an objective function which will allows us to determine the optimal membership.

Defuzzification Process To achieve this task, we make use of a priori knowledge about the physics of ultrasound imaging : as mentioned earlier, ultrasound imaging enhances the difference between acoustical impedances and because of the great difference of the acoustic impedances of the bone and its surrounding soft tissues, almost the entire ultrasound wave is reflected at the surface of the bone so that no imaging is possible beyond it. Dealing with that in image processing, this means that, for a column of the image, the pixel of the osseous interface related to a membership value μ_{ref} is the last (from the top) pixel which has a membership equal or greater to μ_{ref}. At the end of this *defuzzification* process, at the most one pixel by column is highlighted. The 'curve' described by these pixels is called *profile* in the rest of the paper.

Evaluation of the Continuousness of the Profile As we mentioned earlier, actual osseous interfaces do not present discontinuities and therefore, the osseous interface we detect should be as smooth as possible. We use this property to determine the optimal defuzzification threshold by computing a function that reflects the continuousness of a computed osseous interface.

The measure of the continuousness of a profile is achieved by applying the wavelet transform to it : the wavelet transform decomposes the profile with a multiresolution scale factor of two providing one low-resolution approximation (A_1) and one wavelet detail (D_1). We then apply the wavelet transform to A_1 and get a second order low-resolution approximation (A_2) and wavelet detail (D_2). The *Detail* signals are then used to quantify the discontinuities of the original profile. Experimentally, we choose the Daubechies-4 wavelet basis (several others basis have been tested and no dependence was pointed out at the exception of the Haar Basis). The wavelet decomposition of the profile is performed twice. To reject small interfaces (4/5 pixels) detected when the membership value used for the defuzzification is unsuitable (i.e. when it is too high), we add a penalization term related to the length of the profile (Pen). The 'amount' of discontinuities in the profile is computed as follows :

$$\varepsilon(\mu) = E(D_1) + E(D_2) + Pen \tag{2}$$

where $E(s)$ represents the energy of a signal $s(t)$ and is computed by :

$$E(s(t)) = \frac{1}{n} \sum_{i=0}^{n} s(t)^2 \tag{3}$$

Finally, $\varepsilon(\mu)$ is normalized (i.e. $\varepsilon(\mu)$ is linearly scaled from $[\varepsilon_{min} - \varepsilon_{max}]$ to $[0\text{-}1]$) and we compute the continuousness of the profile as :

$$C(\mu) = 1 - \varepsilon(\mu) \tag{4}$$

As one can see (Fig.4-a), the continuousness function $C(\mu)$ presents several local maxima. Each of them locates a membership degree μ where the associated profile is more continuous than the profiles of its neighbors and so each of them may be the optimal defuzzification threshold. We detect them by computing the watershed transform of $C(\mu)$. For each local maxima, the image is defuzzed to the corresponding membership degree μ and the local contrast is computed.

Local Contrast Computation For each pixel p belonging to a profile (i.e. the pixel p is highlighted after the defuzzification process related to a given μ), the local contrast

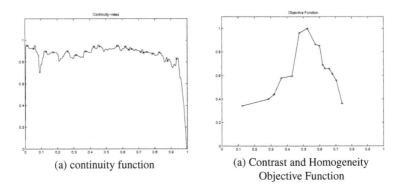

(a) continuity function

(a) Contrast and Homogeneity Objective Function

Fig. 4. Objective Functions

$LC(p)$ is computed between the above and the underneath areas of 10 pixels long. The local contrast associated to the pixel p is computed by :

$$LC(p) = \frac{\overline{Up} - \overline{Down}}{\overline{Up} + \overline{Down}} \tag{5}$$

where $\overline{Up}$ (resp. $\overline{Down}$) is the mean value of the above (resp. underneath) area. This definition of the local contrast gives us a way to determine whenever the pixel p is in the vicinity of the osseous interface because the bone appears in the image as a 'light' area followed by a 'dark' area i.e. a positive local contrast. We then obtain a cost function $Contrast(\mu)$ related to the global contrast along the profile and defined by :

$$Contrast(\mu) = \sum_p LC(p) \tag{6}$$

Because the contrast along the profile is homogeneous, we also compute a measure of the homogeneity of the contrast along the profile. This is achieved by computing the standard deviation of the values of the contrast along the profile (this criterion was used as homogeneity measure by [17]) and gives us a function $StdDev(\mu)$

Optimal Defuzzification Threshold Determination The optimal membership degree $\mu_{Optimal}$ is chosen so that it maximized $Cost(\mu)$ (Fig.4-b) defined by :

$$Cost(\mu) = Contrast(\mu) + \frac{1}{StdDev(\mu)} \tag{7}$$

4   Results

The method was originally designed for sacral osseous interface delineation. Because the method tries to reproduce the expert's reasoning and because the a priori information we make use are not specific to a part of the human body, the method appears to be usable on ultrasound images of different bones which are in relationship with various current research projects in CAOS. This section first presents the results of sacral images segmentation and then shows some results of vertebrae images segmentation.

4.1 Sacral Images Segmentation

The proposed method has been tested on ultrasound images of sacrum coming from cadaver datasets or patient datasets : about 250 images have been processed. For each image, the manual segmentation of the expert is available and constitutes our bronze-standard.

For each image within a dataset, we compute the differences between the manual segmentation and the segmentation computed by our method per image column. We then compute the mean error for each image (Table 1-column 1) and the Hausdorff distance and mean absolute distance (average of all the maximum errors within a subset) (Table 1-column 2). In order to evaluate the ability of the proposed method to delineate the osseous interface in strongly corrupted images, we also compute the Signal-to-MSE ratio (Table 1-column 3), which corresponds to the classical Signal-To-Noise ratio computed in the case of additive noise, and is defined as [18] :

$$S/mse = 10 * log_{10}\left(\frac{\sum_{i=1}^{K} S_i^2}{\sum_{i=1}^{K} (\widehat{S}_i - S_i)^2}\right) \tag{8}$$

where

S is the original image
$\widehat{S}$ represents the denoised image
and K is the number of pixels (i.e. 90308 for a 214×422 image).

$\widehat{S}$ is obtained by filtering S with a 5x5 median filter. As one can easily see from Equ. 8, the less S/mse ratio, the noisier the image.

Dataset	Segmentation Error mean/SD (pixel)	Max Errors mean/max (pixel)	S/mse mean/SD (dB)
Patient 1 (51 images)	7.808 / 1.995	12.137 / 22	5.052 / 0.185
Patient 2 (49 images)	8.807 / 3.177	16.905 / 25	5.206 / 0.428
Patient 3 (69 images)	4.545 / 3.874	17.0789 / 35	8.905 / 0.283
Cadaver 1 (37 images)	3.495 / 1.931	9.830 / 36	8.786 / 0.340
Cadaver 2 (41 images)	2.679 / 1.456	7.294 / 19	9.019 / 0.259
Cadaver 3 (39 images)	4.056 / 3.213	12.14 / 38	7.984 / 0.177

pixel size is 0.112mm × 0.109mm

Table 1. Segmentation errors

As one can see (table 1), as compared to the manual delineation of the expert :

• the mean error of segmentation is always less than 10 pixels (i.e. 1mm) even on highly corrupted images. However, it is clear that the accuracy of the delineation is correlated within the amount of noise and therefore, we think that taking into account the noise (measured by the S/sme ratio by example) during the fusion and/or delineation process may be a way to improve the delineation. This could be done by weighting the *Fuzzy Intensity Image* values by a factor depending on the noise (as described in [19]).

• The maximum error still remains substantial but, according to us, it is not the error we should focus on : we point out that these errors occur at more or less one pixel on complex shapes (such as medial sacral crest or sacral hiatus) giving thus an important maximum error relatively to the manual delineation but the overall error on the global shape still remains negligible and has very limited impact on the registration step which follows.

• The proposed method is also sufficiently fast to be used during the intra-operative stage of a CAOS : the time needed to delineate one image is less than 4 s. The processing of large datasets such as *Patient 3* takes about 4 minutes (on a standard PC, Pentium III-800Mhz) whereas it took more than 30 minutes in the case of a manual delineation (according to [20]).

4.2   Spine Image Segmentation

42 images of the L4-vertebra were acquired on a healthy volunteer and processed. In order to see a large part of the spinous process, we use a linear US-probe of 80 mm large working at a frequency of 7.5 MHz. The image size is 768×576 pixels and a subimage (346×467) is extracted before processing and one image is processed in less than 6 s.

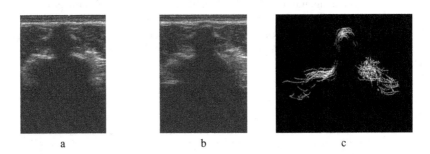

a   b   c

Fig. 5. vertebra image segmentation

One can clearly recognize the spinous process on Fig. 5-a and Fig.5-b. The overall shape of the vertebra is also clearly visible on Fig. 5-c which is a 3D point cloud computed from the delineation of the vertebra surface in the ultrasound images.

5   Discussion

Recently, lots of methods dedicated to the *indirect* delineation of the bone surface in ultrasound images have been proposed in the literature [3, 12, 21] but these methods have not been tested on real patients' datasets yet. Moveover, the ultrasound imaging is constrained by the use of a mechanical system [3, 21] ; and a good initial estimation of the rigid registration matrix between the CT and US datasets is often required to achieve the bone surface segmentation in the ultrasound images [2, 12].

The method described in this paper does not require neither a dedicated ultrasound images acquisition system nor an estimation of the rigid registration matrix between the CT and US datasets to perform the delineation of the osseous interface in ultrasound images. Moreover, it has been extensively tested on images acquired on cadavers (about 120 images) and on real patients (about 170 images).

Although the method is sensible to noise, the mean errors are still acceptable : we measure a maximum mean error of 8.8 pixels (i.e. 0.8 mm) with a S/mse ratio of 5.206 dB which corresponds to a highly corrupted image (according to [18]).

We think that an important point have also to be made clear : the validation, based on the comparison to a single expert segmentation, may appear limited. However, segmenting bones on ultrasound images is very unusual for physicians and it is difficult to find several expert users. Moreover, gold-standard does not exist and tests on phantoms or isolated bones would not allow to draw conclusion and we then consider that this evaluation is just a first step.

Finally, we did not notice any dependence of the accuracy to the visualization parameters tuning, i.e. the different gains (proximal, distal) the physician can play with to enhance the contrast of the image on the ultrasound scanner. The only condition is that the osseous interface should not get bogged down in noise and according to us, it is an acceptable condition since the physician has to validate the images during the acquisition stage and this validation can only be done if he is able to localize approximatively the osseous interface.

6   Conclusion

In this paper, we present a method for automatic delineation of the osseous interface in ultrasound image. The method is based on the fusion of the pixels intensity and gradient properties in a first step and then on the fusion of information extracted from the physics of ultrasound imaging and a priori knowledge.

Tests were performed with images coming from patients or cadaver studies. The method has been used to delineate osseous interface in ultrasound images of the sacrum which may present several shapes ; we also use it to delineate the osseous interface in vertebrae images and good results were obtained in all cases so that it's independent of the shape to be recovered and that's why we think that the described method is a first step toward robust delineation of the osseous interface in ultrasound images.

References

[1] J. Tonetti, L. Carrat, S. Blendea, Ph. Merloz, J. Troccaz, S. Lavallée, and JP Chirossel. Clinical Results of Percutaneous Pelvic Surgery. Computer Assisted Surgery using Ultrasound Compared to Standard Fluoroscopy. *Computer Aided Surgery*, 6(4):204–211, 2001.

[2] G. Ionescu, S.Lavallée, and J. Demongeot. Automated Registration of Ultrasound with CT Images : Application to Computer Assisted Prostate Radiotherapy and Orthopedics. In *CS Serie, Springer Verlag, MICCAI*, volume 1679, pages 768–777, 1999.

[3] B. Brendel, S. Winter, A. Rick, M. Stockheim, and H. Ermert. Registration of 3D CT and Ultrasound Datasets of the Spine using Bone Structures. *Computer Aided Surgery*, 7(3):146–155, 2002.

[4] A. Krivanek and M. Sonka. Ovarian Ultrasound Image Analysis : Follicle Segmentation. *IEEE Transactions on Medical Imaging*, 17(6):935–944, 1998.

[5] SD. Pathak, DR. Haynor, and Y. Kim. Edge-Guided Boundary Delineation in Prostate Ultrasound Images. *IEEE Transactions on Medical Imaging*, 19(12):1211–1219, 2000.

[6] I. Mikic, S. Krucinski, and JD. Thomas. Segmentation and Tracking in Echocardiographic Sequences : Active Contours Guided by Optical Flow Estimates. *IEEE Transactions on Medical Imaging*, 17(2):274 –284, 1998.

[7] JG. Bosch, SC. Mitchell, BPF. Lelieveldt, F. Nijland, O. Kamp, M. Sonka, and JHC. Reiber. Automatic Segmentation of Echocardiographic Sequences by Active Appearance Motion Models. *IEEE Transactions on Medical Imaging*, 21(11):1374–1383, 2002.

[8] F. Lefebvre, G. Berger, and P. Laugier. Automatic Detection of the Boundary of the Calcaneus from Ultrasound Parametric Images using an Active Contour Model ; Clinical Assessment. *IEEE Transactions on Medical Imaging*, 17(1):45–52, 1998.

[9] P. He and J. Zheng. Segmentation of Tibia Bone in Ultrasound Images using Active Shape Models. In *Proceedings of the 23rd Annual International Conference of the IEEE Engineering in Medicine and Biology Society*, 2001.

[10] BH Sollie. Automatic Segmentation and Registration of CT and US images of Abdominal Aortic Aneurysm using ITK. Master's thesis, Norwegian University of Science and Technology. Faculty of Information Technology, Mathematics and Electrical Engineering, 2002.

[11] A. Roche, X. Pennec, G. Malandain, and N. Ayache. Rigid Registration of 3-D Uultrasound with MR Images : a New Approach Combining Intensity and Gradient Information. *IEEE Transactions on Medical Imaging*, 20(10):1038–1049, 2001.

[12] D.V. Amin, T Kanade, A.M. DiGioia III, and B. Jaramaz. Ultrasound Registration of the Bone Surface for Surgical Navigation. *Computer Aided Surgery*, (8):1–16, 2003.

[13] T. Langø. *Ultrasound Guided Surgery : Image Processing and Navigation*. PhD thesis, Norwegian University of Science and Technology, Trondheim, Norway, 2000.

[14] C. Barbe, J. Troccaz, B. Mazier, and S. Lavallée. Using 2.5D Echography in Computer Assisted Spine Surgery. In *Proceedings of the 15th Annual International Conference of the IEEE Engineering in Medicine and Biology Society*, pages 160–161, 1993.

[15] V.Daanen, J.Tonetti, J. Troccaz, and Ph. Merloz. Automatic Determination of the Bone-Soft Tissues Interface in Ultrasound Images. First Results in Iliosacral Screwing Surgery. In *Proceedings of Surgetica-CAMI 2002*, pages 144–151, 2002.

[16] Z.Chi, H.Yan, and T.D. Pham. *Fuzzy Algorithms : with Applications to Image Processing and Pattern Recognition*, volume 10 of *Advances in Fuzzy Systems - Applications and Theory*, section 2. World Scientific, 1996.

[17] M. Garza, P. Meer, and V. Medina. Robust Retrieval of 3D Structures from Image Stacks. *Medical Image Analysis*, 3(1):21–35, 1999.

[18] A. Achim, A. Bezerianos, and P. Tsakalides. Novel Bayesian Multiscale Method for Speckle Removal in Medical Ultrasound Images. *IEEE Transactions on Medical Imaging*, 20(8):772–783, 2001.

[19] S.Vial, D. Gibon, C. Vasseur, and J. Rousseau. Volume Delineation by Fusion of Fuzzy Sets Obtained from Multiplanar Tomographic Images. *IEEE Transactions on Medical Imaging*, 20(12):1362–1372, 2001.

[20] L. Carrat, J.Tonetti, S. Lavallée, Ph. Merloz, L. Pittet, and JP. Chirosset. Treatment of Pelvic Ring Fractures : Percutaneous Computer Assisted Iliosacral Screwing. In *CS Serie, Springer Verlag, MICCAI*, volume 1496, pages 84–91, 1998.

[21] O. Schorr and H. Wörn. A New Concept for Intraoperative Matching of 3D Ultrasound and CT. In *Proceedings of MMVR : Medecine Meets Virtual Reality*, pages 446–452, 2001.

Multi-label Image Segmentation for Medical Applications Based on Graph-Theoretic Electrical Potentials

Leo Grady* and Gareth Funka-Lea

Siemens Corporate Research — Department of Imaging and Visualization
Leo.Grady@scr.siemens.com

Abstract. A novel method is proposed for performing multi-label, semi-automated image segmentation. Given a small number of pixels with user-defined labels, one can analytically (and quickly) determine the probability that a random walker starting at each unlabeled pixel will first reach one of the pre-labeled pixels. By assigning each pixel to the label for which the greatest probability is calculated, a high-quality image segmentation may be obtained. Theoretical properties of this algorithm are developed along with the corresponding connections to discrete potential theory and electrical circuits. This algorithm is formulated in discrete space (i.e., on a graph) using combinatorial analogues of standard operators and principles from continuous potential theory, allowing it to be applied in arbitrary dimension.

1 Introduction

One of the greatest challenges of automated medical image analysis is how to best take advantage of input from the technician or medical practitioner who will be performing the analysis. The current state-of-the-art is such that few automated image analysis techniques can be applied fully autonomously with reliable results. Consequently a person must evaluate the results of any automated process. In general, this person is currently performing the analysis manually. The goal of the automation is to shorten the time and improve the reliability of the analysis.

Frequently a medical image acquisition device is used for multiple medical indications and studies. In this case the goal of image analysis varies with the patient symptoms and history. For example, a cardiac image admits several "correct" segmentations depending on the nature of the region of interest: the entire heart or a specific ventricle or atria. The knowledge of the goal for the analysis is entirely with the user but by specifying the number of segments and by providing small samples of each segment the goal of the segmentation can be better defined for an automated approach.

---

* Leo Grady is with Siemens Corporate Research, Department of Imaging and Visualization, 755 College Road East, Princeton, NJ 08540.

M. Šonka et al. (Eds.): CVAMIA-MMBIA 2004, LNCS 3117, pp. 230–245, 2004.

In this paper we propose a novel algorithm to perform semi-automated image segmentation, given medical practitioner or computer pre-specified **labels**. Assume that the medical practitioner has provided K labeled voxels (hereafter referred to as **seed points** or **seeds**). For each unlabeled pixel, we could now ask: Given a random walker starting at this location, what is the probability that it first reaches each of the K seed points? It will be shown that this calculation may be performed exactly without the simulation of a random walk. By performing this calculation, we assign a K-tuple vector to each pixel that specifies the probability that a random walker starting from each unlabeled pixel will first reach each of the K seed points. A final segmentation may be derived from these K-tuples by selecting for each pixel the most probable seed destination for a random walker. In a uniform image (e.g., all black), a segmentation will be obtained that roughly corresponds to Voronoi cells for each set of seed points. We term this segmentation the **neutral** segmentation since it does not take into account any information from the image. By biasing the random walker to avoid crossing sharp intensity gradients, a quality segmentation is obtained that respects object boundaries (including weak boundaries). Analytical properties of the algorithm are listed at the end of the introduction.

In our approach, we treat an image (or volume) as a purely discrete object — a graph with a fixed number of vertices and edges. Each edge is assigned a real-valued weight corresponding to the likelihood that a random walker will cross that edge (e.g., a weight of zero means that the walker may not move along that edge). Formulation of the algorithm on a graph allows the application of the algorithm to surface meshes or space-variant images [1, 2]. Regardless of the dimensions of the data, we will use the term *pixel* throughout this paper to refer to the basic picture element in the context of its intensity values. In contrast, the term *node* will be used in the context of a graph-theoretical discussion.

It has been established [3, 4] that the probability a random walker first reaches a seed point exactly equals the solution to the Dirichlet problem [5] with boundary conditions at the locations of the seed points and the seed point in question fixed to unity, while the others are set to zero. The solution to the discrete Dirichlet problem on an arbitrary graph is given exactly by the distribution of electric potentials on the nodes of an electrical circuit with resistors representing the inverse of the weights (i.e., the weights represent conductance) and the "boundary conditions" given by voltage sources fixing the electric potential at the "boundary nodes". For the remainder of the paper, we will adopt the terminology of circuit theory to describe the algorithm, with a potential, x_i^s, indicating the probability that a walker starting at node v_i first reaches a seed point with label s. A function that solves the Dirichlet problem for a given set of boundary conditions (i.e., the random walker probabilities) is known as **harmonic**. Figure 1 illustrates the harmonic functions (and subsequent segmentation) obtained for a 4×4 graph with unit weights in the presence of three seeds with different labels.

In light of the connection between random walks on graphs and discrete potential theory, one may calculate the probability that a random walker starting at pixel v_i first reaches a seed with label s, by solving the circuit theory problem that corresponds to a discrete analog of the Dirichlet problem [6]. Ground (i.e., fix the potential to zero) all seed points belonging to labels other than s and establish a unit voltage source with ground that fixes the s-labeled seeds to have a unit potential. The electric potentials established at each unlabeled node provide the probabilities that a walker originating from that node will first reach the seed with label s. These electric potentials may be calculated through the solution of a system of sparse linear equations, as described in section 2.2. The full K-tuple may be calculated by finding the potentials established through switching "on" (providing a unit voltage source to) each labeled collection of nodes and "off" (grounding) the remaining labeled nodes. Therefore, $K - 1$ systems of linear equations must be solved. By linearity (i.e., the principle of superposition in circuit theory), the potentials so calculated must sum to unity. This allows us to avoid solving for one of the systems by subtracting the sum of the calculated potentials from unity to find the last entry in the full K-tuple.

There exists a small literature that addresses the problem of multi-label image segmentation without resorting to recursively applied binary segmentation (see [7] for a discussion on some concerns about recursive bisection) using both automated [8, 9, 10, 11, 12] and semi-automated [13, 14, 15] methods. Existing automated methods operate by defining K-way clustering heuristics over the image values or values derived from another processes (e.g., spectral coefficients). These methods attempt to cluster the image into K clusters with either a pre-defined K or a K chosen to satisfy a given criterion. As fully automated methods, there is no user interaction. In addition, spectral methods are not guaranteed to produce a unique solution and, indeed, may lead to a fully degenerate problem [2]. One should not be confused by the random walker interpretation of spectral methods [16] and the present method. In the former, it is illustrated that spectral methods may be interpreted as finding a subset of the nodes with cardinality equal to half the nodes in the graph, such that a random walker starting in the set is least likely to cross into the set complement. As mentioned above, this subset may not be unique, no user constraints are introduced and only a binary (i.e., 2-way) segmentation is obtained, without resorting to recursion or clustering on the spectral coefficients.

Semi-automatic methods with a similarity to our proposed algorithm also exist [17, 15]. The K-way max-flow/min-cut algorithm of [17] attempts to find the cuts with smallest value (as defined by image gradients) that separate each labeled region from all others using K-way graph cuts. Although this problem is NP-Hard, one may obtain a solution that is within a proven bound of the optimal. Our proposed algorithm has two main advantages over this semi-automated approach. First, given single pixel labels (or labels with a small boundary cost), graph cuts will produce small partitions that segment solely the labeled region from the remainder of the image. Second, our algorithm provides a confidence rating of each pixel's membership in the segmentation. An additional difference between our random walker approach and the graph cuts algorithm is that the solution obtained by the random walker approach is guaranteed to be unique, by the uniqueness principle for harmonic functions [4], while the minimum boundary cost criterion of max-flow/min-cut may have multiple solutions (although the graph cuts algorithm of [17] always finds one of these solutions). An algorithm independently developed for machine learning by Zhu et. al [15] also finds clusters based upon harmonic functions, using boundary conditions set by a few "known" points (i.e., user-specified labels). However, by the nature of their problem domain, they employ different methods for finding similarity measures between points in feature space than are appropriate for computer vision and medical image analysis.

Additional properties of our approach that will be established later include:

1. Each segment is guaranteed to be connected to seed points with the same label, i.e., there are no isolated regions of a particular label that contain no seed points.
2. The K-tuple of probabilities at each pixel is equal to the weighted average of the K-tuples of neighboring pixels, with the weights given by walker biases.
3. The solution for the potentials is unique.
4. The expected value of the probabilities for an image of pure noise, given by identically distributed (not necessarily independent) random variables, is equal to those obtained in the neutral segmentation.
5. The expected value of the probabilities in the presence of random, uncorrelated walker biases is equal to the probabilities obtained by using walker biases equal to the mean of each bias.

This paper is organized as follows. Section 2 gives a simple weighting function to use, derives the set of linear equations that must be solved, establishes some theoretical results about the algorithm and provides implementation details. Section 3 illustrates the behavior of the algorithm in the presence of weak object boundaries and demonstrates results on real-world medical images. We conclude in Section 4 with a summary of the algorithm presented and a discussion of future work.

2   Exposition of the Algorithm

This section describes four aspects of the algorithm: Generating the graph weights, establishing the system of equations to solve, proving theoretical results about the algorithm performance and the practical details of implementation.

We begin by defining a precise notion for a graph. A **graph** [18] consists of a pair $G = (V, E)$ with **vertices (nodes)** $v \in V$ and **edges** $e \in E \subseteq V \times V$. An edge, e, spanning two vertices, v_i and v_j, is denoted by e_{ij}. A **weighted graph** assigns a value to each edge called a **weight**. The weight of an edge, e_{ij}, is denoted by $w(e_{ij})$ or w_{ij}. The **degree** of a vertex is $d_i = \sum w(e_{ij})$ for all edges e_{ij} incident on v_i. In order to interpret w_{ij} as the bias affecting a random walker's choice, we require that $w_{ij} > 0$. The following will also assume that our graph is connected.

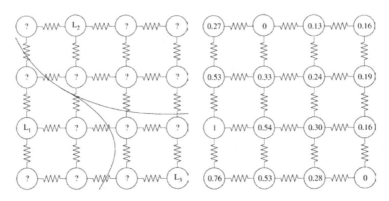

(a) Seed points with segmentation

(b) Probability that a random walker starting from each node first reaches seed L_1

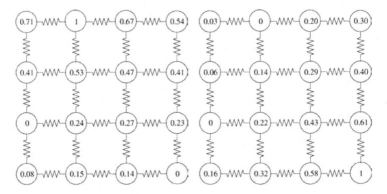

(c) Probability that a random walker starting from each node first reaches seed L_2

(d) Probability that a random walker starting from each node first reaches seed L_3

Fig. 1. Illustration of the approach to segmentation. With three seed points representing three different labels (denoted L_1, L_2, L_3), alternately fix the potential of each label to unity (i.e., with a voltage source tied to ground) and set to zero (i.e., ground) the remaining nodes. The electric potentials calculated represent the probability that a random walker starting at each node first reaches the seed point currently set to unity. Figure 1(a) shows the initial seed points and the segmentation resulting from assigning each node the label that corresponds to its greatest probability. For illustration, all the weights (resistors) were set to unity. In the case of an image, these resistors would be a function of the intensity gradient. The reader can verify that the probabilities at each node sum to unity (up to rounding).

2.1   Edge Weights

In order to represent the image structure (given at the pixels) by random walker biases (i.e., edge weights), one must define a function that maps a change in image intensities to weights. Since this is a common feature of graph based algorithms for image analysis, several weighting functions are commonly used in the literature [19, 17, 2]. Additionally, it was proposed in [15] to use a function that maximizes the entropy of the resulting weights. In this work we have preferred (for empirical reasons) the typical Gaussian weighting function given by

$$w_{ij} = \exp\left(-\beta(g_i - g_j)^2\right), \tag{1}$$

where g_i indicates the image intensity at pixel i. The value of β represents the only free parameter in this algorithm.

Later, we will discuss some principles for the design of an ideal weighting function for this algorithm.

2.2   Discrete Dirichlet Problem

The discrete Dirichlet problem has been discussed thoroughly in the literature [20, 4] and a convenient form for the solution in the context that we are concerned with is given in [21]. We will now review the method of solution.

Define the discrete Laplacian matrix [22] as

$$L_{v_i v_j} = \begin{cases} d_{v_i} & \text{if } i = j, \\ -w_{ij} & \text{if } v_i \text{ and } v_j \text{ are adjacent nodes}, \\ 0 & \text{otherwise}, \end{cases} \tag{2}$$

where $L_{v_i v_j}$ is used to indicate that the matrix L is indexed by vertices v_i and v_j.

Partition the vertices into two sets, V_M (marked/seed nodes) and V_U (unmarked nodes) such that $V_M \cup V_U = V$ and $V_M \cap V_U = \emptyset$. Note that V_M contains all seed points, regardless of their label. Then, we may reorder the matrix L to reflect the subsets

$$L = \begin{bmatrix} L_M & B \\ B^T & L_U \end{bmatrix}. \tag{3}$$

Denote the probability (potential) assumed at each node, v_i, for each label, s, by x_i^s. Define the set of labels for the seed points as a function $Q(v_j) = s$, $\forall v_j \in V_M$, where $s \in \mathbb{Z}, 0 < s \leq K$. Define the $|V_M| \times 1$ (where $|\cdot|$ denotes cardinality) marked vector for each label, s, at node $v_j \in V_M$ as

$$m_j^s = \begin{cases} 1 & \text{if } Q(v_j) = s, \\ 0 & \text{if } Q(v_j) \neq s. \end{cases} \tag{4}$$

As demonstrated in [21], the solution to the combinatorial Dirichlet problem may be found by solving

$$L_U x^s = -B m^s, \tag{5}$$

which is just a sparse, symmetric, positive-definite, system of linear equations with $|V_U|$ number of equations and the number of nonzero entries equal to $2|E|$. Since L_U is guaranteed to be nonsingular for a connected graph [6], the solution, x^s, is guaranteed to exist and be unique. Therefore, the potentials for all the labels may be found by solving the system

$$L_U X = -BM, \tag{6}$$

where X has columns taken by each x^s and M has columns given by each m^s. Therefore, there are $K - 1$ sparse linear systems to solve, where K is the total number of labels.

2.3   Theoretical Properties of the Algorithm

We now establish the properties of the algorithm outlined in the introduction.

The following propositions have a few practical consequences. First, if an "interpolation" is desired between the solution for a particular image and the neutral solution, this may be achieved through the addition of a constant to the weights. This situation might occur if the image data was known to be very poor and an almost semi-manual segmentation was desired by the medical practitioner. Second, the ideal weighting function would produce weights, such that the presence of independent random noise at the pixel level would produce uncorrelated multiplicative noise at the level of the weights. If such a weighting function were used, then the expected value of the potentials (and hence, the solution) in the presence of independent noise would equal the potentials found in the presence of no noise. The weighting function used in (1) does convert additive pixel noise to multiplicative noise on the weights. However, those weights are not, in general, uncorrelated. Finally, we know that the segmentation obtained with this algorithm in the case of pure noise (and presumably very close to pure noise) is the neutral segmentation, which seems appropriate.

The following two properties are discrete analogues of properties of continuous harmonic functions [5] and may be seen directly by viewing the solution to the combinatorial Dirichlet problem as a solution to the discrete Laplace equation (with Dirichlet boundary conditions), where the potential of each unlabeled node must satisfy

$$x_i^s = \frac{1}{d_i} \sum_{e_{ij} \in E} w(e_{ij}) x_j^s, \tag{7}$$

where the $x_j^s \in V$ (i.e., may include seed points).

1. A potential $0 \le x_i^s \le 1$, $\forall\, i, s$ (maximum/minimum principle)
2. The potential of each unlabeled node assumes the weighted average of its neighboring nodes (the mean-value theorem).

Proposition 1. *If the final segmentation is determined from the potentials using the above rule (i.e., node v_i is assigned to segment, s, only if $x_i^s > x_i^f \ \forall f \ne s$), then each node assigned to segment s is connected through a path of nodes also assigned to segment s to at least one of the seed points with label s.*

A restatement of this proposition is that the connected components generated by the final segmentation must contain at least one seed point bearing that label.

Proof. Note, this proof is similar to that given in [2].

The result follows if it can be shown that any connected subset, $P \subseteq V_U$, assigned to segment s must be connected to at least one node that is also labeled s.

A block matrix form of (7) may be written

$$L_P x_P^s = -R_P x_{\overline{P}}^s, \tag{8}$$

where $x^s = [x_P^s, x_{\overline{P}}^s]^T$, L has been decomposed into the block form

$$L = \begin{bmatrix} L_P & R_P \\ R_P^T & L_{\overline{P}} \end{bmatrix}, \tag{9}$$

and $\overline{P}$ denotes the set complement of P in V. For example, in the case of $P = \{v_i\}$ in (7), $L_P = d_i$ and $-R_P x_{\overline{P}}^s = \sum_{e_{ij} \in E} w(e_{ij}) x_j^s$.

If $x_P^s > x_P^f$ $\forall f \neq s$, then $x_P^s - x_P^f > 0$ and $-L_P^{-1} R_P (x_{\overline{P}}^s - x_{\overline{P}}^f) > 0$. The entries of R_P are nonpositive by definition of L. Since L is an M-matrix, any block diagonal submatrix of an M-matrix is also an M-matrix, and the inverse of an M-matrix has nonnegative entries (see [23] for the previous three facts), then $-L_P^{-1} R$ has nonnegative entries and therefore, some $x_i^s \in \overline{P}$ must be greater than $x_i^f \in \overline{P}$. Furthermore, since the entries of R_P are zero for nodes not connected to P, the nodes in $\overline{P}$ satisfying the inequality must be connected to a node in P. □

Proof of the remaining propositions rest on following lemma

Lemma 1. *For random variables, X, A and B, such that $X = \frac{A}{B}$, $E[X] = 0$ if $E[A] = 0$ and $B > 0$.*

Proof. By the Hölder inequality [24], $E[A] = E[XB] \leq E[X]E[B]$. By the same inequality, $E[X] = E[\frac{A}{B}] \leq E[A]E[\frac{1}{B}]$. Therefore, $\frac{E[A]}{E[B]} \leq E[X] \leq E[A]E[\frac{1}{B}]$, and the result is proved. □

Since the time of Krichhoff [25], it has been known that there is a relationship between the potentials solved for in (5) and the weighted tree structure of the graph. The following relationship for the potential at node v_i in the presence of unit voltage sources (tied to ground) is given in [6, 26]

$$x_i^s = \frac{\sum_{TT \in TT_i} \prod_{e_{ij} \in TT} w(e_{ij})}{\sum_{TT \in TT_G} \prod_{e_{ij} \in TT} w(e_{ij})}, \tag{10}$$

where TT_i is the set of 2-trees present in the graph, such that node v_i is connected to a seed with label s, and TT_G is the set of all possible 2-trees in the graph. A **2-tree** is defined as a tree with one edge removed. Note that $TT_i \subseteq TT_G$ $\forall v_i$ with equality holding if v_i is a seed point labeled as s. Therefore, to restate (10) in prose, if you sum over the product of the weights in every 2-tree that has v_i connected to a seed with label s and divide that sum by the sum of the product of the weights of the edges in every 2-tree that exists in the graph, that ratio is equal to the potential found by solution of (5). Although (10) is not very useful for computation of (5) (due to the massive number of 2-trees involved in any sizable graph), we can use it to prove some interesting results about the behavior of x_i^s under different choices of weights.

If the weights are uniform, the neutral case, by (10), yields potentials satisfying

$$x_i^s = \frac{|TT_i|}{|TT_G|}. \tag{11}$$

Now we are in position to prove a series of propositions about x^s under different conditions. We also note that if the weights are all multiplied by a constant, k, there will be no effect on x_i^s, since it is clear by (10) that the constant will divide out of the numerator and denominator.

Proposition 2. *If the set of weights, w_{ij}, are identically distributed (not necessarily independent) random variables, with $w_{ij} > 0$, then $E[x_i^s]$ equals the potential obtained in the neutral segmentation.*

Proof. We proceed by simply verifying this proposition using Lemma 1. Denote the potential for label s at v_i for the neutral segmentation by n_i^s. Denote the complement of TT_i in TT_G as TT_C, such that $TT_i \cup TT_C = TT_G$ and $TT_i \cap TT_C = \emptyset$. For brevity of notation, denote $S_{TT_i} = \sum_{TT \in TT_i} \prod_{e_{ij} \in TT} w(e_{ij})$.

$$E[x_i^s - n_i^s] = E\left[\frac{S_{TT_i}}{S_{TT_i} + S_{TT_C}} - \frac{|TT_i|}{|TT_i| + |TT_C|}\right]. \tag{12}$$

Since each of the 2-trees will contain an equal number of edges, $(n-2)$, and all of the weights are identically distributed, S_{TT_i} will contain the sum of $|TT_i|$ identically distributed random variables. Let μ denote the mean of the distribution of these new variables.

After combining terms, the numerator of (12) is given by

$$E[S_{TT_i}(|TT_i| + |TT_C|) - |TT_i|(S_{TT_i} + S_{TT_C})] = $$
$$\mu|TT_i|(|TT_i| + |TT_C|) - |TT_i|(\mu|TT_i| + \mu|TT_C|) = 0, \tag{13}$$

and the denominator of (12) must be strictly positive, since all the w_{ij} are guaranteed to be positive by construction.

Therefore, the conditions of Lemma 1 are satisfied for the left hand side of (12) to be equal to zero, and $E[x_i^s] = n_i^s$. □

Since the same technique as above may be used to verify the following two propositions, the proofs are left to the reader.

Proposition 3. *If the set of weights, w_{ij}, are uncorrelated (not necessarily independent) random variables with corresponding means μ_{ij}, then $E[x_i^s]$ equals the potential obtained by setting $w_{ij} = \mu_{ij}$.*

Proposition 4. *If* $w_{ij} = k_{ij}y_{ij}$, *where the* k_{ij} *are (not necessarily equal) constants and* y_{ij} *are identically distributed random variables, such that* $y_{ij} > 0$, *then* $E[x_i^s]$ *equals the potential obtained by setting* $w_{ij} = k_{ij}$.

With a similar approach, we may prove

Proposition 5. *If* $w_{ij} = k_{ij} + r$ *where* k_{ij} *are (not necessarily equal) constants and* r *is a constant added to all weights,* $\lim_{r \to \infty} x_i^s = n_i^s$, *where* n_i^s *is the potential obtained in the neutral segmentation.*

Proof. We may write the potential for node v_i as

$$x_i^s = \frac{\sum_{TT \in TT_i} \prod_{e_{ij} \in TT} (k_{ij} + r)}{\sum_{TT \in TT_G} \prod_{e_{ij} \in TT} (k_{ij} + r)} = \frac{|TT_i| r^{N-2} + \mathcal{O}(r^{N-3})}{|TT_G| r^{N-2} + \mathcal{O}(r^{N-3})}, \qquad (14)$$

where $\mathcal{O}(\cdot)$ indicates a term of order no greater than the argument. By l'Hôpital's Rule,

$$\lim_{r \to \infty} x_i^s = \frac{|TT_i|}{|TT_G|} = n_i^s. \qquad (15)$$

$\square$

2.4 Numerical Practicalities

Many good sources exist on the solution to large, sparse, symmetric, linear systems of equations (e.g., [27, 28]). A direct method, such as *LU* decomposition with partial pivoting has the advantage that the computation necessary to solve (6) is only negligibly increased over the amount of work required to solve (5). Unfortunately, current medical data volumes frequently exceed $256 \times 256 \times 256 \approx 16e^6$ voxels, and hence require the solution of an equal number of equations. Furthermore, there is no reason to believe that the resolution will not continue to increase. The memory capabilities of most contemporary computers simply do not have enough memory to allow an *LU* decomposition with that number of equations.

The standard alternative to the class of direct solvers for large, sparse systems is the class of iterative solvers [29]. These solvers have the advantages of a small memory requirement and the ability to represent the matrix-vector multiplication as a function. In particular since, for a lattice, the matrix L_U has a circulant nonzero structure (although the coefficients are changing), one may avoid storing the matrix entirely. Instead, a vector of weights may be stored (or computed on the fly, if memory is at a premium) and the operation $L_U x_U^s$ may be performed very cheaply. Furthermore, sparse matrix operations (like those required for conjugate gradients) may be efficiently parallelized [30, 31], e.g., for use on a GPU. Because of the relationship of (5) to a finite differences approach to solving the Dirichlet problem on a hypercube domain, the techniques of numerical solution to PDEs may also be applied. Most notably, the algebraic multigrid method [32, 33] achieves near-optimal performance for the solution to equations like (5).

For simplicity, we have implemented the standard conjugate gradients algorithm with Jacobi preconditioning, representing the matrix-vector multiplication implicitly, as described above on an ™Intel ™Xeon 2.40GHz dual-processor with 1GB of RAM. Solution of (5) using conjugate gradients (tolerance = 1e^{-4}, sufficient for the algorithm) for a 256×256 image with two randomly placed seed points required 4.831 seconds.

2.5   Algorithm Summary

To summarize, the steps of the algorithm are:

1. Obtain a set, V_M, of marked (labeled) pixels with K labels, either automatically or through the intervention of a medical practitioner.
2. Using (1), map the image intensities to edge weights in the lattice.
3. Solve (6) outright for the potentials or solve (5) for each label except the final one, f (for computational efficiency). Set $x_i^f = 1 - \sum_{s<f} x_i^s$.
4. Obtain a final segmentation by assigning to each node, v_i, the label corresponding to $\max_s (x_i^s)$.

We note that other options might be explored for assigning a label to each pixel based on the potentials (e.g., applying a clustering algorithm to the K-dimensional vectors at each node).

3   Algorithmic Results

3.1   Weak Boundaries

We will prefer the term object *boundary* to the traditional computer vision term *edge* (e.g., "edge detection") to avoid confusion with the edge set of the graph (e.g., $e_{ij} \in E$). Unlike region growing approaches, one aspect of the random walker motivation for this algorithm is that weak object boundaries will be found when they are part of a consistent boundary. Consider the situation of Figure 2, where a random walker starting on one side of a weak boundary wanders until first striking one of the two labeled nodes. On a four-connected lattice, the walker has three initial steps that keep it on one side of the boundary. Since other nodes on that side of the boundary are all very likely to reach seed 1 (filled circle), this walker is also very likely to first reach seed 1. For the same reasons, a walker on the other side of the weak boundary is also very likely to first reach seed 2 (open circle). Consequently, there will be a sharp potential drop (i.e., voltage) over the entire boundary, resulting in the correct segmentation. Figure 3 shows the segmentation obtained for a synthetic image with four areas of varying sizes and convexity with weak boundaries and few labeled nodes.

3.2   Segmentation of Real Images

Figure 4 shows the segmentation results on two CT cardiac images and two MR brain images. The images and seeds were chosen to demonstrate the general applicability of the semi-automated segmentation approach on objects of varying

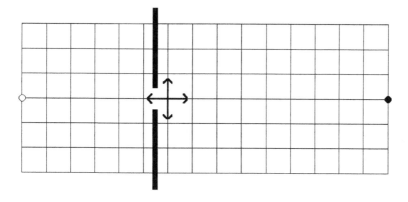

Fig. 2. Illustration of why the segmentation obeys weak image boundaries. Consider the 16 × 7 image consisting of just one hard boundary with a hole, represented by the thick black line, and two seed points placed at the white and black circles at the far ends of the image. A random walker starting at the pixel next to the weakness in the boundary (the center of the arrows) has 3 out of 4 chances on its initial step to enter into the region that is likely to be labeled as belonging to the black circle. Since the same holds true on the other side of the weak boundary, there will be a sharp drop in the probabilities and consequently, the segmentation will respect the boundary, even though it is weak.

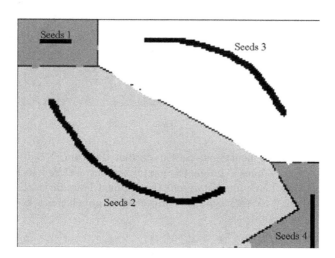

Fig. 3. Demonstration of the algorithm response to weak boundaries of different types, large/small regions and nonconvex regions on a synthetic image consisting of only black and white pixels. The thin black lines represent the "object" boundaries in the image, the thick black patches represent the labeled seeds of four different types and the shaded regions correspond to the resulting segmentation.

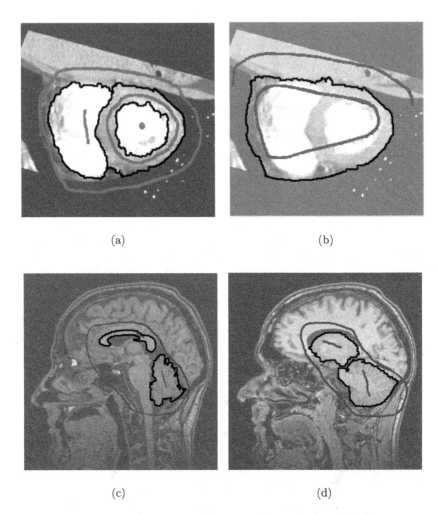

(a)   (b)

(c)   (d)

Fig. 4. Examples of segmentations on CT cardiac data and MR brain images. The thick, dark gray lines (chosen to maximize contrast) represent the seed points and the thick black lines represent the segment boundaries. For clarity of exposition, seed points of each type are connected, although this is not necessary. $\beta = 900$ for all segmentations.

uniformity, size, shape, contrast and topology. The first two figures, 4(a) and 4(b), demonstrate the segmentation results on two CT cardiac images. Figure 4(a) uses four groups of seeds, corresponding to the left ventricle, right ventricle, myocardial wall and the background, while Figure 4(b) segments the entire heart from the background. The two neural MR images have three segments each. Figure 4(c) shows the corpus callosum and cerebellum segmented from the background and Figure 4(d) shows the thalamus and cerebellum segmented from the background. In each segmentation, the value of the one free parameter, β in (1), was kept constant, despite the different image characteristics of CT and MR images. Space constraints limit us from showing 3D segmentations, but we stress that the algorithm is defined on a lattice of arbitrary dimension.

4   Conclusion

We have presented a novel algorithm for general image segmentation based on a small set of pre-labeled pixels. These pre-labeled pixels may be either generated automatically for a particular purpose, or they may be given directly by a medical practitioner. The algorithm functions by assigning each unlabeled pixel to the label of the seed point that a random walker starting from that pixel would be most likely to reach first, given that it is biased to avoid crossing object boundaries (i.e., intensity gradients). Because the algorithm is formulated on a general graph, and produces segmentations based on the separation of quantities defined at the nodes (i.e., potentials), the graph (lattice) may represent any dimension or topology.

We have demonstrated this approach on real images and shown that it provides a unique, quality, solution that is robust to weak object boundaries and that the solution respects the medical practitioner's pre-labeling choices. Furthermore, there is only a single free parameter, β in (1), and all of the segmentations shown in this paper were used with the same choice of that parameter. Of course, this approach could also be combined with pre-filters (e.g., median) or post-filters (e.g., clustering) to produce enhanced, problem-specific results.

The connections between random walks, combinatorial potential theory and electric circuits allowed us to prove that the segments are guaranteed to be connected (i.e., smooth), and that the segmentation approaches the neutral segmentation (i.e., Voronoi-like) as increased amounts of random noise are introduced. Furthermore, the direct correspondence with analog electric circuits opens the possibility for a hardware (e.g., VLSI) implementation of the algorithm, where the physics of the circuit perform the same "computation" as the standard CPU, except at the extremely fast speed of the natural world. Finally, since our PDE (effectively the Laplace equation with Dirichlet boundary conditions) is formulated on a graph, there are no concerns about discretization errors or variations in implementation that sometimes cause problems for other PDE-based approaches.

Future work will concentrate on a faster implementation, clinical evaluation, systematic comparison with other techniques, the use of prior information in the segmentation and leveraging the theoretical results to produce a more effective weighting function.

Acknowledgments

The authors would like to thank Marie-Pierre Jolly and Yuri Boykov for advice and criticism during the preparation of this manuscript.

References

[1] Wallace, R., Ong, P.W., Schwartz, E.: Space variant image processing. International Journal of Computer Vision **13** (1994) 71–90

[2] Grady, L.: Space-Variant Computer Vision: A Graph-Theoretic Approach. PhD thesis, Boston University, Boston, MA (2004)

[3] Kakutani, S.: Markov processes and the Dirichlet problem. Proc. Jap. Acad. **21** (1945) 227–233

[4] Doyle, P., Snell, L.: Random walks and electric networks. Number 22 in Carus mathematical monographs. Mathematical Association of America, Washington, D.C. (1984)

[5] Courant, R., Hilbert, D.: Methods of Mathematical Physics. Volume 2. John Wiley and Sons (1989)

[6] Biggs, N.: Algebraic Graph Theory. Number 67 in Cambridge Tracts in Mathematics. Cambridge University Press (1974)

[7] Simon, H.D., Teng, S.H.: How good is recursive bisection? SIAM Journal of Scientific Computing **18** (1997) 1436–1445

[8] Chan, P.K., Schlag, M.D.F., Zien, J.Y.: Spectral k-way ratio-cut partitioning and clustering. IEEE Transactions on Computer Aided Design of Integrated Circuits and Systems **13** (1994) 1088–1096

[9] Alpert, C.J., Yao, S.Z.: Spectral partitioning: the more eigenvectors, the better. In: Proceedings of the 32nd ACM/IEEE conference on Design automation conference, ACM/IEEE, ACM Press (1995) 195–200

[10] Zhu, S.C., Yuille, A.: Region competition: Unifying snakes, region growing, and Bayes/MDL for multiband image segmentation. IEEE Transactions on Pattern Analysis and Machine Intelligence **18** (1996) 884–900

[11] Yu, S.X., Shi, J.: Multiclass spectral clustering. In: Ninth IEEE International Conference on Computer Vision. Volume 1 of International Conference on Computer Vision., Nice, IEEE Computer Society, IEEE COmputer Society (2003) 313–319

[12] Bar-Hillel, A., Weinshall, D.: Learning with equivalence constraints and the relation to multiclass learning. In: 16th Conference on Learning Theory, Washington DC (2003) 640–654

[13] Boykov, Y., Jolly, M.P.: *Interactive graph cuts* for optimal boundary & region segmentation of objects in N-D images. In: International Conference on Computer Vision. Volume I. (2001) 105–112

[14] Boykov, Y., Veksler, O., Zabih, R.: Fast approximate energy minimization via graph cuts. IEEE Transactions on Pattern Analysis and Machine Intelligence **23** (2001) 1222–1239

[15] Zhu, X., Lafferty, J., Ghahramani, Z.: Combining active learning and semi-supervised learning using gaussian fields and harmonic functions. In: Proceedings of the ICML 2003 workshop on The Continuum from Labeled to Unlabel Data in Machine Learning and Data Mining. (2003) 58–65

[16] Meilă, M., Shi, J.: Learning segmentation by random walks. In: Advances in Neural Information Processing Systems. Volume 13. (2000) 873–879

[17] Boykov, Y., Veksler, O., Zabih, R.: A new algorithm for energy minimization with discontinuities. In Pelillo-M., H.E.R., ed.: Energy Minimization Methods in Computer Vision and Pattern Recognition. Second International Workshop, EMMCVPR'99, York, UK, 26-29 July 1999. (1999) 205–220

[18] Harary, F.: Graph Theory. Addison-Wesley (1994)

[19] Shi, J., Malik, J.: Normalized cuts and image segmentation. IEEE Transactions on Pattern Analysis and Machine Intelligence **22** (2000) 888–905

[20] Biggs, N.: Algebraic potential theory on graphs. Bulletin of London Mathematics Society **29** (1997) 641–682

[21] Grady, L., Schwartz, E.: Anisotropic interpolation on graphs: The combinatorial Dirichlet problem. Technical Report CAS/CNS-TR-03-014, Department of Cognitive and Neural Systems, Boston University, Boston, MA (2003)

[22] Merris, R.: Laplacian matrices of graphs: A survey. Linear Algebra and its Applications **197,198** (1994) 143–176

[23] Fiedler, M.: Special matrices and their applications in numerical mathematics. Martinus Nijhoff Publishers (1986)

[24] Feller, W.: An Introduction to Probability Theory and its Applications. Second edn. Volume II. John Wiley and Sons, Inc. (1971)

[25] Kirchhoff, G.: Ueber die auflösung der gleichungen, auf welche man bei der untersuchung der linearen verteilung galvanischer ströme geführt wird. Poggendorf's Annalen der Physik Chemie **72** (1847) 497–508

[26] Chen, W.K.: Applied Graph Theory: Graphs and Electrical Networks. 2nd edn. Applied Mathematics and Mechanics. North-Holland Publishing Company (1976)

[27] Golub, G., Van Loan, C.: Matrix Computations. 3rd edn. The Johns Hopkins University Press (1996)

[28] Press, W.H., Teukolsky, S.A., Vetterling, W.T., Flannery, B.P.: Numerical Recipes in C: The Art of Scientific Computing. 2nd edn. Cambridge University Press (2002)

[29] Hackbusch, W.: Iterative Solution of Large Sparse Systems of Equations. Springer-Verlag (1994)

[30] Dongarra, J.J., Duff, I.S., Sorenson, D.C., van der Vorst, H.A.: Solving Linear Systems on Vector and Shared Memory Computers. Society for Industrial and Applied Mathematics, Philadelphia (1991)

[31] Gremban, K.: Combinatorial preconditioners for sparse, symmetric diagonally dominant linear systems. PhD thesis, Carnegie Mellon University, Pittsburgh, PA (1996)

[32] Shapira, Y.: Matrix-Based Multigrid: Theory and Applications. Volume 2 of Numerical Methods and Algorithms. Kluwer Academic Publishers (2003)

[33] Dendy, J.E.: Black box multigrid. Journal of Computational Physics **48** (1982) 366–386

Three-Dimensional Mass Reconstruction in Mammography

Ling Shao, Michael Brady

Department of Engineering Science
University of Oxford
Parks Road, Oxford OX1 3PJ, UK
{shao, jmb}@robots.ox.ac.uk

Abstract. In this paper, we present a novel method for reconstructing the 3-D shapes of masses. We first use the Shape from Silhouettes technique to get an approximation to the 3-D shape of the mass. We calculate the centroid of the mass in the 2-D images and back-project them to get their intersection in 3-D. We then apply a novel iterative method, which is derived from ART (Algebraic Reconstruction Technique), to refine the 3-D shape of the mass. The thickness of the masses is calculated according to the h_{int} representation. We use the thickness of the masses in the CC and MLO or LM views to refine the 3-D approximation to the reconstructed shape of the mass. We find that the mean deviation rate of the reconstruction of a pair of benign masses is much larger than that of malignant masses, which can be used as a criterion of classifying a mass into malignant or benign.

1   Introduction

A localised abnormality in the breast is called a 'mass'. Masses may be benign, such as cysts (composed primarily of fat and water), which have a soft, spongy feel; or fibro adenomas, which are composed of swollen fibrosis tissue. Conversely, masses may be malignant, in which case they are called tumours. There are several different kinds of tumours, which vary in shape and composition. The surest way to diagnose a tumour is to biopsy it and to inspect it pathologically. This is expensive, invasive, and traumatic for the woman, and anyway most masses are benign. After a mass is detected, radiologists try to classify it as malignant or benign. Generally, the shapes of malignant lesions are more irregular than benign ones. Masses may be circumscribed, irregular or spiculated in shape. Circumscribed lesions are mostly considered to be benign and irregular and spiculated masses have more chance of being malignant. Shape information is key in the classification of masses as benign or malignant. However, due to screening practice in mammography, we only have two 2-D views projected from the 3-D breast, namely cranio-caudal (CC)-"head to toe", and medio-lateral oblique (MLO)-"shoulder to the opposite hip" or lateral-medio (LM)-"shoulder to the opposite shoulder". Depth information of the 3-D mass is lost in

M. Šonka et al. (Eds.): CVAMIA-MMBIA 2004, LNCS 3117, pp. 246-256, 2004.

projection. We conjecture that, after the 3-D shape of a mass is reconstructed, we could classify it more accurately as benign or malignant, because we would have a more informative representation of their shape.

In this paper, we present a novel method for reconstructing the 3-D shapes of masses. We first use the Shape from Silhouettes technique to get an approximation to the 3-D shape of the mass. We calculate the centroid of the mass in the 2-D images and back-project them to get their intersection in 3-D. We then develop a novel iterative method, which is derived from ART (Algebraic Reconstruction Technique), to refine the 3-D shape of the mass. We calculate the h_{int} representation (see below) of the region corresponding to the mass in the CC and MLO projections, and convert the h_{int} representation into the thickness of the masses according to the X-ray attenuation coefficient ratio between masses and interesting tissues. We use the thickness of the masses in the CC and MLO or LM views to refine the 3-D approximation to the reconstructed shape of the mass. This procedure is repeated until the difference between the thickness computed from the 3-D reconstruction and the thickness converted from the h_{int} representation of the mass regions is smaller than a previously indicated threshold.

In this paper, we restrict attention to manually segmented masses, because our focus is on the 3-D reconstruction problem. It turns out that the segmentation accuracy massively influences the accuracy of the 3-D reconstruction, because the reconstruction algorithm relies strongly on the boundaries of the 2-D mass segmentations. Highnam and Brady [4] mentioned: "If we have accurate calibration, then we can use the absolute h_{int} values as quantitative features. Otherwise, it is better to use features that involve local difference or gradients to remove any calibration-induced uniform shifts in the h_{int} values." Here, we use the absolute values of h_{int}, which affect the accuracy of our reconstructed 3-D mass.

2   What Is the h_{int} Representation?

The visual quality of a mammogram is always subject to variations in the imaging conditions. In order to develop robust and reliable algorithms for mammographic image analysis, we need first to understand and model the imaging process itself. Highnam and Brady [4] studied the mechanism of how an X-ray mammogram is formed and modelled the physics of the X-ray imaging process to develop a normalised mammographic representation – the h_{int} representation, which discards various undesirable image degrading factors, such as scatter and extra-focal radiation.

In the h_{int} representation, each pixel value represents the thickness of "interesting" (or non-fatty) tissue, compressed between the compression plate and the imaging surface, above that pixel. Quantification of the amount of interesting tissue above each pixel allows robust image features, which are invariant to the actual imaging conditions but related only to the breast anatomy, to be extracted and analysed. As a result, the mammographic image analysis algorithms developed based upon the h_{int} representation are much less sensitive to changes due to different imaging parameters than those applied to ordinary intensity images. For a more detailed description of the h_{int} representation, refer to [4].

3 Algebraic Reconstruction Technique

The Algebraic Reconstruction Technique was first introduced by Gordon, Bender, and Herman[3]. They used it to reconstruct three-dimensional objects from electron-microscopic scans and X-ray photography. In [2], Gilbert proposed another reconstruction algorithm, namely the Simultaneous Iterative Reconstruction Technique(SIRT), which updated the 3-D object grid after each iteration, unlike in ART, where every voxel was updated for every ray back-projection. Andersen and Kak [1] combined the positive aspects of the above two methods and presented the Simultaneous Algebraic Reconstruction Technique (SART).

In the following few sections, we recall the basics of ART. For more detailed description of ART, refer to [3][6].

3.1 The Formulation of ART

We assume that we are given M images each with Q pixels and represent the given data as a vector P. ART can be formulated as a matrix equation: $\mathbf{WV} = \mathbf{P}$, where: $\mathbf{V}$ is the $N \times 1$ ($N = n^3$) column vector to be solved for, and which represents the values of the voxels in the $n \times n \times n$ reconstruction grid; $\mathbf{P}$ is a $R \times 1$ ($R = M \times Q$) column vector storing the values of pixels of all M projection images, each of Q pixels; and $\mathbf{W}$ is a $R \times N$ weight (or coefficient) matrix, in which an element w_{ij} measures the influence that voxel v_j has on the ray r_i passing through pixel p_i. We can expand $\mathbf{WV} = \mathbf{P}$ into the form of linear equations:

$$w_{11}v_1 + w_{12}v_2 + w_{13}v_3 + \cdots + w_{1N}v_N = p_1$$
$$w_{21}v_1 + w_{22}v_2 + w_{23}v_3 + \cdots + w_{2N}v_N = p_2 \tag{1}$$
$$\cdots$$
$$w_{R1}v_1 + w_{R2}v_2 + w_{R3}v_3 + \cdots w_{RN}v_N = p_R$$

From this set of linear equations, we see that the weight matrix W is crucial to the solution of this equation system. The weight matrix links the unknown 3-D reconstruction object V to the known 2-D projection images P. Each weight element w_{ij} must accurately represent the influence a voxel v_j has on the ray r_i passing through pixel p_i, in order to get an accurate solution of the linear equations. Gordon, Bender, and Herman [3] represented the voxel grid using a raster of squares. A weight w_{ij} was given a value 1 if a ray back-projected from pixel p_i passed through the voxel cube v_j and set to 0 otherwise. Nowadays, the ray beam is usually represented as a thin linear ray r_i and weight w_{ij} is determined by the length of the ray r_i passing through the voxel v_j (see **Fig. 1**).

3.2 Solving the Linear Equations

We now attempt to solve the linear equations (1). In the most common case, $N > R$, so many solutions exist that satisfy $\mathbf{WV} = \mathbf{P}$. ART attempts to find the "closest" solution to represent the 3-D object from which the 2-D projection images were obtained.

We start by guessing the initial value of the voxel vector, $\mathbf{V} = V^{(0)}$. Currently we do that using the Shape from Silhouette method. At each iteration, we use a correction equation to update the volume vector $\mathbf{V}$. At iteration step k, the value of $p_i^{(k)}$ is measured as projected from the present state of the volume vector $V^{(k)}$. The difference between p_i and $p_i^{(k)}$ is then back-projected to the 3-D volume object which generates $V^{(k+1)}$ to make sure that if $p_i^{(k+1)}$ were computed from $V^{(k+1)}$, it would be closer to p_i than $p_i^{(k)}$.

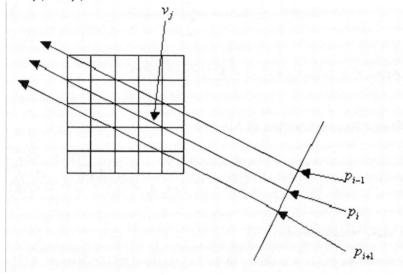

Fig. 1. A ray back-projected from pixel p_i passes through voxel v_j a weight element w_{ij} is represented by the length of ray passes through the voxel cube

The correction equation can be written as:

$$v_j^{(k+1)} = v_j^{(k)} + \lambda \frac{p_i - \sum_{n=1}^{N} w_{in} v_n^{(k)}}{\sum_{n=1}^{N} w_{in}^2} w_{ij} \qquad (2)$$

In this equation, λ is the relaxation factor, which is usually chosen to be much less than 1.0, in order to dampen the correction process. The correction procedure is applied to each element of the vector $\mathbf{V}$ and iterated until a convergence condition is met.

3.3 Simultaneous ART (SART)

SART differs from ART only in the correction function. In SART, grid correction is not performed for each pixel separately. Instead, an entire projection image is first computed, then each voxel in the reconstruction grid is corrected by an accumulated correction term that is due to all pixels in that projection image [6].

Mathematically, the correction equation can be expressed as follows:

$$v_j^{(k)} = v_j^{(k-1)} + \lambda \frac{\displaystyle\sum_{p_i \in P_\varphi} \left(\frac{p_i - \displaystyle\sum_{n=1}^{N} w_{in} v_n^{(k-1)}}{\displaystyle\sum_{n=1}^{N} w_{in}} \right) w_{ij}}{\displaystyle\sum_{p_i \in P_\varphi} w_{ij}} \tag{3}$$

P_φ represents the projection image at the orientation of φ.

4 Shape Reconstruction of Masses

The 3-D shape reconstruction of masses is composed of two steps. The first step is to get a shape approximation to the mass using the Shape-from-Silhouettes method. The second is to refine the shape using an iterative method, which is derived from ART.

4.1 Shape from Silhouettes

The method we use here is similar to the methods used by Maidment et al [5] and Yam [7]. We first compute the centroids of the segmented mass regions in the CC and MLO/LM views and align the two regions according to their centroids. Suppose (X_{cen}, Y_{cen}) are the coordinates of the centroid in one mammographic view. They can be calculated as follows:

$$X_{cen} = \frac{1}{N} \sum_{(x_i, y_i) \in M} x_i \tag{4}$$

$$Y_{cen} = \frac{1}{N} \sum_{(x_i, y_i) \in M} y_i \tag{5}$$

where (x_i, y_i) represent the coordinates of one pixel within the mass region, M represents the mass region, and N is the number of pixels within the mass region.

The silhouette of the mass region in each view is then back-projected towards the X-ray source. The voxels in the intersection of the back-projected rays form a three-dimensional volume. Each voxel in the volume is then projected into the silhouette images to determine whether or not it intersects with the silhouettes. If the projection of the voxel intersects with both silhouettes in CC an MLO/LM views, the voxel is marked 1. Otherwise, the projection of the voxel does not intersect with at least one silhouette, the voxel is marked 0.

4.2 Iterative Procedure

In the second step, we refine the 3-D shape approximation according to the boundaries and thickness of the mass regions in CC and MLO/LM views. We first compute the thickness of the mass (h_m) according to the *ratio* of the attenuation coefficient of the masses to that of the interesting tissues. To define a background area, we use a disc which covers the region of a mass and is a little larger than the region of the mass. The centre of the disc coincides with the centroid of the mass region. The average h_{int} value of the background region is computed as follows:

$$h_{int}^{background} = \frac{\sum_{k \in B} h_{int}^{k}}{N_B} \tag{6}$$

where B denotes the background region, N_B represents the number of pixels in the background region. The thickness of a mass can be expressed as follows:

$$h_m = \frac{h_{int}^{mass} - h_{int}^{background}}{ratio} \tag{7}$$

In practice, the attenuation coefficient of the tumours is similar to that of interesting tissues. We can approximate this *ratio* to be 1. Thus, the thickness of a mass can be revised as:

$$h_m = h_{int}^{mass} - h_{int}^{background} \tag{8}$$

Let v(i, j, k) be the 3-D reconstructed object image, i = 1, …, n, j = 1, …, n, k = 1, …, n, which is a discrete three-dimensional image that represents a binary object A and the background $\overline{A}$:

$$v(i, j, k) = \begin{cases} 1, \text{ if } (i, j, k) \in A \\ \\ 0, \text{ if } (i, j, k) \in \overline{A} \end{cases} \tag{9}$$

Here, we assume that the mass lesion to be reconstructed is incompressible and that the attenuation coefficient within a mass is constant. For this reason, we represent the reconstructed object as a binary three-dimensional image.

Let $P_{CC}(r, c), P_{MLO}(r, c)/P_{LM}(r, c)$ represent the mass regions in the CC and MLO/LM views and the background, r = 1, …, n, c = 1, …, n.

$$P_{CC}(r,c), P_{MLO}(r,c)/P_{LM}(r,c) = \begin{cases} h_m, \text{ if (r, c) belongs to the mass region} \\ \\ 0, \text{ if (r, c) belongs to the background} \end{cases} \quad (10)$$

Then, we convert $v(i, j, k)$ into v_j, $j = 1, 2, ..., n^3$. We also convert $P_{CC}(r,c)$ into $P1_i$, $i = 1, ..., n^2$, $P_{MLO}(r,c)$ into $P2_i$, $i = 1, ..., n^2$, respectively. As in ART, we can write the linear equations as follows:

$$w_{11}v_1 + w_{12}v_2 + w_{13}v_3 + \cdots + w_{1N}v_N = P1_1$$
$$w_{21}v_1 + w_{22}v_2 + w_{23}v_3 + \cdots + w_{2N}v_N = P1_2$$
$$\cdots$$
$$w_{n^2 1}v_1 + w_{n^2 2}v_2 + w_{n^2 3}v_3 + \cdots w_{n^2 N}v_N = P1_{n^2}$$
$$w_{(n^2+1)1}v_1 + w_{(n^2+1)2}v_2 + w_{(n^2+1)3}v_3 + \cdots w_{(n^2+1)N}v_N = P2_1$$
$$\cdots$$
$$w_{(2n^2)1}v_1 + w_{(2n^2)2}v_2 + w_{(2n^2)3}v_3 + \cdots w_{(2n^2)N}v_N = P2_{n^2}$$

$$(11)$$

w_{ij} represents the influence of a voxel v_j on a ray r_i passing through pixel p_i and it is determined by the length of ray r_i in voxel v_j.

The correction procedure is only applied to the boundary voxels, because our reconstructed object is a binary volume image and solid. Let $b(V)$, $b(\overline{V})$ be the boundary voxels. When $v_j = 1$, and its six neighbouring voxels have both 0s and 1s, $v_j \in b(V)$. On the other hand, When $v_j = 0$, and its six neighbouring voxels have both 0s and 1s, $v_j \in b(\overline{V})$. Here, one voxel's six neighbouring voxels mean the above, below, left, right, front and back voxels of the current voxel. In fact, a voxel should have 26 neighbouring voxels, but into order to accelerate the calculation speed, we only use six of them. The correction procedure can be expressed as follows:

- If $v_j \in b(V)$, and $\dfrac{\sum\limits_{i=1}^{2n^2}(P_i - \sum\limits_{n=1}^{N} w_{in}v_n)(w_{ij} > 0?1:0)}{\sum\limits_{i=1}^{2n^2} w_{ij}} < -Threshold$,

change v_j from 1 to 0;

- If $v_j \in b(\overline{V})$, and $\dfrac{\sum\limits_{i=1}^{2n^2}(P_i - \sum\limits_{n=1}^{N} w_{in}v_n)(w_{ij} > 0?1:0)}{\sum\limits_{i=1}^{2n^2} w_{ij}} > Threshold$,

change v_j from 0 to 1.

Suppose the reconstruction is the exact 3D shape from two projections, except that one voxel $v_j \in b(V)$ is an error, then:

$$\frac{\sum_{i=1}^{2n^2}(P_i - \sum_{n=1}^{N} w_{in}v_n)(w_{ij} > 0?1:0)}{\sum_{i=1}^{2n^2} w_{ij}} = -1; \tag{12}$$

similarly, assume $v_j \in b(\overline{V})$ is the only error in the reconstructed 3D shape, thus:

$$\frac{\sum_{i=1}^{2n^2}(P_i - \sum_{n=1}^{N} w_{in}v_n)(w_{ij} > 0?1:0)}{\sum_{i=1}^{2n^2} w_{ij}} = 1. \tag{13}$$

We set *Threshold* as 0.5 in the current reconstruction procedure. The above procedure is applied recursively, until the reconstruction converges to a particular shape.

In this section, we applied the iterative algorithm to refine the shape approximation from the Shape-from-Silhouette method. In each iteration, we updated the shape according to all the pixels in both views and all the voxels of the previous iteration. As a result, our reconstruction method converges much faster than ART and SART.

4.3 Evaluation Method

We evaluate the reconstruction method using the cranio-caudal (CC) and medio-lateral oblique (MLO) views in pair. Due to the low contrast of the h_{int} image files, we use the intensity images instead. We first obtain the contours of the masses within the images. The pixel values within the contours are filled by h_m, calculated as described in 4.2.

5 Results and Discussion

In order to show the 3-D shapes of the reconstruction algorithm, we select four representative pairs of CC and MLO views, which are displayed in **Fig. 2**. The masses in Figure 2(a), 2(c) and 2(d) are malignant, and those in Figure 2(b) are benign.

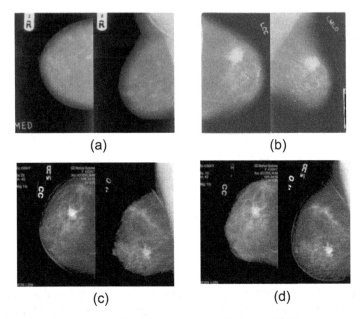

(a)   (b)

(c)   (d)

Fig. 2. 4 sets of mammographic images of CC and MLO views, which have masses in them

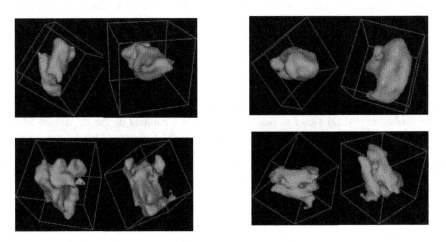

Fig. 3. The reconstructed 3D mass shapes of **Fig. 2** using the iterative method

The masses in Figure 2(a), 2(c) and 2(d) are malignant, and those in Figure 2(b) are benign. Firstly, we reconstruct the masses from the pairs of views using Shape from Silhouettes method. After that, we use the iterative method described in Section 4.2 to refine the initiative 3D shapes getting from the Shape from Silhouettes method, which results in the reconstructed 3D mass shapes in **Fig. 3**. The reconstructed 3-D objects are displayed using Visualisation Toolkit (VTK).

Usually, the projection angles between the CC and MLO views are not recorded in screening systems. The angle is some value between 20 and 60 degrees. Here, we assume the angle between CC and MLO views to be $45°$, which is not only approximately correct but also more efficient to implement. In order to test the influence of the selection of angle on our reconstruction algorithm, we also do some experiments using other angles from 30 to 60 degrees. The results show that errors of reconstructions are almost invariant with those using angles around 45 degrees to be the smallest.

From the final reconstructed mass shapes, we can see that they have very complicated structures on the surface. In order to evaluate the accuracy of the reconstructed algorithm, we project the reconstructed objects to two planes, which are parallel to the CC and MLO views, respectively. That is, the two planes make an angle of $45°$. Let $I_1(x,y)$ and $I_2(x,y)$ be the projections of the reconstructed 3D masses. The mean deviation rate of the projections of the reconstructed masses from the original $h_m's$ can be expressed as follows:

$$\varepsilon = \frac{\sum_{x=1}^{n}\sum_{y=1}^{n}\left|I_1(x,y)-h_m^{CC}(x,y)\right| + \sum_{x=1}^{n}\sum_{y=1}^{n}\left|I_2(x,y)-h_m^{MLO}(x,y)\right|}{2n^2 \cdot \overline{h}} \tag{14}$$

where $\overline{h}$ represents the mean intensity (or h_m) value of the mass regions to be reconstructed. The mean deviation rates (ε) of the projections of 10 pairs of malignant masses and 10 pairs of benign masses are drawn in **Fig. 4**.

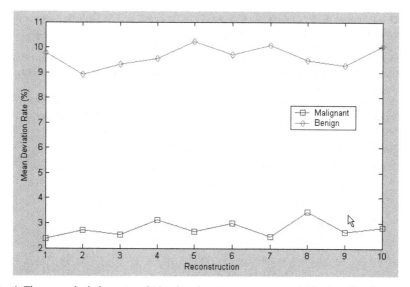

Fig. 4. The mean deviation rates of 10 pairs of malignant masses and 10 pairs of benign masses

From **Fig. 4**, we can see that the mean deviation rate of a pair of benign masses is much larger than that of malignant masses. This is reasonable because benign masses are compressible, and our reconstruction algorithm is based on the assumption that the masses are incompressible. If the assumption is violated, the error rate of the reconstruction will exceed the average value. Therefore, we can use this characteristic to classify the masses into malignant or benign. If the error rate is smaller than a particular value, we classify it as malignant; otherwise, benign. We will do further research on this topic in future work.

There a one drawback to the reconstruction method described above, that is the accuracy of the 3D reconstruction is highly dependent on the accuracy of the segmentation in CC and MLO views. Due to the usually very low contrast of the X-ray mammographic images, it is very difficult to segment the mass lesions accurately. In future work, we will investigate the technique of segmenting mass lesions automatically

References

1. A. H. Andersen and A. C. Kak: Simultaneous Algebraic Reconstruction Technique (SART): A Superior Implementation of the ART Algorithm. Ultrasonic Imaging, Vol. 6, 81-94 (1984)
2. P. Gilbert: Iterative Methods for the Three-dimensional Reconstruction of an Object from Projections. Journal of Theoretical Biology, 105-117 (1972)
3. R. Gordon, R. Bender. G. T. Herman: Algebraic Reconstruction Techniques (ART) for Three-dimensional Electron Microscopy and X-ray Photography. Journal of Theoretical Biology, 471-481 (1970)
4. R. Highnam and M. Brady: Mammographic Image Analysis. Kluwer Academic Publishers (1999)
5. A. D. Maidment, E. F. Conant, S. A. Feig, C. W. Piccoli, and M. Albert: 3-dimensional analysis of breast calcifications. In Proc. 3rd International Workshop on Digital Mammography (IWDM), 245-250 (1996)
6. K. Mueller: Fast and Accurate Three-dimensional Reconstruction from Cone-beam Projection Data Using Algebraic Methods. Dissertation, Department of Computer and Information Science, Ohio State University (1998)
7. M. Yam: Detection and Analysis of Microcalcification Clusters in X-ray Mammograms Using the h_{int} Representation. PhD thesis, Engineering Science, Oxford University, UK (1998)

Segmentation of Abdominal Aortic Aneurysms with a Non-parametric Appearance Model

S.D. Olabarriaga[1], M. Breeuwer[2], and W.J. Niessen[1]

[1] University Medical Center Utrecht, Image Sciences Institute,
Heidelberglaan 100, 3584 CX Utrecht, NL
{silvia,wiro}@isi.uu.nl
[2] Philips Medical Systems, Medical IT - Advanced Development, Best, NL
marcel.breeuwer@philips.com

Abstract. This paper presents a new method to segment abdominal aortic aneurysms from CT angiography scans. The outer contour of lumen and thrombus are delineated with independent 3D deformable models. First the lumen is segmented based on two user indicated positions, and then the resulting surface is used to initialize the automated thrombus segmentation method. For the lumen, the image-derived deformation term is based on a simple grey level appearance model, while, for the thrombus, appearance is modelled with a non-parametric pattern classification technique (k-nearest neighbours). The intensity profile along the surface normal is used as classification feature. Manual segmentations are used for training the classifier: samples are collected inside, outside and at the given boundary. During deformation, the method determines the most likely class corresponding to the intensity profile at each vertex. A vertex is pushed outwards when the class is inside; inwards when the class is outside; and no deformation occurs when the class is boundary. Results of a preliminary evaluation study on 9 scans show the method's behaviour with respect to the number of neighbours used for classification and to the distance for collecting inside and outside samples.

1 Introduction

Contrast CT angiography images (CTA) of abdominal aortic aneurysms (AAA) provide information about the aortic anatomy, making it possible to visualize lumen, calcifications, and thrombus (Fig. 1). A patient-specific model of the abdominal aorta based on these data can be used, for example, for simulation or for pre-operative planning and post-operative follow-up of AAA repair surgery (e.g. [1]). While several methods for lumen segmentation and tracking are reported in the literature (e.g. [2, 3]), only a few researchers have addressed the more complex issue of thrombus segmentation in CTA data. Due to the low contrast between thrombus and surrounding tissue in CTA images, segmentation methods have difficulty to delineate the correct boundary. Approaches based on image gradient often fail because strong responses from neighbouring objects,

M. Šonka et al. (Eds.): CVAMIA-MMBIA 2004, LNCS 3117, pp. 257–268, 2004.

such as the spine and lumen, distract the method from finding the correct boundary. Threshold-based approaches are also prone to fail, since the same intensity value is found inside the thrombus and in the neighbouring structures.

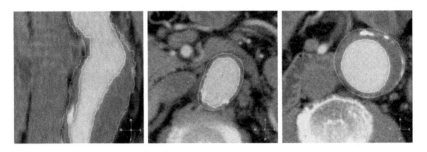

Fig. 1. Slices of abdominal CTA scans showing lumen (inner) and thrombus (outer) contours delineated by experts: coronal and axial slices.

A few attempts to segment the thrombus have been reported in the literature ([4, 5, 6]). The method proposed by De Bruijne et al. in [4] is based on a slice-by-slice approach. The user has to draw a contour in one slice, and this contour is propagated to the adjacent slice based on the similarity between the grey values in both slices. At any time, the user can correct a contour generated automatically and resume propagation. The method proposed by Subasic et al. in [5] is based on the level-set technique. A sphere positioned by the user inside the lumen initializes a deformable model that segments the lumen using image gradient as image feature. This result is used to initialize the thrombus segmentation method, which uses specific image features derived from a pre-processing step (threshold, morphological operations, and image gradient). Another method proposed by De Bruijne et al. in [6] consists of a 3D active shape model in which the appearance of grey values is modelled with a non-parametric pattern classification technique. As initialization, the user has to draw the top and bottom contours, as well as to indicate an extra position corresponding to the approximate aneurysm centre.

The above mentioned methods suffer from two shortcomings. In [4] and [6], the reported results are accurate (in average, 95% of volume overlap with a gold standard), but the amount of user intervention is significant. Typically, a large number of contours must be manually drawn in [4], and two contours in [6]. Moreover, in both cases the lumen and thrombus are handled separately, requiring extra interaction for the reconstruction of a complete AAA model. In [5], user intervention is limited to indicating the centre and radius of the initial sphere, but the reported results do not seem sufficiently accurate (no comparison with a gold standard was presented in that paper).

In this work we perform the segmentation of lumen and thrombus in a combined manner, as in [5]. First the lumen is segmented based on minimal interaction, and then it serves as initialization for the automated thrombus segmentation method. Segmentation in both cases is accomplished with discrete deformable models based on simplex meshes [7]. For the lumen, a simple threshold-based image force is sufficient to obtain accurate results. For the thrombus, a non-parametric appearance model built from training data is used as image-based deformation force, as in [6]. The method was evaluated on 9 patients, and compared with manual segmentations performed by one expert.

The paper is organized as follows: the deformable models used for lumen and thrombus segmentation are described in Sect. 2, the initial evaluation study is described in Sect. 3, and the results are presented in Sect. 4. Section 5 contains a discussion and preliminary conclusions.

2   Materials and Methods

Figure 2 provides an overview of the segmentation method. First the user clicks two positions inside the lumen, which are used to define the volume of interest (VOI) and to create a tube roughly located inside the lumen. Secondly, the tube is used to initialize the deformable model for lumen segmentation. Finally, the segmented lumen is used to initialize another deformable model that automatically determines the thrombus boundary.

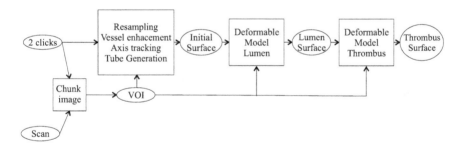

Fig. 2. Overview of the lumen and thrombus segmentation method.

2.1   Discrete Deformable Model

In deformable model-based segmentation, an initial boundary is deformed under internal (shape-based) and external (image-based) forces until an equilibrium is achieved (see [8, 9] for reviews). This work adopts the discrete deformable model proposed by Delingette [7], where the object boundary is represented by a polygonal mesh with particular topology (2-simplex). The deformation process, with discrete time steps t, is determined by the evolution equation:

$$\mathbf{x}_i^{t+1} = \mathbf{x}_i^t + (1 - \lambda)(\mathbf{x}_i^t - \mathbf{x}_i^{t-1}) + \alpha_i F_{int}(\mathbf{x}_i) + \beta_i F_{ext}(\mathbf{x}_i), \qquad (1)$$

where λ is a damping factor, F_{int} and F_{ext} are respectively the internal and external forces acting on the vertex $\mathbf{x}_i$, and α_i and β_i indicate their relative importance in the deformation process.

As in any method based on deformable models, the success of segmentation is dictated by the initial boundary, the stopping criterion, and the internal and external deformation forces. The initial boundary in the proposed method is generated with minimal user intervention and, at the same time, is located as close as possible to the desired result. For the lumen, the initial mesh is generated from two positions provided by the user (see Sect. 2.2). The initial mesh used for thrombus segmentation is the lumen boundary. A simple convergence criterion is used to stop the deformation: the difference in the object volume between two iterations. The deformation is interrupted when this difference is smaller than a given threshold (0.1% in this case). The adopted internal force (continuity of mesh mean curvature in a neighbourhood of a given size) enforces mesh smoothness and regularization, both for the lumen and the thrombus boundaries.

In this paper we focus on the external forces, which attract the mesh to image positions where certain boundary properties are found. In a typical case, as in many deformable model implementations, the object boundary is assumed to be located at a sharp transition of image intensity, and first-order image features are used as external force. In the case of the abdominal aorta, however, this assumption does not hold entirely. Firstly, several other neighbouring structures (e.g. spine, calcifications and other enhanced vessels) appear with strong contrast in an abdominal CTA image, and might attract the boundary to the wrong position. Secondly, the contrast between thrombus and background can be extremely weak in some cases (e.g. near the bowels), so that the first-order filter response at such locations cannot be easily distinguished from noise.

Here F_{ext} corresponds to an inflating (or shrinking) force along the vertex normal $\mathbf{n}_i$ as defined by (2):

$$F_{ext}(\mathbf{x}_i) = \begin{cases} S\mathbf{n}_i & : \quad \mathbf{x}_i \text{ is inside the object} \\ -S\mathbf{n}_i & : \quad \mathbf{x}_i \text{ is outside the object} \\ 0 & : \quad \mathbf{x}_i \text{ is at the object boundary} \end{cases} \tag{2}$$

where S is the maximum force strength (or deformation step size). Furthermore, a shrinking force is always generated when the vertex is outside the VOI. For the lumen, a threshold-based approach is used to classify the vertex $\mathbf{x}_i$ as "inside" or "outside" (see Sect. 2.2), while a more complex appearance model is adopted for the thrombus (see Sect. 2.3).

2.2   Lumen Segmentation

The two positions clicked by the user at the proximal and distal slices of the vessel segment to be delineated are used for two purposes: (1) to determine the volume of interest (VOI), in particular the slice interval where both lumen and thrombus are visible, and (2) to determine the lumen axis used to generate the initial surface for the deformable model.

A rough approximation of the lumen axis is calculated with the approach proposed by Wink et al. [10], where vessel axis tracking is performed by finding a connected path between two points in a cost image such that the total cost along the path is minimum. Here the path extremities correspond to the points given by the user, and the cost is given by the reciprocal response of a vessel enhancement filter proposed by Frangi et al. in [11]. For improved lumen enhancement, the VOI intensity is first windowed to the expected values corresponding to contrast medium. For efficiency, the VOI is downsampled to voxels of 4 x 4 x 4 mm, allowing for fast vessel enhancement and axis tracking, as well as favouring lumen axis stability under variation of the given positions. Although the resulting line is not necessarily central to the lumen, it is sufficiently accurate for the generation of a tube used as initial mesh for the deformable model. The tube has circular cross-sections of constant radius (5 mm).

The initial tube is deformed into the final lumen surface based on the following image force – see also (2):

$$F_{ext}(\mathbf{x}_i) = \begin{cases} S\mathbf{n}_i & : & T_l \leq I(\mathbf{x}_i) \leq T_u \\ -S\mathbf{n}_i & : & \text{otherwise} \end{cases} \tag{3}$$

where T_l and T_u correspond to lower and upper thresholds defining the intensity interval of voxels inside the lumen and can be adjusted interactively.

Note that a threshold-based force is sufficient in this case because the contrast between lumen and surrounding tissue is high in CTA scans. An exception occurs in the presence of small calcifications, which, due to the partial volume effect, are represented with intensity values similar to those found in contrasted blood. In such cases, the smoothness constraint plays the important role of preventing the surface from erroneously embracing the calcifications.

2.3   Thrombus Segmentation

The thrombus segmentation method is initialized with the lumen boundary. Thrombus segmentation, however, is a complex problem, and a deformable model adopting simple forces based on image intensity threshold, even when initialized close to the target boundary, is prone to generating incorrect results.

The image-based force adopted is inspired by the appearance modelling strategy proposed by De Bruijne et al. [6]. A non-parametric statistical pattern classification approach, k-nearest neighbours (kNN) [12], is used for grey value modelling. In this supervised learning technique, the arbitrary probability density functions for each class are estimated by dividing the feature space into cells of variable size. A cell corresponds to the k "neighbours" (or closest training points) of a given feature point $\mathbf{y}$. The posterior probability of $\mathbf{y}$ belonging to class ω_j is determined by the density of training points with a given label in the cell:

$$P(\omega_j|\mathbf{y}) = \frac{k_j}{k} \tag{4}$$

where k_j is the number of points belonging to class ω_j among the k nearest neighbours of $\mathbf{y}$. The point is then assigned to the class with largest probability.

As in [6], three classes are sampled from training data: *inside* the object (ω_I), *outside* the object (ω_O), and at the object *boundary* (ω_B). The classification features are image intensity values (or intensity profiles) collected along the vertex normal vector $\mathbf{n}_i$. Figure 3-left illustrates how the training samples are obtained at the boundary position $\mathbf{x}$ and at two shifted positions inside and outside the thrombus, respectively at $\mathbf{x} - d\mathbf{n}$ and at $\mathbf{x} + d\mathbf{n}$. Note that the distance parameter d affects only the classifier training stage, by regulating how far from the correct boundary the other non-boundary samples are collected. Figure 3-right illustrates how the intensity profiles (or features) are sampled at each vertex during training and deformation. Two parameters, the profile length l and the sampling spacing δ, determine the number of classification features.

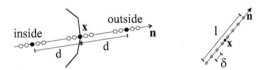

Fig. 3. Intensity profiles at a boundary position $\mathbf{x}$: the normal vector $\mathbf{n}$ and the distance d for sampling inside/outside classes (left); and profile length l and spacing δ (right).

During deformation, the intensity profile $\mathbf{y}_i$ sampled at the vertex $\mathbf{x}_i$ is used to determine the image force as follows:

$$F_{ext}(\mathbf{x}_i) = \begin{cases} Sc\mathbf{n}_i & : & j = I \\ -Sc\mathbf{n}_i & : & j = O \\ 0\mathbf{n}_i & : & j = B \end{cases} \tag{5}$$

where S is the maximum force magnitude, $c = P(\omega_j|\mathbf{y_i})$ is the confidence in the classification step, and j indicates the class (inside, outside, boundary) with largest posterior probability given by $\max_{j \in [I,O,B]} P(\omega_j|\mathbf{y}_i)$. Note that the force magnitude is reduced when the intensity profile pattern does not clearly indicate the situation at hand.

This deformation approach differs significantly from that proposed in [6]. In that case, a few new positions in a search area are considered during deformation for each vertex, which is displaced to the location with the highest $P(\omega_B|\mathbf{y})$. That scheme requires the search area to be large enough to include the target boundary, or the initialization to be close enough to the target. Moreover, multiple intensity patterns must be evaluated (classified) for each vertex at each deformation step. Finally, that approach does not take into account the information available when the intensity pattern is more similar to one of the other two classes. In our approach, the classification step is only performed once for each vertex, and the most likely class directly (and efficiently) indicates the deformation direction. Additionally, the requirements on the distance between the initial and target boundaries can be minimized in our approach by choosing proper training data (value of parameter d, see Fig. 3).

3   Performance Assessment

As a first performance assessment, the method is tested on nine (9) contrast-enhanced CTA scans of different patients. In all cases, no stents or other implants are present and the AAA is located in the aortic segment between the branching to the renal and to the iliac arteries. The scans are part of a random sample of patients from the University Medical Center Utrecht, NL (UMCU) endovascular aneurysm repair programme [13]. All images were acquired with Philips Medical Systems, Best, NL (PMS) spiral CT scanners (Tomoscan series). The images have resolution of $0.5 \times 0.5 \times 2$ mm and contain circa 125 slices of 512×512 voxels.

Since lumen segmentation is quite straightforward due to the high contrast with the background, the analysis of results generated with the proposed method is limited to visual inspection. The deformable model parameters are set as follows: $\lambda = 0.8$, $\beta = 0.4$, $\alpha = 1 - \beta$ (see (1)); and $S = 0.2$ mm, $T_l = 100$ and $T_u = 250$ Hounsfield units (see (3)).

For the thrombus segmentation method, the behaviour with respect to variation of k in the kNN classifier ((4)) and the quality of results obtained when the inside/outside training patterns are collected at different distances (d, Fig. 3) are analysed. The training samples are collected based on the boundary position given by manual segmentations performed by experts of the Department of Vascular Surgery and the Image Sciences Institute, UMCU, using the PMS EasyVision workstation contouring facilities. The original manual contours are used to reconstruct 3-D meshes, which are then smoothed and resampled. The leave-one-out strategy is used, i.e., the segmented scan is never part of the training set. The training sets contain circa 110 000 profiles.

The profile configuration is constant in all experiments, with $l = 5$ mm and $\delta = 1.0$ mm (in total 6 features per sample). This configuration was fixed based on the observation that smaller profiles ($l = 3$ mm) often provide wrong results, and larger profiles ($l = 7$ and 9 mm) do not provide better results, but demanded more computation time. Wherever omitted, $k = 21$. The thrombus deformable model parameters are set as follows: $\lambda = 0.8$, $\beta = 0.3$, $\alpha = 1 - \beta$ (see (1)); and $S = 1$ mm (see (3)).

Results are evaluated based on an error measure corresponding to the distance D_i from the vertices $\mathbf{x}_i$ in a mesh generated with our method to the (triangular) faces M_j in the reconstructed mesh corresponding to the manual segmentation:

$$D_i = \min_j d(\mathbf{x}_i, M_j), \tag{6}$$

where $d(.)$ is the distance measured along the face normal. The quality of results is discussed based on the mean distance (μ_D) for all vertices in a given mesh.

4   Results

Figure 4 illustrates the quality level of lumen segmentation results, which were considered satisfactory for all scans. The lumen boundary is delineated successfully even when the initial tube is not completely inside the structure. When calcifications are present near the lumen boundary, however, the threshold T_u must be chosen carefully for successful segmentation.

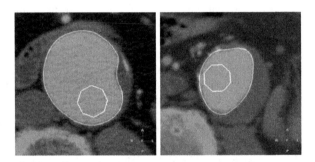

Fig. 4. Illustration of lumen segmentation results at selected cross-sections, showing the initial tube (octagon) and the result generated automatically.

Figure 5 presents the average thrombus segmentation error for results obtained in all scans with varying k. Results are rather insensitive to the number of neighbors in a large range ($k \in [20, 150]$). These results were obtained with $d = 3$ mm, but the same trend is observed for different d.

Table 1 and Fig. 6 present the segmentation error for varying distance $d \in \{0.5, 1, 3\}$ mm. In most scans, the difference between results obtained with $d = 1$ and $d = 0.5$ mm is very small. Better results are typically obtained with $d = 3$, specially when the thrombus is large; with smaller d, often the surface does not deform far enough from the lumen. Figure 7 provides an impression of the results obtained with the proposed method with $d = 3$. Results are plausible in the large majority of cases, with the surface determined automatically being located near to the manually delineated boundary. The method, however, has difficulty to place the thrombus surface at the correct position near the bowels and veins in scans where there is no intensity contrast at the boundary.

5   Discussion and Conclusions

The thrombus segmentation method presented here is inspired by approaches in which an appearance model is fitted to the data, based on grey value information learned from a training set. The most notable example of such approaches is the active shape models (ASM) introduced by Cootes et al. [14]. In the conventional

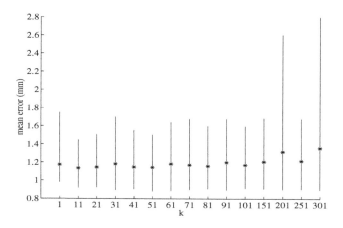

Fig. 5. Mean segmentation errors obtained with varying k for all scans: mean μ_D (stars), maximum μ_D and minimum μ_D (errorbars).

Table 1. Segmentation error (mm) for varying d: $\mu_D \pm$ standard dev. for 9 scans.

Scan	$d = 3$ mm	$d = 1$ mm	$d = 0.5$ mm
1	1.0 ± 0.5	3.8 ± 4.4	3.8 ± 4.2
2	1.2 ± 0.8	1.0 ± 0.8	1.1 ± 0.9
3	1.5 ± 1.4	0.8 ± 0.5	3.9 ± 5.4
4	0.9 ± 0.5	1.1 ± 1.2	1.1 ± 1.2
5	1.0 ± 0.5	2.8 ± 4.0	3.0 ± 4.1
6	1.0 ± 0.6	0.8 ± 0.5	6.1 ± 6.5
7	1.5 ± 1.4	3.6 ± 3.8	3.6 ± 3.8
8	1.2 ± 0.7	4.1 ± 4.2	4.2 ± 4.3
9	1.1 ± 0.6	3.3 ± 4.4	3.6 ± 4.5

ASM approach, a simple grey value model is used, namely a parametric statistical model describing image features measured along the normal direction to the deforming boundary. Such a simple model is not applicable here because the contrast between thrombus and surrounding tissue is typically low and largely varying. More powerful techniques are therefore desirable to model the complex nature of image intensity patterns at the thrombus boundary. Examples of such modelling techniques are found in the methods proposed by De Bruijne et al. [6] and Pardo et al. [15]. In [6], the grey level model is trained based on samples collected at correct and at displaced boundary positions inside and outside the object. A non-parametric pattern classification technique is used during deformation, namely k-nearest neighbours. In [15], the grey level model is trained at the 2-D contour in one slice and propagated to the next slice in the sequence. A

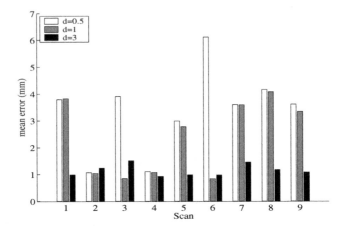

Fig. 6. Segmentation error μ_D (in mm) obtained with varying d for 9 scans.

bank of Gaussian filters is used as classification features for points at the boundary and non-boundary positions. The most discriminating features are selected using Fisher linear discriminant analysis and used during deformation in the neighbouring slice.

In all the methods mentioned above [14, 6, 15], the deformation is driven by a quality of fit that only measures the likelihood of a given intensity pattern belonging to the boundary class. In this work we extended the approach proposed by De Bruijne et al. [6] to explicitly use three classes of intensity patterns, namely the boundary, the inside, and the outside of the structure of interest. These classes are used not only during training, but also to steer deformation more efficiently by determining the direction that is likely to produce the highest impact towards the desired boundary configuration.

The method was evaluated on 9 scans using a leave-one-out strategy, and results compared to manual segmentations. Starting from 2 positions indicated by the user, the lumen is automatically segmented in a satisfactory manner (Fig. 4). The lumen surface is used to initialize the thrombus segmentation method, which produces plausible results (Fig. 7). In an initial study, the method's behaviour with respect to two main aspects has been investigated.

Regarding the behaviour with respect to variations in the number of neighbours for the classifier (k), results are robust in a large range of values. This behaviour enables the choice of a small k (21 in the experiments shown here) and, consequently, faster processing.

With respect to the distance to obtain samples for inside and outside patterns (d), smaller segmentation errors are obtained when the training profiles are sampled at a larger distance ($d = 3$ mm). The advantage of using a larger d is more noticeable when the thrombus is large: the non-boundary intensity pat-

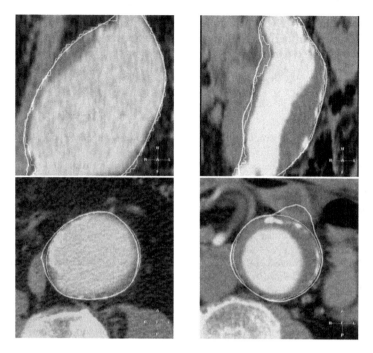

Fig. 7. Illustration of segmentation results obtained with $d = 3$: smaller μ_D (left, scan 4) and larger μ_D (right, scan 3). The manual segmentation (jagged line) and the automatic contour (smooth line) are shown on selected cross-sectional images.

terns collected too close to the boundary (small d) might not be representative of those encountered during the deformation process and cause the method to produce a wrong result.

Although more investigation is needed to tune the profile configuration parameters (length and sampling interval) and the training parameters (distance for non-boundary samples) for this application, the results obtained so far are considered promising. We believe that this approach could be valuable in other difficult problems in medical image segmentation as well.

Acknowledgments

We thank Prof. Dr. J. Blankensteijn and M. Prinssen, formerly with the Dept. of Vascular Surgery at the UMCU, for kindly providing datasets, manual segmentations, and application support. We also thank Dr. M. de Bruijne for the valuable inspiration, discussions and suggestions. Finally, we are grateful to the developers of several libraries used in the implementation: 3D Active Objects, by Philips Research Paris (J.M. Rouet and M. Fradkin); Approximate Nearest

Neighbors (ANN), by Dept. of Computer Science, Univ. of Maryland (S. Arya and D. Mount); and isiImage library, by Image Sciences Institute, UMCU (L. Spreeuwers). This research is partly funded by Senter (Dutch Ministry of Economic Affairs).

References

[1] J.J. Wever. *CT Angiographic follow-up after endovascular aortic aneurysm repair.* PhD thesis, Utrecht University, 1999.
[2] O. Wink, W. J. Niessen, and M. A. Viergever. Fast delineation and visualization of vessels in 3-D angiographic images. *IEEE TMI*, 19(4):337–346, April 2000.
[3] M. Tuveri A. Giachetti and G. Zanetti. Reconstruction and web distribution of measurable arterial models. *Medical Image Analysis*, 7(1):79–93, March 2003.
[4] M. de Bruijne et al. Active shape model based segmentation of abdominal aortic aneurysms in CTA images. In *SPIE Medical Imaging*, volume 4684, pages 463–474. SPIE, 2002.
[5] M. Subasic, S. Loncaric, and E. Sorantin. 3-D image analysis of abdominal aortic aneurysm. In *SPIE Medical Imaging*, pages 1681–1689. SPIE, 2002.
[6] M. de Bruijne et al. Adapting active shape models for 3D segmentation of tubular structures in medical images. In *IPMI*, volume 2732 of *LNCS*, pages 136–147. Springer, 2003.
[7] H. Delingette. General object reconstruction based on simplex meshes. *Intl. Journal of Computer Vision*, 32(2):111–146, 1999.
[8] C. Xu, D.L. Pham, and J.L. Prince. Image segmentation using deformable models. In *SPIE Handbook on Medical Imaging*, volume 2. SPIE, 2000.
[9] T. McInerney and D. Terzopoulos. Deformable models in medical image analysis: A survey. *Medical Image Analysis*, 1(2):91–108, 1996.
[10] O. Wink, W. J. Niessen, and M. A. Viergever. Minimum cost path determination using a simple heuristic function. In *ICPR*, 2000.
[11] A.F. Frangi et al. Multiscale vessel enhancement filtering. In *MICCAI*, pages 130–137. Springer Verlag, 1998.
[12] R. Duda, P. Hart, and D. Stork. *Pattern Classification.* John Wiley & Sons, 2001.
[13] M. Prinssen et al. Concerns for the durability of the proximal abdominal aortic aneurysm endograft fixation from a 2-year and 3-year longitudinal computed tomography angiography study. *J Vasc Surg*, 33:64–69, 2001.
[14] T.F. Cootes et al. The use of active shape models for locating structures in medical images. *Imaging and Vision Computing*, 12(6):355–366, 1994.
[15] X.M. Pardo, P. Radeva, and D. Cabello. Discriminant snakes for 3d reconstruction of anatomical organs. *Medical Image Analysis*, 7(3):293–310, 2003.

Probabilistic Spatial-Temporal Segmentation of Multiple Sclerosis Lesions

Allon Shahar and Hayit Greenspan

Department of Biomedical Engineering, Tel-Aviv University, Tel-Aviv, Israel 69978
hayit@eng.tau.ac.il; http://www.eng.tau.ac.il/~hayit/

Abstract. In this paper we describe the application of a novel statistical video-modeling scheme to sequences of multiple sclerosis (MS) images taken over time. The analysis of the image-sequence input as a single entity, as opposed to a sequence of separate frames, is a unique feature of the proposed framework. Coherent space-time regions in a four-dimensional feature space (intensity, position (x,y), and time) and corresponding coherent segments in the video content are extracted by unsupervised clustering via Gaussian mixture modeling (GMM). The Expectation-Maximization (EM) algorithm is used to determine the parameters of the model according to the maximum likelihood principle. MS lesions are automatically detected, segmented and tracked in time by context-based classification mechanisms. Qualitative and quantitative results of the proposed methodology are shown for a sequence of 24 T2-weighted MR images, which was acquired from a relapsing-remitting MS patient over a period of approximately a year. The validation of the framework was performed by a comparison to an expert radiologist's manual delineation.

1 Introduction

Detection and tracking of objects in image sequences are regarded as two of the most challenging problems in the field of computer vision and image processing. A novel statistical space-time (video) modeling scheme was recently proposed [1]. We extend the scheme and apply it to the automatic detection, segmentation and tracking of lesions in MR images of the brain, in particular, multiple sclerosis lesions.

Multiple sclerosis (MS) is a neurological disease primarily affecting the central nervous system. The disease is characterized by the presence of areas of demyelination and perivascular inflammation in the brain's white matter (WM), also known as multiple sclerosis lesions (MSL). Usually, MSL can be detected visually due to their appearance as regions with increased signal intensity on T2- and PD-weighted MR images. In cases of relapsing-remitting MS, which is the most common variant of the disease (about eighty percent of the patients [2]), the signs of demyelination and inflammation appear and disappear periodically [3].

The analysis of MR images may be done qualitatively, by visually estimating the disease's progress, and/or quantitatively. The most common quantitative parameter is the burden (or load) of the disease, i.e., the overall volume of the lesions. This parameter is indicative of the patient's current state when analyzing a specific scan, and is also of clinical importance as an indication of temporal pathological processes.

M. Šonka et al. (Eds.): CVAMIA-MMBIA 2004, LNCS 3117, pp. 269-280, 2004.
© Springer-Verlag Berlin Heidelberg 2004

To make a quantitative analysis of the brain scans of the patient, the clinician is required to perform manual segmentation of the multiple sclerosis lesions present in those scans. Because of the vast amount of data presented by the MRI modality, manual analysis is very time-consuming. Furthermore, high inter- and intra-observer variability has been demonstrated in several studies [4]. These shortcomings were the motivation for introducing automated techniques into the process of MSL segmentation and tracking in time.

Works in the field of multiple sclerosis image processing can be categorized into two main groups. One group focuses on brain image segmentation while the second focuses on lesion tracking in time. Prominent works in the field of statistical MSL segmentation include the algorithm presented by van Leemput et al. [4], and the algorithms for automated segmentation and the identification of brain structures introduced by Warfield et al. [5] and Wei et al. [6]. The above works focused on the segmentation of an individual image frame (scan). Image intensity was used as the single feature of interest. In order to introduce spatial considerations to the segmentation scheme, an anatomical atlas was incorporated into their framework. The atlas was also used to determine required initial parameters.

The task of tracking lesions over time is closely related to the segmentation problem. Kikinis et al. [7] applied frame-by-frame modeling and segmentation as a means for handling the space-time domain. Tracking mechanisms need to be incorporated in order to find correspondences across frames in the sequence and to extract the space-time profiles of the lesions. Other research groups incorporate the temporal data into the detection stage. In Gerig et al. [8] the focus is on using the temporal change of voxel features for the identification and segmentation of MSL. No segmentation procedures were applied to individual scans. For every voxel, a feature vector was calculated based on the temporal evolution of its intensity, described by the intensity vs. time graph (the voxel's temporal profile). Rey et al. [9-10] presented two approaches to the problem of lesion tracking. In [10], lesion evolution was detected by comparing two consecutive images at a time, based on optical flow considerations. In [9] a parametric model for the intensity change of a pixel on a whole set is derived and used for candidate pixel detection. In all the works described above, a voxel-based analysis is pursued. Spatial constraints based on connectivity principles are required as a post-processing stage to extract *regions* that are suspected to be lesion regions.

The objectives of the proposed probabilistic framework include three main tasks:

1. Detection of regions pertaining to relapsing-remitting multiple sclerosis lesions (i.e., lesions that change in size over time), in a sequence of two-dimensional MR scans of the brain.
2. Delineation of these regions, or in other words, segmentation of the lesions
3. Tracking of the segmented regions through the sequence, thus producing the temporal profile of the size of each dynamic lesion (a separate size vs. time plot for each lesion).

2 Methodology

In this section the mathematical tools at the core of our framework are presented. The first subsection is dedicated to the assumptions and apriori knowledge that motivate the design of the framework. The utilization of a GMM for modeling the image-sequence in a chosen feature-space and for statistical segmentation is described in the second subsection.

2.1 Model Assumptions and Apriori Knowledge

Multiple sclerosis lesions have several typical visual features. An example of a T2-weighted image with MSL is given in Figure 1(a) (one of the lesions is marked by a surrounding circle). The most distinct of the lesions' visual features is their relatively high intensity. In addition, lesion regions are usually convex. Lesions are known to appear in the brain WM [2]. Therefore, it can be assumed that lesions are rarely on the brain's vertical centerline (the line that goes through the corpus callosum) and that high-intensity regions connected to the brain's boundaries are not lesions [7]. The intensity, shape and location characteristics are used as apriori knowledge in the design of the proposed modeling framework.

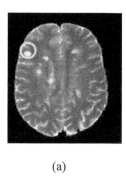
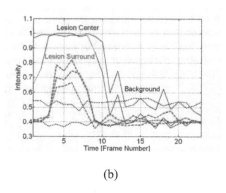

(a)   (b)

Fig. 1. (a) An example of a T2-weighted image of an MS patient. One of the lesions is circled. (b) Evolution in time of pixel intensity for different pixels in the encircled region in (a): lesion-center (*solid line*), lesion-surround (*dash line*), and non-lesion tissue (*dot line*).

The underlying assumption of the suggested methodology is that a Gaussian mixture model (GMM) generates the image intensities and their space-time distribution. The model is based on the following observations:

1. Gaussian behavior of the intensity feature – regarding this issue, we follow previous works that suggest modeling brain intensities by a GMM ([4-5], [7]).
2. Spatial convexity of the lesion regions.

3. Distribution of the intensity feature in time – Figure 1(b) shows the intensity vs. time plots of several pixels taken from the center of the marked lesion in Figure 1(a), from its surround and from the background. Unlike the background pixels that demonstrate noisy fluctuations around their mean intensity, the lesion pixels present a clear relapsing-remitting pattern.

Figure 1(b) teaches us of an important distinction between lesion center and lesion surround characteristics in time. While lesion-surround pixels present a pattern of behavior similar to that of the central pixels, their peak intensity is lower and the time interval in which they show a relapsing-remitting behavioral pattern is shorter. The differences may be attributed to the fact that the lesion-surround often includes a mixture of lesion and edema or lesion and normal WM ([7]). We employ this knowledge to provide a more accurate delineation of the lesion region, as will be described in the section 3.

2.2 GMM for Image Representation and Segmentation

In order to construct a GMM for a given sequence of images, a transition is first made from the image domain to a selected feature-space. Following the feature extraction, each pixel is represented by a feature-vector and the image-sequence as a whole is represented by a collection of feature-vectors in the feature-space. Note that the dimensionality of the feature-vectors and the feature-space is dependent on the chosen features and may be reduced or augmented in a modular way, as needed.

Learning a Gaussian mixture model from the feature data is, in essence, an unsupervised clustering task. The EM algorithm is used to determine the GMM parameters according to the maximum likelihood principle [11]. Following the learning process, a correspondence can be made between the coherent regions in the feature space and homogeneous regions in the image plane. The probabilistic affiliation of pixel x to cluster (Gaussian) j is given by:

$$p(Label(x)=j) = \frac{\dfrac{\alpha_j}{\sqrt{(2\pi)^d |\Sigma_j|}} \exp\left\{-\dfrac{1}{2}(x-\mu_j)^T \Sigma_j^{-1}(x-\mu_j)\right\}}{\displaystyle\sum_{j=1}^{K} \dfrac{\alpha_j}{\sqrt{(2\pi)^d |\Sigma_j|}} \exp\left\{-\dfrac{1}{2}(x-\mu_j)^T \Sigma_j^{-1}(x-\mu_j)\right\}} \qquad (1)$$

K indicates the number of Gaussians in the learned model. The model parameters include the mean (μ_j), covariance matrix (Σ_j) and relative weight of each Gaussian (α_j); these parameters are characterized as follows:

$$\alpha_j > 0 \ , \quad \sum_{j=1}^{k} \alpha_j = 1$$

$$\mu_j \in R^d \ , \quad \Sigma_j \ is \ a \ d \times d \ positive \ definite \ matrix$$

Segmentation maps are generated by assigning each pixel in the sequence to the most probable Gaussian cluster, i.e., to the component j of the model that maximizes the a posteriori probability (Equation 1).

3 Proposed MSL Spatial-Temporal Segmentation Framework

Figure 2 presents the four-stage framework proposed (a preliminary three-stage framework was introduced in [12]). The first stage is a preprocessing stage, in which the framework's regions of interest (ROIs) are extracted (registration and bias field correction are not part of the current framework; we assume that these operations were performed on the input sequence prior to the application of our framework). In the second stage, a Gaussian mixture model (GMM) models the sequence in space-time. Space-time regions pertaining to dynamic lesions are detected, segmented and tracked in time in the third stage based on the features of the Gaussian clusters of the model. The final stage is aimed at producing a more complete delineation of the lesions via model adaptation.

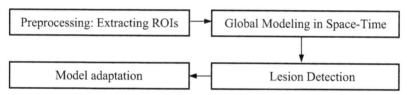

Fig. 2. The framework proposed for dynamic lesion detection & tracking

3.1 Preprocessing: Extracting Regions of Interest

One of the most distinct visual features of MSL is their high intensity. We start by focusing on the intensity feature and model the entire sequence by an intensity-based GMM. The model parameters are determined via the EM algorithm. Initial values for the EM algorithm can be obtained by incorporating a priori knowledge (e.g., via an anatomical atlas) or by extracting the values from the data itself, as performed in our framework by employing the K-Means algorithm. The model order, K, is usually chosen within the range of 3-6, so as to reflect the number of different tissues present. K can be determined by an optimization criterion, such as the Minimum Description Length (MDL) [13].

Each component of the model represents coherent intensity clusters in the feature domain. Following the model generation, a correspondence is made between the coherent regions in the feature space and homogeneous regions in the image plane. Each pixel of each frame is assigned to the most probable Gaussian cluster, i.e. to the component of the model that maximizes the a-posteriori probability (Equation 1).

Our goal in this stage is to extract the high-intensity clusters that correspond to the high-intensity regions in the sequence. We define these regions as our regions of interest (ROIs), since they include the pixels that pertain to MS lesions. The segmented regions that correspond to the two highest-mean-intensity Gaussians clusters are extracted and are used as the input data for the following stages. We choose to extract two clusters and not just one in order to ensure that pixels pertaining to lesion-surround (typically of lower intensity, as shown in section 2.1) are included in the ROIs. In order to eliminate potential false positives (mainly pixels of a skull-CSF Partial Volume Effect) a region growing procedure removes hyper-intense regions on the boundaries of the brain.

3.2 Modeling and Segmenting the Sequence in the Space-Time Domain

A global space-time model is generated next. The ROIs are modeled in a four-dimensional feature space: intensity, spatial position (x,y) and time expressed by the frame's index within the sequence. In the global model, each Gaussian corresponds to what we call a "space-time blob" [14]. The learning process of the model provides us with the parameters that characterize each blob of the model. The blob characteristics of each tracked region are stored for the lesion identification stage that follows.

Attention should be given to the fact that in the proposed methodology, a unique set of blobs is used for modeling the entire frame-sequence. The same blobs are also used in the segmentation of the sequence, as each pixel in the sequence is probabilistically affiliated to one of the blobs in the set. Connecting all the pixels in a specific frame, which were labeled as pertaining to a certain blob, yields a segmented region. Moreover, because a space-time model is used and the sequence is processed as a single entity, a certain region is marked by the same label in all the frames in which it is present. A by-product of the segmentation process is, therefore, the *temporal tracking* of regions, since their region of support is known from the segmentation maps in each frame. The unification of segmentation and tracking in our scheme is unique when compared to other works in the field [7-10].

3.3 Lesion Detection

Criteria for the identification of blobs pertaining to lesions are applied to the *parameters* of the GMM. While current schemes detect lesion-voxels based on voxel-level rules (e.g., [8-10]), in this work we propose a unique set of criteria that incorporate region-based (blob) features. Such features are attainable in a direct manner from our global model, as each blob in the model corresponds to a space-time region in the sequence. Therefore, the parameters of a blob represent the intensity and space-time features of its corresponding region. Furthermore, the segmentation maps enable the incorporation of region-level features, such as the segmented region's size-profile along the sequence.

Based on context-specific knowledge, two criteria for the identification of blobs pertaining to MSL (lesion-blobs) are applied:

1. A constraint on the mean intensity of the blob; MSL appear hyper-intense in T2-weighted MR images.

2. A constraint on the blob's size variability in time; dynamic changes in the size is characteristic of MSL, since the structures of normal tissue remains relatively constant during the time period that is typical to our case.

3.4 Model Adaptation

Lesion-center and lesion-surround regions have different characteristics (section 2.1). In an unsupervised modeling scheme, the entire region of the lesion is likely to be assigned to more than one blob. In order to produce a more accurate delineation of the lesion region, we suggest a merging process to combine the lesion-center pixels with those of the lesion-surround. In this stage it is assumed that all the lesion-center blobs were accurately detected in the lesion-detection stage (section 3.3). The merging procedure requires identification of lesion-surround blobs. For each lesion-center blob, a lesion-surround blob is detected according to the following criteria:

1. Mean spatial features (x,y) close, in terms of Euclidean distance, to the mean spatial features of the lesion-center. This criterion ensures the merging of spatially close regions.
2. Mean-intensity above a certain threshold, which ensures that no regions pertaining to background-blobs, erroneously included in the ROIs, are merged.
3. Temporal overlap with the lesion-center blob. This criterion ensures that in a case of two lesions appearing in the same place, but at different time-points, lesion-surround blobs are affiliated only with their corresponding lesion-center blob. Blobs that are sequential in their temporal extent, i.e. there is an interval of one frame between the disappearance of one blob and the appearance of the other are also considered as temporally overlapping.

Following the extraction of lesion-center and lesion-surround blob pairs, the segmented regions corresponding to these blobs are merged to produce an updated lesion region.

4 Experiments and Results

The framework was applied to a T2-weighted serial data set received from Harvard Medical School and Brigham and Women's Hospital in Boston [8]. In our experiment, a single slice from each set of 54 scans was considered. Each slice is 3-mm thick and holds a 256×256 resolution, thus resulting in voxel dimensions of $0.48×0.48×3$ mm^3. The time series includes 24 frames acquired over a period of approximately a year. The data sequence underwent several preprocessing procedures [6], including sequence registration with respect to the first frame of the series, extraction of the intracranial cavity and the correction of intensity inhomogeneities.

In Figure 3 the results of the detection and merging stages are presented for four example frames (Figure 3(a)). In the preprocessing stage an intensity-based model with five components was learned. The high intensity clusters that were extracted

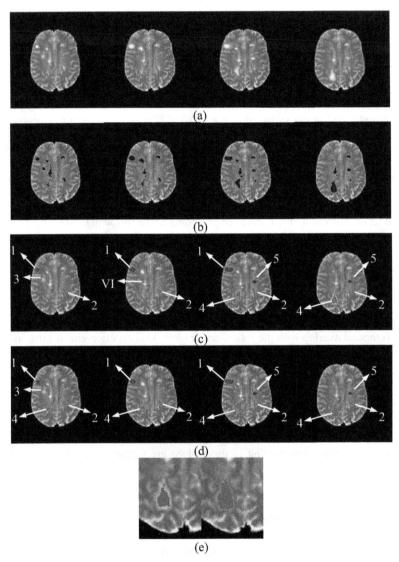

Fig. 3. Detection and merging results. (a) Frames [1 3 8 20] of the original sequence. (b) ROI extraction. Potential lesion-regions that were extracted in preprocessing are marked in dark color. (c) Spatial-temporal segmentation of the *dynamic* lesions. Detected regions are color marked and labeled. Static lesions are not colored. (d) Model adaptation via region merging. (e) Zoom on lesion 4 in frame 20, before (left) and after (right) model adaptation.

from the sequence in this stage represent an estimation of the lesion burden present in the input. In Figure 3(b) these ROIs are darkened (this figure corresponds to the results following the removal of potential false positives). It can be noticed that all the lesions that are clearly visible in Figure 3(a) were marked, i.e., the results hold no false negatives. The regions in Figure 3(b) correspond to both static and dynamic lesions and cover the MS presence in the example frames. In Fig. 3(c) and 3(d) *only* regions that correspond to lesion-blobs that were detected as pertaining to *dynamic MSL* are color marked and labeled.

Following the preprocessing stage a space-time global GMM was constructed. The model order, K, was empirically chosen to be 75. In Figure 3(c) the results of the detection scheme are presented for the example frames. Six of the 75 extracted blobs were identified as potential lesion-blobs (five of which are shown in these frames). Each lesion-blob, which was detected by the dynamic lesions detection scheme, is marked by a different color and labeled.

Figure 3(c) demonstrates the ability of our framework to unite segmentation and tracking in time. While lesions, which show a significant size change, are all marked in at least one frame, static lesions (e.g., the one labeled 'VI') are rightfully undetected and unmarked. Even though there are no false positives in the results, lesions were not identified in some of the frames. Furthermore, the delineations of the lesions do not seem accurate as the identified blobs failed to cover the full extent of the lesion (note lesion 4).

Results at the output of the model adaptation process are shown in Figure 3(d), using the same pseudo-colors and number labels as in Figure 3(c). The set of criteria applied to each blob in the results of Figure 3(c), in order to determine if it is a lesion-surround blob, includes: (1) A distance of less than 4 pixels between the blob center and the center of a detected lesion blob; (2) Mean intensity higher than 0.6; (3) Temporal overlap with the closest (criterion 1) center-lesion blob.

The more accurate segmentation of lesions achieved by the model adaptation process is clear. A distinct improvement can be seen in Figure 3(e), which shows lesion 4 before and after the merging (image corresponds to frame 20). Overall, the results demonstrate that the proposed scheme is effective in confronting the task of tracking highly dynamic MS lesions.

Figure 4 presents a plot of lesion area (in pixels) versus time for the lesions numbered 1 (triangular labeling) and 4 (circular labeling) in Figure 3. We observe a temporal evolution characteristic of relapsing-remitting MS lesions. The size estimation for these two lesions in the first ten frames of the sequence is given in Table 1.

Assessing the automated segmentation (and tracking) accuracy is problematic in the absence of a "ground truth". We validated our results by comparing them to the output of an expert's manual segmentation. All six dynamic lesions marked by the expert were detected by our framework. The expert's estimation of the size evolution of lesions 1 and 4 is given in Figure 4 alongside the framework's results and in Table 1. Although the expert typically marks larger areas, the two plots show the same pattern of disease progress, and are, therefore, clinically compatible.

5 Conclusions

In the presented study, the space-time content of an MR brain image-sequence is described using a statistical parametric methodology. We chose to model the se-

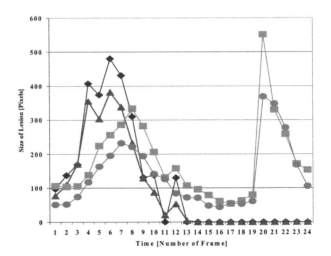

Fig. 4. Quantitative results and validation. The evolution in time of the size of lesions numbered 1 and 4 in Figure 3 is shown (triangular/circular labels). Results are compared to an expert's manual delineation of the same lesions (diamond /rectangular labels).

Table 1. Quantitative results and validation. The size estimation of lesions numbered 1 and 4 in Figure 3 is presented for the first ten frames of the sequence. The size is calculated in number of pixels and refers to the given resolution. The framework's results (the FW rows) are compared to an expert's manual delineation.

Les.		1	2	3	4	5	6	7	8	9	10
1	Exp.	97	137	169	407	374	480	431	310	131	137
	FW	77	109	170	355	303	394	338	232	129	87
4	Exp.	106	104	105	138	224	256	286	333	282	206
	FW	51	52	74	117	163	195	232	221	194	141

quence in this work by using a four-dimensional feature space (intensity, spatial position and time). While current schemes detect lesion-voxels based on voxel-level rules, in this work we propose a unique set of criteria that incorporate region-based (blob) features. Region-based features, such as the size-profile, are attainable in a direct manner from our global model, since each blob in the model corresponds to a space-time region in the sequence. This region-level analysis can be regarded as compatible to the definition of a lesion as a spatially connected entity with a unique space-time profile. Following the detection, segmentation and tracking of lesions are performed simultaneously in a unified stage of spatio-temporal segmentation, and not separately as in other works. Adding a model adaptation stage improves the framework's results, as it enables the detection of lesions at extreme points of their temporal existence and suspected edema regions around lesions.

Model initialization is critical for the capability to produce a representation of image-sequence regions that delineates accurately regions of interest and distinguishes between static and dynamic regions. The most crucial element in the initialization process is the determination of the number of blobs. In the case of a global model, K needs to be chosen as the number of expected homogeneous space-time regions in the sequence. However, this number may be large and its range unpredictable, and, therefore, it is impractical to use such criteria as the MDL to establish the model's order. We confronted the problem by suggesting a scheme that includes context-based masking as a preprocessing step, followed by an empirical choice of K. The initial masking provides a reduced region of interest for the image modeling stage, and, as a result, blobs are more likely to fit and accurately model lesion regions.

Overall, the results and their validation by comparison to manual estimation demonstrate that the proposed scheme is effective in confronting the task of tracking dynamic MS lesions. In future work, we plan to investigate larger datasets and expand the framework to volumetric data.

Acknowledgements

We would like to thank Dr. Warfield of Harvard Medical School and Brigham and Women's Hospital in Boston for providing the multiple sclerosis image data and Prof. Gomori of Hadassah Medical Center in Jerusalem for manually marking the lesions in our data.

References

1. Greenspan, H., Goldberger, J., Mayer, A.: Probabilistic Space-Time Modeling via Piecewise GMM. *IEEE Trans. Pattern Analysis and Machine Intelligence* **26:3** (Mar. 2004) 384-396
2. Grossman, R.I., McGowan, J.C.: Perspectives on multiple sclerosis. *American Journal of Neuroradiology* **19** (Aug. 1998) 1251-1265
3. Noseworthy, J.H., Lucchinetti, C., Rodriguez, M., Weinshenker, B.G.: Multiple Sclerosis. *The New England Journal of Medicine* **343:13** (2000) 938-952
4. Van Leemput, K., Maes, F., Vandermeulen, D., Colchester, A., Suetens, P.: Automated segmentation of multiple sclerosis lesions by model outlier detection. *IEEE Trans. on Medical Imaging* **20** (Aug. 2001) 677-688
5. Warfield, S., Dengler, J., Zaers, J., Guttmann, C.R.G., Wells, W.M., Ettinger, G.J., Hiller, J., Kikinis, R.: Automatic Identification of Grey Matter Structures from MRI to Improve the Segmentation of White Matter Lesions. *Journal of Image Guided Surgery* **1:6** (1995) 326-338
6. Wei, X., Warfield, S.K., Zou, K.H., Wu, Y., Li, X., Guimond, A., Mugler III, J.P., Benson, R.R., Wolfson, L., Weiner, H.L., Guttmann, C.R.G.: Quantitative Analysis of MRI Signal Abnormalities of Brain White Matter with High Reproducibility and Accuracy. *Journal of Magnetic Resonance Imaging* **15** (2002) 203-209
7. Kikinis, R., C.R.G. Guttmann, D. Metcalf, W.M. Wells, G.J. Ettinger, H.L. Weiner, Jolesz, F.A.: Quantitative follow-up of patients with multiple sclerosis using MRI: technical aspects. *Journal of Magnetic Resonance Imaging* **9:4** (1999) 519-530

8. Gerig, G., Welti, D., Guttmann, C.R.G., Colchester, A.C.F., Székely, G.: Exploring the discrimination power of the time domain for segmentation and characterization of active lesions in serial MR data. *Medical Image Analysis* **4:1** (Mar. 2000) 31-42
9. Rey, D., Stoeckel, J., Malandain, G., Ayache, N.: A Spatio-temporal Model-based Statistical Approach to Detect Evolving Multiple Sclerosis Lesions. In *IEEE Workshop on Mathematical Methods in Biomedical Image Analysis (MMBIA'01)*, Kauia, Hawaii, USA (Dec. 2001) 105-112
10. Rey, D., Subsol, G., Delingette, H., Ayache, N.: Automatic Detection and Segmentation of Evolving Processes in 3(d) Medical Images: Application to Multiple Sclerosis. *Medical Image Analysis* **6:4** (Dec. 2002) 163-179
11. Dempster, A., Laird, N., Rubin, D.: Maximum Likelihood from incomplete data via the EM algorithm. *J. of Royal Statistical Society* **39:1** (1977) 1-38
12. Greenspan, H., Mayer, A., Shahar, A.: A Probabilistic Framework for the Spatio-Temporal Segmentation of Multiple Sclerosis Lesions in MR Images of the Brain. In *Proceedings of SPIE International Symposium on Medical Imaging,* San Diego, USA (2003) 1551-1559
13. Cover, T.M., Thomas, J.A.: *Elements of Information Theory.* Wiley Series in Telecommunication, John Wiley and Sons, New York (1991)
14. Carson, C., Belongie, S., Greenspan, H., Malik, J.: Blobworld: Image Segmentation Using Expectation-Maximization and Its Application to Image Quering. *IEEE Trans. on Pattern Analysis and Machine Intelligence* **24:8** (Aug. 2002) 1026-1038

Segmenting Cell Images: A Deterministic Relaxation Approach

Chee Sun Won[1], Jae Yeal Nam[2], and Yoonsik Choe[3]

[1] Dept. of Electronics Eng., Dongguk University, Seoul, 100-715, Korea
cswon@dongguk.edu
[2] Dept. of Computer Eng., Keimyung University, Daegu, 704-701, Korea
[3] Dept. of Electrical and Electronics Eng., Yonsei University, Seoul, 120-749, Korea

Abstract. Automatic segmentation of digital cell images into four regions, namely nucleus, cytoplasm, red blood cell (rbc), and background, is an important step for pathological measurements. Using an adaptive thresholding of the histogram, the cell image can be roughly segmented into three regions: nucleus, a mixture of cytoplasm and rbc's, and background. This segmentation is served as an initial segmentation for our iterative image segmentation algorithm. Specifically, MAP (maximum a posteriori) criterion formulated by the Bayesian framework with the original image data and local variance image field (LVIF) is used to update the class labels iteratively by a deterministic relaxation algorithm. Finally, we draw a line to separate the touching rbc from the cytoplasm.

1 Introduction

There are three major regions in the cell images of the human blood: leukocyte (white blood cell), red blood cell (rbc), and background. Among them leukocyte plays an important role in recognizing various pathological conditions. Note that leukocytes have a number of different sub-groups such as neutrophil, eosinophil, basophil, monocyte, and lymphocyte. The population of each sub-group in the human blood is one of the most important information for the pathological measurements. Therefore, the identification and classification of the various leukocytes via cell image segmentation is an essential requirement for the pathology [1][5]. One of the features to classify leukocytes into different sub-groups is the ratio between the nucleus and the cytoplasm in it. Also, the textural features of the nucleus play an essential role in differentiating different sub-groups of the leukocytes. This implies that the separation of the nucleus and the cytoplasm regions from the blood cell images is indeed an important task for hematologists and pathologists.

Note that, for a cell image acquired by a light microscope, the nucleus region is normally dark and the background is bright [2][4][9]. The intermediate level of brightness corresponds to cytoplasm and rbc [2]. Also, obviously, the boundary pixels of the nucleus have high contrast. We basically make use of these clues to segment the cell image into three regions: the nucleus region, a mixture region of cytoplasm and rbc's, and the background. The initial segmentation of

M. Šonka et al. (Eds.): CVAMIA-MMBIA 2004, LNCS 3117, pp. 281–291, 2004.

this three-region-partition is obtained by a histogram thresholding method. Note that, normally, there are three or four clusters in the histogram of cell images. The first and the last clusters correspond to background and the nucleus, respectively. Therefore, the first bottom after the first peak and the last bottom before the last peak of the histogram can be used as the thresholds to separate initial three regions. The initial segmentation roughly locates the three regions in the cell image. Now, our next step is to refine the initial segmentation using the contextual information of the image. To this end, we employ maximum a posteriori (MAP) segmentation criterion based on the Markov random field (MRF) models [3][8]. The clique potentials of the MRF model are designed to exploit the smoothness constraint of the segmented regions and the high gradients at the region boundaries. To extract the high frequency components in the region boundaries, we use the local variance image field (LVIF) [7]. It has been shown that the LVIF can locate the boundary pixels in the spatial image domain quite well. Since we already have a rough initial segmentation, our algorithm for the MAP criterion is a deterministic relaxation. Specifically, by iteratively updating the class labels of the pixels in the direction of increasing the MAP criterion, the interior homogeneous regions are expanded or shrunk to the region boundaries with high gradients within tens of iterations.

Having segmented the cell image into three regions, we finally need to separate the cytoplasm from the rbc's. This can not be done only with the brightness information. Instead, one can exploit the connection status to the separation. Specifically, if the rbc and the leukocyte do not touch each other, the cytoplasm is the immediate connection of the nucleus. That is, since the nucleus is surrounded by the cytoplasm, the area of the cytoplasm can be defined by simply grouping the connected pixels between the nucleus and the background. However, there are cases where the rbc touches the cytoplasm. In this case, since the rbc and the cytoplasm often have similar brightness, it may not be possible to differentiate them by the brightness and gradients. Instead, we may draw the boundary line between two concave points formed by the contact points of the cytoplasm and the rbc [6].

2   Overall Structure of the Segmentation Algorithm

As shown in Figure 1, the proposed segmentation algorithm consists of three steps: initial three-region segmentation, segmentation with a deterministic relaxation, and separation of the cytoplasm from the touching rbc. In the first two steps, the cell image is segmented into three regions: nucleus, a mixture of cytoplasm and the rbc's, and the background. The cytoplasm and the rbc are separated in the final step, resulting in 4-region segmentation of nucleus, cytoplasm, rbc, and the background.

3   Initial Segmentation Using the Histogram Thresholding

As already mentioned, there are three regions in the cell images acquired by a light microscope, which are roughly separable by the gray level distribution.

They are nucleus, a mixture of cytoplasm and the rbc's, and the background. For example, as shown in Figure 2, the histogram of the cell image normally has three or four clusters. The first cluster includes mostly the pixels in nucleus, the second one (and possible the third one) includes those of cytoplasm and the background, and the final one has the brightest background in the image. Since they are relatively well separated, the bottom of the histogram between two peaks can be used as the threshold for the segmentation. However, since the intermediate cluster formed by the cytoplasm and the background may and may not have separated clusters in the histogram, they are not differentiable by the histogram thresholding. Thus, for our initial segmentation using the histogram thresholding, three regions are separated, needing two thresholds T_1 and T_2. Here, T_1 separates the background from the rest of image regions and T_2 extracts the background. The remaining regions are cytoplasm and the rbc's.

Before we determine T_1 and T_2, we need to smooth the histogram $H(i)$, $i = 0, \cdots, 255$ to remove the noise. The histogram smoothing adopted in this paper is a 9-point averager

$$\bar{H}(i) = \frac{1}{9} \sum_{k=-4}^{4} H(i+k).$$

Our strategy to find T_1 is to detect the first concave after the first peak of the histogram. This can be equivalently done by detecting the point, where the first decreasing of the difference $\bar{H}(i) - \bar{H}(i-1)$ terminates. That is, scanning from $i = 0$ to 255, we set the flag to 1 when it starts to satisfy $\bar{H}(i) - \bar{H}(i-1) < 0$ and holds it as long as the condition is satisfied. With the flag equals to 1, we set $T_1 = i^*$ for the first point that satisfies $\bar{H}(i^*) - \bar{H}(i^* - 1) \geq 0$. Similarly, T_2 is determined by scanning the histogram in the reverse order: from $i = 255$ to 0. This time, the flag is set to 1 while $\bar{H}(i) - \bar{H}(i+1) < 0$. If the flag is 1, we set $T_2 = i^*$ for the first point that satisfies $\bar{H}(i^*) - \bar{H}(i^* + 1) \geq 0$. The result obtained by T_1 and T_2 is used as an initial segmentation for the MAP segmentation in the next section.

4   Segmentation with a Deterministic Relaxation

For those cell images with slowly varying brightness in the background, the cluster for the background with high gray levels in the histogram is not well separated (see Figure 3-(b)). As one can expect, the result of the segmentation using the histogram thresholding explained in section 3 is unsatisfactory (see Figure 3-(c)). To solve this problem and to smooth out the erroneous region (e.g., small holes in Figure 3-(c)), we need to refine the initial segmentation obtained in section 3. Our refinement is based on the contextual information of the image space such as the smoothness constraint and the high gray level variance (i.e., high contrast) in the region boundaries. These clues are incorporated into the MAP segmentation framework for the refinement.

Let us denote $z = \{z(i,j) : (i,j) \in \Omega\}$ as the set of all gray levels in $N_1 \times N_2$ 2-D image space $\Omega = \{(i,j) : 0 \leq i \leq N_1, 0 \leq j \leq N_2\}$. For notational convenience, we sometimes denote $z(i,j)$ as z_t for $t = (i,j) \in \Omega$. Also, let us denote $\hat{z}$ as the image obtained by the processing of the histogram equalization of z. The histogram equalization is a necessary process to adopt the fixed thresholding values for all types of input images for the detection of the boundary points. Now, we can define the following local variance σ_t^2 as a measure of the local gray level contrast at a pixel $t \in \Omega$:

$$\sigma_t^2 = \frac{1}{|\zeta_t|} \sum_{s \in \zeta_t} (\hat{z}_s - \bar{z}_t)^2, \tag{1}$$

where ζ_t is the set of pixels including pixel t and its neighboring pixels, $|\zeta_t|$ is the cardinality of ζ_t, $\hat{z}_s$ is the (histogram equalized) gray level at pixel s, and $\bar{z}_t$ represents the average gray levels in ζ_t. Obtaining local variances for all pixels and quantizing and limiting them into integer values from 0 to 255, we have the LVIF $y = \{y(i,j) : (i,j) \in \Omega\}$ for all pixels in the set Ω with

$$y_t = \begin{cases} \langle \sigma_t^2 \rangle, & \text{if } \langle \sigma_t^2 \rangle \leq 255 \\ 255, & \text{if } \langle \sigma_t^2 \rangle > 255 \end{cases} \tag{2}$$

where $\langle \sigma_t^2 \rangle$ takes the nearest integer value of σ_t^2. Note that each pixel in the LVIF takes a value $y_t \in \{0, \cdots, 255\}$. As y_t increases, higher contrast of the original gray levels in the vicinity of t is expected (see Figure 3-(d)).

The maximum a posteriori (MAP) criterion formulated by the Markov random field (MRF) modelling is the criterion adopted for the region and boundary based segmentation. In addition to the random fields Z for observed gray levels and Y for the LVIF, we also define the random field $X = \{X(i,j) = x(i,j) : (i,j) \in \Omega\}$. Here $x(i,j) \in \{0,1,2\}$ is the labelling for the nucleus (i.e., $x(i,j) = 0$), for a mixture of the cytoplasm and the rbc (i.e., $x(i,j) = 1$) and for the background (i.e., $x(i.j) = 2$). Then, our goal is to find an optimal class label x^* such that

$$x^* = \operatorname*{argmax}_{x} P(y, z | x)$$
$$\propto \operatorname*{argmax}_{x} P(z|x) P(y, x). \tag{3}$$

Since we already have a rough initial segmentation $\hat{x}^{(0)}$, an approximation of the optimization of (3) can be done by adopting a deterministic relaxation method [8]. Specifically, for each pixel visit on Ω and at the nth iteration, we update the current class label $\hat{x}_t^{(n)}$ to $\hat{x}_t^{(n+1)}$ via the following criterion:

$$\hat{x}_t^{(n+1)} = \operatorname*{argmax}_{x_t} P(z_t|x_t) P(x_t|\hat{x}_{\eta_t}^{(n)}, y_t, y_{\eta_t}), \tag{4}$$

where $P(z_t|x_t)$ is assumed to have a Gaussian distribution with mean μ_{x_t} and variance $\sigma_{x_t}^2$ and the local conditional probability $P(x_t|\hat{x}_{\eta_t}^{(n)}, y_t, y_{\eta_t})$ has a Gibbs distribution with the previous class labels $\hat{x}_{\eta_t}^{(n)}$ and the LVIF y_t and its neighborhood y_{η_t}. The Gibbs distribution of $P(x_t|\hat{x}_{\eta_t}^{(n)}, y_t, y_{\eta_t})$ is given as follows

$$P(x_t|\hat{x}_{\eta_t}^{(n)}, y_t, y_{\eta_t}) \propto \exp(U_t), \tag{5}$$

where

$$U_t = \sum_{c \in C_t} V_c(x_t) \tag{6}$$

and C_t is the set of the cliques at $t \in \Omega$. For the second-order neighborhood system with pair cliques [8], we define the clique potential for a clique c at a pixel t as follows:

$$V_c(x_t) = \begin{cases} \beta, & \text{if } x_t = \hat{x}_s^{(n)} \text{ and } |y_t - y_s| < T_3, \text{ for } t, s \in c \\ -\beta, & \text{if } x_t \neq \hat{x}_s^{(n)} \text{ and } |y_t - y_s| > T_4, \text{ for } t, s \in c \\ 0, & \text{otherwise.} \end{cases} \tag{7}$$

According to (7), not only the homogeneity of the class labels in the cliques but also the smoothness of $y(,)$ values in the clique are required to generate high (positive) clique potentials for the continuity of the class labels. Also, if the pixels in the clique take nonidentical class labels and any absolute difference of the LVIF values (i.e., $y(,)$) in the clique is large enough (i.e., T_4), then we regard that pixel as a boundary point and we give a negative potential to discourage the region expansion or shrinkage. Note that there are also cases where the clique potential $V_c(x_t)$ takes a value zero for those that do not satisfy the above two conditions, which may be considered as a "don't care" state.

In summary, given an initial segmentation $\hat{x}^{(0)}$, we update the class labels iteratively with the following steps:

(i) Let $n = 0$.
(ii) For given current class labels $\hat{x}^{(n)}$, calculate (μ_0, σ_0^2), (μ_1, σ_1^2), and (μ_2, σ_2^2) for the class labels 0, 1, and 2, respectively, by calculating sample means and sample variances.
(iii) For all $t \in \Omega$, update $\hat{x}_t^{(n+1)}$ by using (4).
(iv) If $n = n_{max}$ or $\hat{x}^{(n)} \approx \hat{x}^{(n+1)}$, stop. Otherwise, $n = n + 1$ and go to step (ii).

Note that n_{max} is the pre-determined maximum number of iterations. The deterministic relaxation algorithm takes less than 30 iterations to converge. Applying the above segmentation algorithm to Figure 3-(c), we have a correct three-region segmentation as shown in Figure 3-(e).

5   Separation of Cytoplasm and rbc

For those cell images with no touching rbc (e.g., see Figure 4), one can easily separate the cytoplasm from the mixed region of the cytoplasm and the rbc's. That is, grouping all the pixels between the background and the nucleus forms a region of the cytoplasm. However, there are also rbc's touching the leukocyte as shown in Figure 2-(a). For those images with touching rbc's, a separation algorithm is required. Our separation algorithm is based on the fact that a pair of sharp concavities are created on the verge of boundary pixels due to the round shape of the cells. These are two boundary points where the cytoplasm and the rbc meet (see Figure 5). Thus, our goal is to identify those concave points and to connect them to delineate the boundary of the cytoplasm. The separation algorithm consists of four steps: boundary smoothing, detection of concavities, finding a pair of concavities to be connected, and the undoing the incorrect partitions. Boundary smoothing is required to remove the noise concavities. One way of detecting the concave points is to measure the ratio of the number of the background pixels (i.e., $x_t = 2$) and the number of the pixels classified as the mixture of the cytoplasm and the rbc's (i.e., $x_t = 1$) within a small window centered at each pixel. At a concavity, the number of pixels with label 1 (cytoplasm plus rbc's) is greater than that of label 2 (background). Identifying the concavities, the next step, is to find a pair of concavities to be connected. If there are multiple touching rbc's, this turns out to be the most difficult problem in the separation. Our method is to examine all possible pairs of concavities and choose the one that satisfies the following conditions:

- the connecting line should not pass through the nucleus,
- pixels on the real connecting lines tend to yield higher average LVIF values than wrong ones.

If an incorrect pair of the concavities is chosen, the connecting line results in partitioning a part of the convex cytoplasm regions. This incorrectly partitioned region normally has thin and long shape, comparing to the almost round shape obtained by the correct partition. This fact is utilized to undo the incorrect partitions, reassigning them to the cytoplasm.

6   Experiments

The proposed segmentation algorithm was applied to 22 cell images, including 4 basophils, 3 eosinophils, 5 lymphocytes, 5 monocytes, and 5 neutrophils. Here, 18 of them have touching rbc's. Note that T_1 and T_2 are determined automatically, but T_3 and T_4 are fixed as 50 and 200, respectively. We set the pair-clique potential for the second-order neighborhood system to $\beta = 0.3$. For all 22 images, the three-region segmentation by the deterministic relaxation yields 100% correct results (see some of them in Figure 4 and Figure 6 - 11). On the other hand, the segmentation accuracy of the separation algorithm is only around 60% with multiple touching rbc's. Figure 12 shows an example of unsuccessful separation.

7   Conclusion

We have proposed a segmentation algorithm for cell images. The distinctive brightness features of nucleus, a mixture of cytoplasm and the rbc's, and the background are used to obtain the three-region segmentation. Also, novel Gibbs energy potentials have been proposed for the region and boundary based image segmentation. Then, the separation of the cytoplasm and the rbc is done using

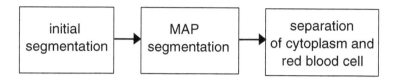

Fig. 1. Three major steps of the proposed segmentation.

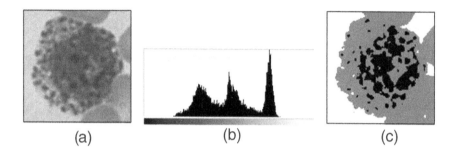

(a)   (b)   (c)

Fig. 2. A cell image with a basophil: (a) original image, (b) histogram, (c) initial segmentation by the histogram thresholding.

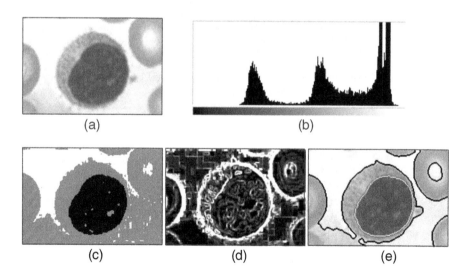

(a)   (b)

(c)   (d)   (e)

Fig. 3. A cell image with a lymphocyte: (a) original image, (b) histogram, (c) initial segmentation by the histogram thresholding, (d) LVIF, (e) segmentation by the deterministic relaxation (white line on the boundary of nucleus, black line on the boundary of the background).

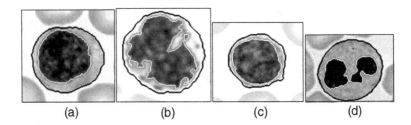

Fig. 4. Segmentation results with no touching rbc (white line on the boundary of nucleus, black line on the boundary of the cytoplasm): (a) Lymphocyte, (b) Basophil, (b) Lymphocyte, (d) Neutrophil.

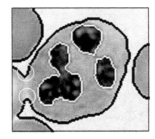

Fig. 5. A pair of concavities (in white circles) created by a touching rbc.

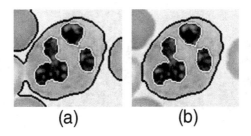

Fig. 6. Segmentation result: (a) after the deterministic relaxation, (b) after the separation.

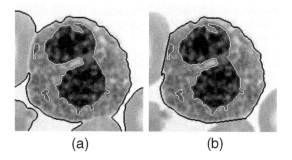

Fig. 7. Segmentation result: (a) after the deterministic relaxation, (b) after the separation.

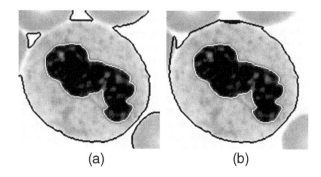

Fig. 8. Segmentation result: (a) after the deterministic relaxation, (b) after the separation.

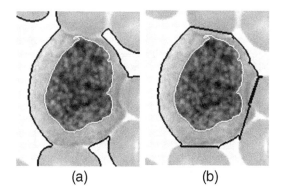

Fig. 9. Segmentation result: (a) after the deterministic relaxation, (b) after the separation.

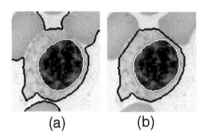

Fig. 10. Segmentation result: (a) after the deterministic relaxation, (b) after the separation.

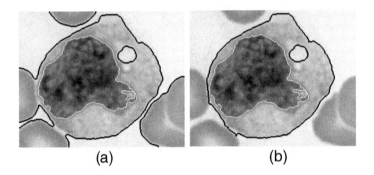

Fig. 11. Segmentation result: (a) after the deterministic relaxation, (b) after the separation.

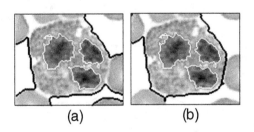

Fig. 12. An example of incorrect separation: (a) after the deterministic relaxation, (b) after the separation.

the concavities of the touching rbc's and the connection status. Experiments show that the three-region segmentation using the deterministic relaxation algorithm yields almost perfect segmentation results, proving our successful MRF modelling using both the smoothness contextual constraint and high contrast constraint at the region boundaries.

8   Acknowledgements

This work was supported by grant No R01-2003-000-10412-0 from the Basic Research Program of the Korea Science & Engineering Foundation.

References

1. Bikhet, S.F., Darwish, A.M., Tolba, H.A., and Shaheen, S.I.: Segmentation and classification of white blood cells, IEEE Proc. ICASSP00,vol. 6, (2000) 2259–2261
2. Cseke, I.: A fast segmentation for white blood cell images, IAPR int. Conf. on Pattern Recognition (ICPR), (1992) 530–533
3. Geman, S. and Geman, D.: Stochastic relaxation, Gibbs distribution, and the Bayesian restoration of images, IEEE Tr. Pat. Ana. Mach. Intel., vol. 6, (1984) 721–741
4. Liao, Q. and Deng, Y.: An accurate segmentation method for white blood cell images, IEEE Proc. of Int. Symposium on Biomedical Imaging, (2002) 245–248
5. Nilsson, B. and Heyden, A.: Model-based segmentation of leukocytes clusters, IEEE Proc. ICPR vol. 1, (2002) 727–730
6. Poon, S., Ward, R., Palcic, B.: Automatic image detection and segmentation in blood smears, Cytometry, (1992) 766–774
7. Won, C.S., Pyun, K., and Gray, R.M.: Automatic object segmentation in images with low depth of field, Proc. of ICIP, (2002)
8. Won, C.S. and Gray, R.M.: Stochastic Image Processing, Kluwer Academic, (2004)
9. Wu, H.-S.,Gil, J., and Barba, J.: Optimal segmentation of cell images, IEE Proc.-Vis. Image Signal Processing, vol. 145, no. 1, (1998) 50–56

TIGER – A New Model for Spatio-temporal Realignment of FMRI Data

Peter R. Bannister[1], J. Michael Brady[1], and Mark Jenkinson[2]

[1] Robotics Research Group, Department of Engineering Science,
University of Oxford, Parks Road, Oxford, OX1 3PJ, UK
{prb,jmb}@robots.ox.ac.uk
[2] Oxford Centre for Functional Magnetic Resonance Imaging of the Brain,
John Radcliffe Hospital, Oxford, OX3 9DU, UK
mark@fmrib.ox.ac.uk

Abstract. We describe a new model which is able to model accurately the characteristics of subject motion, a dominant artefact in Functional Magnetic Resonance Images. Using the model, which is based on specific knowledge regarding the nature of the image acquisition, it is possible to correct for this motion which would otherwise render activation detection on the images invalid. We also present an initial implementation based on the model and are able to demonstrate that the corrections available under this new scheme are significantly more accurate than existing approaches to the problem of subject motion, enabling a far more accurate analysis of the patterns of brain activation which these images seek to capture.

Key words: Motion correction, slice-timing correction, FMRI, registration, spatio-temporal re-alignment.

1 Introduction

Functional Magnetic Resonance Imaging (FMRI) is a relatively recent development of Magnetic Resonance Imaging (MRI) and is a non-invasive technique which can be used to form images of neural activation. The technique can answer questions about the way in which the brain works and can also characterise deficiencies due to illness or injury. The modality is based on measurements of the magnetic behaviour associated with blood flow change due to metabolic activity which can be observed using an MRI scanner.

Images are acquired using a multi-slice Echo Planar Imaging (EPI) protocol which raster scans k-space. While this achieves the necessary acquisition speeds for individual slices which are grouped along the z-axis to form volumes (typically a volume must be acquired every 3 seconds so that the temporal dynamics of the haemodynamic response can be captured), the signal-to-noise ratio (SNR) suffers and as a consequence image resolution must be lowered. This makes it much harder to reliably detect activation and dynamic behaviour in a subject's

M. Šonka et al. (Eds.): CVAMIA-MMBIA 2004, LNCS 3117, pp. 292–303, 2004.

brain. Also, because this detection is based on the statistical comparison of many scans of the same sections of the brain, the situation is further confounded by the adverse effect of subject motion at even very low levels of a few millimetres or less. This situation is exacerbated by the fact that clinical patients will generally move far more than cooperative volunteers while in the scanner. Echo Volumetric Imaging is the full extension of EPI to 3-D which means that the full volumetric image is acquired in a single shot. It is extremely difficult to carry out in practice and results in a very low resolution image (currently, about $32 \times 32 \times 16$ voxels) with large levels of distortion due to an even lower SNR than is typical of multi-slice EPI.

Given that SNR considerations limit FMRI to stacked-slice acquisitions in practice, the problem of temporal offsets within a volume due to the successive acquisition of slices remains a significant confound to motion correction. Previous attempts to correct FMRI data for artefacts introduced during acquisition have considered spatial realignment and slice-timing correction as two distinct and separate stages in the processing chain. We discuss the problems inherent in such an approach in section 2, and go on to propose a new method, which we have called Temporally Integrated Geometric EPI Re-alignment (TIGER). We present the initial results from an implementation based on this model and conclude by describing a more sophisticated realisation based on this model which may be applied to real FMRI studies.

2 Existing Approaches to Motion Correction in FMRI

While the need for slice-timing is acknowledged widely, these corrections are not always performed in practice on FMRI data. Applying the two corrections separately is convenient, not least because it facilitates the use of existing tools such as MCFLIRT [3] and SPM [2] for rigid-body motion correction along with separate temporal interpolation of each voxel time-course to re-shift slice-timings. There are fundamental errors in the assumptions underlying this distinction, however, regardless of the order in which the two steps are performed. Clearly, if no subject motion has occurred, it is sufficient simply to apply slice-timing correction as a series of temporal interpolations over each voxel time-course in turn, where the amount of shift is proportional to the temporal offset associated with the slice containing the voxel being considered. However a complete lack of subject motion is unlikely to occur in real data, so the interaction between motion and acquisition delays must be modelled in order to correct fully for the resulting artefacts in the data.

Assuming that motion correction is carried out before any temporal corrections, data which may not correspond to acquisition at a consistent point in time will be co-registered. If slice-timing correction is applied after the initial realignment, the corrected images will contain data from several discrete sample times within individual slices. This is because, in the general case of through-plane motion, spatial registration will realign the data so that intensity values from individual slices in scanner space are distributed across several slice locations

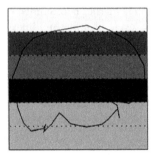 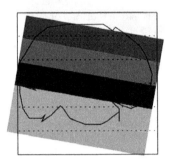

Fig. 1. In this figure the shaded bars, fixed to the same reference frame as the brain, indicate the acquisition timings associated within each slice. Even in the case of rigid-body motion, spatial realignment (in this case correcting a simple pitch of the head) will lead to a breakdown in the correlation between slice location used to determine slice-timing correction (marked with dotted lines) and associated acquisition timings (shaded bars).

in the corrected data. This is illustrated in figure 1. Specifically, if rigid-body realignment is performed, subsequent slice-timing will make the incorrect assumption that data within individual slices will have been acquired at the same time-point. In this situation, it is necessary to keep a record of the slice in which the data were originally acquired, and then apply the appropriate timing correction, a step which is usually omitted. It might, therefore, seem obvious that temporal re-sampling should be carried out before motion correction. An obstacle to such a re-sampling is that in order to carry out slice-timing correction by temporal interpolation of a particular voxel, the time-course of that voxel must be known. If the subject has moved, there is no guarantee that a voxel in object space will be in constant alignment with a voxel in scanner coordinates. This creates a cyclic problem where motion correction is needed in order to determine slice-timing before motion correction. Recognising this inter-dependency is by no means original; but prior to this work there have been no attempts to utilise knowledge about the acquisition sequence in order to correct the situation.

The situation is worse when considering a voxel on an intensity boundary (for example on the interface between two tissue types or on the perimeter of an activating region), since in such a case the voxel described by a particular set of scanner coordinates may rapidly switch between two different intensity regions in object space, thus creating a physically implausible (uncorrected) time-course on which to base temporal interpolation.

In general, if a rigid-body model is assumed, the motion correction stage will also ignore the fact that there may not be a parallel correspondence[3] be-

---

[3]That is, it is no longer correct to assume that the relative movement between slices is consistent across different volumes.

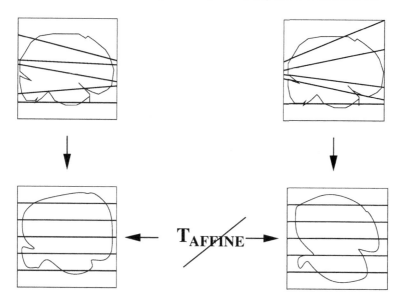

T_{AFFINE}

Fig. 2. Local distribution of slices within different volumes may force the motion correction problem to require a non-rigid solution.

tween the slices from different volumes if motion has occurred during or between activations, such as the example in figure 2. Thus a rigid-body spatial realignment will inevitably attempt to compute pair-wise voxel comparisons on data which originates from different spatial locations in the subject's brain. It is also possible that the slices will remain unaligned, even when the volumetric optimisation has reached a minimum. In conclusion, movement throughout a scan will lead to different displacements in individual slices. This is ignored by volumetric corrections, such as MCLFIRT, which assume a rigid-body transformation over the entire volume. These observations show that the separate application of slice-timing and motion correction cannot accurately account for motion artefacts in FMRI. For this reason, we propose an integrated approach to these two corrections that is able to cope with the potential spatial non-linearities in the data.

If the subject has moved during acquisition of that volume, a quite likely possibility, as previously noted, is that there will be redundancy at some locations yet sparseness and/or voids at other points of the volume. This is due to a particular location in the object having moved sufficiently quickly between slice acquisitions to have been captured either more than once or not at all, as shown in figure 3. This observation is not new in the FMRI literature: incorrect assumptions about spatial distribution of slices have already been identified as the cause of errors in the realignment of FMRI data [6, 1].

At a more basic model level, because subject motion may occur more markedly during some volume acquisitions than in others, the initial motion correction

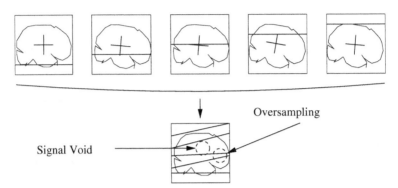

Fig. 3. Movement during the acquisition of a volume (in this case a simple nodding motion is depicted) may cause acquisition redundancy and voids.

stage may be trying to infer an affine relationship between two volumes which do not have the same overall morphology (such as the example shown in figure 2). Another flaw in applying standard intensity-based volumetric registration in this situation is that each volume will contain a unique spatio-temporal distribution of voxels. While all the voxels within each scanner slice are temporally aligned, it is not possible to say before motion estimation which physical locations in object space these voxels relate to or whether this object-to-scanner correspondence is consistent across all volumes. A method that registers individual slices to a single anatomical volume has been proposed in [4] but this does not take into account the timing issues and requires a cross-modal registration. The latter condition is particularly confounding as any 2-D to 3-D registration of this kind is bound to be poorly constrained (the most pathological example of this would be to trying to match a circle to a unique plane within a sphere) and even more so in a cross-modal application where one of the modalities is low resolution EPI, with all its inherent distortions.

Estimation of slice-timing and motion inevitably relies on voxel intensities acquired through a relatively low resolution modality (including activation-related signal changes of interest), so a spatio-temporal scheme offers the additional advantage that it may be possible to combine information over a large number of images to give more robust conclusions than those normally available from pair-wise realignment of EPI volumes.

3   Spatio-temporal Model

The new model described in this section is intended to bypass the shortcomings of the primarily sequential methods described above. The acquisition process is modelled as a set of discrete time-points within each volume, one corresponding to each slice, so as to allow changes in the orientation of the head for each slice. A practical approximation to this process is to express the orientation of each slice as a fraction of the estimated gross motion contained in the volume. This is done by estimating the motion between two volumes and decomposing this motion into a set of evenly-spaced rotations about a common axis [7]. It should be noted that the associated increase in DOF is only a total of 6 additional parameters for the whole time-series. Thus the assumption of an even distribution of slices along some postulated rotational axis is the key to keeping the subsequent optimisation problem manageable. This is discussed in more detail below. Due to the increase in the number of DOF for the registration problem, however, it is necessary to devise a method which is able to efficiently cope with the permitted flexibility in the data and which applies constraints and some global cost invariant over the data as a whole.

The proposed method can generally be divided into 3 separate sections: the initialisation stage, which transforms the images from volumetric data into distributed, discrete slices; the cost function optimisation, with its requisite spatial interpolation choices, which serves to refine the initial image pose estimates by exploiting spatio-temporal similarities in the data; and, finally, the temporal interpolation which implements spatially-integrated slice-timing corrections and includes the estimation of intensity values associated with voxels which are deemed not to have been acquired as a result of inter-slice movement.

3.1   Slice Pose Estimation

Given two volumes which have been acquired one after the other in an FMRI time-series, it is possible to estimate the total motion of the subject's head within the first volume V_n, as the rigid-body transformation $\mathbf{T_n}$ which relates V_n to the second volume, V_{n+1}. This is the approach adopted by MCFLIRT and other rigid-body motion correction schemes. Although this estimate can only be an approximation in the case of an independent-slice model, since the movement is intra-scan rather than volumetric, it provides a useful initial approximation which can then be refined progressively throughout a subsequent optimisation process. It is assumed that T_n is smoothly varying (sudden intra-scan movements within the volume are possible; but in this first study the model will avoid this additional level of complexity in the interests of testing the underlying hypothesis of significant inter-slice motion) so that the transformation can be decomposed into a rotation θ about some common axis [7] $\mathbf{q} = q_x\mathbf{i} + q_y\mathbf{j} + q_z\mathbf{k}$. This formulation, or 'screw decomposition', makes it possible to construct a set of incremental rotations about $\mathbf{q}$ by allowing the angle of rotation to range as $\theta_s = s.\Delta\theta$ where $\Delta\theta = \frac{\theta}{S}$, where s is the current slice number and S is the number of slices. Similarly the translational component $\mathbf{t} = t_x\mathbf{i} + t_y\mathbf{j} + t_z\mathbf{k}$ can be applied in increasing fractions up to the full (rigid-body) value.

These slice-based transformations can be written as $\mathbf{T_{n,s}}$ where $s = 1, .., S$. By applying each incremental transformation to the corresponding plane in scanner space it is possible to form an independent-slice representation of the volume. This is illustrated in figure 4. This decomposition provides a more realistic interpretation of the data in each slice with respect to the subject's head than the standard stacked-slice model [4, 5].

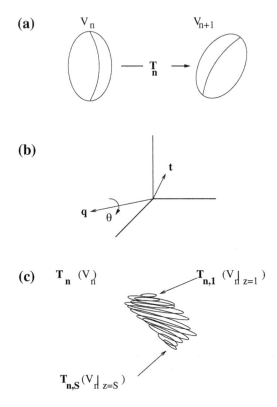

Fig. 4. By expressing the rigid-body transformation $\mathbf{T_n}$ relating volume V_n to volume V_{n+1}, shown in (**a**), as a rotation θ about a single axis $\mathbf{q}$ and a translation $\mathbf{t}$, depicted in (**b**), it is possible to determine a set of transformations $\mathbf{T_{n,s}}$ which describe the local movement of n individual slices. These can be applied to each slice of volume V_n, written $V_n|_{z=s}$ where $s = 1,..,S$, to give volume $\mathbf{T_n}(V_n)$ shown in (**c**), where each slice is transformed by progressively greater fractions of the original transformation, $\mathbf{T_n}$. This provides a more accurate model of the data acquired on a slice-by-slice basis within each volume.

Furthermore, because the distribution of slices is determined by a limited number of parameters (specifically $\mathbf{q}$, θ and $\mathbf{t}$ - all of which are derived from the rigid-body matrix $\mathbf{T_n}$) it is possible to update the orientation of the slices by varying only $\mathbf{T_n}$, thus limiting the complexity of a correction scheme based on this model. This is an important aspect of the model, given the dimensionality of the spatio-temporal data and the number of sample points.

An important corollary to this observation is that by altering $\mathbf{T_n}$, and thus the slice distribution within the test volume V_n, the distribution of slices within the adjacent reference volume V_{n+1} will also be affected. This may be thought of as an 'accordeon' effect where the first slice of the test volume and the final

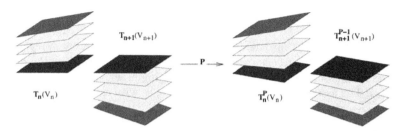

Fig. 5. At each optimisation step for a volume V_n, a perturbation $\mathbf{P}$ is applied to $\mathbf{T_n}$ and the new slice distribution $\mathbf{T_{n,s}^P}(V_n)$ tested. Throughout this optimisation step, the end slices of the volume pair $[V_n, V_{n+1}]$ shown in light grey are kept fixed. In effect what $\mathbf{P}$ does is to vary the mid-point slice between these two volumes, shown in dark grey. Thus, for every perturbation applied to V_n it is necessary to apply the inverse $\mathbf{P^{-1}}$ to $\mathbf{T_{n+1}}$ (giving $\mathbf{T_{n+1}^{P^{-1}}}(V_{n+1})$) to maintain the constraint on the end (light grey) slices.

slice of the reference volume are constrained while the midpoint slice is varied, thus altering the spacing of slices within each volume. An illustration of this relationship between volumes is given in figure 5 . For example, if $\mathbf{T_n}$ relates slice 1 of V_n to slice 1 of V_{n+1} and $\mathbf{T_{n+1}}$ relates slice 1 of V_{n+1} to slice 1 of V_{n+2}, then if slice 1 of V_{n+1} moves by $\mathbf{P}$, the transformation $\mathbf{T_n}$ followed by $\mathbf{P}$ will map slice 1 of V_n to the (now perturbed) slice 1 of V_{n+1}. If the updated rigid-body transformation associated with V_n is written

$$\mathbf{T_n^P} = \mathbf{P} * \mathbf{T_n} \tag{1}$$

where $\mathbf{P}$ describes the parameter updates determined by optimisation (the *perturbation matrix*), then the rigid-body transformation T_{n+1} describing the orientation of the next volume V_{n+1} (which is based on its relative position with respect to V_n) must be adjusted. To understand this, consider the relationship between the newly perturbed slice 1 of V_{n+1} and its original orientation in the example above, which equals $\mathbf{P^{-1}}$. Therefore, the updated $\mathbf{T_{n+1}}$ becomes $\mathbf{P^{-1}}$ followed by the original $\mathbf{T_{n+1}}$. According to the relationship between V_n and V_{n+1} described in section 3.1, this update can be written:

$$\mathbf{T_{n+1}^{P^{-1}}} = \mathbf{T_{n+1}} * \mathbf{P^{-1}}. \tag{2}$$

This ensures that the product $\mathbf{T_{n+1}} * \mathbf{T_n}$ is the same, independent of the application of $\mathbf{P}$, which is necessary as the product of the two transformations describes the mapping between slice 1 of V_n and slice 1 of V_{n+2}, neither of which have moved. By performing this slice-wise decomposition for every image in the series, it is possible to obtain an initial approximation to the data as a more realistic representation of the subject's head in scanner coordinates, rather than a volume corrupted by a single volumetric transformation (illustrated in figures 2 and 3).

3.2   Cost Function Optimisation

Having constructed the initialised distributed-slice time-series by applying the model from section 3.1 to each volume, the next stage in correcting the data is to construct a cost function which attains a minimum when the 4-D time-series is aligned. The assumption underlying this stage, as with conventional intensity-based rigid-body schemes designed to work on FMRI data, is that there will be a small level of intensity variability restricted to a small number of voxels. These voxels are assumed to correspond either to regions of the subject's brain which have activated under the stimulus of the experiment or those areas which have been affected by an acquisition artefact. The intensity of the remaining voxels should remain broadly constant in object coordinates so the correction should seek a realignment over the 4-D data which minimises this variance. A Least Squares metric [3] is used to reduce the likelihood of local movement patterns dominating the evaluation of a minimum. An example of such a situation would be where there is no appreciable motion throughout two adjacent volumes but where those two volumes are significantly offset from the rest of the time-series. By generating a reference image from the entire remainder of the time-series, there is a much smaller possibility of the presence of an adjacent (similarly mis-aligned) volume driving the evaluation of the cost function. When interpolating intensity values after registration, sinc interpolation is applied to the original data. Currently multi-dimensional optimisation using the golden section method is used to search for cost function minima, with the order of rotation searches being permuted to avoid local minima traps. More sophisticated optimisation strategies are considered in section 5.

In order to enforce the anatomical constraint, that is, that the realigned data should represent the data in object space, not simply in a pose which satisfies the cost function, it is necessary to include at least one volume which contains little or no inter-slice movement. While this may seem to be a very specific case of the likely input data, it is relatively easy to select such a volume from within the time-series by examining the relative RMS difference between each volume, as estimated by MCFLIRT. In the case where the relative movement between two volumes is very low, an assumption can be made that little or no inter-slice movement occurred over the course of the acquisition of either. Thus the images will hopefully contain a physically-consistent representation of the brain, even if its global pose is not entirely co-incident with the coordinate axes.

Either of these two internally static images can then be used as a canonical reference volume for the spatio-temporal realignment. An appropriate modification to the realignment scheme is to select the static volume using the procedure described above and to then allow the adjacent volume to perturb according the the model shown in figure 5. Once this second volume has been realigned with respect to the first static volume, it is then possible to use both these volumes as a reference image in the variance cost for the realignment of the third volume. In this way, the reference image is built up iteratively but anatomical constraints are enforced by virtue of starting with a volume which has been measured as the most likely to contain little in the way of inter-slice movement.

In addition to the intermediate interpolation described above, care must also be taken when performing the temporal re-sampling applied to each voxel time-course after spatial realignment. The underlying acquisition process should ensure that once optimisation is complete, all the voxels within each slice of scanner space should contain intensity values acquired at the same time. Unlike existing rigid-body schemes which are inappropriately used with slice-timing, the spatial realignment of the data resulting from the proposed slice-based model allows the application of appropriate temporal interpolation. However, care must be taken to deal with situations where there may be no acquisitions for a given voxel at a particular volume's time-point. In order to apply a shift to reflect the temporal offset of each slice it is necessary to have at least one sample for each voxel location and time-point. If reconstruction of the data has concluded that the particular voxel was 'missed' during acquisition as a result of subject motion, its intensity value is estimated using Hermite splines. By maintaining a record of the slice from which each transformed intensity value originated, it is then trivial to apply the appropriate temporal shift using sinc or other interpolation basis functions.

4   Testing and Results

The method described above has been implemented and applied to synthetically-generated test data, based on a single high resolution EPI image to minimise the effect of interpolation artefacts when re-aligning the data to simulate motion. Two datasets were constructed which contained a static initial volume followed by 20 volumes which contained motion. The first dataset simulated a nodding motion distributed over the individual slices of each volume up to a maximum of 2 degrees, while the second dataset contained a nodding design of the same magnitude, centered on the centre of mass of the original image.

An initial analysis of the cost function behaviour on this test data revealed that the cost function was not at a minimum, even when the images were perfectly re-aligned using the independent slice model. We believe that this discrepancy is due to the extremely high levels of accuracy which are required for the spatial interpolation of comparatively sparse data. Testing the spatio-temporal optimisation on the shaking dataset revealed that the realignment scheme was able to reduce the average RMS error within each volume from an un-corrected value of 1.9331 millimetres to 0.2829 millimetres. The deviations from ground truth in the parameter estimates were noted to consistently follow the observations made in the initial cost function analysis.

Qualitative examination of the realigned data revealed that very little perceptible global motion remained within each slice. Of potentially greater interest was the presence of local detail variation between time-points. This reflects the changing role played by interpolation across a range of slice poses and further reenforces the earlier hypothesis that interpolation is responsible for much of the error with respect to zero motion observed in the cost plots. While deviations from zero were still observable in the parameter estimates for the nodding data, the realignment was able to reduce the average RMS error from 2.1863 millimetres to 0.7451 millimetres.

The current implementation takes approximately 72 hours to process a 20 volume time-series on a 64-bit ES40 667MHz Alpha platform, approximately 80% of which is dedicated to the additional parameter permutation searches.

5   Conclusions and Future Work

It has been shown that an implementation of the TIGER model can be applied in order to provide corrections which are known to be fundamentally more accurate than existing rigid-body and separate slice-timing methods. In the case of both nodding and shaking motion, the scheme was able to significantly reduce the levels of motion in the data to a sub-millimetre level which is necessary for accurate activation detection.

Given that the dominant source of error in the above implementation was interpolation accuracy, an improvement in the spatial estimation of the TIGER framework is likely to result from the inclusion of a more sophisticated inter-polation technique. The issue of accuracy of interpolation has been highlighted repeatedly as a fundamental factor in the reliability of motion correction, even more so than in conventional medical image registration [3]. It is possible that advanced forms of spatial interpolation, such as Markov Random Fields could be adapted to include the robust estimation of inhomogeneous sampling rather than having to use a separate spline interpolation stage. An alternative approach to the problems caused by inaccurate interpolation might alternatively involve deriving the interpolated values from the original k-space data. By interpolating in k-space, before the data is Fourier transformed into cartesian image space, it might be possible to achieve more accurate interpolation by avoiding the errors associated with interpolating truncated data in the form of images.

Furthermore, necessary step in making the scheme practical for use on real data, which may contain inter-slice motion over several axes, will be to incorporate a more advanced optimisation framework. This optimisation method should be able to search the cost function space in a quasi-exhaustive manner so that the best minimum is always located. Possible candidates for this scheme include simulated annealing and parallelised gradient descent.

6   Acknowledgements

The authors would like to thank Christian Beckmann, Stuart Clare, Stephen Smith and Mark Woolrich for a number of helpful discussions on this research. Financial support from the MRC and EPSRC is gratefully acknowledged.

References

[1] R.W. Cox. Motion and Functional MRI: Informal notes for the Boston '96 workshop on functional MRI, 1996.

[2] K.J. Friston, J. Ashburner, C.D. Frith, J.-B. Poline, J.D. Heather, and R.S.J. Frack-owiak. Spatial registration and normalization of images. *Human Brain Mapping*, 2:165–189, 1995.

[3] M. Jenkinson, P.R. Bannister, J.M. Brady, and S.M. Smith. Improved optimisa-tion for the robust and accurate linear registration and motion correction of brain images. *NeuroImage*, 17(2):825–841, 2002.

[4] B. Kim, J.L. Boes, P.H. Bland, T.L. Chenevert, and C.R. Meyer. Motion correction in fMRI via registration of individual slices into an anatomical volume. *Magnetic Resonance in Medicine*, 41:964–972, 1999.

[5] L. Muresan, R. Renken, J.B.T.M. Roerdink, and H. Duifhuis. Position-history and spin-history artifacts in fMRI time-series. In A. V. Clough and C.-T. Chen, edi-tors, *Proc. Medical Imaging 2002: Physiology and Function from Multidimensional Image*, volume 4683, pages 444–451. Proc. SPIE, 2002.

[6] D.C. Noll, F.E. Boada, and W.F. Eddy. Movement correction in fMRI: The impact of slice profile and slice spacing. *International Soc. of Magnetic Resonance in Medicine*, page 1677, 1997.

[7] R.L. Paul. *Robot manipulators*. Series in Artificial Intelligence. The MIT Press, 1981.

Robust Registration of 3-D Ultrasound Images Based on Gabor Filter and Mean-Shift Method

Feng Cen[1], Yifeng Jiang[1], Zhijun Zhang[1], H.T. Tsui[1], T.K. Lau[2], and Hongning Xie[3]

[1] Department of Electronic Engineering
{fcen,yfjiang,zjzhang,httsui}@ee.cuhk.edu.hk
[2] Department of Obstetrics and Gynaecology
The Chinese University of Hong Kong, Shatin NT, Hong Kong
[3] First Affiliated Hospital, Sun Yet-sen University, Guangzhou, China

Abstract. A novel robust method is presented for the registration of 3-D ultrasound images. The proposed method improves the performance of the voxel property-based affine registration in two aspects. First, a set of wavelet-like Gabor filters is used to extract the texture and edge features of the voxels. By using these features, the smoothness of the similarity function in large scale can be improved. Furthermore, adopting edge information can improve the registration accuracy. Second, a robust maximization method based on the mean-shift algorithm and Powell's direction set method is proposed. The implicitly embedded smoothing process of the mean-shift algorithm can effectively remove the local fluctuation of the similarity function and significantly improve the robustness of optimization. Experimental results demonstrate the robust and accurate performance of the proposed method in the registration of 3-D ultrasound fetal head images.

1 Introduction

Ultrasound imaging has been one of the most widely used medical imaging tools in healthcare for diagnosis, planning treatment, guiding treatment. This is because it is safe, non-invasive, real time, low cost and easy to use. However, comparing to other radiological imaging modalities, such as computed tomography (CT) and magnetic resonance imaging (MRI) etc., one of the limitations of the conventional ultrasound examination is the two-dimensional (2-D) imaging nature. Three-dimensional (3-D) ultrasound imaging, the most recent advance in ultrasound imaging, aims to overcome that limitation. Two types of 3-D ultrasound imaging solutions are being developed. One is dependent on the new special 3-D probes to produce a 3-D image of a volume inside the body. The other is based on conventional 2-D images to construct a 3-D data set. Since some technical challenges have yet to be solved for the 3-D probes, currently, the latter solution is actually the preferred choice for most 3-D ultrasound imaging systems used in clinical practice. The emergence of 3-D ultrasound imaging significantly encourages the research on the field of ultrasound image registration.

M. Šonka et al. (Eds.): CVAMIA-MMBIA 2004, LNCS 3117, pp. 304–316, 2004.

This is important as registration is a key step to reconstruct the 3-D ultrasound volumes of the tissues and organs from the consecutive 2-D ultrasound images. Accurate wide field-of-view (FOV) of 3-D ultrasound volumes can also be obtained. Moreover, the registration of different 3-D ultrasound data set permits the comparison of serial examinations performed on the same patient.

Although medical image registration has been a very active field of research, little has been published on the registration of ultrasound images. Apart from the obstacle caused by the 2-D imaging nature of ultrasound examination, this may also be due to the relatively poor image quality of ultrasound images comparing to other medical imaging modalities. Medical image registration methods can be divided into two main classes: feature-based methods and voxel property-based methods. Since the accurate detection of the image features in the noisy ultrasound images is still a very difficult task, the voxel property-based methods seem more suitable for ultrasound image registration.

Rohling *et al*[2] were among those who first attempt to use the voxel property-based method for the registration of ultrasound volumes. They used the correlation coefficient of gradient images for the rigid registration of the human gall bladder images acquired by freehand 3-D ultrasound scan. Meyer *et al*[3] applied the mutual information measure to affine and elastic registration of 3-D ultrasound images in gray-scale and color flow. Shekhar *et al*[1] investigated using the preprocessing of median filter and intensity quantization to improve the robustness of the registration of 3-D cardiac ultrasound images under the affine transform framework. Xiao *et al*[4] study the correlation coefficient based block matching methods for elastic registration of 3-D freehand breast ultrasound images. Gee *et al*[5], proposed to impose the constraint of the mechanics of freehand scanning process on the warp's degree to reduce the computational load in non-rigid registration.

The major procedures involved in voxel property-based methods include: extraction of voxel property, selection of similarity measure, definition of the transformation and the choice of an optimization approach. One of main difficulties in ultrasound image registration is the poor image quality primarily caused by speckle noises. The poor quality of ultrasound images may introduce many local maxima in the similarity measure. Consequently, it is difficult to obtain the desired solution in the following optimization procedure. Hence, when trying to devise a robust voxel property-based registration method of 3-D ultrasound images we use two techniques: reducing the fluctuation of the similarity function varying with the transformation parameters and enhancing the robustness of the optimization method to the local fluctuation of the similarity function.

In this paper, we propose first to use the wavelet-like complex Gabor filter banks to extract the voxel features for the similarity measure in the registration of ultrasound images. Then, we employ the mean-shift algorithm combined with the Powell's direction set method[6] to search through the affine transformation for the strong local maximum of the similarity function. This is expected to be the location of the desired registration solution. The paper with a similar focus to ours is that by Shekhar *et al*[1]. There are two advantages of the proposed

method. First, by using the Gabor filter bank for the preprocessing, we can reduce the fluctuation of the similarity function in large scale without any sacrifice
in accuracy due to the localization property of the Gabor filters. Further, it can
also incorporate the edge information of 3-D ultrasound images to improve the
accuracy of registration. Second, the implicitly embedded smoothing process of
the mean-shift algorithm can significantly improve the robustness of the optimization through directly smoothing the surface of similarity function. Based on
the proposed preprocessing and optimization method, the accuracy and the robustness of three prevalent similarity measures for the registration of ultrasound
images are tested in this paper.

The paper is organized as follows. Section 2, the voxel feature extraction
by Gabor filter is presented. Section 3 introduces the similarity measure. The
optimization method based on mean-shift algorithm is described in section 4.
Experiment and conclusion are given in section 5 and section 6, respectively.

2   Voxel Feature Extraction

Although the ultrasound images are of poor quality degraded by heavy speckle
noises, they are highly textured. The speckle noises are able to be viewed as in an
irregular and complex texture pattern[9]. This fact inspires us to employ the Gabor filter, an excellent and extensively studied multi-channel filtering method for
texture analysis, for the preprocessing of the registration of ultrasound images.
The attractive properties of Gabor filter include its optimum joint spatial/spatial
frequency localization and the ability to simulate the behavior of 2-D receptive
field of simple cell in the visual cortex by isolating specific frequencies and orientations.

A 2-D complex Gabor filter represented as a 2-D impulse response is given
by[8]

$$h(x, y) = g(x', y') \exp(j2\pi F x'), \tag{1}$$

where $(x', y') = (x \cos \theta + y \sin \theta, -x \sin \theta + y \cos \theta)$ are rotated coordinates, F is
the radial center frequency, and

$$g(x, y) = \frac{1}{2\pi\sigma_x\sigma_y} \exp\left\{-\frac{1}{2}\left[\frac{x^2}{\sigma_x^2} + \frac{y^2}{\sigma_y^2}\right]\right\}, \tag{2}$$

where σ_x and σ_y are the space constants of the Gaussian envelope along the x
and y axes and can be calculated by

$$\sigma_x = \frac{\sqrt{\ln 2}\left(2^{B_F} + 1\right)}{\sqrt{2}\pi F\left(2^{B_F} - 1\right)},$$

$$\sigma_y = \frac{\sqrt{\ln 2}}{\sqrt{2}\pi F \tan(B_\theta/2)},$$

where B_F is the frequency bandwidth and B_θ is the angular bandwidth. To
enhance the texture separability of the Gabor filter, a Gaussian smoothing filter, $g(\gamma x, \gamma y)$, is used to post-filter the output amplitude for each channel. The

$g(\gamma x, \gamma y)$ is set to have the same shape as the corresponding channel filter but greater spatial extents, because it can yield results that are still spatially well localized. The spatial extent is controlled by γ.

Because of the complexity and irregularity nature of the speckle texture, a predefined set of Gabor filters, so-called Gabor filter bank, covering the spatial frequency domain, is a reasonable choice for the extraction of texture features in ultrasound images. The Gabor filter bank can be generated by varying four free parameters $(F, \theta, B_F, B_\theta)$. In our implementation, the selection of the parameter set follows the suggestion in [7], i.e., the frequency spacing and bandwidth is one octave and the orientation spacing and bandwidth is 30°, and γ is set to 2/3, because the Gabor filters generated with this parameter set have the optimal texture separability. The response of Gabor filter bank, generated with our parameter set selection, in spatial frequency domain is shown in Fig. 1.

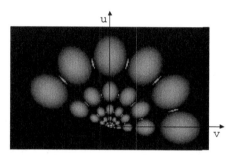

Fig. 1. The responses of Gabor filter bank in spatial frequency domain. Only the portion larger than the half-peak magnitude is shown for each filter

Directly applying a 3-D Gabor filter bank for 3-D ultrasound volumes is computationally intensive. To save the computation time, we take two banks of 2-D Gabor filters located at the orthogonal planes as an approximation. Since in our experiment, the 3-D ultrasound volume is reconstructed from a sequence of 2-D images, which are closely parallel to each other (this is also true for most of prevalent 3-D ultrasound system), one of the two planes is set parallel to the ultrasound echo plane, i.e., the same plane as the 2-D ultrasound images (we define as x-y plane), the other is adapted perpendicular to the ultrasound probe.

By using the two Gabor filter banks designed above, we can obtain four sets of outputs: $\{H_{s,k}^r(\boldsymbol{X})\}$, $\{H_{s,k}^i(\boldsymbol{X})\}$, $\{P_{s,k}^r(\boldsymbol{X})\}$, $\{P_{s,k}^i(\boldsymbol{X})\}$, for each voxel $\boldsymbol{X} = (x, y, z)$ corresponding to real and imaginary parts of parallel plane and perpendicular plane filter banks, respectively. Here, $s = (0, ..., S-1)$ and $k = (0, ..., K-1)$ denote the scale and orientation of the outputs, respectively. The DC component is set to zero as the mean local gray level does not make sense for the texture feature.

The four sets of the outputs of Gabor filter banks, in a high dimensional feature space, are not suitable to be directly used as the voxel properties for the similarity measure. Therefore, we sum the real part and imaginary part outputs separately, and get

$$G^r(\boldsymbol{X}) = \sum_{s,k} H^r_{s,k}(\boldsymbol{X}) + \sum_{s,k} P^r_{s,k}(\boldsymbol{X}), \tag{3}$$

$$G^i(\boldsymbol{X}) = \sum_{s,k} \frac{H^i_{s,k}(\boldsymbol{X})}{\boldsymbol{n}_k \cdot \boldsymbol{u}} + \sum_{s,k} P^i_{s,k}(\boldsymbol{X}), \tag{4}$$

where $\boldsymbol{n}_k$ is the unit vector of the center frequency of Gabor filter in k's direction, and $\boldsymbol{u}$ is the unit vector of the ultrasound beam direction.

In fact, as the amplitude of ultrasound echo is proportional to the difference between successive tissue layers, the interfaces between anatomical structures present as enhanced edges in ultrasound images. So, incorporating edge features into the similarity measure can improve the accuracy of the registration of ultrasound images. Actually, the imaginary parts of the Gabor filters are of the representation of the intensity variation of ultrasound images in multi-scales and multi-orientations[10]. Therefore, using both the real parts and imaginary parts of the Gabor filters is a nature way to combine the texture and edge property of the voxel for the registration of ultrasound images. However, the amplitude of ultrasound echo is also approximately proportional to the projection of the interface direction on the ultrasound beam direction. As a consequence, the edges closely parallel to the ultrasound beam direction are weak and blur, which is a undesirable effect for most ultrasound image processing, including registration. So, in order to partially compensate the degradation of parallel edges in ultrasound images , we propose to divide the imaginary responses of the Gabor filter by $\boldsymbol{n}_k \cdot \boldsymbol{u}$, the projection of the unit vector of Gabor filter direction on the ultrasound beam direction. But we only carry out this compensation in x-y plane for the reason that the beam direction is hard to determine in perpendicular plane.

In addition, the small responses in the imaginary parts of Gabor filters, which are mainly produced by the noises, should be eliminated so that the edge information can be represented more accurately. Define the mean and standard deviation of $G^i(\boldsymbol{X})$ over the entire 3-D volume as $\widetilde{G^i}$ and σ_{G^i}, respectively, we use the following process to remove the imaginary responses caused by noises,

$$E^i(\boldsymbol{X}) = \begin{cases} G^i(\boldsymbol{X}), & \text{if } G^i(\boldsymbol{X}) - \widetilde{G^i} > \sigma_{G^i} \\ \widetilde{G^i}, & \text{if } G^i(\boldsymbol{X}) - \widetilde{G^i} \le \sigma_{G^i}. \end{cases} \tag{5}$$

To be easily adopted into the similarity measure, in our experiments, the double-valued texture and edge feature of the voxel, $\{G^r(\boldsymbol{X}), E^i(\boldsymbol{X})\}$, are quantized by 256 levels. Due to the robust local maximum searching method in Sec. 4, the selection of the number of quantization levels does not significantly affect the registration performance.

Note that the above preprocess also performs like a multi-scale wavelet denoising procedure, which effectively suppresses the speckle noise and at the same time preserves the useful details.

3   Similarity Measure

When the affine transformation, T, is adopted in the voxel property-based registration, there are three prevalent similarity measure: correlation coefficient (CC), correlation ratio (CR)[11] and mutual information (MI)[12]. Denoting the reference image by I^r and the floating image by I^f, typically, the respective cost function can be written as:

$$\eta(I^r, I^f \circ T) = \begin{cases} H(I^r) + H(I^f \circ T) - H(I^r, I^f \circ T) & \text{MI} \\ \frac{Var[E(I^f \circ T|I^r)]}{Var(I^f \circ T)} & \text{CR} \\ \frac{Cov(I^r, I^f \circ T)}{\sqrt{Var(I^r \circ T)}\sqrt{Var(I^f \circ T)}} & \text{CC} \end{cases} . \quad (6)$$

The underlying differences between these similarity measures are the different assumptions they make on the relationship between the two images to be registered. Among three similarity measures, the CC is the most restrictive criterion, assuming that the two images are related by an affine mapping. The MI is the most general criterion, only assuming a statistical relationship between the two images (which means the two image are only need to be predictable). The CR is in between, assuming a functional relationship[14].

After the preprocessing of Gabor filters, two sets of maps: the texture maps, $G^r(I^r)$ and $G^r(I^f)$, and the intensity variation maps, $E^i(I^r)$ and $E^i(I^f)$ can be obtained. Here, we propose to use linear method to combine the similarity measures of these two map sets for , i.e.,

$$\eta(I^r, I^f \circ T) = \eta(G^r(I^r), G^r(I^f) \circ T) + \alpha\eta(E^i(I^r), E^i(I^f) \circ T), \quad (7)$$

where α is a weighting constant.

In our study, we test the robustness and accuracy of all three similarity measures and observe that the registration performs more robustly with CR measure than with CC and MI measures, as there is a wider capture range for CR measure. But, little difference is shown in registration accuracy. Therefore, we propose to use CR measure in our method.

4   Mean-Shift Based Optimization

Generally, the desired solution in voxel property-based registration is related to a strong local maximum of the similarity measure but not necessarily the global maximum. So, we suppose that the start alignment of two ultrasound volumes, which is set by a human interactive procedure, is in the vicinity of the desired solution and the strong local maximum closest to the start position corresponds to the desired solution. Here, "strong" not only refer to the magnitude of the local maximum, but also means the large extent of the cost function surface. Therefore, in our method, the optimization is restricted to search for the strong local maximum closest to the start position.

According to mean-shift algorithm, a vector (named mean-shift vector) at location pointing towards the gradient ascent direction can be obtain by[13]

$$m(\boldsymbol{x}) = \frac{\sum_{\boldsymbol{s}\in\Omega} K\left(\frac{\boldsymbol{s}-\boldsymbol{x}}{\lambda}\right)\omega(\boldsymbol{s})\boldsymbol{s}}{\sum_{\boldsymbol{s}\in\Omega} K\left(\frac{\boldsymbol{s}-\boldsymbol{x}}{\lambda}\right)\omega(\boldsymbol{s})} - \boldsymbol{x}, \tag{8}$$

where K is a suitable kernel function, and the summation is performed over a local window of Ω with a window radius λ around the current location x. An important property of the mean-shift algorithm is that the mean-shift vector is always point towards the gradient ascent direction of the convolution surface given by

$$C(\boldsymbol{x}) = \sum_{\boldsymbol{s}} H\left(\frac{\boldsymbol{s}-\boldsymbol{x}}{\lambda}\right)\omega(\boldsymbol{s}), \tag{9}$$

where H is the shadow kernel of K.

There are two advantages for using the mean-shift algorithm in optimization procedure. First, by choosing a smoothing kernel H, which can effectively eliminate the local fluctuation on the surface of similarity function, a robust local maximum searching procedure can be achieved with the mean-shift algorithm. For simplicity and effectiveness, we choose the kernel K as a flat kernel, and the corresponding shadow kernel is the Epanechnikov kernel respectively given by

$$K(\boldsymbol{x}) = \begin{cases} 1 & \text{if } \|\boldsymbol{x}\| \le 1 \\ 0 & \text{if } \|\boldsymbol{x}\| > 1 \end{cases}, \tag{10}$$

$$H(\boldsymbol{x}) = \begin{cases} \frac{1}{2}c_d^{-1}(d+2)(1-\|\boldsymbol{x}\|) & \text{if } \|\boldsymbol{x}\| \le 1 \\ 0 & \text{if } \|\boldsymbol{x}\| > 1 \end{cases}, \tag{11}$$

where c_d is the volume of the unit d-dimensional sphere. An example of mean-shift optimization in one dimension is shown in Fig. 2. Second, by varying the kernel scale λ from large scale to small scale progressively, the optimization can be run robustly and accurately in a coarse-to-fine strategy.

In high dimensional space, performing an entire mean-shift search is infeasible due to excessive computation cost. To reduce the computational load, we incorporate the mean-shift method with the Powell's direction set method[6] by adopting the mean-shift as the sub-line optimization procedure. Although, the method we proposed here is not actually equivalent to the multidimensional mean-shift method in mathematics, the advantages of smoothing the surface of the similarity function and searching for the strong local maximum in a coarse-to-fine strategy can also be achieved with acceptable computational complexity.

5   Experiments and Results

Two sequences of fetal head ultrasound images from a woman with 19-week pregnancy were used in our study. The images were collected from Voluson 730, a real-time 3-D ultrasound system manufactured by GE company, in two sweep scans with different resolutions. Before applying the method to 3-D ultrasound

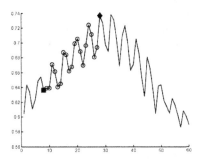

Fig. 2. Searching for maximum with mean-shift method in one dimension. The start position is marked with a solid square, the intermediate steps are shown by hollow circles and the final result is represented by a solid diamond

volumes, we first use 2-D ultrasound images to demonstrate the characteristics of the proposed method.

Both two 2-D images used in registration involve the Biparietal Diameter (BPD). The BPD, a most widely used ultrasound parameter in the estimation of gestational age, is the maximum diameter of a transverse section of the fetal skull at the level of the parietal eminences. It can be precisely identified by experts. So, the selected 2-D images, as shown in Fig. 3(a), stand for the same anatomical structure precisely. The size of 2-D image is 256×256. Meanwhile, Fig. 3(b) and (c) show the texture maps and the intensity variation maps produced by the Gabor filter bank.

The smoothing effect of using the voxel features extracted with Gabor filter bank on the similarity function is given in Fig. 4. From Fig. 4(b), we can see that the undesired local maxima in large scale have been effectively smoothed and removed when using the texture maps for similarity measure. Furthermore, we show the improvement of the registration accuracy in Fig. 5, when incorporating the edge information into the similarity measure. It is observed that the skull profiles match more precisely in Fig. 5(b).

In our implementation the affine transformation is approximated by a series of successive elementary transformations: shearing, scaling, rotation and translation. The units of searching step in optimization are set to: 1 pixel for translation, 1% for scaling, 1 degree for rotation and shearing. The weighting parameter α in Equ. 7 is set to 1.

To compare the robustness when adopting different cost function, we randomly start registration from the fixed range of initial misalignment and estimate the percentage of successful registration. Three random sets of the start misalignment, 200 positions in each of them, are generated with the maximum misalignment of 10, 20 and 30 steps in each degree of freedom, respectively. Because the ground truth is not known for our experiment, visual assessment is used for the identification of correct registration. From Table. 1, it is evident

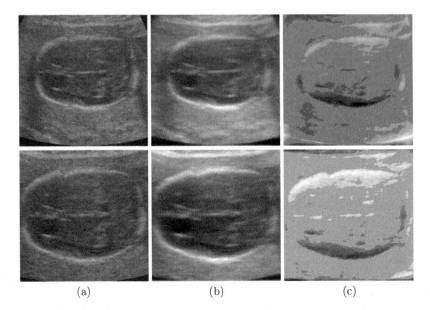

(a)   (b)   (c)

Fig. 3. Results of Gabor filter preprocessing for reference image (top row) and floating image (bottom row).(a) Original ultrasound images. (b) Texture maps. (c) Intensity variation maps.

that the capture range of CR measure is larger than CC and MI measure. We also compare the accuracy of the registration, when adopting different similarity measure. However, we can hardly observe the difference with visual assessment.

Table 1. Comparison of the ratio of successful registration for MI, CC and CR measures

Range (steps)	10	20	30
MI	100%	74.5%	-
CC	100%	100%	81%
CR	100%	100%	92%

The effects of interpolation are also investigated, but little difference in the performance of registration is shown between the bilinear, cubic and partial volume interpolation. This is expected, since the implicitly embedded smoothing process of the mean-shift algorithm can effectively remove the local fluctuation on the surface of the cost function caused by interpolation.

Finally we apply the proposed method to 3-D ultrasound volumes. The size of ultrasound volumes are $256 \times 256 \times 106$ and $256 \times 256 \times 92$ for floating volume and

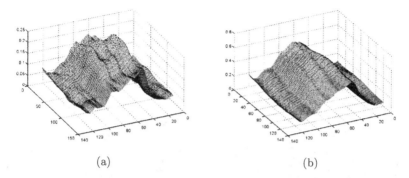

(a)   (b)

Fig. 4. Correlation Ratio as a function of misalignment caused by translation in y axis and scaling in x axis for (a) the original image pair and (b) the texture maps of the image pair.

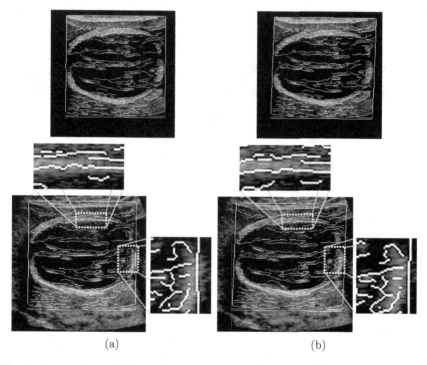

(a)   (b)

Fig. 5. Comparison of the registration results for using (a) texture maps, (b) texture maps and intensity variation maps. The white curves superimposed on each images are the edges detected by Canny edge detector in the corresponding texture maps of the floating images. The top row shows the floating images when registered and the bottom row the reference images. Parts of images are enlarged to show the improvement of the registration accuracy clearly.

reference volume, respectively. Fig. 6 shows three image slices of the reference volume fused with the floating volume before and after registration. We can observe that even with a large start misalignment, two ultrasound volumes are aligned correctly.

Skull in floating volume

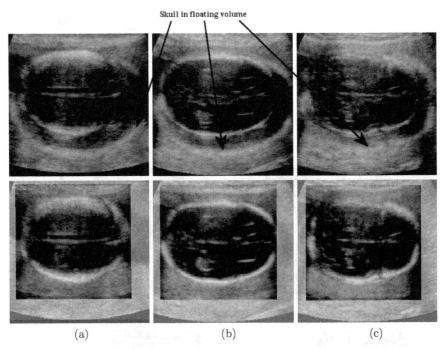

(a)   (b)   (c)

Fig. 6. Image slices of the reference volume fused with floating volume before (top row) and after (bottom row) registration in x-y plane. Three images correspond to the (a) 25th, (b)50th and (c)75th slices in reference volume, respectively.

6   Conclusion

In this paper, a novel robust approach for the registration of 3-D ultrasound images has been proposed. Wavelet-like Gabor filter banks are used for the extraction of texture features and edge features. The use of both texture features and edge features facilitates the smoothness and accuracy of the similarity function. Furthermore, on the assumption that the correct registration is related to a strong local maximum of the similarity function, a mean-shift based optimization method is proposed to robustly search through the affine transformation for the desired solution. Since the proposed optimization method is robust to the local fluctuation on the similarity function, the selection of interpolation method, a difficult task in other registration method, becomes less important. From the experiments on the registration of the ultrasound images of the fetal head, we can conclude that the proposed method is robust and accurate for the affine registration of the ultrasound images. Our future work will focus on improving the efficiency of the approach and extend it to the registration of multi-module medical images.

Acknowledgement

The work described in this paper was supported by a Central Allocation Grant from the Research Grants Council of the Hong Kong Special Administrative Region. (Project no. CUHK1/00C)

References

1. R. Shekhar and V. Zagrodsky. Mutual Imformation-Based Rigid and Nonrigid Registration of Ultrasound Volumes. *IEEE Trans. Medical Imaging*, 21(1):9-22, 2002.
2. R. N. Rohling, and A. H. Gee, and L. Berman. Automatic Registration of 3-D Ultrasound Images. *Ultrasound Med. Biol.*, 24:841-854, 1998.
3. C. R. Meyer, J. L. Boes, B. Kim, P. H. Bland, G. L. Lecarpentier, J. B.Fowlkes, M. A. Roubidoux and P. L. Carson. Semiautomatic Registration of Volumetric Ultrasound Scans. *Ultrasound Med. Biol.*, 25:339-347, 1999.
4. G. Xiao, M. Brady, J. A. Noble, M. Burcher and R. English. Nonrigid Registration of 3-D Free-Hand Ultrasound Images of the Breast. *IEEE Trans. Medical Imaging*, 21(4):405-412, 2002.
5. A. H. Gee, G. M. Treece, R. W. Prager, C. J. C. Cash and L. Berman. Rapid Registration for Wide Field of View Freehand Tree-Dimensional Ultrasound. *IEEE Trans. Medical Imaging*, 22(11):1344-1357, 2003.
6. W. H. Press, B. P. Flannery, S. A. Teukolsky and W. T. Vetterling. Numerical Recipes in C, 2nd ed. *Cambridge, U. K.: Cambridge Univ. Press*, 1992.
7. D. A. Clausi, M. E. Jernigan. Designing Gabor Filters for Optimal Texture Separability. *Pattern Recognition*, 33:1835-1849, 1999.
8. A.C. Bovik, M. Clark and W.S. Geisler. Multichannel Texture Analysis Using Localized Spatial Filters. *IEEE Trans. Pattern Anal. Machine Intell.*, 12(1):55-73, 1990.
9. C. M. Chen, H. H. Lu and K. Han. A Textural Approach Based on Gabor Functions for Texture Edge Detection in Ultrasound Images. *Ultrasound Med. Biol.*, 27(4):515-534, 2001.
10. D. Shen, Y. Zhan and C. Davatzikos. Segmentation of Prostate Boundaries from Ultrasound Images Using Statistical Shape Model. *IEEE Trans. Medical Imaging*, 22(4):539-551, 2003
11. A. Roche, G. Malandain, X. Pennec and N. Ayache. The Correlation Ratio as a New Similarity Measure for Multimodal Image Registration. In *Proc. of First Int. Conf. on Medical Image Computing and Computer-Assisted Intervention (MICCAI'98)*, 1115-1124, Oct 1998.
12. F. Maes, A. Collignon, D. Vandermeulen, G. Marchal and P. Suetens. Multimodality Image Registration by Maximization of Mutual Information. *IEEE Trans. Medical Imaging*, 16(2):187-197, 1997.

13. Y. Cheng. Mean Shift, Mode Seeking, and Clustering. *IEEE Trans. Pattern Anal. Machine Intell.*, 17(8):790-799, 1995.
14. A. Roche, G. Malandain and N. Ayache. Unifying Maximum Likelihood Approaches in Medical Image Registration. *International Journal of Imaging Systems and Technology: Special Issue on 3D Imaging*, 11(1):71–80, 2000.

Deformable Image Registration by Adaptive Gaussian Forces

Vladimir Pekar[1] and Evgeny Gladilin[2]

[1] Philips Research, Röntgenstr. 24-26, D-22335 Hamburg, Germany
vladimir.pekar@philips.com
[2] Zuse Institute Berlin, Takustr. 7, D-14195 Berlin, Germany
gladilin@zib.de

Abstract. This paper introduces a novel physics-based approach to elastic image registration. It is based on applying Gaussian-shaped forces at irregularly distributed control points in the image, which is considered to be an infinite elastic continuum. The positions of the control points, the directions and magnitudes of the applied forces as well as their influence areas, and the elastic material properties are optimized to reach a maximum of the similarity measure between the images. The use of the adaptive irregular grid potentially allows to achieve good registration quality by using fewer parameters as compared to regular grids, e.g. B-splines. The feasibility of the proposed approach is tested on clinical images, and open problems and directions for future work are discussed.

1   Introduction

Image registration is an important procedure in medical image analysis, aimed at obtaining complementary information from different representations of the same anatomy. The goal of image registration is to find a transformation bringing the anatomy in the source and target image into the best possible spatial correspondence.

Many classification schemes of registration algorithms exist [1,2]. One of the most general classification criteria is the transformation type. Algorithms using rigid and affine transformations are significantly simpler than those using nonlinear transformations. On the other hand, the application range where rigid and affine transformations are sufficient is limited. Rigid and affine registration has successfully been applied for many clinical applications, and the corresponding software is commercially available from the vendors of medical image processing equipment. However, the situation is quite different in the area of non-linear (deformable) registration, where only few potentially feasible solutions exist despite many years of active research.

A challenging problem in deformable image registration is coping with the complexity of the underlying non-linear transformations, often resulting in prohibitive computational costs for the practical use. The use of non-parametric transformations may, for example, lead to optimization problems with several

M. Šonka et al. (Eds.): CVAMIA-MMBIA 2004, LNCS 3117, pp. 317–328, 2004.

million unknowns, where only a few efficient solutions are known in the literature [3,4]. An advantage of parametric methods is the ability to represent non-linear transformations with a moderate number of parameters. One example is deformable registration based on regular B-spline grids [5,6]. However, their performance is highly dependent on the grid resolution, with fine grids leading to a high-dimensional search space and coarse grids leading to improper registration of small structures. To circumvent this problem, an appealing approach has recently been proposed based on an irregular grid of radial basis functions with compact support [7], which only deforms misregistered image areas, but leaves the already registered image parts untouched.

In many clinical applications, it is important to obtain physically plausible non-linear transformations. The introduction of physics-based deformable registration in the pioneering work of Bajcsy et al. [8,9] was a first step in addressing the modeling of real-world deformations of biological tissue. Since that time, several physics-based registration approaches using different physical models (elastic, viscous fluid, etc.) have been proposed [10,11,12,13,14].

The aim of the present work is to approach the idea of deformable image registration by adaptive irregular grids of control points with limited influence areas using a physics-based elastic deformation model. The approach introduced in this paper uses a linear elastic deformation model, assuming that Gaussian-shaped forces are applied at several control points irregularly distributed in the source image. The positions of the control points, the magnitudes and directions of the applied forces as well as their areas of influence, and the elastic material properties are optimized to reach a maximum of the similarity measure between the images. This formulation is related to the elastic body splines [13,14] with the differences being that no explicit landmark correspondences are used, and the influence area of each force application point is controlled individually. Our primary goal is to demonstrate the ability of the resulting deformation field to cope with complex deformations arising in registration of clinical data.

In the remainder of the paper, we present the theory of elastic deformations, including the derivation of the closed-form solution of the Navier equation for a Gaussian force, describe the registration approach based on application of adaptive Gaussian forces, and present experimental results with clinical data. We conclude the paper with a discussion of open problems and directions for future research.

2   Theory

2.1   Physics-Based Deformable Registration

In physics-based registration images are modeled as physical continua (elastic solids, fluids, etc.) deforming under the application of external forces. The problem of physics-based registration can be formulated as finding the elastic deformation $\varphi : \bar{\Omega} \to \mathbb{R}^3$ in a spatial domain Ω with the boundary $\partial\Omega$ ($\bar{\Omega} = \Omega \cup \partial\Omega$) by solving a (generally non-linear) partial differential equation (PDE) of the type: $\mathcal{L}(\mathbf{u}) = \boldsymbol{f}$ with the appropriate boundary conditions. Here $\boldsymbol{f} : \Omega \to \mathbb{R}^3$ denotes the vector of the applied forces acting on the underlying physical medium, $\mathbf{u} : \Omega \to \mathbb{R}^3$ is the displacement field, and $\mathcal{L}$ is an operator defining the response of the material. The connection between the elastic deformation and the displacement field is given as $\varphi(\mathbf{x}) = \mathbf{x} + \mathbf{u}(\mathbf{x})$. The optimal elastic deformation is determined as maximizing a certain similarity measure M between a source image $I_S(\mathbf{x})$ and a target image $I_T(\mathbf{x})$.

2.2   The Linear Elastic Model: The Navier Equation

The elasticity operator $\mathcal{A}$ defines the response of a three-dimensional elastic medium to external forces. Assuming the elastic material to be isotropic and homogeneous, the elasticity operator is of the form [15]:

$$\mathcal{A}(\mathbf{u}) = -\mathbf{div}\left\{(\mathbf{I} + \nabla\mathbf{u})\sigma(\mathbf{e}(\mathbf{u}))\right\}, \tag{1}$$

where $\sigma(\mathbf{e}) = \frac{E}{1+\nu}\left(\frac{\nu}{1-2\nu}\mathrm{tr}(\mathbf{e})\mathbf{I} + \mathbf{e}\right)$ is the stress tensor, and $\mathbf{e}(\mathbf{u}) = \frac{1}{2}(\nabla\mathbf{u}^\mathrm{T} + \nabla\mathbf{u} + \nabla\mathbf{u}^\mathrm{T}\nabla\mathbf{u})$ is the strain tensor. The two constants $E > 0$ and $\nu \in]-1; 1/2[$ are known in elasticity theory as Young's modulus and Poisson's ratio. They describe the elastic properties of the material (stiffness and compressibility).

A common linearization approach is expanding (1) at the origin:

$$\mathcal{A}(\mathbf{u}) = \mathcal{A}(0) + \mathcal{A}'(0)\mathbf{u} + O(\|\mathbf{u}\|^2) \approx \mathcal{A}'(0)\mathbf{u}. \tag{2}$$

The linear PDE $\mathcal{A}'(0)\mathbf{u} = \boldsymbol{f}$ is known as the Navier equation and can be written as:

$$\Delta\mathbf{u} + \frac{1}{(1-2\nu)}\nabla(\nabla \cdot \mathbf{u}) = -\frac{2(1+\nu)}{E}\boldsymbol{f}. \tag{3}$$

The linear elastic model is limited to applications with small deformations. Formally, the criterion for a small deformation can be given by: $\max(|\omega_i|) < \epsilon$, where ω_i are the eigenvectors of the displacement gradient matrix $\nabla\mathbf{u}$, and ϵ denotes the linearization error threshold.

The Navier equation can be solved analytically only for a few special cases. In the context of image registration, it is typically solved numerically, leading to non-parametric registration approaches [9,11].

2.3   Solution of the Navier Equation for a Point Force

The solution of the Navier equation (3) for a point force: $\boldsymbol{f}^* = \mathbf{f}\delta(r)$, where $\delta(r)$ is the Dirac delta function, and $r = |\mathbf{r}|$ is the distance from the force origin (see Fig. 1), is known as Green's function of linear elasticity and is given by [16]:

$$\mathbf{u}^* = \frac{1+\nu}{8\pi E(1-\nu)r}\left\{(3-4\nu)\mathbf{f} + (\mathbf{f} \cdot \mathbf{e}_r)\mathbf{e}_r\right\}, \tag{4}$$

where $\mathbf{e}_r$ is a unit vector pointing in the direction of $\mathbf{r}$. This solution contains a singularity at the origin which results in an infinite displacement at the force application point: $\mathbf{u}^*|_{r=0} = \infty$.

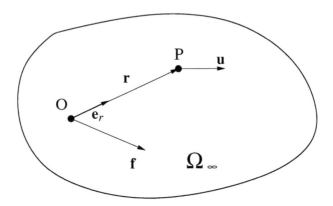

Fig. 1. Point force in an infinite elastic medium.

2.4   Solution of the Navier Equation for a Gaussian Force

In image registration, it is advantageous to distribute a force field in a limited area surrounding the control points to compensate for global and local deformations. This corresponds to regularization of the point force with a smooth function $g(r)$ with the property $\int_\Omega g(r)dx = 1$, which quickly approaches zero for increasing r, i.e. $\lim_{r\to\infty} g(r) = 0$, and approaches the Dirac delta function for decreasing r, i.e. $\lim_{r\to 0} g(r) = \delta(r)$. The regularized solution is obtained by solving the Navier equation for the force field given in the form of a scaled smoothing function: $\boldsymbol{f} = \mathbf{f}g(r)$.

In this work, we use the 3-D Gaussian as the smoothing function:

$$g(r) = \frac{1}{(\sqrt{2\pi}\sigma)^3} \exp\left(-\frac{r^2}{2\sigma^2}\right). \tag{5}$$

In the following, we outline the derivation of the solution of the Navier equation for a Gaussian force as proposed by one of the authors [17].

The Navier equation for a Gaussian-shaped applied force is given by:

$$\boldsymbol{\Delta u} + \frac{1}{(1-2\nu)}\nabla(\nabla \cdot \mathbf{u}) = -\frac{2(1+\nu)\mathbf{f}}{(\sqrt{2\pi}\sigma)^3 E} \exp\left(-\frac{r^2}{2\sigma^2}\right). \tag{6}$$

Analogously to the derivation of the solution for a point force [16], the solution of (6) is considered to be of the form: $\tilde{\mathbf{u}} = \mathbf{v} + \mathbf{w}$, with $\mathbf{v}$ satisfying the Poisson equation:

$$\boldsymbol{\Delta v} = -\frac{2(1+\nu)\mathbf{f}}{(\sqrt{2\pi}\sigma)^3 E} \exp\left(-\frac{r^2}{2\sigma^2}\right). \tag{7}$$

For the radial component of (7) we get:

$$\Delta_r v_r = -\frac{2(1+\nu)f_r}{(\sqrt{2\pi}\sigma)^3 E} \exp\left(-\frac{r^2}{2\sigma^2}\right), \tag{8}$$

with Δ_r being the Laplace operator in spherical coordinates: $\Delta_r = \frac{1}{r^2}\frac{d}{dr}\left(r^2\frac{d}{dr}\right)$. By taking the derivatives, we obtain the ordinary differential equation:

$$v_r'' + \frac{2}{r}v_r' = -\frac{2(1+\nu)f_r}{(\sqrt{2\pi}\sigma)^3 E}\exp\left(-\frac{r^2}{2\sigma^2}\right). \tag{9}$$

The solution of (9) is sought in the form: $v_r = C\frac{\mathrm{erf}(r/\sigma\sqrt{2})}{r}$, where C is a constant. By substituting this into (9), we get: $C = \frac{(1+\nu)f_r}{2\pi E}$, and the solution of the Poisson equation (7) is given by:

$$\mathbf{v} = \frac{(1+\nu)\,\mathbf{f}\,\mathrm{erf}(r/\sigma\sqrt{2})}{2\pi E}\frac{1}{r}. \tag{10}$$

When substituting $\mathbf{v} + \mathbf{w}$ into (6) we get:

$$(1-2\nu)\Delta\mathbf{w} + \nabla(\nabla\cdot\mathbf{w}) = -\nabla(\nabla\cdot\mathbf{v}), \tag{11}$$

or taking into account: $\Delta\mathbf{w} = \nabla(\nabla\cdot\mathbf{w}) - \nabla\times(\nabla\times\mathbf{w})$:

$$2(1-\nu)\nabla(\nabla\cdot\mathbf{w}) - (1-2\nu)\nabla\times(\nabla\times\mathbf{w}) = -\nabla(\nabla\cdot\mathbf{v}), \tag{12}$$

When applying a curl operator to both sides of (12), it can be shown that $\nabla\times\mathbf{w} = \mathbf{0}$ [16], so that $\mathbf{w}$ can be written in the form: $\mathbf{w} = \nabla\phi$, with ϕ satisfying the equation:

$$\nabla\{2(1-\nu)\Delta\phi + \nabla\cdot\mathbf{v}\} = \mathbf{0}. \tag{13}$$

Taking into account (10) and introducing $\xi = r/\sigma\sqrt{2}$ yields:

$$\phi = -\frac{(1+\nu)\mathbf{f}}{4\sqrt{2\pi}\sigma E(1-\nu)}\nabla\psi, \tag{14}$$

where ψ is the solution of the equation: $\Delta\psi = \mathrm{erf}(\xi)/\xi$. Solving this equation by integration and substituting the result into (14), we obtain finally:

$$\mathbf{w} = -\frac{1+\nu}{4\sqrt{2\pi}\sigma E(1-\nu)}\left\{\left(\frac{\mathrm{erf}(\xi)}{\xi} - \frac{3}{\xi^3}\int\xi\,\mathrm{erf}(\xi)d\xi\right)(\mathbf{f}\cdot\mathbf{e}_r)\mathbf{e}_r + \right.$$
$$\left. \frac{\mathbf{f}}{\xi^3}\int\xi\,\mathrm{erf}(\xi)d\xi\right\}. \tag{15}$$

The solution of the Navier equation for a Gaussian force is thus given by:

$$\tilde{\mathbf{u}} = \frac{1+\nu}{8\pi E(1-\nu)}\left\{\Phi_1(\xi)\mathbf{f} + \Phi_2(\xi)(\mathbf{f}\cdot\mathbf{e}_r)\mathbf{e}_r\right\}, \tag{16}$$

with

$$\Phi_1(\xi) = \frac{1}{\sigma\sqrt{2}}\left\{\frac{(3-4\nu)\,\mathrm{erf}(\xi)}{\xi} + \frac{\mathrm{erf}(\xi)}{2\xi^3} - \frac{\exp(-\xi^2)}{\xi^2\sqrt{\pi}}\right\},$$
$$\Phi_2(\xi) = \frac{1}{\sigma\sqrt{2}}\left\{\frac{\mathrm{erf}(\xi)}{\xi} - \frac{3\,\mathrm{erf}(\xi)}{2\xi^3} + \frac{3\exp(-\xi^2)}{\xi^2\sqrt{\pi}}\right\}. \tag{17}$$

In contrast to the solution for a point force (4), the solution of the Navier equation for a Gaussian force does not contain a singularity at the origin and is proportional to the applied force:

$$\tilde{\mathbf{u}}|_{r=0} = \frac{(5 - 6\nu)(1 + \nu)}{3\left(\sqrt{2\pi}\right)^3 \sigma E(1 - \nu)} \mathbf{f}. \tag{18}$$

With increasing distance from the origin ($r \gg \sigma$), the Gaussian solution (16) converges to the solution for a point force (4) as $\Phi_1 \to (3 - 4\nu)/r$ and $\Phi_2 \to 1/r$.

3   Deformable Registration by Adaptive Gaussian Forces

We assume that Gaussian-shaped forces are applied to a set of control points in the source image modeled as an infinite homogeneous elastic continuum. The total displacement field is obtained as a superposition of the displacement fields produced by all Gaussian forces. This corresponds to a parametric elastic deformation $\boldsymbol{\varphi}(\mathbf{x}, \mathbf{a})$, where $\mathbf{a} = (\mathbf{p}_i, \mathbf{f}_i, \sigma_i, \nu)^{\mathrm{T}}$, $i = 1, \ldots, N$ is the parameter vector. Here $\mathbf{p}_i$ are the positions of N control points in the source image, $\mathbf{f}_i$ are the vectors of the applied forces, σ_i denote the Gaussian width corresponding to each force application point, and ν is the Poisson ratio. We assume the image to be modeled by a homogeneous elastic material, and the Poisson ratio does not vary spatially. The use of the Poisson ratio as an extra parameter for optimization means that the "best" elastic material is selected for each concrete registration task. The Young modulus E can be considered as a proportionality factor between the force and the displacement and does not need to be optimized separately.

In this work, we consider the most general elastic registration approach, maximizing a similarity measure M between the source image $I_S(\mathbf{x})$ and the target image $I_T(\mathbf{x})$ over a $(7N + 1)$-dimensional parameter space:

$$\mathbf{a}_{\mathrm{opt}} = \arg\max_{\mathbf{a}} M\left(I_S(\boldsymbol{\varphi}(\mathbf{x}, \mathbf{a})), I_T(\mathbf{x})\right). \tag{19}$$

The resulting objective function is complex, and the optimization problem (19) is generally difficult to solve due to many local maxima. A multi-resolution strategy can be applied to accelerate the optimization process and to reduce the risk of becoming trapped by local maxima.

The convergence speed of optimization depends strongly on the number of evaluations of the similarity measure required to reach an optimum. This, in its turn, is directly related to the type of the similarity measure used for the registration and in particular its differentiability. In this work, we use the cross-correlation coefficient, which is a commonly used similarity measure in mono-modal image registration [1]:

$$M_{CC} = \left(\frac{\left(\sum_{\mathbf{x} \in \bar{\Omega}} (I_S(\mathbf{x} + \mathbf{u}) - \hat{I}_S)(I_T(\mathbf{x}) - \hat{I}_T) \right)^2}{\sum_{\mathbf{x} \in \bar{\Omega}} (I_S(\mathbf{x} + \mathbf{u}) - \hat{I}_S)^2 \sum_{\mathbf{x} \in \bar{\Omega}} (I_T(\mathbf{x}) - \hat{I}_T)^2} \right)^{1/2}, \tag{20}$$

where $\hat{I}_S$ and $\hat{I}_T$ denote the average gray value intensities in the source and target image.

4   Experiments

The goal of the experiments presented in this section was to demonstrate the ability of the proposed registration approach to cope with complex elastic deformations by using only a small number of control points. We considered, for the sake of simplicity, the 2-D case only, where the image was modeled as a 2-D slice of an infinite 3-D elastic medium. The z-component of the force field was respectively set to 0. (Note that 2-D and 3-D solutions for a Gaussian force differ [17], and the 2-D solution cannot be extended to 3-D by simply increasing the dimensionality of the force and displacement field.)

The optimization was performed by applying the downhill simplex algorithm [18], which is a simple derivative-free local optimization method, showing good results in finding the optimum of the objective function in our case. Its drawback is the slow convergence, resulting in the computation time of about 10-30 min., depending on the image size and tolerance threshold.

In the first experiment, we registered a slice of a PET transmission map with a pseudo-transmission map generated from the corresponding CT image (see Fig. 2). Prior to the experiment, the 3-D datasets were pre-registered rigidly. The size of both slices was 128×116 pixels, and the in-plane resolution was 4 mm. We used a multi-resolution strategy with 3 resolution levels and started with a regular equidistant grid of 9 control points at the coarsest level (32×29 pixels). The initial values for σ_i were all set to 4 mm, and $\nu = 0.25$. In order to avoid topology violations due to small values of the Gaussian width w.r.t. the force strength and physically unacceptable values for the Poisson ratio, a constrained optimization was carried out for $\sigma_i \geq \frac{1}{2}|\mathbf{f}_i|$ and $-1 < \nu < 1/2$. It can be seen in Fig. 2 that moderate elastic deformations were required to compensate for most of the differences between the images. Note that only 7 of 9 control points were located within the image boundaries after the registration.

In the second experiment, involving larger deformations, two slices of a 3-D MR knee image in a bent and a straight position were registered (Fig. 3). The size of the slices was 256×256 pixels, and the in-plane resolution was approx. 1 mm. As the slices were taken from a 3-D dataset, they only approximately correspond anatomically due to through-plane movement. Here we used 4 resolution levels and again started with a regular grid of 9 control points at the coarsest level (32×32 pixels). Since larger deformations were expected in comparison to the previous experiment, the start values for σ_i were all set to 6 mm, and $\nu = 0.25$. The central row of Fig. 3 shows the registration result and the end positions of the control points.

A summary of the experimental results is presented in Table 1. It can be seen that relatively high values of the similarity measure were achieved by only using 9 control points. Note that the values for the Poisson ratio differ, indicating in particular that the use of highly compressible elastic material was encouraged

Experiment	M_{CC} (unregistered)	M_{CC} (registered)	Poisson's ratio
PET-CT	0.6867	0.9105	0.03
MRI knee	0.4904	0.8803	0.47

Table 1. Summary of experimental results.

for the PET-CT case, and almost incompressible material was advantageous for the MRI knee case. This corresponds very well to the highly inhomogeneous deformation field encountered in the PET-CT case compared to the smooth deformation in the MRI knee case.

5   Discussion

5.1   Relationship to Radial Basis Functions

There exist analogies between the proposed approach and deformable registration methods based on radial basis function (RBF) grids [19,7], where the displacement field is modeled as a linear combination of basis functions distributed over the image domain: $\mathbf{u}(\mathbf{x}) = \sum_{i=1}^{N} \mathbf{c}_i \phi(\mathbf{x} - \mathbf{x}_i)$, where $\mathbf{c}_i \in \mathbb{R}^n$ are the weights, $\phi : \mathbb{R}^n \to \mathbb{R}$ is a RBF, and n is the problem dimensionality. An optimization scheme can be applied, where the weights $\mathbf{c}_i$ and the locations of the RBF centers $\mathbf{x}_i$ are determined to maximize a gray value based similarity between the images. By using RBFs with compact support [20,7], the influence areas of each RBF can be limited, which also improves the computational efficiency.

The principal difference to our method lies in the nature of the generated deformation field. i) The solution of the Navier equation for a Gaussian force is, in contrast to RBFs, not spherically symmetric and is thus more advantageous for modeling of inhomogeneous and anisotropic deformation fields. ii) It directly encapsulates elastic material properties and thus produces deformation fields which are closer to physical reality. It would be useful to carry out a comparative validation study of the existing RBF approaches and our method in order to better assess the feasibility of both strategies w.r.t. the registration of real clinical images.

5.2   Future Research

A limitation of our method in its present form is the complexity of the optimization problem, resulting in high computational costs. In this section, we discuss several future research directions aimed at increasing the computational efficiency of the method.

One important issue is the choice of the optimization algorithm, where a tradeoff exists between the global methods, which are computationally expensive but are in most cases able to yield the global maximum of the similarity measure, and the local methods, which are more computationally efficient, but on the other hand may converge to an inappropriate local optimum. The downhill simplex algorithm used in this work yields satisfactory results, but it requires a large number of objective function evaluations. We plan to investigate the applicability of more efficient local optimization methods, e.g. Levenberg-Marquardt.

The computational performance of our approach can be considerably improved by using prior knowledge to reduce the search space for optimization. This prior knowledge can include, e.g., the initial constellations of the control points and Gaussian width estimates based on anatomical features or correlations with the similarity measure. In order to avoid potential topology violations due to the linearity of the deformation model, it can be useful to couple the Gaussian width to the force strength: $\sigma_i = K(|\mathbf{f}_i|, \nu)$, where the exact functional form for K can be derived, for example, taking the orientation preserving condition for the deformation (positiveness of the deformation gradient: $|\nabla \varphi| > 0$) into account. Lastly, the Poisson ratio can be fixed for concrete registration applications after determining its optimal value by test runs.

The performance of the proposed method is also limited by the fact that the elastic material response is not compact. As a consequence, an arbitrary image point is in general influenced by all control points. However, since the displacement field approaches zero with the increasing distance to the force application point, the deformation field is basically restricted to a limited area around the control point. Thus, the contributions of certain remote control points can be neglected.

The approach can potentially be extended to inhomogeneous elastic materials, which allows to model the elastic behavior of the biological tissue more accurately, for example, in order to prevent deformations of rigid structures.

6   Conclusion

We have introduced a new physics-based approach to deformable image registration. We assume that Gaussian-shaped forces are applied at control points irregularly distributed in the source image, which is modeled as a homogeneous infinite elastic medium. By adjusting their positions, as well as directions, strengths, and influence areas of the applied forces, a maximum of a gray value based similarity measure can be obtained.

This work is aimed at demonstrating the ability of the proposed approach to cope with complex registration tasks. The practical applicability of our method is currently limited by the optimization time. Several strategies have been discussed, which potentially allow to significantly increase its computational efficiency. Their implementation will be the subject of future work. We also plan to investigate the extension of the approach to inhomogeneous elastic materials to model the biological tissue more accurately.

Acknowledgments

The PET and CT data used in this work are courtesy of the University of Pennsylvania.

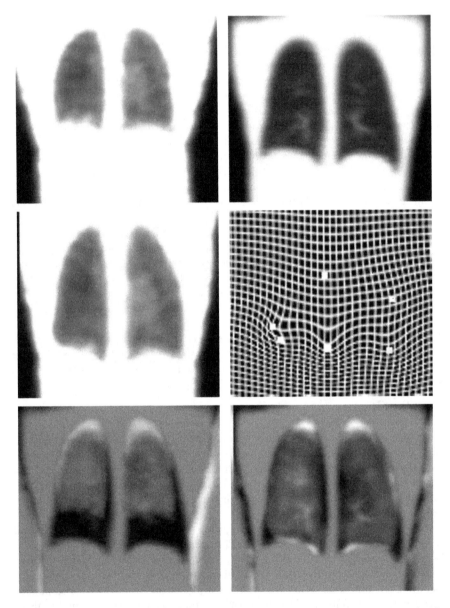

Fig. 2. PET-CT registration example. Top row: PET transmission map (left) and CT pseudo-transmission map (right). Central row: Deformed transmission map and deformed grid with end positions of the control points. Note that only 7 of 9 points lie within the image boundaries and two points in the center of the grid almost coincide. Bottom row: Difference image before (left) and after (right) registration.

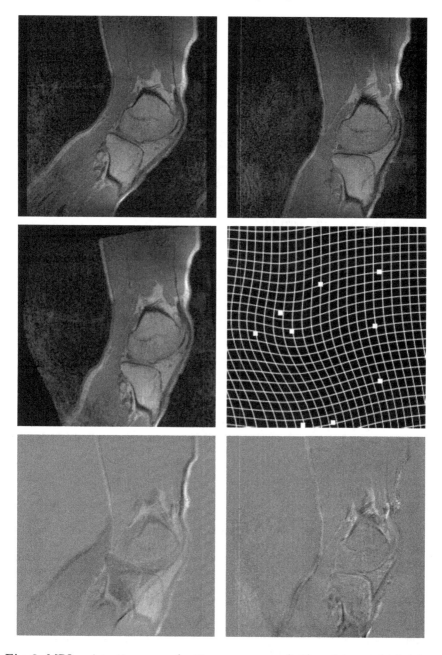

Fig. 3. MRI registration example. Top row: source (left) and target (right) image. Central row: Deformed source image and deformed grid with end positions of the control points. Bottom row: Difference image before (left) and after (right) registration.

References

1. Maintz, J., Viergever, M.: A survey on medical image registration. Medical Image Analysis **2** (1998) 1–36
2. Modersitzki, J.: Numerical Methods for Image Registration. Oxford University Press (2004)
3. Bro-Nielsen, M., Gramkow, C.: Fast fluid registration of medical images. In: Proc. Visualization in Biomedical Computing (VBC'96), Hamburg (1996) 267–276
4. Fischer, B., Modersitzki, J.: Fast image registration - a variational approach. In: Proc. of the Int. Conf. on Numerical Analysis and Computational Mathematics (NACoM'03), Cambridge (2003) 69–74
5. Rueckert, D., Sonoda, L., Hayes, C., Hill, D., Leach, M., Hawkes, D.: Nonrigid registration using free-form deformations: Applications to breast MR images. IEEE Transactions on Medical Imaging **18** (1999) 712–721
6. Kybic, J., Unser, M.: Fast parametric elastic registration. IEEE Transactions on Image Processing **12** (2003) 1427–1442
7. Rohde, G., Aldroubi, A., Dawant, B.: The adaptive bases algorithm for intensity-based nonrigid registration. IEEE Transactions on Medical Imaging **22** (2003) 1470–1479
8. Bajcsy, R., Broit, C.: Matching of deformed images. In: Proc. 6th Int. Conf. on Pattern Recognition, München (1982) 351–353
9. Bajcsy, R., Kovačič, S.: Multiresolution elastic matching. Computer Vision, Graphics, and Image Processing **46** (1989) 1–21
10. Christensen, G., Rabbitt, R., Miller, M.: Deformable templates using large deformation kinematics. IEEE Transactions on Image Processing **5** (1996) 1435–1447
11. Davatzikos, C., Prince, J., Bryan, R.: Image registration based on boundary mapping. IEEE Transactions on Medical Imaging **15** (1996) 112–115
12. Hagemann, A., Rohr, K., Stiehl, H., Spetzger, U., Gilsbach, J.: Biomechanical modeling of the human head for physically based, nonrigid image registration. IEEE Transactions on Medical Imaging **18** (1999) 875–884
13. Davis, M., Khotanzad, A., Flaming, D., Harms, S.: A physics-based coordinate transform for 3-D image matching. IEEE Transactions on Medical Imaging **16** (1997) 317–328
14. Kohlrausch, J., Rohr, K., Stiehl, H.: A new class of elastic body splines for nonrigid registration of medical images. In: Proc. Workshop Bildverarbeitung in der Medizin 2001, Lübeck (2001) 164–168
15. Ciarlet, P.: Mathematical Elasticity. Volume I: Three-Dimensional Elasticity. North-Holland, Amsterdam (1988)
16. Landau, L., Lifshitz, E.: Theory of Elasticity. Volume 7 of Course of Theoretical Physics. Butterworth-Heinemann, Oxford (1986)
17. Gladilin, E.: Theoretical and experimental study of linear elastic boundary element method for registration of medical images. Master's thesis, University of Hamburg (1999) In German.
18. Nelder, J., Mead, R.: A simplex method for function minimization. Computer Journal (1965) 308–313
19. Davis, M., Khotanzad, A., Flaming, D.: 3D image matching using a radial basis function neural network. In: Proc. of World Congress on Neural Networks, San Diego, CA (1996) 1174–1179
20. Fornefett, M., Rohr, K., Stiehl, H.: Radial basis functions with compact support for elastic registration of medical images. In: Proc. Workshop on Biomedical Image Registration (WBIR '99), Bled (1999) 173–185

Statistical Imaging for Modeling and Identification of Bacterial Types

Sigal Trattner[a], Hayit Greenspan[a,*], Gabi Tepper[b], Shimon Abboud[a]

[a]Department of Biomedical Engineering, Faculty of Engineering,
Tel-Aviv University, Tel-Aviv 69978, Israel
*hayit@eng.tau.ac.il; http://www.eng.tau.ac.il/~hayit/
[b]Spring Diagnostics Ltd., shin ben-zion 51, Rehovot, Israel, 76472

Abstract. An automatic tool is developed to identify microbiological data types using computer-vision and statistical modeling techniques. In bacteriophage (phage) typing, representative profiles of bacterial types are extracted. Currently, systems rely on the subjective reading of the profiles by a human expert. This process is time-consuming and prone to errors. The statistical methodology presented in this work, provides for an automated, objective and robust analysis of the visual data, along with the ability to cope with increasing data volumes. Validation is performed by a comparison to an expert manual segmentation and labeling of the phage profiles.

1 Introduction

The need to analyze vast amounts of microbiological data requires computer modeling and automation. Current manual procedures are prone to large variability within and across the human experts due to natural fuzziness present in the microbiological data. These procedures are time consuming and are of great cost. Reducing the amount of human intervention in the data analysis is crucial in order to cope with the increasing volume of data and to achieve more objective and quantitatively accurate measurements as well as to obtain repeatable results. In this work we combine image analysis with statistical modeling tools in a general framework for visual array analysis. We focus on microbiological data and bacterial type modeling.

Bacteria are known as the main cause for disease outbreaks [1]. Defining an effective treatment requires characterizing the disease outbreak by identifying its pathogens. A bacterial type diagnosis is required, i.e. the identification of pathogens below the species level [1-2], for controlling the disease. Sub-grouping of bacterial species to bacterial types is used for many important pathogenic bacteria, such as the Staphylococcus aureus (S. aureus). The S. aureus species is a major cause of infections as well as farm animals' diseases such as mastitis of lactating cows [1], [3]. This bacteria tendency to develop resistance to antibiotics raises the importance of its identification via typing.

M. Šonka et al. (Eds.): CVAMIA-MMBIA 2004, LNCS 3117, pp. 329–340, 2004.

Phage typing is a method used for defining the types of a species via the species reactivity to a set of selected bacteriophages (phages) [1]. A phage is a bacterial virus activated by specific bacterial surface constituents of the checked species. The phage receptor binds to a bacterial surface component, invades and multiplies in the bacterial host. When a phage infects a layer of bacterial cells, a zone of lysis produces a plaque, viewed as a clear area in the bacterial lawn, such as the full circles (spots) in Figure 2(a). These represent positive reactions to different phages. When the phage receptor does not recognize any of the tested bacterial surface constituents, no plaque is formed and it is defined as a negative reaction. In this case no surface change is visible. The set of phages active against a culture of bacteria isolates, form a unique profile specific for each bacterial type. We term this profile the "phage profile".

The identification of a bacterial type phage profile belongs to the general task of image array analysis. Analysis of image arrays is comprised of two important tasks: spot finding and spot analysis. Our research includes spot finding as well as spot categorization (labeling spots into positive and negative reactions) and phage profile extraction. A preliminary report of this work has appeared in [4]. To the best of our knowledge, no previous work has been done on automatic spot analysis for phage typing. Related work on spot finding has been described for microarrays and macroarrays, both on rigid slides and on flexible membranes. Many works on spot finding are found in the domain of cDNA microarray data analysis, where the goal is to identify the locations and extents of labeled DNA spots in a scanned microarray image [5], [6].

The spot finding task usually involves two objectives of image segmentation and grid positioning. A preliminary grid overlay [e.g. 5-8] separates the signal from the background. The grid partitions the image plane into windows, rectangular units uniformly spaced in an array overlayed on the image plane, such that each window contains a single reaction (spot). The windows are analyzed locally, each one separated into a spot region and a background region. Grid placement is commonly achieved with human intervention. Various methods have been used to segment each window, including histogram-based segmentation [8-10], seeded region-growing [11], shape-based segmentation [7, 12, 13] and more. Human intervention is important in most of the above-mentioned methods. Manual input consists of roughly circling the spot regions, a-priori setting the grid partitions and in determining parameter settings, such as intensity thresholds, shape and size of spots.

The proposed framework is comprised of the following main features: (1) A major focus of the work is on spot categorization and analysis, which was not previously done in the domain of phage typing; (2) The spot finding task is composed of global image segmentation into signal vs. background regions via unsupervised clustering, followed by a gridding procedure that provides localization of the individual spots. Note that most works in the field use localized processing only, and thus require a gridding process as a crucial first step of the system; (3) Statistical analysis of the spot region characteristics enables probabilistic categorization of the spot reactions and the transition from spot categorization to phage profiling per bacterial type.

In section 2 input data characteristics are presented. The methodology involving computer-vision and statistical modeling is presented in section 3. Experimental results on the S. aureus are shown in section 4. Discussion of the results is conducted in section 5.

2 Data Characteristics

Gray-level images of phage typing arrays are the visual input to the proposed system. The images are scanned using a UMAX scanner, Powerlook2 model, with a transparency adaptor. Each image is of size 532x532 pixels. An example of scanned images is presented in Figure 2(a). The petri-dishes seen in the images contain a surface of S. aureus species. Reactions to 60 different phages are present on the surface of the dish. The reactions are organized in a fixed array and known order. An *image-group* contains a set of images. A given database consists of image-groups, each group representing a particular S. aureus bacterial type.

A significant variability between the scanned images and irregularities in each image exist within a given database. Image contrast and dynamic range is considerably different across the image-group. Reaction shapes and sizes are irregular, both within an image as well as across the images. Reactions are not positioned in a uniform layout. Finally, the background, i.e. the dish surface, also exhibits non-uniformity due to inevitable differences in experimental conditions, and variability in the pigmentation of bacterial isolates.

3 Methods

Figure 1 presents the general framework proposed in this work. Visual array data is processed via two stages: a segmentation stage and a follow-up categorization stage. Statistical modeling via Gaussian Mixture Models (GMM) and Expectation-Maximization (EM) learning are utilized in both stages of analysis. A transition is made to phage profiling and the final output is a probabilistic signature of phage-reaction profile (phage profile) per image-group.

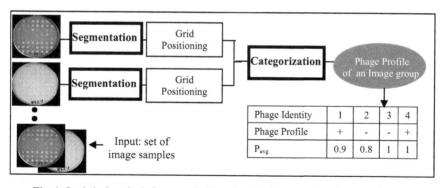

Fig. 1. Statistical analysis framework: from the visual array to the phage profile.

3.1 Statistical Modeling

In modeling image data, an initial transition is made from the raw pixel input to a selected feature space. Each pixel is represented by a feature vector and the image as a whole is represented by a collection of feature vectors. The underlying assumption is that a mixture of Gaussians generates the image features' distribution. The distribution of a random variable, $x \in R^d$, is a mixture of k Gaussians if its density function is:

$$f(x \mid \theta) = \sum_{k=1}^{K} \alpha_k \frac{1}{\sqrt{(2\pi)^d \mid \Sigma_k \mid}} \exp\left\{ -\frac{1}{2}(x - \mu_k)^T \Sigma_k^{-1}(x - \mu_k) \right\}, \qquad (1)$$

such that the parameter set $\theta = \{\alpha_k, \mu_k, \Sigma_k\}_{k=1}^{K}$ consists of:

$$\alpha_k > 0 \quad , \quad \sum_{k=1}^{K} \alpha_k = 1$$

$$\mu_k \in R^d \ , \quad \Sigma_k \ \text{is a } d \times d \ \text{positive definite matrix}$$

where α_k is the prior probability for Gaussian k, and μ_k, Σ_k are the mean vector and covariance matrix of Gaussian k, respectively.

Given a set of feature vectors $X_1, ..., X_N$ the maximum likelihood estimation of θ is:

$$\hat{\theta}_{ML} = \underset{\theta}{\text{argmax}} \ f(X_1, ..., X_N \mid \theta) = \underset{\theta}{\text{arg max}} \prod_{n=1}^{N} \sum_{k=1}^{K} \alpha_k f(X_n \mid \theta) \qquad (2)$$

The EM algorithm is an iterative method to obtain the parameter set θ_{ML} increasing the likelihood function in each iteration [14].

The probabilistic affiliation of feature vector X_n to cluster (Gaussian) k is given by:

$$P(label(X_n) = k) = \frac{\alpha_k f\left(X_n \mid \mu_k, \Sigma_k\right)}{f(X_n \mid \theta)}. \qquad (3)$$

Each feature vector, X_n, is assigned to the most probable Gaussian cluster, i.e. to the component of the model that maximizes the a-posteriori probability:

$$Label(X_n) = \underset{k}{\text{argmax}} \ P(label(X_n) = k). \qquad (4)$$

3.2 Image Segmentation: Signal Vs Background

The objective of the segmentation phase is to extract a probabilistic separation of the data, per image, into the spot region and the background region. The segmentation is performed globally on the entire image plane (rather than window by window). The segmentation task is treated as an unsupervised clustering task using the intensity feature, with two main clusters to be found. The image is represented by a mixture of two Gaussians ($k=2$), one Gaussian represents the image signal, the other represents the image background intensity distribution. The choice of k is based on apriori analysis of the data at hand. Once the model is learned, the probabilistic affiliation of each feature vector, the image pixel intensity, with each of the Gaussians in the model ($k=1,2$) can be computed (equation (3)), and each pixel of the original image, X_n, is then affiliated with the most probable Gaussian cluster (equation (4)). The result of the segmentation phase is a binary image in which an estimate of the signal region is given.

3.3 Grid Positioning: From the Image Plane to Image Spots

A transition is made from the global image signal to localized reactions, or spots. Extracting local areas of interest in an input image is accomplished by partitioning the data into windows via a grid. In this work we position the grid automatically based on the segmentation results. The grid-positioning algorithm is as follows: Starting with its original state, each binary (segmented) image is rotated in intervals of 1° between +10 and –10 degrees. For each angle of rotation, ϑ, a projection (sum) over the x-axis and the y-axis is computed. Thus, for each ϑ we get two projection functions, $f_\vartheta(x)$ and $f_\vartheta(y)$ for the x-axis and the y-axis, respectively. The angle α by which the image has to be de-rotated is determined by the angle for which a maximum projection value is found:

$$\alpha = \arg\max_\theta \left[f_\theta(x), f_\theta(y) \right]; \quad \vartheta \in \left[-10...+10 \right] \tag{5}$$

The set of maximal-strength signal values is extracted from the x and y-profiles of the de-rotated image. The location, for which the maximum projection value for the x-axis and the y-axis is achieved, serves as an anchor point from which the grid is defined. The grid interval is calculated as the average maximal-strength signal values. Utilizing the grid, spot finding is accomplished; a transition is made to local image analysis and further spot processing.

3.4 Spot Categorization

A categorization of each spot to positive or negative reaction is pursued. A set of feature vectors extracted per image-group is analyzed statistically for modeling positive and negative reactions. Using the learned model a categorization of each spot into the positive and negative clusters is enabled. A reaction is defined as positive, when there is a sufficient number of pixels of high-intensity present and a circular structure is evident. A transition is thus made from the raw pixels to a feature space that accommodates the signal strength and morphology criteria. The labeling task becomes a clustering task within the selected feature space. The following features are extracted from each spot:

(1) Normalized Area (*NA*). The area of a spot, A, is the sum of pixels that comprise the spot. This sum is normalized by the average spot size within the image. For the average, only spots with an area above a certain threshold, T, are considered:

$$\frac{A - Avg(A > T)}{Avg(A > T)} * 100, \tag{6}$$

with the threshold value T empirically set to 200. The normalization factor is important in order to achieve invariance to the variability in the positive reaction area across the images in the dataset. The normalized area feature is therefore an estimate of the relative size of a reaction per spot.

(2) Shape Index $(SI) = \dfrac{4\pi A}{P^2}$, $\qquad\qquad$ (7)

where A is the area of signal and P is the perimeter of the signal (sum of edge pixels per spot). This feature is used in the literature as a measure of circularity [15]. High values of SI represent spots with higher circularity and less graininess.

Feature vectors, $X_1,..., X_N$, ($X_n = (NA, SI)$) are extracted from all spots, $n=1...N$, across all the images in a given image-group. Clustering of the features is pursued using GMM and EM. A two-cluster partition is used ($k=2$) to separate the space into the positive and negative reaction categories. The choice of a two class partitioning is motivated from the biological categorization of the spots into two reaction groups. Utilizing the learned GMM model, the probabilistic labeling of each spot is enabled (equation (3)). The affiliation of each spot to the most probable Gaussian cluster (equation (4)) produces image spot categorization.

3.5 From Spots to Phage Profiling

We next shift from the level of spot categorization to the level of phage profiling per image-group. Each phage (G_i) is probabilistically affiliated with the positive and negative reaction categories (k), by averaging across the corresponding spot probabilities:

$$Pavg(label(G_i) = k)) = \frac{1}{N} \sum_{n \in G_i} P(label(X_n) = k), \tag{8}$$

with the averaging performed over the spots, X_n, $n=1...N$, related to the same phage, G_i, for all images in the image-group. The phage label is determined by the higher average probability of the two:

$$label(G_i) = \arg\max_k P(label(G_i) = k). \tag{9}$$

A standard-deviation measure is computed over the spot probabilities to estimate the variability in the spot reactions within the image-group. The phage profile is taken as a collection of phage labels along with the average probabilities per phage, extracted in a pre-defined order across the image array.

4 Experiments and Results

We present experimental results for both spot and phage level analysis. The dataset used consists of 4 image-groups, each from a different farm. Each farm corresponds to a particular bacterial type. Three image-groups (#1, #2, #4) consist of 40 images. Group #3 contains 260 images. A central sub-array of 6*6 (36) phages is analyzed per petri-dish image, to avoid edge effects. Four petri-dishes are input at a time, thus a total of 144 (36*4) phages are considered in a phage profile.

The segmentation and gridding processes are exemplified in Figure 2 The segmented images in (b), are shown following de-rotation. Note that pixels that are affiliated with the "signal" Gaussian are displayed in white, while pixels that are affiliated with the "background" Gaussian are displayed in black. The separation between the signal and background regions is evident. The graininess present in the segmented images is due both to the low contrast input (as in image #1) as well as to biological reactions (as in image #2). The dark-particle noise evident in image #2 is removed in the segmentation process while the bright noise artifacts are interpreted as signal. Results of the gridding process and the transition to image spots are shown in in Figure 2(c).

Spot analysis and categorization (section 3.3) is demonstrated in Figure 3 and Figure 4. The GMM learned from all feature-vector samples, using the shape index (SI) and normalized area (NA) features, for a particular image-group, is shown in Figure 3. A clear separation between the two major modes is evident, with one cluster (Gaussian) representing positive reactions and the second cluster representing the negative reactions. The spread of each cluster defines the variance in each group.

Spot *categorization* is achieved by computing the probabilistic spot affiliation to each of the Gaussians of the learned GMM, and then determining the most probable Gaussian cluster (equations (3) and 4)). Figure 4 presents an example of image with spot categorization. The reaction category is indicated (+/-), along with its probability. Spots that are perceptually very clearly categorized (into positive or negative reactions) are supported with higher probabilities than spots for which the reaction category is visually questionable.

Table 1. Correlation and statistical results of expert-based categorization versus automatic categorization

Category	True Positive	False Negative	False Positive	True Negative
Number of spots	5100	105	340	2807

Sensitivity (True Positive Categorization)	98%	(True Negative Categorization)	89%	Correlation with	95%
Predictive Value	98%	Negative Predictive Value	96%		

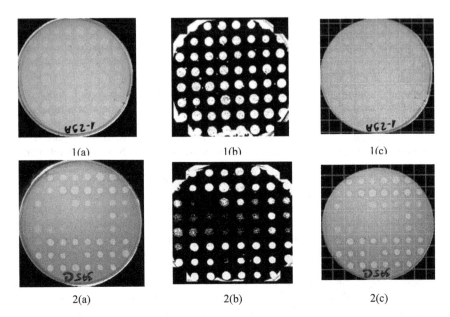

Fig. 2. Examples for segmentation and gridding: (a) Original images; (b) Segmented images; (c) Images overlayed with grid (de-rotated)

Prior to proceeding to the phage-level analysis, we wish to validate the spot categorization results. The validation process included a comparison of a large set of categorized spots to human-expert labeling as ground-truth. Results are given in Table 1 for 7992 spots, which were ascribed a label of positive and negative reactions by an expert. The algorithm achieved a correlation of 95% with the supervised categorization. A 98% correlation was achieved with the supervised positive categorization (sensitivity) and an 89% correlation was achieved with the supervised negative categorization (specificity). The positive predictive value, i.e. the probability that the spot reaction is manually categorized as positive when the automatic categorization is positive, is 98%. The negative predictive value is 96%.

4.1 Phage Profiling and Analysis

An example of a phage profile is shown in Table 2 (equations (8) and (9)). The categorization of each phage is given in the second row. The corresponding average probability, P_{avg}, and standard deviation (*std.*) are listed in the third and fourth rows, respectively. A high average probability indicates a similar (and strong) spot reaction in the particular image location, across the images in the image-group. For example, consider phage #7 in Table 2. The category is the negative category (-), P_{avg} is 100 with a std. of 0. We can conclude from this that all spots in the image-group have a negative response at 100% probability. A low average probability indicates either that the spot reactions (per phage) are not similar, which will be evident in a large *std.* value, or that for each labeled spot, the affiliation probability is low (equations (3) and (4)). Phage #14 in Table 2, for example, has a P_{avg} of 50% and a large *std.* The spot reactions for this phage are in fact split, with half of the spots having a large probability for the positive reaction and half having a large probability for the negative reaction.

Table 2. An example of a phage profile (19 out of 144 phages). Each phage is identified by a serial number and is affiliated with a reaction type (+ or -). The average probability for the reaction type is shown, along with the corresponding standard deviation

Phage Identity	1	2	3	4	5	6	7	8	9	10	11	12	13	14	15	16	17	18	19
Phage Profile	+	+	+	+	+	+	-	-	+	+	-	+	-	-	-	-	-	+	-
Pavg	84	95	91	94	94	99	100	97	83	67	81	78	79	50	100	85	60	98	53
STD	0.37	0.21	0.28	0.23	0.24	0.05	0.00	0.18	0.38	0.47	0.39	0.42	0.41	0.50	0.00	0.36	0.49	0.12	0.50

The phage profiles are used in this work as a basis for analyzing similarities and differences of bacterial types. An assumption that serves as the ground-truth, is that an image-group corresponds with a particular bacterial type. In validating the phage profiles generated by the proposed system, profiles that are extracted from image-groups of a similar bacterial type are expected to have a similar signature, while phage profiles that are extracted from image-groups of different bacterial types, are expected to show large profile variations. The comparison between phage profiles is measured as the percentage of similar categorization (PSC) between the phages.

Two experiments are conducted to validate the extracted phage profiles. In the first experiment, a given image-group of 260 images is divided into seven image subgroups. A phage profile is generated for each image-subgroup and PSC values are computed across the profiles. Utilizing the full profiles (144 phages) results in a PSC value across the seven subgroups of 78%. Close examination reveals that phages for which the reaction category is not consistent across the profiles, have low average probabilities. Thresholding the phage profiles, using an average probability threshold value of 80%, results in a reduced size profile of 96 phages. Within this phage-profile set, the PSC is 100%, i.e. a full similarity is achieved across the seven profiles.

In a second experiment, phage profiles for the four image-groups in the dataset are investigated. Table 3 presents the phage profiles generated for the four image-groups. The phage profiles indicate a difference between groups #1, #3 and #4, with a similarity between groups #2 and #3. Figure 5 displays corresponding PSC values. The similarity percentage is plotted vs the percentage of profile thresholding. Three curves are shown, each representing PSC values for a particular pair of image-groups. The curve representing groups #2 and #3 has a high percentage of similarity of above 90% without any thresholding, and an increased value of 100% following profile thresholding. A similarity percentage of less than 60%, without thresholding, is seen in the comparison between groups #1 and #3, and groups #4 and #3. The distinct groups remain mostly around the 60% and 70% range throughout. From these results, it may be concluded that different bacterial types are present in groups #1, #3 and #4. The same type is most likely present in groups #2 and #3.

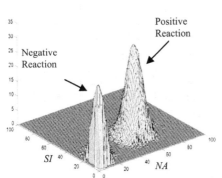

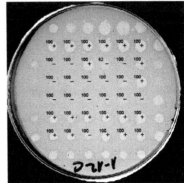

Fig. 3. The learned GMM for the input data. The two modes represent positive and negative reactions, respectively

Fig. 4. Spot categorization along with corresponding probabilities

5 Conclusions

In this work we developed an automatic tool which analyses microbiological data and extracts bacterial types as probabilistic phage profiles. Image array analysis is used to analyze spots by advanced computer vision algorithms, with minimal human intervention. Automation of biological analyses is of importance for efficient and accurate research and production, especially as the amount of data is constantly increasing.

In the current work visual array data was segmented and categorized utilizing statistical imaging methods (GMM and EM). The output of the system is a probabilistic phage profile representing the input image-group. Supervised validation was used in the spot categorization task. Strong correlation, of 95%, was found with the human expert labeling (Table 1).

An important objective of the work is the ability to identify similarity and distinction amongst phage profiles within and across image-groups. Examples of phage profiles are shown in Tables 2 and 3. In the first experiment conducted, PSC values reached 100% for a comparison across subgroups, i.e. originating from a single image-group. Figure 5 shows the percentage of similar phage categorization, for different pairs of image-groups. The PSC is seen to correspond with the given ground-truth. These results are encouraging in that the automated extracted phage profiles seem to be able to validate hypothesis about bacterial types present in a given dataset.

Our study suggests a generic tool that aids the microbiologist in transforming and supplementing data into useful information for analysis. An objective and consistent processing is provided. The expert can effect the evaluation by determining a (optional) probability threshold, for the compaction of the representative profile into the set of the more probable profile reactions. Probabilistic phage profiling can provide a strong basis for further analysis and bacterial type classification. The methodology presented includes general processing steps that may be applicable regardless of scale: from the micro-array to the macro-array. It should be noted, that in each case, adaptation is needed to the data characteristics, and the required level of accuracy. Related domains include phage therapy, a developing domain related to drug discovery, and the domain of cDNA microarray data analysis.

Table 3. Profiles (19 out of 144 phages) from four image-groups

Phage no.	1	2	3	4	5	6	7	8	9	10	11	12	13	14	15	16	17	18	19
Group #1	-	-	-	+	+	+	-	-	-	-	-	-	-	-	-	-	-	-	-
Group #2	+	+	+	+	+	+	-	-	+	-	-	-	-	-	-	-	-	+	-
Group #3	+	+	+	+	+	+	-	-	+	+	-	+	-	-	-	-	-	+	-
Group #4	+	+	+	+	+	+	+	+	+	+	+	+	+	+	+	+	+	+	+

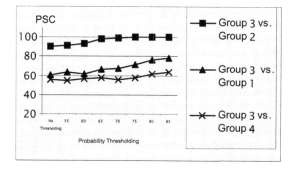

Fig. 5. The PSC (percentage of similar categorization) in different pairs of image-groups vs the percentage of profile thresholding

References

1. Emori T.G, Gaynes R.P.: An Overview of Nosocomial Infections, including the Role of the Microbiology Laboratory. Clinical Microbiology Reviews 6 (1993) 428-442
2. Tenover F.C., Arbeit R.D., Goering R.V.: How to Select and Interpret Molecular Strain Typing methods for Epidemiological Studies of Bacterial Infections: a Review for Healthcare Epidemiologists. Infection Control and Hospital Epidemiology 18 (1997) 426-439
3. Spring Diagnostics. http://www.itek.co.il/spring
4. Trattner S., Greenspan H., Teper G, Abboud S. Automatic Identification of Bacterial Types Using Statistical Imaging Methods. Proceedings of SPIE International Symposium on Medical Imaging, San Diego, USA (2003).

5. Yang Y.H., Buckley M.J., Dudoit S., Speed T.P.: Comparison of Methods for Image Analysis on cDNA Microarray Data. Journal of Computational and Graphical Statistics 11(1) (2002) 108-136
6. Smyth G.K., Yang Y.H.: Statistical Issues in cDNA Microarray Data Analysis. In Functional Genomics: Methods and Protocols. Brownstein M.J. and Khodursky A.B., Eds., Methods in Molecular Biology series, Humana Press, Totowa, NJ (2003)
7. Ideker J., Haynor T., D.: Dapple: Improved Techniques for Finding Spots on DNA Microarrays. University of Washington CSE Technical Report UWTR (2000)
8. Chen Y., Dougherty E.R., Bittner M.L.: Ratio Based Decisions and the Quantitative Analysis of cDNA Microarray Images. Journal of Biomedical Optics 2 (1997) 364-374
9. QuantArray Analysis Software. http://lifesciences.perkinelmer.com
10. Scanalytics MicroArray Suite. http://www.scanalytics.com
11. Adams R., Bischof L.: Seeded Region Growing. IEEE Transactions on Pattern Analysis and Machine Intelligence 16 (1999) 641-647
12. Eisen M.B., ScanAlyze User Manual. Stanford University, Palo Alt, http://rana.lbl.gov (1999)
13. Wang X., Ghosh S., Guo S.W.: Quantitative Quality Control in Microarray image Processing and Data Acquisition. Nucleic Acids Research 29(15) (2001) e75
14. Bishop C.M.: Neural Network for Pattern Recognition. Clarendon Press, Oxford (1996)
15. Sonka M., Fitzpatrick J.M.: Handbook of medical imaging, Vol. 2: Medical Image Processing and Analysis, SPIE Press, Washington (2000)

Assessment of Intrathoracic Airway Trees: Methods and In Vivo Validation

Kálmán Palágyi[1,2], Juerg Tschirren[2], Eric A. Hoffman[3], and Milan Sonka[2]

[1] Dept. of Image Processing and Computer Graphics,
University of Szeged, H-6720 Szeged, Hungary
`palagyi@inf.u-szeged.hu`
[2] Dept. of Electrical and Computer Engineering,
The University of Iowa, Iowa City IA 52242, USA
`{juerg-tschirren,milan-sonka}@uiowa.edu`
[3] Dept. of Radiology,
The University of Iowa, Iowa City IA 52242, USA
`eric-hoffman@uiowa.edu`

Abstract. A method for quantitative assessment of tree structures is reported allowing evaluation of airway tree morphology and its associated function. Our skeletonization and branch–point identification method provides a basis for tree quantification or tree matching, tree–branch diameter measurement in any orientation, and labeling individual branch segments. All main components of our method were specifically developed to deal with imaging artifacts typically present in volumetric medical image data. The proposed method has been tested in a computer phantom subjected to changes of its orientation as well as in repeatedly CT-scanned rigid and rubber plastic phantoms. In this paper, validation is reported in six in vivo scans of the human chest.

1 Introduction

Tubular structures are frequently found in living organisms. The tubes – e.g., arteries or veins are frequently organized into more complex structures. Trees consisting of tubular segments form the arterial and venous systems, intrathoracic airways form bronchial trees, and other examples can be found. Computed tomography (CT) or magnetic resonance (MR) imaging provides volumetric image data allowing identification of such tree structures. Frequently, the trees represented as contiguous sets of voxels must be quantitatively analyzed. The analysis may be substantially simplified if the voxel-level tree is represented in a formal tree structure consisting of a set of nodes and connecting arcs. To build such formal trees, the voxel-level tree object must be transformed into a set of interconnected single-voxel centerlines representing individual tree branches. Therefore, the aim of our work was to develop a robust method for identification of centerlines and bifurcation (trifurcation, etc.) points in segmented tubular tree structures acquired in vivo from humans and animals using volumetric CT or MR scanning, rotational angiography, or other volumetric imaging means.

M. Šonka et al. (Eds.): CVAMIA-MMBIA 2004, LNCS 3117, pp. 341–352, 2004.

Many researchers focused on this task in the past [2,3,6,7,8,11,13,14]. Despite of the wealth of previous work, no perfect skeletonization technique exists to date. Our new approach that is presented below is attempting to overcome most of the existing problems. Since our work is driven by the need for quantitative analysis of intrathoracic airway trees from multidetector CT images, we concentrated on developing a method serving this purpose. However, the resulting approach is widely applicable to a variety of medical image data.

2   Methods

The reported method allows to quantitatively analyze tubular tree structures. Assuming an imperfectly segmented tree was obtained from volumetric data in the previous stages, the presented technique allows to obtain a single–voxel skeleton of the tree while overcoming many segmentation imperfections, yields formal tree representation, and performs quantitative analysis of individual tree segments on a tree–branch basis. The input of the proposed method is a 3D binary image representing a segmented voxel–level tree object. All main components of our method were specifically developed to deal with imaging artifacts typically present in volumetric medical image data. As such, the method consists of the following main steps:

1. *Topological correction of the segmented tree*: Internal cavities (i.e., connected "0" voxels surrounded by "1" voxels), holes (i.e., "0" voxels forming tunnels), and bays (i.e., disturbances without a topological change) are eliminated by sequential forward and backward scanning (instead of the conventional object labeling) and morphological closing.

2. *Identification of the tree root*: In the pulmonary CT images, the center of the topmost nonzero 2D slice in direction z (detected by 2D shrinking) defines the root of the formal tree to be generated and belongs to the trachea. The detected root voxel acts as an anchor point during the centerline extraction (i.e., it cannot be deleted by the forthcoming iterative peeling process).

3. *Extraction of the 3D centerlines – skeletonization*: A sequential 3D curve–thinning algorithm was developed for extracting both geometrically and topologically correct centerlines.

4. *Tree pruning*: False segments are removed by using both the length and depth information.

5. *Identification of branch points*: In a centerlines, three types of points can be identified: endpoints (which have only one 26–neighbor [5]), line–points (which have exactly two 26–neighbors), and branchpoints (which have more than two 26–neighbors) that form junctions (bifurcations, trifurcations, etc.).

6. *Generation of a formal tree structure*: The centerlines are converted into a graph structure (each voxel corresponds to a graph node/vertex and there is an edge between two nodes if the corresponding voxels are 26–adjacent. A similar structure is assigned to the branchpoints. In the branch-tree, a path between two branch– or endpoints is replaced by a single edge.

7. *Tree partitioning*: All voxels of the elongated binary tree (after the topological correction) are partitioned into branches — each voxel is assigned a branch–specific label. A gray–level image is created, in which value "0" corresponds to the background and different non–zero values are assigned to the voxels belonging to different tree branches/partitions.

8. *Calculating associated measures*: For each partition/branch of the tree, the following quantitative indices are calculated: branch length, branch volume, branch surface area, and branch radius.

The entire process has been described in [9,10], therefore, only the critical steps are now described in more detail.

2.1   Centerline Extraction

One of the well-known approaches to centerline determination is to construct a 3D skeleton of the analyzed object. However, some of the properties of 3D skeletons in discrete grids are undesirable. Specifically, in the case of 3D tubular objects, we do not need the exact skeleton, since a 3D skeleton generally contains surface patches. We need a skeletonization method that can suppress creation of such surface patches. As a solution, a 3D curve–thinning algorithm was developed that is preserving line–end points and can thus extract both geometrically and topologically correct centerlines. As part of this process, a novel method for endpoint re–checking was developed based on comparisons between the centerline configuration at some stage of thinning and the previous object configuration.

Thinning is a frequently used method for producing an approximation to the skeleton in a topology–preserving way [5]. Border points of a binary object that satisfy certain topological and geometric constraints are deleted in the iteration steps. In case of tubular 3D objects, thinning has a major advantage over other skeletonization methods. Curve–thinning (i.e., iterative object reduction preserving line–end points) can directly produce one voxel wide centerlines.

We proposed a sequential curve–thinning algorithm [9,10]. One iteration step of the object reduction process is decomposed into six successive sub–iterations according to the six main directions in 3D. Each sub–iteration consists of two phases; at first the border points according to the actual deletion direction that are simple (i.e., their deletion does not alter the topology of the image [5]) and not line–end points are marked as potential deletable. Then marked points are checked: a marked point is deleted if it remains simple and is not a line–end point after the deletion of some previously visited marked points. In addition, in some special cases, simple points are also deleted if they have become line-end points. That endpoint re–checking process statistically decreases the number of unwanted/false side branches in the created centerlines [10].

It can produce maximally thinned (i.e., 1-voxel wide) centerlines (see Fig. 1, since all simple points are deleted. The produced centerline is topologically equivalent to the original elongated object, since simple points are deleted sequentially. Our algorithm is topology-preserving by definition of simple points, therefore, the proof is self-evident.

Additionally, our method allows an easy and efficient implementation. It is much faster than the thinning algorithms employed, e.g., in [13].

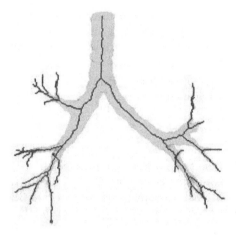

Fig. 1. The segmented volume of a human airway tree and its centerlines extracted by the proposed curve–thinning algorithm

2.2   Pruning

Unfortunately, each skeletonization algorithm (including ours) is rather sensitive to coarse object boundaries or surfaces. As a result, the produced (approximation to the) skeleton generally includes false segments that must be removed by a pruning step. Applying a proper pruning method that would yield reliable centerlines is critical in all tree-skeletonization applications. An unwanted branch causes false generation numbering and consequently false measurements corresponding to the individual segments of the tree (including length, volume, surface area, etc.).

We have developed a centerline pruning that uses both the branch length and the distance-from-surface (depth) information for the identification of the following pruning candidate: all branches are deleted if their lengths are shorter than a given threshold t_l and their associated branchpoints are not closer to the border/surface of the elongated tree (after topological correction) than a given threshold t_d:

The pruning process can be repeated for different pairs of thresholds (t_l, t_d). In our experience, 2 to 4 iterations typically provide satisfactory results for in vivo airway trees. The result of our pruning is demonstrated in Fig. 2.

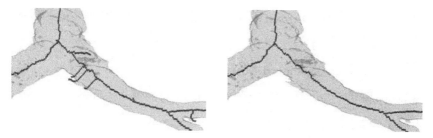

Fig. 2. A part of a segmented tree and its centerline before pruning (left) and after pruning (right). The applied pruning technique can delete unwanted long branches from thick parts and unwanted shorter ones from thinner parts, while correct branches are typically preserved throughout the tree

2.3   Tree Partitioning

The aim of the partitioning procedure is to partition all voxels of the binary tree into branches — each voxel is assigned a branch-specific label. There are two inputs into the process — the binary image after topological corrections, and the formal tree structure corresponding to the centerlines. The output is a gray–level image, in which value "0" corresponds to the background and different non-zero values are assigned to the voxels belonging to different tree branches/partitions (Fig. 3).

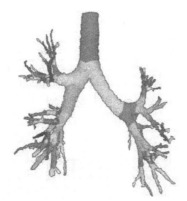

Fig. 3. The the partitioned volume of a human airway tree close to total lung capacity (TLC)

The automated partitioning consists of two steps. First, only the voxels in the centerlines are partitioned so that each branch/partition of the centerlines has a unique label. Non-skeletal tree voxels are then partitioned by isotropic label propagation — each voxel in the tree gets the label of the closest skeletal point.

2.4 Calculating Associated Measures

For each partition/branch of the tree, the following measures/indices are calculated:

- branch length — defined as a Euclidean distance between the parent and child branchpoints (in mm),
- branch volume — defined as a volume of all voxels belonging to the branch (in mm^3),
- branch surface area — defined as a surface area of all boundary voxels belonging to the branch (in mm^2),
- branch radius — derived from the branch length and the branch volume assuming "cylindrical" partition (in mm):

$$radius = \sqrt{\frac{volume}{\pi \cdot length}}.$$

Determining the first three indices is fairly straightforward, but calculating a reliable approximation to the branch radius is rather complicated. The two ends of a partition/branch are "conic", therefore, they must be suppressed to get measurements only from the "cylindrical" partitions.

3 Experimental Methods

Performance of the reported method was assessed in 343 computer phantom instances subjected to changes of its orientation, in a rigid plastic phantom CT-scanned under 9 orientations, in a rubber plastic phantom CT-scanned under 9 orientations, and in six in vivo scans of human lungs.

3.1 Phantoms

The computer phantom [4] is a 3-dimensional structural model of the human airway tree (Fig. 4a). The model consists of 125 elongated branches and its centerlines have 62 branchpoints and 64 endpoints (including the root of the tree) — all positions of the branchpoints are known. The generated object is embedded in a $300 \times 300 \times 300$ binary array containing unit-cube voxels. Independently, the phantom was rotated in 5 degree steps between -15 and $+15$ degrees along all three axes.

The second phantom is a hollow rigid plastic one (Fig. 4b), derived from an in vivo scanned human bronchial tree, transformed in a computer graphics representation, and built by a rapid prototyping machine. The third phantom is a hollow rubber plastic one (Fig. 4c), casted from a normal human bronchial tree

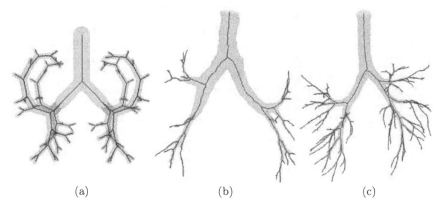

(a)   (b)   (c)

Fig. 4. The computer phantom (a), the rigid phantom (b), and the rubber phantom (c) in their neutral orientations and their centerlines

and consists of about 400 branches and 200 branchpoints. The physical phantom was embedded in potato flakes (simulating lung tissue). The rigid and the rubber phantoms were imaged in 9–9 orientations using multi-row detector computed tomography (4-slice spiral CT, Mx8000, Philips Medical Systems) with voxel size $0.439 \times 0.439 \times 0.5$ mm and $0.488 \times 0.488 \times 0.5$ mm, respectively. The volume sizes were $512 \times 512 \times 300 - 400$ and $512 \times 512 \times 500 - 600$ voxels, respectively. The rotation angles defined 9–9 phantom orientations in the scanner, the orientations were separated by $15°$ intervals in the $x - z$ and $y - z$ planes.

From the 9–9 CT phantom images, segmentation was performed to separate bronchial airways from the lung parenchyma yielding a binary image used as an input to the reported skeletonization algorithm. For each of the $342 + 9 + 9 = 360$ phantom trees, skeletonization was performed fully automatically and the resulting skeletons were not interactively edited. For each instance of the computer phantoms, the branchpoint position error was determined. It was defined as a Euclidean distance between the skeletonization-determined and true coordinates of the corresponding branchpoints.

For a subset of 9 computer phantoms, the 9 rigid and the 9 rubber phantoms, the above introduced quantitative indices were determined for the first 5 generations of the matched trees. Here, the reproducibility was determined by assessing differences between the reference tree and the tree analyzed in different orientations, after registering the analyzed tree with the reference tree. The quantitative measurements described above were compared in different orientations.

3.2   In Vivo CT Scans

The method was tested in six in vivo scans of the human chest. For each subject, a scan close to total lung capacity (TLC) was acquired by multi-detector row spiral computed tomography with voxel size $0.683 \times 0.683 \times 0.6$mm^3 (4-slice spiral CT,

Mx8000, Philips Medical Systems). The volume sizes were $512 \times 512 \times 450 - 550$ voxels. The segmented in vivo trees are not isometric (i.e., the voxels are cuboids instead of cubes) and contain numerous "thin" branches. To facilitate reproducibility assessment, a "more regular" reference tree was constructed for each segmented subject (see Figs. 5-6). The reproducibility analysis was performed in the reference trees artificially rotated in 8 different ways.

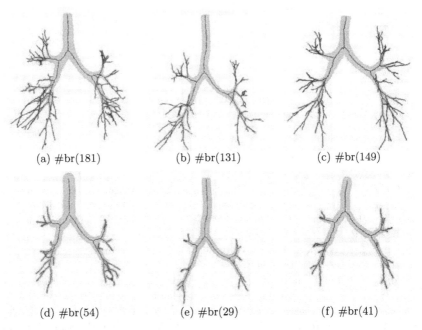

(a) #br(181)   (b) #br(131)   (c) #br(149)

(d) #br(54)   (e) #br(29)   (f) #br(41)

Fig. 5. The first three in vivo TLC trees (a-c) and the corresponding reference trees (d-f) (#br means the number of branches)

The reference tree construction consisted of the following steps:

- Centerlines from the segmented in vivo tree were extracted and the formal tree structure with the associated measures was created. Let S be the set of the skeletal voxels and let $radius(s)$ denote the radius of the branch containing $s \in S$ (in voxel).
- A new tree $R_t(S)$ is formed in the following way:

$$R_t(S) = \bigcup_{s \in S,\ radius(s) > t} \{\, r \mid d(r, s) \leq radius(s) \,\},$$

where $t \geq 0$ is an integer threshold for suppressing "thin" branches and $d(r, s)$ denotes the Euclidean distance between r and s (in voxel).

In other words, the reference tree is a collection of spheres in which the center of each sphere is a skeletal voxel in a "thick" branch of the original tree and the radius of a sphere is derived from the (cylindrical) radius associated with the corresponding branch of the original tree. Note, that the dimensions of the original and the reference volumes are the same and the reference volume is isometric (unit cube voxels 1 mm^3).

The extraction of the centerlines from each segmented tree was driven by the same pruning parameters. For each of the 6 in vivo trees, skeletonization was performed fully automatically and the resulting skeletons were not interactively edited. Each of the 6 reference trees was created by the same thickness parameter ($t = 2$). Figs. 5-6 show the original and reference trees and their centerlines. Note, that the reference trees are "more cylindrical" and contain much smaller number of branches than the original ones.

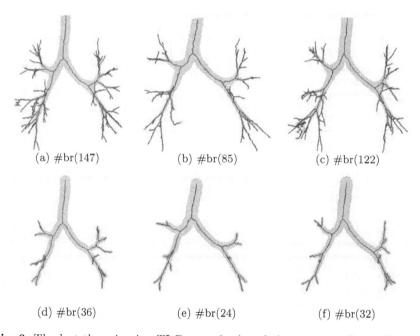

(a) #br(147)   (b) #br(85)   (c) #br(122)

(d) #br(36)   (e) #br(24)   (f) #br(32)

Fig. 6. The last three in vivo TLC trees (a-c) and the corresponding reference trees (d-f) (#br means the number of branches)

For each reference tree, 8 rotated instances were created, the orientations were separated by 15° intervals in the $x - z$ and $y - z$ planes. For each of the 6 trees, a set of 9 trees (i.e., the reference tree in neutral position and its 8 rotated instances), skeletonization and quantitative analysis were performed fully automatically using the same parameters setting for all 54 trees. Again, the quantitative measurements described above were compared in different orientations.

3.3 Statistical Assessment

The reproducibility results are reported separately for the three phantom studies and for in vivo data. The average branchpoint positioning errors are only calculated for the computer phantom for which the true branchpoint positions were known. These errors are presented as mean ± standard deviation and reported in voxels. All other reproducibility indices were compared using Bland-Altman statistic for which the average value of all corresponding measurements was used as an independent variable. The reproducibility showing 95% confidence intervals are presented in the form of Bland-Altman agreement plots [1].

4 Results

In the computer phantoms, the average branchpoint positioning error showed subvoxel accuracy of 0.93 ± 0.41 voxel size [10].

The reproducibility of the associated in the tree kinds of phantoms is discussed in [9,10].

The reproducibility of the quantitative tree morphology indices in in vivo CT scans are given in Fig. 7. In all cases, the relatively large differences between the surface and volume indices are to be expected due to a high sensitivity of these measures to minor partitioning errors, especially in short branches. Compare with the high reproducibility of the branch diameter and length measures.

5 Conclusion

The presented automated method for skeletonization, branchpoint identification and quantitative analysis of tubular tree structures is robust, efficient, and highly reproducible. It facilitates calculation of a number of morphologic indices described above as well as indices not considered in this work — branch angle, curvature, and many others.

The developed approach is built on the following novel concepts and skeletonization algorithm: fast curve-thinning algorithm to increase computational speed, endpoint re-checking to avoid generation of spurious side branches, depth-and-length sensitive pruning, exact tree-branch partitioning allowing branch volume and surface measurements, identification of non-branching tree segments, achieving sub-voxel accuracy of branch point positioning, and performing extensive validations on complex phantoms and in vivo scans.

Acknowledgments

This work was supported by the NIH grant HL–064368.

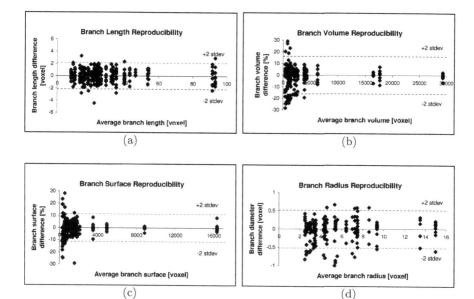

Fig. 7. Reproducibility in the 54 "reference" trees derived from in vivo CT data. a) Branch length, b) Branch volume, c) Branch surface area, and d) Average branch radius

References

1. J.M. Bland, D.G. Altman: Statistical methods for assessing agreement between two methods of clinical measurement. Lancet **1(8476)** (1986) 307–310
2. Z. Chen, S. Molloi: Automatic 3D vascular tree construction in CT angiography. Computerized Medical Imaging and Graphics **27** (2003) 469–479
3. G. Gerig, Th. Koller, G. Székely, Ch. Brechbühler, O. Kübler: Symbolic descriptions of 3–D structures applied to cerebral vessel tree obtained from MR angiography volume data, In: Proc. 13th Int. Conf. Information Processing in Medical Imaging, IPMI'93, Lecture Notes in Computer Science **687**, Springer (1993) 94–111
4. H. Kitaoka, R. Takaki, B.: A three-dimensional model of the human airway tree. Journal of Applied Physiology **87** (1999) 2207–2217
5. T.Y. Kong, A. Rosenfeld: Digital topology: Introduction and survey. Computer Vision, Graphics, and Image Processing **48** (1989) 357–393
6. M. Maddah, A. Afzali–Kusha, H. Soltanian–Zadeh: Efficient center–line extraction for quantification of vessels in confocal microscopy images. Medical Physics **30** (2003) 204–211
7. K. Mori, J. Hasegawa, Y. Suenaga, J. Toriwaki: Automated anatomical labeling of the bronchial branch and its application to the virtual bronchoscopy system. IEEE Trans. Medical Imaging **19** (2000) 103–114
8. I. Nyström: Skeletonization applied to magnetic resonance angiography images. Proc. Medical Imaging 1998: Image Processing, SPIE Vol. 3338 (2003) 693–701

9. K. Palágyi, J. Tschirren, M. Sonka: Quantitative analysis of three-dimensional tubular tree structures. In: Proc. Medical Imaging 2003: Image Processing, SPIE Vol. 5032 (2003) 277–287

10. K. Palágyi, J. Tschirren, M. Sonka: Quantitative analysis of intrathoracic airway trees: methods and validation. In: Proc. 18th Int. Conf. Information Processing in Medical Imaging, IPMI 2003, Lecture Notes in Computer Science 2732, Springer (2003) 222–233

11. J. Toriwaki, K. Mori: Distance transformation and skeletonization of 3D pictures and their applications to medical images. Digital and Image Geometry, Lecture Notes in Computer Science 2243, Springer (2001) 412–429

12. Y.F. Tsao, K.S. Fu: A parallel thinning algorithm for 3–D pictures. Computer Graphics and Image Processing **17** (1981) 315–331

13. S.Y. Wan, A.P. Kiraly, E.L. Ritman, W.E. Higgins: Extraction of the hepatic vasculature in rats using 3-D Micro-CT images. IEEE Trans. Medical Imaging **19** (2000) 964–971

14. S. Wood, A. Zerhouni, J. Hoford, E.A. Hoffman, W. Mitzner: Measurement of three-dimensional lung tree structures using computed tomography. Journal of Applied Physiology **79** (1995) 1687–1697

Computer-Aided Measurement of Solid Breast Tumor Features on Ultrasound Images

Miguel Alemán-Flores[1], Patricia Alemán-Flores[2], Luis Álvarez-León[1],
José Manuel Santana-Montesdeoca[2], Rafael Fuentes-Pavón[2], and
Agustín Trujillo-Pino[1]

[1] Departamento de Informática y Sistemas
Universidad de Las Palmas de Gran Canaria, 35017, Las Palmas, Spain
[2] Sección de Ecografía, Servicio de Radiodiagnóstico
Hospital Universitario Insular de Gran Canaria, 35016, Las Palmas, Spain

Abstract. This paper presents a new approach in the application of
computer vision techniques to the diagnosis of solid breast tumors on
ultrasound images. Most works related to medical image analysis for
breast cancer detection refer to mammography. However, radiologists
have proved the significance of some aspects observed on ultrasound images, among which are spiculation, calcifications, ellipsoid shape, dimensions, echogenicity, capsule, angular margins, lobulations, shadowing and
ramifications. We have developed a common framework for the analysis
of these criteria, so that a series of parameters are available for the physicians to decide whether the biopsy is necessary or not. We present a set
of mathematical methods to extract objective evidence of the presence or
absence of the diagnostic criteria. This system is able to extract the relevant features for solid breast nodules with high accuracy and represents
a very valuable help in the assessment of radiologists.

1 Introduction

There are certain criteria which are used by the physicians to determine whether
a solid breast nodule is benign or malignant. This work uses the computational
techniques for the study and classification of shapes and textures to help the
physicians in the early diagnosis of breast tumors on ultrasound images. Contrary
to other works which deal with mammographies, this one is based on the analysis
of ultrasound images, in which a series of diagnostic factors can be observed.
Some previous works try to adjust the parameters of the ultrasound systems
to help in the decision making process [1], segment the tissues [2], or deal with
certain particular aspects of the nodules, such as texture [3] or general shape
[4]. The analysis of ultrasound images that we propose allows performing precise
measurements of a series of diagnostic factors in order to characterize each nodule
according to the values of the parameters which have been obtained.

Spiculation, taller than wide shape, angular margins, markedly hypoechoic
appearance, acoustic shadowing, calcifications, ramifications and microlobulations are considered as malignant findings which lead the physicians to carry

M. Šonka et al. (Eds.): CVAMIA-MMBIA 2004, LNCS 3117, pp. 353–364, 2004.
© Springer-Verlag Berlin Heidelberg 2004

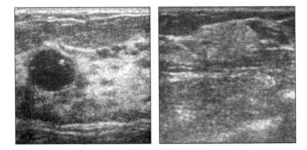

Fig. 1. Markedly hypoechoic nodule (left) and hyperechoic nodule (right)

out a biopsy. On the other hand, hyperechogenicity, ellipsoid shape, two or three gentle lobulations as well as a thin and echogenic capsule suggest the benignity of the nodule [5].

It is not always easy for a human observer to measure some of these features and provide objective evidence of the benignity or malignancy of the tumor. However, computer vision techniques may help detecting some of them and supplying numerical measurements of the presence and relevance of these factors, in such a way that the risk of overlooking a malignant nodule can be reduced [6] [7]. The purpose of this work is not the substitution of the human observer or the physician's interpretation, but the addition of a precise, objective and invariant examiner which can draw the specialist's attention to those areas where each diagnostic factor is likely to be present.

2   Description of the Diagnostic Criteria

In this section, we will describe each one of the criteria that will be considered in the diagnosis of the nodules, both malignant and benign. These criteria have been extracted and adapted from [5]. We will also present some examples of the results provided by the computer-aided system.

First, we will consider the generation of echo by the nodule and the area around it. The hyper or hypoechogenicity of a nodule, i.e. the excessive or defective generation of echoes by that nodule, is measured with respect to the echogenicity of the fat of that particular woman, since it is the relative intensity and not the absolute one that determines whether it is hyper or hypo-echoic. This feature is considered because of the hyperechogenicity of some benign tumors and the marked hypoechogenicity of malignant nodules. In fact, the central part of two-thirds of malignant solid breast nodules is very hypoechoic with respect to fat. In Fig. 1, we can see an example of a markedly hypoechoic nodule (left) and a hyperechoic nodule (right).

Not only the generation of echo within the nodule is relevant, but also how the region under it is affected. A nodule is said to produce acoustic shadow if the ultrasound is attenuated when crossing through it. In this case, the region

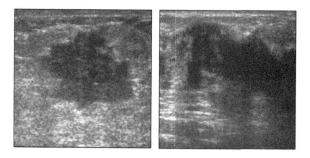

Fig. 2. Nodule without acoustic shadowing (left) and with acoustic shadowing (right)

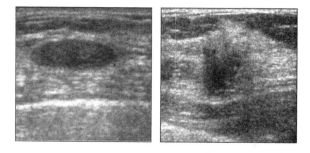

Fig. 3. Wider-than-tall nodule (left) and taller-than-wide nodule (right)

beyond the nodule, from the point of view of the ultrasound emitting device, is darker than the region at the same level which is not under the nodule, since its emission of echo is not altered by the nodule's being in between. In Fig. 2, we observe how a nodule can leave the generation of echo unaltered (left) or interfere it (right). The generation of shadowing is considered as a malignant factor.

We will now focus on the general shape of the nodule. A nodule is said to be taller than wide when it is greater in the direction normal to the skin than in the parallel ones. When this ratio is quite high, the possibility of being analyzing a malignant nodule increases, since this reflects that the nodule is growing across normal tissue planes. On the other hand, benign nodules usually affect a single tissue and appear perpendicular to the direction of the ultrasound signals. Figure 3 shows a wider-than-tall nodule (left) and a taller-than-wide one (right).

An ellipsoid shape increases the probability of the nodule's being benign, and even if a nodule does not present an ellipsoid-like shape, it is considered as benign if it presents two or three smooth, well circumscribed and gentle lobulations. Figures 4 and 5 present a nodule with elliptical shape and a nodule with two smooth and gentle lobulations, respectively, as well as the ellipses extracted by the computer-aided system to help classifying the nodules.

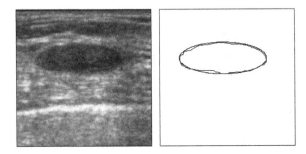

Fig. 4. Ultrasound image of a solid breast nodule (left), contour and ellipse extracted from that contour (right)

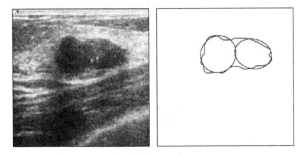

Fig. 5. Ultrasound image of a solid breast nodule (left), contour and combination of two ellipses extracted from that contour (right)

Contrary to the elliptical shapes described above, malignant breast nodules may present projections from the surface of the nodule which extend radially within a duct towards the nipple (duct extension) and/or within ducts away from the nipple (branch pattern). Figure 6 shows a nodule with ramifications, which have been signaled by the system.

Some other factors do not refer to the general shape, but to local variations of the contour. For example, the finding of angular margins makes the nodule suspicious of being malignant. Angular margins refer to the contour of the junction between the hypoechoic or isoechoic solid nodule and the surrounding tissues. The entire surface of the lesion must be surveyed, since they may involve only a part of it. Similarly, microlobulations are observed as small ellipsoid arcs in certain regions of the contour and are frequently associated with angular margins. Figures 7 and 8 show the angular margins and microlobulations extracted for a nodule, respectively.

Spiculation consists of contrasting lines radiating out perpendicularly from the surface of the nodule. Figure 9 shows the spiculated areas extracted for a nodule.

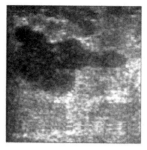

Fig. 6. Ultrasound image of a solid breast nodule (left), contour and ramifications extracted by the system (right)

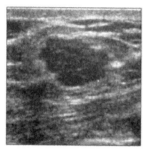

Fig. 7. Ultrasound image of a solid breast nodule (left), contour and angular margins extracted from that contour (right)

Finally, the presence of echogenic calcifications within a solid breast nodule is worrisome for malignancy. Calcifications are identified as highly contrasting white points inside the nodule. Figure 10 shows an example of a nodule with calcifications and where they are located by the computer.

In the following section, we show how the ultrasound images have been processed to analyze these factors on them.

3 Computer Processing of the Diagnostic Criteria

In this section, we will show how the criteria described above have been processed by the computer-aided system. First, we will explain how the nodule has been segmented, then we will present the processing of the intensity-related criteria, and finally we will explain how the shape of the nodule has been analyzed.

3.1 Image Segmentation

Before measuring the diagnosis criteria on the nodule, it must be located and delimited. Thus, we must segment the interesting area and the background in

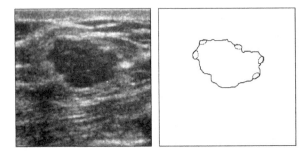

Fig. 8. Ultrasound image of a solid breast nodule (left), contour and microlobulations extracted from that contour (right)

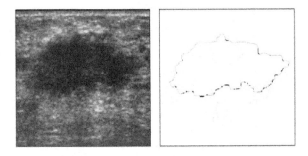

Fig. 9. Ultrasound image of a solid breast nodule (left), contour and spiculations extracted from that contour (right)

order to identify the regions which will be processed in the further studies. The segmentation of the images to separate the nodule from the surrounding tissues is performed by means of a truncated median filter, a balloon algorithm and a dilation process. Due to the presence of Rayleigh distributed noise, which characterizes ultrasound images, the mode filter could be appropriate to denoise the images, since it eliminates the spurious negligible points. However, its performance depends strongly on the size of the window in which the filter is applied and, if it is not large enough, it may result in modeless regions or quite arbitrary values. That is why we have used the truncated median filter, which produces quite good results in a few iterations. In this filter, the median is calculated in each iteration and the further values are eliminated, so that the median and the mode approach. For a given pixel (x, y), the process is as follows: let f_n be the histogram of the grayvalues in the wxh window from $(x-(w-1)/2, y-(h-1)/2)$ to $(x + (w - 1)/2, y + (h - 1)/2)$ (n ranges from 0 to 255), and let m be the median of such histogram, i.e. $\sum_{k=0}^{k=m-1} f_k < (w*h)/2$ and $\sum_{k=0}^{k=m} f_k \geq (w*h)/2$, those values which differ from m more than the minimum of m and $255 - m$ are

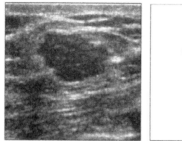

Fig. 10. Ultrasound image of a solid breast nodule (left), contour and calcifications extracted from that contour (right)

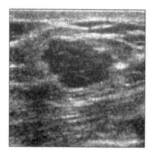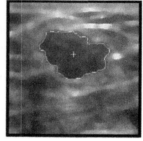

Fig. 11. Ultrasound image of a nodule (left), contour and center on the filtered image (right)

eliminated and the median is recalculated [7]. After a few iterations, the median can be considered as a good approximation of the mode.

From a seed into the nodule, which must be entered to the system by the user, a balloon algorithm allows filling the interesting area as connected intensity-similar pixels. The pixels which are connected to the already selected ones, whose intensity is similar to theirs and inside a certain interval are included into the selected region. If given two thresholds for intensity and difference, no more points can be incorporated, the thresholds are increased until no point is added in a given iteration or the added region is larger to the previous one, since the latter might mean that the background has been connected to the nodule.

Due to the difficulty that many of these images present, the user is allowed to correct the result of the automatic segmentation in case it does not fit the area covered by the nodule. Thus, adding and subtracting regions in the segmentation will produce a more reliable delimitation of the nodule to proceed to its analysis. Fig. 11 shows an example of the ultrasound image of a nodule (left), the filtered image, the contour and the center of the selected region (right).

3.2   Intensity-Related Features

In this section, we consider those factors which refer to the graylevels of the image, which represent the echo produced at each point when the ultrasound reaches it. These are the echogenicity of the nodule, the presence of acoustic shadow under the nodule, the microcalcifications and the observation of a thin echogenic capsule around the nodule.

Using the binary segmented image as a mask, we calculate the mean intensity of the region covered by the nodule. This is its mean echogenicity and, similarly, a fat region is selected by the user to extract its echogenicity and compare them. This comparison will help determining whether the nodule is hypo or hyperechogenic.

To determine whether the nodule is producing acoustic shadowing, we compare the region under the nodule and the region at the same level which is not covered by the nodule. As done before, we calculate the mean intensity (echogenicity) of both regions. The comparison of both mean intensities allows determining whether the nodule is absorbing the ultrasound or not.

By using the structure tensor method, we have estimated the magnitude of the gradient in every point inside the nodule. Those points where the intensity and the magnitude of the gradient is quite high have been selected as calcifications (see Fig. 10). In order to estimate the magnitude of the gradient, we first calculate an initial estimation for every point using the following mask for the horizontal component and its transpose for the vertical component:

$$u_x = \frac{1}{4h} \begin{pmatrix} -(2-\sqrt{2}) & 0 & (2-\sqrt{2}) \\ -2(\sqrt{2}-1) & 0 & 2(\sqrt{2}-1) \\ -(2-\sqrt{2}) & 0 & (2-\sqrt{2}) \end{pmatrix} . \tag{1}$$

For every point, we select an area around it and build the following matrix from the estimations of the gradient (x_n, y_n) in those points:

$$\begin{pmatrix} \sum_{i=0}^{N} y_i^2 & -\sum_{i=0}^{N} x_i y_i \\ -\sum_{i=0}^{N} x_i y_i & \sum_{i=0}^{N} x_i^2 \end{pmatrix} . \tag{2}$$

The eigenvector associated to the minimum eigenvalue is the estimation of the orientation of the gradient, and the maximum eigenvalue is the square of the norm of the gradient estimation.

The capsule of the nodule is extracted by eroding the selected region and analyzing the eroded points. The echogenicity of the capsule is measured, as the previous ones, from the mean intensity of the region.

3.3   Shape-Related Features

This section deals with those factors which refer to the shape of the nodule. The proportion of the width and the height of the nodule, the presence of angular margins, the ramifications which may appear, the number and size of lobulations and the ellipsoid shape are considered as benign or malignant factors.

On the binary segmented image, we calculate the mean width and the mean height of the nodule and the quotient of both measures indicates its disposition. Besides, those points whose vertical distance to the center is larger than the mean width indicate the areas where the nodule is growing vertically. When studying whether the nodule has ellipsoid shape or not, we extract the ellipsoid for which the distance from the points on the contour is minimum. This yields the one which best represents the set of contour points (see Fig. 4). When the mean distance is low enough, the nodule has a clearly ellipsoid-like shape. On the other hand, the higher the distance, the more dissimilar the nodule and the ellipsoid are.

The usual techniques to estimate the ellipse location in an image are based on the Hough transform or the principal axis estimation [8][9]. We propose an algorithm to estimate, in a very accurate way, the ellipse location in an image by minimizing the mean distance from a set of points to the ellipse. This minimization criterion has a more physical meaning and provides a very accurate estimation.

An ellipse depends on 5 parameters $\Theta = (x_0, y_0, a, b, \theta)$, where (x_0, y_0) is the center, (a, b) are the sizes of the principal axes and θ is the orientation. We parametrize an ellipse in the following way:

$$e_\Theta(t) = \begin{pmatrix} x_0 + \cos(\theta)a\cos(t) + \sin(\theta)b\sin(t) \\ y_0 - \sin(\theta)a\cos(t) + \cos(\theta)b\sin(t) \end{pmatrix} \quad t \in [0, 2\pi] \ . \qquad (3)$$

In the following lemma, we compute the distance from a point to an ellipse:

Lemma 1. *Let $(x, y) \in R^2$, and let $e_\Theta(t)$ be an ellipse. The distance from the point (x, y) to the ellipse is denoted by $d((x, y), e_\Theta(.))$. Such distance is attained in a point $t_0 \in [0, 2\pi]$. If $z = \cos^2(t_0)$ then z is a root of the polynomial*

$$l^2 z^4 + 2mlz^3 + (k + 2ln + m^2)z^2 + (2mn - k)z + n^2 = 0 \ . \qquad (4)$$

where

$$\tilde{x} = \cos(\theta)(x - x_0) - \sin(\theta)(y - y_0)$$
$$\tilde{y} = \sin(\theta)(x - x_0) + \cos(\theta)(y - y_0)$$
$$l = -(b^2 - a^2)^2, \ m = (b^2 - a^2)^2 + a^2\tilde{x}^2 - b^2\tilde{y}^2, \ k = 4\tilde{x}^2\tilde{y}^2 a^2 b^2, \ n = -\tilde{x}^2 a^2$$

Proof: A straightforward calculation.

Given a set of points $X = \{(x_i, y_i)\}_{i=1,\dots,N}$, we define the mean distance from an ellipse to the set of points X as

$$d(X, e_\Theta(.)) = \frac{1}{N} \sum_{i=1,\dots,N} d((x_i, y_i), e_\Theta(.)) \ . \qquad (5)$$

Next, we minimize the distance from X to the ellipse with respect to the parameters of the ellipse Θ. We propose a gradient descent method to perform the minimization procedure. We start with an initial approximation for the ellipse parameters which could be provided by the Hough transform or another simpler method. Then, we iterate the scheme:

$$\Theta^{k+1} = \Theta^k - \lambda \nabla_\Theta d(X, e_{\Theta^k}(.)) \ . \tag{6}$$

The step λ is adapted in each iteration using the following criterion: We initialize $\lambda = \lambda_0$, we compute Θ^{k+1} from Θ^k using (6). If $d(X, e_{\Theta^{k+1}}(.)) < d(X, e_{\Theta^k}(.))$, we update $\lambda = 10\lambda$. If $d(X, e_{\Theta^{k+1}}(.)) > d(X, e_{\Theta^k}(.))$, we update $\lambda = 0.1\lambda$ and we recompute Θ^{k+1}. We stop the iterative scheme when $\Theta^{k+1} - \Theta^k$ is small enough, or when we cannot reduce $d(X, e_{\Theta^k}(.))$ after a number of attempts. The distance is divided by the square root of the area of the nodule to normalize it. If the nodule has not ellipsoid shape, we must determine if it has two or three gentle lobulations. We proceed as in the previous case, but instead of searching for an ellipsoid which fits the whole contour, we search for large lobulations which fit a large region of the contour each, which together cover the whole contour, whose axes do not differ strongly in their lengths, and whose centers are clearly separated (see Fig.5).

To analyze whether the nodule presents ramifications, we locate those points whose distance to the ellipsoid which best fits the nodule is large. Since the ellipsoid covers the most representative part of the nodule, when it has ramifications, they appear as branches projecting out from this ellipsoid. The number and dimensions of these ramifications is strongly considered to characterize the nodule.

In order to prevent the ramifications from influencing the position and dimensions of the main ellipse, an iterative scheme has been used in which the points which are very far from the ellipse are eliminated and the ellipse is recalculated. After a few iterations, the ellipse which is extracted is much more representative of the central region and the ramifications are more clearly identified (see Fig. 6).

We can locate angular margins by searching for pseudo-straight lines on the contour of the nodule. In order to adjust a set of N points to a straight line, we proceed as follows:

Let (u, v) be a point, and let $r = x + ay + b$ be a line, the distance from (u, v) to $x + ay + b$ is:

$$d(m, r) = \frac{|u + av + b|}{\sqrt{1 + a^2}} \ . \tag{7}$$

If we minimize with respect to a and b, we obtain the values which best extract the supporting line for a set of planar points.

When a point joins two straight lines with different orientations, an angle is signaled. In order to select those angles which are significant for the study, the lines must fit the contour, i.e. the mean distance from the points on the contour to the line must be low, they must be long enough in order to neglect small variations in the orientation of the contour, and the difference in the orientation must be less than $\pi/2$, i.e. they form an acute angle (see Fig. 7). For every candidate to be a pseudo-corner, the line which adjusts the points before it in the contour and the line which adjusts the points after it, considering the contour as a sequence, must be extracted and compared.

Besides angular margins, we may find microlobulations. For this feature, a similar technique as the one used when extracting the general ellipsoid is applied. However, in this case, we search for segments of the contour which can be approximated by a part of an ellipse and whose size and axes are small. In order to avoid the duplication of the lobulations by extracting overlapping ellipses, only those whose centers are clearly different are selected (see Fig. 8).

To locate the areas where spiculation appears, we extract the orientation of a window around every contour point. As done with the calcifications, the structure tensor method has been used, though, in this case, not only the magnitude of the gradient, but also its orientation is significant. When the orientation in that region is quite dissimilar to the one of the contour in that point, it is marked as a spiculation zone (see Fig. 9). Non-spiculated nodules present a clearly defined contour along which the orientation varies softly. Similarly as done when we calculated the magnitude of the gradient for the localization of the calcifications, we now extract the magnitude and the orientation.

We have tested the measurements extracted for the different criteria by considering ultrasound images of 40 solid breast nodules. To estimate the relevance of the information provided by each factor in the diagnosis, we have calculated the area under the ROC curve for each one of them. This curve relates the sensibility and the specificity of a diagnostic criterion, and the closer to 1 the area is, the more powerful the criterion is. The best results were obtained for microlobulations (0.854), angular margins (0.849), ellipsoid shape (0.794) and ramifications (0.789).

4   Conclusion

In this paper, we have presented a new approach in the field of breast cancer early detection. We have dealt with a very difficult type of images, those generated by ultrasound devices, which present a dense and intense kind of noise and whose interpretation is quite difficult, even for a human observer.

The definition of a series of objective and reliable criteria for the discrimination between benign and malignant solid breast nodules and their relation to visual characteristics of a region have made it possible to apply those techniques used in shape and texture analysis to the description of those nodules.

A wide range of techniques, such as truncated median, seed segmentation, shape adjustment, ellipse location or structure tensor, have allowed reaching very satisfactory results in terms of quantitative and qualitative description of the criteria that the physicians take into account when diagnosing a nodule.

The possibility of providing objective numerical measurements of the presence of the diagnosis criteria represents a remarkable progress in the classification of the nodules.

These results emphasize the importance of the introduction of computer vision techniques in the processing of medical images, not to substitute the role of the physicians, whose skills can only be imitated in a hard and limited way, but to aid the decision making process.

References

1. Kuo, W.J., Chang, R.F., Moon, W.K., Lee, C.C., Chen, D.R.: Computer-Aided Diagnosis of Breast Tumors with Different US Systems. Acad Radiol **9** (2002) 793-799
2. Kaufhold, J., Chan, R., Karl, W.C., Castanon, D.A.: Ultrasound Tissue Analysis and Characterization. Battlefield Biomedical Technologies, H.H. Pien editor, Proc. SPIE **3712** (1999) 73-83
3. Chen D.R., Chang, R.F., Juang, Y.L.: Computer-Aided Diagnosis Applied to US of Solid Breast Nodules by Using Neural Networks. Radiology **213** (1999) 407-412
4. Cheng, C.M., Chou, Y.H.,Han, K.C., Hung, G.S., Tiu, C.M., Chiou, H.J., Chiou, S.Y.: Breast Lesions on Sonograms: Computer-Aided Diagnosis with Nearly Setting-Independent Features and Artificial Neural Networks. Radiology **226** (2003) 504-514
5. Stavros, A.T., Thickman, D., Rapp, C.L., Dennis, M.A., Parker, S.H., Sisney, G.A.: Solid Breast Nodules: Use of Sonography to Distinguish between Benign and Malignant Nodules. Radiology **196** (1995) 123-134
6. Sonka, M., Hlavac, V., Boyle, R.: Image Processing, Analysis, and Machine Vision. PWS-ITP (1999)
7. Nixon, M.S., Aguado, A.S.: Feature Extraction and Image Processing. Oxford Newnes (2002)
8. Ahn, S.J., Rauh, W., Warnecke, H.J. Least-Squares Orthogonal Distances Fitting of Circle, Sphere, Ellipse, Hyperbola, and Parabola. Pattern Recognition, Elsevier **34** (2001) 2283-2303
9. Halíř, R., Flusser, J. Numerically Stable Direct Least Squares Fitting of Ellipses. In Proc. of WSCG 98 (1998) 125-132

Can a Continuity Heuristic Be Used to Resolve the Inclination Ambiguity of Polarized Light Imaging?

Luiza Larsen and Lewis D. Griffin

Imaging Sciences, King's College, London, UK
{luiza.larsen,lewis.griffin}@kcl.ac.uk

Abstract. We propose the use of a continuity heuristic for solving the inclination ambiguity of polarized light imaging, which is a high resolution method of mapping the spatially varying pattern of anisotropy in biological and non-biological samples. Applied to the white matter of the brain, solving the inclination ambiguity of polarized light imaging will allow the creation of a 3D model of fibers. We use the continuity heuristic in several methods, some of which employ the simulated annealing algorithm to reinforce the heuristic, while others proceed deterministically to solve the inclination ambiguity. We conclude by explaining the limitations of the continuity heuristic approach.

1 Introduction

There exist materials with an anisotropic and spatially varying, structure. Among them are specimens like crystals, liquid crystals, amorphous and semi-amorphous materials and polymers. Some biological tissues also show anisotropic properties. For example brain white matter, cardiac tissue and bone tissue.

There exist applications for which it would be useful to map the spatial pattern of the anisotropy. The most challenging of these are biological applications where resolving the 3D pattern of anisotropy is essential. Two important examples for biology are mapping the orientation of axons in the white matter of the brain, and mapping the orientation of muscle fibers in cardiac tissue. We will focus on the first of these here.

Understanding the architecture of the human brain has many clinical applications, such as surgery, targeted drug delivery and improved stroke recovery. Detailed white matter fiber mapping is also important because defects in the white matter structure lead to complex neuropsychological deficits.

One widely used method for mapping 3D fiber orientation is DT- MRI (Diffusion Tensor Magnetic Resonance Imaging) [5], [11], [16]. Its operation is based on the fact that diffusion perpendicular to the neuronal fiber orientation is more restricted than diffusion parallel to it [19]. Such anisotropic water diffusion causes different signal intensities depending on the direction of the MR gradient pulses applied. Thus water diffusion can be measured and fibers visualized [11]. However the DTI method of mapping fiber orientation has some limitations, the main being relatively low reso-

M. Šonka et al. (Eds.): CVAMIA-MMBIA 2004, LNCS 3117, pp. 365-375, 2004.

lution. An anisotropic resolution of $(39\mu m)^2 \times 156\mu m$ and an isotropic resolution of $(156\mu m)^3$ are the best that have been achieved, but both used 9.4T scanners and were of the mouse brain, which is only approximately 10mm in size [6], [24].

An alternative method of mapping fiber orientation, with potentially higher resolution, is polarized light imaging. The resolution is limited by the capability of the light microscope used (in the plane of the sample) and the thickness of the prepared section.

By passing polarized light through thin sections of anisotropic tissue such as brain white matter, fiber orientation in a plane of the sample can be mapped [1-5], [9], [12], [13], [20], [22]. This method can and has been used for characterizing all kinds of transparent microscopic specimens including organic tissues such as muscle, bone and brain, as well as polymers and mineral samples [10].

The polarized light imaging method is based on the optical phenomenon of birefringence, which results from optical anisotropy within the sample. The direct cause of birefringence is the fact that the speed of light through the sample varies with the plane of polarization of the transmitted light. Refractive index is different across and along the fibers, thus polarized light can be used to probe the orientation of fiber tracts.

The basic polarized light imaging method is the method of crossed polars. A polarization filter, (the polarizer), is placed into the beam of light before it passes through the sample, and a second polarization filter, (the analyzer), is put into the beam of light after it has passed the sample. Polarizer and analyzer transmission axes are oriented perpendicular to each other. The amount of light which passes the analyzer, is dependent on the orientation of the anisotropic structures in the sample in relation to the orientation angle of the polars. If it is assumed that that the two polarizers are perfect and perfectly crossed, no light should pass through this system unless the sample changes the polarization state of the light. As the polarizers are rotated, transmitted light intensity, measured in each point of the sample, varies depending on the angle between polarizers, and thus can be used to infer local fiber orientation. Between the sample and the polarizer a quarter wave plate, which imposes a phase shift of quarter of a cycle on the light wave, can be introduced as a compensator.

2   Statement of Problem

The local 3D orientation of fibers can be described by a pair of angles. The *direction* which is the angle in the plane of the section (*xy* - plane), and the *inclination* which indicates the elevation of the fibers perpendicular to the plane of the section (*z*-direction) [4].

Polarized light imaging methods can produce images describing fiber orientation in the plane of the section (Figure 1). The direction of fibers can be unambiguously obtained by measuring the intensities of light passing through the sample whilst varying the angle of the polars, to find the angle of the polars for which there is the lowest intensity. The inclination of fibers can be estimated from how the amplitude of the transmitted light varies with the orientation of the polars. The steeper the inclination angle of the fibers the less the variation.

In the MetriPol picture (Figure 1) [18], where the unambiguous fiber directions (in the xy plane) are shown, the colors indicate fiber directions in each pixel. Fiber directions are also represented by short lines which are averaged across several pixels for clearer visualization.

Fig. 1. Image of a rat brain section taken by the polarized light microscope imaging system "MetriPol" [18]. The short lines show orientation of the fibers in the plane of the section. The size bar shown in the legend of the picture describes in plane resolution. Thickness of the slice used was 80μm.

However, as illustrated in figure 2, the polarized light imaging method, as described, is completely unable to distinguish between positive and negative angles of inclination, e.g. 30° and -30° (Figure 2). In each site therefore there are two possible inclinations to choose from. Choosing the right one is a discrete combinatorial problem.

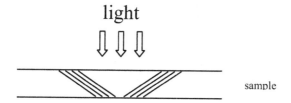

Fig. 2. Inclination ambiguity resulting from polarized light imaging methods. For both orientations of the fibers, measured light intensity is identical.

Solving the inclination ambiguity is a 3D problem, however in this paper all simulations are performed in 2D as this is sufficient for understanding the pros and cons of the approaches we propose and much easier to visualize. Furthermore all proposed approaches can be easily implemented in 3D.

3   Proposed Solution

In this article we propose a continuity heuristic for solving the inclination ambiguity. The heuristic we propose is that: 3D orientations in adjacent locations are more likely to be similar than different. We make use of the continuity heuristic in several algorithms. First we discuss a single scale simulated annealing approach, and then two multi-scale approaches; one that proceeds from fine to coarse levels of detail, and the other from coarse to fine levels. Inadequacies in the performance of each algorithm motivate the next in the sequence. The final algorithm performs so well that it enables us to characterize fundamental limitations of the use of the continuity heuristic.

4   Algorithms for Finding Solution

We assume that the most continuous solution is the solution which is most likely to be correct. The continuity of the solution is calculated as the sum of squared angle differences between adjacent pixels. 8-neighbour connectivity was used but the significance of diagonal connectivity was attenuated by using a $2^{-\frac{1}{2}}$ weighting. This definition was used in all of the proposed approaches.

4.1   Single Scale Simulated Annealing

Here, in order to solve the inclination ambiguity by maximizing continuity, simulated annealing has been used. The name simulated annealing comes from an analogy with the process of annealing metals by slow cooling in stages, which allows atoms plenty of time to form ordered crystal structures and a state of minimum energy to be achieved but without precipitantly locking into a sub-optimal solution that cannot further be revised (e.g. quenching) [7].

The simulated annealing algorithm is simple. The initial state of a system is chosen randomly. Its energy is calculated and denoted E. The temperature is initialized to some high value T. The initial configuration is then perturbed – the new trial solution is generated - and the change in energy dE is computed. If the change in energy is negative the new configuration is accepted. If the change in energy is positive it is accepted with a probability given by the Boltzman factor $e^{\frac{dE}{T}}$.

This process is repeated a sufficient number of times for the current temperature. Then the temperature is reduced and the entire process repeated until a frozen state is achieved at T≈0.

The procedure of setting an initial value for temperature depends on the application. As a starting point the initial temperature can be set to be the mean of the energy changes due to random steps from the start. Then the other parameters can be adjusted. An example of the results of the algorithm is shown in Figure 3.

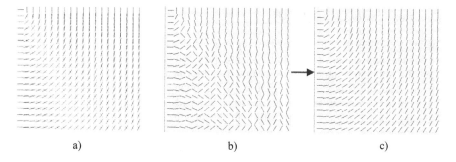

a)   b)   c)

Fig. 3. Simulated annealing algorithm. a) At each location the two possible inclinations are shown superimposed. b) The random starting configuration for the simulated annealing algorithm – at each location one of the two possible inclinations has been chosen. c) Solution found by the algorithm.

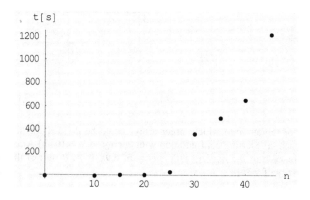

Fig. 4. How elapsed time t (in seconds) increases with the size of the array n.

For small arrays like the one shown in Figure 3, composed of 20x20 pixels, simulated annealing is very fast. The minimal score 6.4×10^4 for this example is reached after 11 seconds from the beginning score of 1.6×10^6. For larger arrays the time lengthens as is shown in Figure 4. For an array twice the size, it takes 10 minutes to find a solution with a minimal energy of 7.5×10^4 from a starting configuration with energy of 6.7×10^6. Figure 4 illustrates only a few experiments and in each instance the parameters have to be adjusted separately and might not be optimal.

Despite the advances in computer technology, running the simulated annealing algorithm on large arrays of data exceeds the power of the systems currently available. Therefore we propose two solutions for solving optimization with simulated annealing for larger arrays. The first approach solves the problem locally and then proceeds to coarser levels, while the second averages data and solves the problem in the more coarse levels and then uses this information to calculate it locally.

4.2 From Fine to Coarse Levels

The array of sites is first divided into regions. An example division is shown in Figure 5a. The regions don't have to be square, they can have varying height and width. Then the simulated annealing algorithm is performed individually on each of the regions. The result is shown in Figure 5b. Following this, the simulated annealing algorithm is performed on the entire array but with the perturbation option being flipping of not a single site, but rather all the sites in the region. The simulated annealing performed for the entire array has different parameters than the one run on the regions. Figure 5c depicts the result of this approach for an example array of 32x32 pixels.

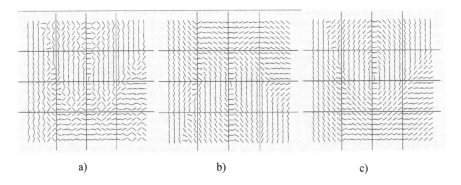

a)   b)   c)

Fig. 5. Example of regions into which larger arrays could be divided for the fine to coarse multi-scale approach. a) Starting configuration with energy of 2.4×10^6 b) After running simulated annealing for each of the regions with energy of 6.9×10^5 c) Result of the fine to coarse approach with energy of 5.3×10^5.

In this example the starting energy of the system was 2.4×10^6. After running simulated annealing for the regions, which took less than one minute, this score improved to 6.9×10^5, and after the final stage of the algorithm reached 5.3×10^5. However the global minimum - energy of 4.8×10^5 - hasn't been found in this case. As the example shows, the disadvantage of the method is that in general the solution depends on the division into regions.

4.3 From Coarse to Fine Levels

The second proposed solution solves the ambiguity on a coarse level and then uses the result to calculate it on a fine level. In this approach every group of 4 adjacent pixels are averaged to form a coarser level of detail. Each group of four pixels results in one in a new array. The process of averaging is performed until the resulting array is small enough to run the simulated annealing algorithm or to solve the optimization problem deterministically. The averaging process for a 32 x 32 array of angles is shown in Figure 6.

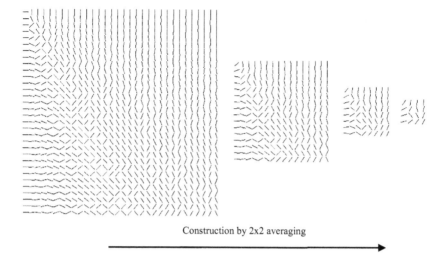

Construction by 2x2 averaging

Fig. 6. Averaging steps for coarse to fine multi-scale approach on larger array.

The small averaged array is subjected to the simulated annealing algorithm or other optimization algorithm. Values in larger arrays are back-calculated based on this result so the angles in each site are closer to the determined direction as shown in Figure 7. After each step, when the whole one-size larger array is filled, the random gradient descent method is performed to smooth the effect of errors when data contains them. Random gradient descent is a gradient descent optimization where each site is visited in random order to find out if the change will improve the final score. Randomness prevents bias.

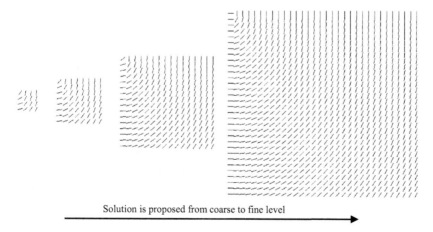

Solution is proposed from coarse to fine level

Fig. 7. Steps of back calculating the larger arrays using the results of simulated annealing run on the smallest array.

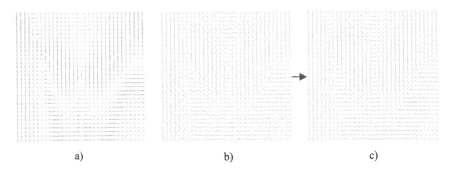

a)   b)   c)

Fig. 8. Coarse to fine approach. a) Inclination ambiguity for a chosen pattern. b) Starting configuration with energy of 4.3×10^6 c) Result of coarse to fine approach. The minimal energy of 5.7×10^5 was reached virtually instantly.

5   Analysis of Failure of Continuity Approach

There is however a problem with the continuity heuristic fiber mapping approach. Both proposed methods can result in the underlying geometry being smoothed more than in reality as shown by the example in figure 8. The achieved score is lower than that of the true solution, so the solution is smoother than the ground truth. Therefore if fiber tracts do in fact make pronounced changes of direction, these changes will become smoothed to the extent that they no longer correspond closely with reality. The true solution is not necessarily the most continuous one. However the simulated geometry in this case is not likely to occur in white matter, as it contains circles. It was chosen specifically to test the behavior of the algorithm with geometries that consist of singularities.

Apart from the problem described above, following the application of the simulated annealing algorithm, the ambiguity inherent in the angle of each site is reduced but not eliminated completely.

Let's consider pairs of adjacent sites. When one out of them is horizontal or vertical the score is unaffected by which inclination is chosen at the other site. So there is no coupling between any such pairs of sites. If the underlying geometry is relatively smooth and the noise level is low the sets of horizontal and vertical sites form closed paths. All the sites encircled by a path are coupled, but the coupling doesn't cross the paths. Therefore all the sites in the block tend to flip together independently of what occurs in other blocks. Because each of the blocks has two possible states, solving this ambiguity requires more information. How clearly blocks are defined depends on how much noise the data contains. Clearly defined blocks result from noise free data whereas with increasing noise the blocks became less well defined. Figure 9.

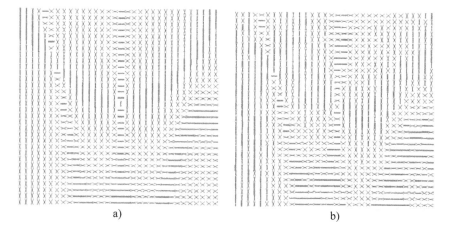

a)   b)

Fig. 9. Ambiguous blocks as a result of running the simulated annealing algorithm. a) Blue lines (thin) show the ambiguity within the blocks while red (thick) lines, representing near horizontal or near vertical sites, form paths when there is no noise added. b) Noise of 40 degrees has been added to the starting configuration. Red lines don't form paths.

6   Use of Continuity Heuristic in Addition to Other Information

The algorithms proposed in this paper as solutions to inclination ambiguity, rely on the continuity heuristic. However we have seen that this is insufficient to resolve the ambiguity.

If we were to know, without doubt, at least one inclination angle from each strongly coupled block, it would enable us to solve the ambiguity for each block and hence for the entire sample.

In addition, estimating how many blocks exist, and their typical size, in a real data sample, (as opposed to the small simulated examples used here), would provide valuable information on how many inclination angles have to be known unambiguously in order to solve the ambiguity for the entire sample.

Extrapolating these examples to three dimensions, which must be done in order to use them in the real world, we can see that there will be 3D blocks which will behave similarly. In order to solve the ambiguity for the entire sample, we must obtain, by other methods, unambiguous inclination angles for at least one site in each block, (the noisier the data the more unambiguous inclination angles will be required for each block). To solve this problem, one in (for example) every 20 slices should be subjected to additional measurements to ensure its inclination angles are known with certainty. There exist polarized light imaging methods which can solve this, but they are much more laborious and time consuming. Therefore the continuity heuristic can be used so that only a small number of slices in a volume need to be subjected to these further methods.

References

1. Axer, H., Lippitz, B. & Keyserlingk, D. Morphological asymmetry in anterior limb of human internal capsule revealed by confocal laser and polarized light microscopy, Psychiatry Res Neuroimaging, 91, (1999) 141–54.
2. Axer H, Berks G, Keyserlingk D. Visualization of nerve fibre orientation in gross histological sections of the human brain Microscopy Res. and Technique 51(5) (2000) 481-492
3. Axer, H. Keyserlingk, D. Mapping of fibre orientation in human internal capsule by means of polarized light and confocal scanning laser microscopy.., J Neuroscience Methods, 94, . (2000) 165–75.
4. Axer, H., Axer, M., Krings, T. & Keyserlingk, D. G. V. Quantitative estimation of 3-D fibre course in gross histological sections of the human brain using polarized light, Journal of Neuroscience Methods, 105 (2001), 121–131.
5. Axer H, Leunert M, Mürköster M, Gräßel D, Larsen L, Griffin LD & Graf v. Keyserlingk D A 3D fibre model of the human brainstem. Comp. Med. Imag. & Graphics 26 (2002) 439-444
6. Basser PJ, , Mattiello, J, Le Bihan D et al. Estimation of the effective self-diffusion tensor from the NMR spin echo. J. Magn. Res., Series B 103 (1994) 259-267
7. Bucci, M.:Optimization with Simulated Annealing.C/C++ Users Journal Vol 19, No.11 (2001) 10-27
8. Coremans J Luypaert R, Verhelle F, Stadnik T, Osteaux M. A method for myelin fibre orientation mapping using diffusion-weighted MR images, Mag. Reson. Imag. 12(3) (1994) 443-454
9. Fraher, J. & Macconai, M. Fibre bundles in the CNS revealed by polarized light., J Anat, 106, (1970) 170.
10. Geday, M. A. Birefringence Imaging Jesus College Oxford. (2001)
11. Jones, D. K., Simmons, A., Williams, S. C. R. & Horsfield, M. A. Non-invasive assessment of axonal fibre connectivity in the human brain via diffusion tensor MRI, Magnetic Resonance in Medicine, 42, (1999) 37-41.
12. Kilossy J & van der Loos H Cholestrol ester crystals in polarised light show pathways in the human brain, Brain Res. 426 (1987)377-380.
13. Kretschmann, H. J. On the demonstration of myelinated nerve fibres by polarized light without extinction effects., J Hirnforsch, 9, (1967) 571–5.
14. Le Bihan, D., Breton, E., Lallemand, D. et al. MR imaging of intravoxel incoherent motions: application to diffusion and perfusion in neurologic disorders, Radiology, 161, (1986) 401-7.
15. Le Bihan, D., Turner, R. & Douek, P. Is water diffusion restricted in human brain white matter? An echo-planar NMR imaging study., NeuroReport, 4, (1993) 887-890.
16. Napadow, V. J., Wedeen, V., Chen, Q. et al. Quantification of Fibre Orientation with Diffusion Tensor MR Imaging and 3D Resolved Two-Photon Microscopy, Paper presented at the ISMRM, Denver (2000)
17. Norris, D. G. The effects of microscopic tissue parameters on the diffusion weighted magnetic resonance imaging experiment, Nmr in Biomedicine, 14, . (2001) 77-93.
18. Oxford Cryosystems http://www.metripol.com/
19. Pierpaoli C, Basser PJ.: Toward a quantitative assessment of diffusion anisotropy. Magn Reson Med. 36(6) (1996) 893-906
20. Sadun AA, Schaechter JD Tracing axons in the human brain; a method utilizing light and TEM techniques, J. Electron Microsc. Techn. 2 (1985) 175-186.
21. Thomsen C Henriksen O, Ring P. e In vivo measurement of water self-diffusion in the human brain by magnetic resonance imaging, Acta Radiologica 28 (3) (1987) 353-361

22. Vidal CB, Mello MLS, Caseirofilho AC, GODO C Anisotropic properties of the myelin sheath, Acta Histochemica 66(1) (1980) 32-39
23. Whitaker S Diffusion and dispersion in porous media, AIChE Journal 13 (1967) 420
24. Zhang J Zijl PCM, Mori S. Three-dimensional diffusion tensor microimaging of the adult mouse brain and hippocampus. Neuroimage 15 (2002) 892-901

Applications of Image Registration in Human Genome Research*

Petr Matula, Michal Kozubek, and Pavel Matula

Faculty of Informatics, Masaryk University
Laboratory of Optical Microscopy
Botanická 68a, CZ-60200 Brno, Czech Republic

Abstract. Fluorescence microscopy has some limitations and imperfections that can affect some types of study in human genome research. Image registration methods can help overcome or reduce the effect of some of them. This paper is concentrated on several applications of image registration that are carried out in our laboratory. The concerned areas are: 1. chromatic aberration correction, which improves precision of colocalization studies, 2. registration of images after repeated acquisitions, which helps to enlarge the number of object types studied simultaneously, and 3. registration of tilted images in micro-axial tomography, which helps to improve optical resolution of light microscopy.

1   Introduction

In human genome research, the spatial organisation of the genetic material inside cell nuclei, relative positions of different genetic loci, organisation of chromosomes, etc. is studied [1,2]. Tasks such as measurement of mutual distance between two targets, determination of position distribution of an object type (e.g. a gene) inside another object type (e.g. a cell nucleus), etc. are solved, nowadays often even in 3D. As a suitable tool for this research fluorescence microscopy is commonly used.

In fluorescence microscopy, fluorescent dyes, which contain fluorochromes, are attached to visualised objects in laboratory with one of the available fluorescent labelling techniques (e.g. Fluorescence In Situ Hybridization (FISH), immunofluorescence, etc.). Each fluorochrome is excited by light with a specific spectrum of wavelengths and a spectrum of higher (visible) wavelengths is emitted and thereafter captured. Several object types are usually visualised simultaneously on a slide. Each object type has its own fluorochrome that is visible in its own colour. Therefore, it is easy to distinguish the objects of different types from each other.

Unfortunately, fluorescence microscopy has some limitations and imperfections that can affect some types of study. For example there are always chromatic

---

* This research was funded by the Ministry of Education of the Czech Republic (Grant No. MSM-143300002) and by the Grant Agency of the Academy of Sciences of the Czech Republic (Grant No. A5004306).

M. Šonka et al. (Eds.): CVAMIA-MMBIA 2004, LNCS 3117, pp. 376–384, 2004.

aberrations to some extent between two images acquired at different wavelengths even if the best microscopes available on the market are used. This can degrade colocalization studies. Another example is anisotropic resolution of optical microscopes (including confocal microscopes), which limits observation of supra-molecular genome structures because the images are more blurred in z-direction than in x- and y-directions.

This paper reviews image registration methods used in our laboratory for overcoming or reducing some limitations of fluorescence microscopy. Its main goal is to show possible applications of image registration methods in human genome research.

2   Image Acquisition Process

Since both the size and the dimensionality of available light detectors are limited, *scanning strategies* are indispensable during image acquisition process. Generally, there are five main dimensions (x, y, z, λ, and t) that can be scanned. The first three ones are the classical spatial dimensions, λ denotes the wavelength of observation and t represents time. Scanning in the spatial dimensions produces 3D images (stacks of optical sections). The time dimension is not concerned here because fixed (dead) cells have mostly been processed in our laboratory so far.

Scanning in the wavelength dimension produces *multi-spectral* images, i.e. a series of greyscale images. The individual greyscale images are called *channels*. The number of channels of a multi-spectral image is always limited in fluorescence imaging because each channel is related to an object type that was visualised with a particular fluorescent dye. The number of simultaneously used fluorochromes on a slide is limited in fluorescence imaging due to spectra overlaps. Therefore, if more than three or four object types need to be studied simultaneously, then restaining techniques are used [3,4]. It means that the slide is removed from the stage, the old set of fluorochromes is washed away and new objects are stained in laboratory. Thereafter, the slide is put back onto the stage, the objects are relocated and a new set of images is acquired.

An example of a multi-spectral image with 5 channels of a human cell nucleus with three stained targets (in this case 3 types of genes) is shown in Fig. 1. Only very limited part ($\approx 15 \times 15\,\mu m^2$) of the whole 3D image $\approx 150 \times 130 \times 12\,\mu m^3$ is shown as maximum projections. In the whole image, there are typically more cell nuclei visible (usually tens) and they contain several stained subcomponents (genes in this example). Their positions can be used for point-based image registration. All five greyscale channels in the figure are shown after registration, therefore there is no misalignment visible. The dotted line indicates restaining of the slide.

The cell nuclei as well as the stained targets are segmented and 3D positions of the segmented objects are computed. Segmentation is mostly based on adaptive thresholding and/or mathematical morphology methods (see [5] for details). The object 3D positions are computed as intensity weighted centres:

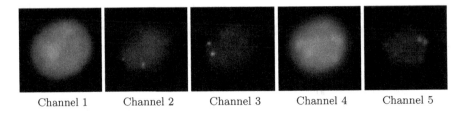

Channel 1	Channel 2	Channel 3	Channel 4	Channel 5

Channel	Object type	Fluorochrome	Emission colour
1	Cell nucleus	DAPI	Blue
2	Gene ABL	FITC	Green
3	Gene BCR	Rhodamin	Red
4	Cell nucleus	DAPI	Blue
5	Gene C-MYC	FITC	Green

Fig. 1. Example of a multi-spectral image

$$c_x = \frac{\sum\limits_{v \in S} v_x I(v)}{\sum\limits_{v \in S} I(v)}, \quad c_y = \frac{\sum\limits_{v \in S} v_y I(v)}{\sum\limits_{v \in S} I(v)}, \quad c_z = \frac{\sum\limits_{v \in S} v_z I(v)}{\sum\limits_{v \in S} I(v)}, \tag{1}$$

where c_x, c_y, and c_z are the x-, y-, and z-coordinates of the centre, S is the set of object voxels, which was determined by a segmentation algorithm, v_x, v_y, and v_z are the x-, y-, and z-coordinates of the voxel v, and $I(v)$ is the intensity of the voxel v.

3   Sources of Misalignment

There are several sources of misalignment in fluorescence microscopy. They can be classified as *inter-channel* and *intra-channel*. An example of the inter-channel distortion is chromatic shifts (Section 4). They are caused by different refractive indices for different wavelengths. Another example is misalignments caused by replacing the slide when it is reacquired after restaining (Section 5). An example of intra-channel registration is the registration of tilted images in micro-axial tomography (Section 6). Micro-axial tomography, generally tilted-view microscopy, belongs to optical resolution improvement techniques [6]. In this case, the misalignment between images is caused by fibre rotation on which the observed objects are fixed. All the given examples are detailed in the following three sections.

4   Chromatic Aberration Correction

Chromatic aberrations are caused by the fact that refractive indices differ for different wavelengths. As a result, the same point in real space being observed in different colours is imaged to different locations. Therefore, certain misalignment between different channels always exists that cannot be neglected in some types of study (e.g. in colocalization studies) and software correction is highly desirable. Considering the example above the affected channel pairs was 1-2, 1-3, and 4-5 (Fig. 1).

The correction function can be computed from a theoretical model of aberration formation or it can be measured experimentally. The latter approach is superior to the former because the chromatic aberrations depend on the overall performance and alignment of all optical components of the given optical set-up and it is practically impossible to describe contributions of all parts of the optical arrangement in any theoretical model. An experimental procedure for chromatic aberration correction has been developed in our laboratory [7].

In the first step, chromatic shifts in the field of view of the microscope are measured using small fluorescence beads, which are spread on a microscope slide and are visible in several colours. Several 3D greyscale images are acquired for each colour, the bead images are segmented by mathematical morphology methods combined with thresholding approach and their positions are computed as intensity weighted centres (1). Only single beads that are visible in the studied colour pair are considered (e.g. red and green). Positions from all acquired images are put into one set. Let $r_i = (r_i^x, r_i^y, r_i^z)$ and $g_i = (g_i^x, g_i^y, g_i^z)$ denote measured positions of i-th bead visible in red and green colours, respectively. Then

$$S_{rg} = \{r_i - g_i \mid i = 1, \ldots, n\}$$

is the set of measured chromatic shifts. The i-th element of the set is the measured chromatic shift between red and green colour at the position (r_i^x, r_i^y) in the field of view of the microscope.

In the next step, the computed shifts are decomposed into x-, y-, and z-components and the correction functions are found by fitting smooth functions to each component separately. The domain of correction functions is naturally the field of view of the microscope. It was observed that plane fitting is optimal for x- and y-components. The best results for z-component were obtained by second order polynomial fitting ($ax^2 + by^2 + cxy + dx + ey + f = 0$).

The correction functions are under certain conditions quite stable and can be used for correction of independent experiments. From image registration point of view, chromatic aberrations are a static distortion and the correction functions can be, therefore, computed in advance and used only when they are needed.

5   Repeated Image Acquisition

There are several situations when it is convenient to repeat image acquisition of the same slide more than once even if only fixed cells are considered. For example the same position on the slide can be imaged in different imaging modes, e.g. in confocal mode, if details in images are required (e.g. for chromosomes) or in wide-field mode (non-confocal), if more light and higher speed is preferred to details (e.g. for small objects such as genes). Because an additional element (a confocal unit) is put into or is removed from the optical path, the image formation process differs in both modes. Consequently, the images are misaligned. This misalignment is a static distortion similarly to chromatic aberrations but the correction function is simpler. In this case, it is a trivial translation. If different imaging modes are used for different colours, the translation must naturally be combined with the appropriate chromatic aberration correction function.

More interesting situation arises when the slide is restained in laboratory between acquisitions in order to overcome the limited number of object types visualised simultaneously. In this case, it is practically impossible to put the slide onto the same place in the microscope stage after restaining. Moreover, the restaining process can change the slide: whole cells that were not firmly fixed can be washed away, they can "resettle" on a new place or some cells can even be damaged. Image registration method must find as precise transformation function between acquisitions as possible and in addition all problematic cells, which have no counterpart or are damaged, must be excluded from further analysis.

The registration method used in our laboratory is again point-based because intensity weighted centres (1) can easily be computed from the image segmentation results, which are needed for the measurements required by biologists in our application. In the first phase the method finds matching of objects in images from different acquisitions. The matching point-pairs are sought using a backtracking scheme (a kind of relaxation method), which exploits knowledge about spatial organisation of points. Shifts within a certain range given by the point-sets are tried. The matching that gives the maximal number of matched pairs is selected. In the second phase, the optimal transformation function is computed from the found matching. The optimal transformation function, in many cases a translation is sufficient, is computed as a difference between centres of gravity of the matched points.

Note that image registration of channels after restaining is combined with other methods. For instance considering the example in Fig. 1, if the mutual position of stained genes is studied the transformation function found between channels 1 and 4 is combined with the appropriate chromatic aberration correction functions.

6   Micro-axial Tomography

Micro-axial tomography is a special technique that makes observation of the same cells from many views possible (Fig. 2). The cells are fixed to a glass fibre that is put into a groove in a glass or plastic slide. The groove is filled with an appropriate embedding medium. One fibre end is glued to a stepper motor shaft so that a computer can rotate the fibre around its axis. An advantage of this set-up is that a cover glass can be used for better imaging properties. From the same reason, only the upper part of the fibre is imaged. The angular range of the tilted images depends on several factors, mainly on the diameter of the fibre and on the working distance of the objective. Tilting devices with angular range up to approximately 120° can be constructed [8].

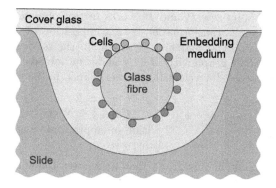

Fig. 2. A cut through a slide in micro-axial tomography.

Major significance of micro-axial tomography lies in suppression of anisotropy of resolution, i.e. the fact that the optical resolution differs for different spatial directions. For instance in classical optical microscopy, axial resolution (i.e. resolution in the direction of optical axis) is much worse than lateral resolution (i.e. resolution in the image plane). By combining several tilted images together the overall resolution can be improved. One of the tested methods [9] works in Fourier domain and its idea is to select the frequencies with the maximal magnitudes to the result. However, image reconstruction methods, in general, require very precise alignment of tilted images, otherwise artifacts can be introduced into their result. It is impossible to reach the required precision without registration based on the image content, because sufficiently precise tilting devices do not exist so far.

Methods that are most often used in this area are based on cross-correlation or phase-correlation [10,11,12]. The main disadvantage of these methods is that they are very sensitive to elongated point spread function (PSF), consequently they may introduce a bias in the alignment. In order to solve this problem, it has been suggested to intentionally reduce the in-plane resolution yielding near-isotropic data-sets before running an alignment algorithm [12]. However, the authors did not attempted this reduction. A further disadvantage is that it is hard to assess registration precision from the shape of the correlation map peak. To overcome the main drawbacks of these methods, a new point-based method has been designed and evaluated on generated images as well as images of fluorescent beads [9].

In the beginning, the images are analysed and 3D positions of small objects (genes, centromeres, fluorescent beads, etc.) are computed (1), i.e. we obtain a set of point-sets $\mathcal{P} = \{P_1, \ldots, P_n\}$, where each point-set P_i corresponds to a different view within the acquired angular range. The registration task is solved for point-sets P_i and P_j. The index i is fixed and the index j iterates, i.e. we try to transform the images into one coordinate system (i usually corresponds to some view from the middle of the angular range).

Registration of point-sets P_i and P_j works in two phases. Coarse registration phase finds rough transformation as a composition of 3D rotation and translation. An appropriate matching is sought in the following way. A complete weighted bipartite graph with $M + N$ nodes in both parts ($M = |P_i|$ and $N = |P_j|$) is constructed. Its weight function is defined in the following manner:

$$w(u_i, v_j) = \begin{cases} 0 & i > M \text{ or } j > N, \\ d_{max} - |x_i - x'_j| & i \leq M \text{ and } j \leq N \text{ and "the points lies} \\ & \text{within an appropriate angular range"} \\ -1 & \text{otherwise.} \end{cases}$$

An optimal assignment in this graph that maximises the sum of the weights on the associated edges is found by Kuhn-Munkres algorithm. Such assignment must be non-negative, because there always exists an assignment with zero sum.

The optimal assignment defines the matching between points. The assignments between the nodes u_i and v_j for $i \leq M$ and $j \leq N$ means that the points $\boldsymbol{p}_i \in P_i$ and $\boldsymbol{p}_j \in P_j$ correspond to each other. Other assignments mean that the corresponding points have no counterpart in the other set. Notice that positive weights can only be between the points within an appropriate angular range, whose x-distance is less than a constant d_{max}. The x-distance weighting works well because the rotation axis is almost parallel to x-axis and the fibre cannot move in the x-direction. The translation and rotation from matchings is sought by the Horn's method [13].

In the second phase, the registration function is refined. First, the matching is refined based on nearest neighbour approach and then the computation of 3D rotation and translation is repeated for several z-scale factors. For each z-scale factor, average distance between matching point-pairs is computed (measured alignment precision). The computed values are fitted with parabola and its minimum indicates the best z-scale factor. The shrink or elongation in the z-direction is a very common phenomenon in optical microscopy and it is caused by the refraction index mismatch. Therefore all registration methods used in this area must take it into account.

The biggest advantage of our method as compared to correlation-like methods is that its real alignment precision can be estimated from its output (the measured alignment precision) and the estimate of the localisation precision of the objects. Real alignment precision is always better than the measured alignment precision from a certain number of matched pairs, because the imprecision of the object localization is compansated. The main disadvantage of the method is that salient points must exist in images and at least about ten point-pairs must be found in images for very good results. This requirement, however, is predominantly satisfied for specimens in human genome research. If it is not, fluorescent beads can be added to the specimen during the fibre preparation.

7   Conclusion

All presented registration methods have been successfully applied in human genome research in our laboratory and most of them are often combined together. For instance, chromatic aberration correction is combined with shifts caused by removing slide during restaining procedure if short distance measurements are performed between channels. The only techniques that cannot be combined from practical reasons are the restaining techniques and micro-axial tomography because objects fixed to a fibre cannot be restained. All the methods can reduce some limitations of fluorescence microscopy.

Although the presented methods mostly work well on our data, some further improvements will be considered in future. For example, distortion of images that comes from deep layers below cover glass is worse than the distortion of images from layers near the cover glass and therefore non-rigid image registration will be required.

References

1. Cremer, T., Kurz, A., Zirbel, R., Dietzel, S., Rinke, B., et al.: Role of chromosome territories in the functional compartmentalization of the cell nucleus. Cold Spring Harbor Symp Quantitative Biology **58** (1993) 777–792
2. Eils, R., Bertin, E., Saracoglu, K., Rinke, B., Schröck, E., Parazza, F., Usson, Y., Robert-Nicoud, M., Stelzer, E.H.K., Chassery, J.M., Cremer, T., Cremer, C.: Application of confocal laser microscopy and 3D Voronoi diagrams for volume and surface estimates of interphase chromosomes. J. Microsc. **177** (1995) 150–161
3. Lukášová, E., Kozubek, S., Kozubek, M., Kroha, V., Marečková, A., Skalníková, M., Bártová, E., Slotová, J.: Chromosomes participating in translocations typical of malignant haemoblastosis are also involved in exchange aberrations induced by fast neutrons. Radiation Research **151** (1999) 375–384
4. Wählby, C., Erlandsson, F., Bengtsson, E., Zetterberg, A.: Sequential immunofluorescence staining and image analysis for detection of large numbers of antigens in individual cell nuclei. Cytometry **47** (2002) 32–41
5. Kozubek, M., Kozubek, S., Lukášová, E., Bártová, E., Skalníková, M., Matula, Pa., Matula, Pe., Jirsová, P., Cafourková, A., Koutná, I.: Combined confocal and widefield high-resolution cytometry of fluorescent in situ hybridization-stained cells. Cytometry **45** (2001) 1–12
6. Gustafsson, M.G.L.: Extended resolution fluorescence microscopy. Cur. Opin. Struct. Biol. **9** (1999) 627–634
7. Kozubek, M., Matula, Pe.: An efficient algorithm for measurement and correction of chromatic aberrations in fluorescence microscopy. J. Microsc. **200** (2000) 206–217
8. Kozubek, M., Skalníková, M., Matula, Pe., Bártová, E., Rauch, J., Neuhaus, F., Eipel, H., Hausmann, M.: Automated micro axial tomography of cell nuclei after specific labelling by fluorescence in situ hybridization. Micron **33** (2002) 655–665
9. Matula, Pe., Kozubek, M., Steier, F., Hausmann, M.: Precise 3D image alignment in micro axial tomography. J. Microsc. **209** (2003)
10. Shaw, P.J., Agard, D.A., Hiraoka, Y., Sedat, J.W.: Tilted view reconstruction in optical microscopy: Three-dimensional reconstruction of drosophila melanogaster embryo nuclei. Biophysical Journal **55** (1989) 101–110
11. Cogswell, C.J., Larkin, K.G., Klemm, H.: Fluorescence microtomography: Multiangle image acquisition and 3D digital reconstruction. In: SPIE. Volume 2655. (1996) 109–115

12. Heintzmann, R., Cremer, C.: Axial tomographic confocal fluorescence microscopy. J. Microsc. **206** (2002) 7–23
13. Horn, B.K.: Closed form solution of absolute orientation using unit quaternions. Journal of the Optical Society of America A **4** (1987) 629–642

Fast Marching 3D Reconstruction of Interphase Chromosomes*

Pavel Matula, Jan Hubený, and Michal Kozubek

Masaryk University, Faculty of Informatics, Laboratory of Optical Microscopy,
Botanická 68a, 602 00 Brno, The Czech Republic
{pam|xhubeny|kozubek}@fi.muni.cz
http://www.fi.muni.cz/lom

Abstract. Reliable 3D reconstruction of interphase chromosomes imaged using confocal microscopy is an important task in cell biology. Computer model of chromosome territories enables performing necessary measurements and consequently making morphological studies. A large number of processed objects is necessary to ensure statistical significance of the results. Therefore an automated procedure is needed. We have developed a successful algorithm for 3D reconstruction of chromosome territories on the basis of well-known fast marching algorithm. The fast marching algorithm solves front evolution problem similarly to deformable models but in an effective way with the time complexity $\mathcal{O}(n \log n)$.

Keywords: fast marching method, deformable models, 3D object reconstruction, biomedical application, interphase chromosome

1 Introduction

Limited knowledge about the spatial organisation of genetic material in human cell nuclei is one of the most challenging problems of modern molecular biology. The complete knowledge of the spatial structure of genes and chromosomes is absolutely necessary for the full understanding of mechanisms of events in cell nuclei and for the detection or reparation of an abnormal state, which can cause a disease of the whole organism, as a result.

Genetic information is coded by double stranded DNA, which is deposited in cell nucleus in the form of chromosomes. Recent evidence has demonstrated that chromosomes occupy distinct domains in the cell nucleus, called chromosome territories [5, 6]. Each territory can be considered as a connected, variably-shaped, three-dimensional structure which is mutually exclusive from other territories.

* This work was supported by the Grant Agency of the Czech Republic (Project No. 204/03/D034) and by the Ministry of Education of the Czech Republic (Grant No. MSM-143300002).

M. Šonka et al. (Eds.): CVAMIA-MMBIA 2004, LNCS 3117, pp. 385–394, 2004.

Nevertheless, the organisation of individual genes inside the chromosome territories is not known so far. Neither the mutual positioning of chromosome territories is known.

Chromosome territories or individual genes can be stained by fluorescence in situ hybridization (FISH) with chromosome or gene specific DNA-probes. Different targets are usually stained by colours of different wavelengths and observed using different combination of emission and excitation filters. Biological specimens are usually transparent and, therefore, serial optical sections can be acquired using confocal light microscopy. The confocal microscope produces gray-scale volumetric image (for each stained target).

Morphological characteristics and mutual position between two different objects need to be studied and therefore an easy-to-use, precise, fast, and automatic method for 3D chromosome reconstruction is badly needed nowadays. For example distance between a specific gene (imaged as a bright point or a very small spot) and the boundary of chromosome territory needs to be measured. Analysis of a large number of objects is particularly important to ensure statistical significance of results. Recently fully automated image acquisition and analysis systems capable of performing a large number of high-resolution measurements on cells have been developed [10].

The following approaches were applied for chromosome territory reconstruction in the past. A computational geometry method based on Voronoi tessellation [2] was adapted for 3D reconstruction of interphase chromosomes in [7, 8]. Also a method based on local thresholding and mathematical morphology methods have been used for chromosome segmentation [10].

This paper describes a different approach to 3D interphase chromosome reconstruction based on the fast marching method [14, 15]. The fast marching method is the special case of a deformable modelling technique known as the level set method [13, 15]. While the level set method computes the solution iteratively, the fast marching method can compute the evolution of the model explicitly with time complexity $\mathcal{O}(n \log n)$, where n is the number of voxels in the input 3D image.

The main idea of level set method is to represent the surface implicitly as level set of a higher-dimensional function. This formulation has several important advantages over the parametric deformable models [9, 3, 4]. It can change the topology of the model completely intrinsic and it is independent of the parametrisation of the evolving surface. Thus there is no need to add or remove nodes from initial parametrisation or adjust the spacing of the nodes.

The limitation of the fast marching algorithm is that the surface can evolve only in one direction (either inward or outward). This paper shows that this limitation is not crucial for the task of interphase chromosome reconstruction and the fast marching algorithm can successfully be applied here.

2   Fast Marching Method

In this section, the fast marching method is briefly reviewed.

2.1 Method Background

The contour[1] $C(t)$ in time t can be advantageously represented as a zero level set of a scalar function $\psi(\boldsymbol{x}, t)$ i.e.

$$C(t) = \{\boldsymbol{x}|\psi(\boldsymbol{x}, t) = 0\}, \tag{1}$$

where $\boldsymbol{x}$ is a point (in $\mathbb{R}^2$ for curves or in $\mathbb{R}^3$ for surfaces).

Let $F(\boldsymbol{x}, t)$ be a scalar function describing the contour speed in its normal direction (speed function). Then, by differentiating $\psi(\boldsymbol{x}, t) = 0$ with respect to t, the following associated equation of motion for level set function $\psi(\boldsymbol{x}, t)$ can be derived:

$$\frac{\delta\psi(\boldsymbol{x}, t)}{\delta t} = F(\boldsymbol{x}, t)\|\nabla\psi(\boldsymbol{x}, t)\|,$$
$$\psi(\boldsymbol{x}_0, 0) = 0, \quad \boldsymbol{x}_0 \in C(0), \tag{2}$$

where ∇ is the gradient operator and $\|\nabla\psi\|$ is the norm of the gradient of ψ. The function $F(\boldsymbol{x}, t)$ often depends on the curvature of the contour and on the input data simultaneously. Algorithms based on (2) are often called level set methods. From the computational point of view it is not necessary to consider the whole $\mathbb{R}^2$ or $\mathbb{R}^3$ space during the iterative contour evolution. It is sufficient to update only points in the narrow band of the contour in each step [1, 15].

If the special case of contour movement with $F(\boldsymbol{x}, t) > 0$ is considered, then each point in a space is visited by the contour only once. Let $T(\boldsymbol{x})$ be the time at which the contour crosses a given point $\boldsymbol{x}$ (arrival time). Then (2) can be rewritten as

$$1 = F(\boldsymbol{x}, t)\|\nabla T(\boldsymbol{x})\|,$$
$$T(\boldsymbol{x}_0) = 0, \quad \boldsymbol{x}_0 \in C(0). \tag{3}$$

The main advantage of this formulation is that a highly effective algorithm exists to solve (3). The algorithm is called the fast marching algorithm.

2.2 Fast Marching Algorithm

We review the fast marching algorithm for time computation of the arrival time function $T(\boldsymbol{x})$ [12, 14].

Input

- Discrete grid $G = \{\boldsymbol{x}|\boldsymbol{x} \in \mathbb{Z}_{n_1} \times \mathbb{Z}_{n_2} \times \mathbb{Z}_{n_3}\}$ of size $n_1 \times n_2 \times n_3 \in \mathbb{N}^3$. Two dimensional grid can be obtained for $n_3 = 1$. Let d denote the dimensionality of the grid.
- Function $F(\boldsymbol{x}) > 0$ for each $\boldsymbol{x} \in G$ (i.e. we assume time-constant positive speed function here),
- Initial contour $C(0) \subset G$.
- Spatial step h_i between two neighbouring[2] grid points in each direction $1 \leq i \leq d$.

---

[1] We use the word *contour* to refer either a curve or surface.
[2] Two grid points $\boldsymbol{x}, \boldsymbol{y} \in G$ are neighbouring if and only if $\|\boldsymbol{x} - \boldsymbol{y}\| = 1$.

Output

- Arrival times $T(\boldsymbol{x})$ for each $\boldsymbol{x} \in G$.

Initialisation

- Set $Trial = C(0)$, $T(\boldsymbol{x}) = 0$ for $\boldsymbol{x} \in Trial$,
- Set $Far = G \setminus C(0)$, $T(\boldsymbol{x}) = \infty$ for $\boldsymbol{x} \in Far$,
- Set $Known = \emptyset$.

Main loop

1. Find $\boldsymbol{u} \in Trial$ having the smallest value of arrival time $T(\boldsymbol{u})$,
2. Exclude $\boldsymbol{u}$ from $Trial$ and include it into $Known$,
3. For each neighbour $\boldsymbol{v} \in G$ of $\boldsymbol{u}$ do
   (a) If $\boldsymbol{v} \in Far$ then include it into $Trial$,
   (b) Compute the new arrival time T' for $\boldsymbol{v}$ according to the following equation:

$$\sum_{i=1}^{d} \max(D^{-i}(\boldsymbol{v}), 0)^2 + \min(D^{+i}(\boldsymbol{v}), 0)^2 = \frac{1}{F(\boldsymbol{v})^2}, \tag{4}$$

   where D^{-i} and D^{+i} are backward and forward difference operators for direction i defined as $D^{-i}(\boldsymbol{v}) = \frac{T' - T(\boldsymbol{v} - \boldsymbol{e}_i)}{h_i}$, $D^{+i}(\boldsymbol{v}) = \frac{T(\boldsymbol{v} + \boldsymbol{e}_i) - T'}{h_i}$, where $\boldsymbol{e}_1 = (1, 0, 0)$, $\boldsymbol{e}_2 = (0, 1, 0)$, $\boldsymbol{e}_3 = (0, 0, 1)$. Equation (4) leads to solution of a quadratic equation.
   (c) If $T' < T(\boldsymbol{v})$ then $T(\boldsymbol{v}) = T'$.
4. Break main loop and stop the algorithm while $Trial$ set is empty.

Equation (4) was obtained from (3) using upwind finite difference scheme where gradient operator was approximated by an entropy satisfying formula [15]. The algorithm produces numerically stable solution and its correctness was proved in [14].

The suitable implementation of operations on $Trial$ set is the key for the effective performance of an algorithm. Main loop is evidently performed at most N times, where N is the number of grid points $(n_1 \times n_2 \times n_3)$. If $Trial$ set is implemented as a min-heap data structure, where finding the minimal node can be performed in constant $\mathcal{O}(1)$ time and inclusion and exclusion of a node in $\mathcal{O}(\log N)$ time, then the whole algorithm works in $\mathcal{O}(N \log N)$ time in the worst case.

Function $F(\boldsymbol{x})$ is usually defined as

$$F(\boldsymbol{x}) = \frac{1}{1 + \|\nabla \mathcal{G}_\sigma * I(\boldsymbol{x})\|}, \tag{5}$$

or

$$F(\boldsymbol{x}) = e^{-\alpha \|\nabla \mathcal{G}_\sigma * I(\boldsymbol{x})\|}, \tag{6}$$

where $I(\boldsymbol{x})$ is the intensity of input image in point $\boldsymbol{x}$ and $\mathcal{G}_\sigma * I(\boldsymbol{x})$ is the convolution of intensity image with Gaussian smoothing filter of variance σ (to reduce noise in the input image). Real parameter α controls the steepness of the function (6). Both definitions slow down the contour movement on object boundaries, where the intensity is rapidly changing (i.e. magnitude of the gradient is high).

3   Fast Marching Reconstruction of Interphase Chromosomes

Fast marching algorithm described in the previous section is very useful for the 3D reconstruction of interphase chromosomes. Healthy human cell nucleus contains one pair of each chromosome, therefore mostly two objects must be segmented in each nucleus. The fast marching method is capable of doing this task, because it can change the topology of contour during the computation in a natural way. Moreover the chromosome territories have relatively simple shapes and the input data acquired by confocal microscope has sufficient quality that enables application of the fast marching algorithm.

3.1   Input Data

Fast marching algorithm was studied on the following material. Targets in biological material (HL-60 cells — blood cells) were visualised by fluorescence in situ hybridization. The chromatin of cells (occupies the whole volume of the nuclei) was stained by DAPI (blue colour). The chromosomes 9 were stained by Rhodamin (red colour) and chromosomes 22 by FITC (green colour). The images of visualised targets were acquired using fully automated high-resolution cytometry system in the Laboratory of optical microscopy, Masaryk university Brno [10] (Zeiss Axiovert 100S inverted fluorescence microscope equipped with a CARV confocal module based on a Nipkow spinning disc). Specimen was observed through a PlanApochromat $63\times/1.4$ oil immersion objective. Stack of 40 2D images (parallel optical sections) was captured with a high-quality digital CCD camera for a ten chosen stage positions (field of views) for each colour. CCD chip of the camera has 1300x1030 pixels; pixel size is 6.7μm. Dynamic range of the camera was 12 bits but only 8 bit integer was used for pixel intensity storage. Axial (z) step between two optical sections was 0.2μm. Lateral (x, y) step is given by the magnification power of the objective and the pixel size of CCD chip and it was $\approx 0.1\mu$m. Each field of view typically contained tens of cells. For each 3D image also maximal intensity projection image in axial direction over all slices, called auto-focus (AF) image, was recorded. An example of a typical microscope field of view is shown in Fig. 1.

3.2   Algorithm

The input images have been processed in two steps:

Cell nucleus segmentation the goal of this step was to segment the large input images covering the whole microscope field of view into small subimages containing only one cell nucleus per image. An algorithm for cell nucleus segmentation based on local thresholding [10] was applied on AF chromatin images and a proper bounding box for each cell nucleus was computed. The nuclei are spread on a microscope glass in one layer and do not occlude. Therefore we can crop all slices in the stacks according to the 2D bounding box computed from AF image.

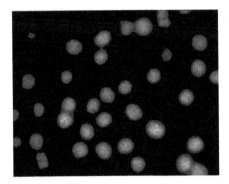 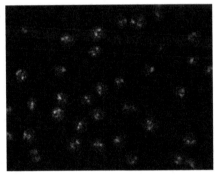

Fig. 1. An example of a typical microscope field of view (1300x1030 pixels). Maximal intensity projection image in axial direction. (Left) chromatin of HL-60 cells stained with DAPI. (Right) Chromosomes 22 stained with FITC.

Chromosome territory reconstruction Fast marching algorithm described in Section 2 was applied for chromosome territory reconstruction in each sub-image. Eight corners of the sub-image were taken as a starting contour $C(0)$. The idea was to initialise the contour outside the object. As the contour is marching through the data it slows down in points with high gradient magnitude and waits there (regardless of the topology changes) for the contour passing the points with gentle gradient magnitude.

We have used equation (5) for the speed function computations. Gaussian $3 \times 3 \times 3$ filter with variance $\sigma = 1.5$ was applied. The step $h_i = 0.1$ was assumed in all directions and the final surface was appropriately stretched at the end for visualisation purposes. The size of sub-images was approximately $120 \times 120 \times 40$ voxels.

Optimal contour level was computed from histogram of arrival time function $T(x)$. The histogram was constructed from integer part (floor) of function $T(x)$ and it maps integer level t to the number of grid points which were visited between time t and time $t + 1$. The number of such grid points is related to the size (surface area) of the object defined by the level t. The goal was to find a level where the contour movement was very slow, i.e. the change of contour size was small (i.e. the first derivative of histogram is minimal). The first level, which has the second derivative lower than predefined constant (we have used 5), was taken as the optimal contour level in our experiments. The histogram was smoothed by Gaussian kernel of size 7 and $\sigma = 0.5$ at the beginning.

4   Results and Discussion

The algorithm described in Section 3.2 was successfully applied on the input data (Section 3.1). The first step produced more than hundred sub-images of individual cells. We took randomly 25 of them for fast marching algorithm testing.

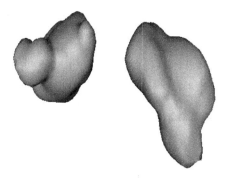

Fig. 2. An example of the final 3D reconstruction of territories of chromosome 22 pair in HL-60 cell nucleus. The fast marching algorithm was applied for 3D reconstruction. Size of the input sub-image containing only one cell nucleus was $111 \times 131 \times 40$. Arrival time for which the proper contour level (in this case value of 25) best approximated the object boundary was computed automatically using histogram analysis. The proper level was visualised using marching cube algorithm [11].

Only green image channel (chromosome 22) of these 3D sub-images was studied. The red image channel (chromosome 9) was overexposed and the image quality was poor.

Results for each sub-image were examined by an expert. The expert had to decide how many chromosome territories was in the nucleus according to the input image (usually two) and whether the algorithm found accurate boundary of them. The expert studied input data, superposition of the final model onto the input data and 3D computer model of territories.

Five images were analysed without any problem. Both number of chromosome territories and boundary position agreed with expert's opinion. An example of typical final 3D reconstruction of chromosome territories of one cell nucleus is shown in Fig. 2. Projection of this final 3D model onto the input data is shown in Fig. 4 and Fig. 5. The figures indicate that the method produces really correct results.

The algorithm found more territories than the expert in 13 cases. This problem is illustrated in Fig. 3. The additional objects computed by the algorithm were very small in all cases and should be removed. Contour position agreed with the expert's opinion in all cases. The additional objects could be removed according to their size in a post-reconstruction phase.

Finally, if two chromosome territories were too close each other, then the algorithm found only one joined object. This situation is illustrated in Fig. 3 right. It occurred in 7 cases (in 4 cases the algorithm found also 1 or 2 small additional objects, which should and could be removed). If the separation of the joined close territories is desired then some more sophisticated method should be

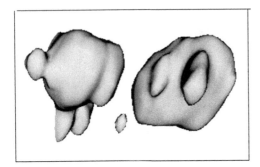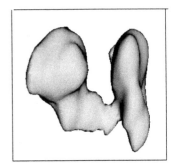

Fig. 3. An example of possible problems during the 3D reconstruction of chromosome territories. (Left) Small additional objects can appear. Post-reconstruction phase can remove them according to their size. (Right) Close territories can be reconstructed as a single joined object.

developed. Note that the expert often was not sure about the boundary between close objects also.

There are many advantages of proposed algorithm. The algorithm is fast, relatively easy to implement, and our experiments have shown that it is also sufficiently robust for the presented application field. The time complexity of the algorithm is $\mathcal{O}(N \log N)$ in the worst case and common PC workstations can analyse one cell nucleus almost in real time. The images of one cell nucleus were processed in 3.3 seconds in average (on Celeron 1.13MHz, Linux 2.4.22) in our experiments.

The constraint on the one directional movement of the contour in fast marching method can bring problems if the input data are noisy. If the method fails then its results can be often corrected using successive application of the general level set method [15]. However, no correction was needed in our experiments due to noise.

The presented algorithm has provided promising results for the chromosome territories reconstruction. However, it is necessary to perform more detailed studies of the algorithm for each biological application. Especially, it is necessary to give evidence that the algorithm and setting of its parameters do not significantly affect the successive measurement (volume, surface area, distances, etc.) and the measurement will be sufficiently precise.

References

[1] D. Adalsteinsson and J. A. Sethian. A fast level set method for propagating interfaces. *Journal of Computational Physics*, 118:269–277, 1995.
[2] E. Bertin, F. Parazza, and J. M. Chassery. Segmentation and meassurement based on 3D Voronoi diagram: application to confocal microscopy. *Computerized Medical Imaging and Graphics*, 17(3):175–182, 1993.

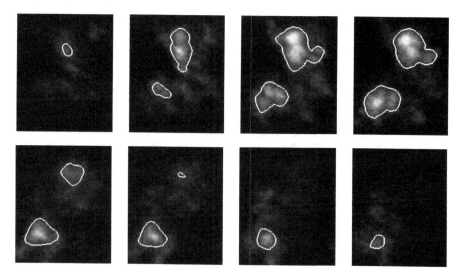

Fig. 4. Projection of the final model from Fig. 2 onto the input data is shown for 8 xy slices (top) $z = 14, 16, 18, 20$; (bottom) $z = 22, 24, 26, 28$.

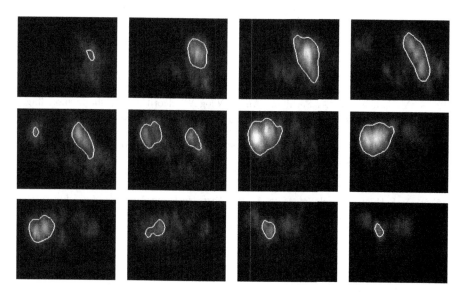

Fig. 5. Projection of the final model from Fig. 2 onto the input data is shown for 12 yz slices (top) $z = 43, 46, 49, 52$; (middle) $z = 55, 58, 61, 64$; (bottom) $z = 67, 70, 73, 76$.

[3] L. D. Cohen. On active contour models and balloons. *CVGIP: Image Understanding*, 53(2):211–218, 1991.

[4] L. D. Cohen and I. Cohen. Finite element methods for active contour models and balloons for 2D and 3D images. *IEEE Transactions on Pattern Analysis and Machine Inteligence*, 15(11):1131–1147, 1993.

[5] T. Cremer and C. Cremer. Chromosome territories, nuclear architecture and gene regulation in mammalian cells. *Nature reviews genetics*, 2(4):292–301, April 2001.

[6] T. Cremer, A. Kurz, R. Zirbel, S. Dietzel, B. Rinke, E. Schröck, M. R. Speicher, U. Mathieu, A. Jauch, P. Emmerich, H. Scherthan, T. Reid, C. Cremer, and P. Lichter. Role of chromosome territories in the functional compartmentalization of the cell nucleus. *Cold Spring Harbor Symp Quantitative Biology*, 58:777–792, 1993.

[7] R. Eils, E. Bertin, K. Saracoglu, B. Rinke, E. Schröck, F. Parazza, Y. Usson, M. Robert-Nicoud, E. H. K. Stelzer, J. M. Chassery, T. Cremer, and C. Cremer. Application of confocal laser microscopy and treee-dimensional Voronoi diagrams for volume and surface estimates of interphase chromosomes. *Journal of Microscopy*, 177(2):150–161, February 1995.

[8] R. Eils, S. Dietzel, E. Bertin, E. Schröck, M. R. Speicher, T. Ried, M. Robert-Nicoud, T. Cremer, and C. Cremer. Three-dimensional reconstruction of painted human interphase chromosomes: active and inactive X chromosome territories have similar volumes but differ in shape and surface structure. *Journal of Cell Biology*, 135(6):1427–1440, December 1996.

[9] M. Kass, A. Witkin, and D. Terzopoulos. Active contour models. *International Journal of Computer Vision*, 1(4):133–144, 1987.

[10] M. Kozubek, S. Kozubek, E. Bártová E. Lukášová, M. Skalníková, Pavel Matula, Petr Matula, P. Jirsová, A. Cafourková, and I. Koutná. Combined confocal and wide-field high-resolution cytometry of FISH-stained cells. *Cytometry*, 45:1–12, 2001.

[11] W. E. Lorensen and H. E. Cline. Marching cubes: A high resolution 3D surface construction algorithm. In *Computer Graphics (SIGGRAPH '87)*, volume 21, pages 163–169, 1987.

[12] R. Malladi and J. A. Sethian. An $\mathcal{O}(N \log N)$ algorithm for shape modeling. *Proceedings of the National Academy of Science*, 93:9389–9392, 1996.

[13] R. Malladi, J. A. Sethian, and B. C. Vemuri. Shape modeling with front propagation: a level set approach. *IEEE Transactions on Pattern Analysis and Machine Inteligence*, 17(2):158–175, 1995.

[14] J. A. Sethian. A fast marching level set method for monotonically advancing fronts. *Proc. Nat'l Academy of Sciences*, 93:1591–1595, 1996.

[15] J. A. Sethian. *Level Set Methods and Fast Marching Methods: Evolving interfaces in computational geometry, fluid mechanics, computer vision, and materials science*. Cambridge University Press, 2nd edition, 1999.

Robust Extraction of the Optic Nerve Head in Optical Coherence Tomography

Artemas Herzog[1], Kim L. Boyer[1], and Cynthia Roberts[2]

[1] The Ohio State University
Signal Analysis and Machine Perception Laboratory
Department of Electrical and Computer Engineering
herzoga@ece.osu.edu, kim@ece.osu.edu
[2] Department of Ophthalmology
roberts.8@osu.edu

Abstract. Glaucoma is a leading cause of blindness. While glaucoma is a treatable and controllable disease, there is still no cure available. Early diagnosis is important in order to prevent severe vision loss. Many current diagnostic techniques are subjective and variable. This provides motivation for a more objective and repeatable method. Optical Coherence Tomography (OCT) is a relatively new imaging technique that is proving useful in diagnosing, monitoring, and studying glaucoma. OCT, like ultrasound, suffers from signal dependent noise which can make accurate, automatic segmentation of images difficult. In this article we propose a method to automatically extract the optic nerve and retinal boundaries from axial OCT scans through the optic nerve head. We also propose a method to automatically segment the curve to extract the nerve head profile that is important in diagnosing and monitoring glaucoma.

1 Introduction

Optical Coherence tomography (OCT) is a relatively new imaging technique [1]. While similar to ultrasound, OCT relies on the detection of backscattered light and time of flight information to produce high resolution, cross-sectional images. OCT has been particulary useful in biological imaging applications such as dermatology, cardiology, and ophthalmology [2, 3, 4]. Specifically in the ophthalmological case, OCT has been used for a variety of purposes which range from measuring corneal thickness in the anterior segment of the eye to measuring the retinal thickness in the posterior segment of the eye [5]. Although limited to relatively shallow imaging depths, approximately 2mm in retinal scans, OCT benefits from being a non-invasive procedure in ophthalmological imaging with a 5-10 micron axial resolution [6]. Thus detailed images of the retinal tissue structure can be obtained with the potential for high tolerance measurements.

Retinal nerve fiber layer thickness is a clinically important measurement in the diagnosis and monitoring of glaucoma [7]. Over time the retinal nerve fiber layer thickness around the optic nerve tends to decrease as nervous tissue is destroyed. It has been estimated that up to 40% of the nerve fiber can be destroyed

M. Šonka et al. (Eds.): CVAMIA-MMBIA 2004, LNCS 3117, pp. 395–407, 2004.

before significant vision loss occurs [8]. The cup-to-disk ratio and the optic cup shape are also important indicators of glaucoma and optic nerve health; however, cup-to-disk ratio is an ill-defined term. The most popular way to measure the cup-to-disk ratio is through direct observation. Here the physician observes the optic nerve through fundus imaging and estimates what he/she believes the cup-to-disk ratio to be. This technique is subjective and variable and provides motivation for an objective method that is more accurate and repeatable. In this paper we propose a method to robustly extract the retinal and optic nerve head boundaries from axial OCT scans of the optic nerve head. With the boundaries extracted, we next propose a method for segmenting the optic cup from the retina and disk.

The eye is divided into two chambers, the anterior chamber and the posterior chamber. The posterior chamber is filled with a relatively homogenous, jelly like substance called the vitreous humor [9]. The retina is the anterior most tissue layer in the back of the posterior chamber. It is here that light rays are focused and processed before being sent via the optic nerve to the brain. We note that the top most layer of the retina is composed of nerve fibers. It is these nerve fibers that are destroyed due to glaucoma. The layer of tissue below the retina is a highly reflective layer called the choroid and is mostly composed of blood vessels which feed the back of the eye.

Finally, the optic disk is the area of the retina where the nerve fiber layers converge to form the optic nerve. The cup is the area of so-called empty space in the central region of the optic disk. In normal eyes the ratio of the cup area to the disk area (cup-to-disk ratio) is small (less than 0.6) [8]. In glaucomatous eyes, the death of nerve fibers causes the size of the cup to increase and thus the cup-to-disk ratio also increases. The shape of the cup can also provide an indicator as to whether or not an individual has glaucoma.

2   Optical Coherence Tomography

Optical Coherence Tomography is similar to ultrasound. Instead of sound, light is sent into a sample and the time of arrival and intensity of the backscattered light is used to form an image. However, because the speed of light is over a million times faster than the speed of sound, coherence based detection techniques are often chosen over nonlinear gating techniques and Kerr shutters [10].

In coherence based detection an interferometer is used to split the energy from a light source $E(t)$ into a reference field $E_r(t)$ and a sample field $E_s(t)$. The sample field travels a total distance l_s and the reference field l_r. The two fields add together at the detector and the total detector photocurrent is

$$I_D \sim \frac{1}{4}|E_r|^2 + \frac{1}{4}|E_s|^2 + \frac{1}{2}|E_r E_s| \cos(2\frac{2\pi}{\lambda}\Delta l) \tag{1}$$

where λ is the wavelength of the light source and

$$\Delta l = l_r - l_s \tag{2}$$

Thus (1) tells us that the intensity of the photocurrent oscillates as a function of the path length difference (2). It can be shown that when a low coherence source is used I_D becomes the cross-correlation function of the sample field with the reference field. The fields are correlated (i.e. interfere constructively) when Δl is less than the coherence length l_c and are uncorrelated otherwise. The coherence length is inversely proportional to the bandwidth of the light source. Because the sample field is relatively constant, we can control imaging depth by controlling the length of the reference beam. Our images were obtained using the OCT

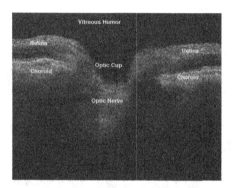

Fig. 1. A typical OCT scan through the optic nerve with labeled structures.

3000 from Zeiss-Humphrey. The typical scan consists of 512 A-scans where each A-scan consists of 1024 pixels. The axial resolution is $< 10 \mu m$ and the transverse resolution is dependent on the scan length. Fig. 1 shows a typical scan through the optic nerve head with various anatomical structures marked.

3   Theory

Segmentation of OCT images is a difficult task. Koozekanani *et al.* [11] proposed a Markov Boundary Model to extract the retinal boundaries from circular scans of the macula. While their method is robust on the macular region of the retina, the model they used fails in the optic nerve head region due to the significant anatomical differences. It is impractical to train a new Markov model because there is considerably more variation in the optic nerve head regions between subjects. We can still, though, rely on the assumption that the retinal/optic nerve head profile is smooth and that significant undulations in the retina are usually the result of eye movement. The optic disk surface also varies slowly, although considerably less so than the retina. We can assume that the imaging technician will discard the image if movement is severe enough to cause significant image distortion or large breaks in the profile. Likewise, if shadowing significantly reduces the visibility of entire image regions, the technician will again discard the images. However, less severe shadow effects, breaks, distortions, and artifacts

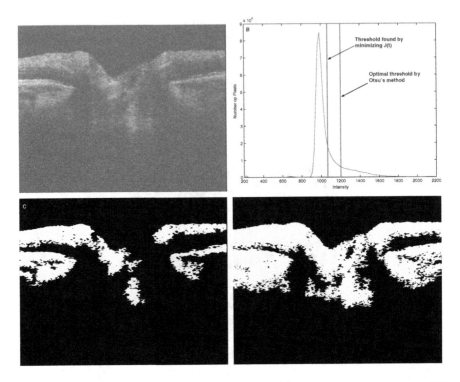

Fig. 2. (A) is a noise suppressed OCT scan. The image histogram is shown in (B) and shows the thresholds obtained using Otsu's method and our method. (C) is the thresholded image resulting from Otsu's method and (D) is the thresholded image using our method.

must be assumed likely and that the OCT technician will keep such images. Thus our method should be robust enough to handle such effects.

The most complicated problem with OCT images is the nonlinear, signal dependent noise that is inherent in coherence imaging techniques. This noise is called speckle due to its appearance in the images. Ultrasound and synthetic aperture radar imaging also suffer from this phenomenon. Speckle arises because of multiple backscattering and forward scattering within the sample volume [12]. Organic tissue is never homogenous and thus a sample volume is highly likely to have multiple scatterers (i.e cells, organelles, fibers, fluids ...). Speckle forms when light from these multiple scatterers reaches the detector out of phase within the coherence time of the source. Thus multiple backscattering causes constructive and destructive interference that alters the wave shape incident the detector. Speckle is both a signal carrier, in that it reveals information about the underlying microstructure, and a source of noise. While distinguishing between noise speckle and information speckle is difficult [10] we need not be concerned. We are only interested in the gross anatomical structure of the retina and optic nerve head and not in its microstructure. Thus both types of speckle can be considered noise for our case.

While some speckle can be reduced through imaging techniques such as spatial compounding and polarization diversity there still remains a significant problem. Because of its signal dependent nature, speckle noise can not readily be decoupled from the signal. Various techniques have been proposed to alleviate the problem with the most common being the use of median filtering [13, 14, 11] or one of its variations. Suvichakorn and Chinrungrueng propose fitting a two-dimensional polynomial using a least squares approach to estimate the actual image intensities [15]. Park et al. rely on an adaptive windowing procedure with adpative filtering based on local statistics [16] and Xiang et al. used wavelet filters incorporating automatic noise thresholds [17].

Observations of retina and optic nerve images reveal that there is a significant contrast difference at the vitreal-retinal boundary. When speckle is suppressed through filtering, the retina becomes a relatively homogenous region and the contrast between the vitreous humor and retina is significantly increased. Define Region 1 to be the vitreous humor and the dark area in the lower portion of the image corresponding to signal loss. Next, define Region 2 as the retina, optic disk, and choroid. Now we assume that there exists a threshold t such that Region 1 is completely separated from Region 2. If such a t exists then the top profile of the retina and optic nerve is just the boundary between the upper portion of Region 1 and Region 2.

Thresholding is a simplistic yet powerful image segmentation tool. The problem with thresholding lies in the selection of the threshold. Assuming that the pixel distributions of the regions are normal, one might consider using Otsu's thresholding algorithm [18] which seeks to minimize the within class variance of the two distributions in a bimodal histogram. This can provide sub-optimal results if there is considerable overlap between the distributions or if the histogram is not bimodal. Rather than rely on the histogram to select the threshold we propose a new method based on edge maximization and smoothness constraints to choose an optimal threshold.

Let $E(r, c)$ be an edge image produced by column-wise, one-dimensional edge detection, $r(t, c)$ be the boundary of interest as a function of the threshold t and image columns, and $r'(t, c)$ be the first derivative with respect to c. Note here that $E(r, c)$ may be a modification of the actual edge image, for instance we could threshold the weaker edges or use only edges of a certain polarity. Furthermore, define $p(t, c)$ to be a function that corresponds to whether an edge exists (we could also use edge strength) for a given $r(t, c)$, that is

$$p(t, c) = E(r(t, c), c) \tag{3}$$

Now we can define a cost function

$$J(t) = \sum_c p(t, c) - \alpha \frac{1}{N_c} \sum_c |r'(t, c)| \tag{4}$$

where α is a constant of proportionality. The optimal threshold given the criteria we have defined can then be found by setting

$$\frac{\partial J}{\partial t} = 0 \tag{5}$$

and solving for t.

The first term of (4) corresponds to the number of edge locations that intersects $r(t, c)$. The second term adds a smoothness constraint based on the anatomical properties of the vitreal-retinal boundary. We expect that the average rate of change of the correct boundary is small (even in the region of the optic cup). Breaks in the boundary due to subject movement or portions of the optic cup may correspond to a high rate of change. However, this will be relative constant over a range of thresholds and should not affect the correct choice of t. This terms adds a degree of robustness to $J(t)$ particularly in the case of shadowing. In A-scans where there is partial occlusion the contrast tends to be lower than the non-occluded A-scans and the second term tends to pull the threshold lower to account for the occlusion. The constant α controls the amount of correction that can occur. Setting α too low results in little or no correction while setting α too high can cause incorrect segmentation. Thus the optimal t maximizes the number of edge locations in $E(r, c)$ located along $r(t, c)$ and minimizes the average rate of change of $r(t, c)$.

Fig. 2A shows an OCT image where the noise has been suppressed by median filtering. Fig. 2B shows the histogram of the image along with Otsu's threshold and the threshold chosen by our algorithm. In this case the distributions do not clearly exhibit a bimodal nature. Fig. 2C shows the result of thresholding based on Otsu's method. Fig. 2D shows the result of minimizing $J(t)$ to obtain the correct threshold.

At first glance (4) resembles the active contour model first proposed by Kass et al. [19] and seen extensively throughout the literature [20, 21, 22, 23]. Indeed, there are some similarities since we are seeking a threshold dependent upon image forces and contour smoothness. The key difference lies in that we have defined a function $J(t)$ in terms of a scalar threshold t. Active contour models seek an entire contour the minimizes a certain functional. In our case, the contour results from finding the threshold that minimizes $J(t)$. Indeed, (4) is less sophisticated and simpler than the active contour model but it suffers less from some of the problems associated with active contour models such as contour initialization and attraction to incorrect minima.

The vitreal-retinal boundary $Y(x)$ can be modeled as a piecewise smooth function consisting of a straight line segment, followed by a parabolic segment, and ending with another straight line segment as follows:

$$P(x) = \begin{cases} a_1 x + b_1 & \text{if } c_1 \leq x \leq c_2 \\ a_2 x^2 + b_2 x + c & \text{if } c_2 \leq x \leq c_3 \\ a_3 x + b_3 & \text{if } c_3 \leq x \leq c_4 \end{cases} \tag{6}$$

while c_1 and c_4 are known since they represent the first and last columns in the image, c_2 and c_3 are unknowns which we will call breakpoints. The parameters for each curve segment are also unknown, but if we are given c_2 and c_3, the parameters for each curve segment can be found using a least squares fit. For instance, in the case of the parabolic segment one needs to solve the matrix equation

$$
\begin{bmatrix} x_1^2 & x_1 & 1 \\ x_2^2 & x_2 & 1 \\ \vdots & \vdots & \vdots \\ x_N^2 & x_N & 1 \end{bmatrix} \begin{bmatrix} a_2 \\ b_2 \\ c \end{bmatrix} = \begin{bmatrix} P_1 \\ \vdots \\ P_N \end{bmatrix} \tag{7}
$$

where x_i and P_i are defined in (6). The solution to (7) is

$$
\begin{bmatrix} a_2 \\ b_2 \\ c \end{bmatrix} = (X^T X)^{-1} X P \tag{8}
$$

where we have used the Moore-Penrose inverse. The parameters for each segment can thus be found provided that c_2 and c_3 are known but the problem is that c_2 and c_3 are not known. In order to find the breakpoints we will need to define a criterion that will provide insight to how well $P(x)$ for a given c_2 and c_3 models the boundary profile $Y(x)$. First let

$$
\bar{c} = \begin{bmatrix} c_2 \\ c_3 \end{bmatrix} \tag{9}
$$

Next, consider

$$
P_i(x) = P(x) \quad c_i \le x \le c_{i+1} \tag{10}
$$

to represent the modeled boundary using the parameters from (6) where i represents the curve segment number. Also define

$$
Y_i(x) = Y(x) \quad c_i \le x \le c_{i+1} \tag{11}
$$

Then we can write the squared error for each curve segment as

$$
e_i(\bar{c}) = \sum_{n=c_i}^{n=c_{i+1}} (Y_i(n) - P_i(n))^2 \quad i = 1 \ldots 3 \tag{12}
$$

Now we can write the total squared error, TE, as a function of $\bar{c}$

$$
TE(\bar{c}) = \sum_{i=1}^{3} e_i(\bar{c}) \tag{13}
$$

$TE(\bar{c})$ gives us an indication of how well our model fits the actual upper retina-optic nerve head profile for a given set of breakpoints. Now we assume that $TE(\bar{c})$ has a global minimum that corresponds to the ideal location of the breakpoints. That is, when $TE(\bar{c})$ is minimized, the model we have proposed has found the edges of the optic cup. Here we will make one further assumption about $TE(\bar{c})$, that is the error function is quadratic and only has one minimum. This is of course a weak assumption. In actuality there are saddle points and local minima on the error surface; however, these local minimum and saddle points are usually much weaker then the global minimum and thus the assumption that $TE(\bar{c})$ is a quadratic error surface is justified. Since we assume that $TE(\bar{c})$ is quadratic we can then use a gradient descent algorithm to locate the correct breakpoints.

4   The Algorithm

4.1   Median Filtering (Step 1)

The first step in our approach is noise suppression. We chose to use a median filter due to its simplicity and its property of preserving the important macrostructure of the image. We applied a 4 x 4 median filter to each image twice. This suppresses most of the speckle and homogenizes the retina and choroid by destroying the underlying microstructure. Because the columns of an image are acquired independently, two-dimensional median filtering tends to introduce artifacts. However, since we are only relying on the edges to choose a threshold, the artifacts are of little consequence. The result of filtering can be seen in Fig. 2A.

4.2   Columnwise Edge Detection (Step 2)

Edge detection was performed on the each A-scan of the filtered image. The lack of registration, the speckle character of the noise, and the dislocations between adjacent columns tend to cause problems in the case of 2-D kernels. Indeed, the transverse and axial resolutions are not identical whereas most 2D kernels are isptropic and rely on the assumption that the transverse and axial resolutions are identical. Columnwise edge detection is similar to the methods of Thune *et al.*[24] and Koozekanani *et al.* [11].

   We chose to use the Marr-Hildreth operator (LoG) which is given below [25]. There is no special reason for this choice as any other 1D kernel, such as the optimal zero-crossing operator proposed by Sarkar and Boyer [26], would have worked as well.

$$E(r) = g''(r) * A \tag{14}$$

where

$$g(r) = \exp(\frac{-r^2}{2\sigma^2}) \tag{15}$$

The edge locations $s_{zc}(r)$, are the zeros crossings of (14). We chose to use a $\sigma = 5$. This provided a compromise between edge position preservation and additional filtering of noisy edges. Edge preservation is particularly important as threshold choice relies on the assumption that a large number of edges lie on the vitreal-retinal border. We can reduce the number of edges in the image by considering only those edges of negative polarity. This is justified because the vitreal-retinal border is a transition from a darker region to a lighter region.

4.3   Optimal Threshold Selection (Step 3)

Using the cost function that we defined in (7) we wish to learn which threshold value t extremizes this function. In this case a gradient descent algorithm can be computationally expensive and slow to converge and is thus undesirable. Instead we sample J(t) for a set of t values which are evenly spaced over a range that typically bounds t. Our observations, over many trials, indicate that $J(t)$

is generally a well behaved parabolic function for the bounded set of threshold values. We then fit a parabola to the sampled $J(t)$ and the extremum for

$$y(t) = at^2 + bt + c \tag{16}$$

occurs at

$$t = -\frac{b}{2a} \tag{17}$$

This is the optimal threshold according to our definition of $J(t)$.

4.4   Boundary Extraction (Step 4)

Using t as found in Step 3 to threshold the image, the matter of boundary extraction is trivial. Noise in the vitreous humor can cause small artifacts to occur in this region of the thresholded image. These are easily removed and the boundary is just the first non-zero pixel in each image column.

4.5   Curve Segmentation (Step 5)

Given the retina-optic disk boundary from Step 4, the final step of our algorithm is to find the edges corresponding to the optic cup in the boundary. Using the model we stated earlier (6) and the cost function (13) we can use a gradient descent algorithm to find the columns that best correspond to the edges of the optic cup. The method of gradient descent updates the current estimate of $TE(\bar{c})$ for each iteration k by

$$\bar{c}(k+1) = \bar{c}(k) - \eta \nabla TE(\bar{c}, k) \tag{18}$$

where η is called the learning rate. The gradient descent algorithm moves along the negative direction of the gradient until the algorithm converges to the optimal value of $TE(\bar{c})$. The parameter η controls the speed of convergence; however, if η is set too high divergence may occur. Although methods exist to calculate the best η and to update it iteratively, we found that $\bar{c}$ typically converged quickly even for small values of η and by making η smaller we can avoid divergence problems. Limitations of this method occur if patient movement is significant enough to severely alter the retina profile. In this case the model that we chose no longer fits the actual profile.

5   Results

The algorithm generally identified the correct vitreal-retinal boundary in the images. The rare exceptions occur when the OCT signal has been severely attenuated due to shadowing. If the shadowing is severe enough in a portion of an image, then the threshold selected will set all of the A-scans affected by the shadowing to zero. In this case, no boundary will be found; however, it is easily identified and measures can be attempted to find the correct boundary.

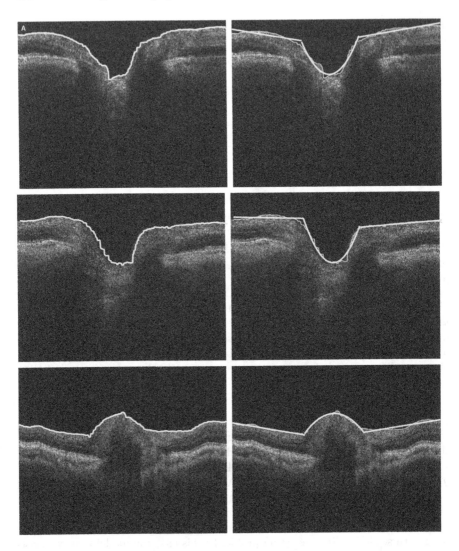

Fig. 3. (A) shows an example of a correctly identified boundary while (B) shows the resulting curve segmentation. (C) and (D) show another pair with correct boundary identification and segmentation. (E) and (F) show the results for a subject suffering from papilla edema. Again we have identified the correct boundary and have achieved correct segmentation.

Our curve segmentation algorithm also produced good results. Exceptions occurred when movement introduced a significant distortion in the boundary profile. Fig. 3 shows some examples of results obtained using our algorithm.

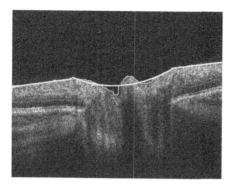

Fig. 4. An example where the boundary curve is not segmented properly due to distortion from subject movement.

Fig. 4 shows an example of curve segmentation when the boundary profile has been affected due to movement.

6   Conclusion

We have presented two significant contributions in this paper. First, we have developed a method to adaptively threshold OCT images of the optic disk in order to extract the vitreous-retinal boundary from the images. Our method relies on maximizing the number of edges that lie on the boundary while minimizing the boundary's average rate of change. Our method proves to be robust even in the presence of noise artifacts and significant shadowing that would normally cause problems in identifying the correct boundary. The second contribution is an accurate segmentation of the boundary profile obtained via our thresholding technique. This curve parsing procedure relies on a piecewise continuous model of the retinal-boundary where the retina/optic disk portions of the boundary are represented as straight lines and the cup portion is represented by a parabola. By minimizing the sum of squared errors for each segment we can find the optimal edge points of the optic cup. Reliable boundary extraction and segmentation of the axial optic nerve head scans are particularly useful in the clinical setting where current diagnostic procedures lend themselves to the subjectivity of the technician. Further work includes finding the boundary regions corresponding specifically to the optic disk so that a cup-to-disk ratio can be calculated and used in a clinical setting.

References

[1] Huang, D., Swanson, E.A., Lin, C.P., et al.: Optical coherence tomography. Science **254** (1991) 1178–1181

[2] Welzel, J., Lankenau, E., Birngruber, R., Engelhardt, R.: Optical coherence tomography of the human skin. J. Am. Acad. Derm **37** (1997) 958–963

[3] Brezinski, M.E., Tearney, G.J., Brett, B.E.: Imaging of coronary artery microstructure with optical coherence tomography. American Journal of Cardiology **77** (1996) 92–93

[4] Hee, M.R., Izatt, J.A., Swanson, E.A., et al.: Optical coherence tomography for ophthalmic imaging. IEEE Engineering in Medicine and Biology **14** (1995) 67–76

[5] Wang, R., Koozekanani, D., Roberts, C., Katz, S.: Reproducibility of retinal thickness measurements using optical coherence tomography. Investigative Ophthalmology and Visual Science **40** (1999) S125–S125

[6] Zeiss-Humphrey: Optical coherence tomographer model 3000: User manual (2002)

[7] Puliafito, C.A., Hee, M.R., Schuman, J.S., Fujimoto, J.G., eds.: Optical Coherence Tomography of Ocular Diseases. First edn. Slack, Thorofare (1996)

[8] Boyd, B.F., Luntz, M.H., eds.: Innovations in the Glaucomas: Etiology, Diagnosis, and Management. First edn. Highlights of Ophthalmology Int'l, El Dorado (2002)

[9] Tasman, W., Jaeger, E.A., eds.: The Willis Eye Hospital Atals of Clinical Ophthalmology. 2nd edn. Lippincott and Williams and Wilkins, Philadelphia (2001)

[10] Bouma, B., Tearney, G.J., eds.: Handbook of Optical Coherence Tomography. 1st edn. Dekker, USA (2001)

[11] Koozekanani, D., Boyer, K., Roberts, C.: Retinal thickness measurements in optical coherence tomography using a markov boundary model. In: IEEE Computer Society Conference on Computer Vision and Pattern Recognition. Volume 2., Hilton Head, SC (2000) 363–370

[12] Schmitt, J.M.: Optical coherence tomography (oct): A review. IEEE Journal of Selected Topics in Quantum Electronics **5** (1999) 1205–1215

[13] Loupas, T., McDicken, W.N., Allan, P.L.: An adpative weighted media filter for speckle suppression in medical ultrasonic images. IEEE Transactions on Circuits and Systems **36** (1989) 129–135

[14] Czerwinski, R.N., Jones, D.L., Jr, W.D.O.: Ultrasound speckle reduction by directional median filtering. In: Proceeding of the 1995 International Conference on Image Processing. Volume 1. (1995) 358–361

[15] Suvichakorn, A., Chinrungrueng, C.: Speckle noise reduction for ultrasound images. In: IEEE APCCAS 2000. (2000) 430–433

[16] Park, J.M., Song, W.J., Pearlman, W.A.: Speckle filtering of sar images based on adaptive windowing. In: Visual Image Signal Processing. Volume 146. (1999) 430–433

[17] Xiang, S.H., Zhou, L., Schmitt, J.M.: Speckle noise reduction for optical coherence tomography. In: Proc. SPIE. Volume 3196. (1997) 79–88

[18] Otsu, N.: A threshold selection method from gray level histograms. IEEE Transactions on Systems, Man, and Cybernetics **9** (1979) 62–66

[19] Kass, M., Witkin, A., Terzopoulos, D.: Snakes: Active contour models. International Journal of Computer Vision (1988) 321–331

[20] Berger, M., Mohr, R.: Towards autonomy in active contour models. In: IEEE: 10th International Conference on Pattern Recognition, Piscataway NJ (1990) 847–851

[21] Cohen, L.D.: On active contour models and balloons. In: CVGIP - Image Understanding. Volume 53. (1991) 211–218

[22] Duta, N., Sonka, M.: Segmentation and interpretation or mr brain images using an improved knowledge-based active shape model. In Duncan, J., Gindi, G., eds.: Information Processing in Medical Imaging, Berlin, Springer Verlag (1997) 375–380

[23] Xu, C., Prince, J.L.: Snakes, shapes, and gradient vector flow. IEEE Transactions of Image Processing **7** (1998) 359–369

[24] Thune, M., Olstad, B., Thune, N.: Edge detection in noisy data using finite mixture distribution analysis. Pattern Recognition **30** (1997) 685–699

[25] Marr, D., Hildreth, E.: Theory of edge detection. Proceedings Royal Society,London **2076** (1980) 187–217

[26] Sarkar, S., Boyer, K.: Optimal impulse response zero crossing based edge detectors. Computer Vision Graphics Image Process: Image Understanding **54** (1991) 224–243

Scale-Space Diagnostic Criterion for Microscopic Image Analysis[1]

Igor Gurevich, Dmitry Murashov

Scientific Council "Cybernetics" of the Russian Academy of Sciences. 40, Vavilov street,
Moscow, GSP-1, 119991, Russian Federation
igourevi@ccas.ru, dmmur@rbcmail.ru

Abstract. In this paper, a new criterion for diagnostics of hematopoietic tumors from images of cell nuclei of lymphatic nodes is presented. A method for image analysis of lymphatic node specimens is developed on the basis of the scale-space approach. A diagnostically important criterion is defined as a total amount of points of spatial intensity extrema in the families of blurred images generated by the given image of a cell nucleus. The procedure for calculating criterion values is presented. Testing of the obtained criterion is carried out using different classifiers. The accuracy of diagnostics is greater than 81% for collective classifiers.

1   Introduction

The visual analysis of microscopic preparations still remains an important component of diagnostics in hematology. One of the perspective trends in image processing is concerned with the development of early diagnostic techniques for automated analysis of morphology of blood cells and hematopoietic organs microscopic images. In this paper, a relatively small sample of images is used for obtaining the criterion for diagnostics of lymphatic system tumors, such as chronic B-cell lymphatic leukemia, its transformation to lymphosarcoma, and primary B-cell lymphosarcoma (according to the classification of A. Vorob'ev and M. Brilliant [9]).

It is known, that specimen cell nuclei of malignant lymphatic node tissue are larger than those taken from patients with the non-malignant tumor diagnose. Thus, an obvious diagnostic criterion is the area of cell nucleus. However, this criterion is unsuitable for the more accurate diagnostics: it is impossible to distinguish the transformation of chronic lymphoid leukemia from lymphosarcoma.

The procedure of searching for a diagnostic criterion includes the following steps. The experts indicate the diagnostically important cell nuclei in the images of lymphatic node specimens of three groups of patients having the diagnosed diseases. These images are considered as an input information. Next, the developed method of specimen image analysis is used for calculating qualitative characteristics from the

---

[1] This work was partly supported by the Russian Foundation for Basic Research (grant NN 02-01-00182, 03-07-90406, 04-07-90202).

M. Šonka et al. (Eds.): CVAMIA-MMBIA 2004, LNCS 3117, pp. 408–416, 2004.

indicated nuclei. The obtained values are analyzed and thus, a criterion for making diagnostic decisions is formulated. The proposed method for specimen image analysis is based on the known scale-space approach [1-3].

2 Properties of Cell Nucleus Images

The image of a lymphatic node specimen is a color image taken by a camera and enlarged by a microscope (24 bpp). The size of the image is 1536x1024 pixels covering a site of 60—100 microns in diameter. The resolution is 0.06 microns per pixel. The analyzed objects are the fragments of the gray-scale images of specimens containing cell nuclei. These images are characterized by inhomogeneous coloring and the presence of dark spots and bright areas representing their internal structure.

To make a diagnosis, experts pay a special attention to the cells of two classes: mature cells, with the mature structure of chromatin (see Fig. 1 (a)), and sarcomatous cells, with the immature structure of chromatin (see Fig. 1 (b)-(d)) [9-11].

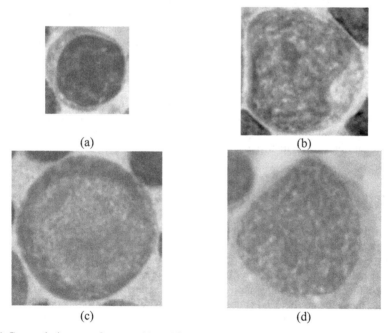

Fig.1 Grayscale images of mature (a) and immature cell tumors of different patterns: fibrous (b), filamentous (c), granular (d)

In the first case (chronic lymphatic leukemia), with few exceptions, the image contains only mature cells. In the cases of sarcomatous transformation of the chronic lymphatic leukemia or primary lymphatic sarcoma, the specimen contains both mature and immature (sarcomatous) cells.It is necessary to take into account the specific properties of cell images, such as low dye quality, instability of specimen characteristics, nonuniformity of light exposure during specimen microscoping, presence of damaged and unsuitable for analysis cells. Mature chromatin is homogeneous with light furrows. Immature chromatin can have a filamentous structure of different patterns, a fibrous or granular structure [11]. The analysis of cell nucleus images should yield quantitative characteristics that capture the structure and pattern of chromatin.

3 Contemporary Approaches to Image Analysis of Cell Nuclei

The quantitative analysis of cytological and tissue specimen images is based on the evaluation of shape, intensity, and textural features. In practice, great attention is paid to automated analysis of chromatin arrangement in cell nuclei. It has been proven in many studies that chromatin distribution corresponds to the state of malignancy [5]. Two basic approaches to analysis of a chromatin constitution are known [5]. Within a framework of the first, structural approach, the chromatin distribution is considered as a local arrangement of fairly small objects of varying intensity. The intensity features of dark and bright particles are evaluated. This approach is substantially heuristic. The second approach, textural, is based on the statistical characteristics of chromatin arrangement and related to analysis of patterns of chromatin structure. The methods for textural analysis applied in practice use grey level dependency matrices [4], co occurrence, run-length features, rice-field operators, watersheds (topological methods) [6], heterogeneity, clumpiness, margination, radius of particles [8] (the Mayall/Young features), and invariant features (polynomial invariants).

The main disadvantage of the known textural methods [5] is their sensitivity to parameters and conditions of image acquisition, to properties of preparations, and to precision of microscope focusing.

4 Method for the Analysis of Chromatin Constitution

Among the contemporary approaches to image analysis, the approach of Gaussian scale-space entirely fulfills the task of cell nuclei image analysis [1-3]. The scale-space technique provides the invariance with respect to shift, rotation, scaling, and linear transformations of intensity. It decreases the sensitivity of the analysis to microscope focusing. An image family $L(x,t)$ is generated (the Gaussian scale-space) from the input image (here $L(x)$ denotes an intensity function of spatial coordinates $x=(x_1,x_2)$). Each image of the Gaussian scale-space is constructed by convolving an input image $L(x)$ with a normalized Gaussian kernel with zero mean and standard deviation $\sigma = \sqrt{t}$ (t is a scale parameter). The family of blurred images [3] $L(x,t)$ satisfies the diffusion equation

$$\partial_t L(x,t) = \Delta L(x,t), \; L(x,0) = L(x),$$

where Δ is the Laplace operator.

As t increases, the blurring appears: the fine details of the image are lost. The properties of the constructed scale space reflect the properties of the initial image and are explored using analysis of neighborhoods of spatial critical points.

The main idea of the analysis is based on the assumption that significant structures in scale-space are likely to correspond to significant structures in the image [3]. The chromatin structure in the nucleus image is represented by a grey-level landscape containing connected bright and dark regions (peaks and valleys). Areas of these regions are characterized by thickness of chromatin filaments and furrows, chromatin centers size, and distances between them. Each of these regions contains at least one point of intensity extremum. One of the quantitative characteristics of chromatin constitution is the amount of chromatin particles represented in the image as grey-level blobs (or amount of associated spatial extrema). The method for blob detection is described in [3]. In this work, we propose an algorithm for approximate evaluation of the amount of chromatin particles based on the topological properties of isointensity manifolds in the neighborhoods of spatial extrema [1].

At some scale parameter value an extremum is encapsulated by isophotes (in 2D case) and curves of nonzero gradient values, topologically equivalent to circles. The intensity value of each of these isophotes is smaller (greater) than the value of maximum (minimum). Thus, isophotes and curves of nonzero gradient values generate the sets of closed curves contracting to an extremum point. The regions bounded by the most distant closed curves enclosing extremum point correspond to the elements of nuclei chromatin constitution.

The algorithm for detection of regions bounded by isointensity curves includes the following steps.

1. Generating scale-space from input cell nucleus image.
2. The following operations are carried out for each image in scale-space (see Fig.2): (a) obtaining gradient images $\nabla L(x, t)$; (b) thresholding the resulting image (threshold value is T=1); (c) removing of nonclosed curves of nonzero gradient values; (d) overlaying a nucleus mask to restrict the region of interest and remove the residual garbage at the peripheries of a nucleus.
3. All scale-space images processed at Steps 1 and 2 are overlaid (using logical "OR" operation). Thus, the duplicates of the same regions in scale-space images are excluded, larger regions cover smaller regions.
4. The morphological operations are applied in order to fill regions bounded by closed curves of nonzero gradient (see Fig.3 (a)) and to remove residual rubbish (using morphological erosion).
5. The coordinates of the geometrical centers of the filled regions (the neighborhoods of extrema) are found (see Fig.3 (b)).
6. The total amount of the centers of the filled regions is calculated.

In Fig. 4 (a) - (c), the cell nuclei with the mature (chronic lymphatic leukemia) and immature (sarcomatous transformation of the chronic lymphatic leukemia and primary lymphatic sarcoma) structure of chromatin are shown. In Fig. 4 (d) - (f)) the corresponding images of extrema neighborhoods obtained at Step 4 are presented. The areas of the nuclei in Fig. 4 (a) - (c) are 92, 244, and 246 squared microns. The amounts of extrema neighborhoods in Fig. 4 (d) - (f) are 39, 108, and 87.

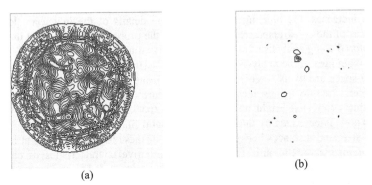

(a)   (b)

Fig.2 Spatial gradient image $\nabla L(x,t)$ at $\sigma = 8$ (a) and extracted closed curves around extrema in a single scale-space image (b)

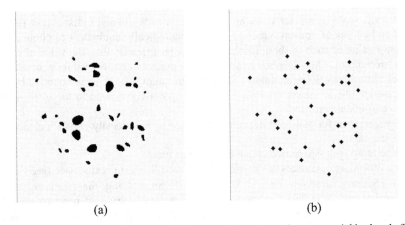

(a)   (b)

Fig.3 Neighborhoods of scale-space spatial extrema (a), centers of extrema neighborhoods (b)

The range of the standard deviation of the Gaussian kernel for scale-space generation was selected for the following reasons. The dependencies of amount of intensity extrema, associated with dark and bright regions, on Gaussian kernel standard deviation has been experimentally found in blurred images of nucleus having different chromatin structure. These dependencies are shown in Fig. 5. Maximum of information about the chromatin constitution is contained in the images generated for $6 \leq \sigma \leq 11$ pixels (for above mentioned resolution).

At smaller σ, fine details and noise disturb the analysis. At $\sigma > 11$, the effect of blurring is too strong and there are few objects left for analysis.

5   Selection of Diagnostic Criterion

The developed procedure was applied to the analysis of scale spaces, generated by images of lymphatic node specimens for diagnoses of malignant (primary B-cell

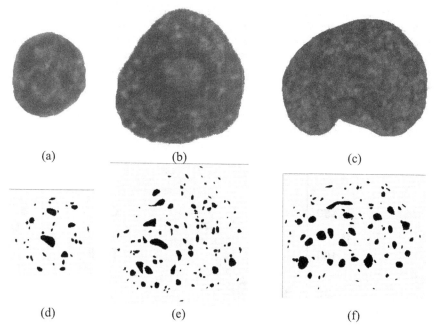

(a)   (b)   (c)

(d)   (e)   (f)

Fig. 4. Cell nuclei with the mature (chronic lymphatic leukemia) (a) and immature (b), (c) (sarcomatous transformation of the chronic lymphatic leukemia and primary lymphatic sarcoma) structure of chromatin and corresponding images of extrema neighborhoods (d)-(f)

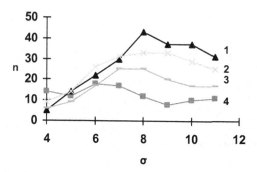

Fig. 5. The dependence of amount of intensity extrema n in blurred nucleus images on the value of kernel standard deviation σ for different types of chromatin structure: granular (curves 1 and 4), fibrous (2), filamentous (3)

lymphosarcoma and transformation of chronic B-cell lymphocytic leukemia) and non-malignant (chronic B-cell lymphocytic leukemia) tumors. 300 images of cell nuclei from 27 patients were analyzed. The families of blurred images for standard deviation of the Gaussian kernel in the range of $6 \leq \sigma \leq 11$ were generated and explored.

Using the results of experiments, the chart displaying the characteristics of cell nuclei images, such as total amount of spatial extrema n and the area of a nucleus s, was created (see Fig. 6). The chart area (see Fig. 6) includes three main parts: (I) the area, located to the left of value s = 137 squared microns and below n = 60; (II) the area, where 137 < s < 200 and n > 60; (III) the area to the right of value s = 200 squared microns.

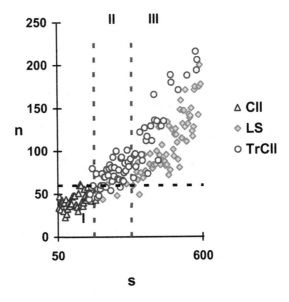

Fig. 6. Distribution of cell nuclei in coordinates "nucleus area","amount of extrema" (s, n)

The first area mainly contains the points corresponding to the diagnosis of chronic lymphocytic leukemia (CLL). In the second area, the transformation of chronic lymphocytic leukemia (TRCLL) is dominating. The third area contains transformation of chronic lymphocytic leukemia as well as lymphosarcoma (LS). For classification of cell nuclei located in area (III), it is possible to construct separating functions.

The results presented in Fig. 6 allow us to conclude that the total amount of spatial extrema in cell nuclei images may be used as a diagnostic criterion.

6   Testing Diagnostic Criterion

Taking into account the results of the computing experiments, the obtained diagnostic criterion was tested. The procedure is as follows.

Using the results shown in Fig. 6, several classifiers were trained: q-nearest neighbors, test algorithm, linear Fisher discriminant, and algorithms for collective solutions (complex committee algorithm c with an average of accessory evaluations, convex stabilizer) [12, 13]. Training sample included 150 cells which were marked in specimen images by experts. Four classes were pointed out: "CLL", "sarcomatous transformation of CLL", "LS", and "Unknown". Further, control sample of 150 cells was presented. For these cells, values of diagnostic criterion were calculated, and the classification with the help of the listed above algorithms was carried out. The results of classification are presented in Table 1. The accuracy of classification is in the range from 72% up to 80% for a single algorithm, 81% for algorithm of the convex stabilizer, and 85,4% for complex committee algorithm. Testing was carried out through the instrumentality of "Loreg" software system [12]. The results of classification showed the efficiency of the obtained diagnostic criterion.

Table 1. Results of classification

Classifier	Accuracy, %
q-nearest neighbors	80
test algorithm	72
linear Fisher discriminant	73
complex committee algorithm	85,4
convex stabilizer	81

7 Conclusions and Directions of Future Research

The results of the research are as follows: (a) the method for analysis of the images of lymphatic node specimens is developed; (b) a diagnostically important criterion is obtained; it is defined as a total amount of spatial extrema in scale space generated by the image of a cell nucleus; the technique for calculating the diagnostic criterion value is developed and implemented in the software system; (d) the results of testing have shown the efficiency of the obtained diagnostic criterion.

The further research will be aimed at increasing the precision of critical points localization, augmenting the sample of cell images, fine tuning and retraining the classifier algorithms.

References

1. Florack, L.M.J., Kuijper, A.: The topological structure of scale-space images. Journal of Mathematical Imaging and Vision, Vol. 12, N1 (2000) 65-80
2. Koenderink, J.J.: The structure of images. Biol. Cybern., Vol.50. (1984) 363-370
3. Lindeberg, T.: Scale-space Theory in Computer Vision. The Kluwer International Series in Engineering and Computer Science. Kluwer Academic Publishers (1994)
4. Weyn B., Van de Wouwer G., Koprowski M., Van Daele A., Dhaene K., Scheunders P., Jacob W., and Van marck E. Value of morphometry, texture analysis, densitometry and histometry in the differential diagnosis and prognosis of malignant mesothelioma, Journal of Pathology, 189 (1999) 581-589
5. K. Rodenacker, and E. Bengtsen. A feature set for cytometry on digitized microscopic images. Anal Cell Pathol, 25(1) (2003)1–36

6. K. Rodenacker. Applications of topology for evaluating pictorial structures. In Reinhard Klette and Walter G. Kropatsch, editors, Theoretical Foundations of Computer Vision, Akademie-Verlag, Berlin, (1993) 35–46

7 K. Rodenacker. Quantitative microscope image analysis for improved diagnosis and prognosis of tumours in pathology. In Creaso Info Medical Imaging, Vol. 22 (1995)

8. I.T. Young, P. Verbeek and B.H. Mayall, Characterization of chromatin distribution in cell nuclei, Cytometry 7(5) (1986) 467–474

9. Vorob'ev A.I., ed. Atlas "Tumors of lymphatic system", Hematological Scientific Center of the Russian Academy of Medical Sciences (2001)

10. Vorob'ev A.I., Vorob'ev I.A., Kharazishvili D.V., et.al. Recognition of lymphatic tumours of a mediastinum. Problems of a tuberculosis, 2 (2001) 21-25

11. Kharazishvili D.V., "Morphometrical analysis of intracellular neoplasms of lymphatic system", Hematological Scientific Center of the Russian Academy of Medical Sciences, Ph.D. thesis, (2001)

12. Zhuravlev Yu.I., Ryazanov V.V., Senko O.V., et. al. "The Program System for Data Analysis Recognition (Loreg)". Proceedings of the 6th German-Russian Workshop "Pattern Recognition and Image Understanding" (OGRW-6-2003), August, 25-30, 2003. - Novosibirsk (2003) 255-258.

13. R.O. Duda, P.E. Hart, D.G. Stork. Pattern Classification (2nd Edition). Wiley-Interscience (2000).

Image Registration Neural System for the Analysis of Fundus Topology

V.K. Salakhutdinov[1], Y.G. Smetanin[2], D.M. Murashov[2], V.A. Gandurin[1]

[1] The Institute of Optico-Neural Technologies of the Russian Academy of Sciences, Vavilov street, Moscow, GSP-1, 119991,
iont@postman.ru
[2] Scientific Council "Cybernetics" of the Russian Academy of Sciences. 40, Vavilov street, Moscow, GSP-1, 119991,
d_murashov@rbcail.ru

Abstract. The developed system is a tool for high aperture imaging of the fundus. The obtained high resolution images preserve the topology of the blood vessels. The system is based on mosaicking a series of distinct low aperture fragments in order to obtain a high aperture image. Mosaicking is implemented by a neural network with stubborn learning taking into account the importance of the information of particular features. In mosaicking, the aberrations of the third order are partly compensated.

1 Introduction

The analysis of the topology of the blood vessels of fundus is an efficient, and in some cases the only possible method of diagnosis of many serious diseases [1 - 4], for example, diabetics. The images of the fundus must be registered with high aperture and with high resolution [5], because early stages of diseases are latent and anomalies of the topology are small and usually localized in peripheral areas of the fundus.

The difficulty is that the optical system of any eye, even a normal one, has considerable individual aberrations. Moreover, in the non-invasive visualization it is impossible to fix the eye with respect to the optical system of the measuring instrument. Hence, the topology of the blood vessels of fundus can be registered either with sufficient resolution but with a small angular aperture, or with a large angular aperture but with low resolution.

Here we present a new method for high aperture and high resolution registration of the topology of fundus. The method is based on the mosaicking of a number of low aperture fragments to form a high aperture image. To implement the method, a new neural network is developed. The neural network is 1-layer recurrent with stubborn learning. It takes into account the importance of particular geometric features in the process of mosaicking.

M. Šonka et al. (Eds.): CVAMIA-MMBIA 2004, LNCS 3117, pp. 417-422, 2004.

1.1 Image Registration System

For the high resolution registration of colour images, an optical system from [6] was used; it is presented in Fig..1. The system includes: a telescope with two confocal objectives (1 and 2) and a tool for speckle elimination; a light source for the illumination of the fundus (LS), which consists of three LEDs with red, blue, and green radiation; a high sensitive BW CCD camera; a PC for video registration and processing and control of peripheral tools. It also includes a small PC-controlled LCD display for angular location of the patient's eye; the display is not presented in Fig. 1.

The pupil of the patient's eye is located in the focus of objective 1. The patient fixes his sight on a point on the LCD display ,and thus his eye is fixed relative to the optical system.

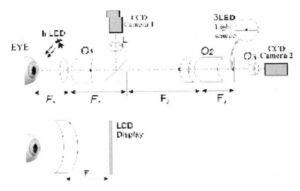

Fig. 1. Optical system

For the illumination of the eye, the radiation from LS is focused by the telescope into a spot in the central area of the eye and homogeneously illuminates the fundus. The diameter of the spot is about 0.5 mm. The light dissipated on the fundus passes through the optical system of the eye and the telescope. It is registered by the CCD camera, and the signal from the camera is stored in the PC.

To form a colour image, each fragment is registered three times: in red, blue, and green light. To register various areas of the fundus, angular location of the eye is changed by a corresponding shift of the location of the light spot on the LCD display. In Fig 2, an image of a fundus with the diameter of the pupil 3.2 mm is presented.

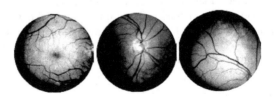

Fig. 2. Input images of the fragments optimised with respect to the contrast and brightness

Thus, the PC registers a series of fragments of the colour image of the fundus together with the information about their relative location and common areas.

2 Image Preprocessing

Unfortunately, a registered image of a fragment in its initial form is poorly applied for automatic processing, in particular, for mosaicking. The difficulties are: low contrast caused by the similarity of specters of adsorption of the blood in the vessels and the rodophsine in the retina, inhomogeneity of the illumination caused by the spherical form of the reflecting surface of the fundus, high level of noise caused by the fine grain structure of the retina. Smoothing procedures result in the loss of important information about small pathologies, i. e. micro aneurisms [3] (Fig. 3).

To enhance input images, an a priori information is used, in particular, about the invariance of the form and size, the homogeneity of the mean optical density. One copy of the registered image was processed by a low frequency spatial filter. As a result, all spatial/specter components with the frequency higher than 2/D, where D is the diameter of the image, are eliminated. This copy is inverted, normalized with respect to the optical density, and multiplied by the second copy, which was not filtered. The product is normalized again.

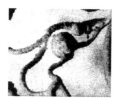 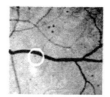

Fig. 3. Images of small pathologies of peripheral vessels of the fundus corresponding to initial stages of NPDR

In Fig. 4, a series of fragments of the fundus after equalization of the optical density is presented.

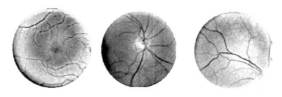

Fig. 4. Images of the fragments after the equalization of the optical density optimised with respect to the contrast and brightness

Fig. 2 and Fig. 4 demonstrate that a priori information about the object considerably enhances the quality of the processed.

3 Mosaicking of Fragments

The last step of image processing is the mosaicking of the equalized fragments. The main problem here is the most precise matching between boundary segments of the juxtaposed image I_1 and the boundary segments of the base image I_0.

The experiments with the algorithm proposed in [7], which is based on pairwise matching of sequential frames using the minimization of metrics demonstrated that it is subject to severe errors. The algorithm based on the parametric irreversible quadratic transformation and hierarchical robust estimation [8] is inefficient because of its computational complexity. Obviously, it is the result of specific noises in non-invasive registration without artificial extension of the pupil.

A new efficient neural method of mosaicking is proposed. The neural network is 1-laer recurrent with non-zero diagonal elements and stubborn learning [9]:

$$v_i(t+1) = F\left(\sum_{j=1}^{n} w_{ij} v_j(t) - w_{i0}\right), \quad t = 0,1,2,..., \ i = 1, ..., n, \tag{1}$$

where v_i are neuron values, w_{ij} are synaptic weights, $F = sgm(\cdot)$ is a sigmoid activation function, v_i is the set of pixels of I_1 within the intersection of I_0 and I_1. The set of pixels of the I_0 within the intersection of I_0 and I_1 gives the template a_i.

The dynamics of the neural network is defined by the equation

$$v_i(t+1) = sgm\left(\sum_{j=1}^{n} w_{ij} v_j(t) - w_0\right) = sgm\left(\sum_{j=1, j \neq i}^{n} w_{ij} v_j(t) + w_{ii} v_i(t) - w_0\right). \tag{2}$$

A specific feature of the developed neural network is that its diagonal elements are non-zero. The factors w_{ii}, define a feedback that prevents the changes of the neuron values. They take into account the fact that various segments of the images have different importance of information. The points of large vessels contain more information and hence have greater weights w_{ii}.

The learning of the proposed model is based on the outer product method with a compulsory procedure of turning of diagonal elements.

Let template vectors $a^1 = (a_i^1), ..., a^p = (a_i^p)$ be given. For each vector, a matrix W^k with elements $w_{ij}^k = a_i^k a_j^k$ is constructed. Obviously,

$$sgm(W^k a^k) = sgm(\sum_{j=1}^{n} a_i^k a_j^k a_j^k) = sgm(a_i^k), \ W^H = \sum_{k=1}^{p} W^k - pI, \tag{3}$$

where I is a unit matrix. Matrix W^H corresponds to the conventional version of the outer product method for the Hopfield model.

To tune the diagonal elements, the following rule is applied: $W^D = diag\left(c_1 \sum_{j=1}^{n} w_{1j}^H, ..., c_n \sum_{j=1}^{n} w_{nj}^H\right)$. The weight matrix of the neural network after learning is $W = W^H + W^D$.

The case $c_1 = ... = c_n = 0$ corresponds to the equal importance of all pixels.

In case $c_i > 1$, the value of the i-th neuron at $(t + 1)$ is defined only by its value at t, i. e. the i-th neuron is a threshold. This case corresponds to the situation when the value is reliable and need not be corrected. The model becomes equivalent to the learning base on the projections onto convex sets [10].

The factors c_i are chosen on the base of the relative importance of the points. In multiple mosaicking, the procedure is reiterated. After each step, the obtained image is used as a new template I_0, and the new fragment is used as a new vector v_i, which corresponds to I_1.

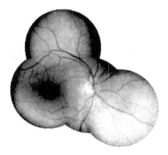

Fig. 5. The result of mosaicking

The proposed neural network with stubborn learning was applied in the mosaicking of images taking into account the topology of the vessels. The size of the fragments is 480×480 pixels. The mean error of mosaicking in the experiments was less than 1.5 pixel. The number of operations in the processing was 2×10^9 FLOPs.

The results of image processing are presented in Fig. 5.

4 Consequences

The developed system gives high aperture and high resolution images of the fundus that preserve the topology of the vessels. It is based on the mosaicking of low aperture images to form a high aperture image. The mosaicking is realized by a neural network with stubborn learning that takes into account the importance of information of various features. The method partially compensate the third order aberrations.

Compared to usual manual mosaicking, the system achieves higher quality. It is also less subjective and more fast.

References

1. F. Zana, Une approche morphologique pour les détections et Bayesienne pour le recalage d'images multimodales: Application aux images rétiniennes, thesis, ENSMP, CMM, May (1999).

2. B. Lay, Analyse automatique des images angiofluorographiques au cours de la rétinopathie diabétique, thesis, ENSMP, CMM, June (1983).
3. T. Spencer et. al., An image processing strategy for the segmentation and quantification of mycroaneurysms in fluorescein angiograms of the ocular fundus, Computers and biomedical research, Vol. 29 (1996) 284–302.
4. P. Massin, A. Erginay, and A. Gaudric, *Rétinopathie Diabéthique*, vol. 1, Paris, Elsevier edition (2000).
5. M. Goldbaum, S. Moezzi, A. Taylor, S. Chatterjee, J. Boyd, E. Hunter, and R. Jain, "Automated diagnosis and image understanding with object extraction, object classification, and inferencing in retinal images", *in IEEE Int. Conf. on Image Processing*, (1996).
6. V. A. Gandurin, V. K. Salakhutdinov. Patent RF no. 2215463 "Fundus camera" (2003).
7. J. Asmuth, B. Madjarov, P. Sajda, J.W. Berger, Mosaicking and enhancement of slit lamp biomicroscopic fundus images. Br J Ophthalmol. 85 (2001) 563–565.
8. A. Can, C. Stewart, and B. Roysam. Robust hierarchical algorithm for constructing a mosaic from images of the curved human retina. In *Proc. CVPR* (1999) 286–292.
9. F. Rosenblat. Principles of Neurodynamics. New York (1962).
10. R. J. Marks and L. E. Atlas Content Addressable Memories: Relationship between Hopfield's Neural Net and Iterative Matched Filter, Rep. no. 51887, Univ. of Washington, Interactive System Design Lab. (1987).

Robust Identification of Object Elasticity

Huafeng Liu[1,2] and Pengcheng Shi[2]

[1] State Key Laboratory of Modern Optical Instrumentation
Zhejiang University, Hangzhou, China
[2] Department of Electrical and Electronic Engineering
Hong Kong University of Science and Technology, Hong Kong

Abstract. Quantification of object elasticity properties has important technical implications as well as significant practical applications, such as civil structural integrity inspection, machine fatigue assessment, and medical disease diagnosis. In general, given noisy measurements on the kinematic states of the objects from imaging or other data, the aim is to recover the elasticity parameters for assumed material constitutive models of the objects. Various versions of the least-square (LS) methods have been widely used in practice, which, however, do not perform well under reasonably realistic levels of disturbances. Another popular strategy, based on the extended Kalman filter (EKF), is also far from optimal and subject to divergence if either the initializations are poor or the noises are not Gaussian. In this paper, we propose a robust system identification paradigm for the quantitative analysis of object elasticity. It is derived and extended from the $\mathcal{H}_\infty$ filtering principles and is particularly powerful for real-world situations where the types and levels of the disturbances are unknown. Specifically, we show the results of applying this strategy to synthetic data for accuracy assessment and for comparison to LS and EKF results, and using canine magnetic resonance imaging data for the recovery of myocardial material parameters[3].

1 Introduction

Quantitative and noninvasive assessment of the intrinsic material properties provides invaluable insights into the objects' physical conditions, i.e. the structural integrity of bridges and the material fatigue states of airplanes. Of particular current interests, there have been plenty studies on living soft tissues, such as heart [2,9], breast [5,10], skin [11], and blood vessels [8], under the clinical assumptions that diseases are highly correlated with changes of local tissue elasticity. From computer vision and medical image analysis perspectives, the goal is to use image-derived noisy observations on the kinematic states to arrive at accurate, robust, and meaningful measurement of the object elasticity distribution, where the recovered information is key to the better formulation and understanding of many physically-based vision problems, including motion tracking, object segmentation, virtual-reality systems, and computer-assisted diagnosis.

[3] This work is supported in part by Hong Kong Research Grant Council under CERG project HKUST6151/03E and by the National Basic Research Program of China (No: 2003CB716104).

M. Šonka et al. (Eds.): CVAMIA-MMBIA 2004, LNCS 3117, pp. 423–435, 2004.
© Springer-Verlag Berlin Heidelberg 2004

1.1   Related Works

The forward processes, which provide the image-derived measurement data on the kinematic states, have strong implications on the reliability of the inverse processes, which recover the material parameters. In addition to reservoir of motion analysis strategies in computer vision, there have been efforts aimed at establishing displacement fields from specialized medical imaging techniques, such as elastography [6] which measures tissue motion induced by external or internal forces, and magnetic resonance (MR) tagging [14] which creates a sparse magnetization grid that tags the underlying tissue and provides tissue movement information through the tracking of the grid deformation.

The inverse algorithms, which are the main focuses of this paper, reconstruct the elasticity distributions from the motion measurement data. The first type of efforts attempt to quantify the material Young's modulus by inverting the measured mechanical responses based on numerical solution of the elasticity equation [4], which describes the mechanical equilibrium of a deformed medium. Ignoring terms related to pressure, the equation becomes a function of the spatial derivatives of the Young's modulus E, which, in principle, could then be used to reconstruct the distribution of E [10]. An related approach re-arranges the linearly discretized equations that describe the forward problem, such that the modulus distribution directly becomes the unknown variables to be solved [7].

The second group of efforts try to minimize criteria that measure the goodness of fit between the model-predicted and data-measured mechanical responses. In [2], finite element (FE) meshes are constructed with loading parameters measured during imaging. FE solutions are then performed using small-strain, small-displacement theory, and corresponding strains are computed independently using imaging-derived data. The material parameters are determined for strain energy functions that maximize the agreement between the observed (from imaging) and the predicted (from FE analysis) strains. Similar in spirit, iterative descent methods are used for various FE models of the elasticity equations to fit, in least-squares sense, a set of tissue displacement fields [5,11].

1.2   Contributions

We present several robust estimation schemes for the recovery of object elasticity parameters from imaging data. Constructing the object dynamics from continuum mechanics laws and finite element method, we convert the system equation into state-space representation, which is further reformulated as a general non-linear system identification problem for the spatially varying material Young's modulus. Within this paradigm, we examine the validity and limitations of the existing works, largely based on the least-square (LS) estimators and the extended Kalman filters (EKF), both of which adopt the minimum-mean-square-error criteria in terms of the reconstructed state, and assume that the noises of the measurement data are Gaussian. We then present two robust strategies, the full-state-derivative information (FSDI) and the noise-perturbed full-state information (NPFSI) methods, which are derived and extended from the $\mathcal{H}_\infty$ filtering principles and provide the minimum-maximum-error (minimax) solutions to the material property estimation problem, without assumptions on the noise statistics. Using synthetic data, we investigate the sensitivity of the algorithms towards noise types and levels, as well as towards system initializations. The experimental results show consistently superior performance of the robust methods, especially the NPFSI form, over the LS and EKF algorithms for non-Gaussian data. We also present EKF and NPFSI estimation results from MR imaging data of a canine heart, both showing good agreement with histological tissue staining of the myocardium, the clinical gold standard.

2   Parameter Identification Problem Formulation

2.1   Continuum Mechanics Model and State-Space Representation

In general, natural objects such as biological tissues have very complicated continuum mechanical properties in terms of their constitutive laws [4]. For computational simplicity and feasibility, we assume that the objects under consideration are nearly incompressible linear elastic solids. For such a material, the strain energy function W has the form $W = \frac{1}{2}c_{ijkl}\varepsilon_{ij}\varepsilon_{kl}$, where ε_{ij} and ε_{kl} are components of the infinitesimal strain tensor and c_{ijkl} is the material specific elastic constant. In our case, the stress-strain relationship obeys the Hooke's law, which states that the stress tensor σ_{ij} is linearly proportional to the stain tensor: $\sigma_{ij} = c_{ijkl}\varepsilon_{kl}$. Under the assumptions that the material is isotropic, where the elastic properties are identical in all directions, and the strain and stress tensors are symmetric, there are exactly two elastic constants which characterize the material and we have the linear isotropic constitutive relationship:

$$\sigma_{ij} = \lambda\delta_{ij}\varepsilon_{kk} + 2\mu\varepsilon_{ij} \tag{1}$$

where λ and μ are the *Lame* constants, and δ_{ij} is the Kronecher's delta function. In matrix form, under two dimensional Cartesian coordinate system, $[\sigma] = [D][\varepsilon]$. Assuming the displacement components along the $x-$ and $y-$axis to be $u(x, y)$ and $v(x, y)$ respectively, the infinitesimal strain tensor $[\varepsilon]$ and the material matrix $[D]$ under plane strain situation are:

$$[\varepsilon] = \begin{bmatrix} \frac{\partial u}{\partial x} \\ \frac{\partial v}{\partial y} \\ \frac{\partial u}{\partial y} + \frac{\partial v}{\partial x} \end{bmatrix} = \begin{bmatrix} \frac{\partial}{\partial x} & 0 \\ 0 & \frac{\partial}{\partial y} \\ \frac{\partial}{\partial y} & \frac{\partial}{\partial x} \end{bmatrix} \begin{bmatrix} u \\ v \end{bmatrix}$$

$$[D] = E \begin{bmatrix} \frac{1-\nu}{(1+\nu)(1-2\nu)} & \frac{\nu}{(1+\nu)(1-2\nu)} & 0 \\ \frac{\nu}{(1+\nu)(1-2\nu)} & \frac{1-\nu}{(1+\nu)(1-2\nu)} & 0 \\ 0 & 0 & \frac{1-2\nu}{2(1+\nu)(1-2\nu)} \end{bmatrix} \tag{2}$$

Here, derived from the *Lame* constants, the Young's modulus E measures of the stiffness and the Poisson's ratio ν measures the compressibility of the material.

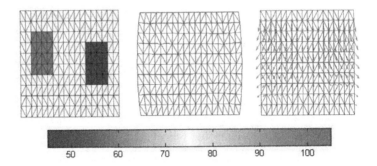

Fig. 1. Generation of the synthetic kinematic data: original state (left), deformed state (middle), and the displacement field (right). The colors of the left figure indicate the Young's moduli of the hard (red), normal (white), and soft (blue) tissues, respectively.

The finite element method is used to discretize the regions of interests into small elements, the Delaunay triangles of the sampling nodes in our implementation. Specifically, an isoparametric formulation defined in a natural coordinate system is used, in which the interpolation of the element coordinates and element displacements use the same basis functions. The nodal displacement based governing dynamic equation of each element is established under the minimum potential energy principle [1], and is then assembled together in matrix form as

$$M\ddot{U} + C\dot{U} + KU = R \tag{3}$$

with mass matrix M, stiffness matrix K which is related to the material Young's modulus E and Poisson's ratio ν, and Rayleigh damping matrix $C = \alpha M + \beta K$.

Equation 3 can be converted into a state-space representation of a continuous time linear system by making $x = (U, \dot{U})^T$ (T denotes transpose) such that:

$$\dot{x}(t) = A(\theta)x(t) + Bw(t) \tag{4}$$

where the material parameter vector θ, the state vector x, the system matrices A and B, and the control (input) term w are:

$$\theta = E \quad x(t) = \begin{bmatrix} U(t) \\ \dot{U}(t) \end{bmatrix}, \quad w(t) = \begin{bmatrix} 0 \\ R \end{bmatrix},$$

$$A = \begin{bmatrix} 0 & I \\ -M^{-1}K & -M^{-1}C \end{bmatrix}, \quad B = \begin{bmatrix} 0 & 0 \\ 0 & M^{-1} \end{bmatrix}$$

Note that, for this particular paper, we are only interested in estimating the Young's modulus whereas the Poisson's ratio is fixed. In principle, however, both E and ν can be estimated simultaneously [9].

2.2   System Dynamics in Parameter Identification Form

Since our goal is to recover the parameter vector $\theta = E$, instead of the more typical problem of estimating the state vector x, the system Equation 4 needs to be reformulated in the form of $\dot{x}(t) = \mathcal{A}_c(x(t))\theta + \mathcal{B}_c$ to facilitate the process. Submitting in $C = \alpha M + \beta K$ and rearranging the system equation to:

$$\begin{bmatrix} \dot{U}(t) \\ \ddot{U}(t) \end{bmatrix} = \begin{bmatrix} 0 & \dot{U} \\ -M^{-1}KU & -\alpha\dot{U} - \beta M^{-1}K\dot{U} \end{bmatrix} + \begin{bmatrix} 0 & 0 \\ 0 & M^{-1} \end{bmatrix} \begin{bmatrix} 0 \\ R \end{bmatrix} \tag{5}$$

we now need to convert all the terms which contain K into functions of E: $KU = G_1 E$ and $K\dot{U} = G_2 E$.

According to the finite element method, the global stiffness matrix K is assembled from the element stiffness K_e:

$$K = \sum K_e = \sum \int_{\Omega_e} B_e^T D_e B_e \, d\Omega_e \tag{6}$$

where Ω_e is the domain of an arbitrary element e, B_e is the local element strain-displacement matrix, and D_e is the element material matrix. The element stiffness matrix K_e can then be stated in terms of its *unknown* Young's modulus E_e:

$$K_e = E_e \int_{\Omega_e} B_e^T D_e' B_e \, d\Omega_e = E_e K_e' \tag{7}$$

Then, the iterative steps of recasting KU to $G_1 E$ (and $K\dot{U}$ to $G_2 E$ in the exactly same fashion) are:

1. Initialize a $N \times N_e$ null matrix G_1 with zero entries, where N = number of system nodal variables and N_e = number of system elements.
2. Initialize a $N \times N$ null matrix K_s with zero entries.
3. For an arbitrary element N_x, construct the local element matrix K'_{N_x} following Equation 7.
4. Using established correspondence between local and global numbering schemes, change the subscript indices of the coefficients in the K'_{N_x} matrix to the global indices.
5. Insert K'_{N_x} terms into the corresponding K_s matrix in the locations designated by their indices.
6. Insert $K_s U$, which is now a column vector reflecting the contribution by element N_x, to the N_x^{th} column of the G_1 matrix.
7. Return to step 2 and repeat this procedure for next element until all elements have been so treated.

Once the numerical procedures of computing G_1 and G_2 are completed, Equation 5 is converted into the parameter identification form which can be used for the estimation of the Young's modulus distribution:

$$\dot{x}(t) = Fx + \mathcal{A}_c(x(t))\theta + B_c w(t) \tag{8}$$

Table 1. Estimated Young's moduli from the synthetic data. Each data cell represents the mean ± standard derivation for the normal (75), hard (105), and soft (45) tissues

Method	Tissue	Noise-Free	20dB(Gau)	30dB(Gau)	20dB(Poi)	30dB(Poi)
	Normal	75.0 ± 0.0	FAILED	74.9 ± 2.9	FAILED	75.1 ± 3.6
LS	Hard	105.0± 0.0	FAILED	106.2± 9.1	FAILED	104.8± 7.9
	Soft	45.0 ± 0.0	FAILED	45.3 ± 3.2	FAILED	44.9 ± 2.8
	Normal	74.9 ± 1.7	76.0 ± 5.5	76.6 ± 3.0	77.1 ± 6.6	75.0 ± 3.6
EKF	Hard	105.2± 1.0	101.8± 10.1	104.2± 3.8	100.6± 23.0	103.8± 9.9
	Soft	46.0 ± 1.8	46.0 ± 3.8	47.1 ± 3.4	50.1 ± 5.7	47.9 ± 3.8
	Normal	75.0 ± 0.0	FAILED	74.8 ± 5.0	FAILED	75.1 ± 3.0
FDSI	Hard	105.0± 0.0	FAILED	106.4± 9.4	FAILED	104.7± 5.8
	Soft	45.0 ± 0.0	FAILED	45.4 ± 5.7	FAILED	44.9 ± 1.3
	Normal	74.8 ± 1.5	73.3 ± 8.4	73.8 ± 3.4	74.8 ± 7.2	73.9 ± 3.1
NPFSI	Hard	104.1± 1.2	100.9± 24.0	102.6± 9.1	100.1± 15.7	102.3± 7.2
	Soft	46.3 ± 2.1	47.0 ± 5.9	44.9 ± 2.7	45.2 ± 4.6	44.8 ± 2.5

where

$$\theta = E, \quad x(t) = \begin{bmatrix} U(t) \\ \dot{U}(t) \end{bmatrix}, \quad w(t) = \begin{bmatrix} 0 \\ R \end{bmatrix},$$

$$\mathcal{A}_c = \begin{bmatrix} 0 & 0 \\ -M^{-1}G_1 & -\beta M^{-1}G_2 \end{bmatrix}, \quad B_c = \begin{bmatrix} 0 & 0 \\ 0 & M^{-1} \end{bmatrix}, \quad F = \begin{bmatrix} 0 & I \\ 0 & -\alpha I \end{bmatrix}$$

3   Parameter Identification Algorithms

3.1   Synthetic Data for Evaluation

In order to illustrate the accuracy and robustness of the material parameters estimates, synthetic data with known kinematics are generated, as shown in Fig. 1. The rectangular testing object, with dimension of 28 (height) x 16 (width) x 1 (thickness), is made of three components of different material elasticities, $E_{hard} = 105$ for the hard (red) part, $E_{normal} = 75$ for the normal (white) part, and $E_{soft} = 45$ for the soft (blue) part, while Poisson's ratio is set to 0.49 for all parts. The elastic medium is constrained to deform 1.2 displacement in the vertical direction at the top side and 0 at the bottom side. Using these boundary conditions, we solve the forward problem and the resulting displacements are labelled as the ideal measurement data. Different types and levels of noises are then added to generate the noisy data.

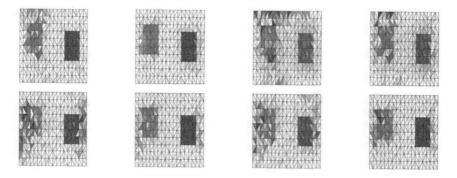

Fig. 2. Estimated elasticity modulus distributions using the EKF (top row) and NPFSI (bottom row) methods for noisy input data (left to right): $SNR = 20dB$ (Gaussian), $SNR = 30dB$ (Gaussian), $SNR = 20dB$ (Poisson), and $SNR = 30dB$ (Poisson).

3.2   Least Squares Approximation

Least-squares algorithms are often considered static, where the uncertainties of the measurements and the system are not of concern. Rearrange Equation 8 as:

$$\mathcal{A}_c(x)\theta = \dot{x} - Fx - B_c w(t) = \dot{x} - \mathcal{B} \tag{9}$$

the parameter vector θ can then be directly estimated from the least-squares approximation:

$$\hat{\theta} = [\mathcal{A}_c^T \mathcal{A}_c]^{-1} \mathcal{A}_c^T (\dot{x} - \mathcal{B}) \tag{10}$$

Method Evaluation Using the synthetic data, the LS estimated Young's modulus values for ideal and noisy inputs of displacement measurements are shown in Table 1. For clean and low noise (30dB) cases, the LS method does give excellent performance. However, when the noise levels (20dB) increase, LS fails to provide any meaningful results. Clearly, the LS strategy does not have the capability to handle uncertainties of the system modeling and the measurement data. Further, it is actually a pseudo-inverse process, and we are going to discuss the more efficient least-square solution based on the Kalman filters.

3.3   Extended Kalman Filter

The EKF approach to parameter estimation in dynamical system has a rather long history. It has the flexibility to easily incorporate both system modeling and measurement uncertainties. The basic idea is to consider system parameters as part of an augmented state vector, and with measurements taken over time, the

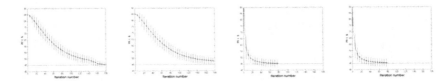

Fig. 3. Converging speed of the average Young's modulus in the soft region using EKF (the two left figures) and $\mathcal{H}_\infty(NPFSI)$ (the two right figures) methods: $SNR = 30dB$ Gaussian inputs and $SNR = 30dB$ Poisson inputs

system response and the parameter estimates are adjusted so that they match the data in an optimal manner:

$$\begin{bmatrix} \dot{x}(t) \\ \dot{\theta} \end{bmatrix} = \begin{bmatrix} Fx + \mathcal{A}_c(x)\theta + B_cw(t) \\ 0 \end{bmatrix} + \begin{bmatrix} v(t) \\ 0 \end{bmatrix} \tag{11}$$

$$y = \begin{bmatrix} I & 0 \end{bmatrix} \begin{bmatrix} x \\ \theta \end{bmatrix} + e(t) \tag{12}$$

This augmented system is nonlinear due to the cross-product between x and θ. If the process noise $v(t)$ and measurement noise $e(t)$ are both white Gaussian with covariances Q_v and R_e respectively, the EKF solution comes from [12]:

$$\begin{bmatrix} \dot{\hat{x}}(t) \\ \dot{\hat{\theta}} \end{bmatrix} = \begin{bmatrix} F\hat{x} + \mathcal{A}_c(\hat{x})\hat{\theta} + B_cw(t) \\ 0 \end{bmatrix} + PH^T R_e(t)^{-1}[y - H\hat{z}] \tag{13}$$

$$\dot{P} = LP + PL^T + Q_v - PH^T R_e(t)^{-1}HP \tag{14}$$

where $P(0) = P_0 > 0$, $H = [I \ 0]$, and $L = \begin{bmatrix} F + \frac{\partial}{\partial \hat{x}}\{\mathcal{A}_c(x)\hat{\theta} + B_cw(t)\} & \mathcal{A}_c(\hat{x}) \\ 0 & 0 \end{bmatrix}$.

One difficulty EKF faces is that there is no general, cost effective theory for choosing optimal R_e, Q_v and P_0. Prior knowledge thus often plays important roles in the *ad hoc* determination of these parameters.

Method Evaluation For measurement data inputs with various noise types and levels, the average EKF based parameter estimation results are tabulated in Table 1, and the recovered elasticity distributions are shown in Fig. 2.

Due to the coupling between the state variables and system parameters, the precision of the EKF estimate for the noise-free case has dropped from the LS result. For input data corrupted by Gaussian noises, however, EKF typically achieves much better results, even though the convergence speed is quite slow (Fig. 3). It is also well known that EKF could be greatly affected by the quality of the initializations. In order to investigate the effect of initial modulus values on the algorithm convergence, experiments have been conducted using $\hat{\theta}(0) = 95$, $\hat{\theta}(0) = 65$, and $\hat{\theta}(0) = 35$ for Gaussian data inputs. As shown in Fig. 4, a faster convergence is achieved when a proper initial value is chosen. However, the

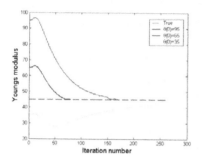 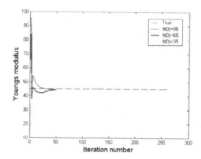

Fig. 4. Convergence sensitivity to different initial values (Gaussian inputs) for the EKF (left) and $\mathcal{H}_\infty$-NPFSI (right) estimation of the soft region.

convergence rates from the upper side and the lower side of the initializations are not symmetric, which hinder the possibility to choose the *optimal* initial values in a symmetric fashion. Further, comparing the estimation results for Gaussian and Poisson inputs (Fig. 5), it is indicative that EKF is far from optimal for non-Gaussian noises and may be subject to divergence, at least during certain period of the iterative process, which motivates us to seek more robust strategies.

3.4 $\mathcal{H}_\infty$ Filters

Because of the deficiency of the LS and EKF methods to deal with noisy inputs, especially the non-Gaussian measurement data, we have developed two robust, mini-max parameter identification strategies based on the $\mathcal{H}_\infty$ filtering principles [3], which assume no specific types of noise distribution. While the full-state-derivative information (FSDI) method takes into account of the process noise $v(t)$ and the initial parameter estimation error $\theta - \hat{\theta}(0)$, the noise-perturbed full-state information (NPFSI) method also considers the measurement noise $e(t)$ and the initial state estimation error $x - \hat{x}(0)$.

FSDI Method We introduce a cost function that measures the worst-case attenuation from the additive process disturbance as well as error in the initial estimate of θ to the estimation error over an interval of interest:

$$sup \frac{\|\theta - \hat{\theta}\|_Q^2}{\|v\|^2 + |\theta - \theta(\hat{0})|_{Q_0}^2} < \gamma^2 \tag{15}$$

where $\theta(\hat{0})$ is an *a priori* estimate of the parameter vector θ, $\| \bullet \|_Q^2$ is a L_2 semi-norm with weighting function Q, $| \bullet |_{Q_0}^2$ is the Euclidean norm of $\bullet^T Q_0 \bullet$, and v is the process noise. Different from $\mathcal{H}_2$ (Kalman) filter based framework, the $\mathcal{H}_\infty$ method has many solutions corresponding to different γ values. Nevertheless,

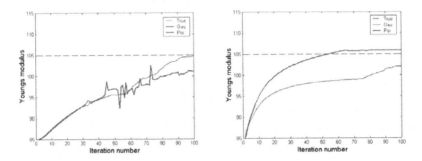

Fig. 5. Estimation sensitivity under different types (Gaussian and Poisson) of noises: EKF (left) and $\mathcal{H}_\infty$-NPFSI (right) methods

if the optimal performance level γ^* does exist [3], the following solutions are optimal in mini-max sense for every $\gamma > \gamma^*$:

$$\dot{\theta} = \Sigma^{-1} \mathcal{A}_c{}^T (\dot{x} - \mathcal{B}) \tag{16}$$

$$\dot{\Sigma} = \mathcal{A}_c{}^T \mathcal{A}_c - \gamma^{-2} Q; \quad \Sigma(0) = Q_0 \tag{17}$$

Hence, the $\mathcal{H}_\infty$ filter of FSDI form can be treated as a more general framework for material parameter estimation from *clean* kinematics measurement. If we let $\gamma \to \infty$, the limiting filter would converge to the aforementioned least-squares estimator. Let $Q = \mathcal{A}_c{}^T \mathcal{A}_c$, we have the following:

$$\gamma^* = 1, \dot{\hat{\theta}} = Q_0{}^{-1} \mathcal{A}_c{}^T (\dot{x} - \mathcal{B}) \tag{18}$$

which is the generalized least-mean-squares filter.

NPFSI Method In practice, inaccuracies are often due to unmodeled dynamics or measurement errors that are not considered when the model is built. To cope with such situations, we introduce a more complete cost function for all $\gamma > \gamma^*$:

$$sup \frac{\|\theta - \hat{\theta}\|_Q^2}{\|v\|^2 + \|e\|^2 + |\theta - \hat{\theta}(0)|_{Q_0}^2 + |x - \hat{x}(0)|_{Q_1}^2} < \gamma^2 \tag{19}$$

Here, $\hat{x}(0)$ is initial estimates for $x(0)$, Q_1 is a weighting factor, and e models the measurement uncertainty. Under this criterion, we come to the solution:

$$\begin{bmatrix} \dot{\hat{x}} \\ \dot{\hat{\theta}} \end{bmatrix} = \begin{bmatrix} F & \mathcal{A}_c(x) \\ 0 & 0 \end{bmatrix} \begin{bmatrix} \hat{x} \\ \hat{\theta} \end{bmatrix} + \begin{bmatrix} B_c w(t) \\ 0 \end{bmatrix} + \Sigma^{-1} H^T (y - \hat{x}) \tag{20}$$

$$\dot{\Sigma} = -\Sigma \begin{bmatrix} F & \mathcal{A}_c(x) \\ 0 & 0 \end{bmatrix} - \begin{bmatrix} F^T & 0 \\ \mathcal{A}_c{}^T & 0 \end{bmatrix} \Sigma + \begin{bmatrix} I & 0 \\ 0 & -\gamma^2 Q \end{bmatrix} - \Sigma \begin{bmatrix} I & 0 \\ 0 & 0 \end{bmatrix} \Sigma \tag{21}$$

In general, it is difficult to determine the optimal γ^*, and it may even be infinite which means that no guaranteed disturbance attenuation level can be achieved. In fact, however, if Q is chosen, γ^* can be obtained analytically. For a fixed γ, it is necessary to have $\Sigma > 0$ for the existence of the identifier. Note that partitioning this matrix as $\Sigma = \begin{bmatrix} \Sigma_1 & \Sigma_2 \\ \Sigma_2^T & \Sigma_3 \end{bmatrix}$, the Schur test implies that $\Sigma > 0$ if and only if $\dot{\Pi} = \Sigma_2^T \Sigma_2 - \gamma^2 Q > 0$, $\Pi(0) = Q_0$ and $\Sigma_1 > 0$. Hence, if $\Sigma_1(0)$ is chosen to be identity matrix and $Q = \Sigma_2^T \Sigma_2$, γ^* will be 1 [3].

Method Evaluation The two $\mathcal{H}_\infty$ methods are evaluated using the synthetic data and the convergence criteria are the same as the EKF one. $\gamma = 3$ has been used in our experiments. The estimated Young's moduli are listed in Table 1 (both FSDI and NPFSI) and shown in Fig. 2 (NPFSI results only). As a generalized LS methods, the FSDI performs well for noise-free and low-noise inputs, but fails to converge for 20dB cases. While underperforming EKF estimator somewhat for Gaussian inputs, it is obvious that the $\mathcal{H}_\infty$-NPFSI framework gives the best overall results when the data noises are not Gaussian. Further, even for Gaussian noises, NPFSI converges much faster than EKF, and it is not affected by the initial values of the Young's modulus (Fig. 4). In Fig. 3, the mean values with standard derivation of the estimates are plotted as a function of iterative numbers. It is evident that NPFSI results in faster and more stable convergence of the estimates for both Gaussian and Poisson inputs.

In a further sensitivity test of the algorithms to different types of noises, the convergence of the Young's modulus estimate for a particular element is given in Fig. 5, where the red and blue curves are generated for the $SNR = 30dB$ (Gaussian) and $SNR = 30dB$ (Poisson) input data respectively. It is clear that EKF has certain desirable optimality properties for Gaussian noisy inputs. However, the EKF results for Poisson noises are pretty bad, with unstable bursts during the convergence process. It seems that if the assumptions on the noise statistics are violated, it is possible that small noise errors may lead to large estimation errors for EKF. On the other hand, very stable convergence results are obtained using the NPFSI method for two sets of data contaminated by different types of noise, showing its desired robustness for real-world problems.

4 Applications and Discussion

4.1 Canine Imaging Data

The displacements of the canine heart wall are reconstructed using the active region model [13] on MR phase contrast images, which also provides the corresponding velocity information. The histological staining of the post mortem myocardium (Figure 7), with the infarct region highlighted, provides the clinical gold standard for the assessment of the image analysis results. Based on the reconstructed displacements and measured velocities (Fig. 6), the $\mathcal{H}_\infty$-NPFSI and the EKF frameworks are used to recover the elasticity modulus distribution,

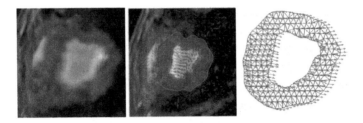

Fig. 6. A mid-ventricle MR image of a canine heart (left), velocity data (middle), and the displacement data acquired from the spatio-temporal active region method (right).

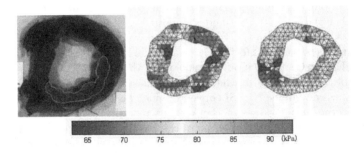

Fig. 7. TTC-stained post mortem left ventricular myocardium with infarcted zone highlighted (left), NPFSI (middle) and EKF (right) estimated Young's modulus maps.

where Poisson's ratio are fixed at 0.47 to model approximate incompressibility and the initial estimates of Young's modulus are set to be 75kPa.

4.2   Results and Discussion

The experimental results obtained with real canine imaging data are presented in Fig. 7, where the middle map depicts the NPFSI results and the right one for EKF results. It is observed that both the estimated Young's modulus distribution patterns agree pretty well with the highlighted histological staining results, i.e. the infarcted myocardium is harder than the normal tissue. As a continuation of this work, future study will be extended to time-varying estimation of the elasticity with more realistic material models.

References

1. Bathe, K.: Finite Element Procedures in Engineering Analysis. Prentice Hall (1982)
2. Creswell, L.L., Moulton, M.J., Wyers, S.G., Pirolo, J.S. et al.: An Experimental Method for Evaluting Constitutive Models of Myocardium in vivo Hearts. American J. Physio. **267** (1994) H853–H853

3. Didinsky, G., Pan, Z., Basar, T.: Parameter Identification for Uncertain Plants using $\mathcal{H}_\infty$ Methods. Automatica. **31** (1995) 1227–1250
4. Fung, Y.C.: A First Course in Continuum Mechanics: for Physical and Biological Engineers and Scientists. 3rd edn. Prentice Hall (1994)
5. Kallel, F., Bertrand, M.: Tissue Elasticity Reconstruction Using Linear Perturbation Method. IEEE Trans. Med. Imag. **15** (1996) 299–313
6. Muthupilla, R., Lomas, D.J., Rossman, P.J., Greenleaf, J.F., Manduca, A., Ehman, R.L.: Magnetic Resonance Elastography by Direct Visualization of Propagating Acoustic Strain Waves. Science. **269** (1995) 1854-1857
7. Raghavan, R.H., Yagle, A.: Forward and Inverse Problems in Imaging the Elasticity of Soft Tissue. IEEE Trans. Nucl. Sci. **41** (1994) 1639–1647
8. Shapo, B.M., Crowe, J.R., Skovoroda, A.R., et al.: Displacement and Strain Imaging of Coronary Arteries with Ultraluminal Ultrasound. IEEE Trans. Ultrason. Ferroelect. and Freg. Cont. **43** (1996) 234–246
9. Shi, P., Liu,H.: Stochastic Finite Element Framework for Simultaneous Estimation of Cadiac Kinematic Functions and Material Parameters. Medical Image Analysis **7** (2003) 445–464
10. Skovoroda, A.R., Emelianov, S.Y., O'Donnel, M.: Tissue Elasticity Reconstruction Based on Ultrasonic Displacement and Strain Images. IEEE Trans. Ultrason. Ferroelect. and Freg. Cont. **42** (1995) 747–765
11. Tsap, L.V., Goldgof, D.B., Sarkar S.: Nonrigid Motion Analysis Based on Dynamic Refinement of Finite Element Models. IEEE. PAMI. **22** (2000) 526–543
12. Weiss, H., Moore J.B.: Improved Extended Kalman Filter Design for Passive Tracking. IEEE Trans. Auto. Contr. **25** (1980) 807–811
13. Wong, L.N., Liu, H., Sinusas, A.J., Shi, P.: Spatio-temporal Active Region Model for Simultaneous Segmentation and Motion Estimation of the heart. ICCV-VLSM03. Nice, France (2003) 193–200
14. Zerhouni, E.A., Parish, D.M., Rogers, W.J., Yang, A., Shapiro, E.P.: Human Heart: Tagging with MR imaging - A Method for Noninvasive Assessment of Myocardial Motion. Radiology. **169** (1988) 59-63

Author Index

Lecture Notes in Computer Science

For information about Vols. 1–3115

please contact your bookseller or Springer